The Best of
Liz Curtis Higgs

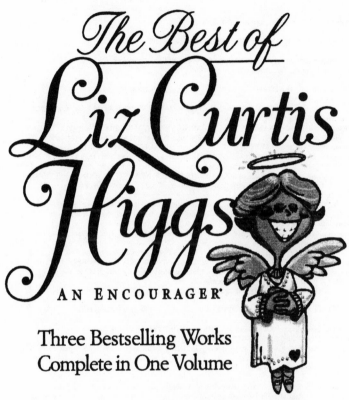

AN ENCOURAGER

Three Bestselling Works
Complete in One Volume

"One Size Fits All" and Other Fables

Only Angels Can Wing It

Help! I'm Laughing and I Can't Get Up

INSPIRATIONAL PRESS
NEW YORK

CONTENTS

"One Size Fits All"

and Other Fables

Dedication

To my husband, Bill Higgs,
who waited almost thirty-four years
to marry this "big, beautiful woman . . ."
your love makes everything possible.

June 1993

Acknowledgments

Heartfelt thanks and many hugs to the hundreds of people who made these pages possible:

To the women whose comments appear here ... thank you for your time, your courage and your honesty.

To: Catherine from Kentucky, Etta from Wisconsin, Melissa from New Jersey, Carla from New Hampshire, Fanny from Tennessee, Cindy from Illinois, Shirley from Arizona, Jan from Indiana, Bonita from Colorado, Mary from Pennsylvania, and Linda from Pennsylvania, who provided the names of each chapter, or "fable." Thank you for your creativity.

To the eleven remarkable women who shared their professional expertise through lengthy telephone interviews: Lynette, Anne, Robin, Kayla, Pat, Kathy, Nancye, Carole, Jeanne, Carol and Alice. Many thanks for sharing your time and talents.

To my friend and encourager, Duncan Jaenicke, with the terrible handwriting and wonderful insights. Thank you for believing in me.

To my National Coordinator, Pam Dennison, who kept our office humming. Thank you for sharing your many gifts (especially, patience!).

To Anne Dorton, who entered into my word processor — without a single typo! — the written responses of more than 200 wonderful women. Thank you for your commitment to getting it right.

To my friends and associates in the National Association of Women's Health Professionals. Thank you for your generous encouragement.

To Sonya Davis, who cared for our little ones, and kept them out of the study so I could press on. Thank you for being Mom #2.

To all my new friends at Thomas Nelson Books. You are simply the best.

To Bob Russell, who was the first to teach me about God's grace. I am ever in your debt.

To my father, D. Curtis Amidon, who always told me I was beautiful. You are, too, Daddy.

To my children, Matthew and Lillian, who make every morning Christmas. Thank you for letting me be your "Mama."

To you, who were kind enough to purchase this book. May it fill your heart!

Contents

Introduction

Back in October 1962, the Four Seasons had a #1 hit record, "Big Girls Don't Cry." Don't you believe it! More tears have been shed over expanding waistlines than all of life's other challenges combined, including departing sweethearts and declining bank accounts.

Each day brings a new diet book, and magazine racks shout monthly, "Lose 20 Pounds in 20 Days!" We buy it, we try it, we cry when it doesn't work. Everyone is dieting, but the only thing we're losing is our self-esteem.

For almost thirty years, my own self-esteem hovered somewhere between poor and pitiful (in the South, that's pronounced "p-i-i-i-tiful!"). Surrounded by my tiny cheerleader friends in school, I always felt fat, even though I was only a few pounds above the norm.

My first diet was at age ten, to be followed by dozens more in the years that followed. I was the classic yo-yo dieter: up and down, up and down.

Like many young women with low self-esteem, I didn't date much, and settled for any guy in pants when I did go out. I dropped out of college and landed in lots of dead-end jobs and going-nowhere relationships.

Call me the Prodigal Daughter. I had to try everything, had to hit rock bottom before I woke up.

That "wake up call" came soon after my thirtieth birthday. Weary of looking for love in all the wrong places, and trying to diet my way into some man's arms, I threw out every scale in the house (both the big kind you stand on and the little ones that weigh food) and announced to the world, "This is the Liz-that-is!"

A funny thing happened. The mountains didn't crumble and the earth didn't stop spinning. Over the next seven years, I bought the wardrobe I needed and deserved (instead of waiting until I was thin enough to "earn" it), married a wonderful man, started my own business, gave birth to two adorable children, bought my dream house in the country and started writing this book.

I am grateful for every blessing from above, but most of all for God's complete and loving acceptance of me, big hips and all. That's what helped me accept myself. That's what made the difference.

There are, at this moment, thousands of women across America who are still trying to diet their way to happiness. Not just big women, mind you, but medium size and thin women! We tell ourselves that if we "just lose 10 pounds" (or 20, 40, 60 or 100 pounds), we will look better, feel better, even be better people.

So much for complete and loving self-acceptance.

I believe that basing our self-worth on what the scale says means programming ourselves for disaster.

Such a heartless and fickle device, that bathroom scale! If we lose a quarter of a pound, we dance all the way to the doughnut store to celebrate. All this for a quarter of a pound. Four liquid ounces. (We could lose that much in a good sneeze!)

On the other hand, if we gain a quarter of a pound, our whole week is up in flames. Nothing but carrot sticks, forever. Bad girl.

Now, this is silly. I say, let's get happy, get healthy and get on with life!

This book is a celebration of who you are right now. If your health (and your doctor) requires you to change your eating habits and increase your exercise, by all means go for it. But . . . you still need the life-changing material in this book.

Too often, we postpone joy until we are, say, a size 10. I've *been* a size 10, and was no more joyful at that size than I am now as a size 22 Tinkerbell. "Thin" does not guarantee health, happiness or a husband. Today, and every day, you need to be assured that you are a woman of immeasurable worth and great beauty "as is," not "when."

Please understand that this business of getting on with our lives does not mean we are giving up, nor does it mean we are living in denial. It's simply an acknowledgment of the truth about dieting, exercise and good health, and an acceptance of the bodies we've been given. Really, it's more than just acceptance, it's a celebration!

The more we learn about how the human body works, the more we are discovering that "healthy" means having a healthy mind and spirit, as well as a healthy body, not to mention having a healthy sense of humor!

Throughout the pages of *"One Size Fits All" and Other Fables*, you're going to meet lots of women — more than two hundred of them — from thirty-seven states across America. They come in all sizes, from 4 to 34, all shapes, all ages, from teens to seniors, and from all walks of life. You'll laugh with them, cry with them, and applaud their insights. In fact, the dozen chapter titles are some of their favorite fables about weight, size and dieting.

Through surveys, interviews and heartfelt discussions with these wonderful, honest women, I've discovered that very few of us (even the size 4's) are happy with our bodies, particularly the amount of flesh attached thereto. Everyone expressed a desire for some encouraging words that would help them accept themselves for who and what they are, regardless of size or shape.

Each chapter is followed by interviews with experts in women's health, fitness, psychology, nutrition, fashion and publishing, who offer further insights for those of us seeking answers to questions like, "Does my size affect my health?" and "Can you be fit *and* fat?" Their responses may surprise you.

Prepare to be encouraged, my friend, because it's time to look at your beautiful body in a whole new light. It's time to embrace all of your lovable self, just as God made you.

It's time to stop crying and start rejoicing!

"There's a Thin Person Trapped Inside You"

Raise your hand if you have ever stood in front of one of those carnival mirrors that make you look thinner. I'm assuming you hustled right past the one that makes everything w-i-d-e-r, until your eyes settled on the Magic One and you took your stance.

There you were, thin. You were also eight feet tall (but a very slim eight feet). If you moved forward or back, you could create the illusion of a nice elongated neck (say, 38 inches), or the waistline of a bird. A flamingo. True, it wasn't your fantasy body, but it was a thinner one.

File that under, "Lies My Mirror Told Me."

What is it about being thin? Why have many of us longed after it with more passion than we've ever poured into our jobs, our friendships, our marriages, our lives?

My Own Journey

Growing up, I surrounded myself with words about being thin. If I close my eyes I can still see those hand-lettered signs taped all over the walls of my navy blue and yellow bedroom:

"Think Thin"
"Thin Is In, Stout Is Out"
"Loose Lips Sink Hips"

I had a little diet and exercise guide that told me I should weigh 128. At 5'9", my 145 pounds seemed obese. A more recent weight chart would have put me right at the middle of the range. I was already the perfect weight.

But that little book said I was 17 pounds overweight. I spent hours reading and re-reading it, convinced that if I thought about it long enough, a thinner body could be mine. When I blew out the candles on my birthday cake every July I had only one wish: to be thin.

You need to know that my scale hasn't registered anything close to 145 for a *long* time! In the years since then, I've traveled the yo-yo road: up, then down, then up some more, then down, then up even more. You know the routine. Maybe you've made that journey yourself.

Do you, like me, remember certain years as "thin ones" or "fat ones?" I carry around in my head an imaginary calendar, with very specific, chronological memories of my trips up and down the scale.

Take 1964. Please. Fifth grade. I was aware that I was both taller and heavier than most kids in fifth grade. I always took solace in knowing there were two other girls in my class who were bigger than I was. How ridiculous that sounds; but some of us still make such comparisons when we walk into a room full of strangers: "Oh, good! She's at least 20 pounds heavier than me!"

I'm embarrassed to admit that at my ten-year high school reunion, I scanned the room for both those classmates to see who was still the biggest. That was a "thin" year for me (remember, I had a reunion to go to), so I was the smallest of the three. For a season, anyway.

When I shot up five inches in sixth grade, my weight was suddenly distributed more evenly, and I would have qualified as "normal." Not thin, mind you, but certainly average or healthy. But that was the year I stumbled on the little book, so guess how I saw myself?

Fat.

Junior high school was where I learned how to diet, in search of that elusive "thin person trapped inside me." I had lots of company. It seems the only subjects my friends and I talked about were diets, calories, boys (which is *why* we said we wanted to be thin) and losing weight. Down two pounds — HOORAY! Up three pounds — UGH.

As recently reported in *USA Today*, child psychiatrist Ann Childress surveyed close to 1600 girls, and found that 50% of eighth grade girls had dieted. Fifty percent! Dangerous stuff, since dieting before adolescence can slow a child's growth. Childress said, "We need to educate parents on how so much of body build is genetic, so they can promote self-acceptance in kids."

If only my parents had heard that message when I was thirteen! Instead, I dieted with gusto. My friend Judy and I lived on sugarless gum, saltines and yogurt. And pizza, served with large heapings of guilt. We would "save our calories" all day, anticipating that pepperoni binge.

I remember the night we sat in front of Judy's TV, watching a beauty pageant—while eating popcorn. When the winner, Cybill Shepherd, announced that she kept herself thin by chewing gum, our faces lit up. Here was the answer!

We chewed gum constantly, certain that it kept anything evil from passing through our lips. (This did not work. We found out that gum could be parked somewhere while we were indulging in chocolate chip cookies. We also found out that chewing gum in school earned you three afternoons in the detention hall.)

Not much has changed. Women still want fashion models, movie stars and beauty queens to tell us all their diet secrets. On a recent trip to my neighborhood supermarket, I found the following two headlines on display at the check-out counter:

"Lose Weight Like a Star:
Weight Loss Secrets of Shrinking Stars."

"50 Stars' Slimming Secrets:
How They Stay So Young Looking—And YOU Can Too."

One of the many stars featured was Cher, who brought in a team of trainers at $5,000 a week, a nutritionist and a personal cook at $1,200 a week, and spent $200,000 in one year for gym equipment and related expenses.[1]

"And you can too"?

My own favorite diet advice comes from a much more authoritative source, and a very big star. Miss Piggy said, "Never eat more than you can lift."

The Truth with a capital T is this: *every woman, whatever her size or shape, is beautiful.* Fight the urge to say, "Not me!" I said that myself for years. The word "beautiful" literally means "good" or "fine," and the definition of the word includes, "a work of art."

Now, you *are* that: a unique creation, one-of-a-kind, divinely designed, a work of art. Instead of falling into the trap of defining your appearance by comparison ("I'm not as pretty as Christie Brinkley"), say, "I am the best me that I can be."

That's what being beautiful really means.

There She Is, Miss America

You are not only beautiful, you are Miss America material . . . and I'll prove it! *USA TODAY* published the vital statistics of the 1989 Miss America contestants, and came up with an average for each category. (I like to make things easy, so if you have even one quality that matches this list, that makes you Miss America material!).

Let's see if any of these fit you:

1. **The average Miss America is twenty-three years old.**
   (Okay, moving right along . . .)
2. **All the contestants are single.**
   (After all, she is MISS America. Since this is my book, I'll let you count "single again," too.)
3. **The majority of contestants have brown hair.**
   (I should raise my own hand on this one, but instead I'll confess that my blonde hair is . . . chemically dependent.)
4. **Most contestants also have brown eyes.**
   (With tinted contact lenses, *you* can be a brown-eyed beauty, too.)
5. **The average height for Miss America is 5'6".**
   (Surprised? I had always imagined them as very tall, like the super models, but the average height is well within the grasp of many of us. Whatever your height, it's not worth wearing tippy-toe heels to catch up!)
6. **Her average weight is 114 pounds.**
   (Uh-oh. Let's try this: I'll count it if you *ever* weighed 114, even if you shot past it in fourth grade! (Back in the good old days, Miss America 1922-23, Mary Campbell, weighed 140.[2])
7. **The average dress size is 6.**
   (Slight consolation: that's not the smallest size on the rack, there are still 2's and 4's. There are even 1's and 3's!)

8. **The average waist of a Miss America is 24 inches.**
   (I consider this unnatural. My daughter, Miss Lillian, is
   an active, adorable four-year-old. Recently, I got out a
   tape measure to see what her waist measurement might
   be. It was 18 1/2", which turned out to equal her chest
   and hip measurements too!)

You'll like the next one better:

9. **Her average shoe size is 7 1/2.**
   (Of course. She hasn't had children yet. I was ready for
   stretch marks and saggy breasts, but nobody warned me
   that my feet would swell during pregnancy and never go
   back down. I went from a dainty size 8 shoe to a defiant
   size 10 in nine months. Ah well. Small price for a baby,
   this.)

The health conscious among us will appreciate the next final
statistic:

10. **None of the contestants have ever smoked cigarettes.**
    (Gold stars and brownie points for you if you can raise
    your hand on this one.)

Here's the amazing conclusion: when these contestants were
asked to rate their physical beauty on a scale of one to ten, they gave
themselves an 8.62.

Wait a minute. A 24 inch waist, a size 6 dress, and twenty-three
years old and *still* not a "10?" When even Miss America doesn't see
herself as "perfectly" beautiful, no wonder the rest of us struggle with
our self image!

Plastic Beauty

We've all heard the tales of beauty contestants who have spent
their hard-earned money (or their parents' money) on breast
enlargement, nose reduction and other plastic surgery. "What price
beauty," we've sighed, shaking our heads.

But, models, movie stars and pageant participants aren't the *only*
women who choose such options. Many "average" women do too.
For example, in 1989, a survey among plastic surgeons found 71,000

of us wanted bigger breasts.[3] Which brings up one of many benefits of being a big woman: when I stopped dieting, I gained a bustline!

Robert Frost said, "A person will sometimes devote all his life to the development of one part of his body...the wishbone." Unfortunately, we want it both ways: tiny waist, no hips, large breasts. That's strictly glossy magazine stuff. In my whole lifetime, I have met perhaps five women who came by that combination naturally. (They, of course, hated their hair.)

That same year, 1989, another 48,000 people wanted their tummies tucked (15% were under eighteen years old — how flabby could an eighteen-year-old tummy be? — and 23% were men).

Harder to believe: 10,000 folks received fat injections,[4] a concept that escapes me completely!

Has it really come to this? Have we allowed ourselves to be turned into objects with removable, changeable parts? Are our bodies construction zones in various stages of repair, with some parts slated for demolition?

Whatever happened to the psalmist's assurance that we are "fearfully and wonderfully made?"[5]

When we look in the mirror, most of us see double chins, lines, wrinkles, blemishes, crow's feet, bags under our eyes, figure "flaws" — the list goes on and on. That's because we seldom look in a mirror unless we are looking for potential problems.

"Does my hair look okay?"

"Do I need more lipstick?"

"Is my slip showing?"

"Do I look fat in this dress?"

No wonder we find things that need fixing.

When I look in the mirror, I simply see a woman: unique, created by God, the only one quite like her. She is not "better than" or "worse than" or in need of an overhaul. She is definitely happy. (And yes, sometimes my slip is showing, too, but that's very fixable.)

When I look at you, sitting out there in the third row at one of my presentations; when I see your upturned face, full of life, ready to laugh, I do not see wrinkles, blemishes or double chins. I do not see "figure flaws." I see a beautiful woman. I see a woman who is radiant, alive, willing to learn, ready to grow, expectant, laughing and anxious to embrace all that life has to offer. You are something else!

That's not me, you may say. I'm not in your third row, I'm here at home and I'm miserable and I hate my lumpy body and radiant is not what I feel.

Understood.

But what I'm talking about transcends feelings and moves into the realm of faith in order to become fact. That radiant, alive woman is in you, even if you can't see her yet. She was in me for thirty years before I realized it, and she is in you now. And she wants out!

I don't believe for one minute that there is a THIN person trapped inside you, as our fable says, waving frantically to get out. But I do believe there is a BEAUTIFUL you trapped inside, one who was created in the image of God. He is all things beautiful, and He created and defined beauty in our world.

Surely He didn't make lovely butterflies, exquisite flowers and gorgeous sunsets, and leave out womankind, the crown of His creation?

When we stop listening to what Madison Avenue and Hollywood tell us is beautiful, and start listening to our hearts, they will not steer us wrong.

Even though we may never look like the ultra-thin models or movie stars (only 5% of us have the physiology to do so), they, poor things, will never get to look like *us*!

Look around you. Women come in all shapes and sizes, large and small, short and tall. In every home, in every workplace, in every social group, in every church, there are as many different sizes, shapes and personalities as there are women.

Thank goodness! If we all looked like Cindy Crawford, she would be out of work and the entire diet and fitness industry would collapse. (What a shame.)

Each of us is different, and those differences are good.

The Audience Speaks

When I invited audience members to be part of *"One Size Fits All" and Other Fables*, I was often surprised at who came forward to fill out my survey, because some of these women were downright thin!

My only requirement was that they be willing to share their thoughts about body confidence, especially if they were having some sort of struggle going on in their lives with weight, dieting, or body image.

I believe for every woman brave enough to step forward, ten more were thinking, "I really ought to fill out that questionnaire too!"

That means this survey can hardly be considered a scientific sampling of American women. But when it comes to speaking from the heart, these women represent us very well.

They come from all walks of life—administrators to x-ray technicians—and all stages of maturity. When they're not working or mothering, these women are busy having *fun*. Their social and leisure pursuits include everything from rollerblading to quilting to sailing to writing poetry. Once again, we are *different*; there are no stereotypes here and many surprises.

Our Above-Average Bodies

The biggest surprise was this: the average dress size turned out to be 18.35! (Does Lane Bryant carry that one?) That's much higher than the size 6 beauty contestant.

DRESS SIZES	% of those surveyed	AGE RANGES	% of those surveyed
Size 4	1%		
Size 6	4%	18–24	3%
Size 8	4%		
Size 10	5%	25–34	21%
Size 12	8%		
Size 14	6 %	35–44	43%
Size 16	11%		
Size 18	11%	45–54	23%
Size 20	14%		
Size 22	11%	55–64	8%
Size 24	10%		
Size 26	8%	65+	2%
Size 28	3%		
Size 30	1%		
Size 32	2%		
Size 34	1%		

As you can see, 72% of us wear clothing in sizes 16+, which means even the smallest town in America *should* have a decent store that features those sizes, though many don't. I was surprised to find such a large jump in percentages from size 14 to size 16 — almost double!

If you've ever felt like you were the only woman who wears a size 20, as you can see, you have lots of company. That was the most popular dress size among these many women.

200+ Women, 200+ Pages of Hope

Each woman's state of residence appears next to her name throughout the book. We have an excellent representation, with only thirteen states missing: Alaska, Delaware, Maine, Maryland, Mississippi, Montana, Nevada, New Mexico, North Dakota, Rhode Island, Vermont, West Virginia and Wyoming.

If your state is among these, why not write me and request a survey? I'll send one to you, no charge of course. When you fill it out and send it back, then I'll know what a woman from your area thinks and feels about this subject.

The most revealing question I asked women was this: "What do you hope *'One Size Fits All' and Other Fables* will include?"

Liz — you've got your job cut out for you. I've read many books about large sizes. I think yours would be a winner if it appealed more to the "normal" size audience.

Melissa from Ohio

Here's what's interesting: the "normal size" these days is actually size 12–14. And our survey respondents averaged a size 18! This book is really for every woman who has ever struggled with her body image (about 95% of us!), and should be especially encouraging for the woman who wears a size 16+.

Make me see that we're all really alike — just different sizes. Make me laugh and be more comfortable with myself. I realize size 16 isn't that large, but everyone else seems to either be a size 10 or a size 20, and I'm heading upward!

Jan from Indiana

Those of us who've either visited or resided at size 16 know just what she means. It does feel like a not-quite-big, not-quite-small size. Since many dress stores carry only up to size 14, and shops for larger women often begin at 18W, it can be tricky. Whether you go up or down, though, you'll still be you . . . which is pretty terrific!

Give us a framework for re-thinking "same size" mentality.
Carla from New Hampshire

I love the words "re-thinking" and "mentality." The mind is indeed where the changepoint occurs. I'm into "brain washing," myself: wash out the old, pour in the new!

I wish you could give a message to those who have "fatphobia."
However, my guess is that only those with some extra weight will
really read and enjoy the book.
Kitty from Kentucky

Take heart! Everyone will read this book (well, at least everyone in my extended family, and forty-some people is a start!). As our surveys indicate and our own ears tell us, the majority of American women think they are overweight.

We're All In This Together

Almost a decade ago, Dr. Susan Wooley, co-director of an eating disorder clinic at the University of Cincinnati Medical College, conducted a well-known survey of 33,000 women for *GLAMOUR* magazine. She discovered that 75% of these women considered themselves overweight. Seventy-five percent! Only 25% actually were above the desired weight according to insurance charts; 25% were at just the right weight; and another 25% were underweight.[6] For all these women, and the people who love them, *"One Size Fits All" and Other Fables* will have some words of wisdom and hope.

I love to read books which are meant to make me laugh and think.
Yes, I would like to lose some weight, but I need to understand I
will never be a size 8 and I should be happy with a size 14 or 16
as long as I'm healthy. Encourage me to take care of myself—
exercise, watch fat intake, but be happy with my size.
Barbara from Kentucky

Encouragement is my favorite task! Because it drains our energy and self-esteem, I'd also like to help women handle that constant nagging feeling of "I ought to be on a diet."

The process that has made sense for me is this: be happy with my size, as is. Genuinely happy. Then, exercise because I enjoy how it makes me feel, because I love doing it. Finally, moderate fats and sugars because I want to take good care of the body God has loaned me, not because I want to lose weight. That's the road to acceptance *and* health.

> *Help alleviate the focus on tiny, small, thin and help me genuinely believe, "It's what's inside that counts!"*
>
> Marlene from Washington

What's inside not only counts, it's the only part of us that's eternal. Most of us don't need a face-lift just a faith lift!

> *People think that only folks with lots of extra weight worry about eating issues and body image. I'm not real overweight by any means but I have a perfectionist ideal that I probably got from my mother. I would be pleased if you'd address the psychological dynamics of getting happy with your body as it is, rather than yearning for an ideal that is so hard to maintain.*
>
> Cindy from Illinois

I am not a psychologist, but I do know something about "getting happy," and a whole lot about dealing with perfectionism. Of this I'm sure: they are not related! A wise soul once said, "Happiness is not in things, it is in us."

> *As self-esteem boosters for more-than-perfect-size women, we need to let all people know that larger women do well at jobs, are loved, have good sex lives, dress attractively, are physically active — that we're just like everyone else, only more so!*
>
> Catherine from Kentucky

I love her "only more so" outlook! Here's another perspective:

> *Everyone thinks I have a great personality, but inside I am very unhappy. I wish my size didn't bother me — but it does. I hope your book will give me some answers to myself.*
>
> Nancy from Indiana

She is not alone. Some days I don't like my body either. But there were also days I didn't like what I saw in the mirror when I wore a size 10. (That's probably because there was a larger person trapped inside me, trying to get out!)

Time for a Change

Psychology Today conducted a survey of 30,000 men and women, asking them, "How do you feel about your appearance?"

In 1972, 25% of the women said they were dissatisfied with how they looked. In 1985, 38% of the women said they were unhappy with their appearance. At this rate, by the year 2005, each of us will be 100% miserable with our appearance!

> *Wouldn't it be wonderful if, after reading your book, women could look in a mirror and celebrate themselves for who they are, not for what they weigh?*
>
> Jude from South Dakota

In a word, Jude . . . yes!

My heart's desire would be for women of all shapes and sizes to live authentically, to stop making excuses or apologies, to do away with blaming others or hating ourselves because of our bodies. We can never expect others to accept who we are until *we* accept who we are.

Let me close this chapter with a true confession. I spent ten years on the radio as an on-air personality; a disc jockey, if you will. Although I couldn't see my audience, I could chat with them on the phone, meet them in person, and get some feedback along the way.

Sometimes they offered encouraging words: "I love your radio show!" And sometimes their words were hurtful: "I never dreamed you'd be overweight!" Ouch. But at least they were honest with me, and I could connect with them in some manner, face to face or by phone.

When I became a professional speaker in 1987, I found out that I loved public speaking even more than working in a radio studio. Now, with a live, in-the-flesh audience, I see their reactions immediately: laughter, surprise, nods, applause, even tears. I feel free to share very openly with them, knowing I can adapt my message to suit each situation.

But this writing thing, this nakedness on paper, without being able to watch your eyes, sense your mood, or hear your laughter — this is much scarier than standing in front of thousands of people. Writing about something as personal, and as life-changing, as the need for women to get off the diet treadmill is risky. It's not a popular view (yet), nor an easy one to live out.

My own body confidence waivers on occasion (daily!), and so it's a constant challenge to "walk my talk." Just knowing you're still with me means everything.

Begin Building Body Confidence Today

1. Do something nice for your body. Rub in a fragrant lotion from head to toe, or give yourself a facial. Take your time. You are worth it.

2. Put on your favorite outfit, head to toe. Wear make-up if you choose, and style your hair the way you like it. Now, stand in front of a full-length mirror, smile and say "Hello, Gorgeous!" Take an inventory of your favorite physical attributes. Find at least twenty.

3. Spend ten minutes reading something that feeds your soul. A book of poetry, a literary classic, whatever will inspire you. I love the book of Proverbs, which includes this verse: "Say to wisdom, 'You are my sister,'/And call understanding your nearest kin."[7]

❤ A Women's Health Educator Speaks . . .

Lynette Neal has been a women's health educator for more than twenty years. Her current position at Providence Milwaukie Hospital in Oregon puts her in touch with women of all shapes, sizes and levels of health.

Liz: What do you see as the most significant problem for women concerning size?

Lynette: *We have unrealistic expectations and will only be satisfied with big results. We don't seem willing to settle for a healthy middle ground. It's a perfectionist, all-or-nothing attitude that says only thin counts, and unless a diet and exercise program can guarantee us a thin body, it isn't worth it.*

Liz: What can a woman who wants to be healthier do?

Lynette: *She needs to really value herself enough to take care of herself. I don't mean lose weight. I mean get enough sleep, take time to relax, maybe get a massage, walk regularly, choose the healthiest foods she can just because they are good for her, not because she will be thinner. Our goals need to change, as well as the motivations behind them.*

Liz: What attitudes do you think need changing?

Lynette: *Women do an incredible amount of self-talking. For larger women, most of it is negative self-talk. That needs to change. And, we need to stop negating everything about our worth simply because of body size. We also need to recognize our individual strengths and build on those instead of focusing on our weaknesses.*

Liz: As a large and lovely woman, you have come to such a place of peace about this issue. What's the key?

Lynette: *Confidence. Knowing that I have value, that I make a contribution to my workplace, my family, my community.*

Liz: What other observations would you offer?

Lynette: *Large women do not allow thin women to have problems. When we see a woman with a nice figure who is complaining about her job or her marriage or whatever, we think, "Gee, you shouldn't be having any problems, look how thin you are." Body size has nothing to do with happiness, unless we erroneously choose to define it that way.*

Liz: Change is so difficult. Where do we start?

Lynette: *Ask yourself this question: "If I can't make a big change, can I make a little one? What one small step toward health could I take?"*

Liz: Why is it taking so long for women to embrace this new, healthier way of thinking?

Lynette: *Most of what we're hearing from size-acceptance advocates is fueled by anger, and is too strident, too militant to appeal to the general population of large women. Therefore, we may discount the good information they are advocating. All of us need to get to a place where big is neither better nor worse, it just is.*

"All It Takes Is a Little Willpower"

This is the fable that cuts to the quick: All it takes to lose weight, stop eating junk food, and stick to a diet is "a little willpower." The late comedienne Totie Fields said it best: "I've been on a diet for two weeks, and all I've lost is two weeks."

We repeat to ourselves over and over: "If I just had more discipline." Never mind that we went to night school while working full time, which took discipline. So what if we get our kids on the school bus every day right on time (well, almost), which takes incredible planning and execution. Forget that we saved hundreds of dollars to buy a house, said "no" to drugs, said "yes" to daily vitamins. As soon as we see that number on the scale, that flesh under our chin, we say, "I have NO willpower!" And so we begin a diet. Oh, do we feel in control of things now! Look out world; I am following this thing to the letter. Four ounces of chicken, no skin, no gravy. No flavor, either, but look at all this willpower!

Why Diets Are Disastrous

The weight loss industry smacks its corporate lips when we get a shot of willpower coursing through our veins. We're talking about those folks who give us lo-cal products, diet books and videos, fitness clubs and weight loss centers. People who benefit when our willpower weakens. It's big business in more ways than one.

In 1990, the diet industry rang up $30.2 billion in sales revenue. We bought more than $13 billion worth of diet soda alone! We spent another $3.5 billion on weight loss centers and hospital-based programs.[1] If we ever figured out how much money we've spent in our lifetime in the name of losing weight, it would probably add up to a few thousand dollars an ounce.

Today, or any day, thirty million American women are on diets of one kind or another.[2] One woman's response to just the word "diet" is telling:

> *High level of effort — low payoff. Dangerous marketing ploy — abusive to women!*
>
> Donna from Kentucky

I remember two of the early diet potions from my childhood. First there was Ayds, a chewy candy-like product that was supposed to control your appetite. It was big in the early 50's, but persisted for years. Remember the full-page ads and before and after photos? I was hypnotized by them.

Then there was Metrecal, which showed up on grocery store shelves in 1959. As is usually the case, this fad was all the rage for about two years, then faded into obscurity.[3] Even so, I can still see the television commercials featuring the Metrecal for Lunch Bunch dancing before my eyes. I was six.

"Go Where?"

Well-meaning friends and family often say, "You should go to such-and-such diet group!" There are plenty to choose from. Many of the weight-loss support groups we know today got their start around the same time. TOPS was first in 1948,[4] then Overeaters Anonymous in 1960, Weight Watchers in 1963, Diet Control Center in 1968 and so on.[5] No wonder we grew up thinking that dieting was the American way of life. According to a poll published in *USA Today*, 65% of Americans go on a diet each year. More than half of those diets only last thirty days. (Can you say "yo-yo?")

I remember my first trip to a diet organization, in 1976. (Just for the record, I weighed 150, but was still shooting for that elusive 128.)

They gave us a sheet of paper with a brick wall drawn on it. The idea was simple: for each hour that you were "legal" (don't you love that one?), you could fill in one of the bricks. Twenty-four bricks for each day, 168 bricks for each week. A brick wall between you and no willpower.

For those of us striving for perfection in our dieting, this brick wall was the ideal way to measure just how well our willpower was holding up. One tiny crumb of chocolate cake and — horrors! — an empty brick.

Even if 167 hours of my week were brimming with willpower, there was always that one empty brick staring me in the face, shouting out the terrible truth: "You just don't have enough self-control!"

No one else ever sees the brick walls we run into trying to lose weight, but it humiliates us just the same. We suffer defeat in silence, alone. We wouldn't dare tell someone else that we think this dieting thing is impossible, because we know what would be written all over their faces: "She has no willpower." So we conclude that everyone else has willpower except us.

Tuesday Night Meetings

For many of us, our mainstay was Weight Watchers. The food plans were fairly healthy, the classes upbeat, the cost was decidedly less than other options. Just one little problem...

> *I can learn to eat and lose weight successfully with Weight Watchers and I have lost 45–50 pounds several times. I've always gained it back, though.*
>
> Phyllis from Tennessee

Interesting how we define "losing weight successfully." Even the most "sensible" diet isn't much like our normal eating pattern. When we return to that pattern, the weight returns too. We sign up again, thinking, "this will be the time..."

In her book *Breaking All the Rules*, Nancy Roberts explains that the reason she kept going back to Weight Watchers again and again was because "it allows people already obsessed with food to develop, enhance and perfect that obsession." It was in fact a "winning combination of group dynamics and sanctioned obsession."[6]

How well I remember those weekly weigh-ins. Women lined up by the dozens to pay someone nine dollars for the worst news of their week. We could have found this out for free in our own bathrooms. But no, we wanted a public flogging. We wanted to be shamed into success, or have the chance to gloat if we'd had a good week.

If you've never been to such a meeting, let me give you the ground rules. At least 99% of the attendees are women. Weigh-in came right after pay-in, and was preceded by one last trip to the potty (and a "pray-in!"). Night meetings were hard for most of us because they meant an entire day of not eating. No wonder we headed for the nearest restaurant when the meeting was over!

Some people wore the same dress week after week, the flimsiest thing they owned, even in the dead of winter. Shoes always came off first — it helped to wear slip-on flats. I watched women linger at the back of the line while they unhooked belts, slipped off jackets, pulled off sweaters, the works.

One night, I stood behind a woman who had obviously had a bad week. As she got closer to the scale, sweat started popping out in little beads on her forehead. She slipped off her earrings, then her watch, then a little skinny gold necklace, two bracelets and her wedding band. (Her wedding band? How much could that weigh?) She dropped them all in her blouse pocket and got on the scale.

Poor dear. I didn't have the heart to tell her why this didn't help, especially when she gained four and a half pounds. The least I could have done was offered to hold her jewelry.

We'd Rather Die Than Diet

I asked women to tell me on the surveys "What thoughts or experiences come to mind when you think of the word 'diet'?" I was amazed to read over and over, in other women's handwriting, the exact same things I have often felt.

> *I just get a very tired feeling. A sad, frustrated, and sort of rebellious feeling. I've been on diets that took the weight off, then it came back and brought along "friends."*
>
> Pat from Wisconsin

Like the old saying goes, sometimes we get "sick and tired" of being "thick and tired." The word "frustrated" showed up on lots of surveys too.

Agony, futility, frustration, hunger, depression, loss of self-esteem.
                                                    Ada from California

Dieting also brings to mind a very specific menu. Barbara from Kentucky admits, "I hate tuna fish and I'm tired to tears of salad." Mary from Pennsylvania has an even more narrow food plan. "Dieting means you're not allowed to eat anything good."

When it comes to willpower, it seems that some people need it and others don't. Now that's not fair!

Our two sons, ages twenty-two and twenty-five, have moved back home after college graduation. They're slim and trim and can eat anything. So I catch myself thinking how fortunate they are to be able to do that.
                                                    Dorothy from Kentucky

Dorothy has hit on something there. Her sons "eat anything." In other words, they have no willpower. But it doesn't matter, because they are slim. They are the fortunate ones.

But the Dorothys of the world are expected to come up with loads of willpower simply because they are *not* "slim and trim." H-m-m.

Here's a similar story:

Dieting is a lifetime commitment I just can't handle. I wish I could control my eating like my sixteen-year-old daughter who's 5'7" and size 3.
                                                    Janet from Kentucky

Again, here's a comparison of our own bodies at age forty-plus to those of our children who have faster metabolic rates and often higher activity levels. They seldom have to worry about groceries, cooking or clean-up, and they've yet to experience the effects of aging and gravity, not to mention childbirth or decades of diet attempts.

"Won't" Power

Willpower concerning food can lead to serious problems. For many of us, exerting power over our eating habits can produce an obsessive need to control food intake which can lead to eating disorders such as anorexia nervosa and bulimia. In other words, willpower is not always a good thing.

Susan Kano, in her outstanding book, *Making Peace with Food*, lists some of the symptoms of anorexia nervosa, bulimia and chronic dieting. They include:

1. Preoccupation with dietary control; chronic attempts to eat less
2. Preoccupation with eating
3. Preoccupation with thinness/fatness and distorted body image[7]

As you can see, the common word is "preoccupation." Many women have dieted, have thought about the next meal, have wanted to lose 10 pounds. The key here is realizing how *much* those things occupy your mind, time, and activities. Willpower taken to the extreme is no power at all.

The truth is, nobody I've ever met (and liked) had endless willpower. Ugh! Who wants to hang around somebody who never bends her will to meet another's need, who never changes her mind, who never gives in to the desire of her heart? Boring!

A funny fellow named Steve Burns has the perfect solution: "Eat as much as you like — just don't swallow it." Of course, we're awfully hard on ourselves when we do swallow it.

I have no willpower. My "magic number" is 140, and I weigh 148. I have never been able to lose more than two pounds and it lasts a couple days!

Barbara from Ohio

Many of us identify with the "magic number" problem. We think only perfect counts, and perfect is always unattainable. Otherwise it wouldn't be perfect!

The Dreaded Treadmill

Which brings up another word that often surfaces when women talk about dieting. It's a word we repeat like a mantra, the most negative, defeating, discouraging word in American English: failure. It comes from a Latin word meaning, "to disappoint." And when we fail, the person we disappoint most is ourselves.

Pain, punishment, failure, deprived. You are on a merry-go-round of failure and you can't get off!

Martha from Ohio

There's that diet treadmill that just keeps going round and round.

Here we go again! Defeat. "Why couldn't I have kept it off?" I wonder how I could be so stupid to fall off the wagon so many times!

Peg from Kentucky

We can all identify with her frustration, even though we know "stupidity" has nothing to do with it. The problem isn't us, it's the "wagon!"

The embarrassment of gaining back lost weight cannot be understood except by someone who has been there. (I have been there!) People do a double-take when they see you and say things like, "I didn't recognize you. Have you cut your hair?" Or they just stutter, speechless. It's easy to beat yourself up when that happens.

For many of us "yo-yo's," we are aware even at the start of Diet #84 that there will be a Diet #85 someday.

Kind of like planned obsolescence — failure is programmed in at the start. When I hear about someone on or starting a diet I feel sorry for the pain and failure they are in for.

Mary Jane from Kentucky

I feel sorry for them, too, although what most just-starting dieters want us to feel is happy for them.

I've been on and off diets — hoping each one would be "IT." It is my biggest problem.

Monica from Ohio

This breaks my heart, maybe because it sounds like the old me talking. Have you ever felt like your weight was your "biggest problem?" When I think of the energy and angst we have spent on this single, narrow area of our lives it truly makes my heart ache.

Medically Supervised Failure

The diets we are willing to endure are endless in their variety, and in their ability to inflict pain.

I once was put on Dexedrine by my doctor. I went fishing with my son. He wanted to go in and get some lunch. I kept saying "just one more worm." I didn't know then that this was what we call "speed" now.

Nora from Ohio

Many of us have used pots of strong black coffee, to try and accomplish the same thing. The following story describes an experience common to many of us "diet warriors" who have tried everything.

They charged an arm and a leg for required blood work ($160), you had to pay an initial fee of $99 for registration, and after my second visit they said I needed to purchase the "maintenance package" in advance for $159. They were unprofessional, I never saw a doctor, and the nurse told me she was only part-time. They also weighed me on a different scale each of the four times I went before I became totally disgusted. I began to feel like a piece of meat being inspected and scolded or praised depending on how my week went.

Vicky Lynn from Ohio

There are plenty more tales where those came from:

I've tried Weight Watchers several times, Take Off Pounds Sensibly, Overeaters Anonymous, American Weight Loss (developed fissures), acupuncture, shots of hormone from the urine of a pregnant cow, Dr. Stillman's Diet (by the seventh day, I was ready to shoot him too!). In recent years, I have learned to be comfortable with myself—no more diets.

Joyce from Virginia

Facing the Bathroom Scale

Those of us who diet at home can be just as ritualistic as "professional dieters." Some women weigh themselves three, four, five times a day. Only one time counts, though, and that's the weigh-in that takes place first thing in the morning.

And, I mean *first* thing: right after a trip to the bathroom, and right before coffee. It's that little "window of opportunity," the thinnest moment in a woman's day.

Fanatics take a shower first to wash off all that heavy dirt. The next step, by necessity, is blow-drying your hair to get out all those pounds of water. Now you approach the scale, totally nude, completely empty, your most svelte self. You check the "0" setting. If the needle is directly over the "0," that's good. If it's ever so slightly to the left, that's even better. Next, you step on the scale, and start moving around. Where is that light spot? Ah. Finally, the last two steps that women of all sizes take: we exhale (air must weigh something), and then we pull in our tummies, the theory being that if you can't see it, it won't weigh anything. (Or, for some of us, so we can see the numbers!)

If we've lost a pound, we celebrate and eat something. If we've had a gain, we console ourselves and eat something. That's dieting the American weigh.

Some of My Best Friends Are Yo-Yo's

When someone tells me they've lost such-and-such pounds on a diet, my next question is always, "How long have you kept it off?" The effectiveness of any weight loss program should be determined by longevity, not how much we can lose or how fast we can lose it. By that measure, the liquid diets would fare pretty well.

Oprah Winfrey showed us on national television how easy it is to lose 67 pounds, and how even easier it is to gain it back.

Read my lips: *She* did not fail! The *diet* failed her!

Oprah has been, and continues to be, a wonderful role model for all women, but especially for the plus-size woman. She dealt a crushing blow to the liquid diet craze, not just for OptiFast, but for all the hospital and physician-based programs, as well as the across-the-counter versions. According to the *Wall Street Journal*, by September 1992, Ultra Slim-Fast sales were down 45% from the year earlier. DynaTrim sales were down 65%. People were discovering what Oprah already knew: Very low calorie diets don't work.

Naturally, any weight loss organization will tell you about their success stories. There are always a few people willing to forgo health and self-acceptance in the name of thinness. But the research statistics released in April 1992 by the National Institute of Health are not pretty: 90–95% of those who lose weight through a low calorie diet *will* gain back most of their weight within two years, and *all* of it within five years.[8] That puts the success rate at about 7%. One five-year study in Denmark logged only a 3% success rate.[9]

The insurance world would call that a poor risk. At the track, it would be a long shot. In medicine, it might be called malpractice.

When I dropped three dress sizes through strict dieting in 1982, I landed at a nice size 10-12, 160 pounds. Was I happy with that? Naturally not, it still sounded fat. It looked mighty slim, but it sounded fat. By then, I had raised my goal weight to a more "reasonable" 135. Forget the elusive 128; now, I was shooting for 135. At 5'9". Sure.

The scale never budged. A pound or two, but mostly 160, 161, 159, 162, 160, for two full years of dieting. I still have the weigh-in cards to prove it. If I was down a half-pound, I drew a smiley face. Good girl. When the scale crept up 3/4 of a pound, I made a firm red line, like I used to make in league bowling when I wasn't doing well and wanted to tell myself, "I'm starting over as of right here."

I kept that weight off very simply: I ate almost nothing. One meal a day, maybe two. Constant weigh-ins. I had a red patent leather belt from my "fat" days that I would try on as a reminder of where my waist would return to if I wasn't careful.

Two solid years of being legal, good, and righteous. Make that self-righteous. I was convinced if I could do this, anyone could. Weight was all a matter of willpower, I thought, and women who were fat ate too much. Period.

Oh, Lizzie. I was only delaying the inevitable. In the spring of 1984 I finally wearied of toting my plastic scale with me everywhere, of visualizing a pack of playing cards to measure a chicken breast, of eating everything with artificial sweetener and imitation butter. I tired of trying to get to 135. Heck, I'd even raised my goal to 145 by then, the weight I'd weighed all through high school, when 145 seemed fat to me.

Dr. Kathy Johnson, a New York psychiatrist, believes that some women "need a number, an outside source, to validate that they're doing okay."[10] I was not doing okay, because my scale was not telling me what I wanted to hear.

When I went back to normal eating — and I do mean normal, not pigging out, not stuffing my face, not three junk food meals a day — I gained back my weight at a steady one pound per week. That train chugged down the track way past the point where I had started my diet two years earlier.

Was my diet a success? I think not. Most research on yo-yo dieting now concludes that I would have been better off if I had never dieted at all. As Dr. Adriane Fugh-Berman of the National Women's Health Network says, "Yo-yo dieting is for yo-yos."[11]

Diet Defined

To be truly successful, a diet would:

1. Contain easily available, naturally healthy foods
2. Be served in quantities sufficient for your body's needs and your appetite's satisfaction
3. Produce a high level of pleasure, good for a lifetime of eating

If you have shared anything remotely like my own experiences, chances are good that you did not fail your diet, your diet failed you. Especially if it:

1. Consisted of expensive, chemical-laden substitute foods
2. Was served in tiny quantities sufficient for the body and appetite of a field mouse
3. Produced no level of pleasure whatsoever (Art Buchwald said of liquid diets, "The powder is mixed with water and tastes exactly like powder mixed with water.")

That's not a diet, that's purgatory. Or worse. Dolores hit the nail on the head when she defined the word "diet":

Deprivation, denial, punishment, sentencing, lack of trust, lack of freedom, lack of choice, embarrassment, explaining why I'm not eating, people saying "Oh, good . . ."
                                                    Dolores from New York

My hat is off to women who have successfully removed the word D-I-E-T from their vocabularies:

That is a four-letter word and we don't talk like that in our house.
                                                    Gwyn from Ohio

How exciting that she may also have a family who is learning about the ill effects of dieting. Many young girls are getting interested in dieting as early as age eight. They need a mom with compassionate concern to teach them that young girls should never diet.

> *[Dieting] doesn't work and it is not a major religion! Nor does it make you superior if you succeed.*
>
> Diana from Kentucky

I was the queen of self-righteousness when I lost weight. It was disgusting really, very us versus them in nature. I honestly thought that anyone who put their mind to it could do it. It was so simple, I reasoned. Just eat less and exercise more. Anybody who wasn't successful with this easy plan was ... was ... was ... uh ... normal. (Finally, I figured that out!)

> *A diet is something you do to war criminals while you keep them in bamboo cells.*
>
> Janet from Virginia

Sounds like the bread-and-water diet, one of civilization's oldest. We all know the word "diet" just means the food you eat, but in the last century it has come to carry a much more definitive, and more negative, connotation.

> *The word "diet" is like the word "problem." It doesn't belong in the English language. I consider myself to have "challenges and opportunities" only!*
>
> Vicki from Wisconsin

Getting Off the Diet Treadmill

When I talk about doing away with dieting, some women get almost fearful looks on their faces. If you've dieted off and on much of your life, the thought of never doing it again *is* scary.

> *I have retrained myself not to diet, but to make conscious decisions about what I put in my mouth. Diets don't work!*
>
> Lisa from Illinois

Note that this was a deliberate move away from the dreaded "D" word. Decisions, yes; dieting, no.

I have finally reached a point of being good to my body, nutritionally, emotionally and physically.
                                                    LaDonna from Oregon

This is a woman who has learned to properly care about and for herself. Here are some specific suggestions for doing that:

Eat nutritionally and keep fats to a minimum. Balance proteins and carbohydrates and give your body enough water to allow natural body function.
                                                    Lauren from Pennsylvania

Then, there's my favorite way to reduce:

Just "diet" from negative people, and you'll be happy!
                                                    Maria from Arizona

I heard from an eighteen-year-old reader of *Big Beautiful Woman* magazine who shared her journey to self-acceptance:

To me, size isn't everything. Three years ago I wouldn't say that. Now some of my friends tell me that they wish they were as comfortable with their bodies as I am with mine.
                                                    Carly from Missouri

How wonderful that she learned that lesson at such a young age. Some of us take a little longer, but we can get there. Elaine was released out of diet purgatory by (surprise! surprise!) her doctor:

One day he said to me, "When are you going to realize you're always going to be like this and quit worrying about it. You're healthy and your husband loves you—so quit worrying!" That freed me, and I don't diet and I'm still healthy!
                                                    Elaine from Ohio

The key words are: "happy" and "healthy." We must focus the power of our will toward achieving those two important goals —

genuine health, genuine happiness — and sell those food scales and bathroom scales at our next yard sale.

Many women are not willing to take such steps because they see it as "giving up." This is not giving up! It is getting off the diet treadmill and "getting on" with a healthier approach to eating, to movement, to life. It is also doing away with denial, and embracing reality with a grateful heart.

Just think: we might find out what it's like to live that "normal" life we've often longed for, without worrying about what we'll be having (or *not* having) for lunch!

Begin Building Body Confidence Today

1. Banish the word "diet" from your vocabulary. Get rid of "reducing," "weight loss" and "willpower" while you're at it. (If it's any consolation, these terms are *not* in the Bible!)

2. Throw out your bathroom scale, calorie counting guides, and fad diet books. Instead buy one good "healthy eating" cookbook. No food plans allowed!

3. If your friends start talking about diets, change the subject. If they start criticizing you or anyone else for gaining weight, change friends!

❤ A Nurse Speaks . . .

Anne Khol, N.D., R.N., has a bachelor's degree in psychology from Michigan State University and a doctorate of nursing from Case Western Reserve University in Cleveland. She is currently director of community health education for Sparrow Hospital in Lansing, Michigan.

Liz: Weight gain among women is on the way up. Why?

Anne: *Two reasons: Women are less active. The day-to-day work that we do requires much less physical activity than, say, a hundred years ago. We used to beat our rugs; now we have a high-powered vacuum. We used to knead bread; now we use bread machines (or we buy it at the store). We are not working our large muscle groups all day long, and we lead far more sedentary lives.*

The second reason is: The fashion industry has chosen to use very tall, thin models. This keeps American women constantly dieting to try and fit those clothes. We lose weight, we buy new clothes. We gain the weight back, we buy new clothes. By the time we lose again, the old clothes are out of style, so we buy new clothes. Madison Avenue loves yo-yos!

Liz: What's the problem with dieting?

Anne: *Research keeps telling us that dieting makes you fatter. Dieting itself is the problem. When you think diet, you think about calorie restriction, unfortunately. Not healthy eating, just less eating. Such dieting means you lose lean body weight, you lose muscle, and so your metabolic rate slows down. If you are an educated person in this regard, you will never "diet."*

Liz: You mean it takes more than "willpower?"

Anne: *[Laughs] All the "will" in the world can't fight your body's natural tendencies! Our bodies are designed to protect us from starvation, so calorie reduction will make the body store fat, not burn it. Eating less food tampers with the body's natural regulator, and we are depriving ourselves of what we really want and need to eat.*

Liz: How can we attune ourselves to our bodies' needs?

Anne: *We have to make a conscious effort to re-educate ourselves. The truth is, when we crave chocolates or sweets, our body is asking for more complex carbohydrates — bread, pasta, potatoes. By paying attention to hunger cravings, giving your body real food packed with vitamins, minerals and complex carbohydrates, over time you can become more discerning, as well as genuinely satisfied. It's also important to drink enough fluids. Your body needs at least 64 ounces (8 glasses) of liquids a day to replenish what your body uses — more if you exercise. If we don't provide liquid nourishment, our bodies will signal for more food to meet that need. We are reaching for food when what our body wants is water!*

Liz: Is food the real issue?

Anne: *No. Exercise is the real issue. Not only does it raise the metabolic rate, it improves your mood and cognitive processes, helps you handle stress and enhances how you feel about yourself. It improves muscle tone and skin tone too! Understand that basic changes in metabolic rate through exercise take more than a year. But the benefits begin immediately.*

Liz: You are certainly a well-educated, successful woman who also happens to be big and beautiful. What are your tips for success?

Anne: *Recognize your unique skills and abilities, and make them known. Don't settle for less. And, dress the part! Put on makeup, spend some time on your appearance. Thin women have to do this, too, so good grooming isn't limited to large women.*

Liz: As a Christian, do you think size is a spiritual issue?

Anne: *To me, it's a question of stewardship. I think it is wrong to diet, and to do so harms our bodies. When the Bible talks about the body being God's temple, I don't think it means,*

"Watch your weight!" I believe it means watch what you are putting into your body — is it healthy or not? And, do you exercise it? God commanded Adam to work by the sweat of his brow. [Laughing] Maybe we need to sweat more!

"You're Just Big Boned"

Dem bones, dem bones, dem BIG bones. . . that's what the problem must be! I even had a doctor tell me that once: "Liz, you're not really fat, you're just big boned." Then, when he had to do a chest x-ray, he came out from behind the screen and said with a look of surprise, "You have small bones, Liz!"

I've known my bone size for years, because I can circle my wrist with my thumb and middle finger, one of the ways you measure how big your bones really are (or aren't!).

Of course, when I was growing up and looking at those insurance charts, I liked the ranges for "large-boned" people better! But the truth is, I inherited long, thin bones with plenty of cushion. That's how my family is built.

One Big Happy Family

I grew up in a large family, or as an only child, depending on how you view things. Most of my brothers and sisters had graduated and gone on to college by the time I was a preschooler. My five siblings are all between nine and nineteen years older than me. Imagine my parents' surprise when, three months before they both turned forty-three, along came this third little girl, a sixth child! Just for the record, I tipped the hospital scales at a nice, normal seven pounds, eight ounces.

The Amidons are, in the truest sense of the word, one big happy family. We're all tall, for starters. And, I don't think I'll be doing my dear brothers and sisters any disservice to say that we've all struggled with weighty issues over the years. I've probably done the yo-yo routine with more gusto, but we've all taken turns going up and down.

Here's the logical question: Am I large because I come from a family of larger people? If so, is it genetics? Lifestyle? Psychological makeup? Learned behavior? Something in the tap water?

In our surveys, 57% of us indicated we have at least one large parent, and 47% have a sibling that's our size (and remember, we received surveys from many smaller women too). If "big bones" run in your family, here are four possible explanations we hear from others (or say to ourselves). All four are grounded in fact, though all four may not fit your situation (or mine).

1. Your family's eating and exercise habits were poor.

Children do model their parents' behavior, as well as that of their older sisters and brothers. If indeed our food choices were unhealthy (and this is a big "if," but it's possible) and if exercise was not encouraged in the family, then this might be a legitimate contributing factor to our size.

Can we unlearn such things? It would be challenging, but yes, it could certainly be done.

2. You've dieted so much over the years that now your metabolic rate has been lowered.

Dieting patterns can be modeled too. My sisters and I were always going on one diet or another. Starvation seemed to work best. We each found our own favorite groups: Weight Watchers, Overeaters Anonymous, and Lean Line. For my sisters in the 50's and for me in the 60's, dieting was a way of life.

My yo-yo experiences have taken me farther both ways than either of my sisters, and although I'm the youngest, I'm also the largest. Have I just incurred more metabolic changes through severe dieting? Maybe.

Dr. Kelly Brownell from the University of Pennsylvania describes dieting-induced obesity:

> During each diet, lean body mass is lost, but is replaced with fat, as weight is regained. Fat tissue is metabolically less active, therefore the metabolic rate slows further. It takes longer to lose weight each time, and the weight is regained much faster.[1]

Sound familiar? I have often wondered what might have happened if I had quit dieting and focused on healthy, normal eating and exercise when I was back at 160 pounds.

It doesn't take a medical genius to see what happens around us every day: friends or family members go on diets, lose weight, gain it back, and are now ten pounds heavier than when they started. That is the precise path to "dieting-induced obesity."

3. *Family members share the same psychological weaknesses that lead to addictions, with food being the family "drug of choice."*

No doubt about it, we all like to eat. But, eating compulsively is something else again. Compulsive overeating means to eat without thinking about what we are consuming. We stuff food in quickly without really tasting it or even caring how much or even what it is we're eating. We are responding to *mouth* hunger instead of *stomach* hunger.

The feeling is loss of control. Not the rational kind, like when you're eating a brownie and telling yourself, "I really don't need this!" Compulsive eating happens outside of rational thought. You literally cannot stop yourself.

Listen carefully now: It's possible to be fat and not be a compulsive overeater. It's also possible to be of average weight and eat very compulsively. Many of us are made to feel that, if we are big, we must be compulsive overeaters. This is simply not always the case.

The common assumption is that all large people overeat from the time they get up until the time they go to bed. Not so! In study after study, research has shown that large people eat less food or equal amounts of food than thin people.

Nobody believes this, so I'll say it again: Ten out of eleven recently conducted research studies indicate that large people eat *smaller* portions and often *fewer* meals than thin people do. Yet when a large person sits in a restaurant eating a normal meal, people may stare, shake their heads and look disgusted. (This is not my imagination — ask any large person if they've had this experience.) A thin woman will seldom solicit a second glance from anyone, even if she's tearing into a gigantic banana split topped with six dips of ice cream!

I've often said to people, "Please spend a day with me and watch what I eat: three meals, few snacks, lots of fruit and other healthy choices." Their lips will say, "Really?" but their eyes say, "No way, Liz. You must eat a dozen doughnuts for breakfast!" Sorry, but not so.

The truth is I have inherited genes that control how my body processes food. Through regular exercise and normal, healthy eating, I may be able to improve that metabolic rate somewhat. But I was created to be a tall, full-bodied, light brown-haired, blue-eyed, long-legged, short-waisted woman.

Which brings us to the fourth possible reason why I come from a big happy family:

4. We are physiologically and genetically disposed to be bigger.

Statistics speak clearly to this. Children with one large parent have a 40% chance of being large. Having two large parents doubles that to an 80% chance of being large. A child with thin parents has only a 7% chance of being fat. Environment? Nope. A study of 540 adopted men and women found their weights most closely matched their biological, not their adoptive, parents.

Big Beautiful Woman magazine's recent health survey of hundreds of readers weighing 40 pounds or more over their range on the weight charts revealed this amazing statistic: 99% of them had one or two large-size parents! And 98% of them had one or two large-size grandparents![2] Those of us who've been saying, "It's all in the genes" now have further proof that it's not in our collective imagination. It's also worth noting that of those large parents, only 10% had high blood pressure, only 5% suffered from diabetes and a mere 3% suffered from heart disease.[3]

Let me demonstrate how much being "genetically disposed to be bigger" scares some people. In 1990, *NEWSWEEK* magazine reported that of two hundred New England couples who were surveyed concerning genetic tests during pregnancy, 11% of them said they would abort an unborn baby simply for being predisposed to obesity.[4]

When I share that statement with my audiences, they always gasp. Well they should.

I love my big, beautiful family and every gene they gave me. I'm so thankful my mother, at forty-three, took a chance for both of us and brought me into this world!

Like Mother, Like Daughter

One of the women who completed our survey told us she often heard this from her mother: "You have your great-grandmother's shape." Mom may be right! Look at your own family tree, then look in the mirror. When I stand nude in front of a full-length mirror (and I'll be honest, I don't ever do this for hours at a time), I see my mother's round tummy. I only had two children, and she had six, but that shape is very familiar. As we've heard and said many times, "A girl will look like her mother in twenty years."

In my case, since I favor my father physically, I also see him when I look in the mirror. Often, we're pleased with our heritage and with the family genes that go along with it:

I'm a big-boned German descendant. My lab values are normal, I walk when the weather is nice, I enjoy people and recognize that I'm a great wife, mother, and friend. I like living.
Marilyn from Missouri

What a sense of peace and balance she's come to! Some of us get mixed feelings when we see our family staring back at us in the mirror:

When my mom lost a lot of weight for health reasons, she gave me a lot of her clothes. When I put one dress on and looked in the mirror, I had turned into my mother! She is lovely, but I'm not ready to be her.
Sandy from Michigan

In her book *The Hungry Self*, Kim Chernin talks about daughters for whom "the act of eating will be fraught with peril. With every bite she has to fear that she may become what her mother has been."[5]

This issue of weight and family is a very sensitive one, especially between mothers and daughters. Sometimes the daughter wants her mom to feel better about herself:

> *I hope [you can] inspire my mother to accept herself for what she is and see that she is just great no matter what size she is (she is only a size 14–16 — not bad for a fifty-five-year-old grandmother!).*
>   Robin from Ohio

Not bad for anybody, I'd say! More often, it's a thin mother agonizing over a larger daughter:

> *My daughter has more of a significant weight problem [than I do] and I hope to share this [book] with her.*
>   Pat from New Jersey

Following my presentations, I'm often approached by tearful mothers who have large, lovely daughters at home. "I wish she could meet you!" they say. "My daughter just hides at home, and I want her to see she can enjoy life and be successful even though she is big like you are."

Time for a true confession. When I call myself "big" or "bountiful" or "large," it feels good, it feels positive. When a thin woman says "big like you are," I must fight the urge to feel offended. I know that's silly, but it's also the truth. Self-acceptance is a process, an ongoing challenge, day in and day out. I now feel much less "inner bristling" when someone else acknowledges my size. After all, there it is. It's merely a fact, not an accusation, and I've already brought up the subject myself.

Voices from the Past

Perhaps one of the reasons we bristle when someone mentions our size is that we've heard it all before, many years ago. Child psychologists agree that our self-image is formed in the first five years of life. In the years that follow, we continue to hear, again and again, the messages we received at a very young age.

If you were to play back those tapes in your head, those self-talk conversations that shape how you feel about yourself, whose voices would be on those tapes? And what would they be saying? I asked women to tell me, "What comments do you receive about your size, and who says them?" Everyone from family members to strangers has made comments about our bodies. Which of these groups makes the most remarks, the majority of them negative? Sorry, Mom. You win.

We mothers are blamed for everything under the sun these days, from our children's low self-esteem to their poor marks in school. I'm not here to provide fuel for the guilt trip every mother embarks on when she checks out of the delivery room. (Remember, I'm a mother too!) Nor am I anxious to blame your own mother for the way you feel about yourself. Such finger-pointing is non-productive, even dangerous.

You're an adult now. The finger of responsibility points in your direction. You can choose to keep repeating those old negative messages, or you can choose how you feel about your body and yourself.

But let's be realistic. You can't erase a tape you can't locate. A therapist or counselor might help some of us find the source of those "old tapes." Meanwhile, by listening to others who struggle as we do, we may hear negative recordings similar to ours and begin to push our own "erase" button.

Pushing the Playback Button

I want to share with you the various messages, the scripts that women are still able to recite for us. Some are old scripts, things we've heard since childhood. Many contain new phrases, feedback that wasn't sought but was offered nonetheless as people around us reacted to our size, weight or body shape.

We'll let Mother get it out of her system first:

When I wear pants, my mother calls me "Thunder Thighs," or calls the pants, "sausage casings."

Jane from Wisconsin

Many mothers would never dream of being so direct. They make their point in more subtle ways:

My mom said, "You should lose weight — you'd feel better — it's for your own good!"

Linda from Ohio

Now, does that sound like a mother, or what? That "for your own good" stuff was practically a maternal litany that followed everything she ever told us. If her plea to "do it for your own good" doesn't work, Mother can always move to the "do it for your kids" approach, combining shame *and* guilt:

> *My mom said: "You should lose weight for your health and think of your kids. What will happen to them if you are sick or dead?"*
> Connie from Wisconsin

If you don't have children, another angle might be, "Watch it, or you'll lose your husband's interest."

Or, maybe this will sound familiar:

> *Mom has always told me I am heavy. I've always been compared to my smaller sister.*
> Heidi from Michigan

Some mothers send mixed messages:

> *There was a constant battle with her over my weight. On the one hand, I was always too fat. On the other hand, every time I did something she liked (making the cheerleading squad in junior high), I got special dinners and pies and cakes as rewards. I was terribly confused.*
> Diane from Tennessee

Let's face it, mothers are sometimes hard to please. They know us so well, watched us grow up, genuinely love us and want only the best for us.

> *I am staring at yet another size 6 petite knit (of all things) suit that my size 4 petite mother has bought for me and said, "With a little effort you could fit into this!"*
> Debra from Kentucky

Forgiveness is your best response, because in almost every case, our mothers really did mean well. The truth is, their own struggles with body image colored everything they ever said to us about our bodies.

I was fortunate to have a father who always found some kind words to say to me about my appearance. That's why I found these comments about fathers discouraging:

Having been "big" for about twenty years, my dad has called me "Lard."

Marcia from South Dakota

I've been fat since age thirteen. Father always looked at me as though he was disgusted.

Monica from Ohio

My dad called me "Bertha Butt."

Sonya from Kentucky

Our siblings like to be helpful, too, like Marcia's brother who asked: "What tent and awning store did you buy that dress from?"

It Rhymes with Cat, Sat, and Pat

Those of us with children often receive some weighty comments, too, though our children's innocence makes such observations less threatening, even laughable.

My children say, "Look Mommy, she's bigger than you!"

Gail from Texas

When my three-year-old son saw an ad on TV for an exercise video that supposedly produces "buns of steel," he said, "Mom, you need that!"

Pamela from Kentucky

One mother shared this common experience:

One of my son's friends made a derogatory comment about my weight. The painful thing about the incident was that I hurt for my son — the realization that his friends laughed at his mother — the embarrassment he might feel because his mom was fat.

Rosanne from Kentucky

I had something similar happen at church when I had nursery duty. A sweet little three-year-old boy said, "You're fat!" And I said,

"You're right!" Then I laughed and he laughed and we went right on tossing a ball back and forth. In that very brief exchange, he learned that fat is not a bad word, any more than "tall" or "short" or "thin" are bad words. They are descriptive words, perfectly appropriate. He also learned that I am already aware of my size and feel okay about it.

Fat becomes a "loaded" word when it's said in a derogatory way, or if it's said in combination with other words that do have a negative connotation. You know them all: "Fat and lazy!" "Fat and stupid!" "Fat and ugly!" "Fat slob!" You can even have a "fat chance" of doing something (which means the same thing as having a "slim chance!?").

We've chosen many words to describe our own bodies. Some of them are affectionate, even funny. Some are a thin veneer for a lot of heartache. When I asked women to tell me, "What words come to mind when you think of your body?" here were some of their responses. First, the funny ones: Heavy duty cutie. Wide load. Hidden valleys. Gravity-bitten.

The painfully honest ones: *Disgust. Disappointment. Embarrassment. Frumpy. Old, fat and gray!*

The practical ones: *Shade in the summer. Warmth in the winter. A wonderful piece of machinery. It washes up nicely and never shrinks.*

The descriptive ones: *An apple on a stick. Shaped like Mr. Peanut. Vertically Impaired — (I'm short). The Goodyear Blimp.*

The positive ones: *Soft, sensual, warm, comforting, sexy. Big and powerful. Strong, big, beautiful, voluptuous. Renoiresque, luscious.*

Our response to our bodies is, as you can see, all over the map. Those of us who love to display our wit will usually look for a funny way to describe ourselves.

I especially love the word, "luscious." A wonderful therapist in Wisconsin organized a workshop she called "Lifestyles of the Large and Luscious." Sadly, only one woman was willing to sign up. Why? Probably because so few of us see ourselves as "luscious."

Size Is Not the Issue

The amazing thing to me was this: if you covered up the dress sizes listed at the top of the surveys and just looked at the answers, they were almost identical *no matter what the woman's dress size!*

The 4's, the 14's and the 24's all said pretty much the same things: "Flabby thighs, big hips, too much tummy."

One woman wrote that her body is "still a little too plump." She wears a size 6. I'd always mistakenly assumed it was just us big girls who struggled; was I surprised to find that the problem is systemic!

When *USA TODAY* asked 8, 000 readers to "grade" their bodies, 40% of both men and women gave themselves a C. That's a passing grade, but it's not honor roll material.

The newspaper survey also asked them to list what they liked about their bodies specifically, and what they didn't like. Here's how the women responded:

Women Liked MOST:	Women Liked LEAST:
1. Eyes	1. Stomach
2. Face	2. Buttocks
3. Hair	3. Legs

Above the neck, we're happy. From the waist down, we're miserable. That may be in part because we spend thirty minutes or more every day on the features we like.

Our hair is cut, styled, colored, permed, washed, set, curled, straightened, as well as combed several times a day. Our faces are scrubbed, creamed, massaged, waxed, masked, and covered with makeup almost daily. Our eyes are tweezed, lined, shadowed, and for many of us, aided by glasses or contact lenses. For the most part, we're happy with our face and hair (as well we should be, considering what we invest in them!).

The stomach, buttocks and legs are a problem for one simple reason: that's where fat deposits land first. How does that favorite saying go? We're "built for comfort, not for speed?" Women are indeed built with childbearing capabilities, and the area of our bodies where we carry that precious cargo is the stomach, buttocks and legs.

I'm Not Fat, I'm Expecting

This is the truth: I loved being pregnant! For the first time in my life, I didn't go around trying to hold in my stomach. For a season I had a bustline that actually matched my hips... such balance! I felt good from head to toe and only craved healthy foods (fresh pineapple and whole wheat crackers). People told me how radiant and beautiful

I was, patted my tummy, told me my ankles looked great (until the 9th month) and in general made me feel terrific about my body.

Of course, after the delivery all that ground to a halt. Six weeks later people were still asking me, "When are you due?" The "going home from the hospital" outfit I bought continued to hang in the closet with the tags still dangling from the sleeves. Suddenly my large, lovely body was supposed to be slimmer and trimmer again, as if nothing ever happened. Ha.

If you've given birth, you know what takes place. Things expand. Not just your abdomen, either. My hands and feet were permanently changed after two pregnancies only twenty months apart. Let me tell you, for the joy of having Matthew and Lillian in my life, I'm happy to buy bigger shoes and have my rings re-sized!

My friends all said, "Think of the weight you'll lose after you deliver! All that water, all that baby, it'll be twenty-five or thirty pounds, easy!" As soon as I could walk to the nurse's station I climbed on that big white scale to find out how I'd done on the have-a-baby diet.

It couldn't be right. I'd only lost five pounds! How can you have an eleven pound twelve and a half ounce baby and only lose five pounds? (Did they put some back?)

Needless to say, I was full of water. Soon it started flowing and I quickly lost about thirty pounds. My total gain was thirty-five — not bad for a baby that size. But I still came out of the whole thing with fuller, droopier breasts, a rounder tummy, bigger hips and thicker thighs. Those extra five pounds all went to the places we women supposedly hate: stomach, buttocks and thighs. And since I was big before I got pregnant, there was already lots of cushion in those three places. By saying we don't like these parts of our bodies, we're really saying, "I don't like being shaped like a woman!" Today's fashion models are usually young women — still girls really, at twelve and thirteen — with flat chests, flat tummies, no hips, no buttocks. They are, in fact, shaped pretty much like young boys. Older models, who fight like mad to compete with these young girls, must diet and exercise vigorously to keep themselves flat, sleek and bulge-free. It's not surprising that the female fashion world introduces men's suits, ties and shirts about every five years (I never see ordinary women wear those outfits, just models and actresses on TV). Those women look great in male clothing because that's the body they have to work with.

In my family, we're curvy. My mother's yearbook called her "buxom." Great word. It means, "full-bosomed, healthy, plump, cheerful and lively." In 1929, the year my mother graduated, that was a *compliment!*

Now, I'm watching to see how the family genes hold up. Just twenty months after giving birth to Matthew, I welcomed Miss Lillian Margaret Higgs into my life. Compared to her brother she was a little petite thing, just ten pounds, three and three quarter ounces.

Will Lillian also be a big, beautiful woman in a narrow, nervous world? Hard to say. Although doctors say that babies triple their birth weight in the first year, both of mine held steady for a long time. They grew at a nice, slow, steady pace, and soon were right in the normal range. Only time will tell whether they will be "big boned" too.

The Gift of Life

From my own observations, I've concluded most young girls don't feel good about their bodies because they have mothers who don't feel good about their own bodies. Many times, unhappy mothers project their own body dissatisfaction onto their daughters, saying, "Don't get fat (like me)! I don't want you to suffer (like I did)!" And so a new diet treadmill is set up for the next generation.

Whether she turns out to be model-thin or mama-size, I can guarantee you Lillian will be loved, hugged, encouraged, praised and made to feel as absolutely beautiful as possible in this house. I know the world will give her a different message, the media will berate her at any size, her friends will be talking diets by her eighth birthday, and someday some jerk might tell her he could really love her if she'd "just lose a little weight." I know all that may be in her future.

But here at home she will find a haven, a resting place. Within these walls, her mother, her first role model, is busy living and loving her own full life. A life without apology for my genes, my choices or my body. This is the Liz-that-is. Whatever size or shape Lillian turns out to have, it's my fervent prayer that she will accept it, even embrace it as God's gift to her.

In a year or two, she will be old enough to read this book. In ten years, she'll be embarrassed to tears that she's in it! I can hear her now: "Aw, Mom!" Between those two stages, I'd like to put this in writing for her, and for all our daughters:

Miss Lillian:

Daddy and I love you. God loves you. And people will love you — the moment you begin to love yourself.

With all my heart,

Mama

Begin Building Body Confidence Today

1. Forgive your family. Any negative messages they may have given you about your body cannot easily be forgotten, but they can be forgiven. In the process, their power to hurt you will diminish. When those memories come to mind, immediately respond, "I forgive you."

2. Forgive yourself. Each of us is doing the best we can with what we've been given every day of our lives. Relax and extend grace to yourself, as you do to others.

3. Embrace your genetic heritage. Concentrate on the things you really *do* like that have been passed down to you. If you see your own physical traits in your children, fight the urge to say, "You look like me, poor thing!" Instead, say "I'm so glad you got my _____!"

♥ An OB/GYN Speaks . . .

Dr. Harriette "Robin" Smith graduated from the University of Louisville School of Medicine and is board certified by the American College of Obstetrics and Gynecology. She has practiced medicine since 1982, most currently at the Louisville Women's Centers.

Liz: What are some special health concerns of larger women?

Robin: *As a rule, their cardiovascular status is not as good because they are not as active. Often their muscle tone isn't great, either, for the same reason. Large patients are more inclined to be diabetic, and have more of a tendency toward high blood pressure.*

Liz: How do those things affect pregnancy?

Robin: *The placenta is a vascular organ, where the exchange of maternal and fetal blood occurs — it's where you put in the good stuff and take out the bad. If the patient has elevated blood sugar, the babies tend to be large. Large infants can be trickier to deliver, and you'll find an increase in the number of cesarean-sections and birth trauma. If the placenta gets prematurely old or stressed because of diabetes or high blood pressure, then there's a risk for stillbirths and for growth retardation. Also, oxygen transfer is not as good.*

Liz: Good grief! Do you have any good news for the large woman who wants to give birth?

Robin: *Absolutely. If you're healthy, you're going to do fine in your pregnancy. I have just as many gorgeous babies from big people as I do from skinny ones. Thin people sometimes smoke or have poor eating habits, so thinness is no guarantee of an easy delivery or a healthy baby.*

Liz: What about women who gain weight during pregnancy and then can't lose it?

Robin: *I see a lot of that! Once you've stretched the abdominal muscles to term size, it's pretty hard to get that muscle tone back. You really have to work at it, and you are usually busy tending that baby. Everything changes: your life style, your eating and sleeping habits, everything. You have to face the fact that you will never have your high school waist again. In pregnancy your ribs expand, your feet expand, all your weight-bearing structures change. And they should! You can't fight Mother Nature. Look what we get out of the process: a wonderful new person! Those body changes are part of growing up, part of life.*

Liz: What about other gynecological issues for large women?

Robin: *Yeast infections can be a problem, particularly for diabetics. Of course, thin women who eat a lot of chocolate can have them, too, or anybody on antibiotics.*

Liz: Any other concerns?

Robin: *Because we have more fat on our bodies, larger women have an abundance of estrogen. That can lead to irregular periods or breakthrough bleeding, and can increase the threat of cancer of the uterus. And, more fat in the diet can increase the risk of breast cancer.*

Liz: Sometimes larger people feel intimidated, even discriminated against, by the medical community. Is that our imagination?

Robin: *The truth is, it's easier to practice medicine on skinny people, logistically. Big people can be harder to examine. I have to be extra careful not to miss something. If, for example, I am not able to adequately feel a large woman's ovaries, I'll order an ultrasound, just to get a better reading. And, it can be more difficult to do surgery on a large person. These procedures certainly can be done, it just takes more time. Unfortunately, a woman who is self-conscious about her size may not go to her gynecologist for her annual pap smear and exam or seek out routine medical care, just because she's concerned about getting on the scale. Of course, I understand that fear.*

Liz: What is it like for you, being a big, beautiful woman doctor?

Robin: *In general, being beautifully abundant is like being a left-handed person living in a right-handed world. Actually, the only real problem with practicing medicine and being large is finding scrub suits that fit! I now carry my own scrubs with me and hoard them in my locker at the hospital. It would be terrible to miss a delivery just because I couldn't find scrub pants in my size! All of us larger docs and nurses hide our scrubs where we know we can find them when we need them, and I keep a couple in my car, just in case.*

Liz: Do you see any advantages to being large?

Robin: *When you are statuesque, it's a lot harder for people to ignore you. When you are able to look them in the eye and say, "I beg your pardon? Say that again?" they do listen. I guess our body language just talks louder! I hate to speak in public, but the few times I've done it, the response has been very positive. Maybe it's been my content more than my delivery, but I think the power and authority of my size has been an asset.*

Liz: Anything we haven't covered?

Robin: *I see a lot of patients who are growing older, women who are peri-menopausal and distressed about the changes in the body habitus: their upper arms have become heavier, their hips are larger, their tummy has gotten poochy, all because of hormonal changes. It's not that they've gained weight, just that it's been redistributed. This can be very traumatic for women of all sizes. These are natural changes, and part of maturity is dealing with these changes. The good news is, if body image is not such a crucial issue to you, these changes will not be that difficult to handle. Coming to terms with your body now can really help. Let's face it, "big" isn't politically correct and "old" isn't politically correct either. The real changes that need to take place will happen between the ears!*

Fable 4

"You Are What You Eat" (If That Were True, I'd Be Yogurt)

After we've worked through our self-esteem issues, dealt with our "old tapes" and learned to let go of the need to wear a size 6, there's yet another issue to deal with: eating. That time-consuming, mind-consuming experience we face three times a day or more, every day of our lives.

Let's Make Dinner

Consider how many steps go into preparing one simple meal, like Sunday dinner (the kind Mom used to make):

1. Plan what you're going to serve.
2. Browse through a few cookbooks for ideas. (Just the pictures make you hungry, so you nibble on some chips while you keep turning the pages. These do not count as real food.)
3. Check the refrigerator and shelves to see what you have on hand. (Vow to do something with the potatoes before they walk out of the pantry by themselves.)

4. Make a grocery list.
5. Go through your stack of coupons (most of which expired in 1985).
6. Find your car keys.
7. Drive to the local Piggly-Wiggly.
8. Spend a good forty-five minutes wandering aimlessly up and down the aisles, because you left your list on the kitchen table.
9. Spend another fifteen minutes at the checkout counter, while your frozen yogurt melts.
10. Haul the groceries out to the car. (One bag tears open while loading it into the backseat.)
11. Pull into your driveway, and drag in all the bags.
12. Put everything away while you toss a few cocktail peanuts in your mouth. The ones you bought for the candy dish—for company.
13. Wash the dishes in the sink, then scrape the crusty gray stuff off the cutting board.
14. Scrub all the fresh vegetables.
15. Make a salad: tear the lettuce, slice the tomatoes, grate the cheese, chop the bacon, cut the cucumber into cute little shapes, and pour on the dressing. Low-cal, not too much, and don't forget the croutons.

Tired yet? We haven't even made it to the main course! It's an amazing amount of work for one meal. We still have vegetables to prepare, meat to fix, biscuits to beat (remember I live in the South), and potatoes to wrestle, not to mention desserts (which is "stressed" spelled backwards!).

Women and the Food Thing

In addition to all the genetic and gender-specific reasons that women deal with the issue of gaining weight, maybe the fact that we're often the ones in charge of putting food on the table is a contributing factor.

My mom, bless her buxom heart, fed as many as six kids and one hubby three meals a day for over forty years. She scribbled a weekly menu on the back of a used envelope, then called in her grocery list to a local meat market that delivered her order in boxes right to our back door (Can you imagine? Now that's what I call convenience food!).

I was the typical spoiled baby of the family and did little more than put the food away for her. Mom did all the cooking and most of the dishes. Think how many hours of her day, of her life, were centered around feeding her family.

Is this a bad thing, a degrading job, a useless activity? Of course not! Every bookstore owner will tell you that their two perennial bestsellers are cookbooks and diet books. (The Bible still holds the #1 spot.)[1] Preparing a delicious meal is at least a specialized skill if not an art form, and the women and men among us who do it well are to be applauded.

In our household, Bill does as much cooking as I do, if not more. Must be a survival move. In truth, I think he actually enjoys cooking. I can take it or leave it (mostly, leave it). It's fun whipping something up for company, but night after night it gets old.

Nonetheless, the "mother is in charge of the kitchen" adage is still going strong in the 90's. If I call Bill at work just to say hello, he often asks me, "What's for dinner?" I, of course, haven't a clue and say so.

"Take some chicken out of the freezer," he suggests. A few hours later, chicken is on the table, thanks to hubby's helpful handiwork. (P.S. No, you can't have him!)

This example sure blows my "women gain weight because they do all the cooking" theory right out of the dishwater. Maybe preparing the food is not the issue. Maybe food itself—both eating and avoiding it—is the issue.

Sophia Loren said, "Everything you see I owe to spaghetti." (Oh, really? Then, why doesn't pasta with red sauce do that to me?)

Women have a thing about food, like men have a thing about sex. We think about it a lot, even fantasize about it. We feel righteous when we abstain, naughty when we enjoy something "forbidden."

I don't think I'm exaggerating when I say that women have a relationship with food. It is a friend and companion, or an enemy, a traitor. It has a powerful emotional component, especially since certain foods evoke strong memories from our childhood.

Food Memories

What foods have a memory link for you? I remember my Grandma Amidon's gingerbread cookies, cinnamon rolls and French bread. If I close my eyes, I can see her slight form at our red kitchen counter, bent over, stirring something wonderful in a yellow ceramic bowl. I can smell it, taste it, feel the flour on her hands, hear the pin rolling over the dough, watch her shaking the red and white can of cinnamon. It's an all-encompassing experience, arousing all my senses. When Pillsbury said, "Nuthin' says lovin' like somethin' from the oven," they knew exactly what they were talking about. Powerful memories, those.

Is it any wonder we turn to food when we're depressed, discouraged, disappointed, defeated? Food takes us back to a happier time, people and places we've loved, memories we cherish. No wonder they call it "comfort food!"

It doesn't have to be a negative emotion that opens the refrigerator door, though. Every celebration also includes food — every party, family occasion, baptism, graduation, wedding, anniversary. When I travel the country speaking at banquets and other special events, I confess to the audience that my whole job can be summed up in just two words: TALKING and EATING!

Those of us in the church really love to eat. Hey, if you can't smoke, drink, cuss, dance or fool around (and why would you want to?), then bring on the potluck dinner! My very first "Ladies Salad Supper" in the summer of '82 was a real eye-opener. Salad, my foot. Oh sure, there was a little lettuce around the edge of the bowl, but in the middle were marshmallows, sour cream, pretzels, jello, fruit, pecans, mayonnaise, whipped topping and who-knows-what-else. A little bit of heaven, right there in the fellowship hall.

Why Do We Eat?

"Well, why *do* I eat?" I've asked myself that many times over the years, and the complexity of the answer leaves me shaking my head. These are some of the reasons I've come up with:

Nourishment. Our bodies absolutely need food, demand food, would perish without it. That's why the methods that work for abstaining from alcohol, tobacco and drugs don't work for food. We can function without those substances. But we have been eating since pre-birth. That's why fasting, VLCD's (Very Low Calorie Diets) and any attempts to interfere with the body's nutritional needs will eventually backfire.

Habit. At 7:00 A.M., Noon and 6:00 P.M., something inside me goes "BONG!" (Sometimes, at 10:00 A.M. and 3:00 P.M., it also goes "ping!") This is not a bad thing, but it is clock-based rather than hunger-based. It is not as good a reason to eat (but then, sometimes, who needs a reason?). As Shakespeare wrote, "How use doth breed a habit in a man." (Or in a woman!)

Social Custom. Wherever I go, it seems food is served. It can be refused, of course, at the risk of offending the hostess. But gatherings and food go together. These are the occasions that feel dangerous to many of us who are trying to get off the diet treadmill. Social eating usually has little to do with real hunger.

Emotional Need. I once kept track on paper of what feelings I was experiencing while I was reaching for food. The answer was simple: all of them. Every emotion, from anger to anxiety, boredom to bereavement, celebration to cynicism. Even when I felt zealous, I reached for food! Do I have a right to do this? Yes. Is it the best thing for my body? Depends. Paul said, "All things are lawful for me, but all things are not helpful."[2]

Taste. I almost forgot this one. We might eat something just to see what it tastes like, or to experience the pleasure of it again. Taste buds like to have fun too! Like Erma Bombeck says, "I am not a glutton. I am an explorer of food."

Why Can't We Stop Eating?

I think the big question is: When is eating a pleasurable pursuit, and when is it compulsive? When you no longer enjoy eating, that's a good reason to stop and re-evaluate it. Not because you want to lose weight, or because you feel fat, or because you want to exert some "willpower." Forget those things. Focus on getting to know your body's needs better. Then you can respond honestly to real hunger versus emotional hunger, and eat because it is fun instead of eating food you don't even remember putting in your mouth. I don't think that eating compulsively is God's best choice for us. His Creation is filled with plants, fruits, vegetables, nuts, the fowl of the air, the fish of the sea, the beasts of the land, and they are primarily there for our nourishment and enjoyment. Period. These, then, are the two best reasons to eat: nourishment and enjoyment. Moliere was famous for saying, "One must eat to live, and not live to eat."

This may be where the fact that we are female comes into the picture. Men as a rule do not struggle with, "Shall I eat?" They eat because their stomach is growling, because it is lunchtime, because food is put in front of them, because it tastes good, because they enjoy eating. The same reasons that we eat, but without the heavy emotional undertones. Much less angst, much less "bad" and "good" foods, a whole lot less "what will this do to my hips?"

Men seldom sit around plotting what they will eat at their next meal, because they probably ate enough at their last meal to hold them a few hours. Women, on the other hand — ever dieting, ever measuring — are often obsessed with what they'll get to eat next *because they are always hungry!*

Talking Cells

Getting off the diet treadmill means taking better care of your body's needs, including feeding your hungry cells! First you have to figure out what they are hungry for. Cells don't talk. Or do they?

When I became pregnant with Matthew in 1986, one of the things I noticed immediately was my cravings. Never mind pickles and ice cream, I wanted green beans. Not dripping in butter or fatback, just fresh, steamed green beans. M-m-m-m. And oranges, mandarin oranges especially. I was good for two cans a day. We fully expected our firstborn to have orange-tinted skin and green ears!

A baby's tiny life has big needs, and God makes sure that we pay attention to them. Those cravings are real, and they are a good example of how our bodies talk to us. We tend to hear them more when we are pregnant because that is a time when we focus on what's happening to our bodies. We notice every subtle (and not so subtle!) change, as well as every movement in our abdomens. It's no wonder we also notice what we're really hungry for.

It's been several years since I carried a baby in my womb, but I still find if I slow down and pay attention, my appetite often leads me to particular preferences, and healthy ones to boot. Until we teach them otherwise, children have very intelligent appetites. Toddlers know when they are hungry, and it has nothing to do with the clock. When we say to them, "Not now, dear, supper is only an hour away," no wonder they start crying! They are hungry right then. My Lillian will say, "My tummy is empty," and that's exactly what she means. She knows when she's hungry and, most of the time, what she is hungry for—bananas, turkey or grapes. (And, sometimes, pizza!)

If our body starts craving complex carbohydrates, for example, we often interpret that as "I want cookies! I want cake!" That may be more sugar than our body was really looking for. When we eat it, it doesn't really satisfy that need. We eat more cookies, more cake, and may end up with that fuzzy-headed feeling, that cloudy sugar high, without ever making our body happy.

Next time your appetite says "cookies," just for fun, slip it something like a warm, delicious baked potato. I know what you're thinking: "I don't have time to bake a potato!" Plenty of fast food places have them, and the old microwave can zap you one in short order. Besides, talk about comfort food! My dear friend Evelyn craved potatoes so much she carried a picture of a big, fluffy baked potato in her wallet throughout her pregnancy. (Ev is a little different. That's why we get along!)

Am I saying don't eat the cookie? This is Liz speaking, your friend. By all means, if the cookie is what you really want, have it. Have several. But getting in tune with your body's nutritional needs should still be a priority for women of all sizes. Good health comes from many things you can't change (heredity and genetics) and a few things you can (nutrition and movement).

Games Dieters Play

If we're honest with ourselves, some of us are pretty adept at food games, especially in restaurants. We order fish ("it's better for me than beef"), but we order it fried. Or we order a chef's salad loaded with cheeses, meat and dressing, but say, "I only had a salad at lunch today!" Maybe we choose a light entree, then splurge on dessert, thinking it will all balance out somehow.

We may walk three blocks on the way to lunch and figure that such an effort should earn us an extra dinner roll or two. Or, we have carrot cake for dessert because that has to be good for us: after all, it's made out of carrots. (Please don't hear one word of condemnation in all this: I took these examples from my own life.)

I love the story of the woman who professed to be dieting, but had eight frozen cheesecakes in her freezer. Her explanation was simple: "They were on sale."[3] Then there's the hostess who kept a candy dish symmetrical by reducing the M & M's to the same number of each color. Or how about the teenager who drinks a diet soda while eating a candy bar?

Get serious. Diet foods are a joke. As one woman said: "Diet foods? I mean, really! Hawaiian Punch Lite?!"

The time has come to stop playing games and be more honest with our eating. By focusing on nutrition and enjoyment, instead of calories and pounds, the experience becomes one of common sense rather than compulsion, of honest emotions rather than stuffed feelings.

No More Games

Here is an outrageous idea: fill your house with healthy foods. Pack the refrigerator with fresh fruits. Keep the crisper filled with veggies, and stock the shelves with whole grains, legumes and pasta. Replace your soda cans with fruit juices, toss some frozen yogurt in the freezer, along with chicken breasts and fish. And, yes, go ahead and throw in some Twinkies, nacho chips, or whatever rings your bell. The things you really do crave on occasion. Then eat what you need, when you need it.

Oh, my stars! I will gain two hundred pounds!

Really? Ever tried it? Spontaneously eating healthy foods is the best thing you can do for your body. Sure, sometimes you'll reach for the stuff with a little less nutritional value. But so what? Everybody does that. Thin people, healthy people, old people, young people. Everybody eats potato chips and nobody has died from them yet.

David Garner, Ph.D. is the director of research at the Eating Disorders Section, Department of Psychiatry at Michigan State University. His advice? "Stop dieting. This means start eating regular meals, including appropriate sweets and snacks. Many people who have struggled for years find that when they give up dieting they do not gain weight."[4]

What's an "appropriate" sweet or snack? Well, it's your body: ask it! When you're hungry, have some healthy choices available for the nutrients they provide, and give your body the fuel it needs to function. (When only a cupcake will make you happy, that's what you should eat, guilt-free.)

Whatever you do, enjoy what you eat! If you are not hungry for carrots, for heaven's sake, don't force them between your lips. One woman said dieting conjured up, "ugly, ugly thoughts of carrot sticks pounded into my heart like a stake."

Transylvania time! Restricted eating, better known as dieting, gets us primed for the day we'll go off that diet and binge on whatever foods we deprived ourselves of. Don't be deceived. The body will not be mocked. This divinely designed machine needs fuel at regular intervals in sufficient amounts. It will run best on the high octane stuff, but is so remarkable a contraption that it will run on almost anything. For a while. Dieting is like driving on fumes. It's hard on the engine. You could run out of gas at any moment. The smart driver keeps her tank filled and her engine tuned up, and she heads out for a spin regularly, just to keep her gears oiled. And, remember: the big Cadillac looks just as sharp on the open road as the little Honda!

3,500 Calories = One Pound

We've all been brainwashed into thinking that by just cutting our calorie intake by 500 calories a day, 3,500 calories a week, we will effortlessly lose one pound a week. Simple arithmetic, right?

That would be fine if we all processed those 500 calories in the same way, but we don't! Our metabolic rates can vary widely. For some folks, 1,500 calories a day would be a strict diet and they'd lose two pounds a week. For the next person, it would only mean one pound of weight loss. Some folks might not lose anything; others could *gain* weight on those same 1,500 calories a day.

On a recent plane trip to Texas, I watched as the flight attendants placed the exact same meal in front of all the passengers. (Maybe "meal" isn't the right word for it; "hot items" and "cold items" would fit better!)

As we all ate these identical foods in almost identical portion sizes, it struck me how differently our individual bodies were going to process that meal. We are not empty jars into which food is poured — just pour in less and there'll be less volume. Instead, we are incredible machines, very complex, each unique. God designed us to be different. And (I'll say it again) different is good!

Often in diet groups I attended, we were told that we would just have to accept the fact that some people could eat more than we did and not gain weight. Resign yourself to a life of reduced calories, they said, because your body needs fewer calories. What if, instead, we accept the fact that our bodies were meant to be, designed to be, bigger! We need healthy foods in healthy amounts. We will never wear a size 6 dress, but could wear a size 16 and be our healthiest, happiest self. Wouldn't that make more sense than semi-starving ourselves, beating ourselves up for not being thinner, and making ourselves and our families miserable? Of course.

Here's a novel thought: when we are dieting, we feel in control of our eating. In reality, we're obsessed with our eating, or non-eating. It's all we think about or plan for. Our lives revolve around it. How many times have you said, "I'll diet when I'm ready" or "I'll diet when the time is right." Exactly. Dieting takes so much effort that it is all you could conceivably do. That is not reality, and not a life worthy of pursuit.

When we put food in the proper perspective – a source of nutrition, energy and enjoyment – that's when we're really in control. Our emotional selves do need nurturing, but not with food! In her terrific book, *Inner Eating*, Shirley Billigmeier states:

> By struggling, withholding food, and putting yourself on restrictive diets, you make life more difficult for yourself. If you separate the two issues (emotions and body care), you can learn to handle both better.[5]

We all have seen examples of thin people who are not in the least bit healthy, who eat all the wrong foods, never exercise, and so forth.

Most of my friends are "small" and in terrible health. Gallbladder, arthritis, diabetes, and so on. Is it possible to be overweight and healthy?

Elaine from Ohio

It's time to say this again: if you are a large woman, you may not be overeating at all. Your eating may not be emotionally based in the least. All of us have different *everything* – metabolic rates, nutritional needs, fat-to-muscle ratios, everything. Relax. My only encouragement to you is to seek honest eating.

One of my college dormitory mates told me that she would never understand why I was overweight. After a few months of living in the same building, she noticed that I rarely snacked or over-indulged. She could not understand this and even asked me if I was a "closet" eater, which I am happy to say I am not. It gave me a better sense of what I was up against.

Mary Ann from New York

Mary Ann found out what many of us have suspected: we do indeed eat normally, we aren't the gluttons we think we are. After all, the word "glutton" means, "one who eats excessively." It comes from a word meaning "to gulp" and has only to do with eating, nothing to do with body size.[6]

In *Making Peace with Food*, author Susan Kano suggests we "enjoy eating, avoid being fanatical or rigid about the choices you make, eat in harmony with your hunger and satiation, and try to keep dieters' mind-set from creeping into your efforts."[7]

Eat in peace, free from games, denial, apology, worry. That stuff weighs a ton! Your body can be trusted today, as is, right now, this minute. Treat it with respect, and watch what happens!

Begin Building Body Confidence Today

1. Start listening to your body for clear directives. What are you really hungry for? Begin keeping your refrigerator and shelves stocked with those items.

2. Whenever your body says, "I am hungry!" give it water first. We need lots of it, and you may just be thirsty. Still hungry? By all means, eat what you are hungry for.

3. Stop comparing notes with others, and eat what makes *you* feel good and function well. Above all, stop dieting!

❤ A Nutritionist Speaks . . .

Dr. Kayla Carruth received her Ph.D. in nutrition from the University of Tennessee. She is now director of program development for health education at the University of Tennessee Medical Center in Knoxville.

Liz: Why are American women getting bigger?

Kayla: *Actually, the whole population is getting bigger! In general, it's fair to say that part of the growth in our body size is that women are beginning to feel freer to be themselves, rather than follow the trends that fashion sets for us.*

Liz: In part, then, it's a social movement. What else?

Kayla: *Once we hit around forty, our muscle mass starts declining. For men, this doesn't happen till about age fifty. So, we have to do something proactive to even maintain muscle, let alone increase the muscle mass. When fat replaces muscle, less energy is used to process the nutrients coming into the cells, and the metabolic rate will lower further.*

Liz: So age enters into the picture. Other factors?

Kayla: *Genetic predisposition plays a big part. When it comes to health, it pays to choose your parents well. I always tell patients to look at their family tree, in particular their mother, sisters, grandmother, and aunts. (Of course, some of us take after the male side of the family tree too.) If everybody in your family is tall, big boned and heavy, you are probably going to be the same way, unless you were adopted.*

Liz: If we are genetically programmed to be larger, why are some of us so unhappy with our bodies?

Kayla: *Our expectations of our bodies have not been very realistic. Social pressures are so great, especially for* younger women, many of whom haven't yet established their own identity.

Liz: Do diets work?

Kayla: *Theoretically, you can lose weight on any diet. But unless you truly change your life style habits through behavior modification, you will indeed gain it back. And changing those habits is very difficult because you developed your current eating pattern – what you eat, how much and how often – over dozens of years.*

Liz: What changes could be made, then?

Kayla: *Forget dieting! Eat healthy foods and really work on the other life style habits, things that make you active. Lower your fat intake significantly and eat a wide variety of foods. Think of this as change for a healthier body, not as punishment. Never go below 1,200 calories a day. Making time for regular exercise each day is equally important.*

Liz: At 4'11", you are a petite woman. How is size an issue for you?

Kayla: *"One size doesn't fit" all for me either! I would say 90-95% of the time I am not aware of being smaller. Only when someone points it out to me am I aware of it.*

Liz: Do any situations like that come to mind?

Kayla: *I can remember walking through an airport and being stared at so intently by a woman that I thought perhaps I knew her, so I spoke to her. She came back with a question: "How tall are you?" When I told her, she explained, "I saw you and said to my husband, 'Look how short that woman is!' and he said I was the same size, and I told him, 'No way!' So, I just had to find out how short you really were."*

Liz: Good grief!

Kayla: *I was angry. I guess it never occurred to her that her story might hurt my feelings. I'm glad my husband was with me. Marrying someone six feet tall has been a big help, because he sees me as being just as tall as he is!*

Fable 5

"All Fat People Are Lazy"

The year was 1978. I was twenty-four years old, 171 pounds. A solid size 14 — a 12, if there was elastic in the waist. I'd signed up for a jazz dance class with an instructor everyone raved about. I loved to dance, always had. From my toddler days when my older sisters taught me how to do the "Twist" at their slumber parties, I loved the way my body felt when it moved across a polished wooden floor, music pounding in the background. I could hardly wait for that first dance class. I wore the standard black leotard and tights (workout gear was not as slinky and colorful in those days), and the black soft ballet slipper. Plunking down my money, I signed my name to the day's roster and stepped into the dance studio.

Mirrors were everywhere. Sunlight poured through the windows, and the wood beneath my feet felt warm. The music began. Rhythmic, energetic, magnetic. My body responded instinctively. Swaying, stretching, bending. Oh, it felt wonderful to move to music again!

I stayed in the back row with the other beginners, carefully watching the women in front, mimicking their every move. One, two, step, step, lunge, back, slide, slide. I'm a quick study and soon could feel my pulse pick up at the excitement of moving again, doing something so right, so good for my body and myself. Then it happened. My eyes caught the instructor following my every move, and she was smirking. No, make that laughing. I looked around. Had

I missed something amusing? I turned back to her with a quizzical look on my face, and she put words to my fears: "You look so funny when you move!" The rest of the class giggled and kept dancing.

That was it. I finished class that day, but I never went back. Not to that class, not to any class until 1982, the year I starved myself down to 155 (for about a week), and joined an aerobics class. The instructor was a friend, and would never have dared say anything more challenging to me than, "Go for the burn!" (That was the big deal in those days, along with "No pain, no gain." Oh brother.)

When the Music Stops

I stopped dancing in those "lost" years, even in the privacy of my own home. (Who was going to see me there? The UPS guy?) Instead, I told people that I had four very effective means of exercise:

1. Jogging my memory
2. Climbing the walls
3. Jumping to conclusions
4. Throwing my weight around

Funny, yes, but sad too. I'd taken one insensitive instructor's pronouncement that I looked silly when I danced, and made it my prison.

In their excellent book, *Great Shape*, Pat Lyons and Debby Burgard state, "this fear of wondering what others will think. . . probably keeps more large women inactive than any other factor, even the fear of injury. It is as if splitting our pants or having someone laugh at us would be more painful than breaking a leg."[1]

It does seem foolish to be fearful of a sideways glance, a giggle or the "rrrr-rip" of a pant seam. But that fear is real for many of us, and not to be discounted. It does not, however, have to be endured; it can be faced and overcome.

When the 1982 diet dissolved into the 1984 gain, I knew I'd never diet again, with a capital D. I was, however, ready to dance! I called all around town until I found a woman willing to give me private lessons at a reasonable price. Out came the black leotards once more (in a larger size, of course).

But no ballet slippers this time. No, something a little noisier, something that fit my ever-growing level of confidence, something that always makes people smile: tap dancing shoes!

A Real Toe-Tapper

Ada Lee is the queen of tap in our town, a veteran teacher of hundreds of second graders slugging their way through "Shuffle One, Shuffle Two." She did not laugh at me. In fact, she told me after our first lesson that if I was willing to work hard and practice, I could be one swell tap dancer.

Well, I tapped all right. All 195 pounds of me worked out on a little patch of wooden floor in my Oak Street cottage. I took my tap shoes into the radio station and tapped live, on the air. When I met Bill in 1985, I greeted him at the door "en tappe," and blew him away. In short, I had a great time and gave my cardiovascular system a dandy workout as well, because tap dancing *is* serious exercise.

When the babies came and my feet swelled, the size 8 1/2 tap shoes were put away for good. But not my spiral notebook with Ada Lee's careful diagrams and instructions. No, that notebook is waiting for a new pair of size 10 tap shoes to show up in my closet!

Maybe this is a novel concept to you: exercise for fun? Not to lose weight? Not to burn calories? Just to... enjoy it? Absolutely. Adriane Fugh-Berman, M.D., board member of the National Women's Health Network, said: "Exercise is as good for your mind as it is for your body—it can lessen depression, anxiety, and insomnia, and is a good all-purpose stress reliever."[2] Not a word there about losing weight, but plenty about good health.

Good for Every Body

Unfortunately, for many of us movement and exercise are deemed valuable for one purpose only: to get some extra pounds off. In addition to those crazy calorie charts we've all memorized, I also spent some early years studying how many calories I'd burn while, say, riding my bike. It was very discouraging. A whole hour biking only burns 175 calories? Good heavens, why bother? Let's have an ice cream cone instead.

What the charts didn't say was, the cardiovascular benefits of biking continue long after the bike is back in the garage. Building muscle mass also contributes to a higher metabolic rate. As Dr. Fugh-Berman notes, "A pound of muscle needs 30 to 50 calories a day just for maintenance, while fat only needs two calories a day to get along."[3]

In *Great Shape*, the authors point out the negative side effects of dieting: "slowed metabolic rate, sluggishness, loss of muscle mass, feelings of deprivation." These are just the opposite of the benefits of exercise: "heightened metabolic rate, increased energy, increased muscle mass—and feelings of well-being."[4] The obvious conclusion: don't diet, exercise!

Recently, after several months of being too busy to exercise (sound familiar?), I jumped up and went for a long walk. Here's what I wrote in my journal when I got home:

> That was one of the most positive experiences I've had all week. It felt good, like coming out of my shell. I saw a neighbor and she smiled. I tried to smile back. My calves started hurting about half way around the block, but that's okay. I did it!

Every time I've ever done something that would qualify as exercise, I've been glad I did it. There may have been times I've regretted (rightly or wrongly) what I ate, but I've never been sorry I exercised! Guilt or regret is never the by-product of movement (unless we try to do too much too soon, and are injured. Be good to yourself and go s - l - o - w.).

If you find yourself dragging at the end of the day, believe it or not, you need *more* movement, not less.

Walk, Don't Run

Walking is my favorite exercise for many valid reasons:

1. I don't need any special equipment, just my feet (which, to be sure, are very special size 10 equipment!).
2. I can walk anywhere, anytime, without planning ahead or making an appointment.
3. It's free!

4. It requires little concentration, so I can take in my surroundings or let my imagination soar.
5. I may break into a sweat, but it usually doesn't mess up my hair. So I can walk whenever the mood strikes, even if I have an important appointment later that day.
6. Walking requires absolutely NO squat-thrusts!

If you diet *without* exercise, you hit your body with a double whammy, and your metabolic rate undoubtedly takes a dive. Not good. If you diet *with* exercise, you'll probably see some good results (mostly from the exercise), and now you'll want to increase your food intake and have more energy. If you exercise without *dieting*, then you're right on target as far as your metabolic rate is concerned.

Your basal metabolic rate, the calories your body burns at rest, accounts for most of your daily calories expenditure. In other words, if you stayed in bed all day and didn't lift a finger, you'd still burn about 70% of your normal daily calories. (I don't recommend this, but wanted you to know how your body works.) Another 10% of calories are burned just digesting and absorbing the foods you've eaten. That leaves 20% of your caloric intake to be burned off with exercise.[5]

The conclusion? Stop thinking about food and start thinking about movement. Is it possible to become too compulsive about exercise? Of course. Since the fitness craze hit in the 70's, we could all probably name someone whose over-commitment to exercise got out of hand. One fitness expert said, "I've begun to worry that the fitness revolution has brought us just a new way to strive for the same unreasonable goals."[6]

Personally, I'm not too worried about developing an obsession with exercise. I try to sneak in a little movement where I can, avoiding the "E" word ("exercise") because it brings back grim memories of gym.

P.E. Stands for Painful Experience

I don't know if it was my instructor—short hair, no makeup, big calves, loud bark—or me, but I dreaded gym for six years running. I'd have graduated with a much higher grade point average, but because of all those C's in P.E. I came in twentieth in a class of two hundred.

Maybe it was that powder blue gym uniform, designed by someone who'd never played hockey while wearing a short dress with a full circle skirt and bloomers underneath. BLOOMERS! With "Liz" stitched on the right cheek. Oh, please.

In team sports I was, as you might expect, the last one chosen for the team. Even my closest friends picked me last, then said, "I'm sorry, but we want to win!" The only exception was basketball, a sport where my 5'9" body was worth something. I played a lot of Saturday ball at the playground, shot baskets after school, and tried out for the junior varsity team in 9th grade. When I made the first cut, I was so happy I cried all the way home. I didn't make the second cut, but that was okay. My body had served me well and done its best.

I tried out for hockey too, but never made it past day one of tryouts. In retrospect, I'm so proud of myself for even trying. The tenacity and courage I developed throughout my teen years has served me well on the playing field of life.

Since most of my friends were cheerleaders (I think they liked to keep me around for comic relief), it was only natural that I'd try out for cheerleading. I knew every cheer, every jump, could do a mean split and by the third year of tryouts, could turn a decent cartwheel.

The cheerleading coach was also my English teacher, which happened to be my best subject. I knew she'd give me a fair shot. It was my freshman year of high school, my third year to try out and, I had decided, my last. The rejection was beginning to take its toll.

I practiced until I had spider veins in my thighs from clapping and slapping. Even my Dad knew all the cheers by heart. My cartwheel was awesome, all legs in motion. I was in great shape, great voice, a 140-pound wonder, the all-American blonde, and I was ready.

Three days of practice, then the main event. White blouse, blue shorts, white socks, saddle shoes. Thankfully, it was a good hair day.

When my name was called, I moved to the center of the gym with confidence and performed my routine with gusto. I can still hear Coach Sally's comment when I finished: "Great voice!"

The kiss of death. Great voices do not great cheerleaders make. Face it, Liz, you just didn't look the part. You were simply too much woman for the job. (I've since read that cheerleaders often ruin their voices for life, and develop a permanent raspiness from too much shouting in their formative years. God must have spared my voice for radio and platform speaking. For that, I'm grateful.)

One interesting point: I dieted and exercised constantly at that time, and still the scale stayed at 140 pounds and wouldn't budge. I was unquestionably fit, but not model-thin, because my body was not built to be a size 6 model! Unfortunately, what I did to my metabolism at age fourteen wasn't smart, healthy, or in tune with my body's needs.

Learning to Move Again

That was then, this is now. We cannot change the past, but we definitely can impact the present. Now, we are no longer given a grade for our exercise efforts (or if we are, it's always an A for attempt!), nor do we have a whole panel of judges watching us when we work out. One of the many joys of adulthood is not having to measure up to anyone's standard of fitness but our own. I think for most of us, the real stumbling block is time. Have you ever found yourself saying, "I'd love to exercise if I just had more time?" That was always my constant refrain. Now, I have a new one: "Can I walk right now? Can I stretch and bend, right here, for five minutes?" The answer is almost always, "Yes, I can!" And so I do. It feels terrific. Will I burn calories, will I lose weight? Good heavens, who cares? Will it improve my muscle tone, circulation, and flexibility? Yes indeed, and make me feel better to boot. That's enough.

Here's another change I'm learning to make. With two young children still eager to please their mother (I know, these days are numbered), it's easy to say to them, "Would you bring Mommy her coat? Would you take this to Daddy?" instead of getting up and doing it myself. On other occasions I've witnessed Bill sprawled across the staircase because he tripped over a pile of things I left on the bottom step for my "next trip up." I'm also notorious for driving around and around a parking lot, looking for the space nearest the door. On a rainy day that's understandable, but on a beautiful sunny day it's unnecessary.

These are the "time savers" I'm learning to undo.

Do I agree with the fable, "All fat people are lazy?" No way! Some of us are so industrious we border on workaholism. The last thing we are is lazy. I do find a pattern in my own life, though, of looking for physical shortcuts and avoiding exertion. It's just habit, not a character flaw, and I am moving toward more movement every day.

In *Making Peace with Food* Susan Kano offers goals for any exercise program, including some we've already talked about: having fun, feeling better and improving health. She also sees exercise as a great way to "promote a less ornamental and more instrumental body view" and to "develop unconditional body acceptance and appreciation."[7] Although a small woman herself, Susan is an advocate for body confidence at any size. Bless her!

From the Publishers of "Lose Weight While You Sleep" . . .

A booklet called *Instant Fitness* caught my eye while I stood in line at the grocery store recently. It was displayed among a whole series of booklets with equally outrageous titles: *Birth Signs to Improve Your Love Life*, *150 Beauty Tricks of TV Stars* and *Know Your Lucky Numbers*. Oh sure.

The back cover of this book declared, "It's fun and it's easy to own a well-proportioned figure! Re-shape yourself into a stunning new body that will have heads turning and make you feel like a new woman!" I knew it was worth the seventy-five cent investment, just for the laughs.

I was not disappointed. The first chapter was "How to Flatten Your Stomach." Their advice was to "try to keep your stomach muscles pulled in at all times." The next chapter was "How to Flatten Your Thighs." (Of all the things in life I've ever yearned for, *flat thighs* are not one of them.) They suggested cutting down on salt intake to achieve the desired results.

The chapter titled "Firm Up Flabby Areas" warned against staying in one position too long, which can cause "molecular stagnation." Horrors. In a section on "Mental Conditioning," the reader is told to "Think about how charming you will be with a slim new figure. Think about the new winning personality that will go with that figure." I guess that means at present, the reader is neither charming nor personable.

The final pages contain this sage advice: "Don't be disappointed if some of your friends fail to praise you for making your figure trim.

Some people are hostile to those who successfully lose weight—because they can't do it themselves." Oh, brother!

All this would be good clean fun if it weren't taken so seriously by the hundreds of women who purchase such guides every week. Even the title is a fable: "Instant Fitness." There is nothing instant about getting fit. And fitness does not rule out fatness. Despite Covert Bailey's insistence that we are either "fit or fat," it's not impossible to be both at the same time.

In an article titled, "Fat and Fit: An Idea Whose Time Has Come," fitness expert and author Pat Lyons, R.N., M.A., states that "regular exercise has been shown to have wonderful health benefits, regardless of whether weight is lost. Exercise is also a prime component in stabilizing weight, a legitimate health goal because it places far less stress on the body than constant fluctuations do."[8]

One of the participants in her "Great Shape" exercise program summed up this approach perfectly: "I feel healthier now than any diet I was ever on, and everyone in class has improved health-wise. And we all smile and enjoy life more."[9]

Exercising for the sole purpose of losing weight tends to be (like dieting) short-term, ineffective and self-defeating. Putting movement in your life to improve health and well-being, and for sheer enjoyment, tends to be (unlike dieting) long-term. Plus, it effectively lowers blood pressure and reduces the need for insulin in some diabetics.

Fitness Fears

The truth is, even with all those healthy benefits, many of us are none too eager to jump into a fitness or sports program. It has nothing to do with laziness. One of our survey questions asked, "Does your size affect your social life?" Several women commented specifically about physical activity.

I'm afraid if I ski, I might fall and then couldn't get up.
                                                    Joann from Michigan

(This reminds me of the TV ad featuring the elderly woman moaning, "I've fallen and I can't get up!") Of course, many of us can identify with her honest fear. The solution? If she really wants to ski, she might take a friend who will be happy to help her get up! Or, she might find another winter sport that would be more fun and less frightening for her. Such fears are legitimate, just because they are hers. Only she can choose how to address them.

> *I used to be very athletic—now I've given up softball because my legs hurt when I play and I'm embarrassed to run—my stomach bounces. I would probably use our neighborhood swim and tennis club if I were smaller. I like to dance—now I become winded easier.*
>
> Joyce from Virginia

It's always easy to offer advice, isn't it? We might be quick to suggest that Joyce do more warm-up exercises so her legs won't hurt, or we might tell her to accept the fact that her windedness may come from age as much as weight. It's easy for us to say, "Put on your bathing suit and hit that swim club!" or "Who cares if your stomach bounces when you run?"

It's obvious that Joyce cares. We women of all sizes need to do less finger-wagging at one another and more hand-holding. If we try some of these activities together, maybe with a woman of our own size and at our level of fitness, the whole thing would become less scary.

Fitness Fashions

Some of us aren't hesitant about sports, dance or exercise because of the movement required, but because of the clothing issue.

> *I don't like to participate in activities that are real physical or require less clothing. (I mean, if I stuffed this body into a bathing suit I would clear the pool.)*
>
> Rosanna from Kentucky

Those darn bathing suits. We're talking about an article of clothing that dominates three entire months of the year, for heaven's sake. How many times has a magazine cover shouted at us, "Get Ready for Swimsuit Season!" It's never "Get Ready for Blue Jean Season" or "Leather Belt Season," but sure enough, June, July and August are "Bathing Suit Season" with a vengeance. Fat women need not apply.

Bathing suits conceal nothing, reveal everything. (They may be "suits," but very few have pockets!) One tabloid collection of the latest in swimwear fashion featured a suit with "adjustable triangles." (What a nice choice for a geometry major!) Those, of course, are not "one size fits all" triangles. (Is that an isosceles triangle or scalene? Obtuse or acute?)

I remember well my first two-piece bathing suit. It was yellow and white gingham check, very conservative, more like large squares than tiny triangles. It had a little modesty panel attached to the top with Velcro, and draped down to the pant leg. Great for covering tummy flab. I was twelve.

One year, I found a great two-piece suit that fit nicely but had, alas, no modesty panel. To make up for the missing panel, I arrived at the public swimming pool with a big beach towel tied around my waist. With practice, I learned to whip off the towel, spread it flat on the grass and lie down on it in one brief sweeping motion, executed with such speed that no one saw The Roll. If someone came by to speak to me, I didn't dare sit up. Instead I flipped over on my stomach and propped my head in my hands to talk while I tanned.

Actually, bathing suits have little to do with exercise, or even swimming, and everything to do with body image. It's not surprising the Miss America pageant features a swimsuit competition, because that's exactly what every American woman faces when she hits the beach: competition.

I say, skip the silly suit, wear shorts and a top or whatever's comfortable, and cavort in the waves all you like. It's truly a mind-over-matter issue: if you don't mind, it won't matter! Enjoy the splash of cool ocean water on your legs. Feel the warm, wet sand squish between your toes, and catch the scent of sea water while you romp on the shoreline. The activity is more important than how you look doing it.

For the local pool or swim club, practical one-piece suits are easily available from catalogues in sizes up to 26. Larger sizes can be custom-made. If swimming is the exercise your body craves, don't disappoint it by "waiting until you're thinner." As the athletic shoe people are fond of saying, "Just do it!"

Body Confidence in Action

Some women are elated to discover when push comes to shove, they do just fine in the exercise department. I love this story from a Virginia woman who found out her body functioned admirably when put to the test by her employer at an outdoor team building session. She and her coworkers had to climb a twenty-foot pole, scale a forty-foot wall and slide down a zip line from a forty-foot pole. Here's what happened:

> *My group of seven ladies who are desk-bound and only walk occasionally for exercise, was with a group of six guys from the shipping area who all work out during lunch at our on-site fitness center. All of us made it, and the guys didn't! We gained new respect.*
> Janet from Virginia

Congratulations, Janet and company! There's no doubt physical achievement of any kind, whether it's receiving a trophy for "Most Improved Bowler" or making it to the top of the steps without getting winded, is an accomplishment worthy of applause. You may have to do all the clapping, but so be it!

No one can do it for you, and no one can take away what you have achieved. Mark Twain put it this way: "Skill and confidence are an unconquered army." Just as education gives you power, an advantage that can't be seen but can be experienced, physical exercise can give you a sense of wellness and body confidence. This may or may not be reflected in firmer muscles, but it's surely reflected in your smiling, confident face!

Professional Help

Speaking of education, you need to know about the Aerobics and Fitness Association of America (AFAA), a professional organization that boasts 50,000 members in seventy-three countries, and calls itself "the world's largest fitness educator." They conduct certification classes all the time, all over the country. One of the courses they offer is a special workshop called "Teaching the Overweight." Now, I love the concept of fitness classes just for us, but I *hate* the name. I called the AFAA toll-free line to tell them so. The woman who assisted me was most sympathetic, and very helpful. This special "Teaching the Overweight" certification can be earned only after an instructor earns the AFAA's Primary Certification. It's exciting to think there are fitness professionals all over America who've invested in our health and well-being by learning how to teach us safely and effectively.

I asked her, "How would I find such an instructor?" She recommended putting a small ad in the newspaper—"I am looking for an AFAA-certified instructor to lead a class for large women"—or post a similar notice on bulletin boards at local fitness centers. She assured me the phone would ring off the hook.

Having found an instructor, she suggested they might know of a class for larger women already underway in my city. The second option, she said, is to organize such a class myself, and advertise it.

The third option might be to find two or three friends and have our own class. The helpful woman from AFAA said the average hourly fee for such group instruction would be $15-$35 an hour, depending on your area of the country. The obvious appeal of these classes is two-fold: safe exercise and zero intimidation!

The Last Word on Moving Your Muscles

Fat people are by no means "lazy." Whether you choose to exercise or not, the decision is yours and should bear no weight of moral consequence.

You're not "bad" if you don't, or "good" if you do add movement to your life. Paul wrote Timothy that "bodily exercise profits a little, but godliness is profitable for all things."[10] Yes, exercise is good for your body, but it doesn't make you a good person. It might make you feel better, it might improve your health, and both are valid. But exercise should never be confused with moral or spiritual goodness. After all, you won't find the word "fitness," as we define it, in the Bible!

When it comes to the body (what the Greeks called "soma"), we can both overestimate and underestimate its value. To pay no heed to our bodies whatsoever is foolish and invites disaster. Sleep, food, water, shelter and moderate exercise are all necessary requirements for life on this planet.

But the Western world has gone overboard in its pursuit of the consummate healthy body; measuring foods by the ounce, fat composition by percentage and bodies by the pound. To our culture's way of thinking, less is always better. Paul asked the Colossians, "Why, as though living in the world, do you subject yourselves to regulations—'Do not touch, do not taste, do not handle,' which all concern things which perish with the using—according to the commandments and doctrines of men?"[11] (Sure sounds like dieting to me!) Paul even declares, "Let no one judge you in food or in drink."[12] Of course, Paul was talking about the many food regulations that the religious types of his time loved to impose on one another. (Then again, for many folks today, being fit and trim *is* a religion, so maybe the analogy works better than one might think!)

We have only so many hours in each day. Assume for the moment you spend eight hours at work, seven hours sleeping, one hour driving, one hour bathing and dressing, one hour on household chores, one hour on the phone, and one hour watching television. That leaves four hours in your busy day. Do you want to spend them shopping, chopping, weighing, measuring, planning, preparing and agonizing over every morsel that goes in your mouth? Or do you want to spend that time stretching your muscles while you enjoy your favorite fun activity? Thirty minutes would be plenty. Less is okay too. Try ten minutes. Five minutes. Just begin.

Maybe you want to spend time with your family, or do something meaningful for the less fortunate around you. Whatever you do, seek out that which tastes like eternity and feels like forever. Like Ziggy says, "The waist is a terrible thing to mind."

Begin Building Body Confidence Today

1. Find a form of movement you can do right where you are, for 10 minutes. Anything counts: arm circles, marching in place, touching your toes. Do it now, for ten full minutes by the clock. (I just tried it and I feel wonderful! How do you feel?)

2. Find a form of movement that is *fun*, perhaps done with a group: a walking club, a dance class, a bowling league. Call about it. Ask them to send you some information.

3. Buy yourself one special item to encourage you: a new pair of sweats, a head band, new shoes, a snazzy leotard, a bathing suit. Make sure it fits now, not a size smaller for "when." Let it be your uniform for having fun!

❤ A Fitness Expert Speaks. . . .

Pat Lyons, R.N., M.A., is the regional health education consultant for Northern California Kaiser Permanente, the oldest and largest HMO in the world. Her background is in sports psychology and women's health, and her favorite sports include tennis, softball, skiing, ice skating and hiking. Pat is the co-author of *GREAT SHAPE: The First Fitness Guide for Large Women.*

Liz: Why do women of all sizes, but especially larger women, need to embrace exercise?

Pat: *It's a fundamental way for women to "come home" to their bodies. Sport, dance and movement help you trust your body again. We have a right to feel good, to enjoy physical strength and well-being.*

Liz: And your focus with *GREAT SHAPE* is on enjoyment, not losing weight, is that right?

Pat: *Yes! We need to stop seeing physical activity as punishment, and a thinner body as the only viable product of exercise. Not true! Being physically active is a way to nourish ourselves.*

Liz: We all know, theoretically, that exercise is good for us. Why don't we do it?

Pat: *The number one reason is, "I don't have enough time." The number two reason is, "I'm too embarrassed to go to a gym or exercise class. People make fun of me."*

Liz: Where do we, the great un-exercised, begin?

Pat: *It's a process of small steps. Find something you enjoy, that feels good to do, that's fun. Maybe something you did as a child, or a sport you played in school. Be creative! Your movement does not have to be an organized aerobics class. It could be square dancing or folk dancing.*

Liz: Or tap dancing!

Pat: *Right! Try different kinds of things, experiment, make enjoyment a priority. Get a buddy. Help each other, be easy on one other. Stay in the moment of the activity. Don't think about, "How much will I lose?" or any of that. Think about how much you are enjoying it. If you are out for a walk, smell the roses along the way!*

Liz: What if a woman says, "I'm too out of shape and too intimidated by group exercise things. I just can't do it."

Pat: *I understand that. The larger woman can't just "slip into" an exercise class unnoticed. And often, she can't keep up with the accelerated pace of a standard aerobics or step aerobics program. Start with climbing the stairs inside your own home. Dance around to your favorite music in the privacy of your living room. It takes a long time to change old habits, so relax. Break it down into really small pieces, and validate every small thing you do. Above all, do not focus on the weight loss benefits, which may be minimal, but rather on the health benefits, which are tremendous.*

Liz: Tell us more about that.

Pat: *Researchers from Stanford University found that exercising ten minutes at a time, three times a day is just as effective for improving health as exercising thirty minutes all at once.*

Liz: Hooray! That takes care of the "we don't have time" problem.

Pat: *Right. Their study was particularly aimed at determining health benefits for those with hypertension and diabetes. And the benefits of exercise are realized most by the people who are most sedentary. Every little effort for the sedentary person is really worthwhile. When it comes to exercise, let go of the results and get into the process. Fitness and health are for everybody. Let's enjoy it!*

"Things Would Be Perfect If I Were a Size 10"

Helen Hunt, who knew a lot about money, said, "There is a myth that if you amass enough wealth, then your life falls into place." Many people I've met over the years would buy into that "money equals happiness" fable, even though our newspapers are filled with stories of how wealth has ruined marriages, torn apart families to the third generation, and made hordes of people nigh unto miserable.

The same thing is true with body size. Lizzie's version is: "There is a myth that if you lose enough weight, then your life falls into place."

People buy into that, too, with every dime in their wallets. Roberta Pollack Seid writes in her book, *Never Too Thin*, that "the quest for a fit, fat-free body . . . is held in almost as much esteem as that older American ideal, making money."[1]

The title of this chapter is one of the most carefully crafted fables of all: "Things would be perfect if. . .". You might end that phrase, "if I were a size 4" or "size 6," or perhaps for you, "size 16" would be perfection. This promise of a happy, easy, carefree life after losing weight is carefully hidden under many "fat-free" product labels, or between the covers of the latest diet book.

"Perfect" is exactly what some of us are aiming for:

I will never be 100% comfortable with my body until it is 100%
perfect, and of course it never will be. I wish I could overcome
this . . .

Lisa from Connecticut

Many of us identify with this desire for perfection. Notice her use
of "100%" — no room for error there! We don't just want to be
comfortable, we want to be 100% comfortable. We don't want to be
merely perfect, but guaranteed-absolutely-positively perfect. With
such a high standard, we can be certain that comfort and perfection
will permanently elude us.

Please reinforce this message: quit trying to be perfect in every
area and love yourself just the way you are. Also, quit judging
others who aren't perfect either.

Barbara from Ohio

Gotcha, Barbara. That's exactly the direction we're moving
toward.

What Every Woman Wants

A promotional letter from an organization called The Winning
Woman advertised a cassette on raising your self-esteem with this
opening statement:

She was over twenty, overweight and overwhelmed by feelings of
insecurity and inferiority. She knew she'd failed at work, at
marriage, at family relationships, at everything.

My friend Anne, who sent me a copy of this "winning" offer,
jotted down two valid questions in the margin:

1. If this were a man, would they have been as likely to point
   out that he was "overweight?"
2. Is this meant to infer that if a woman is overweight, she is a
   failure at work, marriage, family . . . at everything?

These subtle (and not so subtle!) messages bombard us every
day, in magazines, on television, even in our mailboxes. The life

style improvements ascribed to bodily perfection are endless: greater happiness, professional success, attention from the opposite sex, ease in shopping, more money in the bank, even cuter kids.

The definition of the perfect body keeps moving down the scale, and not in our direction. In the early 60's, the average model weighed just 8% less than the average American woman. In the late 80's, the average model weighed 23% below the average weight of American women.[2]

Not a good trend.

Miss Perfect on Campus

The desire for a model-thin body has kept many women from pursuing their dreams.

> *When I was in high school, our state's largest newspaper used to print photographs of pretty, slender co-eds at our state's colleges every week. I was so convinced I wouldn't fit in there because I was fat that I never tried to get a college education.*
>
> Pat from Wisconsin

This is a heartbreaking comment to read, because the situation was so avoidable. If only someone had been an advocate for this woman in her post high school years. If only a sister, friend or parent had stepped in and said, "You can do this!" It might have made all the difference for Pat and many others of us.

My own college degree was handed to me in May 1990, a full fourteen years after most of my high school buddies graduated from college. I'd simply been too busy with my radio career and didn't bother to finish my college education. When I finally went back to college in 1986, I found it to be altogether fun, fairly challenging, and highly worthwhile.

True confession: I did not fit in those wrap-around classroom desks, especially when I was pregnant in 1987 and 1989! No problem. I just brought in a regular straight back chair from another room. You can adapt. If you aren't embarrassed about making such concessions, no one else will even notice or care.

When I graduated on Mother's Day 1990, I wore the flat hat with the tassel and the black graduation robe. It was, of course, "One Size Fits All!" Actually, I'm probably the only graduate whose gown really was my size. It zipped right up and fit like a dream. (I would have worn it home, but solid black is not my color!)

Did it feel good to earn that bachelor of arts in English after eighteen years and three colleges? You bet. Did I have a perfect 4.0 grade point average? Heavens no! I did my best, earned perfectly fine (though not perfect) grades, and most important of all, graduated. As in many things in life, the key is to get it done, to the best of your ability. Period.

Not-So-Perfect Is Still Terrific

One woman's stumbling block—being less than perfect—is another woman's key to success:

> *My imperfection makes me more accessible and safe to admit "fears" to. I am less threatening.*
> Sandra from Missouri

My own experience as a speaker bears that out. Complete strangers come up and throw their arms around me after one of my presentations. What fun to give them such "permission!" I suppose it is a combination of body language, demeanor, dress, or style. But they can see I'm not perfect, don't expect *them* to be perfect, and that I'm there to help them have a good time. (Plus, I have a very huggable body, just like you do!)

Some of us have at least one perfect attribute:

> *Everyone makes fun of me because I'm a perfect hair person. It's like they never see the rest of me. My favorite comment is that if I took as much time worrying about my rear end as I do my hair, I'd have the best looking rear end in town!*
> Gail from Kentucky

Now, there's a woman I can relate to: funny and human. That's something we can all aspire to!

A Sizeable Impact at Work

It's one thing to want to be perfect for yourself. I don't advocate it, but at least it's your choice. What is definitely a no-no is when an employer expects you to meet some standard of perfection concerning appearance that has nothing whatsoever to do with your job performance.

One of the most revealing questions on my survey for this book was, "Does your size have any impact on your job? If so, please explain." Here are their responses. (Prepare to get angry!)

> *I believe that I was passed over for a job for someone with the same qualifications, but less experience, because of my "image."*
>
> Kitty from Kentucky

Many employers hide behind the word "image" because it is conveniently vague. While I am all in favor of dressing well and looking our best, our body size and shape and facial characteristics should never enter into the job placement picture.

But, they *do* enter into the picture, in subtle and not so subtle ways. Dr. Esther Rothblum conducted an employment study at the University of Vermont. Students were given identical job resumes, one with the photo of a woman weighing about 120 pounds, the other with a photo of a woman who weighed 150 pounds. Hardly a large woman, just a bit heavier than the social norm. The students' response? They consistently rated the 150-pound woman as lower on supervisory potential, self-discipline, professional appearance, personal hygiene, and determined that she deserved a lower starting salary![3] All this because of thirty pounds? Two dress sizes? Unfortunately, yes.

In the workplace we are, without a doubt, up against deeply ingrained misconceptions and old stereotypes that won't go away. We've seen such struggles before:

> *Back around 1945 when discrimination was raging, I had two strikes against me: I was black and I was fat. I was only seventeen-years-old. The pressure made me suicidal.*
>
> Martha from Ohio

That reminds me of a statement former Congresswoman Shirley Chisholm once made. She said that between being black and being female, being female was the greater challenge to her career. For Martha, being large may have been a third, even greater challenge. My hat is off to her for not only surviving, but thriving!

The competition in the workplace today is volatile enough without tossing in the size issue. But let's face it, size is an issue.

I think I have to work harder to win people over by being either knowledgeable, very nice and sincere, or funny.

Joyce from Virginia

Job discrimination because of size is a serious problem, one that was being addressed at various national levels even as I was writing this book. In the meantime, I firmly believe that our best defense is a positive offense. A woman who is confident about her knowledge and skills will project that confidence far beyond the boundaries of her body.

A Dilemma in Women's Health

Much of the work I do as a professional speaker is in the field of health care. Nurses, technicians, medically related associations, and hospital-sponsored events for the public are some of the health-oriented audiences I have the privilege of addressing each year.

Many of my clients kindly completed surveys for this book, and I was surprised to see a very definite pattern to their answers concerning, "Does your size affect your job?" These are all women, employed specifically in women's health departments, usually as R.N.'s or directors. Here are some of their replies, with names omitted (since they *are* my clients!). Note the similarities in their answers, which I've taken the liberty of capitalizing:

The PERCEPTION is that people in the health care field should be thin, trim and the PICTURE of health.

People PERCEIVE or think because I'm in health education I should be perfect. Perfect body, perfect eating and exercise habits, non-smoker.

I didn't get a job as a nurse recruiter because they felt my IMAGE wasn't what they wanted projected from the hospital.

It's essential to LOOK fit and healthy when you work in health care.

APPEARANCE is very important. (Especially when representing a hospital.)

If I FEEL overweight, I think I am delivering an unhealthy message to my clients. (This is the result of brainwashing, I know.)

Oh, dear friend, you are quite correct there! If these women had stated, "I must have low blood pressure, a healthy heart and low cholesterol levels to do this job," we might think it unusual. But we could at least say, "well, they must be in good health to help others be healthy." That's not reality, but it would at least make sense. Yet, none of them said they had to *be* healthy, just *look* healthy (read: thin).

Am I blaming these fine professionals? Not in the least. They are the product of the same society we are, one that equates perfectly thin bodies with perfect health, imperfect-looking bodies with imperfect health. One thin counselor who works with women struggles with what almost amounts to reverse discrimination because of her "image":

> *My big, beautiful clients hate me; and my narrow, nervous, eating-disordered (anorexic) clients think I'm just like them. Clients often assume that I'm "perfect" because they think my size is "perfect."*
>
> Cindy from Missouri

Or, how would you like to be a lecturer for a weight loss center and live up to these requirements?

> *I must remain within 4 pounds of goal weight or risk losing my job. It's hard to focus on whether you even feel well when you have a constant pink slip in your future.*
>
> Cynthia from Michigan

We have a long way to go, in health care and every other profession, toward ending size discrimination. After all, our goal is for everyone to *be* healthy, not just look the part.

Our Own Worst Enemies

Without question, there are whole professions that are size-biased, and some individual employers as well. There are times, however, when we "shoot ourselves in the foot," as my husband likes to say. By believing so completely that only thin women can compete in the workplace, we stop believing in ourselves.

I may hesitate to approach a potential client because of insecure feelings about the reaction to me.

Louise from Georgia

It's easy to brush away such concerns on paper. But, we all know Louise's hesitance is common. The trick is to develop sufficient body confidence to handle such insecurities head-on.

You'll hear it again and again in these pages: People will accept you only to the extent you accept yourself. If you have confidence in your abilities, they may have confidence in you too. I've spent ten years moving from holding back to pushing full steam ahead, and I'm here to tell you: it's up to you!

Practical Considerations

Even if you have all the confidence a woman could want, there are still some everyday hassles that need to be addressed when you're venturing forth into a world made for smaller people.

I think the audience may not accept or believe me if I'm too big.

Patty from California

This wonderful woman also happens to be a professional speaker (and a friend). The part about the "audience may not accept or believe me" fascinated me because that's not been my own experience at all. I think attitude is everything. I accept myself and dress appropriately. Audiences always applaud enthusiastically, and sometimes they stand up! I take that as acceptance of both the message and the messenger.

Then again, another speaker who conducts training sessions got this reaction from someone in her audience:

One day my husband came home from work and was telling me what one of his colleagues said about me. His coworker mentioned how smart I was and that as soon as I started talking, people started listening and didn't even think about what I looked like.

Joyce from Virginia

Her husband thought it was meant to be a compliment, and it was. Sort of.

Here are some other practical concerns women voiced about life on the job:

> *Getting around hospital furniture and physical therapy equipment is hard.*
>
> Andi from California

And, many of us can identify with this woman's challenge.

> *Getting in and out of my car is difficult in a compact car space in the parking structure.*
>
> Mary Ann from California

These things are definitely a nuisance. In some cases, we can simply arrange things to make life easier for ourselves and other larger people. Or, we may just need to enlist someone else for assistance:

> *Every time something is needed that's in a "tight" spot — I'm elected to "squeeze" in and get it because I'm a size 6!*
>
> Mary Anne from Indiana

I am always grateful when I'm seated next to the Mary Anne's of the world when I'm in this situation:

> *I'm embarrassed on airplanes because my arms touch the other person.*
>
> Janice from Idaho

Oh, Janice! I could do a twenty-minute routine on my experiences with airline seats. As a frequent flyer on six carriers, let me offer some words of wisdom for handling the hassle of flying.

Helping Delta Be "Ready When You Are"

Here are a dozen tips for making air travel more bearable, even enjoyable:

1. Use a great travel agent, someone who knows the business and is empathetic to your needs. If you aren't already a frequent flyer on the airline with the most flights in and out of your nearest airport, fill out their simple form

now. It doesn't cost a dime, and I've found that being a Delta Royal Medallion Member gets me extra good service.

2. Book thirty days in advance for the best choice of seats (and usually, the lowest airfares).

3. Get an aisle seat on the three-seat side, as close to the front as possible, but *not* the bulkhead seat. (They have solid stationary sides.) Ask for a row that doesn't have a passenger seated in the middle seat. (They can't guarantee it will remain that way, but you can at least begin with the best situation.)

4. Try to fly during off times (middle of the week, middle of the day, Saturdays) rather than the busiest times (mornings, Fridays). There is always more room and better service when you're not flying peak.

5. Arrive at the gate at least thirty minutes before the scheduled departure time. When the agent is checking your ticket, ask, "Is the seat in the middle still vacant?" I usually have a little fun with them, and add, "You see, I like to travel with both my hips, and thought I'd see if there's room for them today!" They always laugh, and they always help me if they can. They'll usually move me to an empty row. On four occasions they've moved me up to First Class at no extra charge, just to be nice! (Don't hold your breath for this. That's four times out of hundreds of flights.) The only time they can't move me is when the flight is booked solid.

6. When you find your seat, get everything up in the overhead compartment so you have as much room around you as possible.

7. Push up the arm rest. If someone is seated in that middle seat (ugh), I say something like, "We will probably both be a little more comfortable with this up. Would you mind?" Sometimes they do mind, most times they don't. It's worth asking.

8. Try the seat belt as soon as you sit down. If it won't extend enough for you, ask the flight attendant, before she gets busy, for a seat belt extension. It's actually one of those little demonstration belts and should help you breathe easier. For some reason, the seat belts on jets are bigger

than those on commuters. I just ask for one as I'm boarding the smaller planes, and they hand me one on the spot. I've never had them even look at me funny, let alone act rude or insensitive. These truly are professionals, and safety is their first concern.

9. When the middle seat is vacant, use that tray table for your soda and peanuts or the "snack" (i.e., frozen solid roll, limp roast beef, cheese wedge, tiny cracker, mushy apple. M-m-m . . .).

10. If all three seats in your row are vacant (you lucky soul!), then switch to the middle seat, and put up both arm rests. The center cushions are invariably softer (less use), and then the attendants won't accidentally crash their beverage cart into your elbow or knee. I flip all three tray tables down and have a branch office in the sky!

11. For hauling luggage, I use one of those little carts on wheels like the flight attendants use. If you fly even twice a year, you'll appreciate having one of these handy helpers. A good one will cost $35-$45, but will last for years.

12. Dress comfortably! I wear flats with cushioned soles, only a light coat year-round, and slacks or a split-skirt for more graceful bending over. Since I'm often met by a client, I send them a little poem that tells them what to expect when they meet me. It says:

> At the airport, should we meet,
> Here's the woman you will greet . . .
> I'll be tall, about five-nine,
> Yellow hair that's short and fine,
> Full of figure, eyes of blue,
> Fair of skin and glasses, too.
> Wearing flats and comfy clothes
> Don't forget those pantyhose!
> Luggage will be one black bag,
> On a rolling cart to drag.
> Smiling, laughing, waving, too —
> I'll be happy to see you!

It features a little caricature of me, so the person meeting me will know me on sight. It also lists the arrival date, time and flight. Just a simple thing, but it takes away some of those meeting-somebody-for-the-first-time jitters.

Go to the Head of the Class

Even if your job doesn't require air travel, your size may mean some similar challenge must be met:

> *It makes it more difficult to haul in my supplies for teaching. I always hope they'll put my class on a ground floor, next to the outside door, by a close parking lot!*
>
> Pat from Wisconsin

Maybe that luggage cart would help here. My guess is, *thin* teachers hope for the same thing. I love this woman's experience:

> *I work with two other teachers — same age as me, but sizes 6 and 8. One day at the end of our classes a sweet little eight-year-old girl gave each of us a hug. She looked at me quite politely and said, "Mmmm! You're soft!"*
>
> Barbara from Pennsylvania

One teacher said that her size did indeed impact her job, because her very presence could "scare the most troublesome kids to death!" Here is another woman who makes the most of her abundant talents:

> *I think my size is reassuring and non-threatening. Occasionally I will have an individual who initially is distant, but I have this wonderful smile and a southern accent. I use them both!*
>
> LaDonna from Oregon

A Skinny Voice

I'm already a fan of a woman named Cookie. She's a sales representative who spends a lot of time on the phone. Size is not an issue for her on the job:

> *I don't have any problem because I have a skinny, young voice!*
>
> Cookie from Texas

Funny you should say that, Cookie. That's what I heard from people back when I was a radio personality. My career on the air spanned ten years (1978-88), seven stations with all kinds of formats (jazz, top 40, disco, album rock, country, oldies, and adult contemporary), in five states (Pennsylvania, Maryland, Indiana, Michigan and Kentucky).

The one constant in all that craziness was that people thought I sounded thin. (What exactly does a thin person sound like?) My voice is fairly low for a woman, and somewhat musical. In fact, one time I had a listener complain about "that woman on the air who sounds like a piano!" Most people were much kinder and said my voice was mellifluous. This I know: many clients were delighted to have me voice their commercials and could have cared less what size or shape I was.

But my regular listeners cared very much. They wanted me to fit an imaginary picture of Liz they had in their mind's eye. When they would finally meet me in person at a promotional event, their responses were pretty predictable:

"Gee whiz! You don't look like you sound!"

"I thought you'd be thinner!"

"Are you sure you're Lizzie?" (No. I'm Cher.)

And, my personal favorite:

"You don't sound *fat* on the radio!"

That one left me speechless (which doesn't happen very often!). Later, I thought of a brilliant comeback: "Ma'am, the Bible says that my body is a temple of the Holy Spirit. He just started a building program that got out of hand!"

(Why can't we come up with that stuff when we need it?)

My Radio Studio "Closet"

To be honest, radio was a great place to hide. I could be a sultry siren or a sophisticated career woman or a young ingenue, and no one was the wiser. With only my voice to work with, I could be anything I wanted. I tried all of the above, with limited success.

My real success in radio came when I was just myself on the air, telling stories and sharing my struggles and discoveries. Still, I was only a voice without a body, an invisible woman.

> *I feel that many women become overweight to become invisible. Society tends to look past and ignore large women. It's safe. A place no one will hurt you anymore, because they don't pay attention to you.*
>
> Sandra from Missouri

I think radio was, initially, safe for me. My last station, one of the finest 50,000-watt clear channel outlets in the country, WHAS-AM in Louisville, was less safe. On-air personalities were expected to do lots of meeting and greeting and frequent promotional appearances. I had to play the music, and face the music when I stepped out of the studio each day.

As scary as that was, it was also the very thing that led me into professional speaking. From 1983 on, people began inviting me to speak to their Kiwanis Club, their church group, their school assembly. Soon the number of calls had grown to ninety a year. Before long, it was obvious that I should move to platform speaking. Who could have guessed that what had once scared me most of all – public appearances – would soon become my main source of income and my favorite way to spend the day?

No More Hiding

I began my speaking business in 1987, with one foot still in radio (in case I "bombed!"). My business grew slowly at first. Not every engagement was fun. I remember standing behind a group of folks at a banquet, trying to think of what I might say to invite myself into their circle. I heard one of the men in the group say, "Hey, have you seen Liz yet? She's a big woman. I mean a B-I-G woman!" Everyone laughed and started looking around. As you might imagine, I wanted to crawl out of that room and never speak publicly again!

But I lived through that night, and many since then. Because my promotional brochure and photos clearly show my clients that I'm a "large and lovely" speaker, they're never surprised. And, since they usually use my photos in their promotion of the event, the audience is seldom taken aback either.

To act as an icebreaker, and to address the size issue immediately, I have some fun with my size as soon as I pick up the microphone. Then we're on to other things. I have found audiences don't want a "perfect" speaker — how intimidating! — but they do want a speaker who is perfectly happy with who she is. Finally, I can say I am.

The conventional wisdom in the speaking profession is "the audience will feel what you feel." I focus on feeling joyful, confident and relaxed. Then, I watch people take on those same attributes. I believe you can apply that same simple formula where you work.

Lest you think I've got it all together on this confidence thing, I'll let you in on some instances when my confidence slipped just a tad.

Sizing Up to the Truth

I delayed designing my first fancy brochure for several months, because I kept thinking (you won't believe this), "Maybe I could lose a few pounds before I visit the photographer." Talk about denial!

An agent I was working with just shook his head when I tried to explain this delay. "Listen to your own message, Liz!" he rightfully told me. The photos were taken. Soon my very own red, black, and ivory brochures came rolling off the press. Ta-da!

I mailed copies of my new brochure to some friends in the business and waited for their glowing remarks. They came. But so did a letter from a special friend, Rosita Perez. She wrote: "In your new brochure, you call yourself a 'Size 16 Tinkerbell.' Liz, having cut the labels out of a few 18's myself, I just cannot believe that you are anything less than an 18 or 20." There was no point to being either mad or offended. First of all, I trust her completely, and second of all, she was right. Well, I did have one size 16 dress that still fit — after a fashion. It had an elastic waist. But most of my clothes were indeed 18's and 20's.

Her letter continued. "I care too much about your success, Liz. The problem is, if the audience does not believe you, it may ruin your credibility in all else that you share." That was the real problem here. Not the dress size, forget that. It was my reputation, my trustworthiness that was important. Rosita knew it, and she loved me enough to confront me. Say what you will, that's a real friend.

I have a new brochure now (with no dress size listed at all), and from the platform I call myself, accurately, a size 22 Tinkerbell. (Just for the record, there are a few 24's in the closet too!) Thanks, Rosita, for making an honest woman out of me.

What I've learned after five hundred professional presentations over the last several years is that success is built on credibility, confrontation and communication. In any endeavor, if we're willing to be true to ourselves, confront untruth when we see it, and share the truth as we know it, amazing things will happen.

A Strategy for Success

I had another "a-ha!" experience in 1990 when I enlisted the services of a strategic planning expert to help me map out my speaking business for the next five years. Stephen Tweed asked me a simple question: "What is your competitive advantage? What makes you unique?"

Without hesitation, I blurted out, "I'm a big, beautiful woman!" Soon I thought of other things: I'm funny and love helping women laugh, I enjoy the selling process, serving my clients, and so on. But the first advantage that came to mind was my size.

Imagine that. What I once considered my biggest problem I now considered to be one of my biggest pluses!

Here are three reasons why I believe any large woman can use her size to her advantage in business (I call this my 3-M theory):

1. Few people have ever seen a big woman standing proud, smiling at the world, employing her gifts, and living life to the fullest without apology. You will, therefore, be MIRACULOUS to people!
2. Because of your uniqueness, you will be MEMORABLE. My clients and audiences may remember me as "that big, funny blonde woman," but they do remember me. They will remember you too!
3. As any marketing expert will tell you, an unusual and identifiable product is very MARKETABLE ... that's you! Any products or services that you provide will sell themselves, because you are sold on you, and so are your buyers.

I used to worry that I alone subscribed to my 3-M theory, and therefore it must be faulty. But each year I meet more women who've learned the same lessons and come to the same conclusion:

[Some folks] think that big people — women in particular — are not in control. The joke's on them. Sometimes our very size puts us in control!

Anne from South Carolina

The Perfect Role Model

It's exciting to find people who are further down the road on this particular journey. Such role models can show us where the potholes are, the smoother paths, the hidden stumbling blocks. We need each other!

I live in a very small town and I need to hear about overweight women who have become successful in their careers and lives, who have been pioneers, so to speak, and done things other people may not have done, even people of normal weight.

Pat from Wisconsin

Let me tell you about Linda, an amazing woman I met while doing a presentation in eastern Pennsylvania. After the program was over, I shook hands and gave hugs and greeted the wonderful members of my audience.

That's when I saw Linda, aboard her mobility aid, waiting on the sidelines to talk to me. She is a big, beautiful woman, with the emphasis on beautiful. Linda has conquered cancer, owns her own business, and volunteers as a fireman and emergency medical responder. Incredible! As she puts it:

Someone whose house is on fire, or who has been in an accident and is bleeding, does not care whether I'm fat, skinny, ugly or beautiful. They just need help!

You might wonder, as I did, how a large woman who isn't able to walk because of various physical challenges, might be of service in an emergency. Here's how:

When the alarm sounds, the adrenal rush blocks all pain, at least for awhile. At fire scenes, I can make sure all the men are properly geared, change air bottles, hold a hose. Accident scenes are a little different. Out here in the boonies, I might have to wait an hour for more highly trained personnel to arrive. Sometimes I go home and straight to bed with my Advil, heating pad, hot water bottle and ice pack. The pain eventually goes away. There is such a tremendous satisfaction in knowing I really counted for something, helped someone in trouble and maybe even helped save a life! Nothing compares with that!

Talk about a positive attitude. Linda's heroic efforts would put most of us to shame. Thankful to be alive, she sums it all up: "What's a little fat among friends?" Perfect.

Begin Building Body Confidence Today

1. Begin replacing any "perfect" goals in your life with healthy, realistic goals. When possible, don't aim for a number. Make your goals small, manageable, measurable (but not in pounds and inches).

2. If there is something you've been putting off until you could do it "perfectly" or until the "perfect time," ask yourself, "Why not today?" Take one small step in that direction.

3. Make a list of three benefits of being your current size.

❤ A Psychologist Speaks . . .

Dr. Kathryn D. Cramer is director of The Cramer Institute in St. Louis, Missouri. She has both a master's degree and Ph.D. in psychology, with specialties in health psychology, adult development and organizational consulting. She is the author of *Staying on Top When Your World Turns Upside Down*, and *Forty, Get Set, Grow!*

Liz: What is the connection between the body image obsession many of us have and perfectionism?

Kathy: *No matter what our body type, many women experience a drive to be perfect through having a body that others find attractive. Our striving to be perfect has two dimensions — a self dimension and a social dimension. Our bodies are one of the most prominent means of interacting with one another. It's normal that someone whose internal standards are to strive for perfection would manifest that in terms of her attitude toward her body. And, it's not surprising that she would seek the approval of others to validate her achievement of that internal standard.*

Liz: Why do we set such high standards for ourselves?

Kathy: *The drive to be perfect is really a misguided but well-intentioned motive. Most of us develop our striving to be perfect out of our desire to please our parents and other authorities whom we depend on and love. It's very rare that we emerge from the womb with a desire to be perfect! When the authorities in our lives keep "raising the bar" in order for us to win their approval, the foundation of perfectionism is established.*

Liz: What leads women to believe that if they were just thinner — shorter, taller, prettier, younger, or older — they would be happier and/or more successful?

Kathy: *This is a frequent error most often made during the first half of life, or until a person reaches their mid-40's. Our culture promises that happiness can be achieved by amassing external, visible success. In America that means money, career, marital status, and the "light look." Most people go through some sort of mid-life awakening which conveys just how hollow this search for happiness along such external lines can be.*

Liz: Mid-life awakening sure beats having a mid-life crisis! What does it produce?

Kathy: *Those women who are open to the kind of wisdom which is truly possible only during the second half of life have a chance to correct such misconceptions. Genuine happiness is linked to the fulfillment of one's unique inner talents and potential and has little if anything to do with culturally defined success. However, up until now there have been very few guidelines for how to live a genuinely happy life.*

Liz: How can a woman change how she feels about herself, and be genuinely happy?

Kathy: *One of the most profoundly powerful tools in self-change is self-nurturing. If women will only apply to themselves the type of coaching and caring they give to their children and other people in need, they would begin to view themselves compassionately. This compassionate self-perception is the fundamental basis for self-change.*

Liz: In order for change to occur, how important is it for us to determine why we think, act and feel the way we do?

Kathy: *For some people, insight into their own motives and "blind spots" gives them a chance to make order out of chaos. Self-understanding should not be the only goal, but for many it is the key to being compassionate about themselves. Such insights are achieved layer by layer, like peeling an onion. Slowly, one begins to understand the complexities involved, especially with something as complex as bodily appearance. For many women, gaining insight into themselves is a powerful, positive step in taking charge of their lives.*

"Large Women Adore Wearing Double Knit" (It's So Flattering!)

There was a time when women's clothing left a lot to the imagination. Covering themselves with yards of fabric from neck to toe, women of another era used undergarments to give them the shape they wanted. Rather than dieting and exercise, stays and corsets were used to produce a tiny waist or slimmer torso. Of course, fashion designers of the last century also *added* to the female form with bustles and hoops. (Almost makes you want those antebellum fashions to come back for another round!)

Back then, big, beautiful women like Lillian Russell were revered. Known as America's sweetheart, she weighed in at 200 pounds by the early 1900's.[1] It wasn't long, however, until designers introduced a new style of dress that required a much leaner body. By 1908, *Vogue* was singing the praises of these new straight-skirted, high-waisted empire fashions: "How slim, how graceful, how elegant women look."[2] Full-figured women would never really be "in vogue" again.

With the new fashions came the necessity to reshape the female form, and so women started counting calories and weighing themselves at home. For the first time, we became number-obsessed. Two books published in 1917, both written by women, paved the way for diet books to follow: *Lose Weight and Be Well* and *Diet and Health, with Key to the Calories.*[3] It's interesting to me that, though new fashions were the impetus for this growing concern with being thin, health was touted as the reason to pursue slenderness. (The more things change, the more they stay the same.)

My mother, born in 1911, always said that the worst day of her life arrived with the advent of sack dresses in the 20's. Those straight, shapeless, just-below-the-knee dresses were not flattering to her full-figured body. They've come back in style from time to time, but never for long. They only look good on hangers and fashion models, not on most mothers.

"What Shall I Wear?"

Miss Manners said, "What shall I wear?" is society's second most frequently asked question. The first is "Do you really love me?"

Both questions are self-esteem issues. I believe if a woman truly loves herself and the body she lives in, she will choose what she wears with care, knowing that her outward attire is often a reflection of her inner being.

The balance between inner beauty and the more visible kind is precarious.

> Do not let your adornment be merely outward — arranging the hair, wearing gold, or putting on fine apparel — rather let it be the hidden person of the heart, with the incorruptible beauty of a gentle and quiet spirit, which is very precious in the sight of God.[4]

No question about it. A woman who is only beautiful on the outside is truly unattractive. If we think a hot new haircut, 24k gold jewelry or an expensive outfit is all it takes to be a beautiful woman, we're sadly mistaken. Haircuts grow out, jewelry is lost or stolen, clothing gets damaged or goes quickly out of style. That stuff *is* corruptible. It doesn't last.

But for a woman radiant on the inside to be dull as dishwater on the outside is also a sad waste of beauty. I have met more women who had gentle quiet spirits, drab clothing and sad faces than I can count.

All women, but especially larger women, need to get their inside and outside selves more in sync. Which one needs the most attention right now? If your outside self is gorgeous but your inner being has been neglected, start nurturing your spiritual self. If your spiritual self is beautifully gentle, then frame that with clothes that mirror your sweet spirit and radiate your light from within.

No "Omar the Tentmaker" Jokes, Please

It has taken years, even decades, but the garment industry has finally created decent fashions for larger women. What in the world took them so long? We've been waiting, credit cards clutched in our fists, for ages.

They've had retail stores for larger men since mid-century. These shops are very sensibly called "Big and Tall Men." The fellas just walk in, find what they need, plunk down their money and head out the door. No stigma attached, no clerk "tsk-tsking" outside the dressing room, no premium price for the larger sizes. Oh, maybe a few dollars extra for more fabric, but nothing outrageous.

Why didn't they create stores like that for women with fuller figures? Easy. They knew we would never walk in a store called "Big Fat Girls!"

So, they stayed up late at night in Merchant Land and came up with lots of euphemistic names for such stores: Added Dimensions. Pretty and Plump. Extra Special. Lots to Love. Large and Luscious. Twice as Nice. (I guess they have a line of Petites called "Half as Nice!") One of my favorites is Great Personality. You can just imagine a man saying, "Well, she may not be a size 10, but she has a great personality!"

Some of the names are quite lovely. Grande Lady has a nice ring to it. I found a Renoir's Lady in Portland that had terrific clothes at discounted prices. And I don't mind thinking of myself as a Rubenesque Woman. One of my favorite names is The Forgotten Woman. Oprah has shopped there. So has Roseanne. So has Lizzie, when I'm speaking in one of the nineteen cities that has The Forgotten Woman (and when I have some room left in my budget!).

Just for Us

The "Women's" sizes are always tucked away out of sight . . . in the back of the building next to customer service and the restrooms. It's almost like they're ashamed of it.

Joyce from Virginia

We've come a long way since those days (although in small towns across the land, that's still the only option). The nicer stores for women who wear sizes 14-26 carry everything we might ever need (well, almost everything: "Where are boots for large women?" Judith from Colorado rightly wants to know). They do carry swimsuits, lingerie, business suits, casual clothes, even sequin-bedecked evening gowns! Catherine from Kentucky said sequined dresses were out for her because "I'm not made for slinky!"

Au contraire, my dear Catherine. At a wonderful store in Oklahoma City, with your very name, "Catherine's," I found not one but two gorgeous knee-length sequined dresses, one purple with gold, one black with gold, very classy, my size and on sale.

You'll remember for years they called themselves Catherine's Stout Shop. No more. They've scaled up their image, dropped the Stout Shop part (though on some store marquees you can still faintly see where the letters were). They've also designed a zingy new logo and added the phrase, "Fashion independence for today's large size woman." Hooray for Catherine's!

Two of the women who completed surveys for this book work in stores for larger women. We made a deal: I bought some clothes, they filled out a survey! Vicki lets us in on why such stores are the perfect place to work:

I need to be full-figured to work where I do! You can't put a size 8 clerk in our store and think a size 22 patron will seriously take a compliment from them.

Vicki from Wisconsin

That reminds me of a big, beautiful woman named Leslie who I met at a convention. It seems the national president of her association was coming to town and had asked Leslie to arrange a shopping trip for her. Apparently the only chance this V.P. ever had to buy clothes was when she traveled. She wanted this plus-size beauty to visit a few stores in advance and have some suits ready for her to try on. The V.P. wore a size 2 or 4 petite.

"Liz," Leslie confided, her eyes twinkling, "can you imagine what these shop owners must have thought when I breezed in, grabbed half a dozen suits in sizes 2 and 4 petite, tossed them on the counter and said, 'Could you hold these for me? We'll be back to try them on at 3:00 P.M.'!"

Sometimes it's easier to catalogue shop: *Just My Size* for comfy sweats and pantyhose, *Silhouettes* for nice, affordable dresses, *Just Right!* for better dresses and suits, *Brownstone Woman* for classy career dressing and the *I. Magnin* catalogue when I just want to drool. You'll find more information about these and other catalogues in the resources section of this book.

Wherever you shop, be daring. Try something new, something that doesn't look like "you." More than once I have been surprised and delighted to find that some off-the-wall-looking outfit does fun things to my big body. You just never know. And, don't be afraid to put on a belt if the outfit calls for it. Carole Shaw of *BBW* magazine was one of the first people to suggest putting belts on larger fashions. Women protested, of course, saying, "But, we have no waist!" Carole makes it sound so simple: "Just bend over. Wherever you crack, that's your waist!"

I am short-waisted and long-legged, so I often have trouble finding pants that look, fit and feel right on my body. Recently I found one manufacturer who must have a mannequin built like me, because their pants fit me perfectly. Of course I bought three pairs: black, royal blue and (look out, world) orange! It's true: colors that compliment your skin and hair will make you look more polished, energetic, and comfortable with your twice-as-nice self.

Store-Bought Confidence

To a certain extent, one can "purchase" a healthy dose of body confidence. I love beautiful clothing, not only for how it makes me look, but how it makes me feel.

I choose things that feel good against my skin. Silk is my favorite, because of how it hangs and drapes, the way it floats and dances around me. As a natural fabric, it breathes, keeping me cool in the summer and warm in the winter. Wool makes me itch, but 100% cotton feels fabulous. Yes, you have to iron it, but after enough washings, it gets less wrinkled.

Clothes that feel good physically can help us feel good emotionally. I don't pretend to understand how this works psychologically, but I'm certain it is a universal experience.

Feeling good about the way I look makes me more confident in my ability.

Cynthia from New Jersey

When we feel that we look our best (*our* best, not someone else's definition) then we can face the world with a smile, confident we have something to offer.

Author Roberta Pollack Seid describes dressing as a "virtual process of self-creation, of self-portraiture. It reveals the way we see ourselves and the way we want others to see us."[5] Sometimes how others view us, though, doesn't accurately reflect the message we are trying hard to communicate:

People say to me, "You dress well for a woman of your size."

Kathryn from Arkansas

They were doing fine till they got to the "for a woman of your size" part. It's obvious they mean such things to be compliments, so the best thing to do is receive them as such. Vow to be more sensitive with others than some people are with you.

The truth is, a well-dressed 16+ woman stands out from the crowd, and I mean in the most positive sense. I tell people that I simply must dress well, in dramatic styles and bold colors, because I have such a large canvas to paint on. It would be a shame to waste one inch of it with something dull and drab!

There are many styles that you must be larger to pull off. I think the wedge dresses of recent years, and especially the swing jackets, look ridiculous with a pair of spider legs hanging out the bottom. You and I fill them out properly and give them panache.

Anne from South Carolina wonders, "Why do manufacturers think that big women want to wear faddish clothes, i.e., short hem lines and ruffles, regardless of how we look in them?"

A legitimate question, of course. Yet there are those of us who love how we look in the shorter skirts and ruffled hems. I'm just glad the fashion folks are giving us some choices, so we can decide. After all, ten women may all wear a size 20 dress and yet look very different in the same outfit. Height, build, and body proportions all factor into the fashion mix. The key is to find a few styles that always make you feel good, always get you sincere compliments. Then, seek out those special styles when you shop. I'm grateful for fashions that make us look well-dressed instead of like we're wearing a shower curtain!

Models and Mannequins

When larger women can look so smashing in the latest fashions, why do you suppose the garment industry insists on showing their clothes on very thin women? It's an aesthetic problem. Fashion designers don't want women's bodies to get in the way of their clothes. Instead, they want mannequins that move, dress racks that dance, hangers that have no "love handles" or anything else to distract the eye of the buyer.

You knew I'd have to mention Twiggy. She graced the cover of *Vogue* four times in 1967, the year I entered junior high and began my love/hate affair with dieting. She was 5'7". She weighed 91 pounds.[6] Even Twiggy herself said, "It's not what you would call a figure, is it?"[7]

No. Most mannequins haven't much of a figure either, averaging a 33 inch bust. The average American woman is at least 3 inches bigger, lots of us are 10 inches bigger. Sharlyne Powell, the founder of "Women At Large" and a producer of excellent exercise videos for larger women, was a guest on the Sally Jesse Raphael show recently. Sharlyne shared a telling statistic: Ten years ago, the average bra size for an American woman was a 34B. Now, it's a 36C. We are getting bigger, including in some of the "right" places.

Fashion Fables

A collection of fables has been passed down to us over the years, untruths which we now have to work through, so that dressing becomes fun again. For example, there's the classic, "Black is a slimming color." This is true if you're a penguin. For the rest of us, black turns our body into one giant, colorless shadow. This isn't to say black can't be made to look good on a larger woman. But it needs some shape, some contrast, some movement, or it will just sit there.

Here's another favorite fable: "Stripes make you look thinner." Can't you hear your mother intoning this one from outside your dressing room while you tried on that striped dress she chose? Vertically striped, of course.

As you might guess, the winning fable at our house is, "One size fits all!" All what? All one leg? Ione from Michigan suggests, "Why don't they make one size fits all tent dresses that can be cut off for any height?" (Isn't that a picture?)

"One size fits all" is such a fashion fable that whenever my book title is announced as part of my introduction before a speech, the audience laughs. Rightly so. It *is* laughable, although not in every situation:

> *One New Year's Eve in an emergency situation I was forced to purchase a pair of "Chubby Chick" pantyhose which were "One Size Fits All." Needless to say, pulling them on and [having them] reach only the top of the thigh made for a very uncomfortable evening.*
>
> Merkin from Pennsylvania

Here are some insights from a smaller sister, a woman for whom "one size fits all" is a fallacy too:

> *I'm 5'3", 93 pounds, with a 24 inch waist. I'm also thirty-six years old and the mother of four children, ages eight to fifteen. I have to find my clothes in the children's department, or buy a girl's size 12 pattern then fight to find fabric that doesn't make it look like a child's dress.*
>
> Danise from Ohio

So much for "life must be easier for petites!"

How Can an 18 and a 38 Be the Same Size?

When I asked women to tell me their dress size, some had trouble answering, and no wonder. Clothing manufacturers can't seem to decide if we are 18-20-22-24-26 or 38-40-42-44-46. For most of us, you can forget suits or any combinations that are sold together. Our bodies aren't made that way. We much prefer to buy such pieces separately.

One label in particular gave me a big giggle: I bought a two-piece suit with a split skirt, and was amazed to discover the label clearly said, Petite. It actually fit very well, because of my short waist. Even so, a size 24 Women's Petite seems a contradiction in terms. I must say, I delight in showing the label to my tiny friends, and saying "See? I'm a Petite too!"

Women have sent me dress labels that are equally amusing. One casual outfit sported a tag clearly labeled "2X-Medium." What fun to be a Medium again!

Sometimes, we don't want anyone to know what size we wear. One woman admitted, "I still cut my old underwear up into many pieces before I throw them away so no one can laugh if they happen to find them at the dump." I must admit, I cut the labels out of my own 100% cotton, full-size briefs the minute I take them out of the package, but only because the labels irritate my skin. Or maybe, like this honest woman, I'd rather not have anyone know I wear 4x underwear. (I mean, what would they say in the hospital emergency room?)

Another woman shared her struggles with shopping with a smaller daughter:

> *My teenage daughter likes for me to go shopping with her. I wait while she selects her size 7's and tries them on and models them. I watch smaller mothers with their daughters trying on the same outfits and sharing dressing rooms and I become depressed. I hate to shop.*
>
> Joyce from Virginia

There's no question about it, the word "dressed" is only two letters away from "depressed!" How about a shopping trip for mom to *her* kind of store with *her* clothes, while daughter watches, comments and applauds? It might be a good learning experience for her.

I always prefer to shop alone, with a great sales clerk to help me try things I might otherwise overlook. I've also shopped with my big, beautiful friend Ann, who talked me into purchasing my first outrageously colorful hand-painted silk dress. She was so right . . . I wear it all the time.

Cleaning Your Closets

Let's talk about your closet for a minute. Do you have whole racks filled with clothes, which haven't fit you in five or ten years or more? If you're ready to take a big step, I have an idea for you to consider: GET RID OF THOSE CLOTHES!

Why? They take up valuable closet space. They're going out of style and becoming less useful to someone (especially you) every season they hang there. They're a constant reminder that you're no longer wearing size 10 (or 6 or 14 or whatever). It's time to clean house. Here's how I did it:

1. I hung all the clothing by sizes in my basement on a big wheel-around rack (we picked it up for a song—$25— when a local discount store went out of business). There they were, hundreds of dollars worth of stylish clothing in sizes 10, 12, 14, 16, 18. (Sigh.) Don't make the mistake that I did, of holding your old skirts up to your hips and getting bummed out. Life is too short. Out with the small, in with the new!

2. Taking a deep breath, I invited smaller friends, one by one, to come over and go "shopping." Yes, a consignment shop might have been less traumatic, but it also made a clear statement to those who love me most: I am who I am, and I'm not likely to ever be a size 10 again. It's very freeing to make this kind of public "confession."

3. I rejoiced when I saw my friends sporting my old favorites. Believe it or not, this was a very healing thing for me. It's also a practical move, and good stewardship to boot. Now, those good clothes are being put to use, instead of making faces at me every time I open the closet door. My friends were thrilled, and it made lots more room in my closets.

If you're still hesitating, thinking "maybe someday these will fit me again," let's be realistic. If you were to, quite by accident, lose a lot of weight, do you really think you'd go back to wearing clothes, colors and fabrics from five or ten years ago? Heck no, you'd want to go out and buy a bunch of new clothes to celebrate your new (though probably temporary) body. Trust me: It's better to get rid of your old clothes, buy some beauties in the size that fits you today, and sally forth!

"Figure Flaws" My Foot!

I'll never forget the poolside fashion show I once attended, which was described in the program as "How to Find a Swimsuit to Flatter Every Figure." Sounded good to me, so I sat near the front and waited to see what I might learn. The first model came out. A size 6. The fashion commentator began: "As you can see, Carol's hips are much bigger than her shoulders, and this suit helps camouflage her out-of-proportion body."

A faint rumbling sound moved through the audience of 250 women. I felt sorry for poor Carol up there, having her hips discussed in such an impersonal, public way, especially when she had (compared to most of us in the audience) no visible hips whatsoever.

The second model came out. Another size 6. "Here is Joanie in a slimming black suit that accentuates her slim torso, but plays down her larger backside." Larger than what? Larger than a bread box, maybe, but smaller than any backside I'd seen in years!

It was soon apparent that all the models were going to be a size 6, that their "figure flaws" existed only in the mind of the commentator, and that the women in the audience were about to explode. Finally, they did. They exploded in laughter.

A word of warning for all fashion industry types: we never want to hear about "How to Hide Your Figure Flaws" again! Our figures are not flawed, they are uniquely ours, all different, and wonderful "as is." Stop asking us to change our bodies to fit your clothes, and start changing your clothes to fit our bodies!

Begin Building Body Confidence Today

1. Look through your current wardrobe and determine your favorite style of clothing — your best colors, fabrics and styles. Make a list, even a sketch, of what you like best, and keep it handy when you shop, along with a list of things you really need to complete an outfit. You'll shop smarter and faster!

2. Call a good dress store or sewing shop and locate a skilled, sensitive seamstress who can alter any clothes you have now to make them fit you better. She can also lower or shorten hems and cuffs on new outfits as soon as you bring them home, and she might be able to create some original, one-of-a-kind outfits for you based on your list of favorites.

3. Check the resources section of this book and have some of those catalogues delivered to your door. No salesman will call! Then, go ahead and try something totally "not you" and see if it isn't indeed the *new* you!

♥ A Clothing Store Owner Speaks . . .

Nancye Radmin is the founder and owner of The Forgotten Woman, a store with top-of-the-line fashions for larger women, located in nineteen cities across America. According to *Working Woman* magazine, The Forgotten Woman does $40 million a year in business.

Liz: Where did the name "The Forgotten Woman" come from?

Nancye: *Sixteen years ago, after giving birth to my son William, I had gained 85 pounds. So I went shopping. Understand, I am a clothes horse, only wore Anne Klein, that kind of thing. I went to my regular store, walked up to my favorite sales lady, and her first words were "What have you done to yourself?" I started bubbling about my new son, how thrilled we were, and she said, "I can't do anything for you until you lose weight." I never stepped in that store again.*

Liz: Many of us can identify with that experience! Then what happened?

Nancye: *I went across the street to another favorite store. Now, what I wanted was not that unusual. Navy gabardine pants, a cream blazer, and a yellow cashmere sweater. That's what everybody was wearing that year, so that's what I wanted. Of course, that store didn't have anything in my size either, and I was only a 14-16. They sent me to Elizabeth Arden, which had a wonderful collection of caftans. I wasn't interested. They sent me to B. Altman's, which featured house dresses. They sent me to Macy's, where I got a nose bleed getting up to the ninth floor to the larger women's sizes. They were right next to the pet center. Amid the squawking and the barking, I found a sea of polyester pull-on pants in four colors: navy, burgundy, black and brown. Stunning. In the same department they had coordinating polyester tops with big flowers. They looked exactly like the maternity clothes I had been wearing for the last nine months.*

Liz: Let me guess. You were fairly discouraged at this point.

Nancye: *Absolutely. I went home, having spent a total of $9. 75, and that was just for parking. I had a pocketbook full of money and all the plastic I needed, but no clothes. I turned to my husband and said, "I am a forgotten woman! You have to give me $10,000. I am going to open a store that sells pretty clothes for fat girls." And that's how The Forgotten Woman was born. We opened our first store in May 1977, on Lexington Avenue in New York.*

Liz: You now have nineteen locations in all. Will you be adding more stores?

Nancye: *Probably in 1994. We'd love to bring The Forgotten Woman to Cincinnati.*

Liz: Hooray, that's near Louisville! You have your own "Nancye" label, yes?

Nancye: *That happened because no one in America was willing to manufacture gabardine clothing for me, so I headed to Brazil. The manufacturer asked me, "Where are your labels?" I had never thought of bringing such a thing with me, so I signed my name, and they made labels for me from my signature.*

Liz: Is there anything today's large woman can't buy for herself, clothing-wise?

Nancye: *Well, she can't buy Anne Klein or Donna Karan. Yet. These designers are not ready to create clothing for the larger woman. It seems their smaller customers are worried that they might be wearing something a larger woman is wearing. I don't understand what the problem is — we all wear the same shoes, carry the same handbags, drive the same cars! When designers have nowhere else to go, they finally think "fat."*

Liz: Why do large size fashions cost more?

Nancye: *Because you have to have a separate pattern made. You can't just "grade up" a smaller pattern or your shoulders would reach out to Asia and your crotch down to China! For example, a size 20 skirt requires about 20%*

more fabric than a size 8 skirt, and about 60% more stitches per inch. These things just cost more. In a bakery, a bigger cake always costs more than a smaller one.

Liz: What makes The Forgotten Woman distinctive?

Nancye: *I always insist on excellent service, and I only carry clothes that I would wear, the beautiful clothes smaller women are wearing. After all, we deserve the best. That's why we have never had a polyester pull-on pant out on the floor . . . and we never will!*

Liz: I also love your dress sizes: 1 through 6!

Nancye: *That's right. The size 14's are a 1, the 16's a 2, right up to 24 at a size 6. My customers tell me they love to drape their jackets over a chair, so that the label clearly shows they wear a size 4!*

"You'll Love Yourself More If You Lose Weight"

Self-image, as the phrase implies, refers to the image, concept or mental picture you have of yourself. It's not how you look, it's how you *think* you look. It's not who you really are, but rather, who you *think* you are.

In his book *His Image, My Image*, author Josh McDowell makes a telling point: "If you can think of anyone you'd rather be than yourself, you probably have a self-image problem."[1] Most of us have travelled that road, and it starts at a very young age.

All through grade school I wanted to be Donna — small, dark-haired, quiet. All through junior high I wanted to be Debbie — petite, cheerleader, the first in our gang to date. All through high school I wanted to be Judy — tall, thin, long brown hair, great big smile.

They were special young women and good friends, but for heaven's sake, what was wrong with Lizzie? I had my own gifts and skills to offer, my own happy smile and sense of humor to bring to the table. But I was not "cute," according to the politically correct version of "cute" in the 60's, and so I was miserable.

In the 90's, we are finding some solutions to such misery. Santa Cruz County, California, has a Task Force to Promote Self-Esteem and Personal and Social Responsibility. Their chairperson, Ardena Shankar, offered this definition of self-esteem: "Appreciation of my own worth and importance, and having the character to be accountable for myself and to act responsibly toward others."[2]

Sure sounds mighty Biblical to me! The Lord, without a doubt, "appreciates our worth and importance," calls us to be "accountable" and expects us to act "responsibly."

Notice how self-esteem, by this definition, has nothing to do with appearance, dress size, or level of "cute." Self-esteem based on such a flimsy foundation could be blown away with one tight button on your skirt. That's why the promise that "you'll love yourself more if you lose weight" is so dangerous. The corollary is, "and if you gain it back, you'll hate yourself forever."

When I became a Christian in 1982, I bought into the "looking good = feeling good = being good" philosophy that was being pandered about those days. I put my own little spiritual twist on it, just for grins. At that time, I was flirting with the 200-pound mark, with few attractive clothes to cover my growing self. So off I went to Weight Watchers again, only this time I told myself I would give God the glory for any changes that took place. Sure enough, my weight came off smoothly, easily and quickly. At 155, I was a svelte size 10 and a smash at church.

"Start a weight loss group!" everyone clamored, and so I did. I called it "WILL POWER," which stood for "My WILL Surrendered to God's POWER." There were lots of similar programs available in Christian circles in those days: 3-D, Overeaters Victorious, The Workshop in Lenten Living and others. Books on the topic filled the shelves of Christian bookstores: *Slim for Him, Free to Be Thin, Weight! A Better Way to Lose* and *More of Jesus, Less of Me.*

Before I tell you all the things that were wrong with WILL POWER, let me share a few "right" things. First of all, it brought me closer to God. Studying the Scriptures and writing messages for our weekly classes helped me get rooted and grounded in my faith as a new believer. I'm most grateful for that. It also got me standing up in front of small groups, which gave me the confidence I needed to begin my speaking career a few years later.

Third, it brought many other women closer to God. During the two years I led WILL POWER classes, we had three hundred different women come through our door, many of whom did not know of God's love expressed through the gift of His Son. As the classes grew from one a week to eventually ten a week, I needed competent leaders for each of those classes. Some of those wonderful WILL POWER leaders became special friends. One in particular, Pam Dennison, came to work for me as my National Coordinator! Today I'm thankful for the valuable lessons and lifelong friendships I found in WILL POWER.

What's Wrong with This Picture?

Here's what was *wrong* with WILL POWER, and most of the Christian diet groups of recent years:

1. We promoted the lie that thin equals righteousness.
2. We heaped additional guilt upon women who felt plenty guilty already.
3. We baptized all these efforts as dieting "unto-the-Lord."

It simply was not Biblical! Our twelve week format meant many women kept signing up again and again, getting more discouraged. Didn't God want them thin? Why wasn't He being more helpful? It just compounded their problem. Now they had to lose weight not only for themselves and their loved ones, but for God too. I was convinced that (this sounds ridiculous in print) every Christian woman who was overweight was disobedient. She was playing Spiritual Jeopardy, and was doomed to lose the game. Oh, I was quite the finger-shaker. The old, "If I can do it, they can do it," kind of thing.

Carole Shaw, founder of *BBW* magazine, made this observation: "If you're a creep at a size 20, you're a creep at a size 9."[3] That's the truth, and we know it. Then why do we let folks tell us "if you're a creep at a size 20, it's just because you are a 20. Diet your way to a size 10 again, and you'll love yourself more . . . and God will, too!" Ugh.

We can be very hard on ourselves about this issue. Even *People* magazine had a January 1992 cover story entitled "Diet Wars: Who's Winning, Who's Sinning." Featured on the cover? Oprah Winfrey, Liz Taylor and Delta Burke. "Sinners," I suppose. The article also featured Roseanne Arnold and Dolly Parton, among others, and closed with these words: "In our society, is there such a thing as fat and happy?"[4]

Excuse me while I shout: "YES!"

Those of us who are concerned about righteousness (as opposed to *self*-righteousness), often take to heart the suggestion that being overweight is sinful. Among our surveys was this comment:

> *Try to convince me I'm not a fat ugly slob. I struggle spiritually with this . . . gluttony is listed in the Word as a sin . . . I can't seem to 'mortify' this as instructed in Romans 8:13.*
>
> Sandy from Pennsylvania

Oh, dear friend from my home state! You are not a "fat ugly slob!" You might simply be a large woman. Is that so awful? Words like "big" and "large" can mean very positive things: powerful, mighty, generous, magnificent, spacious, vast, towering, impressive, boundless, substantial, stately and great!

As to her spiritual struggle, I have looked through all the Bible translations I have on hand, and I find there are lots of references to "appetite." However, many times it is not referring to just food, but all the fleshly desires. And those appetites can be found in thin people too.

What the Bible does speak against is overeating to the point of being unable to function or drinking until one is drunk. In Proverbs, it says:

> Do not mix with winebibbers,
> Or with gluttonous eaters of meat;
> For the drunkard and the glutton will come to poverty,
> And drowsiness will clothe a man with rags.[5]

Sinful to be fat? I don't think so. This verse is speaking to the practical, not the spiritual. If you are too "drunk" with wine or food, it *is* hard to function. Sort of how we feel after Thanksgiving dinner, when we really have eaten too much and want to lie on the couch all day! Both the Great Physician and the doctor of the 90's would agree: "all things in moderation." As we've said again and again, being large does not mean you are a glutton. Some of us overeat, some don't. An athlete who eats 5,000 calories a day is not a glutton, because that person's body will burn every one of those calories. It is not how much you eat, but what you do with your body that matters.

What Does God Think About Fat?

There are more than ninety references to "fat" in the Bible, but most of them refer to fat offerings burned unto the Lord. You may remember Abel, of Cain and Abel fame, whose fat offering found favor with the Lord. Also in Genesis is the story of the "sleek, fat cows" versus the "lean, ugly cows." Don't you love that wording? (If anyone ever has the audacity to call you a "fat cow," smile and thank them for knowing beauty when they see it.)

When you think of fat people in Scripture, the name of Eglon, King of Moab may come to mind. After all, right there in Judges 3 it says, "Now Eglon was a very fat man." He was stabbed by Ehud, whose knife disappeared into Eglon's ample belly "and the fat closed over the blade." One dead Eglon. He was the first of 10,000 Moabite men killed by the Israelites. By no means was this king killed because he was fat, nor his men because they were "all stout men of valor." They were oppressing God's people and simply had to go.

The prophet Isaiah spoke of the time when "the glory of Jacob will wane and the fatness of his flesh grow lean." They were not into skinny in those days, because, it seems to me, it would've been downright dangerous. One never knew when a drought or famine might appear on the horizon, so it paid to have some flesh on your bones.

I looked everywhere in Scripture to find an example where fleshiness itself was a problem. Certainly we never hear about anyone's dress size. What size did Ruth wear? Her very name means "beauty," but her size and shape are not mentioned. Her character, on the other hand, is discussed at length. The woman at the well... a size 14? A size 10? Maybe a 22? Who knows? Who cares? The question is: what did she *do* with her life and how did she honor God?

Matthew recorded in his gospel account these words of Jesus:

> The Son of Man came eating and drinking, and they say, "Look, a glutton and a winebibber, a friend of tax collectors and sinners!" But wisdom is justified by her children.[6]

I love this passage because it illustrates perfectly the same kind of hassle we deal with today: People see us eating dessert in a restaurant and jump to the conclusion that we are gluttons or, as we say in the 90's, compulsive overeaters! Jesus was doing nothing wrong, but because He was "different," because people didn't like His message of truth, they looked for something negative to say: "He eats too much, drinks too much, and hangs out with the wrong crowd!"

The last line is the kicker: "But wisdom is justified by her children." Look at the fruit that Jesus' wise choice of companions produced: He gathered together twelve disciples, frankly a bunch of misfits, who changed the world by obeying His commands. (Just for the record, the sizes of their tunics do not appear in any verse.)

The Things That Matter Most

I am not in any way diminishing the spiritual struggles some of us have concerning weight. Having worked through both sides of that issue, I'm here to say without a doubt that the Lord cares a great deal about who we *are* and very little about what we look like.

> For the LORD does not see as man sees; for man looks at
> the outward appearance, but the LORD looks at the heart.[7]

The number of verses on those two subjects — the body and the heart — is living testimony to which one matters most to God. You'll find a half dozen references to "sleek and fat" (but most of the time the writer was talking about cows!). The character issues, lifestyle issues, how-you-spend-your-days issues, the stuff that really matters — these are discussed a lot more than a handful of times. God cares so much about "love" it shows up more than five hundred times. He wants us to have His "joy," and He talks about it more than two hundred times. "Peace" flows like a river through the Bible another couple hundred different times.

But, Weight Watchers? Not in there, nor any other "Lose Ten Pounds in Ten Days" scheme. Yes, fasting *is* in Scripture, not for the purpose of dieting, but for devotion. No aerobics in the wilderness, no diet aids in the desert, no rocks springing forth with Ultra Slim Fast.

Even Queen Esther, whose beauty carried her to an earthly throne, spent "six months with oil of myrrh, and six months with perfumes and preparations for beautifying women."[8] But nowhere does it say, "And she did two hundred leg lifts every morning, and a thousand sit-ups at night!"

In fact, when you look up all those who "wasted away" in Scripture, you find out pretty quickly that losing weight usually indicated death was right around the corner. So, all my sisters in Christ and especially those whom I unintentionally misinformed during my WILL POWER days: please forgive me and accept God's complete and unconditional love for you. Enter into the joy of your Master, and accept His peace!

Positively the Pits

Let's be honest about something.

There's not a woman alive, including me, who can sail through every minute with a totally optimistic attitude, filled with love, joy and peace. That is just not reality. Even Lizzie, your advocate, the woman who finally found peace at the far end of the dress rack — even I sink deep into the pit again from time to time.

Here's one of my journal entries from one very bad day in August 1992 (yes, a full ten years after I gave my life to God):

> I am sick of being fat.
> I am sick of thinking about it,
> tired of speaking about it. I don't want to write about it.
> I am in pain and denial.
> I don't know how to change.
> I don't want to ask for help.
>
> Look at all these negatives, Lord!
> What happened to Lizzie?
> Why won't this hurt go away?
>
> I can't seem to find a "cause" for it.
> A decision of the will to MAKE it go away
> seems very temporary.
>
> One day I think, "Terrific! I can embrace my fat self,
> and get on with life!" The next day (next hour?),
> I am feeling awful about who I am, what I look like,
> what I FEEL like.
>
> I'm going for a walk. Don't go away, Lord.
> I need You.

I'm glad every day isn't like *that* day. Being a Christian does not mean that our lives will be perfect, that problems are easily solved, or that we'll be filled with joy twenty-four hours a day. Everybody slips into a funk now and again, but I'm on a mission to make sure we don't live there. Our hope lies not in perfection, but in perseverance.

Besides, however awful you feel, it could be worse; you could be on a diet! David Garner, Ph.D., a specialist in eating disorders, states: "Dieting and weight loss may have negative psychological effects, including depression, anxiety, irritability and social withdrawal (and) profoundly negative effects on self-esteem."[9]

Depending on your particular personality type, you may slide down the emotional scale pretty easily. Relax. Emotions change, but the truth does not. This book is about truth, about forgetting the fables and finding out the facts. This chapter is meant to drive home one very important fact: God loves you exactly as you are!

Looking for Love in All the Wrong Places

When it comes to helping women develop a positive self-image, I have a very definite goal in mind: our daughters. Not just the ones some of us gave birth to, but all young women. When we feel good about who we are, it produces a double harvest: our own positive self-esteem *and* the chance to be a positive role model for young women who cross our paths. Unfortunately, we can also offer them a discouraging word.

> *My mother (who is a size 8) says, "You would be so much happier if you were thin."*
>
> Barbara from Ohio

Here is how dangerous I believe low self-esteem is for a young woman. I will attest, absolutely, that negative feelings about her body will drive her to go to extreme lengths to be affirmed by someone. Her mother nags her to go on a diet. Her tiny friends live on 600 calories a day and whine about their flabby thighs. Who will tell this young girl that she's attractive?

Her boyfriend.

What will she do to express her gratitude for his attention? You guessed it.

I'm not speaking to you as a psychologist, a Ph.D., or a certified anything. I am speaking to you as a woman who still has a hard time addressing this subject, but believes it simply must be done. In my heart, I know that if you've made it with me to Chapter Eight, then you're ready to hear what I'm about to share with you.

I had my first sexual experience when I was 16. It was his idea, but I'd read *Everything You Ever Wanted to Know About Sex (but were afraid to ask)*, so I thought I was ready. I remember crying afterward and feeling like I had ruined my life for something that wasn't even fun.

Why did I, a woman from a good family, stray from my parents' teachings? I wasn't overwhelmed with passion, or even curiosity. I just wanted somebody to tell me I was pretty.

I soon discovered that boys were very interested in a girl who would "let them," so I just let them. One after another. I counted for a long time, then gave up at well over two hundred. I decided sex was one thing I could excel in, something exciting and dangerous. It made me feel wanted, part of life, even if I knew deep down that it was sleazy and awful and the men didn't care a thing about me.

Oh, how I tried to please them! I hoped that then they would tell me what I wanted to hear: "Liz, you are desirable! You are beautiful! You are wanted!"

I don't know if every woman who grew up struggling with her body image found solace in the arms of appreciative men, but this woman did.

The opposite sex wasn't the only place I looked for acceptance and escape from my pain. By the time I went to college, I was experimenting with drugs. Just pot and hash and pills, no LSD, no acid. This wasn't because I was choosy, but only because, thank goodness, I never ran into any of those particular drugs at a party. Otherwise, I would have tried them, no questions asked.

By my early 20's, I'd found a new friend that was 100 proof. I began drinking regularly. It felt so good to just slip away, to feel so loose and carefree. At my first college frat party, I drank nineteen beers, one for each of my nineteen years. Eventually I passed out, and someone rolled me under a picnic table just so I wouldn't get stepped on.

Blackouts were to become a more common occurrence as the years went by. Some weekends I'd wake up at noon in some stranger's apartment in another city, and I'd have to ask them to drive me home.

It seems unbelievable now, but it was the life I considered normal then. About the only thing that was normal (i.e., acceptable) during this period was my weight. I had gradually dieted myself down to 135, and I stayed there simply because I had only seven dollars a week to spend on groceries. The rest was spent on clothes, pot and bar-hopping.

Shopping was another means of affirming my worth, and a legal "high." Through my mid-20's, I owned twelve credit cards, all run up to the maximum limit and then some. Clothes shopping, especially while stoned, was a favorite pastime, even after my weight had climbed to pre-diet limits. The clerks would giggle at my dazed expression. But I just had them put all those nice size 16 outfits on hangers, and I drifted out into the mall.

When the radio station I was working for suddenly changed format, I took the first available job and headed for my present home in Louisville. Cocaine wasn't as available in this smaller city, but the homegrown pot was cheap and effective. I spent every evening the same way: a joint to relax me, then a drink of Southern Comfort and soda to keep me mellow for six hours in front of the tube.

I seriously contemplated suicide one sunny afternoon after a terrible day at work when I'd screamed at everyone within earshot. But I couldn't think of a method of killing myself that wouldn't hurt. Thanks to my basic fear of pain, and thanks to Tim and Ev Kelly, I'm alive.

A Change of Heart

Tim and Ev came into my life in the fall of 1981. They were a dynamic radio duo who moved to Louisville to do the morning show at my station. I loved them immediately, because they had everything I ever wanted: looks, talent, money, professional credentials, a house in the country, a beautiful daughter and a Mercedes (well, it was leased, but it was nice!). The only thing I wasn't too crazy about was the fact that they called themselves Christians. Ugh. I'd been around enough church people in my life to be wary. They didn't talk about church, though. They talked about Jesus — like they knew Him. More important to me at the time, they loved me, accepted me, invited me into their home, fed me Thanksgiving dinner, and didn't judge me for the life I led. When I would light up a joint, they'd start talking about a "better way."

"A better high?" I said, with interest.

"Yes, sort of," they assured me. "And you'll never have a hangover!"

When they finally did invite me to church, I was ready to find out if there were any other people as warm and weird and wonderful as these two.

There were. Pews full of them!

It didn't take me long to realize that here was the source of love that I had been searching for. God, my creator, who knew me and loved me completely, had been waiting for me all along. On those days when my mirror said "Ugh!" God said, "Ahh!" Hallelujah! Shalom!

The changes in my life, thanks to this new spiritual dimension, were amazing. I unplugged my television for a season and started reading the Bible and singing in the choir. I let the booze and pot run out and never felt the need to replace them. A nice enough young man that I was dating (and sleeping with) was sent on his merry way, and I cut the credit cards up into dozens of tiny pieces.

As you've already read, then I did the WILL POWER number. Down the scale for a two-year stint at thin, then up again for good. We're talking major self-esteem collapse at this point, because I'd put the cart before the horse by believing the fable: "Lose weight, and you'll love yourself more." Wrong! If anything, the reverse might be true: If you love yourself more, you might (accidentally, of course) lose weight. Or you might not lose weight. But either way, you end up loving yourself.

Judy Simon, M.S., is a registered dietitian from Michigan, with a slim body but a sympathetic heart. In her presentation, "Women's Struggle with Body Image," she made this statement:

> Body image is quite independent of physical characteristics. Changing your body itself does not improve your body image or your self-esteem. [But] changing your body image by accepting yourself allows you to increase your self-esteem and make changes in your physical appearance in a healthy and loving manner.[10]

Or, I might add, *not* make changes in your physical appearance, depending on your body's needs. For some of us, it was the heart changes that made the biggest difference of all.

You Took the Words Right Out of My Mouth!

From 1984 to 1986, I lost all that supposed willpower, and gained back all my lost weight and much more. I was very embarrassed about the whole thing. I avoided eye contact with my former students, though many of them were gaining too. I couldn't bear the public scrutiny.

I remember getting a phone call one very down day from a woman in a nearby city. She began the call somewhat hesitantly, and addressed me by my maiden name. Certain it was some telemarketing person, I snapped back at her, "Ma'am, I've been married for several years, and my name is no longer Amidon!"

"Oh!" she was stammering now. "I've been trying to track you down for a long time. I belong to a church here in Lexington, and I wanted to know more about your WILL POWER program."

I felt something go "zing" in my chest as I almost shouted, "WILL POWER? There is no such thing! It doesn't work! It never did! Tell the women of your church to stop dieting and start living!"

Long silence. "Okay," she said. More silence. "Well, thank you very much for your time. I'm sorry that I bothered you, Liz." I mumbled something, then hung up the phone. To say I didn't handle that opportunity to encourage her is the understatement of a lifetime. Lord, forgive me when I have my foot so firmly planted between my teeth I can't talk right.

My overreaction to her request was just another indication that my self-esteem, and self-control, had hit rock bottom. That's what it took for me to get to the truth. My worth could not be measured by any scale, any bank account, any dress size, anything other than my complete acceptance of God's love, Bill's love, my children's love, unconditional love. Do I wish I had never gained back all those pounds? Not this woman. What I have gained in understanding, humility (sometimes!), and compassion is worth every inch.

The fun part is, all across America other women are making the same discovery: self-worth is of much greater value than net worth:

> *Since I hold little hope of ever becoming "slim et trim," I look for encouragement to help me stay positive. The Lord created us — creatures great (big) and small. I'm okay with that, and I love and serve the Lord just as well as any skinny person could.*
> Glenna from Illinois

If we've moved forward on the path to self-acceptance, gained some understanding of why we think, feel and act the way we do, and given up on "perfect" then we're ready for the next step: *being* perfected, which means "completed, finished." It's a process, not a place or destination.

Getting my "insides" right helps me accept my outside self too. Body confidence is a product of self-confidence, which is a product of spiritual confidence in the One who loves me even if I never lose an ounce. That's why they call it "Amazing Grace."

Begin Building Body Confidence Today

1. Write a working definition of self-esteem in twenty words or less. Choose your words carefully. Craft this definition to best meet your needs. Let it be both a statement of where you are now and where you're going. Put it where you'll see it today and every day.

2. Start a journal. Any old notebook will do, or type it into the computer like I do. Don't make it a "have to" thing, another daily grind. Let it be a place where your innermost thoughts can be recorded for your eyes only. Sometimes you may need to share them with someone, as I have shared some of my deep, dark stuff with you. If someone is willing to listen, it can be very freeing for you.

3. Make a list of the places that you have looked for attention, affection and affirmation. Did they consistently provide that? Do you believe God might fill that need for you?

💜 A Fashion Magazine Editor Speaks . . .

Carole Shaw is the founder of *BBW*: *Big Beautiful Woman* magazine, the first and only fashion magazine for the large size woman.

Liz: How did *BBW* happen?

Carole: *It was 1978, and I had suddenly realized after thirty years of dieting that I had gained fifty pounds. [Laughing] I decided right then that I wasn't going to diet anymore. Instead of buying temporary clothes, I went off with a fistful of cash to buy real clothes. Was I disappointed! The selection was awful . . . bullet-proof polyester pants and maternity tops. Ugh. I came home crying. What options did I have? Diet again? No way. Go through my life in fat lady clothes? No thanks. My husband said, "Stop crying and do something!" "Okay!" I said. "I'll do a magazine for big women!" To this day, I don't know where that thought came from. A few days later, he said, "Let's do the magazine!" "How?" I asked. "You'll think of something," he said.*

Liz: So you two were in on this thing together from the beginning.

Carole: *And we're still a team today. We broke all the fat lady fashion rules. We took the clothes that were available at the time—polyester pantsuits, mostly—and did the unthinkable. We belted them! Of course, there were no belts to be found, so we used curtain ties. We tucked in blouses, we used colors other than black. And our models, all of whom were size 16 or larger, wore lovely makeup and hairstyles, which was a no-no. Big women were supposed to be invisible.*

Liz: You went national with the second issue of *BBW*. What really made it take off?

Carole: *I did a half-hour with Tom Snyder on the old* Tomorrow *show. At the end, he gave me a big kiss. That kiss easily got us 7,000 subscriptions.*

Liz: Did you do any test marketing for this concept?

Carole: *None. I had lived in this body for many years, and I knew what hurt my feelings. What I needed and what drove me crazy was the same for BBW's all over the country. It was all instinct. And it worked. We just celebrated fourteen years in print, and we now publish 200,000 copies per issue.*

Liz: Your background was not in journalism, but in show business.

Carole: *That's right. I was a performer, a singer. My hit record was on the Verve label, called "Careless." I was travelling, doing shows all over the country—radio, television, Ed Sullivan, the works. But when I came out of the television studio, I never asked, "How did I sound?" I asked, "Did I look too fat?" I was always on a diet, always agonizing over my weight. Recently, I got to see some of those old TV clips, and I got so angry at myself. I was not fat! My goal with* BBW *magazine is to see that our next generation of young women doesn't waste time and energy dieting and messing up their metabolism.*

Liz: You have two daughters. Are they also big, beautiful women?

Carole: *Beautiful, yes, but they're thin. I like them anyway! We appeared on the Sally Jesse Raphael show together, talking about mothers and daughters and the weight issue. My daughters say they are "fat blind."*

Liz: You have a wonderful sense of humor. How does that fit into your life as a big, beautiful woman?

Carole: *I think anyone who has survived any kind of hardship or challenge in life has to develop a sense of humor about it. I'm not talking about the "jolly fat lady" approach. The* *ability to see humor in life has no size attached. I use humor as a teaching tool. And, I do THIN jokes!*

Liz: What has been the most satisfying thing about *BBW*?

Carole: *Personal appearances are my favorite because I love watching women change both their attitudes and style of dressing right before my eyes. The "fat lady costume" is gone forever! I also love when I'm sitting in an airport and a woman comes over, hugs me and says, "Thank you." That is very moving for me, and makes all the effort worthwhile.*

Liz: What has been your biggest challenge as editor-in-chief?

Carole: *It has taken some time to win over Madison Avenue. The people who manufacture clothes for the larger woman love us, of course, but those who make other products for women — shampoo, cosmetics, and the like — seem to hesitate about buying advertising in* BBW, *for fear women might think they'll gain weight if they use that product! It's silly. I tell them, once the dollars are in the till, you can't tell the fat money from the thin money.*

Liz: What areas in the fashion industry still need to wake up to this underserved population?

Carole: *Big, beautiful teens need clothes just like their contemporaries, and those are still hard to come by. Supersize women, women over size 24, need more options. And maternity clothes for the larger woman are awful!*

Liz: How well I remember! You are doing some things to improve our options, with *BBW* Pattern Collection for Simplicity up to size 32, with your own book, *Big Beautiful Woman: Come Out, Come Out, Wherever You Are!*, even with your own perfume, "Confidence!"

Carole: *It has been an incredible experience — exciting and fun and humbling all at the same time. I would urge every woman of any size to give herself permission to be happy and successful!*

"Big People Are Always Jolly" (Ha!)

One day, I was having my upstairs bedroom wallpapered. There is a floor heating vent in that room, and after the men left, my mother said, "I'm going to clean out that vent. Be careful, I have the top grate off."

Minutes later, I walked into the bedroom with an armload of laundry. The men had left newspapers all over the floor, and a screwdriver was hidden underneath them. Guess who stepped on it, went flying into the air and down into the vent?!

My legs were hanging through the downstairs ceiling, my arms and head were in the upstairs bedroom and I couldn't move. My mother, scared to death, kept yelling, "Be careful, or you'll fall through!" I told her, "No way! I'm stuck — and as soon as I can stop laughing, I'll try to get out and pick the splinters out of my tail!"

Betty from Kentucky

I love that story. Such experiences for us big women can either be hysterically funny or just hysterical. It's all in how you look at things.

It's always an encouragement to know that I'm not alone. Many women struggle with their size. It'll be nice to laugh about it, even though the tears are always hiding behind my laughter.

Rosanna from Kentucky

I have both laughed until I cried, and cried so much that I finally started laughing again. My dear friend and a consummate speaking professional, Rosita Perez, says, "Laughter comes from a very deep need not to cry." From her years in social work, she learned firsthand how people use laughter as a coping mechanism. After all, there are much worse ways to handle pain! Drugs, alcohol, violence — those are the negative means of dealing with life's indignities.

Laughter, on the other hand, offers some of the same qualities: it is addictive and habit-forming: it gives us a "high"; it's a release for pent-up emotions; and, it can be noisy and disruptive. The big differences are: laughter is good for your body, mind and spirit, it hurts no one, and it entertains everyone within earshot. Not bad, for free!

Don't Make Me Laugh!

Some of us have been so afraid of the "jolly fat person" stereotype that we've tried to prove just how serious we can be. In the process, we may be missing the wonderful release of pain, anger and frustration that laughter provides.

Humor is important. I'm not interested in an "us versus them" attitude, rather in something that helps me feel like a valid member of humanity and helps me laugh at my own foolish attitudes and those of others . . . while recognizing I'm different, the point is that we're more the same.

Mary Jane from Kentucky

Humor is the great leveling agent. It pulls down the haughty and picks up the humble. People all over the world love to laugh. It's one of the qualities we humans have that separates us from the beasts. It is, along with music, one of God's most generous gifts to His creation.

Henri Bergson said, "Laughter needs an echo." We do like to laugh *with* someone. As a means of communication, it is the purest, most honest, trusting expression of ourselves we could give one another. When you've laughed wholeheartedly with someone, you've been completely yourself. As you probably found out one Halloween, you can't laugh with a mask on!

I had some nifty refrigerator magnets made up with these words from Konrad Lorenz: "Heartily laughing together at the same thing forms an immediate bond." So true! When we've shared a big laugh together, some invisible walls have come down between us, and we've taken our relationship one step higher.

A Flight of Fancy

Comedians always begin, "Have you heard the one about...?" Well, I know you haven't heard this one, because only two women in the world know it happened. (When you finish reading this, there will be three of us!).

I had just walked into the passenger terminal at the Indianapolis airport and was looking for somewhere to land until they called my flight. Almost every seat was filled. At the end of one of the rows were two seats joined together on a T-shaped base. On one of those seats sat a very thin young lady who barely took up half of her side. "Perfect!" I thought, heading toward the other vacant side.

I sat down carefully, smiled at her, and began to arrange my packages around me. As I was leaning over to close my briefcase, this little slip of a woman apparently stood up. Unfortunately, she was my ballast.

Seconds later, I was shouting out something like, "G-r-r-a-a-a-a-k-k!" I turned the entire double seat completely over sideways and I went tumbling, tails over teacups. Needless to say, this attracted the attention of the men at the ticket counter, who rushed over to help.

They couldn't get me off the floor. Not because of my size (after all, there were three of them), not because I was pinned under the chair, but because I was laughing too hard. All my muscles were so relaxed I was like a large, limp Raggedy Ann doll on roller skates.

They kept asking me, "Are you okay, Miss? Are you okay? Shall we call a doctor?" Well, that just made me laugh harder, until I was almost gasping for air. Finally, they helped me get to a standing position and steered me toward the seat, back on its T-shaped feet again. I very carefully sat down in the middle of the T and took a deep breath.

Assuring everyone around me that I was just fine, I began to pull my coat together and stuff some things back into my carry-on bag.

Every few seconds, I had to stifle another giggle. Pulling out a small mirror to check and see if my lipstick had survived my unscheduled "flight," I caught a glimpse of another large woman seated near me who was watching me with great interest. Her lips were so tightly pinched together, she looked like she had swallowed a large cat.

I sized her up as a "sister" immediately, leaned over to her and whispered, "I'm just thankful I didn't flip that little woman up in the air."

That was all it took. This woman exploded with the loudest "H-a-a-a-w-w-w-w!" I've ever heard, before or since. Having just barely recovered myself, I was right in there with her, howling and snorting and slapping my knee. People would not even look in our direction.

I may never see her again, but that woman and I are now joined at the funny bone for life!

Humor That Heals

Every now and then, a woman attending one of my presentations will slip a note in my hand before she slips out the door. Others will drop a letter in the mail later. Such correspondence is always precious to me. This one in particular, from a woman in Wisconsin, was especially touching:

> *I am a size twenty-four, and have always felt that I had to hide except in coming to work. I am forty-seven and have hidden within my fat, dying to escape into the fun world to do all that I think I cannot because of my size. You showed me such insight into having a good time, by laughing and being sure of yourself and all a mere size twenty-two . . . I just cannot begin to tell you the impact you had on me.*

What a blessing, and how humbling, to be in the right place at the right time for this woman. In sharing so honestly with me (and now, anonymously, with you), she has given us a great gift: herself.

Rosita Perez says, "The older we get, and the more comfortable we get with ourselves, the easier it is to laugh. I once was speaking and looked down to discover a run in my stocking. I told the audience, 'Fifteen years ago, this run would have ruined my day. Isn't it wonderful that today, it doesn't really matter?'"

I have gained more than just a dress size or two these last few years. I have gained quite a bit of knowledge about the subjects of dieting and humor, plus a few insights about myself. Here is the summary of all I have learned:

> Fat, miserable women go on diets and cry.
> Big, bountiful women eat intelligently and LAUGH!

Each day I ask myself, "Liz, to which do you aspire?" I like the second approach better.

False Advertising

I once ordered a book with a most promising title, *Laugh It Off*. It was billed as the "new humor strategy of weight loss," and since I love to laugh and love to hear the latest theories about weight loss, comical and otherwise, I ordered it. By page four, I was not a happy reader. The author insisted: "FAT brings me ILL health, ILL feelings, an ILL nature and ILLusions."[1]

Later she states, "The human body is made to THIN specifications." Oh, is that a fact? Has God shown her His blueprint for humankind? One glance around our globe makes it pretty clear that small is not all there is! What I thought would be, at the very least, a fun book was in fact yet another dreary, All-Fat-People-Are-Compulsive-Overeaters book. Ugh.

To genuinely "lighten up" doesn't mean weighing less on the scale, but having a lighter heart. What is usually lifted from our hearts is pain. My best humor comes out of pain, because it's at that heartfelt level I connect with my audience. Our century's greatest clown, Red Skelton, said: "No matter what your heartache may be, laughing helps you forget it for a few seconds."

The rules are clear on this: I can turn my own pain into humor, but I cannot and should not turn *your* pain into humor. The first is funny, the second is sick and usually passes as R-rated comedy. As Nancy Loving said, "The richest laugh is at no one's expense."

Finding Humor at Every Turn

I write all my own humor, most of it based on real-life stuff from my diary. When I began speaking full-time in 1987, I was constantly shopping for stories to build my repertoire, looking for humor in all the off-the-wall things that happened in our little honeymoon household.

Bill would cringe every time he did something that made me laugh, and say, "Don't tell me that's going to end up in your speech Friday night!" If he really meant it, of course I didn't include it. Now, several years and two kids later, the situation has changed drastically.

These days Bill comes home from work, saying, "Oh, I did this really goofy thing today. Do you want to hear about it? Maybe you could use it in your next speech." I think my hubby has decided he likes being the star of my stories.

In her book, *Sizing Up*, author Sandy Summers Head lists the six qualities that beautiful women of all sizes, from all over the world, seem to share:

- Acceptance
- Sensuality
- Health
- Grooming
- Style
- Sense of Humor[2]

Although there are some parts of her book that I'm not thrilled with (too much dieting advice), in this analysis she is right on target. These are all qualities that every woman can pursue regardless of weight, body type, age, color, or any other characteristic. The easiest one to work on (and the one that won't cost you a dime) is your sense of humor.

> *I'm always working on improving myself by understanding who I am — then not taking myself so seriously and DEVELOPING MY SENSE OF HUMOR!*
>
> Cindy from Kentucky

A sense of humor is like any other sense: with time and effort, it can be developed. For example, you can't improve your hearing, but you can improve your listening skills. In the same way, you can't really learn to be funny, but you can learn to recognize and utilize humor. Usually those of us who value humor have found some way to keep it ever-handy when we need it.

We've all enjoyed those "office handouts," as I call them. It's that stuff that shows up at the copy machine one day and soon every part of the building has a copy of it posted on the bulletin board. More than once, a handout has centered around dieting. Alas, these things never list authors or sources or references or copyrights, so I'll have to give credit for this one to the Great Copy Machine in the Sky. It was labeled, "The Rules of Dieting," and featured, among some old standbys, this new favorite: "Cookie pieces contain no calories, because the process of breaking them causes calorie leakage." A classic.

I'll bet you've seen one of those ubiquitous greeting cards with the little lamb on it that says, "Ewes not fat, ewes just fluffy." Is this supposed to make me feel better? Sheep are not too bright, don't smell very nice, get lost easily and have almost no initiative whatsoever. They get fleeced annually and end up as lamb chops! I'll stick with being fat.

A Big Sense of Humor

So what does it mean to be a large and funny woman? Are we all Roseanne Arnold? No. Truly funny people aren't stereotypes at all, nor are they copycats. They're original. Off beat. Dabbling in the unexpected. Above all, they have to be confident in their ability to communicate their view of the world in such a way that others see the humor in it too.

Give a chuckle now and then. Life is heavy enough just being heavy weight-wise. But upbeat doesn't have to be Richard Simmons — a person can be positive without always flying two feet off the ground!

Linda from California

(Armadillos fly two feet off the ground when they are startled by the oncoming lights of an automobile, and look where it gets *them*!)
We all need more humor in our lives (especially those who are "lean and mean"). Everybody needs to laugh. We need to laugh at our bizarre bodies, our funny experiences, our strange little personality quirks, our odd idiosyncracies, the ill-harbored anxieties we barely contain. Whatever will connect us to other human beings, that's going to be our best source of humor.

I need to be able to laugh at my size (more). To be more candid about it (like you). Give me inspiration on days when I need it.

Marcia from South Dakota

Laughter can be used to cover up *or* to disclose our true selves.

Eye to Eye, Heart to Heart

If you haven't already, you'll meet humorist Jeanne Robertson at the end of this chapter, a T-A-L-L woman with an even taller sense of humor. She has turned her unusual physical characteristic — being 6'2" (make that 5'14") in her stocking feet — into a hilarious platform for her humor. Her height is not all she speaks about, by any means. It just gives her a good launching pad, a way to connect with her audience.

Although everyone may not be 6'2", everyone does have something different about them that they can't change and need to accept, even laugh about. Jeanne helps them do that by leading the way. As Gail from Kentucky says, "[I need] humor and words of wisdom from successful women in all walks of life who know that size is a very small part of a total person."

Our size is a small part of who we are. It just happens to be the part people see first. But once they've fully processed that fact, I believe our size becomes much less of an issue.

A Sense of Humor, A Sense of Self

During the opening moments of my program, I almost always have a little fun with my size. After all, it's the thing an audience is likely to notice first about me, so I address it up front in a humorous way.

I have two reasons for doing this. One is to help people relax and start laughing. They always look sort of relieved, as if to say, "Oh, she *knows* she's big!" I'm also giving them permission to laugh at themselves a little, to see their own differences and celebrate them.

I often tell them about the letter I received from a group of prisoners during my radio years. They wrote:

Dear Lizzie:

The guys in Cell Block D have taken a bet on what you look like. We think you have olive skin, long, dark straight hair, that you're about 5'2" and weigh 105 pounds. Are we close?

Your friends at
Kentucky State Reformatory

So I wrote them back and said, "Gosh, fellas, I can't believe how . . . CLOSE you were!" (I hope they're in for fifteen years-to-life.)

Ethel Barrymore said, "You grow up the day you have your first real laugh — at yourself." I've been laughing at myself for decades, and I've learned I'm not alone:

I usually say to people, "I used to have a dynamite figure. Then, I exploded." That puts them at ease and we all laugh and get on with things.

Dorothy from Kentucky

Sometimes such humor is called "self-deprecating." I agree with Jeanne Robertson, who says, "I don't like the term 'put-down' humor or 'self-deprecating humor.' I see it as a humor born of self-confidence and self-acceptance." Rosita Perez echoes that, saying a woman who can laugh at herself is "intelligent, confident, at ease with herself, contemplative. She can dissect her life, then come up with something that's shareable."

I'll often say during a presentation, "I'm a big, beautiful woman in a narrow, nervous world." The audience always responds positively, because it is obvious from my word choices that I feel good about who I am ("beautiful") and sorry for others ("narrow," "nervous") who were not as abundantly created.

The voluptuous Mae West, who always looked like she was poured into her dress and forgot to say "when," was famous for stating, "Too much of a good thing can be wonderful."

The best one [I've heard] so far is "You are horizontally gifted."
Nancy from Wisconsin

Another comment along those lines is "gravitationally challenged!" The key is, it's perfectly permissible for us to laugh at ourselves in any fashion we're comfortable with. What's not appropriate is others making comments about our size. The first indicates self-acceptance; the second suggests insensitivity.

Stepping Over the Line

Not all fat people are the happy, jolly, always funny people. We also have emotions and fat jokes hurt our feelings just like everyone else.

Connie from Wisconsin

There is a very fine line between having a little fun with your size, and overdoing such humor. I've crossed the line myself more than once, and the audience always lets me know in a very simple way: They stop laughing. In their eyes, I've moved from self-acceptance to self-effacement. Instead of being happy for me, they feel sorry for me. It's critical for all of us who use humor in any form, to understand the difference and stay on the right side of this line.

I may use what Carole Shaw calls "thin jokes!" Without speaking unkindly about those who are smaller, it's possible to offer a gentle jab in their general direction. When I speak of my daughter Lillian, I say, "I don't know whether Lillian will grow up to be built like her mother or not, but I've promised God that if she's thin, I'll still love her." No one is the butt of this joke, and everyone laughs at it. Another good example of this kind of humor comes from Kathryn Grayson, who said: "The worst kind of reducing pill is the one who keeps telling you how she did it."

Humor about ourselves is a female phenomenon. Psychologist Judith Tingley notes that women like humor of such a personal nature, but men don't. Men often respond to more hostile jokes about "the other guy," and women do not. We'd rather laugh at ourselves and our own foibles.

For example, if I'm speaking to a mixed audience, I might poke a little fun at some fellow's tie, along the lines of "Did your wife pick that one out for you? Oh, you picked it out? That explains it." Everyone laughs at this kind of thing, including the man wearing the tie. The truth is, he probably loves being the center of attention. But, to reverse the roles, I would never in a million years choose a woman out of the audience and say, "Will you look at that skirt? Where did you get such an ugly thing?" The audience would be appalled, she would be mortified, and I would soon be looking for another profession. It's just not done.

Can I explain this male/female difference? Nope. It's just a social reality. We women feel more comfortable laughing at ourselves, and feel equally at ease with another woman who's doing the same thing. One study of male and female comics found that 63% of the comediennes included self-disparaging comments, while only 12% of male comics did so.[3]

Humorist Hope Mihalap, a Greek woman who is married to a Russian professor and lives in the South (you can see where she finds her material!), thinks that when a woman has a little fun at her own expense, it "denotes a little more security. She knows that she is loved, and is confident that people love her for who she is. Therefore, she has the freedom to laugh at herself."

In fact, developmental psychologist Dr. Paul E. McGee believes that "self-disparagement may play a unique role in the establishment of a female sense of humor."[4] This is for all women, of course, not just larger women. Tall humorist Jeanne Robertson commented, "Some people say, 'If you woke up short, you'd be nothing.' That's not true. If I woke up short, I'd just write new material."

Most folks who are funny for money are delighted to have some natural material to work with. Watch any stand-up comic, male or female, and they will invariably poke fun at their bald head, big nose, skinny legs, large ears, wide hips, whatever physical characteristic that's obvious to the audience. Then, they'll often switch to humor about their personality or emotional self, or some other unique traits we may not be able to see, but will identify with immediately.

That's really the whole point of using humor: identification. Connecting with one another on some basic level. Laughter tears down walls and builds bridges. How we laugh and what we laugh about reveal a great deal about who we are and how we feel about ourselves. Allen Funt of *Candid Camera* fame, made this observation:

> I think that a sense of humor is deeply involved with a person's self-image. If you like yourself, you have a chance to observe and enjoy situations around you without being threatened or feeling inferior.[5]

The Best Medicine

Not only is laughter important for a healthy self-esteem, it helps us have a healthier body too. One of my favorite programs to present is called, "One Laugh to Live!" It's a 90-minute romp through the latest theories on the health-enhancing, stress-relieving power of humor. Flocks of people always come when this program is offered, which simply means we all yearn to laugh more.

It wasn't *Reader's Digest* who decided that "Laughter is the Best Medicine." Thousands of years ago, Solomon wisely wrote, "A merry heart does good, like medicine."[6]

Did you know, for example, that a big, hearty laugh actually raises your heart rate a bit, then drops it below the starting level? True! Laughing has the same effect on blood pressure, elevating it just slightly, then dropping it back to a new, improved level.

Of course, I realize you could accomplish the same two things with exercise. Theoretically. I always like to follow the advice of comedy writer Robert Orben, who cautions, "The important thing to remember about exercise is to start slow, and then gradually taper off."

Here's another body benefit: laughing massages your organs. Things like your kidneys, pancreas, and spleen. I mean really, have you thought about your spleen lately? It's been thinking of you, saying, "Boy, I could use a good workout." Laughing hard does just that. Norman Cousins called it "internal jogging."

Fifteen facial muscles get into the act when you let loose with a big laugh. If you've ever laughed so hard your cheeks hurt, that's why! Your sore cheeks are trying to tell you, "Please do this more than once a year." Laughing hard also oxygenates the body. In order to laugh out, you have to take air in, and that oxygen exchange is vital. In fact, with a big laugh, you can exhale up to seventy-five miles per hour (which suggests it might be a good idea not to sit in front of somebody with false teeth!).

Josh Billings said it best: "There ain't much fun in medicine, but there's a heck of a lot of medicine in fun!"

Stress Buster

The greatest benefit of laughter for many of us is its ability to help us handle stress. My friend Dr. Clifford Kuhn of the University of Louisville, a psychiatrist and a stand-up comic, says, "Humor won't cure anything, but it does improve a person's resources for dealing with the stresses of life."

Stress really is the disease of this decade. For me, the most stressful privilege I undertake each day is mothering my two precious children. The neat thing is that, although kids may add a little stress to your life, they also bring with them an antidote for stress: they laugh all the time. Babies laugh on average of four times an hour, and toddlers laugh fifteen times an hour!

Until we get our hands on them: "Don't you laugh at that, young man! You think you're so funny. It is not appropriate to giggle during the sermon!" And so on. Pretty soon, children get the idea that Mother has no sense of humor.

If you were to get a letter from me, you would see at the bottom of my stationery a little quote which I made up. It summarizes my philosophy on this subject: "The head thinks, the hands labor, but it's the heart that laughs."

As I travel all over America, I find women of all sizes who are incredibly good at using their heads. We are so bright we can do anything! We're good at using our hands, too, and are gifted and skilled beyond measure. But sometimes we get so busy using our heads and our hands, we forget to exercise our hearts.

I don't only mean in a cardiovascular sense (though as a volunteer for the American Heart Association, I know that's important too). I mean nurturing yourself at the deepest level of who you are, your emotional, spiritual self. That's the part of you that responds to humor, and that's where a laugh takes place. Something funny travels through your eyes or ears, then on through your brain, but it isn't until it hits your heart that a laugh comes out.

Real laughter is not at all premeditated. Nobody is sitting there saying to themselves, "I think I'll laugh in thirteen seconds." The laughter catches us by surprise, gives our heart a little workout, and chases away stress for a season.

Here's an example of how laughter turned a stressful situation into a happier one. Last spring, I tried on a large, plaid suit. We're talking big plaid, big suit. It was gorgeous, my size exactly and a perfect fit. But when I looked in the mirror, I didn't look so much dressed as I did upholstered. Big covered buttons, the whole routine. Just put a skirt around my ankles and stick me in your living room!

Not only is humor available everywhere, great for your body and good for your soul, it is actually dangerous *not* to laugh. Think of all the pent-up stress clogging your arteries! Think of all those stressed-out muscles trying to keep up your pantyhose. Without question, the woman of the 90's must laugh loud and laugh often, or risk the inevitable. As Fred Allen puts it, "It is bad to suppress laughter. It goes back down and spreads to your hips."

Begin Building Body Confidence Today

1. Think of a funny incident when your size factored into the
   hilarity of the moment. Write it down, then share it with
   a friend. (While you're at it, I'd love to read it too! Mail
   me a copy, and I'll try and include it in a future
   publication, credited to you.)

2. Begin collecting your favorite humorous anecdotes, cartoons,
   and one-liners. You might record them in a loose-leaf
   notebook, a humor journal, whatever suits your style. The
   key is to have it ready to go when the need for laughter
   strikes.

3. If you don't already have a quick, clever, put-everyone-
   at-ease comeback to someone who mentions your size,
   begin working on such a comment. By having it on
   hand, you'll relax about such situations a little more and
   increase your ability to laugh at life and yourself while
   you chase away stress!

♥ *A Humorist Speaks . . .*

At 6'2" in her stocking feet, Jeanne Robertson was the tallest woman to ever enter the Miss America contest. (She's happy to point out that she was also the tallest woman to ever lose the Miss America contest!) Since her pageant days in the 60's, Jeanne has entertained audiences all over America with her tall tales and southern-spun humor. A past-president of the National Speakers Association, Jeanne is the author of *Humor: The Magic of Genie*.

Liz: What do people say when they meet you for the first time?

Jeanne: *I was 6'2" at age thirteen, so people have been commenting about my height for most of my life. Let's face it, height and weight are both very noticeable things, and people feel free to make some remark about them when they meet us. When I was young, people always said, "My, how you've grown!" It got to be a joke with my family, such that when we went to visit our relatives in Auburn, my parents would say, "How many times do you think you'll hear, 'My how you've grown'?" We'd even place bets on it. Then, when the comments would come, instead of being embarrassed, I would cut my eyes at my mother and we would nod: "That's one! That's two!" It was funny, and helped me through a very awkward time. Later, they encouraged me to mention it myself, so I'd jump out of the car and say, "My, how I've grown!"*

Liz: Do you think people are intentionally trying to hurt us when they make such comments?

Jeanne: *I really don't. That's why the best response is a humorous one, laughing at yourself, rather than looking for the curt comeback, the one-line zinger. Just recently, I realized that I do something unintentionally that's really very inappropriate. When I'm around a larger man who I know, I'll sometimes poke him in the stomach with my index finger. Of course, it's done in fun, but it's still not right. Unfortunately, we often do such things without really thinking about how it might make the other person feel.*

Liz: What are some of the less funny things, the drawbacks, of being a tall woman?

Jeanne: *The big problem is shopping for clothes. You can't buy anything at the last minute. I've always envied women who can start shopping on Wednesday for a dress they need Saturday night. I have to plan way ahead, and I always have to have things altered. Those of us who are bigger or taller than average almost always spend more money on our wardrobe, and end up with a lot of things we don't wear. If I pass a tall woman coming out of the mall with a big package, my first thought is, "Well, whatever was worth buying, she found it first." If I see a woman in the tall girl store looking through my size, I practically hyperventilate. When I do find something that fits, I always buy it, figuring "I'd better get it today, it may not be here later." I suppose I could find a good tailor, pick out fabrics and so forth, but I'm too busy for all that.*

Liz: It's amazing to me how similar our challenges are in that regard. Now, what are some of the advantages of being tall?

Jeanne: *When you are 6'2", there's no way you won't be noticed when you walk into a room. There is in fact nothing you can do in the way of clothing that will make you not be noticed. Flat shoes look ridiculous with an outfit that calls for heels, so I wear the heels. For the most part, the taller woman looks good in her clothes. She can make a statement, hopefully a positive one. Those of us who are not a "normal" size have a common bond. We can see each other across the room and start grinning, because we know we've had many of the same experiences. Women who are extra large, extra tall, even extra short, all share some of the same challenges. I believe that larger and taller women who develop a high degree of self-confidence command more respect and attention and have more presence about them. I really do think size can be an advantage!*

Liz: Does one size ever fit your all?

Jeanne: *NO! Well, that's not true. I had a One Size Fits All umbrella once that was a good fit.*

Liz: Is the rest of your family tall, too?

Jeanne: *Not my parents or siblings, but my husband is 6'6" and my son is 6'8". One of the challenges of raising a tall teenager is finding clothes that are in style. Yes, you can find him jeans, but not the "in" jeans. An adult may not care about the label thing very much, but it matters a lot to a teenager. I remember the time my son and husband were trying to buy a blouse for me, and the clerk asked what size foundation I wore. My son said, "11-B," thinking she meant my shoe size. We all got a big laugh out of that one!*

Liz: Do you see any connection between your size and your sense of humor?

Jeanne: *Yes, but I credit my parents for that. They helped me see the humor in it at an early age, and taught me how to use humor to help others be as comfortable with my height as I was. There's a big difference between being self-deprecating — always bringing up the size issue yourself in a negative way — and having fun with your size when the situation calls for it.*

Liz: You often say, in print and in person, that you weigh 160 pounds. That's actually low for your height, isn't it? Yet do people seem surprised?

Jeanne: *Yes, it seems big to them, especially if they are 5'2" and weigh 120 pounds! One advantage of being taller is I can gain five pounds and no one notices except me.*

Liz: What encouragement would you offer a woman who is struggling with her size and self-esteem?

Jeanne: *Two suggestions. First of all, it's an acceptance thing. You have certain things you either have to change or* accept about yourself, and size is one of those things. For example, I could probably change my southern accent, if I really wanted to and thought it was worth the effort. But I don't want to, so I accept it and learn to have fun with it. Second, I recommend using your sense of humor. Now remember, a sense of humor is not telling jokes. It's laughing at yourself and at life, seeing the humor in your circumstances. A person who has a sense of humor can usually handle anything. Fortunately, that is not a gift you receive at birth, it is a choice. A sense of humor is not inherited, it's developed. And I, for one, think it's worth developing, especially by us "larger-sized" folks.

"You'll Never Get a Man"

A few years ago, I was hunched over my Delta Air Lines tray table, writing an article called, "What Makes Women Laugh?" The fella next to me studied the title at the top of my legal pad and chuckled. "That's easy!" he said. "Men!"

Well, since you brought it up, sir, sometimes we do find men laughable. Loveable, too. But sometimes we fear they won't love us back because we don't fit the size and shape of American beauty.

According to a 1988 Gallup Poll commissioned by *American Health* magazine, the average American man doesn't even think in terms of dress sizes when he's envisioning the kind of woman he would like to call his own. What he wants is a woman with an ample rear end, medium hips, a small-to-medium waist and medium-sized breasts. An average, not thin, body is his preference, and softer tone, not muscular.

Isn't it nice to know the "hard body" look is not particularly appealing to most men? For those of us whose size is well above average, do not despair! Remember, this is just the *average* response from men, which means others would have chosen bigger everything (and would therefore love us!).

Here's another fun note from my mailbox, written by a woman in Indiana. It seems this woman went on a cruise with three thin, tanned female friends. She was married (with a very trusting husband at home) and they were all single. Whom do you suppose got the flowers delivered to her room, got invited to exotic places and in general was the belle of the ball? Our plump note-writer, of course. She decided that Caribbean men like women who are "meaty!" Almost everywhere except the United States, women with more flesh are found to be more attractive.

I remember when I was trying to find a plus-size wedding gown and was getting desperate. At the eleventh hour, I considered finding a good seamstress to make one for me. I was referred to a sweet German woman who asked my dress size. "Twenty," I gulped.

"Oh, good, then you'll have a pretty neck and bosom!" she exclaimed. "We could do something nice and off the shoulder for you." Fascinating. To her foreign (literally) way of thinking, ample flesh was definitely an asset. Maybe we were all meant to be European!

Men and Size Preferences

If you looked only at polls like the one mentioned above, or glanced at the personals section of any newspaper where all the ads request thin women, it would be easy to surmise that ALL men want a small woman — or an average woman — but not a big woman. Oh, really? Then how do you explain all the men who are happily married to large women? A fluke? A mistake? Hardly. These men love their women who happen to be larger women.

> *My husband says nothing but positive stuff, which means a lot to me.*
>
> Mary Jane from Kentucky

These men may love their wives or girlfriends *because* of their size (and indeed, some men are "Fat Admirers," who simply are attracted to larger women).

> *My husband is a rare breed — he prefers large women. He thinks I'm still a little thin at 180 pounds.*
>
> Jill from Ohio

Or, a man may love his sweetie in spite of her size (perhaps she gained weight after marriage, and he has wisely chosen to accept it).

My #1 wonderful husband says he doesn't love me for my size — that I'm still precious and desirable.

Rosanne from Kentucky

Size is a non-issue with some men, and they would love us at any weight.

My husband says, "You're the prettiest girl in the world."

Sherry from Missouri

Hubby says, "More to love."

Bonita from Colorado

The Great Manhunt

Women who are single but long to be married often think they're doomed to remain unwed if they're not pencil thin. Most of them work at getting or staying lean for those hard-to-lasso hunks:

Since I am not married, I try to stay in shape to catch a man and because I want to.

Robin from Ohio

For the rest of us who may not be "in shape" but definitely are "shaped out," we sometimes conclude we're single *because* we're larger:

I don't have any relationships due to the fact that I'm fat. Always a friend, but never a girlfriend.

Lucia from Louisiana

I have not dated in several years. I assume this is because of my size although I'm not actively pursuing any men.

Debra from Washington

I certainly would have found myself agreeing with these women in 1985, when I hadn't dated in almost three years. I had finally "taken my name off the list," as it were. I was sick to death of being "fixed up" by my friends, as if I were somehow "broken," instead of just single.

Growing up, I always assumed I'd get married someday. It might have helped if I dated the right kind of men. Before becoming a Christian, all the men I dated were either married, separated, or happily single and avoiding commitment. Maybe they cared about my size, maybe they didn't. For certain, they didn't care enough for me to say, "I do."

After my conversion at age twenty-seven, you'll remember I dieted myself down to a slinky size 10. Men were still not beating a path to my door. So much for the, "If I lose weight, I'll get a man" theory. I stayed single and, for the most part, dateless until I met Bill in 1985, just before my thirty-first birthday.

What happened in those three man-free years? I gained weight! And, I gained self-confidence. They didn't come together as a package, but rather in sequence. When I put my weight back on, I lost all the false body confidence that comes from dieting. I had to develop, from ground zero, a whole new foundation of body confidence. This time, though, it was built on things that last and matter: God's love for me, and my love and respect for myself.

I never intentionally skipped marriage, it just happened that way. I woke up on my thirtieth birthday and said, "Oh my word, I forgot to get married!" The women in my church were always fussing over me, trying hard not to feel sorry for me, though they obviously did. "A-w-w-w-w," they'd say. "No husband? No children? Poor thing!" More than once, they intoned, "God has a man for you." (To which I always said, "Hey! He knows my address, what's the holdup?")

But, they were right. God did have a man for me. And He wisely waited until I was at peace with myself. He waited until I had a close relationship with Him, until I no longer needed a man in order to be happy. Then, Bill walked into my life. Great timing. I didn't overwhelm him with an eager, "Oh boy! A live one!" attitude.

I was initially introduced to Bill at a concert one warm June evening. I liked him immediately. He has an easy way about him—friendly, laid-back, warm. He was obviously bright, had a nice deep Kentucky twang and freckles all over. We met only briefly, but I thought, "What a nice man! I hope our paths cross again!"

They did. At a wedding. (No, not ours!) Just three weeks later, I dragged myself to a ceremony for two good friends. I say "dragged" because when you are single, weddings are lethal. We're talking big time bummer for days afterwards.

It just so happened the woman getting married was named "Liz," so the whole time she was taking her vows, I took them with her. (Just practice, you understand, in case I got to do it myself someday.) When the minister said, "Do you, Liz, take Doug?" I whispered under my breath, "I do!"

(After all, he was good looking — even if already spoken for by the other Liz!)

When the ceremony ended and I looked around the church to see who else I might know, there in the sea of pairs was a spare about two rows back: Bill! I studied his handsome, prematurely silver hair that was on full retreat from his forehead and thought, "I wonder how old he is? Thirty-five? Could be. Forty-five? Fifty-five? Whatever he is, he's just right!" I headed enthusiastically in his direction.

We talked until the church was empty. We talked at the reception until everyone else had gone home. I gave him my business card (with my home phone number on the back), and told him to "call me sometime."

"Sometime" came about five days later. Our first date was July 15, 1985. By October, we were in love. By Thanksgiving, engaged. At Christmas, I got my diamond ring (is this sounding too sappy?). We were married at 7:00 P.M., March 14, 1986. Three hundred people came to our wedding (probably to see if it would really happen!). It happened. Seven years later, it's still happening. I am more crazy about this man today than the day I married him.

A Better Class of Man

> *[Tell me] how to get a man to like you for your brain and humor, not for your looks.*
>
> Lori from Florida

Not all men are as wonderful as my Bill. Some are so short-sighted they can't see your intelligence and sense of humor. Too bad, because those things will last a lifetime. "Looks" as we define them grind to a halt somewhere between age sixteen and . . . well, too soon, anyway.

Carole Shaw of *BBW*, advises women: "If you want to meet a better class of man, put on twenty pounds!" Her point is well taken: the kind of man you want will not be so focused on body shape and size that he misses your wonderful mind and big, beautiful heart.

More than one woman can tell the sad tale of how she lost weight, hooked a man who loved her thin body, gained the weight back, and lost that shallow man.

Men are far more friendly when I'm at my low weights.
                                                    Michele from Indiana

My husband says, "Honey, you just sparkle when you lose a few pounds."
                                                    Jeddie from South Carolina

I grow weary of all these "what will a man think?" approaches to weight loss motivation. In an article titled, "The ABC'S of How to be Hungry and Like It," the author quotes Dr. Peter Miller of the Sea Pines Behavioral Institute at Hilton Head, South Carolina: "Imagine that your boyfriend is flirting with a slender, attractive girl instead of talking to you because you are eating an ice cream cone and your bulges are showing."

I say, stick the ice cream cone down his bathing suit and move on!

Don't Love Me (or Leave Me) Because of My Body

The fact is, men not only date, but also fall in love with and marry women who wear a size 16 or bigger. I admit when I looked at wedding pictures of my custom-built size 20 gown, I heaved a big sigh. No, I had never imagined myself as a big bride. But if Bill loved me "as is," I had married the right man, and *that* was something to celebrate!

My husband says he loves ME, not my dress size.
                                                    Diane from Tennessee

We are lucky, Diane. More than one husband does not affirm his wife or her body:

"You're so pretty — if only you would lose weight!" These are my husband's favorite words!
                                                    Barbara from Pennsylvania

Because large men are more tolerated in our society than large women, an unusual double standard can be employed:

My husband (who happens to have a big tummy) calls me "Fat Back" and is constantly telling me I need to diet.
                                                    Sally from Missouri

Other women wrote about husbands who called them, "Porky," "Fatty Fingers," "My Little Chubby One," "Big Boss," and "Miss Piggy."

My ex-husband always laughingly called me "Bubble Butt." He didn't seem to know or care that it hurt.
                                                    Sherry from Missouri

My ex-husband had several favorite nicknames he used to call me: Thunder Thighs, Tons of Fun, Mammoth Petite.
                                                    Vicky Lynn from Ohio

(One wonders if such nicknames were part of the reason these last two are "ex" husbands!)

The Double (Chin) Standard

Some husbands use our weight as their excuse to bail out:

[My size] was one of the reasons my ex-husband left, except I was only about 40 pounds overweight.
                                                    Janet from Kentucky

Good grief! If women left their husbands because *they* gained 40 pounds, the divorce rate would be at about 80%! People would think it shameful (and rightfully so, I might add), but society seems to accept the reverse. They'll put the blame on a woman, shake their heads and say, "Well, she shouldn't have let herself go."

If I lost 40 pounds, I'd have to spend all my time fighting men off with sticks.
                                                    Kathy from Michigan

What is this thing about "40 pounds?" Any man who would begin a relationship with you if you were 40 pounds thinner, but not today, is a dolt. Trust me, I dated plenty of them.

One young man in particular assured me that he would be happy to introduce me to his family and friends "just as soon as I lost 50 pounds." My self-esteem was so low at the time, I just shrugged and said, "I'll keep trying." Even now, as I write these words, I feel the pain of that moment and it makes me so angry I could spit.

If we allow men to hold such sway over our lives that we starve our bodies to attract them, and they subsequently desert us when we begin to eat again, then something is desperately wrong with both them *and* us.

We don't even like to eat around men. Think about your dating years. The guys got popcorn at the movie: we had two bites, they ate the rest. We stopped at McDonald's on the way home: they got a burger and fries, we got a diet drink. A single man in his early thirties once said that he knew a relationship with a woman was getting somewhere "when she was willing to eat more than a spinach salad in front of him."[1]

Thank Goodness for the Good Ones

Lest this appear as some strident attack against men, it's truly not. I like men. I have a father and three brothers. I married a man. And I gave birth to a male. Men are terrific (and quite necessary for the perpetuation of humankind!). Sometimes, they see us more accurately than we see ourselves:

My husband thinks I'm beautiful and I'm really not.
                                        Connie from Pennsylvania

If he thinks you're beautiful, don't argue! Congratulate him on having the good sense to marry you.

It's time to hear from the Good Guys, the significant sweeties who are willing to love us "as is":

My husband says, "Your body is a testament of your life and I love it."
                                        Carla from New Hampshire

My husband says don't worry about it. You look good to me.
Betty from Kentucky

My significant other thinks I'm beautiful.
Tami in Nebraska

My Bill always tells me (and sometimes with actions instead of words) that he finds me very attractive. If he did absolutely nothing else in his whole life, loving me when I sometimes resist it might be his most amazing accomplishment.

Those of us who grew up with (or grew into) a false belief that we couldn't possibly be appealing to a man are always amazed when one breaks through our self-imposed barriers and climbs into our hearts. When they love us, an amazing thing happens: we are set free to completely love ourselves and return their love as well.

Listen to Vicky Lynn's journey on this road:

When I discovered that I was going to have to face the world alone, I was heartsick thinking that no one in their right mind would want a "fat and forty" date. Then, at a Christian fellowship singles event, I realized my size was not that critical and what I had going for me was an infectious sense of humor. Strangers actually like me for who I am. . . and you know what? I LIKE ME!
Vicky Lynn from Ohio

Hooray for her! Whether or not she "gets her man," this woman has found joy, peace and fellowship. In the bargain, she's also discovered she has a lot to offer this world. Chances are, with a personality like that, she *will* have to "fight men off with a stick!"

Begin Building Body Confidence Today

1. Imagine yourself a writer of romance fiction and create a story in your mind of a big, beautiful, brilliant woman who is wildly pursued by a handsome, wise and witty man. They both weigh at least forty pounds over the insurance table desired weights and are having the time of their lives. Hollywood will never produce this story, so you will have to do it in your head. You decide . . . what's the happy ending?

2. Think of the men in your life who said, "I'd love you more IF . . ." or "IF you'd just lose some weight, I'd marry you . . ." or whatever conditional lines you may have heard. Forgive yourself for letting such messages pierce your heart. Forgive them for saying such unkind things. Not because they deserve it. Because you deserve to be set free from the pain that those comments still inflict when they bubble up unexpectedly.

3. Know that any man worth having in your life will find you desirable exactly as you are right now. If a man tells you that you're beautiful, believe him!

❤ *A Husband Speaks . . .*

My husband, William Robert Higgs (better known as Bill), has a Ph.D. in Hebrew from Southern Baptist Theological Seminary and is a computer systems specialist for a television station in Louisville. (You're right, those two areas do not compute. I call him my Renaissance Man!) Bill responded to the following questions on paper while I was presenting a program in Memphis. I asked him to be completely honest, in order to help us all better understand how men think.

Liz: What were your first thoughts when we were introduced on that June evening under the stars at Iroquois Amphitheater?

Bill: *It was only a fleeting meeting, but I was impressed immediately by your warmth and spirit, and by your confidence. You seemed very comfortable with who you were. I had dated a number of women who seemed to expect me to provide all their self-confidence for them. In your case, self-confidence was apparent from the outset.*

Liz: Did my size make any impression on you?

Bill: *Not in any particularly negative sense. What struck me was that your personality and confidence level did not match what I had come to associate with larger women. You didn't fit that image at all. Some men say they are turned off by larger women, and this may be so for a few. I would venture to say that their negative impression is mainly due to an attitude shown by some larger women rather than size itself. For me, at least, my attitude toward a woman is based mostly on her attitude toward herself.*

Liz: What made you decide to ask me out to dinner the following month?

Bill: *I liked you the minute we met and felt immediately comfortable around you. You were someone I needed to know better on a personal level, whether a long-term relationship grew out of it or not.*

Liz: Had you ever dated a larger woman before?

Bill: *Yes, although I had dated women of all shapes and sizes. Remember I was in my early thirties when we met, so my dating experience had been long and varied. For what it's worth, the last three women I dated before our meeting were all petite.*

Liz: After we became friends, did your view of my appearance change at all?

Bill: *Perhaps, but in a positive way. As I fell more and more in love with you, I became less and less aware of size. Other things had become much more important. In that sense, you had given me permission. Size had become a non-issue.*

Liz: Do you ever find yourself wishing I were thinner, or that I would go on a diet?

Bill: *Not often, and only if I sense your self-confidence is sagging or if you have indicated that you want to lose weight. There is a fine line between supporting someone in their desire to lose weight and making them feel as though they are unaccepted otherwise. I have walked that line a few times during our marriage, as you have struggled with whether to diet or not. If losing weight were truly your desire, I would support you in it. BUT, if I felt you were doing so because you no longer felt you met my expectations, I would probably discourage you from dieting.*

Liz: Are you ever embarrassed to introduce me to someone as your wife?

Bill: *Never. I am very proud of you.*

Liz: You have gained a few pounds since we married (though not as much as I have!). Has your size had any effect on how you feel about yourself? Any effect on our relationship?

Bill: *I don't feel it has affected either in any particular way. I wouldn't mind losing a few pounds, but I don't think my self-esteem has suffered any from my weight gain. For*

*men, the pressures are not so much from the standpoint of
appearance, but rather physical prowess or ability. I have
never been much of an athlete, nor have I had any
particular obsession with looking slim and trim. If losing
weight would give me a bit more stamina or ward off future
health problems, I might give it more thought. My guess is
that turning forty has probably had more effect on my
energy level than gaining weight. I am one of those men
who spent most of their youth trying to gain weight rather
than lose it — I did not reach my "textbook" weight until I
was nearly thirty. As far as our relationship is concerned,
I haven't noticed any particular effect. It just makes it
easier to let you throw out my old pants that don't fit
anymore!*

Liz: What would you say to a man who says, "No woman of
mine will ever be fat!"

Bill: *To a married man I would say, "You may not have that
choice, because your wife may not have that choice." To
a single man I would say, "You've severely limited your
options." Unfortunately, this kind of attitude is typical of
a certain male viewpoint which still sees a wife or
girlfriend as a possession, or worse, a status symbol.
Possessions and symbols, by their very nature, are
transient and can be discarded at will. The problem is a
basic misunderstanding of what a relationship is supposed
to be. Such a man can expect problems in a relationship
with any woman, large or small. I wonder what he might
say to a woman who declared, "No man of mine will ever
be bald!" Physical attributes change over time for both
men and women. Maybe he should forget women and buy
a dog instead. He'd be happier!*

Liz: How would you encourage a man to love his wife, no
matter what her size?

Bill: *Never make love conditional on her physical appearance
(or anything else, for that matter).*

Liz: How would you encourage a woman to please her beloved,
no matter what her size?

Bill: *Always assume that you are attractive to him, whether you feel attractive or not. If he says you are beautiful, he's right. If a woman's husband rejects her appearance, this would certainly be tougher for her. I would still say, however, that the key is believing you are desirable. You alone are master of your image and personality. Don't let anyone else (Hollywood, husbands or fashion) define them for you.*

"You Can Lose It If You Really Want To"

One spring, I presented a luncheon program for a small group of executive wives while their husbands conducted business down the hall. They were a fun bunch, beautifully dressed, well-educated, witty and warm. But all they talked about at lunch was how FAT they were. Not one woman in the room could have weighed more than five to ten pounds over the standard weight chart statistics for her height and age, but to them that was positively obese.

The woman sitting directly across from me waited for the right moment to announce that she had just lost 80 pounds.

"Imagine," she said, "I used to wear a size 22 jacket and a size 24 skirt!" Everyone gasped, then praised her for her dieting success.

There I sat, their invited guest speaker, wearing a size 22 jacket and a size 24 skirt. I didn't know whether to laugh or cry. Maybe, I thought, I should ask her if she has any old clothes she'd like to share with me! Before long, she was looking me straight in the eye and saying, "Anyone can lose 80 pounds if they want to badly enough."

"I'm not sure that's true," I said softly. "I believe metabolically and genetically, it would be almost impossible for me to lose and keep off 80 pounds."

She shook her head and rolled her eyes in disgust. "You just haven't really tried," she insisted. It was obvious I wasn't about to change her mind, so I simply smiled and let it drop, praying that the women around us would soon find another topic of conversation.

They didn't.

"Say What?"

What do you say when people suggest, boldly or in a roundabout way, that you could or should lose weight? Society seems to delight in presenting this option to us at every turn, as if we haven't already thought it through and tried dozens of diets. Dr. Albert Stunkard, an obesity researcher at the University of Pennsylvania, found that, "There's that implicit assumption that you really could lose weight if you settled down and stopped being such a fat slob."[1] Dr. Stunkard knows better, and so do we.

Judith from Colorado echoed that false conclusion people often make. "'If large women don't like it, they would lose it.' Get real." The societal assumption is that: 1) We don't know we are fat, so they have to point it out to us. 2) We haven't *really* tried to lose weight.

My first exposure to self-acceptance came almost a decade ago when I tried to start a diet group at work. One woman I was certain would want to sign up immediately said, "No thanks!" I was shocked. She was the first larger woman I'd ever met who was comfortable with her self. She didn't live each day apologizing for her size or vowing to start back on a diet next Monday. She's the same size today she was ten years ago. I think she's on to something!

Most of the time, when people suggest the "D" word to me, I smile and say, "I've decided that diets don't work, and so instead I'm learning to accept myself at this size."

They usually respond with something like, "That's great!" and quickly change the subject. If they come back with, "But what about your health?" I share some of the statistics included in this book.

As Carole Shaw pointed out: "Look in a hospital. Do you think in every one of those rooms is a fat person?" Sometimes a simple statement like that can get a person's mental wheels turning. Another favorite quotable quote from Carole, also from her appearance on the

Jenny Jones show: "In a hundred years, all of us are gonna weigh the same!"[2]

Give people time to accept where you are. Look how long it's taken some of us to wake up to the truth about dieting, weight-loss scams and health risks (or the lack of them). We have a long way to go before we convince the average American woman that we know what we're talking about. Patience will be required to make it through this educational process.

The Last Straw

There are times when I run out of the virtue of patience. An example comes to mind: It was the first day I met with my talented, red-headed editor from Thomas Nelson – the man who believed my message and in my ability to put it into words.

Duncan and I were enjoying lunch in a busy open-air restaurant in La Jolla, California, on a lovely Sunday afternoon in August. The sun was shining, the breeze was blowing, and we were having a wonderful time tossing ideas back and forth about this book-in-progress.

A woman seated at the table next to us kept eyeing me and smiling in my direction. Finally, she came over and introduced herself. "My name is Barb, and I couldn't help overhearing your conversation." (That's probably true, because neither Duncan nor I talk softly!)

She continued, "I thought you might like to know about a product I sell that offers an all-natural approach to weight control."

I have never done this before or since, but I did it that day. "Ma'am, YOU might like to know that I am highly offended that you would be so bold as to suggest that I need, or want, to lose weight!"

She started doing a very quick social two-step. "Oh, I didn't mean to suggest that you need to lose weight, I... uh, just thought with the book you were discussing, you needed to know about this."

Right. It was very obvious what she was suggesting. People are so certain fat people want to be thin people, they think nothing of accosting complete strangers and offering their sure-fire "solutions."

Admittedly, I embarrassed her terribly. (My editor ended up apologizing on my behalf!) But sometimes, enough is enough.

Laura Eljaiek, now Program Director of the National Association to Advance Fat Acceptance, tells the story of having a man behind her on the bus suggest, "You could use some Slim Fast." Her quick comeback? "You could use some manners!"[3]

File It Under "They Meant Well"

When strangers say rude things, we can ignore it, nail them with a caustic reply, or laugh. In any case, soon they are out of our lives, and the sting of their words is quickly dulled.

But when friends comment on our size or weight, the knife is sharper, cuts deeper, and leaves a more gaping wound. In almost every situation, friends are trying to say the right thing, and instead step on their own tongue (and our toes):

> *My pseudo friends say, "Isn't it a shame you're so large — you're so attractive!"*
>
> Diana from Kentucky

> *Women say, "You don't act like a big person." (Figure that out!)*
> Melissa from Ohio

They may watch us for diet signals, so they can be sure to offer just the right word of encouragement:

> *If I'm hungry and I don't eat, my coworkers ask, "Are you on a DIET? Are you trying to lose WEIGHT?"*
> Dolores from New York

If you need a reason to tell people why you have given up on dieting, here's one of the best ones: Diets are a no-win, no-lose proposition. In a recent newspaper survey of local weight loss centers, one center admitted that 75% of their clients had to return to their program. "After two or three years, almost everybody comes back."[4]

What kind of success record is that? And what damage has been done to clients' self-esteem and metabolism in the meantime? At least that particular program was being honest. Of the seven interviewed, four stated that the data on returnees was "not available."[5] Uh-huh.

Even weight control programs that include behavior modification and a full year of maintenance don't fare well. In one study, women participated in a sixteen-week weight loss program, followed by a twelve-month maintenance program. At the start, their average weight was 214. Thirty months after the program, their average weight was 217.[6] Something is wrong here, and it's not the women.

A recent issue of the newsletter *Obesity and Health* took a strong stance against many of the methods of weight loss being offered in today's marketplace. "Exploitation, deception, greed and fraud are common. Many treatments are health-threatening, causing injury and even death."[7]

Some women have a deceptively simple way to "diet": they smoke cigarettes. About 10% of women who start smoking do so to lose weight. Some 25% of women who now smoke use cigarettes to control their weight and are therefore afraid to quit.[8] Because smoking makes the heart work harder, it does raise your metabolic rate a bit. But more than 400,000 Americans died from cigarette smoking in 1991 alone.[9] As diets go, smoking is a killer.

This may be the hardest thing I'll ever say, but by putting it in print, I'll be duty-bound to honor it. I'm never going to diet again. Period. As author Rita Freedman says, "Dieting entails narcissistic self-preoccupation and masochistic self-denial."[10] Neither one of those sound like the path to righteousness that "shines ever brighter unto the perfect day."[11] In fact, it sounds downright gloomy!

When someone starts singing their, "But, what about your health?" tune, why not offer some statistical proof that *dieting* can be hazardous to your health, often more so than carrying extra weight.

Specifically, Freedman warns that "the chronic dieter may suffer from malnutrition, gastric problems, irritability, anxiety, lethargy, fatigue, tension, insomnia and depression."[12] The more drastic the diet, the more dangerous. For example, 25% of people on very low calorie diets (like the liquid kind) develop gallstones.[13] No fun.

Those of us who gain, lose, gain, lose are taking the most risks of all. Research shows that people with high weight variability (us "yo-yo's") are 25-100% more likely to experience heart disease and premature death than people whose weight remains stable.[14] Even those who are data-resistant and refuse to let a little thing like research get in the way of an old belief system would have to pause at that chilling statistic on the dangers of weight cycling.

Guess Who's *Not* Coming to Dinner

What do you say when someone tells you they are on a diet? I don't want to encourage them, but naturally I don't want to *dis*courage them, either. My solution is to say, "I will love and respect you whether you lose, gain or stay the same. Just for the record, you're an attractive and wonderful person right now!"

I also fight the urge to talk someone into eating something they don't want to eat. After all, whether I agree with them or not, they have the right to choose what foods they put in their body. The whole subject of eating and dieting is a very personal one. I do, however, stand ready to support a friend when, as so often happens, the diet doesn't work. At that time of discouragement, a kind word, assurance that they have lots of company (95% of dieters) and a reminder it's not their "fault" can be welcome words. The key is to offer unconditional love.

I recently picked up a brochure on the latest fasting-based diet (I read such things for amusement) and couldn't help noticing that these women looked better in their "before" pictures than they did in their "after" photos! They looked so gaunt and frail after their "doctor-supervised" fasts that you wanted to sit them down to a decent meal and help them regain their strength.

David the psalmist saw the same phenomenon: "My knees are weak through fasting,/And my flesh is feeble from lack of fatness."[15]

There's No Denying It

There's more than one form of denial.

Some women deny that they are fat. They run past mirrors, dress in the dark, wear very loose clothing and just pretend it's not there. They cut out the labels in their clothing, stick to sizes that end in X, and list their dress size as 14-16, when the truth is they haven't worn a size 14 for many years. They do *not* read *BBW* magazine, they read *Ladies Home Journal* or *Redbook*.

Another kind of denial: Some women would call themselves "overweight," but temporarily so. They think they can diet it off anytime, like the smoker who says she can quit anytime, but never gets around to it. These women subscribe to *Weight Watchers* magazine, and go on a diet the first Monday of almost every month. They've joined weight groups half a dozen times, but never made it to the diamond pin. They see their weight as a sign of laziness or lack of willpower. As soon as they have more time, they'll get the weight off.

A third kind of denial: These women are former fat women who have dieted themselves down to an almost-acceptable weight. I say "almost" because I've never met a woman who actually weighed her goal weight. They always say to another woman, "Just seven more pounds to go!" These women are often very self-righteous. They unwittingly look down their noses at every woman who weighs ten pounds more than they do. "I'll never be like that again," they think to themselves. They read *Self* and *Glamour*, and walk past the mirror often. (It's really not their fault they have this attitude, it's just the lack of nutrition. Like Sherry from Michigan says, "Stay out of my way when I'm dieting! I'm grouchy!")

Where did my definitions of these three forms of denial come from? The research project called My Life. Please don't hear judgment in my words, just the truth as I see it.

Here are my findings: being fat does not necessarily mean a person is living in denial; being thin is definitely no guarantee against living in denial. The reality is that all of us are in a state of denial about something. There's no denying this, though: God loves us in whatever state we are in (geographical or spiritual).

The View from the Other Side

Of the more than 200 surveys compiled for this book, only one was from a woman who had recently lost quite a bit of weight. Because she is a dear friend of mine, she was willing to complete the survey anyway. I love her too much to include her name here, but I want to share her words. When I lost 45 pounds back in 1984, this is almost exactly what I might have written myself:

> *The difference between weighing 205 and 135 is so great it can't be explained. Everyone — from store clerks you don't even know to your own husband — treats you differently, more respectfully, when you're thin. And because we are products of the same society we are part of, we treat ourselves differently when we can smile at the reflection in the mirror.*

What is wrong with this picture? Store clerks should treat you with respect no matter what you weigh (whatever happened to "the customer is always right?"). Of all people, your husband should respect you, thick or thin. The Bible commands it: "Husbands, love your wives." Period. No parenthetical, "but if she weighs 205 pounds, treat her like dirt." No way.

Most importantly, we need to smile at the reflection in the mirror *no matter what the size of the woman smiling back*! Because here is the awful truth, and the reason dieting is so dangerous to our emotional well-being: If we gain back some or all of the weight we lost (and remember the odds of that happening are 19 in 20), then how will we feel about that woman in the mirror? What kind of treatment will we think we deserve from our husbands and loved ones? What kind of grief will we put up with from store clerks who are rude to us?

Society will *not* change how it views or treats us until *we* change how we view ourselves and how we treat one another. Susan Wooley, Ph.D., the woman who did the *Glamour* survey in 1984, said, "If shame could cure obesity, there wouldn't be a fat woman in the world."[16]

Look Who's On Our Side

Support for body acceptance, for letting go of perfect, is beginning to come from all corners of our world, both statistical support as well as emotional. Even the medical community is coming around, although slowly. I love the note I received from an Ohio woman who told me about her mother's trip to the hospital at age forty-five. Her tall, skinny doctor ordered his large, lovely patient to go on a 600 calorie a day diet, and instructed the nurse to keep a close eye on her. One week later, without cheating one iota, the woman had gained two pounds. Now, twenty-seven years later, she still has the same doctor, and he has never mentioned her weight again. Bravo!

Here's some authoritative support from an unexpected place. The Smithsonian Museum in Washington, D.C., had an exhibit on display a few years ago titled "Clothes, Gender and Power." It included a whole display cabinet full of diet books, diet products, diet pills and fitness videos. Near the cabinet was displayed this poster:

FAT

- There is no known cause of obesity.
- There is no known cure.
- Obese people do not on the average eat more than anyone else.
- Ninety percent of Americans who lose weight through dieting gain it back within two years.
- There is little scientific evidence to prove that obesity causes high blood pressure or heart disease.

- Slightly overweight people live longer than thin people.
- Taking amphetamines, fasting, undergoing gastric stapling or constantly gaining and losing weight are dangerous to your health.[17]

Thank you, United States Government!

Begin Building Body Confidence Today

1. Decide exactly how you want to respond to people who suggest that you should lose weight. If you plan what you want to say in advance, you are less likely to hurt their feelings or have your own damaged. Something gentle, loving, firm, even informational might work for you.

2. Choose the right way to respond to someone who tells you that *they* want to lose weight. Don't encourage dieting, but do affirm their decision. Again, sensitivity is the key, and perhaps offering some information (or a copy of this book!).

3. Find your own support network, *not* a diet group, to help you grow in the right direction. A circle of friends, a walking group, a Bible study, a weekly lunch gathering, whatever works for you. What matters is that you love and encourage each other without any conditions or judgments.

♥ A Support Group Leader Speaks . . .

Carol Johnson is the Founder and President of Largely Positive, Inc., in Milwaukee, Wisconsin. She earned her master's degree in applied sociology from Kent State University in Ohio. She is a certified psychotherapist, and is currently doing research in mental health.

Liz: Tell us about your journey toward becoming Largely Positive.

Carol: *I am a lifelong larger woman. About five years ago, I was browsing through a bookstore for a new diet book to try and stumbled on* The Dieter's Dilemma: Eating Less and Weighing More *by William Bennett, M.D., and Joel Gurin. The title really intrigued me, because I sure was in a dilemma! I thought it would finally tell me what was wrong with me, why I couldn't lose weight. When I finished reading the book, I just wanted to find the authors and kiss them! It seemed my weight struggles were not my fault after all.*

Liz: What happened next?

Carol: *I started reading all the research on obesity (ugh, I hate that word, but that's what they call it in the medical community), and I began discovering many research findings that no one had ever told me about. It really made me angry, especially at my doctors, because the information wasn't even brand new, it had been around a while. I've since discovered that what most people believe about obesity and what the research really says are two entirely different things.*

Liz: [Laughing] It's been an educational process for most of us, rethinking the whole diet thing. Where did the Largely Positive idea come from?

Carol: *I remember the night it was born. I had been going with a friend to Diet Workshop (you know, one I hadn't tried yet), and I was losing my usual quarter to half pound a week. The woman weighing me kept giving me these "you're not really trying" looks, but I had read all the research and knew that losing slowly was much healthier than losing five pounds a week of water. Anyway, the 4th of July was coming up, so that night she decided as a group exercise, "Let's make a list of all the freedoms we lose when we are overweight." Something snapped. I raised my hand and asked, "Why are we doing such a negative thing? Why are we doing this to ourselves?" I went home that night and said, "That's it! No more negative stuff. I want to go to a place that makes me feel positive about myself!"*

Liz: Who encouraged you to start your own support group?

Carol: *I owe a debt of gratitude to two Milwaukee area doctors. Drew Palin, M.D., president of Competitive Edge Sports Medicine, was also my husband's doctor. Fearful that Dr. Palin might tell my husband that his problems were all due to his weight, I armed my husband with Largely Positive literature and said, "If he says anything about your weight, give him this!" Imagine my amazement when my husband called me later that day and said, "Dr. Palin would like to meet you. He thinks your stuff is great." He's been collaborating with me ever since. One interesting note: Dr. Palin used to work with the Optifast program, but quit when he realized that all his patients were regaining their weight.*

Liz: What about the second doctor who helped you?

Carol: *That's Dr. Anthony Machi, a highly respected physician who treats patients with eating disorders. He was in the audience at one of my programs and afterwards approached me and said, "Is there anything I can do to help you?" Of course, I said, "Yes! I want to start a support group and we need somewhere to have our meetings." He convinced the hospital to provide not only space, but also marketing support and reimbursement for professional facilitators. We meet weekly at Milwaukee Psychiatric Hospital. In addition to Dr. Machi, the hospital has a wonderful team of therapists, all of whom support and promote our group to their patients. I consider Shay Harris, M.S.W., a larger woman herself, as my partner in Largely Positive.*

Liz: How many people have come through your door?

Carol: *I have five hundred names on our mailing list, and about 125 people who subscribe to our quarterly newsletter, On a Positive Note. An average meeting for our weekly discussion night might include twenty to twenty-five people. Our monthly meetings with a guest speaker will draw forty to fifty people.*

Liz: What kinds of issues do you address in your support group?

Carol: *We primarily talk about self-esteem and living a healthy lifestyle. The issues of social prejudice, as well as problems with how large people are depicted in the media, also come up in our discussion groups. We don't talk about dieting, but we had an enlightened dietitian come in and talk about nutrition, as well as an exercise physiologist who spoke about how to exercise without getting hurt. Our emphasis is on wholeness and health. If, in the process of eating healthy foods and beginning to exercise, we become somewhat thinner, okay. If not, that's okay too. Weight loss is not our goal. Being positive about ourselves, and disassociating our self-esteem from our weight is our goal.*

Liz: How has your own body confidence developed?

Carol: *I no longer wear coats in the summertime! I now go to a pool three nights a week, and I'm no longer self-conscious about wearing a bathing suit.*

Liz: That is a big step!

Carol: *It breaks my heart when I see women weigh themselves before and after they exercise, as if that is the only way they can measure the value of swimming.*

Liz: Do you still weigh yourself?

Carol: *No, I threw my scale away years ago. I have a pretty good idea what I weigh and actually have lost some weight since starting Largely Positive. I never worry about* numbers. _We know from research that heredity plays a big part, and I had two wonderful, fat grandmothers, one who lived to eighty-five, one to ninety._

Liz: How's your own level of self-esteem now?

Carol: _Before, I was trying to hide my bigness. Now I celebrate it! I wear big, bold jewelry, bright colors, and am not afraid to be expressive and dramatic._

Liz: What is the heart of your message to larger women?

Carol: _Get out there and live your life. Don't postpone it until you get thin. That day may never come and you will have missed out on some wonderful adventures. Don't let anyone tell you you're not a worthwhile person just as you are. Like other groups who have been treated unfairly, we must demand to be treated with respect, dignity and understanding._

"One Size Fits All"

Here's the biggest fable of all: that one size *anything* would fit a woman who is 5'1", 105 pounds *and* fit a woman who is 5'11", 270 pounds. To even suggest it is ridiculous. Oh, maybe a handkerchief would work for both of them, but not much else! As one survey respondent stated,

> *We are all individuals and "one size fits us all" very differently.*
>   Judy from Ohio

Some manufacturers are wising up, and their labels now read, "One Size Fits Most." That still does nothing for my self-esteem, since I'm not one of the "most."

I received a Christmas catalogue last year featuring a pair of holiday pantyhose with jingle bells and holly stitched up and down each leg. (So professional-looking, this item.) The catalogue stated: "One Size Fits All (We Know, Because We All Tried Them On)."

Really? That's not very comforting to me. First of all, I've never visited that company and don't know if they have a woman on staff who is my exact size or not. And second of all, who wants used pantyhose?!

Another item that debuted last Christmas did ring my bell: the "Happy to Be Me" doll. Cathy Meredig of High Self-Esteem Toys Corporation wanted a doll for young girls that would look like a real person. Hooray for Cathy! If you gave the typical fashion doll a 36 inch bust, her measurements as a full-grown woman would be 36"-18"-33". Not too realistic, I'd say, and a terrible role model for our daughters.

The "Happy to Be Me" doll has a thicker waist and bigger feet than Barbie, and a shorter neck and legs. Plus, her feet fit sensible shoes (not just tippy-toe heels), and her arms bend in a more natural way. Will it help us teach the next generation to love their bodies "as is?" It couldn't hurt!

Someone might also consider revamping store window mannequins, whose average measurements are 33"-23"-34". Talk about one size that fits almost no one! Erma Bombeck says, "'One size fits all' is not listed in my dictionary under 'O.' This is because the phrase exists only in the maniacal minds of manufacturers."[1]

The Good Old Days

Maybe we were just born during the wrong period of history. In the 1600's, one diet specialist wrote that "Every thin woman wishes to put on weight."[2] Can you imagine? The paintings of the era, and the years that followed, cast an adoring eye on round, soft, full-of-flesh women. The works of Rubens in the early 1600's and Renoir in the early 1900's are famous for their display of feminine flesh. The first time I saw one of their paintings, I gasped out loud: "That's me!"

Ann Landers said it best: "What we need is a high-powered campaign to glorify the Rubenesque woman and get off the 'thin is in' kick."[3] You can imagine the letters of support she received on that one.

Although dieting and fitness fanaticism as we know it is a post-WWI phenomenon, women have been agonizing over society's expectations for their bodies for a long time. One woman bemoaned the narrowing of the American ideal saying, "When we see a woman made as a woman ought to be made, she strikes us as a monster."[4] Gloria Steinem? No, Harriet Beecher Stowe, circa 1830.

The time has come for the pendulum to swing back toward reality. I heartily applaud fitness expert Pat Lyons for announcing, "It is time to stop the merry-go-round of self-hatred, dieting and despair and work together to create a more size-accepting world for us all."[5]

Actually, one size has *never* fit all, because our bodies are shaped so differently. Since the 1930's, one of the most widely used means of body typing is called, "somatotyping," designed by William Sheldon. According to his methodology, there are some 2,197 possible body types.[6] (More than just pears and apples, it would seem.) These are genetically-determined body types, not just adult bodies with too many, or not enough, burgers and fries. Size acceptance should be everyone's goal since we all have a size that's uniquely our own.

Mind Over Matter

I've always wondered, who exactly we were trying to be thin for? Our parents? Our husbands? Our friends? Our employers? Ourselves? Society as a whole? Who held such sway over our bodies that we saw fit to starve ourselves into acceptance? I think the whole issue is one of mind over matter — if you don't mind, it won't matter!

Many of the two hundred plus women we surveyed have come to that same conclusion:

Now that I'm almost forty, I have become very happy and comfortable with my size. My kids are too. They love to tell me that I look just like Jane Fonda to them.

Jerri from Indiana

It's apparent that her good feelings about herself have extended to her family. In years to come, those children will have a positive role model to emulate when deciding how they feel about their own bodies.

The wonder and joy of life that is experienced by larger women is the same for all — one size does truly fit all in the whole scheme of things.

LaDonna from Oregon

We just need to look at the big picture. Joy certainly fits us all, love is plenty big enough for everybody, and peace could cover the earth, if we let it. In the meantime, we can work on bringing those qualities into our own lives and the lives of those we care about.

Putting What We Believe into Motion

Since I've become more self-assured, I rarely encounter people who judge me for my size.

Joyce from Virginia

Isn't it amazing how, if we feel okay about who we are, so does everyone else? Gwen from Ohio says, "I have learned to like who I am (no, love who I am). I feel good about me!"

Our call to action is beautifully stated by Sherry from Missouri, who said:

"Until Big, Beautiful Women change how they see themselves, there's no way the world will change how they see us. We need to stand up and be heard."

She's so right! I had to change how I saw myself before I could write this book. You had to be willing to change how you saw yourself to read it. Now, it's time to "stand up and be heard!" In America, we no longer openly tolerate racism (though of course it still rears its ugly head), and we have been fighting sexism more or less successfully for the last twenty-five years or so. Now, ageism is being defeated, as more and more baby boomers hit middle age and realize they want fair and equal treatment through retirement and beyond.

It's time to face, head on, the most insidious "ism" of all. Fatism. It's everywhere—on radio and television, in magazines and in newspapers, in the workplace and the classroom. Comedians still have a field day with fat jokes, doctors still hand out diets and dire predictions, parents still send their kids off to fitness camps, praying that they won't end up (heaven forbid) as fat people.

Fatism needs to be seen as the prejudicial problem that it really is. Author Charles Roy Schroeder notes that it would be helpful "if the term 'fatism' was listed in dictionaries along with the equally sinful traits of racism, sexism and ageism."[7] Amen.

One Size Fits No One

As we learned from the interview with tall humorist Jeanne Robertson, some of the challenges larger women face are not limited to those of us with additional poundage. "Big" doesn't just refer to weight. Tall women have their own struggles that closely match ours.

> *(Being) an Extra Large doesn't necessarily mean that you are big. Height takes up a lot of room in a shirt too!*
>
> Harriet from Louisiana

And, small women don't live on Easy Street, either!

> *People say things like, "How tall are you anyway?" or "What size shoe do you wear?" Children ask me, "When will you be full grown?"*
>
> Rose from South Carolina

> *My coworkers tell me I'm small, petite, cute — and disgusting.*
>
> Jeanie from Ohio

Mark Twain said, "I can live for two months on a good compliment." Maybe if we started offering kinder comments to one another, we could live longer. I know we'd all live happier.

Real winners (that's us!) know that success is not measured in inches and pounds. The first producer for the late Helen Hayes told her when she arrived in Hollywood, that "if you were just four inches taller, you would be a great actress." So much for that advice.

Several years ago, when Lillian was a newborn, I presented my program of this same title, "'One Size Fits All' and Other Fables," to a wonderful audience of eight hundred women of all ages, sizes, shapes and colors. When I finished, the woman who introduced me pulled a poem out of her briefcase. She thought it "suited perfectly" my message of self-acceptance. "You'll want to share it with your daughter when she's older," she said.

Since then, I've shared that verse from a poem by Douglas Malloch with thousands of women across America, as well as with Miss Lillian:

> If you can't be a highway, then just be a trail,
> If you can't be the sun, be a star.
> It isn't by size that you win or you fail,
> Be the best of whatever you are!

We're Not Alone

Among the many challenges that plus-sized women face — tight theater seats, hard-to-find fashions, and pantyhose disasters — the biggest one of all is a feeling of aloneness or isolation. It's not that we're hiding in our houses, it's just that we seldom have a place to go where we feel safe talking about some of these issues. At least one of the times I joined Weight Watchers, it was because I wanted to be in a roomful of women who weren't all thin! Unfortunately, since they were all trying to *get* thin, I didn't find the camaraderie I was hoping for.

According to your surveys, you, too, wanted to find fellowship among these pages:

> *Help me know I'm not alone in this never-ending battle to be slim, trim and gorgeous. Since I was born a Chubette and went straight to Full Blown it's not been easy.*
> Cory from North Carolina

No, it's not easy! We can say that here and know that those reading will understand. (For my money, I'd rather be full-figured than half-figured, any day!)

> *As with other women's issues, the consciousness-raising aspect is important — knowing we are not alone and that the barrier of shame is a greater handicap than a person's weight.*
> Fran from Illinois

"The barrier of shame" is a very accurate description of what many of us feel. Take note: guilt and shame are non-productive states. Guilt leads to hopelessness, defeat, and despair. Shame leads tc isolation, separation, and a feeling of worthlessness. Enough of that. Enough for a lifetime, I'm certain.

A Benediction

> *This book will let all of us who read it know that our struggle is the same all over. And that we can make it through the hard times by laughing at things, rather than crying. If this had been around thirty*

years ago I would have not wasted my teen years hiding out from
the big bad world — wearing a black coat.

Lynda from California

I wish I could have written it for you thirty years ago, Lynda. That was right about the time I first began thinking about dieting. May the young women who follow in our footsteps be spared our pain (or at least *this* pain!).

By the way, I still wear a black coat, but it's a zippy one. I also have a red one, a purple one and a camel one, and they only get worn when it's cold or wet! No more hiding.

As I come to the conclusion of this labor of love, a project that kept me up late, got me up early, stole precious hours from my family, brought tears to my eyes and joy to my soul, I wanted to tie it all together with a ribbon of prayer.

Dear God,

I want to be healthy, happy and whole.
I want to be all Yours, all Bill's, all my children's, all my audience's and ALL MINE.

Not all things to all people, Lord.
Just all there.

Bless those who have kindly read these pages.
I pray these words have given them encouragement, hope and a lighter heart.

Lord, may Your beauty and love shine through us all, and give us confidence of mind, body and spirit — at any size!

Amen

❤ A Size Acceptance Leader Speaks . . .

RADIANCE: The Magazine for Large Women has been published quarterly since 1984. Its creator, founder, editor, publisher and soul is Alice Ansfield of Oakland, California.

Liz: How did *RADIANCE* begin?

Alice: *It began a week after I found myself in an exercise class for plus-size women in 1984. I had been searching for a place to move my body in a setting where I felt safe and supported. Once I found it, I decided I wanted to do a little newsletter for the women in my exercise class. It was apparent that the class members weren't sure where to shop, how to find larger exercise clothes, and needed help feeling better about themselves. So, RADIANCE was born.*

Liz: Except it didn't remain a "little newsletter" for very long.

Alice: *That's right! Within two months, I had a twenty-page publication with twenty-eight advertisements! My initial intent was to distribute it just in the Oakland area, but as I began assembling names and addresses, I thought, "Why not keep going? Why not send copies all over the country?"*

Liz: How many copies of that first issue did you print?

Alice: *We printed five thousand copies in October 1984. People understood our concept right away, and the* San Francisco Chronicle *covered it. Soon, subscriptions started pouring in. We now have six thousand paid subscribers from all over the world.*

Liz: And, it's a bigger magazine too.

Alice: *Yes. Fifty-two glossy, radiant pages!*

Liz: I'm sure readers' responses are very important to you.

Alice: *They keep me going. When a new subscriber sends in an order, I'm the one who types their information into the computer. It keeps me connected to my readers. The very first letter I received was from a fifty-five-year-old woman in Maine who wrote, "Hurry up and send RADIANCE! I've been hiding in my house for six years." I love to see what people write on their gift cards. They are always such loving, supportive comments like "I want the best for you," that kind of thing.*

Liz: Have you received any criticism over the years?

Alice: *[Laughing] Of course! Especially early on. The first time I put a supersize woman on the cover — a very successful San Francisco attorney — I got a lot of flack from the fashion community in L.A.: "Large women want to see the fantasy of what they can look like, not the reality of what they do look like," they said. Over the years, we've heard that we have too much fashion, others say not enough. Or, that we're too political, or not political enough. I do listen to such feedback, but I have to stick with what feels right to me. I must be true to myself, to my aims and my goals.*

Liz: What are some of the problems larger women face?

Alice: *A sense of shame. Self-hatred. Lack of support, lack of trust in ourselves and our bodies. Rejection. Fear of putting ourselves out there. There are some practical challenges, too, like not being able to fit in restaurant booths, theatre seats, airplane seats. Once, I was trying to get into a health club and had trouble fitting through the turnstile! We have a lot of work to do in our society!*

Liz: Are there any advantages to being a large woman?

Alice: *To me, being a large woman is just who I am. It's a part of me. I also have a large heart and a large capacity for fun. My experiences with my body have brought me more in touch with myself, my feelings, needs, visions, and abilities. My body has brought me opportunities to be creative, learn about others and contribute to people's lives. There are advantages to embracing all parts of yourself — whatever situation you're in. And I might add that it's getting easier to be a large person today — with all the support groups, clothing manufacturers and various services just for us!*

Liz: What do you say when people comment, "Well, what about your health?"

Alice: *In my eight years of doing* RADIANCE, *I have heard more often than I can tell you the line, "dieting has made me fatter." I don't think you can achieve a state of positive health while hating your body. Emotional health and social well-being are two factors directly related to physical health. Ending discrimination of all kinds will do more for the health of large people than any new diet plan or well-meaning doctor. People need to find out what helps them feel good — what foods they enjoy, what types of movement their bodies are yearning for, what friends, jobs and activities bring pleasure. Health, obviously, is much more than how much you weigh or what size your waist is.*

Liz: What is the first step to accepting ourselves, "as is?"

Alice: *Self-acceptance is not an easy process. It's difficult to turn around our insecurities, attitudes and fears. Just take it one step at a time. Read one book, attend one lecture, find and talk to one other woman dealing with similar body issues. Try one thing and follow your heart.*

A Perfect Fit

"One Size Fits All" is
Just a fable,
There's no truth to it at all.
Your heart knows it,
Your eyes see it
In the mirror on the wall.

Look around you!
Friends and strangers
Come in every shape and size.
Each one special,
Each one worthy,
In their loving Maker's eyes.

Fight the urge to
Start a diet,
Starving body, heart and soul.
Seek instead
A healthy balance,
Self-acceptance as your goal.

Try some movement,
Add some color,
Paint your canvas bold and bright.
Make the most of
This, your body.
Bet you'll find it fits just right!

— Liz Curtis Higgs
June 1993

Resources

Catalogues for Larger Women . . .

JUST MY SIZE Catalog
P. O. Box 748
Rural Hall, NC 27098-0748

SILHOUETTES
340 Poplar Street
Hanover, PA 17331

JUST RIGHT!
P.O. Box 1020
Beverly, MA 01915-0720

BROWNSTONE WOMAN
Brownstone Studio
P. O. Box 25367
Shawnee Mission, KS 66225

Magazines for Larger Women . . .

BIG BEAUTIFUL WOMAN
P.O. Box 458
Mt. Morris, IL 61054-9806

Organizations of Interest to Larger Women . . .

Largely Positive
ATTN: Carol Johnson
P.O. Box 17223
Glendale, WI 53217

National Association to Advance Fat Acceptance (NAAFA)
ATTN: Sally E. Smith, Executive Director
P.O. Box 188620
Sacramento, CA 95818

Other Books of Interest . . .

Never Too Thin: Why Women Are at War with Their Bodies,
Roberta Pollack Seid, Ph.D., Prentice Hall, 1989.

Bodylove, Rita Freedman, Harper & Row, 1988.

Great Shape: The First Exercise Guide for Large Women,
Pat Lyons and Debby Burgard, Bull Publishing, 1990.

Fat Is Not a Four-letter Word, Charles Roy Schroeder,
Ph.D., Chronimed Publishing, 1992.

Making Peace with Food, Susan Kano, Harper & Row,
1989.

Breaking All the Rules, Nancy Roberts, Penguin Books,
1985.

Inner Eating, Shirley Billigmeier, Oliver-Nelson Books,
1991.

Big and Beautiful, Ruthanne Olds, Acropolis Books Ltd.,
1982.

Overcoming the Dieting Dilemma, Neva Coyle, Bethany
House, 1991.

Don't Diet, Dale Atrens, Ph.D., William Morrow &
Company, 1988.

Rethinking Obesity, Paul Ernsberger and Paul Haskew,
Human Sciences Press, 1987.

Overcoming Fear of Fat, Laura S. Brown and Esther D.
Rothblum, Harrington Park Press, 1989.

The Obsession: Reflections on the Tyranny of Slenderness,
Kim Chernin, Harper & Row, 1981.

The Dieter's Dilemma, William Bennett, M.D., and Joel
Gurrin, Basic Books, 1982.

Never Satisfied, Hillel Schwartz, The Free Press, Macmillan, Inc., 1986.

The Hungry Self: Women, Eating and Identity, Kim Chernin, Harper & Row, 1985.

The Beauty Myth, Naomi Wolf, Anchor Books, 1992.

When Food Is Love, Geneen Roth, Penguin Books, 1992.

The Survey

Here are the questions we posed to the 200+ women featured in *"One Size Fits All" and Other Fables!*

1. Please circle your age range:
   18-24   25-34   35-44   45-54   55-64   65+

2. Please state your dress size:

3. How long have you been this size?

4. Is anyone in your family also your size? Who?

5. What words come to mind when you think of your body?

6. What comments do you receive about your size, and who says them?

7. What thoughts or experiences come to mind when you think of the word "DIET?"

8. If you are employed, what is your occupation?

   Does your size have any impact on your job? If so, please explain:

9. What are your favorite hobbies, social activities, etc.?

Does your size have any impact on your social life?
Please explain:

10. What are some of the challenges you face because of your
size?

11. How might *"One Size Fits All" and Other Fables* be most
helpful to you? What do you hope it will include?

12. Additional thoughts for *"One Size Fits All" and Other Fables*
(personal discoveries, funny stories, memories, or your
own "encouraging" words):

Here's a Bonus Question: What are the 3 biggest
"fables" about weight/size?

1. _____

2. _____

3. _____

Send to: Liz Curtis Higgs
P. O. Box 43577
Louisville, KY 40253-0577

Notes

Fable #1: "There's A Thin Person Trapped Inside You"

1. "Cher: Fit & Feisty at 46," *National Enquirer*, January 1983 Swimsuit Special, 51.
2. Roberta Pollack Seid, Ph.D., *Never Too Thin* (New York: Prentice Hall, 1989), 97.
3. "Plastic Surgery—for Under-Forties," *Self*, September 1989, 228.
4. Ibid.
5. Psalm 139:14.
6. Seid, *Never Too Thin*, 27.
7. Proverbs 7:4.

Fable #2: "All It Takes Is a Little Willpower"

1. "Growth and Recession in the Diet Industry, 1989-1996,"*Obesity and Health*, January/February 1992.
2. "Let Them Eat Cake," *Newsweek*, 17 August 1992, 57.
3. Seid, *Never Too Thin*, 105.
4. Ibid, 107.
5. Ibid, 138.
6. Nancy Roberts, *Breaking All the Rules* (New York: Viking Penguin, 1987), 34.
7. Susan Kano, *Making Peace with Food* (New York: Harper & Row, 1989), 3.
8. Sally Squires, "Which Diet Works," *Working Woman*, October 1992, 92.
9. Carol Johnson, "Fasting: The Problem Lies in the Fast Part," *On a Positive Note*, February 1990, 3.
10. Janice Kaplan, "Regardless of How Fit Women Are, We Still Want to be Thin," *Self*, September 1989, 195.

11. Adriane Fugh-Berman, M.D., *The National Women's Health Network News*, May/June 1992, 3.

Fable #3: "You're Just Big Boned"

1. Carol Johnson, "Fasting: The Problem Lies in the Fast Part," *On a Positive Note*, February 1990, 4.
2. "Medical Myths Debunked," *BBW*, April 1993, 44.
3. Ibid, 43.
4. "Special Edition," *Newsweek*, Winter/Spring 1990, 100.
5. Kim Chernin, *The Hungry Self* (New York: Harper & Row, 1985), 42.

Fable #4: "You Are What You Eat"
(If That Were True, I'd Be Yogurt)

1. Seid, *Never Too Thin*, 4.
2. 1 Corinthians 6:12.
3. Mimi Sheraton, "Figures Can't Lie but ...," *Time*, 20 January 1986, 63.
4. David Garner, Ph.D., "Rent a New Thinner Body?" *Radiance*, Winter 1991, 42.
5. Shirley Billigmeier, *Inner Eating* (Nashville: Thomas Nelson, 1991), 162.
6. *The Random House Dictionary of the English Language* (New York: Random House, 1969), 562.
7. Kano, *Making Peace*, 203.

Fable #5: "All Fat People Are Lazy"

1. Pat Lyons and Debby Burgard, *Great Shape* (Palo Alto: Bull Publishing Company, 1990), 169.
2. Fugh-Berman, *The National Women's Health Network News*, 3.
3. Ibid.
4. Lyons and Burgard, *Great Shape*, 41.
5. Ann Diffily, "Weighty Matters," *Cross and Crescent*, Summer 1990, 33.
6. Kaplan, *Self*, 195.
7. Kano, *Making Peace with Food*, 55.

8. Pat Lyons, "Fat and Fit: An Idea Whose Time Has Come," *The National Women's Health Network News*, May/June 1992, 5.
9. Pat Lyons, "Improving the Health, Fitness and Body Image of Large Women," Presentation to the American Public Health Association Annual Meeting, 12 November 1991.
10. 1 Timothy 4:8.
11. Colossians 2:20–22.
12. Colossians 2:16.

Fable #6: "Things Would Be Perfect If I Were a Size 10"

1. Seid, *Never Too Thin*, 3.
2. Ibid, 15.
3. Dr. Esther Rothblum, "Weight and Social Stigma," *N.A.A.F.A. Newsletter*, November 1992, 6.

Fable #7: "Large Women Adore Wearing Double Knit" (It's So Flattering!)

1. Seid, *Never Too Thin*, 71.
2. Ibid, 81.
3. Ibid, 95.
4. 1 Peter 3:3–4.
5. Seid, *Never Too Thin*, 44.
6. Lois Anzelowitz, "You Call This Progress?" *Working Woman*, October 1992, 95.
7. Michael Cader, *Eat These Words* (New York: Harper Collins, 1991), 13.

Fable #8: "You'll Love Yourself More If You Lose Weight"

1. Josh McDowell, *His Image, My Image* (San Bernardino: Here's Life, 1984), 11.
2. Ardena Shankar, "Self-Esteem and Personal Responsibility," *N.A.A.F.A. Newsletter*, May/June 1992, 6.
3. Carole Shaw interviewed on the *Jenny Jones Show*, 8 April 1992.

4. "Some Folks Are Born To Yo-Yo," *People*, 13 January, 1992, 76.
5. Proverbs 23:20–21.
6. Matthew 11:19.
7. 1 Samuel 16:7.
8. Esther 2:12.
9. Garner, *Radiance*, 37.
10. Judy Simon, M.S., R.D., "Women's Struggle with Body Image," Presentation for the Mid-Michigan Regional Medical Center "Just Between Women" program, November 2, 1991.

Fable #9: "Big People Are Always Jolly" (Ha!)

1. Jane Thomas Noland, *Laugh It Off* (Minneapolis: CompCare, 1991), 4.
2. Sandy Summers Head, *Sizing Up* (New York: Simon and Schuster, 1989), 21.
3. Paul E. McGee, Ph.D., *Humor: Its Origin and Development* (San Francisco: W. H. Freeman, 1979), 206.
4. Ibid, 205.
5. Joel Goodman, "Smile! You're On, Allen Funt!" *Laughing Matters*, Volume 3, Number 1, 10.
6. Proverbs 17:22.

Fable #10: "You'll Never Get a Man"

1. Kaplan, *Self*, 195.

Fable #11: "You Can Lose It If You Really Want To"

1. Gina Kolata, "The Burdens of Being Overweight," *The New York Times*, 22 November 1992, 38.
2. Carole Shaw interviewed on the *Jenny Jones Show*, 8 April 1992.
3. Gina Kolata, *The New York Times*, 38.
4. Beverly Fortune, "Diet Centers: A User's Guide," *Lexington Herald-Leader*, 17 January 1993, J-1.
5. Ibid, J-2.

6. Carol Johnson, "I Thought You'd Tell Me How to Lose Weight and Keep It Off...," *On a Positive Note*, September 1992, 1.
7. Ibid.
8. Kaplan, *Self*, 194.
9. Charles Roy Schroeder, Ph.D., *Fat Is Not a Four-Letter Word* (Minneapolis: Chronimed Publishing, 1992), 140.
10. Rita Freedman, *Beauty Bound* (London: Columbus Books, 1988), 151.
11. Proverbs 4:18.
12. Freedman, *Beauty Bound*, 151.
13. Carol Johnson, "Research Review," *On a Positive Note*, March 1992, 6.
14. Carol Johnson, "Research Roundup," *On a Positive Note*, June 1992, 7.
15. Psalm 109:24.
16. Quoted by Pay Lyons in interview with author, January 1993.
17. Alicia Sandhei, "There is Change," *N.A.A.F.A. Newsletter*, June 1991, 3.

Fable #12: "One Size Fits All"

1. Erma Bombeck, *The Erma Bombeck 1992 Desk Calendar*, (Kansas City: Andrews and McMeel, a Universal Press Syndicate Company), 11 May, Monday.
2. Schroeder, *Fat is Not a Four-letter Word*, 28.
3. Ann Landers, "Society Gives Women Unreal View of Perfect Body Image," *Detroit Free Press*, 6 July 1992, 2D.
4. Schroeder, *Fat is Not a Four-letter Word*, 49.
5. Pat Lyons, "Fat and Fit," 5.
6. Schroeder, *Fat is Not a Four-letter Word*, 110.
7. Ibid, 298.

ONLY Angels CAN Wing It

To my husband, Bill Higgs,
Ph.D., DAD, and Director of Operations:
Bless you for always being there
to straighten my halo,
dust off my wings,
tune up my harp,
and nudge me off my cloud.
I love you, Sweet Bill!

February 1995

Acknowledgements

My husband Bill once observed that "it takes about ten people to do Lizzie!" Sure enough, none of us do what we do without the help of friends and associates. Never is that more true than when writing a book.

Heartfelt thanks, then, to the eight hundred women who completed surveys, offered stories, and shared their lives with me and, therefore, with all of us. You are a blessing!

Hugs to my friends and heroines in the world of speaking and writing: Florence Littauer, Marita Littauer, Jeanne Robertson, Naomi Rhode, Rosita Perez, Elizabeth Jeffries, Gail Wenos, Luci Swindoll, Patricia Fripp, Maureen Mulvaney, Jolene Brown, Janie Jasin, Cathy Fyock, Connie Podesta, Nancy Coey, Sue Thomas, Patsy Clairmont, Joanne Wallace, Hope Mihalap, Marilyn Heavilin, Linda Pulliam, Pat Vivo, Barbara Johnson, and especially my petite "sister" and precious friend, Glenna Salsbury. Your care-filled craftmanship with the spoken and written word is a joy to behold and a beacon for the rest of us to follow.

A big, beautiful hug to my editors at Thomas Nelson Books: Lonnie Hull DuPont in San Francisco and Sheryl Taylor in Nashville. I appreciate you more than even *words* can say!

Special thanks to my friends at *Today's Christian Woman* magazine, Jane Johnson Struck and Ramona Cramer Tucker, who've also helped me find my "voice" as a writer. Bless you both!

Peace and love to my professional manuscript reader, Lois Luckett, MSW, LCSW, who offered much needed direction, feedback, and encouragement. Your caring touch is on every page.

Grateful bows to my clients and friends in the National Association of Women's Health Professionals who've given me so many opportunities over the years to humor and encourage the women they serve. In particular, I'm indebted to my NAWHP readers: Patricia Thomas, Joyce Kieffer, Evelyn Freeman, and Susan Sanders, who allowed my lengthy manuscript to invade their holidays. Ho ho ho!

Many thanks to Sonya, Pat, Debbie, and especially to Anne Dorton and Pamela Dennison, who, at various times and in numerous ways, held my office together for more than a year while I played at the word processor. You really *are* earth angels!

Finally, a lifetime supply of hugs and kisses to my dear children Matthew and Lillian, who give me a reason to soar a little higher.

Contents

You Deserve to Know . .

This book is *not* about how to do more, how to do it better, or how to do it faster; it's not even about how to *do* it, period.

This is a book about putting aside perfectionism so we can embrace grace. To light the way, we'll take a fresh look at an age-old role model from Proverbs. (Good news: she's not perfect, either; she just practices the right things.)

This is also a book full of laughter, stories, and insights offered via surveys completed by eight hundred women from all fifty states. They, too, long for lives that are less stressful, better balanced, and more fun.

This is a book to keep by your nightstand for the end of another had-to-do-it-all day, when the most your weary self can handle is some real-life humor and a gentle tug at your heart. No tips, no lists, no how-tos—you're busy enough already.

This book is what every woman (including me) wants: assurance that we're not alone, we're not crazy, and we're doing the best mortal women can do.

So . . . let's kick off our shoes, find a comfy chair, and start smiling!

1

Measuring Our Wingspan

wing it (an American colloquialism):
to act, speak, etc., with little or no
planning or preparation; improvise
**Webster's New World Dictionary of
American English**

I have been winging it for forty years.

Well, there was that one really organized year when I managed to keep nearly a hundred houseplants alive, walk to work every day, and whip up lots of healthy home-cooked meals because I had no money and steamed vegetables were cheap. That was 1976; it's been downhill since then.

A decade later, I married at thirty-two. The next year brought motherhood and my own business. A second child, a move to the country, and I've been tired ever since. Not only is winging it not working, but my feathers are starting to drop off. Must be hormonal.

Here we are, standing at the threshold of a new millennium, and I'm not sure I've got enough left in me to start another century. The 1950s were too cheerful, the '60s too strange, the '70s too disco, the '80s too driven, and the '90s too politically correct to be any fun. And what are we going to name the next decade . . . the 00s? If we go around calling it *2,001*, I'll keep expecting HAL the computer to show up.

Flying by the Seat of Our Skirts

Depending on when you read this, we may still have time to mend our wings and take some flying lessons from one another before the new century begins. What Sandy from Michigan hopes to find among these pages is "encouragement to keep going when there aren't any other options" and to do so "joyfully, gracefully, and humorously!" Thank goodness she didn't say "perfectly" because, rest assured, angelhood is not my goal; it never has been. We weren't created to be angels. That's their job title alone.

Billy Graham, who should know, says the "concept of angels with wings is drawn from their ability to move instantaneously and with unlimited speed from place to place."[1] I know what you're thinking. That's us, zipping across town in our minivans, clutching directions in one hand and lunch in the other. It makes us amazing, but it doesn't make us angels.

Angels are perfect because God designed them that way. No one has ever worked up to being an angel. They are created beings who can't *not* be angels, but they also can't be human—that's our task. Because they are never lost, they don't need to be found, and they have no need for a shepherd. I'm glad I'm not an angel. I'm very glad I'm a woman.

If angels are messengers—and they are—here's a message from them to us: relax! By design, we are "a little lower than the angels" (Heb. 2:7 NKJV). Perfect is out of the question; practice is just common sense.

What We Need Is an Un-Do List

"People call me an angel because I 'wing it' all the time! Hope your book includes a guilt release!" wrote Jerrie from Tennessee. Guilt is the grease that keeps us sliding toward depression when we should be soaring heavenward. I'm learning to let go of guilt. Conviction? Of course. Contrition? Often. But if "guilt is the gift that keeps on giving," then I intend to leave no forwarding address.

Sara from Colorado made this request: "We can't 'wing it' today—life requires organization. How about some tips on balancing faith, family, and work?" Sounds like a terrific book, but I'm not sure it's this one. Tips, lists, ideas, suggestions, things to check off, tasks to put in motion—most of us already have more of that stuff than we could ever find time to actually do. The August 1994 issue of *Redbook* featured the cover headline, "115 Ways to Be Thin, Rich, Loved . . . and Happy." That's us, looking for joy by the numbers. We tell ourselves, "Just let me get to Tip #115, and I'll be home free!" Oh, sister.

Our purpose here is to stand back from it all for a moment: reevaluate; hold on to what works, and discard what doesn't; consider some proverbial wisdom from the past as we retool for the new century. On second thought, maybe we *will* be talking about balancing faith, tamily, and work after all. But no tips—just stories. Yours and mine and those of eight hundred kindred spirits. The youngest woman to respond was Stacy from Oregon at age twenty-two; the most mature was Irene from Kentucky, a youthful eighty-seven, who said she had no interest in marriage right now because "I enjoy not having to answer to anyone!"

The Day the Earth Stood Still

Sylvania from Missouri is counting on this book to include "humorous war stories." Can do. I'll affectionately call this one, "The Business Trip from the Bad Place." It was to be my first public presentation of *Only Angels Can Wing It,* in Albany, New York. An audience of nearly six hundred women had assembled, with another six hundred turned away at the door. Numbers don't make me nervous, but a new topic can get me completely unglued.

I planned, I prepared, I practiced. I made sure all the bases were covered on the home front: "Honey, do you have anything going May 24?"

"No," my husband, Bill, assured me, "it's just a regular work day, nothing unusual. I'll be happy to drive the kids to and from school. No problem."

Two weeks before the Big Day, Bill came to me looking sheepish. If he'd worn a hat, it would've been in his hands. "May 24 is primary election day," he informed me. That meant a sixteen-hour grind for him at the television station handling election coverage.

"Time to move to Plan B," I said. "We'll call Mom and Dad."

Bless the in-laws, they could come and stay with the children
after school. We were all set.

One week to go, and a note came home in Matthew's back-
pack: "Be sure to mark your calendars for the evening of Tuesday, May 24, for the Elementary School Music Program!" A
small part of me died inside. Not only would I miss our first-grade
son's performance, but so would his dad. Well, Mamoo and Papoo
and his little sister, Lillian, would be there, so it would be all
right. In fact, it would be *special*. Okay, we're fine.

Tuesday morning, May 24: my notes were in order, my
clothes were packed, the kids were in school, the baby-sitter was
ready for carpool pickup, the grandparents were en route, Matthew's costume was finished, and I was off to the airport, feeling
smug. I am Woman, hear me roar.

The flight went smoothly, my kind client deposited me at my
hotel room, and at 4:30 I sat down to make the usual touch-base
phone call home. That's when it all began to unravel.

The strain in Mamoo's voice on the phone was the first clue.
It seemed Lillian had thrown up in the baby-sitter's car on the
way home from preschool and was now "hot as an oven."
(Understand, my kids are *never* sick except when I travel. Is this
a sign?) I sent Mamoo to the kitchen cabinet for the fever-reduc-
ing medicine; she returned to the phone to inform me that the
bottle was there . . . empty. Directions to the nearest drugstore
ensued as I felt my internal hinge about to spring. Promising to
call back in an hour, I hung up and tried Bill at work, knowing he
was up to his ears in election coverage pandemonium. I got his
voice mailbox. At the beep, I almost shouted, "Lillian is sick, and
I've got to go speak! Start praying!"

When it comes to prayer, Bill is an old pro. Before the night
was over, the program in Albany had gone smoothly, thanks to
a gracious God and an awesome audience, Papoo had applauded
Matthew's performance in the school gym; and Lillian's fever
had dropped, so she could sleep through the night (at least
someone did!). In the morning her daddy took her to the pediatrician, who pronounced her completely well, while Mama
winged her way home.

In other words, we survived. And, as Dawn from Oregon pointed out, "Reality is always funny eventually."

Dr. Kevin Leman, the author of *Bonkers*, offered this list, in order, of "Six Major Areas of Stress for Women": children, time, husbands, money, housework, and career.[2] Sure enough, in one twenty-four hour period I had experienced stress in all six of those areas and had learned how to spell G-U-I-L-T with even more gusto.

When women have one of "those kind of days," we often wonder how other women seem to manage better than we do. We chastise ourselves for not measuring up to some angelic ideal, based on a mishmash of images from childhood, *The Donna Reed Show*, and home ec class. We think our husbands want us to be Julia Child in the kitchen, Mother Teresa at church, and Mae West in the bedroom; that our children expect a cross between Amy Grant and Mary Poppins; and that our employers are counting on Mary Kay Ash at a bargain price. To which we must say, "Ain't no way, baby." We've come a long way, but now it's time to make sure we're going in the right direction.

Performance, Perfection, Permission

Alexander Pope said, "Fools rush in where angels fear to tread." What in the world was he talking about? Angels don't tread, they fly, and who ever heard of a "scaredy angel"? Angels have nothing to fear because they only go where they are sent. Ah . . . there's a lesson in that.

Marybeth Weston said it better: "Fools rush in and get all the best seats." For this season, the best seat is in the back row, where we can sit quietly in the dark and let the past few years of our lives play out on the stage before us: single woman, married woman, working woman, mother woman, friend woman, volunteer woman, widow woman, wonder woman, funny woman. But no "perfect woman," unless we follow Wordsworth's definition of us as "yet a spirit still, and bright, with something of angelic light."[3]

"I try to be perfect—I have a feeling this book will tell me that no one is perfect—not even me!" moaned Martha from Florida.

Let's shoot for perfectly wonderful and leave it at that, joining with Arlette from Pennsylvania in seeking "reassurance that our life journeys are filled with lots of 'practice' sessions!"

Most of us want precisely what Louise from Georgia re quested: "Permission to be what I am, without feeling like I'm coming up short." We are "taller" than we think! God gives us permission to be ourselves. In fact, the only way to be certain we are walking in grace is to be our very human, often not very angelic, selves and to lean on God to bridge the gap between human possibility and divine perfection.

More than anything, we want "some indication that I'm not the only woman in this world whose life is upside down," as Cheryl so aptly put it. "Just let me know I'm normal' ' Mickey pleaded. "Help me realize there are others like me," wrote Kathleen. I can attest that there are at least eight hundred women who from time to time feel that same isolation, those same shifting priorities, that same lack of balance in their lives.

In forty years I've learned that balance does not mean we are good at everything. It means we do what we do well and get help with the rest. It means we do not make the mistake of lighting the candle at both ends and putting a match to the middle. One of the definitions of balance is "the power or ability to decide."[4] Well, we all have that

Same Wisdom, Different Century

The saying goes that "practice doesn't make perfect, it makes permanent." So, as we mend our wings and plot our course for beyond 2000, it would seem wise to choose carefully not only our destination but also the road map we use for directions. Barbara Walters cautioned, "Whenever there are the kinds of choices there are today, unless you have some solid base, life can be frightening."[5]

Our solid base for this journey together is an ancient manuscript from two millennia ago, known simply as the book of Proverbs. It has thirty-one chapters in all, but we'll focus on the last chapter, a favorite of women through the centuries because it talks about our many roles in life The experts can't agree on precisely when this section was written—200 B.C., 700 B.C., 950 B.C.—so we'll just call it old wisdom and keep going.

Cervantes said, "A proverb is a short sentence based on long experience." Although Proverbs 31 begins, "The words of King Lemuel" (NKJV), don't be fooled. We're not learning from his experience, we're learning from someone else who'd been around a generation longer, someone who laughed and cried, gave birth and gave advice: his mother.

The full first line says, "The words of King Lemuel, the oracle which his mother taught him" (NASB). This fine son, who is never mentioned by this name anywhere else in the Bible, had the good sense to pay attention when his mother spoke and to write down her words for future generations. As one commentator said, "Mothers, especially queen mothers, were looked upon with great veneration, and treated with marked respect."[6] Those were the good old days.

We know little about this queen mum. Not her name, not her husband's name, not her age, her dress size, nor her target heart range. But we do know two very significant facts:

- She loved God, because the name she chose for her son means "dedicated to God."[7] (I took a page from her book when I named my own long-awaited son "Matthew," which means "gift of God.")

- She loved her son, because she cared enough to teach him not just the ABCs and the 123s but also her values. Jean Fleming, author of *A Mother's Heart,* calls values "an ever present pair of tinted eyeglasses [that] color life for us."[8]

After admonishing her kingly son to stay away from loose women and alcohol (seems to me I mentioned the same thing to Matthew last week!), she encouraged him to speak out for the unfortunate, judge righteously, and defend the rights of the needy. We can almost hear this model mother saying, "Make me proud of you, son!"

But this is all preamble to her real message for Lemuel: how to find a suitable woman with whom to share his life and throne. The twenty-two verses that bring Proverbs to a close are what is known as an acrostic when read in the original Hebrew. Each verse begins with a different letter of the Hebrew alphabet, in order. Just like we might teach a child something important by tying it to A-B-C-D-E, Lemuel's mother followed good oral tradition and sent her son into the world looking for the perfect daughter-in-law, carrying her weighty words with him in his heart.

Onward and Upward

Taunie from Utah expressed her longing for these pages to hold "a balm for the past, encouragement for today, and hope for the future." I can't think of anything better to meet that heartfelt need so many of us share than the wisdom of Proverbs. Although I can't promise to provide what Penny from Alaska requested— "Complete instructions!"—I can help us all focus on *growth*, which is positive, rather than on *improvement*, which suggests that we are something less than fabulous now. We know better.

Each line of the Proverbs poem is different: one paints a humorous word picture, another speaks of deep truths; one may be aimed at the mothers among us, another points to the work place. That means each chapter will have its own unique tone and direction. Don't let that throw you. Like life itself, this ancient passage travels many roads en route to one destination

I'll also offer some therapeutic humor, the kind that comes from real life, not joke books. Joyce Kieffer, a women's health professional and treasured friend, described the healing power of laughter divinely: "Laughter is angel music for the soul. We take ourselves too seriously, and laughter gives us wings."

So it is that our journey through the hearts and lives of eight hundred women begins, with frequent stops in Proverbs along the way and a long visit on my own front porch. Stay alert now, because as Richard Purdy Wilbur said, "Outside the open win dow, the morning air is all awash with angels"!

2
Too Good to Be True

An excellent wife, who can find?

Proverbs 31:10 NASB

Define the Perfect Wife:

Never complains. Is able to leap tall laundry baskets, and is faster than a car pool mom. A chauffeur, who works 40+ hours a week bringing home mega $$. Cooks a huge breakfast and a four-course dinner. Softly reads and puts the children to bed by 8:00, then waits on the sofa in her lingerie ready to please her man all night long. —Alice from Michigan

Ask eight hundred women to define "the perfect wife," and you'll get eight hundred answers with one conclusion: she doesn't exist. Gloria described her as "having no flaws, making no mistakes. There is no such thing!" Susan is sure she is a "nonmortal being that lives in our imagination, setting a standard that is not humanly possible to achieve." Then there's Dauna who wrote, "the definition of a perfect wife eludes me, but I think every woman needs one!"

So, what was Lemuel's mother thinking of, sending him looking for an "excellent" wife? The list of qualities and skills she rattles off for him to look for in a woman is exhausting: self-confident, trustworthy, good with money, devoted to her husband, creative, a gourmet cook, a land developer, strong in character and muscle, sensitive and discerning, hardworking, generous, an expert seamstress, a terrific home decorator, well dressed, self-employed, quick to laugh, never idle, loved by her children, praised by her husband, faithful to God, and well respected by the entire community. LaJoyce Martin, author of *Mother Eve's Garden Club,* says, "She was voted B.C. 1015's top of the top ten. The honor came complete with halo and wings."[1]

"Give me a break!" you say? Happy to. In Jill Briscoe's book *Queen of Hearts,* she refers to this perfect woman of Proverbs 31 as a "Statue of Liberty," which means she is a symbol, larger than life, *not* a real, living, breathing woman who once roamed the earth.[2] One scholar said, "It is a mistake to assume that all the virtues in this section are likely to be embodied in any one woman."[3]

We know. We've tried.

We had some terrific ideas about what constitutes a perfect wife today: "She balances the serious with the humorous, and the responsibilities with the fun," wrote Diana. "Has the ability to meet her spouse's needs because she has met hers first!" were the words of wisdom from Marcia. Rosalind defined the perfect wife as "a woman whose self-confidence is so high she can give freely of her love and talents without doubt, fear, or insecurity."

The proverbial description of womanhood we're about to walk through was meant to be a composite, a "best of" listing. If we made a tally of the finest qualities of each of our ten closest friends, that would most resemble what Lemuel's mother was trying to impress upon her son. Like the '60s song said, "My mama told me . . . you better shop around!"

One Powerful Word

My husband, Bill, "shopped" for me for thirty-four years with the Proverbs 31 description stuffed in his mental back pocket. He had an advantage over most of his fellow shoppers because he knew the original language in which Proverbs was written. We're talking about a man who went to college for twelve years, full time—four years of undergraduate work, eight years at seminary—to earn his Ph.D. in Hebrew. I can imagine what you're thinking: "Say, there's a marketable skill!" Although his current profession as a computer systems specialist does not make much use of those hard-earned credentials, his talents come in handy when studying the Old Testament.

This opening verse about "an excellent wife" has also been translated as "a wife of noble character" (NIV) or, even better, "a capable, intelligent, and virtuous woman" (AMPLIFIED BIBLE). That's us, all right! The Revised Standard Version just says "a good wife." Good grief.

Enter Bill's expertise. It seems the Hebrew word *chayil* that describes this wonder woman is sometimes interpreted as "virtuous" or "excellent" but more commonly means "wealthy, prosperous, valiant, boldly courageous, powerful, mighty warrior." Now, that's a *lot* more than "good"! And the word for *wife,* in Hebrew, *ishshah,* simply means a "mature female." In other words, if you're a single woman, there's something of value for you here too.

I spent nearly five years sitting alone in the pews as a single woman, and the How-to-Be-a-Good-Wife-and-Mother sermons grew ... tiresome. I knew they were truthful and wise, they just didn't apply to me at that point in my life. The first time I heard this Proverbs 31 passage, I mentally checked out after the opening line, "an excellent wife." Not for me.

Then came the verse about her marketplace skills and entrepreneurial abilities and my ears perked up. Something for never-married, career-driven me after all? Finally, the point of the passage dawned on me: these were the qualities of a virtuous and valiant *single* woman, a woman considered worthy of praise for who she was, not for whom she might marry. The kind of woman who brought tons of talent and crateloads of character to the bargaining table. A woman who was, therefore, an excellent choice for a wife because of the full life she was already leading in her singleness.

It seems this passage was for me after all.

What about the Perfect Husband?

If you're beginning to chafe at the thought of a shopping list for an excellent wife but not for an excellent husband, I understand. Personally, I've always wanted a Proverbs 32 chapter for the guys, something nice and succinct to wave in their faces on Father's Day. As Carol from Texas said when asked to define the perfect wife, "It's the same as 'the perfect husband.' Why should it be different?"

Don't worry, there are plenty of verses throughout Scripture telling men how to be a good husband. Two of my favorite commandments are: "Husbands, love your wives" (Eph. 5:25 NKJV) and "Rejoice with the wife of your youth" (Prov. 5:18 NKJV). Unfortunately for us, these directives are scattered throughout the Bible and harder to point to in a hurry, but they're there. We'll offer our numerous definitions of perfect husband-hood in Chapter 21 and see how our own men "measure up."

Meanwhile, Marilyn knows how the perfect wife might be defined from the man's point of view: "Never says no. Doesn't like to go out to eat. Doesn't like to shop." Rose thinks men want a woman who "earns in the six-figure range and loves football." (I may never earn in the six-figure range, but over the years I've had a six-figure wardrobe: Small, Medium, Large, Extra Large, Queen Size, and Never Mind!)

Some of us think our husbands were hoping for a wife like Donna Reed who, according to Debby, "cooks, cleans, volunteers, supports her husband and kids through every crisis, and does it all in a dress and heels!" And wearing pearls, too, I might add. Mary from Indiana sees *herself* as the perfect wife (good for her!), noting, "We've been working on this arrangement for twenty-nine years to perfect it!"

In all, my eight hundred surveys produced eight hundred different responses, but one pattern became clear: we expect more of ourselves than any one woman could possibly deliver and more than any one husband would honestly want. In response to the survey question, "As a wife, how do you measure up to your own standards?" we gave ourselves a 6.8 as wives, compared to the 7.4 we gave our husbands. But that doesn't tell the whole story. Twenty percent of us awarded ourselves a *higher* rating than we awarded our husbands (knowing full well they would never see the survey!).

Laughing Aloud Allowed . . . and Encouraged

On one thing we agreed: The perfect wife needs to have a strong sense of humor. Donna listed "sensitive, humorous, loving. Also romantic and can stand snoring." Judith knew we'd need "a sense of humor and adventure when slogging through the drudge." And Kay from Iowa insists that when it comes to the perfect wife, there's "no such person—but it's fun to try, laugh at ourselves, and know someone loves us no matter what."

I take great solace in those two areas—laughing at myself and knowing someone loves me—when I remember a particular incident a few springs ago. I was to present an after-dinner program here in Louisville, and Bill was able to join me, a real treat. They seated us at the head table and put me in my customary spot right next to the lectern.

Here's how this usually works: dessert is served and immediately the meeting planner leans over to me and says, "Why don't you go ahead and start your program?" When I stand up to begin, I can see out of the corner of my eye that my dessert is melting into oblivion. Soon, they clear it away, and it's gone forever.

So that night when they put dessert in front of me, I grabbed my spoon and—woosh!—it was history. Thank goodness it was chocolate mousse—I barely needed my teeth. As I looked around the room, I noticed that at most of the tables, dessert hadn't even been served yet. *Good,* I thought, *I'll have enough time to dash off to the ladies' room and get my act together before I speak.* Whispering, "I'll be right back" into Bill's ear, I slipped out of the auditorium and headed for the door marked *Women.*

It was a little "one-seater." Just a toilet, a small sink with a mirror, and a locking door. I pushed in the button to lock the door, stepped up to the mirror, and put on a new layer of Chili Pepper Red lipstick. After fluffing my hair and pinching my cheeks (if it's good enough for Scarlett, it's good enough for me), I sat down to "take care of business," as my mother would say.

While seated, I glanced at my nails. I usually wear a bright red polish to match my lipstick, and my hands look great the day I put it on. But, let a couple of days go by, and I look like a hussy—the ends get all worn and big hunks fall off. Sure enough, that night I realized *I had hussy nails!* I don't know how I'd gotten out of the house with my polish in such bad shape, but there was no question that I would have to do something about it right then and there. No way was I going to stand in front of an audience looking so "unpolished."

I got out my bottle of Daytona Red, which I always carry with me for emergencies, and quickly put on a top coat. I'm an old pro at this, and it didn't take me more than sixty seconds to do both hands. What an improvement!

Then I looked down and felt the color leave my face. My pantyhose were around my ankles.

I was in deep trouble. There are only so many things one can do with wet nails, and pulling up your pantyhose is not one of them. Oh sure, you can wave at a friend or make a phone call—if you have a pencil to push the buttons. And you can drive a car; we've all seen women at red lights with their fingers carefully spread across the top of the steering wheel. Sure, you can drive with a fresh manicure.

But you cannot pull up your pantyhose with wet nails. You'll ruin the polish for sure, or you could get *stuck* there. I was now on full-tilt panic, imagining my client stepping to the lectern any minute to introduce me: "Our speaker tonight . . . ," while the speaker was sitting on the commode with wet nails and pantyhose around her ankles. Help!

It was at that moment of panic that I looked across the ladies' room and saw the hand dryer. *That's it!* I thought, as I struggled to my feet and shuffled over to the metal dryer on the wall. Starting the thing with my elbow, I parked my nails underneath it and thought, *I'll be out of here in a flash!* My manicurist has since explained to me that I was doing the worst possible thing to my nails. The heat actually melts the polish and keeps it sticky.

There I was, cooking my nails. Those dryers are really loud, so it wasn't until it shut off that I realized someone was pounding on the door. It was Bill. "Honey, you're on! You're on! Get out here! Get out here!" he shouted, desperation in his voice.

A plan began to formulate in my mind. "B-i-i-l-lll . . ." I sang out slowly, turning toward the door. "Could you step in here for a minute?"

"Do *what?*" came his muffled reply.

"Don't worry, it's just us, just a one-seater, just a minute!" I said with assurance, doing a tricky side-step toward the door.

I released the button lock and in came Bill, looking wide-eyed. After all, he'd led a pretty sheltered life in seminary and hadn't spent a lot of time in women's rest rooms. He didn't know what he was going to find. What he found, of course, was me. He looked at my face. He looked at my feet. He looked at my face again, and assessed the situation correctly.

"I'm going to have to pull them up, aren't I?" he asked with a groan, as his pivotal role in this unfolding saga became very clear.

And so he began tugging. Our half dozen years of marriage were paying off because soon Bill got the hang of it. All was going well until he hit the control top part. Let's face it, every woman of any size has her own little dance routine about this point, right down to the last kick. But Bill did not know the steps to my dance. I was wiggling; he was waggling. We couldn't get it together, so I started shouting out orders. "No! No! Pull here, do this, try that!"

We were so serious, and the situation so intense, until suddenly I had what you'd have to call an "out of body" experience: I mentally floated above this scene, saw how ridiculous it all was, and exploded with laughter. Sweet Bill, who had been waiting seven minutes to have permission to laugh, was now in hysterics. That just made me laugh harder. And now we were nonfunctional. We couldn't do anything right. We laughed so hard that our muscles were in a complete state of relaxation and therefore useless.

We were soon laughing *so* hysterically that we ceased making any noise at all. Just occasional wheezing sounds. That was when we heard a timid knocking at the door, and the voice of the woman who hired me: "Are you . . . through yet?" she asked faintly. Without even thinking about how this might sound to her, we called out in unison, "Just a minute!"

In Search of a Role Model

One thing is certain: King Lemuel's mom did *not* expect an

excellent woman to wear panty hose! She *did* say of her prospective daughter-in-law: "who can find?" Such powerful, noble, courageous, mighty warrior women *are* hard to find! We don't stand on street corners with a big V on our chest for "virtuous." We're busy accomplishing capable, intelligent, valiant deeds, just like our Proverbs 31 sister. LaJoyce Martin wrote of her, "All of us need an ideal and a heroine. She is our mentor, our sampler."[4]

 ## An excellent wife, who can find?

Near the end of my survey, I posed the question, "Who serves as a role model for you . . . and why?" Of those who responded, nearly 10 percent specifically wrote "none" in all three categories—professional life, family life, spiritual life. It isn't that we don't want role models—we are desperate for them. But everywhere we look are people who disappoint us, people who keep lowering their own standards, people who teach us more about how *not* to act than how to act.

That's why this excellent woman in Proverbs 31 is so appealing to me. She has withstood the test of time, wrinkle free. Her truths are eternal, and her wisdom spans the ages. She is not perfect, but she is excellent. And, above all, she has a sense of humor! In the pages that follow, we'll discover together how her life speaks to us in these last years of the twentieth century. And remember . . . no tips, no hints, no to do lists.

Jean Ann from Utah was describing her vision of the perfect wife, but in truth, it fits our proverbial role model like a glove:

> Honest with herself and others. Takes care of her needs, sets boundaries, nurtures herself, knows she is wondrously made and precious in God's sight. Has a sense of humor, adventure, and love. Has an inner peace, serenity, and joy.

Now that's the kind of excellence I could aspire to!

3
The Six Million Dollar Woman

For her worth is far above jewels.
Proverbs 31:10b *NASB*

The very idea that the angelic woman of Proverbs 31 had great worth—in the Hebrew: "value, merchandise, or price"—was an incredible statement for that time and place when women were worth little more than cattle and were never worth as much as men. There it is, as bold as you please in Leviticus 27:3–4: the value of a male slave was fifty shekels; the value of a female, thirty shekels. The equal-pay-for-equal-work struggle goes w-a-y back.

Not all women have a lower price tag attached. Robert Redford was willing to pay Demi Moore a cool million for one night of silver-screen romance. It was indeed an *Indecent Proposal,* yet the movie brings to mind an old story about a man who offered a woman a million dollars if she would spend the night with him. "A million dollars?!" she gasped, then added, "well . . . yes, I guess I will." "How about fifty dollars?" he asked. "Sir!" she retorted, "what kind of woman do you think I am?" "Oh, we've already established that," he assured her, "now we're just talking price." Hm-m-m.

The "Looking Good" Route to Self-Worth

For many of us, our worth is tightly wound around some kind of earthly measurement rather than a heavenly one. Sometimes they are very specific measurements. Becky thought the perfect wife would be "36-24-36"; Gail described her as, "Size 6, exercises three times a week." Molly was sure Ms. Perfect would "never have a 'bad hair' day," and Linda described her as "Sophia Loren at dusk."

What do we think would please our husbands in the appearance department? Some women decided it revolved around clothing: "Dressed sexy," said Linda; "Never wore clothes at home," suggested Sara. Vicki thought her mate would be thrilled if "I flattened my tummy or won the lottery!" Well, at least she has a choice, though the odds of either one happening are slim! The dangers of wrapping your self-worth around your physical appearance were addressed at length in my book, *"One Size Fits All" and Other Fables.* so I'll not cover the same ground here. Suffice it to say that if we measure our value by anything so temporal as the smoothness of our skin, the tightness of our tummy, or the size of our thighs, we'll be spending a great deal of money and time on something that will cease to matter once we're put in a pine box, if not sooner.

No one begins a eulogy for the dearly departed by saying, "She was so faithful to her aerobics classes, skipped desserts every chance she got, and maintained a Size 8 figure throughout her marriage." Get real. It's the example we set, the character we demonstrate, and the love we instill in others that will contribute to our sense of worth now and to our sense of contributing to future generations when we've gone on to glory. Luci Swindoll says, "When you love yourself and accept yourself for who you are, you have nothing left to prove."[1]

If self-worth were measured by the inch, Michelle from Ohio, at 6 feet in height, would rise head and shoulders above many of us. After being involved in a minor car accident she said, "I realized my neck was sore and I was dizzy, so the officer called for an ambulance. They arrived, put me on the stretcher, and loaded me into the ambulance. The next thing I heard was the driver saying, 'Could you pull her up? I can't close the door—her feet are sticking out.' This one comment got me through all the whiplash pain, as I imagined what we would have looked like, careening down the street with the doors flapping open, like something from the Keystone Cops!"

If self-worth were measured by the pound, Janet from Virginia's "plus-size personality" would be worth its weight in gold. "One winter, three coworkers and I decided we wanted 'beach bods' by the summer," she wrote, "and we agreed that Weight Watchers was the answer to our dilemma. At the time, Weight Watchers was having their meetings at our local Holiday Inn. We figured we'd visit their All-You-Can-Eat buffet before going to the meeting. [Makes sense to me!]

"We entered the lobby, and I walked up to the desk clerk and said, 'Excuse me.' He turned, took one look at us, and said, 'Upstairs, first door to the left.' I gave him a startled look and replied, 'Pardon me?!' He said, 'You're here for Weight Watchers, aren't you?' I responded in a huff, 'No, we're not. We're a wrestling tag team and were interested in a room, but after that comment, we'll go elsewhere!' and promptly walked out."

And had a good laugh, I'm sure.

When it comes to her sense of worth, an excellent woman is much more than the sum of her parts. For our value to be "far above jewels," it must be far above dress racks, diet clubs, and beauty salons as well.

The "Credentials after Your Name/Money in the Bank" Route to Self-Worth

Some women use other means of measuring worth numerically: in dollars and cents and/or by the number of letters after their names. Few of us, including me, escape the allure of degrees, awards, titles, and other credentials that the world esteems.

For years, when the only letters after my name were the three I'm most proud of—MOM—I still tried to prove my worth using an old-fashioned method: money. I would never have told a soul my dress size, but I'd find some way to hint at my annual earnings at the drop of a hat. Tacky, Liz.

It's been said that "The real measure of our wealth is how much we would be worth if we lost all our money." No doubt about it, many of us seem to confuse net worth with self-worth As Paula Rinehart, author of *Perfect Every Time,* put it, "[Our] fragile sense of worth is directly attached to abilities and achievements."[2]

These days, it's letters I'm after. In the speaking profession, we have an earned designation called CSP, for Certified Speaking Professional. It takes five years to earn, requires 250 paid presentations for at least 100 different clients, twenty referral letters . . . oh, the list goes on and on.

I couldn't wait to earn my CSP. Because it would mean more income for my family budget? No. Because it would increase my speaking opportunities? Not really. Because it would make me a better speaker, a better servant to my audiences? Not likely. I wanted those three letters after my name so I would be viewed as *somebody* among my professional peers and would impress my clients and audiences. There, I've said it. It looks as bad in print as it feels in my heart.

This is not to say that letters after our names are inherently bad. By no means. I just know that my motives are often not very pure. It's another way to silently say, "I'm better than you." To help me *not* have that attitude when I use those respected letters, I'm going to mentally remind myself of what my real goals are as a CSP: to be Caring, Serving, Purposeful.

I have so much respect for my highly educated husband who is very quiet about his hard-earned letters, Ph.D., and is almost embarrassed when someone calls him Dr. Higgs. His humility speaks volumes to me.

For a man so humble about his own talents, it must be a nuisance to be married to a woman so vocal with her own, especially one who is in the public eye. For example, Bill regularly donates blood to the American Red Cross. One afternoon, sitting in the donor chair, he waited patiently while the nurse checked his temperature, blood pressure, and so forth before she launched into the usual battery of questions.

"Mr. Higgs, have you ever shot up illegal drugs by needle, even once?" Bill shook his head. "Tested positive for the AIDS virus?" "No," he replied as she continued. "Have you been given money or drugs for sex anytime since 1977? Had sex even once with a man? Had sex with a female prostitute?" "No," he assured her, "none of the above!"

As she began swabbing his arm, the nurse asked tentatively, "Uh . . . are you married to Liz Curtis Higgs?" "Yes," Bill responded. She was elated and said, "Oh, I was going to ask you earlier, but I didn't want to get too personal!"

The "Aren't My Children Adorable?" Route to Self-Worth

The best thing I ever did for my husband was give him children. Although there are times when their whining makes his hair (what's left of it) stand up on end, on the whole, he is a model father. Lillian especially knows just how to melt his heart. Sometimes when she sweetly asks him to do something for her, he looks over at me and draws an invisible string around his little finger because that's exactly where she has him wrapped . . . right around her little finger! I can just imagine her saying what Rita from Pennsylvania's daughter did when she came upon her father, fast asleep and snoring loudly. She opened her two-year-old eyes wide with awe and said, "Mommy, listen to Daddy purring!"

Without question, our children can boost our self-esteem. Matthew's first grade class made Mother's Day cards that had a fill-in-the-blank format. I saved mine (of course): "My Mom is smart! She even knows <u>math.</u> I like to make her smile by <u>letting her throw me on the couch.</u>" (Don't get the wrong idea, he likes this!) "My Mom is special because <u>she's in *Today's Christian Woman* magazine.</u>" And, finally, "My Mom is as pretty as a <u>Jewel Sapphire.</u>" What do you know . . . maybe my worth really is "far above jewels!"

But what children give, they can take away. Quickly. Susan from North Dakota remembers her first Sunday at a new church. When she and her family rose for the opening hymn, her daughter whispered none too softly, "Oh, Mommy, don't sing! It's too hard for you!"

My ability to produce two stellar kids for my parents and in-laws to fuss over definitely adds to my sense of value. When Matthew was born, we proudly purchased for Bill's parents (first-timers) one of those bumper stickers that says, "Ask Me About My Grandchildren." Out of a sense of honesty (or maybe a lack of faith in my fertility!) they cut off the last three letters, so it just read "Grandchild." Harrumph! When Miss Lillian showed up twenty months later, we made them scrape off the old sticker and put on a new, plural one.

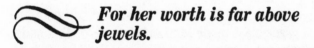

For her worth is far above jewels.

Is my pride in birthing two beautiful babies a bad thing? Well, not as long as I acknowledge what a gift from God children are and that it is his goodness, not mine, that breathed life into their forms. Those among us who are unable to conceive or cannot bear children can feel incredibly deficient as women, even though we have no control over how our bodies are made and little control over how they work. Yet, "a malfunctioning reproductive system is a threat to self-esteem in a way that a failed kidney or a collapsed lung can never be."[3]

Although we no longer use words like *barren* or *cursed,* the childless woman who longs to bear children can feel like those old labels still fit Should that be you, seek the encouragement and understanding that only another woman in the very same shoes can provide. And please forgive the insensitivity and foolishness of those of us with kids. Since we've not walked your path of pain, we often put our feet firmly in our mouths.

For those of us with children, we are called to strike a fine balance between experiencing pride and joy in their existence, and drawing too much of our own self-esteem from their accomplishments. I like Bernie from Pennsylvania's view of the balanced woman as one "who puts her family first without putting herself last."

Model Moms

One of the reasons that the job of mother is valued by so many of us is because of the important place our own mothers had in our lives. Of the hundreds who answered the question, "Who serves as a role model for you in your family life?" more than two hundred of us listed our mothers. Christine remembers, "She raised five children alone and instilled a wonderful set of values and confidence in all." Mary acknowledged that her mom "has lived through much in her life and still finds beauty and laughter—at eighty she is still learning, bowling, cooking, and volunteering!" Our mothers didn't have to be flawless to earn our respect. Shirley wrote, "She was not a perfect mom, so I can learn from her mistakes."

Then there's this story from Cathy in Kentucky. She spent Mother's Day 1993 with her own mother first and then with her husband's mother. After a long day of meals and gifts, they finally walked in the door of their home and parked their eight-month-old son on the kitchen floor. While she and her husband were carrying things in from the car, the baby found the telephone, started playing with it, and hit the redial button. Of course, they didn't know that . . . yet.

Cathy's husband remarked that he thought the day went well. Cathy did not agree. "I rarely lose my temper, but this time I started into him. We had given his mother a $75 gift, and I told him we were never going to spend that much money again because she never thanked us, never commented whether she liked it, just opened her gift and went on. I must have ranted and raved about this for fifteen minutes.

"About then, I asked my husband if he had seen the Barney bag, because it had my aspirin in it and at this point I definitely needed some aspirin. 'You must have left it at your mother's,' he said, so I jumped in the car and drove the ten minutes it takes to get there.

"My mother greeted me at the door and asked me if I'd come for the Barney bag. 'Oh, did you find it?' I asked. 'No,' she said, 'I just heard about it.'" Literally.

It seems that when their son hit redial on the phone, he'd reached her mother, who had listened in on the whole conversation. "We laughed and laughed," Cathy said, "but were *very* grateful he'd called my mother and not my mother-in-law!" Too close for comfort, that one. A sitcom in the making.

The "I Can Do It All" Route to Self-Worth

Judy from Massachusetts had one request for this book: "Convince me that most people don't really do everything naturally with no effort." Like the duck who appears to glide serenely on the lake while paddling like mad to stay afloat, many of us make the "I-can-do-it-all" approach to life look easy—while we put in twenty-hour days to pull it off.

Workaholism and its twin, perfectionism, are an increasing problem as we rush toward the new millennium. Paula Rinehart wrote, "Our culture seems increasingly geared to let such excesses masquerade as virtues."[4] Working mothers are especially good at playing the "my stress is bigger than your stress" game as we compare calendars like grandmothers compare photo brag books: "Mine has more in it than yours!"

A dear friend in my profession described her urge to put too much on her calendar: "I discovered that it had little to do with financial need. It was an inner drive that pushed me to *do*, to *perform*, to *have*, to *show that I could do it!* All wrapped up with self-esteem issues. It was a very lonely realization." Now she has posted next to her phone a copy of one crazy month's schedule from a few years back with a banner headline at the top: *"Never again! Say no!"*

Sometimes I look at my speaking calendar and cry. The tears well up from two sources: gratitude for the opportunities *and* concern for my ability to pull it all off. Believe me, I love making audiences laugh and making clients happy. But sometimes. it comes at the cost of my own laughter and my own happiness. Not to mention my family's joy and contentment Ugh.

Very slowly, I am learning that not only is it okay not to "do it all," it's dangerous to try.

Some of us even wrap our self-worth around service to the church, thinking, "If it's for God, it must be worthwhile; therefore, I am worthwhile too!" Peg Rankin, in *How to Care for the Whole World and Still Take Care of Yourself,* listed some of the seductive messages we hear concerning our spiritual areas of service:

- Take on more than you can handle. You can never do enough for God.

- Set goals and push yourself to achieve them. You want to hear "well done" on Judgment Day.

- Gauge the effectiveness of your service by concrete evidence. If you don't see results, there probably aren't any.[5]

Ouch! These hit too close to home for this woman, especially that last one about looking for tangible, measurable results. It's hard for me to remember that, in matters of faith, invisible growth is the best kind.

Enough Is Enough

Carol from Maryland expressed her need to know "how to recognize enough is enough." *Enough* for me now means quitting an activity *before* it hurts me emotionally, physically, or spiritually. *Enough* means getting my needs met elsewhere, so I'm not looking for self-worth in inappropriate places, such as my to do list. *Enough* means asking for help from a therapist, a friend, a mate, a child, a minister, or—best of all—from God himself. *Enough* means sanity, serenity, and sincerity. *No* still works, if we mean it.

For our worth to be "far above jewels," we must set our price so high that we cannot be bought—not for beauty, money, fame, or letters after our names. Then, when we give ourselves to those whom we love most, we are opening up a treasure chest and not an empty box.

4
Trust Me!

The heart of her husband safely trusts her.

Proverbs 31:11 NKJV

*I*t took me nearly thirty-two years to find a man who trusted me with all his heart, in part because most of the men I met *I* wouldn't trust, not even with my cat, let alone my emotions.

Despite the carefree, glamorous picture the media paints of singleness, most of us who've been there know the truth: it can be tough to be single, especially if you're over thirty, and even more so if you've never been hitched. I remember somewhere near my thirty-first birthday having dinner at a local restaurant with five other never-married friends and laughing hysterically at the thought of all our biological clocks, loudly ticking away in that crowded booth. The more we thought about it, the harder we howled.

Your married friends don't find singleness funny, they find it . . . sad. "Seeing anyone?" they'll ask tentatively, pity in their eyes. When you say, "Not right now," the look on their faces is, "Awwwww, poor thing!"

The assumption or married people is that single people are on constant alert for a possible mate. The truth is, single women have good days and bad days. Days when you are so thankful to be enjoying your singular existence that the very concept of a man cluttering up your apartment and your life would be unthinkable. Then there are those other days, lonely days, when the thought of having a nice, warm fella to curl up with to watch an old movie sounds like nirvana.

"At forty-four, I feel I have found Mr. Close—I'm old enough to know he's not perfect!" wrote Charlotte from Oklahoma. Some of us would be happy with a Mr. Close, and others of us aren't even interested in a Mr. Perfect. One of the questions included in the survey was, "If you are not married now, how important is having a husband to you and why?" On a scale of one to ten, the 136 single women who responded were ambivalent about wanting a husband. Their responses averaged 5.4, but nearly a third gathered toward the No Thanks end of the scale, and exactly the same number—28 percent—leaned toward the Now, Please side of things.

The less-than-enthusiastic crowd had some very good reasons for their choices: "I believe that it is possible to be a whole, happy, fulfilled person without being married, and right now I am one," said Kim from Florida. Barbara from Kentucky wrote, "I'm emotionally still defining what my needs are, so finding someone compatible will have to come after I've completed this process." "The men in my life cost me both financially and emotionally and I feel I'm better off without a man. All they're good for is lifting heavy things," responded Nancy from North Dakota.

Oh, men have a couple of good qualities beyond heavy lifting, but there are few women alive who haven't shared those same feelings about the male of the species at one point or another. Dauna's sage advice is, "If your husband leaves you and it teaches you to never trust or love again, then you've lost much more than a husband."

Some women longed to be married enough to circle Now, Please! They have their own reasons for wanting a partner ASAP:

"I think life is hard to do alone! Would be great to have a kindred spirit around the house."

Patt from Minnesota

"Someone to laugh with, wake up with, make *me* breakfast in bed and share life with."

Martha from Florida

"I am tired of dating. I go out with too many boyfriends and I call them by the wrong names. Disaster!"

Gloria from Washington

Gee, my dating life never got that crazy! If anything, I kept calling them by my cat's name. (Just FYI, men don't react well to being called Big Cat.)

Sometimes our lives are already very full, and there isn't much room or time or need for marriage. Sandra from Wisconsin wrote, "I have freedom, a good job, make my own decisions, am busy and active, have a variety of friends and great support from other women and my grown children. Frankly, I'm not sure I have much left to give to another relationship in my life."

Finally, sitting in the middle of the No Thanks and Now, Please crowds is Linda from Missouri, whose balanced response may come from some hard-won experience: "With the right person, having a husband can be heaven on earth. The wrong person can destroy your entire essence as a person."

Eight Winning Traits

I am fortunate to have chosen the right person. But I believe strongly you have to *be* the right person yourself, first. God in his wisdom did not bring Bill and me together until we were older, wiser, and had a handle on the stuff that really matters. I definitely needed time to work on being the kind of woman who would thrill the heart of the first-class kind of guy I wanted. In other words, I made a list of the qualities I was looking for in a man, then set out to develop them in myself. That way, if I didn't end up finding a good man, I could still be an "excellent woman!"

Here's my list, taken in part from Proverbs 31 and included in our survey:

Flexibility	Creativity
Trustworthiness	Focus
Generosity	Organization
Confidence	Joyfulness

I asked eight hundred women, "How would you rank these, in order of importance to you today?" So now I'll ask you to do the same. Which would be number one for you? Number two? Number three, and so on?

More than one woman jotted a note in the margin, saying "This is hard!" or "They're all important!" Exactly so. Ranked on a scale of one to eight, one being the highest, here's how we stacked them:

1. Trustworthiness

2. Joyfulness

3. Confidence

4. Flexibility

5. Generosity

6. Organization

7. Creativity

8. Focus

Trustworthiness was markedly higher than its nearest competitor, joyfulness (which I expected to come in first!). Lemuel's mother would've agreed with our assessment, which is why she pointed her son toward finding a trustworthy mate. My sense is that the kind of man we want to share our lives with today would also rank the above qualities in much the same way. Thousands of years later, good stuff is still . . . good stuff.

Here Comes the Groom

Not to sound sappy, but my dear Bill truly has those eight traits, and about in that order. (Okay, organization might be shaky.) People always ask me, "Where did you meet such a great guy?" We met at a wedding. Not our own. I mean we had a short courtship, but not that short.

This particular wedding united two friends of mine (and of Bill's, I would find out later). The groom worked in radio and knew us both; the bride was a member of my church, which is where the wedding took place.

As a never-married, over-thirty woman, I didn't care for weddings. No, it was stronger than that. I *hated* weddings. I would sit in the pew, watching the church fill up like the loading of the ark—two by two—all the while moaning under my breath, "Where's *mine?*"

The woman getting married was named Liz, which meant the whole time she was taking her vows, I took them with her. You know, just in case I never got to actually say them myself *or* as a means of practice, if someday I did marry. When the ceremony concluded, I noticed a handsome, smiling man about two rows back, all by himself. No ring on his left hand. Hm-m-m. I knew vaguely that he worked at the radio station with Doug, the groom, but little else. Determined to learn more, I headed in his direction, thinking, *Well, I can at least say "hello"!*

So, I did. And he did. Nice smile, warm handshake. Then he asked me, "What is that sculpture up in front of the church?" That sculpture was a very free-form artistic interpretation of a cross, not an unusual thing to have in front of a church. But then it suddenly struck me: *This guy may not go to church. He may not know what a cross is. Hey, he may not know who God is! Maybe I ought to introduce the two of them.* Off I went, describing the cross itself, repentance, baptism, Acts 2:38, regeneration, everything this guy needed to know.

I went on and on, as only I can, while he was smiling and nodding and smiling and nodding. *I've got a live one here!* I thought to myself. Then slowing down to catch my breath, I said, "So, tell me a little about yourself."

"Well . . ." he said slowly, "I'm an ordained minister."

I was speechless. (This is rare.) "A minister?" I finally said, as a smile slid up one side of his face. "No kidding!" I stammered. "Did I get everything right?"

"You did well," he assured me, and we both laughed.

One thing Bill found out about me right away was that I cared more about his relationship with God than any potential relationship with me. And that was exactly what attracted him to me. That, and my level of self-acceptance. And my laugh!

We stood there and talked in the sanctuary until it was empty, and I realized I didn't have the faintest idea where the wedding reception was. Bill had saved the directions and said, "Why don't you follow me?" Happy to.

At the reception, we kept an eye on each other as we mingled around the room, finally ending up at the same table. (Imagine that.) More talking, more sharing, then finally we exchanged business cards, and I said, "Call me sometime."

Now came the Big Wait. Four or five days later (not wanting to appear overanxious, he said), Bill called. I wasn't home, but my answering machine was. I can still remember coming in and finding the usual 0 replaced with a 1. For a single woman who had not dated in years, any night without a goose egg on the machine was a good night!

The message was short and sweet. A warm voice with a Kentucky twang said, "I wondered if you might like to go to dinner sometime next week?" I might. "Please give me a call back, Liz," were his final words. Not wanting to appear overanxious either, I waited four or five seconds before dialing his number.

Our first date came two weeks later; our wedding date was exactly eight months after that. (The only reason we waited that long is it takes a while to special order a custom-built Size 20 wedding gown!) We'll be forever grateful to Liz and Doug for inviting both of us to their wedding, never dreaming that one ceremony would lead to another.

On Bended Knee

For Linda from Indiana, that first meeting with her future husband was even more unusual than our ceremonial one. "One of the guys on my bowling team, Bob, asked me if I'd like to go on a blind date with his brother. I said okay, and he gave his brother my phone number. This guy called and we went on a date.

"During the evening, I asked him why he and his brother were both named Bob. He said he didn't have a brother named Bob. Getting suspicious, I asked him where he got my phone number. 'From Stan.' 'Who's Stan?' I asked. 'I thought Stan was *your* brother,' he said.

"It turned out that Stan was the first Bob's brother, who really didn't want to go out on a blind date, so he passed my number along to Bob number 2. I guess it was meant to be, because the second Bob is my husband!"

It's fun to hear not only how people met, but also where the proposal actually occurred. Pat from Michigan received her proposal of marriage in the shirt aisle at a Target store. Her husband-to-be was down on his knees supposedly looking for a shirt in his size and said, "Pat, come here, I've found one." As she rounded the corner, he put his hands together and said, "Honey, will you marry me?" Her response, of course, was: "You crazy nut!"

 The heart of her husband safely trusts her.

Dearly Beloved

Let's face it: you can fall in love, but you can't fall in trust. Trust doesn't come from romantic dinners and kisses on the doorstep. Trust, unlike love, is not blind. Trust is based on time, experience, and year-in, year-out faithfulness. It takes a few turns of the calendar before "her husband has full confidence in her" (NIV).

My own trust in Bill had to grow quickly after our short eight-month courtship, especially after we had the rolls of film developed from our honeymoon. The first photos, taken a few months before we met, featured Bill with his arm around another woman! You should've seen his face when I pulled out those photos. . .

After nearly a decade, I can say with assurance that we trust each other completely. He trusts me with our money, the mutual care of our children, and all our possessions, even the riding lawn mower and the remote control. Most of all, he trusts me with his *heart*, his emotional center, even though, as his best friend these many years, I know all his tender spots, pressure points, and fault lines.

Of course, the reason mutual trust works so well is because our men have plenty of dirt on us too. When I asked women to finish the sentence, "My husband would be so proud of me if I . . . ," Lynne said, "was always ready to go fifteen minutes before he is"; "arrived home when I said I would," thought Laurie; "parked the car straight in the garage," guessed Laura, and Doris was certain of this: "got caught up—just once!"

Rosita Perez, a wonderful speaker and friend from Florida, tells a story that has a very familiar ring to it.

One morning I baked a two-layer cake, frosted with chocolate, intending to serve it that night for dessert. I wanted to taste a little bit to see if it was moist enough. It was. It was delicious. So I took another sliver. The sliver became a slab. I ended up cutting a two-inch channel right in the center of the cake, all the way across. Then I could put the two sides together and refrost it so no one would be the wiser. The problem was, I couldn't stop. I kept putting those sides together all afternoon, and I eventually ended up with something that was shaped like a very long, very thin football. I couldn't let my husband see what I had done, so I ate the football. When he arrived home from work, I served him his dinner, and he asked, "Aren't you eating?" And I said, with my best Poor Me face, "No-o-o . . . I'm not very hungry."

Bless His Heart

A group of my friends gathered with me to study Proverbs 31 while this book was in progress, and one week I gave them a homework assignment. "Ask your husband, 'What speaks love to you?' Don't worry, he'll know what you mean." They came back with their research, and we found the answers to be very different than we expected. One husband said he sensed her love for him by "the look in your eyes when I enter the room"; another said, "the way you address me in conversation"; a third answered, "the sacrifices you are willing to make on our behalf." With answers like that, it's a question worth asking.

In our marriage, there is a question that Bill poses several times a week. He knows just when I need to hear it, just when my to do list is on tilt, and I'm feeling overwhelmed. He simply says, "What can I do to bless you tonight?" And he means specific tasks, something he could do to make my life easier—the dishes, the laundry, the groceries, whatever. Do I deserve a man this good? Absolutely not. But I don't deserve grace either, and I'm grateful to have that poured over me daily.

Thank you, Lord, for grace. And for Bill. Help me be worthy of his trust and his love.

5

Money Is the Root of All Shopping

He has no lack of honest gain or need of dishonest spoil.
Proverbs 31:11b AMPLIFIED BIBLE

I remember the day Bill told me, wide-eyed with horror, about a friend whose wife would hide her purchases in the trunk, then sneak them into the house when he wasn't there. I tried to appear shocked as I made a mental list of all my friends who had done exactly that. (Is there a woman alive who hasn't, at least once, had to do a two-step when asked by her husband, "Is that a new dress?")

So, how did Bill respond when I asked him about spending money? "Just make sure we can afford it." He doesn't just mean, "Is there enough in our account to cover this?" He means, "Do we really need it? Is it a good value for the price?" and, especially in Bill's case, "Is it marked down 50 percent or more?" He gives *tightwad* a whole new meaning. We're perfectly paired, since I am the very personification of the term *spendthrift*.

"No lack of gain" has nothing to do with putting on weight. It means we don't spend all the household money. (Who says the ancient wisdom of Proverbs isn't right on time for the '90s?) Our surveys indicate that we have a pretty good notion of what our husbands prefer in the area of finances: "Pinch pennies until they scream," wrote Vanessa from Nebraska. "Live within the budget," said Judy from Alabama.

Elma knew what would please her man: "Cut up all my charge cards." For Debbie, he'd be happy if she'd "balance the checkbook more than once a year." And Dawn Marie understood what it would take to really make her husband smile: "Quit spending money, of course!"

If men trust us not only with their hearts, but also with the family checkbook, we "earth angels" owe it to those we love to practice some fiscal responsibility. Because it's literally a dollars and cents issue, sometimes it can be the easiest area of our lives to work on, as opposed to "act more loving" or "don't whine." On the other hand, the whole earning/spending/saving issue is reported to be the single thing married couples argue about the most.

Mean Green

When it comes to cash, there never seems to be enough of it. As Richard Armour said, "That money talks, I'll not deny; I heard it once, it said, 'Good-bye!'" My experience is that when payday comes, the check goes in the bank, the balance looks terrific, I spend twenty minutes writing checks to pay the bills, and the balance is right back where it was when I started. In theory, one would think that if we earned just a little more money, it would solve that problem. My own life tells me that when we make a little more, we spend a little more—sometimes before we even earn it! Elsewhere in Proverbs are these words of wisdom:

> Do not weary yourself to gain wealth,
> Cease from your consideration of it.
> When you set your eyes on it, it is gone.
> For wealth certainly makes itself wings,
> Like an eagle that flies toward the heavens.
> (Prov. 23:4–5 NASB)

When I asked women to tell me what they wanted more of and less of in their lives, many said, "More money (without being

greedy)" and "Less fear of not being able to pay the bills." Maybe
Joe E. Lewis was right: "It doesn't matter if you're rich or poor,
as long as you've got money."

Bill does better when funds are tight than I do. Like many
families, we have a good car and a second car, meaning it has
more wear and tear and fewer miles left on it. Poor Bill always
gets the second car because I need the more reliable one for
longer speaking jaunts. He's always endured the clunker car
with a sweet spirit. When I asked him how the current one was
holding up, he smiled brightly and said, "I stepped out on faith
today and filled the gas tank!"

"How Much Was That Again?"

Since the Proverbs woman was so trustworthy, especially in
financial matters, Bill and I agreed from the beginning to stick
to a joint checking account and one credit card, and I would carry
both the checkbook and credit card in my purse. Uh-oh. The
verse clearly says that the husband "lacks nothing of value"
(NIV), but Bill was definitely going around empty-handed!

It was hard for both of us to adjust to a two-income, one-check-
ing-account marriage. After being in graduate school for so many
years, Bill was used to being broke. After eight years of a
successful radio career, I was used to having, and spending, lots
of money, no questions asked.

Funny thing about husbands. They ask questions. "What is
this credit card slip for? 'Merchandise'? What does that mean?"
I would sigh and try to remember what I bought where, and he'd
shake his head and grumble. Finally, we agreed that we would
tell each other when we were going to buy something. I found it
to be a nuisance, but it did keep financial peace in our marriage,
so I tried to be very faithful about reporting expenditures.

But there was this one Saturday morning. I did a presentation
for a very small group of women at a local church and was
surprised and delighted when they generously gave me a check
at the end of our time together. Would you not consider that
"found money"? The kind that's not in the budget? A gift straight
from heaven to your wallet?

Well, I took that nice check, hit the bank machine to cash it, and bought a small cut glass window for our honeymoon home. I almost danced in the door with it, sure Bill would be as pleased as I was. "Did the women of the church give you that?" he asked as soon as he saw the window. "Wel-l-l-l," I began, "sort of!" His face darkened. "What do you mean, 'sort of'?" he wanted to know. "Well," I said, "they gave me a check and this is how I spent it! Isn't it beautiful?"

"Liz!" he said with his I'm-not-happy sigh. "That should have been spent on groceries." I was tempted to make him eat it. "Okay, okay, I'll ask first next time," I assured him, still smarting from his ingratitude over my find. It was days before the glass window was hung because it had caused such a fuss.

As the weeks went by, I did a better job of checking with Bill about this purchase and that. Soon, he began to relax as he understood that I could indeed be trusted, and that there really were sufficient funds on hand to cover a few whimsical acquisitions. Bill, however, still consulted me about every little expense. I remember one day when he called, saying, "I saw this computer magazine while I was out at lunch today. It's $2.95. Do you mind if I buy it?" I'm thinking, *Is this a good time to tell him about the couch?*

Filthy Lucre

Dianna from Oklahoma had a knack for tossing money around too. "One Christmas, while entering the mall, I noticed a lady taking donations for a mission project, using a big red cup. After I finished my shopping, I was leaving the store in a hurry (as usual). I reached into my purse, grabbed some coins, walked up behind the lady with the cup, and dropped it in. Instead of hearing the usual jingle of change hitting metal, I heard a curious 'plop.' I had deposited my money in a stranger's soft drink! I was so embarrassed, I practically ran to my car!" It makes me wonder whether the person (a) finished the soda with the dirty money in it and/or (b) rinsed the coins off and saved them. Speaking of laundering cash, Carole from Utah has managed as many as seventeen different companies at one time and admits, "I need more laughter in my life." Sometimes her own customers provide that opportunity. One day, a woman came into Carole's storage business to pay her rent and proceeded to take off her sock and dump the cash on the counter.

"Oh, I better wash it for you!" she said and headed for the rest room. When she brought the wet money back, Carole's understanding employee simply spread the bills across the radiator to dry. No "lack of honest gain or need of dishonest spoil" there! Just an iron, perhaps.

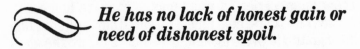

He has no lack of honest gain or need of dishonest spoil.

Then there was last June, when Bill was giving his brand new riding lawn mower a spin around the property. There he sat looking like Mr. Green Jeans, tooling around the backyard, totally unaware of the disaster that lurked right behind him.

Slowly, his shiny new leather wallet began inching its way out of his back pocket. Every time the mower took a bounce, it sneaked out a little bit more. When Bill hit a gopher hole, the wallet was properly launched while its owner rode on. Moments later he made the turn and drove that shiny new blade right over the top of his wallet full of credit cards, car registrations, a driver's license and other Very Important Papers. Thanks to Bill's miserly ways, there was only one dollar in the billfold.

Of course, he didn't miss his wallet until the next day, after an overnight thunderstorm had put the finishing touches on the scene. We looked in the house, we looked in the car, we even looked in the pockets of all his pants—which is when the horrific possibility dawned on him. Pale around the ears, he headed for the back door, saying, "Let me just check something." He came in moments later with that something in his hands. A stray Chevron here, a partial Sears there, but otherwise it was hard to tell what was what, the cards and papers were so gnarled beyond recognition.

We always handle such disasters by beginning with the phrase, "The good news is . . ." In this case, the good news was: this husband had entrusted his wife with duplicates of all those credit cards, the checkbook, and most of the cash. "The heart of her husband safely trusts her" . . . to keep her wallet safely in her purse.

When I told Bill I planned to share his experience in this book, he said, "No one will believe you."

"Why not?" I whined. "It happened, didn't it?"

"Sure, but it also happened in a TV commercial," he informed me, "and your readers will think you borrowed it."

"Nonsense," I told him, "the commercial people obviously lifted the story from *you!*"

Living on Less

When Bill and I married, we set up housekeeping on a property so small that we didn't even need a lawn mower. Cutting the grass meant a Weed Eater and ten minutes, and you were done. Money was tight in the early years, and on paper there was no way Bill and I could pull off starting a business *and* starting a family, financially.

But we did it. Sometimes it meant borrowing money from a loved one for a season, or paying back our obligations v-e-r-y slowly. Most of the time it meant doing without. Peanut butter was a daily fare (until it got so pricey), and dining out meant we split a Happy Meal at McDonald's, and Matthew got the prize!

For fun, we went for long drives up and down the neighboring streets in the evening while Matthew snoozed in his car seat. As the houses got bigger and more expensive, we would marvel at their size and guess at their value. After a few blocks, my eyes would start gleaming, green with envy. So, to keep our covetousness in check, we would turn down streets where the houses and yards were smaller, the cars at the curb were older, the clothes on the line were more modest.

Finally, we would pull into our own driveway and say, "Oh, what a mansion! Thank you, God, for our beautiful home!" It was more cottage than castle, but it was ours (and the bank's), and we were most grateful. We had no "lack of honest gain" and plenty of unmerited grace.

6

The Best
of Intentions

She does him good and not evil.
                                                        Proverbs 31:12 *NKJV*

*O*ne problem here: this verse doesn't leave any room
for "she puts up with him!" She not only does NOT
do evil, but she does only good things. That's a lot of
pressure for us less-than-angelic wives, who try hard but stumble. The Amplified version helps us understand even more
clearly that the woman who loves her man "will comfort, encourage and do him only good."

If your reaction is, "How come he doesn't have to be good to
ME?!" don't worry. He does. There are plenty of verses that
point to the equality of the marriage relationship, the concept of
serving one another, belonging to one another, etc. Meanwhile,
doing good, and not evil, to the men we love just makes sense.

"Good" and "Evil" and Apples
Matthew learned the difference between doing good rather
than evil one fateful day in first grade. On the classroom wall was
a large colorful tree with each child's name, written on an apple,
hanging from the branches. If a child misbehaved—horrors!—
his apple was dropped from the tree and into the basket below,

where it stayed until the next day. If the apple stayed in the tree all week, the child was rewarded with a trip to the prize box.

Our mild-mannered Matthew never dropped his apple. Week after week he came home with something from the prize box and a note from his teacher: "Your son is such a nice boy." Music to a mother's ears.

Until the day I picked him up from school, and the first words out of his mouth were, "Mom, I dropped my apple!" I couldn't help it—a tear slid out of the corner of my eye, knowing how disappointed he must be. "I'm sorry, Mom!" he said, shedding a few tears of his own as he clung to my coat.

"I know just what to do," I assured him, wiping away our tears as we headed to the car. "Matthew, before we even drive away, let's tell God what happened. You'll feel much better after we do."

Sitting in the front seat next to me, Matthew bowed his sweet, round, Charlie Brown-shaped head, folded his hands in mine, and waited.

"You have to go first," I whispered.

He took a deep breath and finally said in a voice filled with juvenile emotion, "Oh, God! I'm such a sinner!"

It took everything in me not to burst out laughing. I patted his hand to get my mind off it, as he continued to tell God what a mistake he had made, horsing around when he should've been listening to the teacher.

When he finished, I said, "Son, I have some good news for you! The Bible says that if we confess our mistakes, God is faithful and just to forgive us completely and wash away our sins. That means we never need to talk about this again, because you're forgiven and it's forgotten! Isn't that terrific?"

His eyes, bright with tears, blinked with astonishment. "Really? That's great!" With that, our discussion moved immediately to other things, and no mention of the dropped apple was made again. Later that evening, when Bill got home from work, Matthew brought it up himself, giving his dad the Cliff's Notes version of the story. "But it's okay, Dad," he assured him, winking at me, "Mom knows a great verse!"

Children really do grasp more than we give them credit for

sometimes. Esther from Illinois remembers when her eleven-year-old daughter was sitting with her older siblings watching an educational program about human reproduction. Soon they began to show footage of the sperm joining with the egg and the announcer stated that the sperm actually attacked the egg. When one of her older brothers stated that maybe she was too young to see that part, she replied, "Oh, I know all about that. That's called 'the battle of the sexes'!" Even at a young age, we females know what a challenge it will be to do men "good and not evil"!

"Hold Your Tongue!"

How do we think our husbands would define such "good" treatment? "Quit nagging!" said Sandy. "Quit arguing!" said Debra. Cass knows he would be grateful if she "would be kind to him," or "would learn to go with *his* flow," wrote Sonya from Oklahoma.

For me, if I could hold my tongue now and again, that would be good enough for Bill. Harlan Miller once said that "the difference between a successful marriage and a mediocre one consists of leaving about three or four things a day unsaid."

Bill and I ate at an Italian restaurant recently and, as is their custom, they served his fettuccine with a large spoon. "Gosh, I've never eaten pasta with a spoon!" he said, trying valiantly to scoop up a spoonful of the slippery stuff. Doing my best not to have an air of superiority in my voice, I said, "Honey, the spoon is for twisting the pasta around your fork."

"Huh?" he said, looking puzzled. "Watch," I told him, as I wound my fork around a few strings of spaghetti, then twisted it carefully into the spoon. In an instant, I had a tidy twirl to pop in my mouth, and did so.

"Hey, that really works," he said, stabbing a large hunk of pasta and beginning to spin it into his spoon. But storm clouds were gathering. The already too-large lump began growing like the proverbial rolling stone gathering moss, only in this case, it was gathering fettuccine and clam sauce with alarming speed. Soon, the better part of his entire serving was on the end of that fork and I feared that soon the red-and-white checked tablecloth would be sucked into its vortex.

When he started to aim the huge blob of pasta toward his mouth, I could keep silent no longer. "Down, Bill, down!" I whispered. Even the best men need mothering occasionally.

Sometimes, in trying to do him "good and not evil," we overdo. As a newlywed, Lynnette from Alaska thought she was doing the right thing by giving her husband the nice, brown toast, the just crisp bacon, and the eggs over easy, keeping the burned toast, black bacon, and hard-cooked eggs for herself. "After about three months, he looked at me from across the kitchen table and asked, 'Why do you always keep the good stuff for yourself, and give me the bad stuff?!' I was dumbfounded and assured him 'Not a problem!'" Apparently, "well-done" in his family meant "overdone" in hers!

Speaking of tasty stories, Bill and I did the traditional "keeping of the top of the wedding cake" to enjoy on our first anniversary. As I recall, we both took one bite and threw it away. Yuck! Major freezer burn. But that's not how things turned out at Leslie's house in Utah. She and her husband dressed up in formal attire to enjoy a delicious anniversary dinner together, with the wedding cake top proudly displayed on a beautiful crystal pedestal cake plate.

"When it was time for dessert, my husband very politely said that he really didn't think he could eat any, but he'd support me if I did. The next thing I knew, he dove head first into the cake! When he lifted his face out, his nose and mustache were covered with frosting. I thought we would die laughing . . . remember, we were still in our formal attire. He then began to coax me to do the same thing. As I leaned toward the cake to take a bite, he very gently pushed my head. Talk about frosting up the nose! It wasn't a pretty sight!"

Maybe we also need a verse that says, "he does *her* good, and not evil!"

Who Is in Control Here?

For some reason, when Bill and I have a disagreement, it usually revolves around home remodeling and repairs (or the lack thereof). Cathy from Iowa remembers the time she was less than helpful to her husband: "He was trying to strip the paint on our kitchen woodwork when it caught on fire. I screamed 'FIRE!' ran some water in a bucket, and proceeded to throw it on him. To add insult to injury, he'd already put the fire out himself. That was almost as bad as the time I put his rubber rainsuit in the electric dryer and it melted!"

My Bill is not a sports fanatic or remote control tyrant, but many women have husbands who are both. Harriet from Kentucky described one Sunday afternoon when she was sitting in the living room reading when her husband came in. He flipped on the football game, watched it for a few minutes, turned to her, and said "Would you watch this for me?" and left the house.

Then there was the time Donna from Ohio got to watch an entire show without any channel surfing because her husband had gone to bed early. When it came time to turn off the television, the remote control was nowhere to be found. Not in the kitchen, the bathroom, or in the Lazy Boy. She gave up, turned the set off manually, and crawled into bed. "Honey, have you seen the remote control?" she asked him, yawning. He slid one sleepy arm down to the floor next to the bed and held up the missing control. Apparently he was still in charge of it, even in his sleep!

She Does Him Good and Not Apple Butter . . .

Bev in Indiana remembers an occasion when her own husband was "in the dark."

My daughter and grandson had come over for the day so we could make apple butter together. We spent the day getting the apples prepared and by late afternoon we had a batch simmering on the stove. We'd discussed the need of a chest of drawers for little Ben's room, and I had promised to buy one if we could get it at a decent price. Looking through the paper, we saw one advertised and decided we'd turn the stove off and head to town to check it out.

So with the house in a mess, I flung off my apron and we headed out the door, leaving dirty dishes stacked high and toys everywhere. We didn't rush, enjoying the time together, and stopped for a few groceries on the way home.

When we pulled into the driveway, it was filled with cars. My immediate thought was, 'Oh no, Rod had a meeting scheduled and forgot to tell me!' Then I realized that *I* was the one who had forgotten about my own Ladies Auxiliary meeting. I ran in the house to find seven of my officers sitting around the table with big smiles on their faces.

I soon learned that my husband had been called out of the shower to answer the doorbell. He said, 'Erma stood there like she thought she belonged so I asked her why she was here,' and that's when he found out about the meeting. More folks kept arriving, so they cleaned up the house and got things set up.

It was unreal. Of course, I hadn't prepared refreshments, but I put out some snack mix and fixed glasses of iced tea for everyone. The biggest laugh came when the chairman picked up her Snoopy glass and read: "There's no excuse for not being prepared!"

A Good Man Is a Good Thing

My own husband has the patience of Job. If we're sitting at a red light, and he's behind the wheel, I'm over on the passenger side with a gas pedal of my own. Sure, it's invisible, but I find myself reaching my foot toward it as I crane my neck to the left and right, ready to take off like a shot.

The light changes, and Bill's foot is still on the brake. "Bill, it's green!" I say, assuming he just didn't see it. Still no forward motion. He's looking around, hands on the wheel at 10:00 and 2:00. "Bill, it's green!!" I say with some measure of desperation.

He turns to me and says, "There'll be another one."

I'm the first to admit that I often have a little fun at Bill's expense, but there are two important considerations: I run every story past him before I use it on the platform or in my writing. If he seems the least bit hurt, it's history. However, 99 percent of the time he loves it and adds another funny line or two of his own. Second, I make certain that for every one of those good-natured ribbings, I share two kinder comments about him.

Women are so used to "male-bashing" humor that I find the more I praise Bill in public, the more women come up to me afterward, conviction on their faces, saying, "Listening to you, I realized that I never say positive things about my husband. That is going to change as of tonight."

We know this truth from experience: "to do good and not evil" to the man we love is not only the right thing, it's the smart thing. Sooner or later, those kind words and deeds just might head back in our direction.

7
Till Death
(or High Water)
Do Us Part

. . . all the days of her life.
Proverbs 31:12b NKJV

True Love knows no age boundaries, according to
Loretta from Kentucky. Her daughter came home
from her first week at kindergarten and announced
that she was in love with a boy in her class. Her father said,
"Don't you think you're a little young?" She replied brightly,
"No, Daddy. He's five and I'm five!"

Bill and I were nearly three decades older when True Love
came a'calling. It was Valentine's Day, 1986, and we were
exactly one month away from our wedding day. On that cold,
wintry holiday evening, Bill had driven seventy miles in a blind-
ing snowstorm to present me with my favorite flowers: red
tulips. In February. No doubt about it, it was True Love.

Not to be outdone, I had spent the afternoon slicing apples
into tiny slivers and rolling out a from-scratch crust to make a
dessert fit for my prince: French apple pie. Classical music,
candlelight on the coffee table. "Wasn't marriage going to be
bliss?" I thought to myself as we cuddled on the couch and
watched the falling snow.

Valentine's Day, 1995: Nine years, several pounds, and two children later. A bigger mortgage, much more laundry, two cars brimming with fast food bags and Sunday school take-home papers. No tulips. No apple pie. No snow. No doubt about it, it was . . . True Love.

Not Hollywood love. Not love at first sight. Not convenient love. Not conditional love. The Real Thing. Love based on commitment, on acceptance, on day-in, day-out, never-mind-the-seven-year-itch perseverance. It's not always exciting. In fact, it would make a dull soap opera script. Barbara Bush once said, "I married the first man I ever kissed. When I tell my children that, they just about throw up." That's True Love for you. Love for the long haul, whenever it begins.

As is the custom now, we had our wedding videotaped. It's a good thing because the entire day was one happy blur. I was so proud of us, both sentimental fools, for not crying a drop. We sang, we laughed, and the guests almost clapped when we turned to be introduced: "Ladies and gentleman, Dr. and Mrs. William Higgs!" It was an evening of transcendent joy.

But now, when I watch the videotape, I cry like a baby. "Look how young we were!" I sniff. The tears really start to roll when we begin repeating our vows. *What were we saying?* I think, shaking my head.

We were saying we would do several outrageously difficult things for the rest of our natural lives, stuff that would be hard to do for a week unless it were really True Love. Here are four of those promises many of us made.

"For Better or for Worse . . ."

This one is easy to say when we don't know how much worse it will get. Our brief, mostly-through-the-mail courtship meant we each could keep up a good "I've got it all together" front right up until we married. Imagine our surprise when we were thrown into a small car on a long honeymoon that nearly ended in divorce. (Well, not really, but for a few minutes there in Roanoke, Virginia, the future of our marriage looked dim.)

Elma from Wisconsin has one vivid memory of her wedding day in February 1958: it was cold. How cold was it? So cold that at their reception, a woman who was helping serve the food came out and announced, "The pickle juice is frozen!" Everyone had to keep their coats on to stay warm, and one man set his scarf on fire getting too close to the heater. When a marriage starts out worse, it can only get better!

If the experts are right, and romance cools 80 percent in the first two years of matrimony, how do we go the distance all the days of our lives? I say, the more surprises we can get out of the way before the wedding day, the better. One of the advantages of marrying a little later in life is it reduces some of the guess-work. In my case, I never have to worry, "Gosh, I wonder what Bill will look like without hair someday?" I already know. He never has to say to himself, "Gee, I wonder what Liz will look like someday if she lets herself go?" I'm already gone.

Melissa in South Dakota admits that she and her husband look enough alike to be related, but not *this* related. After finishing a meal in a restaurant, they were asked by their waitress how they'd like the bill divided. Melissa's husband said, "Put them both together" and paid for it by check. The waitress looked at the check and said, "Oh! You're husband and wife. I thought you were brothers." Melissa said, "We couldn't help laughing, but if it's true that the longer a couple is together, the more they look alike, we could be in trouble. After all, I don't want to lose my hair too!"

Bill and I knew that we had finally moved beyond the honeymoon stage of our relationship when one evening he suggested, "How about we tuck the kids in early and pay bills?"

Water, Water, Everywhere . . .

Dr. Joyce Brothers reminds us, "Marriage is not just spiritual communion and passionate embraces; marriage is also three meals a day, sharing the workload, and remembering to carry out the trash." Or, in our case, carrying out the water.

We can trace almost every *really* hairy moment in our relationship to an excess of water. In one house that had ground level casement windows, a hard rain guaranteed water in the basement. Not a puddle, a lake. We tried nailing the windows shut, caulking them shut, sandbagging them shut, but when the rains came, the water came in. Bill threatened to build an ark in our basement to hold not two of every species but all the soggy boxes full of books, clothing, and toys that he invariably found floating in the flood.

In that same house, the hot water heater didn't just stop working, it collapsed one day, pouring forty gallons of water all through that same wet basement. Not long after, a leaky sink put nasty water stains on the ceiling of our back bedroom. Then, when we had a second floor bath put in, the plumber punctured the hot water pipes in the wall and . . . well, you get the idea. It was always water. I started calling Bill "Noah."

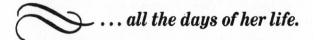 *. . . all the days of her life.*

One month before Matthew was born, I was sent home from work by my doctor. She said, "Liz, you have got to get those ankles up in the air!" Not straight up, you understand, but elevated above my hips so the swelling would go down. A necessary move, because my ankles did look ridiculous. "Squisshh! Squisshh!" they went when I walked. I couldn't wear open-toed shoes, or the water ran out.

So there I was one afternoon in my ninth month, ankles dutifully up, as I sat in an appropriately overstuffed chair and chatted on the phone with my friend Debra. In the laundry room a few feet away, I'd just put in a load of clothes. The washer was sounding unusually loud, and I knew I should put the phone down and check on it, but that would've required getting out of the chair, a seven-minute ordeal of huffing and puffing. Instead, I reached over and shut the door to the laundry room and kept right on talking. For an hour. (This is not difficult for me.)

When I finally hung up the phone, I knew something was very wrong because the washer was still running. Even on the longest cycle, it doesn't go an hour. I struggled out of the chair, made my way to the laundry room, and opened the door.

It was not a pretty sight. The washer hose was loose and spraying hot water everywhere, as it had been for an hour. The walls, the curtains, the ironing board, the piles of clean laundry, *everything* was dripping wet. But, that's not all. This laundry room had a hardwood floor, so the water had also gone through the cracks and down through the subfloor and right into my husband's basement office. That same office where he had, days earlier, gotten organized for the first time in our short married life and put up nice neat shelves with all his books and papers.

Afraid to look, but knowing I had to, I waddled to the top of the basement steps and peered down. Just as I had feared, all his books and papers were floating around about the second step.

Of course, I had to call him. "Bill!" I wailed into the telephone, summoning all my prenatal hysteria for a sympathy vote. "Bill! There's . . . there's water everywhere!"

He almost shouted into the phone. "I'll meet you at the hospital in five minutes!"

"For Richer or for Poorer . . ."

By the time our wedding day arrives, most of us have a pile of gifts that would fill two station wagons, an envelope stuffed with cash and checks from loved ones, not many bills yet, probably two incomes, and few financial worries. The grass looks greener indeed when we leap over the matrimonial fence. But eventually, things change.

Over the years, Bill and I have created budgets based on plentiful and budgets built around pitiful. The day we married, we had two incomes. Two months later, we dropped to one salary when his one-year teaching contract expired. It was not an unexpected situation, but the ensuing financial frustrations were. Add to that the stress of looking for work and our desire to start a family, and we were up to our elbows in newlywed tension.

A job was found, the money picture brightened, and we were back on an even keel for a few months. Then, I got pregnant. Hooray! Uh-oh. Now what? We saved like mad, only to watch the government take it all away at tax time.

The summer of 1987 will be remembered for three major monetary moves: I left my full time radio career, saying good-bye to 75 percent of our family income; I started my speaking career and immediately needed money for a brochure; and our first child was born.

The good news: a young mother who is home, breast-feeding her child, and handling all the household duties, does not spend much money. We were amazed at how little we missed the additional income. I continued to do a weekend radio show to keep some steady money coming in (and to have five hours to myself!). That was the best thing I could ever have done for all three of us. I got to keep my foot in the door of my old career while I established my new one, Bill got thrown into parenting every Saturday and learned How to Do Dad, and our precious baby got to have some uninterrupted time with his father. Except for not having much cash, we were very rich.

"In Sickness and in Health . . ."

Other than the usual aches and pains of moving into midlife, Bill and I have been blessed with good health and little sickness, unless you count the eighteen months of our marriage that I spent "with child."

The physical state known as pregnancy may be healthy for the baby, but it can be rough on Mom—and no picnic for Dad, either, in his role as Coach. Morning sickness, an itchy tummy, backaches, headaches, indigestion, stretch marks—the list of maladies goes on and on. With gratitude we note that it *always* ends—eventually.

My memories of being pregnant neatly divide into the three trimesters. The first trimester featured the exhaustion phase. All I wanted to do was *sleep*. So I did, anywhere I could get away with it. At my desk, on the phone, in the tub, at red lights, you name it.

During the second trimester, all I wanted to do was *eat*. As Dave Barry points out, a pregnant woman is indeed eating for two, but the other one is not Orson Welles.[1] Near the end of those middle three months were some exciting tests to assure everyone that, yes, that was a baby in there. I heard the heartbeat go "sshhwwoooop! sshhwwoooop!" Then, I felt the baby move and spent the next several weeks grabbing Bill's hand and saying, "Here! Here! Can't you feel it?"

During my visits to the doctor, I also discovered an interesting comparison game going on. I found myself feeling superior to those newly pregnant women sitting around the waiting area who looked merely tired and a bit overwhelmed. Then I'd look at the women who were further along than I was and feel humbled by their obvious seniority in these matters. Complete reverence was reserved for those women who were back in the office for their post-partum check-up, babe in arms, who clearly had made it to The Other Side.

"Till Death Do Us Part . . ."

Some people say, "As long as we both shall love," but Bill and I decided to go for a life term and stuck with the traditional, "till death do us part." The phrase "all the days of your life" shows up in Scripture two dozen times, reminding us some choices really are forever.

When we make this vow, we do so blissfully ignorant of the promise we're making and often ill-equipped to fulfill that pledge when serious illness or death comes our way.

I have a friend whose husband was diagnosed with multiple sclerosis just when their children were about to leave the nest and they were ready to be a twosome again. They are . . . but not as she had hoped.

> I'm a widow whose husband hasn't died yet. It's been a grim series of adjustments—deny, accept, accommodate—over and over again. My lover and friend are now neither. He is waiting to die, and my life is in neutral. "For better or for worse" comes to mind each time I feel I want to run away from this. Lost dreams haunt both of us, and time ticks away. We are both trying to do what is right. I find hope and solace in laughter. I try to see every beautiful thing that passes my way. Whenever my mouth upturns, I know it's good.

The Amplified version says, ". . . as long as there is life within her." For this woman, the signs of life are good, if not always joyful. By honoring her vows, even in such difficult circumstances, she earns our respect and deserves our applause.

8
Sew
What?

**She seeks wool and flax, / And
willingly works with her hands.**
Proverbs 31:13 NKJV

With this verse, Lemuel and his mother have left me behind in the dust. I'm allergic to wool, and "flax" sounds like what my two kids give me when I tell them it's time for bed (flack x 2 = flax). I can't sew a straight line without raising my voice, and my attempts at dressmaking look "homemade" not "handmade." I managed a C in junior high home ec only because our teacher graded on a generous curve.

Those on the higher end of the curve are still sewing today. I am friends, it seems, with most of them, who lavish me with their handiwork at holiday time. Had I lived during biblical times, sewing would have been a necessity, not merely a pleasurable pursuit. Today, many women—by choice!—quilt, sew, crochet, macrame, knit one, pearl two, embroider, cross-stitch, smock, appliqué, and create lace *from scratch* (or whatever you make lace from).

Shirl from Kentucky remembers leaving on a long trip and taking her afghan-in-progress to keep her occupied. As they drove along, she mentioned to her husband, "The car heater seems to have something wrong with it. It's getting warmer and warmer in here." Not wanting to discourage her, he suggested, "Maybe you might like to make a smaller project." Looking down, she realized that the harder she worked, the more the afghan grew and—of course—the hotter she got!

Intent on learning the fine art of quilting, I once signed up for a six-week course with a master quilter. I made it through the first hour, during which she handed out templates and fabrics and tiny needles and a hoop and directions in such small print they gave me a headache. Finally, when we took a fifteen-minute break, I gently handed back all her materials and asked: "Can I just buy the quilts?"

I Was Needled into It

Not that I don't keep trying to teach my hands new tricks. A few years ago, I bravely attended a weekend retreat for women who are craft conscious. This was a loosely knit affair (pun intended), a gathering of women whose sole intent was to talk, eat, and quilt for two days—no classes, no breakout sessions, no speakers (although they did make me stand up and tell a funny story).

At first, I loved seeing their works-in-progress: exquisite comforters, delicate baby clothes, intricate tatting. By Saturday morning, I was beginning to feel a bit out of the loop, so a friend and I slipped away after breakfast and headed to a nearby craft supply store. I found the perfect project for my skill level: "Counted Cross-Stitch for the Inept," it was called. The finished size was 3" by 3", and it featured a single color of floss on 11-point Aida cloth. My partner assured me, "Anybody can do counted cross-stitch," so I paid for my stash and we headed back to the retreat. I practically danced through the door; finally, I would feel like "one of the girls."

I'm sure many a woman there had to stuff her face in a pillow to keep from laughing as I struggled with the oversized needle and long black strands of floss. Tentatively, I began to poke at the cloth. *Down, up. Down, up.* Look at the pattern again. *Down, up. Down, up.* Does it matter what it looks like underneath? *Down, up. Down.* Uh-oh. A knot. A knot! Now what?

Three hours of that nonsense and the whole mess went back

in the paper bag, where it has been lying dormant ever since. That was 1992. Stay tuned.

Treasured Possessions

These dear friends and others who have gifted me with their creations over the years could only guess at how their handwork has touched my life. Over a desk in our office is the cross-stitched phrase: "Working for the Lord doesn't pay much, but the retirement plan is out of this world!" Mary Jane did that in 1982. It's still there, still beautiful. On the bulletin board is a heart-stopping embroidered heart in red-on-ivory, my "corporate colors," done by Sandi, an incredible client who *paid* me too! An upstairs bedroom displays framed calligraphy done by a radio listener years ago, to commemorate the birth of Matthew in 1987: "A son is a grin with sneakers." In our bedroom sits a basket handwoven by my mother-in-law, Christmas 1988. The quilt our realtors gave us when we moved into our new/old house hangs in my son's room. The birdhouse wreath from the women of the UMC in Elizabethtown graces an upstairs window. And my feet stay warm in furry handstitched slippers from some Alaskan sisters, who retreated with me one October weekend.

And angels, lots of angels, in fabric, ceramic, corn silk, wood, stained glass, even one made from an old quilt. These gifts are so personal, so infused with love and care, that you can be sure they'll never end up in a closet, let alone a yard sale.

That's not to say there haven't been some unusual handcrafted items that have crossed my path over the last decade. One favorite comes to mind. When I helped some firemen kick off a safety campaign many years ago, they presented me with a steel hatchet, mounted on a big wooden plaque. It weighed a ton, but I felt obliged to hang it on my office wall. After all, if I'd left it tucked under my desk, I could've been arrested for concealing a deadly weapon.

Bloom Where You Are Planted

Then there was that trip to Illinois a few years ago. After speaking all day for a women's event, I was gathering up my goodies and commenting on how beautiful all the silk floral decorations had been. An enthusiastic woman stepped forward to tell me she had designed them herself. "They really are exceptional!" I assured her, which prompted her to grab a huge arrangement at the registration table and hand it to me. "Enjoy!" she said, beaming. The colors were my favorite, red and ivory, and I knew they would be just the thing for my living room. I thanked her many times as we headed for the door.

When Bill and I arrived home the next afternoon, I began walking my new silk arrangement around the house, looking for the perfect place to put it. The dining room turned out to be the best choice, but the milk glass vase was all wrong for my decor. Replacing it with a tall basket that had gone begging for attention, I tossed the milk glass vase in the kitchen wastebasket and forgot all about it.

Two days later, the phone rang. It was the generous woman from Illinois, in a major panic. "Remember the floral arrangement I gave you?" she began, almost gasping for air. "You're welcome to keep the flowers, but that vase is a valuable antique of my mother's, and she just called me and asked me if I'd seen it. Would you mind very much sending it back?"

Mind? Would I mind? Dear friends, my *mind* was blank. Where had I put that bumpy little vase? "Why, of course I'd be happy to return it, but it may take me a few days to find . . . just the right box for it," I stammered, buying time while my mind was whirling. I jotted down her address, hung up the phone, and began tearing the kitchen apart. Retracing my steps from the moment The Arrangement entered the house, I soon realized where the vase went.

I am a blessed woman. The trash bags were still by the curb, not yet picked up by the sanitation crew, so I headed out to hunt for my buried treasure. Rather than stick my hands down into that nasty collection of who-knows-what-all, I began rubbing the outside of all the Hefty bags, feeling for the familiar shape of a vase, the telltale bumps of milk glass. Bag after bag I went, rubbing and squeezing. (Months later, while collecting donations for the American Heart Association, a neighbor confessed she watched me from her window that day, squeezing my trash bags, and laughed till she cried.)

At last, I found the vase. Ripping through the plastic to pull it out, I was relieved to see that it was still in one piece and none the worse for two days in trashland. A thorough scrubbing and it was good as new . . . for an antique.

Happy Hands

The list of things I'm *not* skilled at doing with my hands is laboriously long, but I can do a few crafty things. Creating small, wooden candle boxes is one of them, especially if you like the primitive look.

For the uninitiated, this means you visit a craft store and buy pine candle boxes, already assembled. You paint them all one color with craft paint, using a large sponge brush that even a four-year-old could handle. When the paint dries, you give the wooden box to your dog to play with for an afternoon, so it gets what craft people call a "distressed" appearance. Ta-da! You've just created a Country Primitive. We gave these as Christmas gifts one year, to rave reviews. (We didn't have a pet at the time, so I "distressed" them myself. Very therapeutic.)

 She seeks wool and flax, / And willingly works with her hands.

Stenciling is another way I work with my hands "in delight" (NASB) and "with eager hands" (NIV). Again, it's child's play. Tape stencil on surface. Rub paint over open holes. Lift off stencil (that's the tricky part), and move to next spot. Tape stencil on surface . . . and so on. My problem is, I never do any craft half way. Once I latch on to it, I start buying things in bulk, visions of having my own booth at the Christmas Bazaar dancing in my head. Bill has caught on to me and insists on "one project at a time" purchases.

Some of us know precisely what tasks our husbands would like us to direct our busy hands toward: "Take better care of my car," wrote Gale; "finish *one* craft project," said Shirley; "fix something electrical!" was Karen's contribution; and Mary Jo knew her husband would be thrilled if she would "refinish all the painted wood in the house."

"If only I had time to pursue such things!" many of us fret. Our "want to do" list is three times longer than our "must do now" list. One woman from Michigan has chosen a full-time career as a homemaker, yet often finds it difficult to justify her choice of occupation to other women. "Everybody acts as though you're a disgrace or an alien, but I enjoy being at home, making things from scratch, sewing and doing crafts. I have time and the desire to develop my God-given talents."

To those who are so called and gifted, I say, "Brava!" I also say, "Any interest in four cases of Williamsburg blue craft paint?"

9

From the Distant Shores of the Piggly Wiggly . . .

**She is like the merchant ships, /
She brings her food from afar.**
Proverbs 31:14 NKJV

Few women could draw much encouragement from being compared to a "merchant ship": bottom heavy and in need of paint! All the translations of this verse were almost identical, though the Living Bible adds some insight: "She buys imported foods, brought by ship from distant ports."

I often bring food from afar . . . literally. When I speak in Texas, I always hit the airport gift shop and buy my husband his favorite "cowboy caviar," a hot salsa stuffed with peppers, corn, jalapeños, and other veggies that make smoke come out of your ears.

Since lots of our foods today, from pineapple to coffee, arrive by boat, that should easily get us off the hook on practicing *this* verse. In fact, my understanding of "she brings her food from afar" in the modern vernacular is "she hits the drive-thru window." In my first book, a little volume of humor called, *Does Dinner in a Bucket Count?*, I concluded that it's the woman who's holding the bucket, and not what's in it, that should matter most to her family!

For good or for bad, I have perfected the art of eating while driving. I can hold a juicy burger in one hand, carefully keeping the foil around it to catch drips, while zipping through traffic. I've even been known to eat coleslaw with a "spork" at 60 mph. After all, isn't that why they call it fast food?

Kim from Kentucky confessed, "We have elderly neighbors who spend their hours looking out the windows. When I pull up at the end of the day, sometimes I hide the Wendy's bag in my purse so they won't wonder if I ever fix a decent meal for my family."

She's not the only one who turns to Wendy or the Colonel. I get help from friends—Mrs. Paul, Sara Lee, and the Jolly Green Giant—whenever possible. Karla defined the perfect wife as "a woman who is creative with leftovers." On my own job resume for "excellent wife," the notes scribbled in the margin read: "can't cook, can't sew, can dance a little."

Food That Sticks to Your Ribs (and Everything Else)

Sandy from Pennsylvania and I are kissing cousins when it comes to our kitchen abilities. She was preparing chicken croquettes—as she describes them, "the ready-made, junk food kind that probably rot your stomach, but my husband likes 'em, so who am I to argue?'" She describes the story as such:

> The croquettes take forty minutes to cook, the frozen french fries he likes with them take twenty. At the end of the first twenty minutes, it was time to put the french fries in there on the other end of the same cookie sheet. Sounds simple, right? With a meal like this, you could figure on not having much mess to clean up, right?
>
> I opened the oven door, set the bag of frozen fries on the open door while I slipped on my oven mit so I could pull out the cookie sheet . . . and then it dawned on me that I had just melted the entire plastic bag onto the inside of the hot oven door! My only recourse at this point, since the croquettes are half-baked (like the rest of us), is to put the salvageable fries onto the cookie sheet and shut the oven door. This bakes the plastic on there even harder. Don't ask me what I would do without my poor overworked, under-appreciated husband, who spent half of the next day with a razor blade getting the words "Ore Ida" off the glass oven door.

It warms my heart when I read mealtime horror stories from other families. Like Rita from Pennsylvania who insisted on saving all the drippings from meats thinking, "I'm going to make something out of this someday." On one occasion, after making steamed clams, she poured the copious amounts of broth into— what else—a juice container. The next morning her husband looked in the refrigerator and thought, "Oh, boy—grapefruit juice! We haven't had that for a long time," and poured himself a tall, frosty glass.

As she tells it, "When this unexpected flavor reached his taste buds, he knew it didn't taste right but figured it was because he had just brushed his teeth, so he kept right on drinking until his taste buds finally got his attention." On other occasions, Rita's ham broth was mistaken for iced tea, and family members made sandwiches using "butter" from margarine tubs that turned out to be storage containers for vanilla icing (well, it *would* look the same). Rita says, "I need a sign on my fridge that says, 'Enter At Your Own Risk!'"

Soup's Off!

Lord Byron once said, "Ever since Eve ate apples, much depends on dinner." Men do enjoy bragging about a wife who cooks well. According to some of our eight hundred women, their husbands would love it if they "would cook wonderful meals—any meals," said Marilyn; "won the Pillsbury Bake Off," wrote Patricia; "cooked more—nagged less," admitted Ila. I thought Bill might say he'd love more home-cooked meals—from someone else's kitchen.

Meal preparation is a real sore spot in many households. Who will shop for it? Who will fix it? Who will clean up the mess? These are volatile subjects in some families. More than one nasty argument has begun with the innocent question, "Honey, what's for dinner?" Among those we surveyed, cooking was handled by the woman of the house 58 percent of the time and by husbands only 6 percent. In 31 percent of marriages, women and men split the cooking duties. (I think the other 5 percent eat out!)

Mary Ann from New York offers some advice from her older and wiser perspective: "When I was married about a year, my husband suggested one day that he bake a cake for dinner. I acted very insulted and asked why he didn't like my baking. Needless to say, he didn't bake the cake and never offered to do so again through thirty-five years of marriage. I wish we could live that day over again—I would have handed him the pans and ingredients!"

Diana from Georgia remembers a hectic time in her life when she was going to college full-time and trying to be mother to her sixteen-year-old daughter and wife to her hard-working hubby. One night when she was studying for finals, her daughter announced there was nothing edible in the house. "It was getting close to 11:00 P.M., I was trying to study, my daughter was doing homework, and my husband was already asleep. I was furious. I marched up the steps, woke him, and demanded that he go to the grocery store *now*. The dear man crawled out of bed, got dressed, came downstairs, and said, 'Where is the grocery list?' I burst into tears!"

I think the whole meal situation could be more manageable

at our house if I did a better job of grocery shopping. Too often we eat out, go the bag/bucket/box route, or have pancakes—that's our "special" meal when the only things in the house are milk, flour, and eggs!—not because I don't want to cook but because the cupboard is bare. I promised you this book would have no tips, but I will share one good idea we've implemented.

I prepared a computerized list of all our favorite grocery items, by category, in the order they appear in the store. (Very organized for my personality type, I know.) By keeping one on the fridge at all times and circling things we need as we run out, it makes a trip to the grocery far more efficient. Bill really doesn't expect me to be Betty Crocker; Betty Boop with a full refrigerator is fine.

It was encouraging to read the comments of other cooking-impaired women who knew their husbands would be so proud of them if they "could plan meals ahead," wrote Wanda, or "remembered to make the coffee the night before," said Sharon, or just "filled the ice cube trays," said Barbara.

She is like the merchant ships, / She brings her food from afar.

Marilyn from Michigan admits, "One of the tasks I always disliked (and, of course, felt guilty about) was packing my husband's lunch. I was always so glad when it was done." One day he came home from work and described biting into his sandwich, only to sink his teeth into the round cardboard from the bologna package. (At least I can say I've never served cardboard—not *real* cardboard, anyway.)

Janine from California wanted her first home-cooked meal to be memorable. It was. Knowing that her new husband enjoyed Jell-O, she made a gelatin mold but added too much water, and it wasn't firming up fast enough. So she put it in the freezer. At mealtime, she took the Jell-O mold out and put it onto a plate. "It was as if the Jell-O had come to life. This large red blob started oozing off the plate on all sides and onto the table, headed in every direction. So much for my perfect dinner!"

Becky from Tennessee's four-year-old once explained to her mother just how to make Jell-O: "Take red sand, mix it with very hot water, add some ice blocks, put it in the refrigerator, and leave it until it can wiggle!"

Make Mine a Happy Meal

Getting our kids to eat what we fix for them is sometimes challenging. Rosi from Kentucky remembers when her four-year-old son wanted a piece of cake but didn't want to finish his dinner first. "Mommy," he asked, "if I don't eat my dinner, what will you do with my cake? Give it to some little boy who'll appreciate it?" That same young child was overheard telling his five-year-old brother, "Jesus might come tonight!" To which his brother replied, "I hope so. Then I won't have to eat my burrito!"

Eating out can produce some fond family memories too. Linda from Arkansas remembers a breakfast trip to a restaurant. Looking at the menu, her younger son saw "poached eggs" and asked his older, smarter brother what that was. His serious reply? "Oh, you know, those are eggs from chickens caught illegally."

Dauna from Ohio remembers the day the kids in her third-grade classroom were cleaning up at the end of the day. "Pick up the debris from your area and put it in the waste can," she told them. One little boy looked puzzled and asked, "What's debris?" "Debris is leftover junk," she replied. "Oh yeah," he said with understanding spreading across his face. "My mom fixes debris for dinner sometimes."

Living Bread

Although I spent the first two dozen years of my life in Lancaster County, Pennsylvania, I had never heard of Amish Friendship Bread. One day a friend brought me a small loaf of it and I was hooked. "Do you want some 'starter'?" she asked. Even though it sounded to me like something you put in your car, I said, "Sure!"

She showed up the next day with a bag of glop and a recipe that had obviously been photocopied dozens of times. The instructions were very clear: "*Do not* use metal spoon or bowl when mixing! *Do not* refrigerate! *Expel air* from bag occasionally." Then this ominous note: "It is *normal* for batter to thicken, bubble, and ferment." And they want me to eat this? Too late. I'd already eaten it.

"Okay, what do I do first?" I asked her.

"Nothing."

"You mean you just set it on the counter?"

"Right. And *do not* refrigerate!"

Got that. "What about tomorrow?"

"Squeeze it."

"You gotta be kidding!"

"Read the recipe. Days Two, Three, Four, and Five it just says, 'Squeeze Bag.'"

Now, this is my kind of baking. Day Six you have to open the bag and add some flour, sugar, and milk. But no fridge. Yuck. Three more days of squeezing, then the contents of the bag move to a big bowl. More flour, sugar, and milk. Then—here's where starter is born—you divide the glop evenly into four Ziploc bags and give three of them to friends.

I am doomed! I do not have three friends who cook! Bill, however, is elated at the thought of taking bags of glop to work and carries three off Monday morning with fresh photocopies of the infamous recipe. Finally, it's time to get serious about turning the glop into bread. I pour the fourth bag of glop into a bowl—*not* metal!—and stir in oil, vanilla, eggs, and baking power. That's not a typo, that's what the recipe said I needed: "1-1/2 teaspoons of Baking Power." Heaven knows, I've needed that for years.

More ingredients are added, including "1 Large Box Vanilla Pudding." One wonders how big they made boxes of pudding when this recipe was first written. At the discount shopping clubs, you can now buy one box of pudding that will feed an entire Middle School. I guess at how large they mean "Large" to be, dump the batter into two pans that have been sugared (not floured), and bake for one hour.

The problem is, you have now baked your starter and you are left with nothing to squeeze for the next ten days, until Friends One, Two, and Three all give you back a new bag of starter (actually, your own starter in another life—hard to believe the Amish would go for reincarnation like this). In theory, the Friendship Bread I'm eating today could have molecules of the original starter from, say, Noah's mother. Imagine: centuries of starter, from Joan of Arc to Joan Baez, all in my mixing bowl. Maybe this is what Mother meant when she said, "Don't touch that! You never know where it's been."

A new, more immediate concern comes into view. Let's say you have a bag of three-day-old starter, plus another one from last week, and a third bag of glop walks in the door. It could take a separate calendar just to keep track of which one to squeeze when, or who needed stirring (*do not* use metal spoon). Or what if someone accidentally made their bread on Day Nine? Would it hold their oven hostage for twenty-four hours? Or, worse, what if you don't get around to tossing the Baking Power in there until Day Twelve? Will the bowl become a small nuclear device?

With a sigh of relief, I get to the final note at the bottom of the recipe: "This bread is forgiving." (Thanks, I needed that.) "If you miss a few days, just squeeze daily until you can bake it." It sounds so heartless, until I realize that's the same method I've used to keep my family happy for the last nine years: a quick squeeze, a kiss on the cheek, an "I promise we'll have more time together soon!" and I'm off to play in other kitchens.

My Amish neighbors may be on to something. Time to bring home my flour from afar and bake some bread. First, I need a friend with starter . . .

10

Rising Is Necessary— Shining Is Optional

She also rises while it is yet night, /
And provides food for her household.
Proverbs 31:15 NKJV

*I*n a book called *Get It All Done and Still Be Human,* authors Tony and Robbie Fanning offered this bit of sage advice: "A stretch of uninterrupted quiet to do something on your own can be hard to find if you live with others. Overlooked solution: Get up earlier or stay up later than everyone else." Wait a minute. That solution has been around at least 2,500 years, and this verse from Proverbs proves it.

My feet have hit the floor early hundreds of mornings, but few of them were by choice. Like those nights when caffeine/adrenaline/hormones/whatever make my eyes pop open at 4:00 A.M. and refuse to close again. I toss, I turn, I engage in a round of Quilt Wars with Bill, and I give up and get up. Once awake, I get tons of work done in that quiet house, but by 11:00 A.M., I'm ready for a little nappie.

Donna from Missouri said her husband would be so proud of her if she "got up at 6:00 A.M. every morning." At our house, you would have to specify, "Kitchen Standard Time," because that's the only clock that is consistently right. The bathroom clock is fast, which means if I'm brushing my teeth and look up at the time, panic ensues. Then, I step into the hallway, which features a clock that runs slow, so I sigh with relief and take my time about putting on my makeup. Arriving downstairs, I see the inerrant kitchen clock and hysteria resumes . . . it's later than I thought! I know what you're thinking: get a watch, Liz. I have six of them, which all move at different speeds. Some aren't even in the same time zone. Maybe I should be like the woman I saw once who was wearing a watch on a choker necklace, high and tight around her neck. Then, I could walk up to people, lift my chin, and ask, "What time is it?"

Baby Time

Time goes out the window when the children arrive anyway. Our firstborn showed up seventeen months after we married . . . and two weeks late. When we pulled into the hospital parking garage, the best parking spaces by the door had big signs: "Labor and Delivery Patients Only—15 Minutes." Beneath which a wise labor and delivery nurse had written, "Push! Push!"

I had my "What to Take to the Hospital" list in hand and a whole sack of goodies, as instructed:

- A small paper bag for hyperventilating (or to blow up and smash when things got dull)

- A plastic rolling pin for backache massage (or for tossing at Bill in a heated moment)

- Sugarless lollipops (good heavens, who is counting calories at a time like that?!)

- Heavy socks in case you get cold feet (that's ridiculous; during labor, it is *much* too late to get cold feet about having a baby!)

- A sandwich or other snack for Dad (Bill ate three complete meals in front of me, while I labored and couldn't touch a bite)

- A bottle of champagne (excellent for giving self-same husband a knot on the head for falling asleep just when the contractions were picking up speed)

- A going-home outfit for the new mother (get real—whatever you wore to the hospital will still fit beautifully)

One research study I read indicated that 85 percent of fathers have a strong fear of getting queasy in the delivery room. In truth, they almost never faint or do anything else to embarrass themselves, but Bill did indeed worry about how he might react to the whole thing.

I'm just glad he was there. As labor progressed, I begged him to find some passage from the Bible to encourage me. My Hebrew scholar consulted the concordance and solemnly read aloud the following passage:

> Pains have seized me like the pains of a woman in labor.
> I am so bewildered I cannot hear, so terrified I cannot see.
> My mind reels, horror overwhelms me.
>   (Isa. 21:3–4 NASB)

Thank you very much. Matthew finally made his entrance after twenty-six hours of labor. (All three nursing shifts went around and the first group came back. "She's still here!")

And what an entrance he made: eleven pounds, twelve-and-a-half ounces. Must've been that last half ounce that slowed things down. Healthy as can be and handsome to boot. I loved standing near the big glass windows of the nursery, incognito in my nightgown, as people would walk by and gawk through the glass. "Look at *that* one!" they would say. One gentleman kept looking at Matthew, then looking at me, then looking at Matthew. Finally he said, "Lady, is that your baby?" "Of course," I responded with a smile, "it's my two-year-old, in for repairs."

One of Each

Bonnie from California saw a sign in the window of her beauty shop that says: "Children by Appointment Only." What a great concept! Parents today often try to have their children spaced perfectly apart and end up perfectly spaced out. Children arrive whenever they please and please whenever they choose. We parents spend the first two years of their young lives trying to adjust to their schedules, and the next sixteen years trying to get them to adjust to ours, usually to no avail.

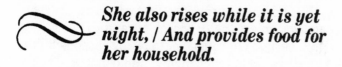

She also rises while it is yet night, / And provides food for her household.

Twenty months after Matthew was born, it was time for Baby Two to make the scene. A few weeks before the blessed day, my doctor ordered an ultrasound to determine the baby's size, maturity, and so forth. Bill and I hoped they could determine another important item while they were looking. We were so close to the delivery date, I thought it would be okay to find out if our new arrival would be the daughter I'd secretly wished for.

The morning of the ultrasound, I wore a pink dress and crossed my fingers. Although we would, of course, be delighted to have another wonderful son, a little sister for Matthew would have been *really* nice. I prepared myself to be jubilant, no matter what the results.

The technician was carefully scanning the screen for the pertinent information, then asked casually, "Would you like to know the sex of your baby?" "Yes!" we both chimed. "Well ..." she said, drawing it out for dramatic effect. "You say you already have a son? Lots of little boy baby clothes? Hm-m-m-m. Looks like you'll need to do some shopping!"

Knowing ultrasounds are not always 100 percent accurate on such things, we kept our news to ourselves (but I bought *lots* of pink). When the Big Day arrived, so did Miss Lillian. A little petite thing, at ten pounds, three and three-quarter ounces. The minute Lillian let out her first wail, my very musical doctor burst into song: "Happy Birthday to You!" Not to be outdone, and under the influence of very good painkilling drugs, I sang right along with her, in harmony, "Happy Birthday, dear Lillian! Happy Birthday to You!"

Gina from Kentucky wrote to ask, "Does childbirth cause memory loss?" Yes, but I don't remember why. Apparently, Gina lives in dread of going off to work and forgetting her child. Not to worry. That's why God gave them sirens. "Wa-a-a-a-a!!"

Which gets us back to "she also rises while it is yet night." Crying babies can and do get their parents out of bed at any hour. In order to be sure we both shared this unique opportunity equally, Bill and I took turns. The first trip to the crib was his, the second was mine, the third was his and so forth. As a nursing mother, certain trips just *had* to be my responsibility, but when it came to rocking, changing, and cuddling, Daddy handled that like a pro. On the other hand, when one of our toddlers started screaming with night terrors, we both launched out of bed so fast our feet didn't touch ground until we reached the hall.

Barbara from Ohio wrote to inform me that "people say the darndest things when you are the mother of triplets!" I'll bet they do. Things like:

- "Did you *want* triplets?" (like you can place an order for multiple gestation!)

- "Are you going to have any more?" (you tell me your reproductive plans, I'll tell you mine!)

- "But you seem so calm" (am I supposed to show them my stark-raving lunatic side right away?)

Whether it's three children or five or one precious child, Kathy from Ohio summed up the motivation we all share to rise and even shine:

> I would walk through fire for my child. No matter what sacrifices, no matter what is thrown at me, my child comes first. She is worth every extra pregnancy pound, every hour of labor, every night I'm tired and just want to sleep, every dirty diaper, every throw-up, every child care dollar. I wouldn't trade her away for all the gold in the world. I bet you'd agree.

Yes, Kathy, I would.

What Comes after Breakfast?

The only directive we're given in this verse is, basically, to get up early and make them breakfast. No problem, I'm a good mother; I make breakfast every morning. Pop Tarts. Even if it doesn't specifically mention it in Scripture, we also need to be sure they scrub their hands and faces. Although, as humorist Fran Lebowitz noted, "Even when freshly washed, children tend to be sticky."

Terry from Pennsylvania wrote, "I always like reading about other moms. It validates that I'm not crazy . . . it's my kids!" Fran said, "Give moms like me the okay to fall somewhere between June Cleaver and Roseanne." Now, that's a wide path. I would say almost all of us fall in the middle, most of the time. Not to say that there haven't been a few frightfully awful days, when I might scream, hiss, bellow, eat my children's Easter candy, or exhibit all manner of beastly behavior.

Leslie from Kentucky may become concerned when she reads this book, since she wanted some "insight on what it would be like to be married, work, and have children . . . I don't know if I want to attempt this!" Oh, by all means, *attempt.* Just be ready to forgive yourself, hug your kids, ask their forgiveness, and keep on going. Dottie is hoping I will "affirm that there is still *hope* for families in this troubled world!" Hope? Absolutely. An easy time of it? Not always.

Betty from Iowa remembers when she was working nights with a new baby, four older children, and *no* washing machine(!). Keeping baby's clothes clean was a problem. She said, "Many times when I was working nights at the hospital, I brought what looked like a bag of crafts but was really baby wash, because we had a laundry there. I felt guilty many times." We mothers gotta do what we gotta do.

The One That Got Away

Sometimes we get so busy, so tired, or so distracted that things just happen. Thank goodness most of the time they have a happy ending. Becky from Indiana confessed to one incident when she and her husband took separate cars to Grandma's house for dinner. Their three-year-old daughter fell asleep, so her father carried her out to the car and moments later both parents drove off for home.

Becky arrived first and went straight to bed, figuring her

husband would be along shortly with their daughter and tuck her
in. Meanwhile, he pulled in the drive and went right to bed, too,
confident that since he had put the little girl in his wife's car, she
had carried her up to bed. At 2:00 A.M., the doorbell rang, and a
tearful three-year-old was begging to get in! "I tried a little
harder after that," Becky admitted.

Mickey from Kansas had a close call on a shopping expedition
with her eighteen-month-old twin girls. She had stopped at a
parking lot plant sale and was pulling along the girls in one cart
and the plants in another. All was going well, the twins were
entertaining each other, and she had found four or five healthy
houseplants and paid for them.

> I was on my way back through all the plants when I saw a nice
> floor plant I'd overlooked before. I stopped both carts to turn
> around and look at this wonderful plant, and when I turned back,
> my babies were heading into the parking lot loaded with cars, and
> my cartful of plants was rolling that way too! Of course, I went
> running to rescue my girls first. [Good mother.] They were hav-
> ing the time of their lives *until* they rammed into the front fender
> of a brand-new pickup truck. The poor owner hadn't even had
> time to get his license plate yet!
>
> The girls weren't hurt but were scared and crying. The man in
> the truck was nice also and handled everything with our insur-
> ance agent (who called to verify that, indeed, two toddlers really
> did damage this man's truck!). By the way, the plant cart struck a
> parked car. Thank heavens for insurance!

"The One Thing I Wish I'd Done Differently As a Mother Is . . ."

This question about mothering produced some very wise,
very poignant answers from women with grown children who
had done the rise and shine routine umpteen times. "I wish I'd
hugged more and yelled less," said Debra from Alaska. "Not
been so strict," shared Joan from Arkansas. "Spent more time
with them in their beginning years," wrote Nancy from Florida.

Many responses fell into the more category: more . . . fun,
hugs, time, reading, playing, listening, accessibility, kisses, posi-

tive reinforcement, consistent discipline, and from Joanne from Montana, "Said 'I love you' more often."

Others, if they could do it all over again, would have done less: less . . . dusting, work, worry, and less emphasis on a perfectly clean house.

If Patricia had a second chance, she'd "have more kids!" Sandi would have "taken more time to enjoy each stage of development." The wisdom of experience shines through Judy's words: "Learn to realize 'teenagers' are a concept that gets better only with time."

When we paint a picture of motherhood that is all rosy, all joyful, we are doing younger women a disfavor. It is not always fun, and it is almost never easy. Shirley Rogers Radl, author of the controversial book *Mother's Day Is Over,* found that facing the realities of motherhood and the less-than-thrilling aspects of the job was an important turning point in her life. She wrote that it "was a new beginning for me—the beginning of self-acceptance, growth, and the rebuilding of my rapidly vanishing self-esteem. It was also a beginning for reaching out and grabbing those joyous times and cherishing them."[1]

Some of us are working without a road map, without family role models to help us find our way. Donna insisted, "I am carving out my own path," and Janet agreed that she and her partner are "making it up as we go!" And Martha cautioned me, "Don't forget single mothers. We are often so overwhelmed with survival that humor eludes us."

Even in two-parent homes, humor can remain hidden. Mary Jane wishes she'd "had more fun with them. Not been as serious." Indeed, Sandy described the perfect parent as "one who is able to smile and relax when the dishes are piled sky high and the weeds in the front yard are up to your waist!" For those of us who feel we don't know enough, or don't do enough, to be an expert parent, pediatrician T. Berry Brazelton says, "A child needs a flexible, humorous parent more than a professional 'child development expert' parent."[2]

Oh, that we could all rise *and* shine and come to the same conclusion someday that Barbara from Utah has reached: "I have no regrets. I did my best."

11

How She Did It All

... and portions to her maidens.
Proverbs 31:15b NASB

Just when we grind our teeth over the poor Proverbs 31 woman who not only has to get up early to feed her family, but must give "portions to her maidens" as well, a little knowledge of Hebrew comes to our rescue: the word *portion* doesn't mean a serving of food, it means "assignments, duties, tasks." In other words, she got up early to *give orders!* Now, that sounds more like it. As The Living Bible puts it, she "plans the day's work for her servant girls." I take this as a biblical directive to hire help! If we're going to "rise while it is yet night," we intend to take a lot of people with us.

Of course, we already have lots more help around the house than our proverbial sister did. Dishwashers, microwave ovens, vacuum cleaners, washing machines—these mechanical marvels have certainly made life easier for us. Or have they? Less time needed for housework should, in theory, mean more time for family fun and leisurely pursuits. A recent advertisement for Whirlpool Home Appliances suggests otherwise: "If only you could duplicate yourself. Imagine how much you'd get done." Even with appliances galore, we still can't seem to plow through all our "home work." Dottie declared, "My husband and I have figured out a really good system about the housework: neither one of us does it."

Hans Hoffman said, "The ability to simplify means to eliminate the unnecessary so that the necessary may speak." Simplification at the Higgs household has meant learning to clearly say no! I can announce with some measure of pride that I have mastered this principle in at least one area: I say no to housecleaning. There are whole businesses built around my willingness to turn this task over to the professionals.

People say, "Oh, you're so lucky you can afford help." Who says we can afford it? Bill and I have agreed that even if we get down to food stamps, an occasional visit from a housekeeper is a good investment in our sanity. For those of us who truly can't afford such help right now, keep in mind the good advice I found on a notepad: "Time management begins with a very large wastebasket."

Washday Blues

Even those of us who use the pros still end up doing our own laundry. There's something about having an outsider flinging around our underwear that just doesn't sit well with me. In order to tackle this thankless task, we observe the following Three Higgs Rules of Laundry:

1. There will always be dirty laundry.

This is very difficult for a "finish-the-job" kind of woman like me to accept. I'm not happy until every piece of clothing is washed, folded, and put away. I've tried lining up my family, collecting everything they're wearing, and stuffing it in the washer, just to have it all done (they are becoming less tolerant of this method). But even then, within minutes another small pile begins to gather in the hamper.

2. If it's clean, it isn't laundry.

With two kids and a husband who all appear to wear six outfits a day, laundry can begin to take over the house. Piles here and piles there, some clean, some dirty, many of uncertain status. Often the scenario goes like this: on my way out the door to a speech, I toss a load of clothes in the washer, push start, and leave. Hours later, my baby-sitter, wanting to be helpful, gathers up a load of wash, opens the washer lid, and . . . uh-oh, clothes. Cold, wet, flat against the sides. "Wonder how long this has been in here?" she thinks. "Better run it through again." In goes the detergent, softener, and water. She pushes start, forgets all about it, and leaves.

That night Bill thinks, "I'll bless Liz and do a load of laundry." So, he collects a pile and flips open the lid . . . yikes! Stuff in there. Cold, wet, flat against the sides. "No telling how long this has been sitting," he thinks. "Better wash it again." More water, more softener, more detergent. Luckily, Bill lives at our house, so he's there when the wash cycle ends and moves everything to the dryer. Whew . . . the clothes are spared!

Except Bill has not had "Folding 101" yet, so when the dryer stops, he stuffs all those nice clean, warm clothes down into a laundry basket and leaves the basket by the machine. When I walk in the door and see that jumble of wrinkled clothes, I sigh, "Better get started on some of this laundry." Into the washer it all goes.

There are outfits that have never escaped. Bill will look at them, finally worn to a frazzle and stuffed in the wastebasket, and say, "I never even saw you in that!"

3. When in doubt, sniff.

This seems the obvious solution. If it smells like Tide, put it on.

Who's in the Kitchen?

We often assume that the female of the species is more concerned with keeping things neat and clean than her male counterpart, but some of our men like it tidy too. "My husband would be so proud of me if I . . . cleaned house every day," said Nancy, or "picked up every object on a horizontal surface," wrote Sandy, or "de-junked the closets, attic, and drawers," said Sue Anne. Then there's Laura who thinks her husband would be thrilled if she "cleaned the litter box." For the cat, I assume.

I was plain curious: who is doing the work around our houses, anyway? Eight hundred women gave me a state of the union on this subject:

- Laundry was more of a she thing than a he thing, falling into our laps 56 percent of the time, and theirs just 3 percent. We share the job 30 percent of the time.

- Dusting and other cleaning sorts of activities fall on our shoulders 39 percent of the time, on his just 4 percent of the time, and are equally shared 24 percent. More than 17 percent of us portion out cleaning duties to hired help. Good news: our kids are also helpful with dusting, at 8 percent.

What did men help with most? Changing the light bulbs. And what did they help with least, of the dozen activities I listed? Cleaning the lint trap in the dryer. (As one wife said, "First he would have to know that such a thing existed!") I was surprised that, despite rumors to the contrary, men do occasionally change the toilet tissue rolls when they are empty—sometimes without even being told to do so.

At our house, I'm the bathroom tissue changer. Had I not portioned this task to myself, in a few months small cardboard tubes with three sheets of tissue still attached would be lurking in every corner of the bathroom, on shelves, and on the back of the toilet. It's simply too important to leave to chance. For the record, 68 percent of us like it to unwind *over,* and 32 percent like it to dispense from *under* the roll. It's not simply an aesthetic decision, since research has shown that the *overs,* on the average, earn $20,000 more each year than the *unders.* It's enough to make you toss down this book and flip over those rolls *right now.*

Training Techniques

The fact is, more men would be willing to help us if they just knew where to begin. They need to be told that there is not a chromosome for domestic skills and that *we* had to learn this stuff, which means they can too! And they need lots of applause. Let's not get huffy or resentful—just start clapping. It also helps to show them exactly how we'd like tasks to be done, describing everything in detail and giving hands-on instruction when needed. Finally, we need to make it worth their while.

I am living with a success story. Bill washes 99 percent of the dishes in our house, virtually every dish! How did I manage this? I am allergic to Joy—not the experience, the dishwashing liquid. (I'm probably fine with Ivory, but I buy Joy.) Plus, Bill does 80 percent of the cooking. This is a survival move, but he also enjoys it. These days, I bring *him* cookbooks from different regions of the country, which he reads like novels then selects a recipe to try for dinner that night. Amazing.

﹏﹏ *... and portions to her maidens.*

Teaching him how to clean the house was not as easy. There are lots of gadgets, sprays, rags, and mops to confuse things. Vacuuming seemed the most "macho" activity of the bunch, so I suggested he give it a try. His blank stare told me I needed to offer more instruction. A good trainer always takes a familiar idiom and grafts it onto the new concept, so that's exactly what

I did—literally. I took an old lawn mower handle, tied it onto the vacuum cleaner, pointed to the carpet, and said, "Mow!" Things were going great until he brought in the Weed Eater.

We all have our own areas of domesticity where we'd like to take advantage of our man's talents. Maryann would love her man to "run the vacuum, wash dishes, do laundry, and send flowers in the same day." Jacki agrees that an ideal husband "helps out without being asked and surprises you by cooking supper (or calling for pizza is fine too!)." For Susan, if he just wouldn't "splash water all over the mirror just after you clean it," she would be happy.

Shelly from Kansas has a helpful hubby, who washes most of their laundry and shares childcare responsibilities. "I'm so fortunate to have a helpmate like him," she wrote. "My friends often ask how I 'changed' him. I didn't change him. He was always willing to help, but he didn't know how. He learned how to do things by watching me and asking questions. I also learned if I wanted his help, I had to be less of a perfectionist! (If the dishes are put away, what does it matter that the measuring cup is on the shelf with the drinking glasses?)"

Our children are woefully underutilized in the home care department. Less than 2 percent help with cooking, about 3 percent help with laundry—this, when easily half the dirty clothes are theirs! Their fault? I doubt it. The truth is, most of us stay up till all hours, washing and folding clothes, feeling every bit the martyr, when our kids could easily be given this responsibility. My own mother never showed me how to use the washer and dryer until I went to college. I don't intend to make the same mistake, although I suppose age five is a tad young for ironing. Drat.

Linda from Pennsylvania received a needlepoint plaque from her daughter that reads, "Dust is a protective covering for furniture." Linda's response was: "Hallelujah! I generally clean only when company is expected and no one seems to mind." Her motto is, "Clean enough to be healthy and dirty enough to be happy."

Anyway, as Barbara Billingsley from *Leave It to Beaver* fame pointed out, "Even June Cleaver didn't keep her house in perfect order—the prop man did it."

12
Across the Fruited Plain

She considers a field and buys it; /
From her profits she plants a vineyard.
Proverbs 31:16 NKJV

*L*ike so many successful women today, some of our
biblical role models were real estate professionals. Women have always had a knack for buying
and developing property. The text doesn't suggest that she
bought and sold fields continually, but she did buy this
particular one.

The Amplified translation sheds a revealing light on exactly
what it meant for her to consider buying that field: "... [expand-
ing prudently and not courting neglect of her present duties by
assuming other duties]."

"Courting neglect?" Well, if that isn't an accurate description
of me! Whenever I take on a new challenge, Bill says, "That's
fine, but what activity are you going to drop in order to make this
one happen?" "Drop?" I ask, with that hand-in-the-cookie-jar
look on my face. "Gosh, I wasn't going to drop anything. I figured
I'd just squeeze it in during the commercials."

Playing "Beat the Clock"

The time management books I've seen (and believe me, *this*
isn't one of them!) all encourage us to maximize every single

waking moment: exercises to do at our desk, Scripture verses to memorize at red lights, language tapes to listen to while we jog, thank-you postcards to carry in our purse for a spare second while standing in line at the bank. Sure, we can accomplish more, but the real question is, "Why?" Is all the energy output worth the information input? No wonder, when asked what we wanted less of and more of in our life, we so often paired them together like this:

We Want More . . .	And Less . . .
Sleep!	Rush, Rush, Rush!
Time off	Deadlines
Energy	Commitments
T•I•M•E	Aggravation
Time for self	Responsibility
Relaxation	60-hour work weeks
Free time	Pressure to do more

The one thing we want *more* of is the one variable we can't change: *time*. More than four hundred of us mentioned it specifically on the surveys. Yet, whether we look back to biblical times, or to the turn of any century, there have always been the same number of seconds in a minute, minutes in an hour, and hours in a day—even if we called them something else.

As the old chestnut goes, "Time flies whether you are having fun or not!" Maybe when we say we need more time, which we can't control, we really mean we need fewer items on our to do list, which we can control. Dolores from New York longed for "more priority-setting ability" and "less hesitance." No doubt about it, *no* isn't hard to pronounce, but it's very hard to say.

We know instinctively that the commitments we have taken on are wearing us out. And we want to change. Bev's words leaped off the page of her survey: "Help me out of being over-committed!" Carolyn said, "Tell me how to manage time—or how I can laugh about not having enough of it!" Kim hoped this book would "provide insight on changing (that is, lowering) your standards. How to say *no* and mean it."

That's a two-part request. First, I don't think *any* woman should really lower her standards. Rather, we should elevate those that matter the *most* and lighten up on the others. For example, as the deadline for this book approached, more and more time was spent at the computer and less and less time was spent with a feather duster in my hand. That was as it should be. The book was more important; the dusting could wait. To my knowledge, the Dust Police are not planning a visit to my house anytime soon.

One could say, "Well, if you wrote for two hours every day for a year, you could still keep the house clean *and* finish the book, and that would be more disciplined." If that's your work style, fine, but it definitely is not mine. I work in Passion Mode. When I get excited and enthusiastic about something, look out. I live, breathe, eat, and drink that subject until it has run its course, then I take a short siesta before diving into the next project.

What this means is that I must plan ahead for when passion strikes (most married women with young children already know how to do this!). In a workload sense, it means blocking out two or three months for writing (or working on whatever special project I might be involved with) during which some extra help, paid or otherwise, will be needed around the house.

By blocking out, by no means am I suggesting we exclude our loved ones. I mean, set aside other outside commitments and tackle one major project at a time. I find that the more consuming that project is, the more I cherish the routine of family life to keep me balanced and to keep my sense of humor intact. Susan from New Hampshire recalls, "One evening, while we were eating dinner, the doorbell rang. My husband left the table to answer it, and of course it was a salesman. When he came back to the table, our four-year-old daughter said, 'Who was it, Daddy?' He replied, 'A stranger.' She quickly asked, 'Did he offer you candy?'"

In the Long Run . . .

In his book, *Bonkers,* Dr. Kevin Leman noted, "Getting your priorities straight and sticking to them is one of the most difficult tasks in life."[1] What makes it easier for me is consciously listening to God's voice, my husband's voice, and my own voice as they all resonate in my heart. This requires ignoring the voices of media and peer pressure and filtering out the you shoulds from well-meaning but ill-informed sources.

Some questions worth asking ourselves might be:

- Will this activity matter one week from today? One month? One year?

- Is there someone who does it better than I do, to whom I might delegate this activity?

- Does it satisfy a heart need for me or someone I love very much?

- What are the ramifications if I *don't* do it?

- What are the outcomes if I *do* do it?

This exercise might be a little much for considering whether you should take out the trash. The answer there is yes! But for any activity that will require even a modest drain on our time/money/energy resources, it could provide the pause we need to reconsider and say, "No, thanks."

My daughter, Lillian, who turned five while I was functioning in Passion Mode for this book, declared, "The next time they ask you to write a book, just tell them, 'No way—I have to tuck my children into bed!'" I laughed, but I listened too. At night when the words flowed most easily, Bill would often kiss them goodnight with a promise that "Mama will see you in the morning." After Lillian's comment, I knew that Passion Mode needed to be parked for a moment while I went upstairs to hug my children and hear their prayers.

After all, look at the five questions above in light of that nightly tuck-in:

- *Yes,* those precious times will matter in years to come, to both of us.

- *No*, there is no one else who can do "Mama" better.

- *Yes*, it satisfies a heart need for me *and* for my loved ones.

- Ramifications if I don't? Disappointment for them. Guilt for me.

- Outcomes if I do? They sleep better, and I work better, knowing I took time to do something that *really* mattered.

(Uh-oh, does this count as a tip or—heavens—a list?!) Just file it under personal experience and my desire to develop good discernment in such matters.

Next to *Time,* We'd Love to Have More . . .

Money, of course, was our second choice after time, but it was a distant second. Elaine St. James, in her book *Simplify Your Life,* observed, "The secret to happiness is not in getting more but in wanting less."[2] Plenty of us feel like we have traded time for money and are now considering the impact it has had on us and our families and the fruit of our efforts to make money and mother as well.

 She considers a field and buys it; / From her profits she plants a vineyard.

According to our surveys, those of us with kids at home are averaging 42.3 hours a week at work. Throw in commuting time, plus any work that's dragged home with us, and that makes for one full week for a working mom. Although we hear plenty about mothers working half-time, part-time, or flex-time, the surveys showed that only 14 percent of working moms put in fewer than thirty hours a week, averaging nineteen hours a week at work. Part-time work often seems like the perfect solution, but Karen Hull, author of *The Mommy Book,* warns that among her friends who tried it, "working at a part-time job was like buying a five-pound turkey. By the time they got rid of the skin and bones—i.e. the hidden expense—there was very little meat left."[3]

At the other end of the scale were the nearly 18 percent of us who work more than 50 hours a week, with some exhausted mothers logging 60, 70, even 80 hours a week at work. Whew!

When asked, "What level of guilt, if any, do you feel about not being with your children full time?" 32 percent of working mothers circled eight, nine, ten, or Guilt to the Max. These women often did not feel comfortable with their childcare arrangements or with their long hours or both. In most cases, they had younger children, when the internal and external pressures to be home are strongest.

Diane notes her guilt "probably is due to outside comments." Melanie feels Guilt to the Max about putting her three children in a childcare center, even though the center is at her work site. She worries that "they spend more waking hours with strangers than at home." Pamela feels a big dose of guilt because "my mother was a full-time mom."

A Hoosier mom poignantly voiced the dilemma that many of us face: "Am I sacrificing important time with my child to provide less important tangible benefits? Are my priorities skewed? Am I being selfish?" This is a woman who loves her work, has her two-year-old son safely cared for by his grandmother, and is frankly not certain she is ready for full-time motherhood. "I'm not sure I could be as excited about mothering if that's all I did twenty-four hours a day."

Even with the best situation for our families, we experience guilt. Donna from Nevada, also with young children, also with a husband to care for them, still circled a nine on her guilt meter, saying, "I should be home, providing them a good environment." Joan admits, "It's hard when they cry when I leave in the morning." She puts her guilt at a seven, even though her kids are cared for by a competent nanny. Lissa, working mother of four, is grateful her children are in the care of their grandparents, but still circled a ten "because I remember the things I missed out on growing up when my mother worked full-time."

Mothers of older kids aren't exempt from guilt, either. Mickey is "afraid I'm missing something" when she is apart from her pre-teenagers and also worries "what others think."

All this to say: If you are struggling with these issues, you are not alone. We are all trying to find our way through the maze and onto the best path—which is not, perhaps, the same path for each of us.

On the Other Hand

Bill and I often send each other greeting cards, not just for the usual occasions, but sometimes just because. He covers them with little personal notes, artistic touches, and inside jokes, so I can't bear to toss them out. One card is dated September 1990—Matthew was three, Lillian was eighteen months old, and my speaking career had suddenly taken off. I was trying hard to gear down my business (funny—still my number one problem today), and Bill's encouraging card included this note: "It's been a long, hard day, and for that matter a long, hard week (for _that_ matter, a long, hard year!!). I love you, Liz, and want to help you find a lifestyle that is fulfilling to you and yet practical for all of us. Let me love you through this tough time." He did, and he does.

As a couple, Bill and I continue to discuss, adjust, negotiate, and hammer out a lifestyle that honors God, his Word, and our own God-given abilities and desires. By staying in tune and in touch with each other, we can keep the guilt meter on low and the fruit meter on high!

Many women surveyed have found out how to do the same. Michele from Indiana circled three on the guilt meter, and wrote, "A working woman is who I am—it's the only kind of mother I know how to be." Becky is able to feel almost guilt-free because of two important considerations: "If I'm not home with the children, my husband is," and "the company I work for allows my family to come first—there are not many companies that do." Not yet, but it's coming.

The other mothers who registered nearly guilt-free are those who have chosen a work schedule that most matches their children's lives (teacher), or who have their own business (selling Mary Kay Cosmetics, Tupperware, or Longaberger Baskets) with flexible hours.

Some of us have found job situations that balance our financial requirements and mothering needs very well. Isabel from New York, whose children are both teenagers, works 20-30 hours a week so she is "there when they are, and when I'm not there, they are learning to be independent and self-reliant." Other women entrust their husbands with childcare duties, like Carol, mother to three youngsters under age five, who insists that "I'd go nutty at home. I like being a working woman . . . my husband does a super job" at home.

Alice, mother of a four-year-old, feels nearly guilt-free because "I give to him completely and easily when we are together because I'm a happy person and love my job." Many mothers echoed that experience of being really focused on their children when they are with them. And other moms wanted their children to have a wider view of life than their own living room. Susan said, "There's a lot more to this world than I alone can give them. I enjoy sharing their daily experiences and talking to them at the end of the day."

Getting Rid of the Guilt

The phrase that kept popping up under the "why I feel guilty" section was I'm too tired to ". . . cook, play, help with homework, taxi to activities, and so on." No wonder we are tired! No generation has tried to accomplish more, been offered as many choices, or faced more negative influences.

And everywhere we turn, we find someone who has The Solution. Or they hold up warning signs that do not fit our situation. Like the sign I saw in a ladies rest room in Winner, South Dakota. On the wall next to the mirror was one of those cloth towel dispensers, where the towel comes down in a loop. Above the towel dispenser was a sign that read: "Warning! Do not attempt to swing from towel."

Wait a minute . . . have you ever stepped into a rest room and found a woman swinging from the towel? The thought had never occurred to me. Now I'm looking at it. How would you do it? Put your arm in the loop? Your leg? One thing is certain: If you ever walk into a rest room now and find a towel draped all over the floor, you've been warned!

Guilt can be a warning sign, too, but it can also simply be an indicator of the need to stop and evaluate. My own approach to guilt is to change the situation or change my attitude but never sit there soaking in guilt stew!

Instead, I pray. And listen. I look at *all* the possible options before me. I put my imagination to work and come up with every method of balancing work and home life conceivable, no matter how wild or impractical they may seem on paper. Then I discuss them with my loved ones and see which ideas should be tossed, and which ones are worth serious consideration.

At some point, we may choose to bring in a professional—a counselor, a career consultant, an accountant, a financial ad- viser—to sort through the specifics. Especially for those of us who may be working outside of the home for only one reason— money—it would be wise to have a tax expert calculate the differences in taxes we would pay with one income versus two. Then we need to figure out exactly what working costs us in childcare, clothing, lunches, commuting expenses, and so forth. The numbers may point to a definite need to work, and that's fine. At least we'll know, and we can begin to let go of the guilt.

For a woman who has a low salary and high expenses associ- ated with her job, it may make more sense to stay home and invest her efforts there, which might significantly lower guilt and raise joy. Until we "crunch the numbers," it's hard to say with authority "I work because we need the money."

The key is to avoid the "good mothers stay home/bad mothers go to work" message, in favor of: "A good mother does what is best for *all* the members of the family, including herself." Melodie Davis, author of *Working, Mothering and Other "Minor" Dilemmas,* thinks "it would be helpful not to think in terms of whether a working mom is 'bad' or 'good' for children. Being a good mom or a bad mom is related to how a woman feels about herself and her children."[4]

Most of us want it to be simpler than that. Those on the conservative end of things insist, "Real mothers stay home because it is our job to care for our children!" Those with a more liberal agenda might say, "Real mothers work, and it's the government's responsibility to provide childcare!" For the vast majority of us who are somewhere in the middle—grateful to be moms, grateful to be working, but not so sure how to pull it all off—it's very confusing.

Elizabeth Cody Newenhuyse, in her book *The Woman with Two Heads,* celebrates the complex nature of life as a devoted mother *and* a devoted career woman. After all, "God created complexity. No one is all one thing. The discovery of complexity, of the pain that comes with many good gifts, can free us from corrosive guilt, worry, frustration, from thinking we should manage our lives better. It's okay not to have all the answers."[5]

Good, because I don't have all the answers. I'm not even sure I'm asking the right questions when I consider the fields before me. I simply focus on serving God, loving people, and doing my best to make a difference in my own spheres of influence. It's not necessary to do more. And it's not satisfying to do less.

13

Personal Best

**She girds herself with strength, /
And strengthens her arms.**

Proverbs 31:17 NKJV

Say it isn't so . . . not aerobics and strength training in the Bible! Relax. King Lemuel's mother was not hoping to get Jane Fonda for a daughter-in-law. She wanted a bride who was "fit for a king," namely, her son. This kind of fitness comes from hard work, not from working out. An excellent woman is ready for action rather than for a life of leisure. The Living Bible says she is "energetic, a hard worker"; and, according to the New International Version, she "sets about her work vigorously." Like Shelly from Kansas described the ideal wife, she's "the 'support beam' in a home. She's the one who sets the tone for rest of the family."

The Amplified version once again gives us the whole picture, defining this strength as "spiritual, mental, and physical fitness for her God-given task." We all know, at least theoretically, how to develop physical fitness: eat healthful foods and exercise our muscles.

I love the classified ad I saw in (of all places) a decorating magazine. It listed an 800 number to call and learn about the "biggest breakthrough in the diet industry in twenty-five years!

Diet one day; eat the next twenty-four hours!" Gee, that's the way I've always done it, haven't you? Besides, as one of my favorite magnets says, "God must have loved calories—He made so many of them."

For mental fitness, we need to feed our minds positive, accurate information and put that knowledge into practice. Eleanor Doan said, "The mind is as strong as its weakest think." We never outgrow the need to expand and educate our minds. With college courses, continuing education programs, and whole libraries full of knowledge waiting for us out there, we are surrounded with food for the intellect. As Beverly Sills said, "There is a growing strength in women but it's in the forehead, not the forearm."[1]

But what about spiritual fitness? The best diet is "the pure milk of the word," (1 Peter 2:2 NKJV), "solid food . . . for the mature" (Heb. 5:14 NIV), the "fruit of the Spirit" (Gal. 5:22 NKJV), and "the bread of life" (John 6:48 NKJV). Having feasted on such fine spiritual food, we are ready to exercise "obedience" (Heb. 5:8 NKJV) and be "clothed with humility" (1 Peter 5:5 NKJV). Even One-a-Day vitamins can't produce that kind of strength in your life!

Endurance Training

I first met Dauna from Ohio through her survey, then from some of her writings, and finally in person at one of my presentations. This woman is the embodiment of how to develop spiritual and mental fitness, a mother who watched her thirteen-year-old daughter deal with the reality of her five-year-old sister's bout with cancer and who grew stronger because of it.

I tried to protect my older daughter from it all and never had her at the hospital with us when her younger sister was so very, very sick from chemotherapy. So all the older one saw was the attention showered on her sister, including hundreds of gifts and cards from friends. I'm certain she was jealous of all of it. Then, during the last round of chemotherapy, she was at the hospital working as a volunteer. It was the first time she saw how grim her little sister's hospital stays really were. It was as though a light bulb went on in her head. I believe sometimes we do a disservice to our children by protecting them from the harsh realities a little too much.

She's right: strength comes from handling adversity, not avoiding it. The strongest women I know got that way by going through, rather than around, life's mine fields. It's a workout, all right, but the spiritual muscles it produces are worth it. As Louisa May Alcott said, "I am not afraid of storms, for I am learning how to sail my ship."

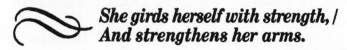 *She girds herself with strength, / And strengthens her arms.*

Nearly half of the speaking I do is for healthcare audiences, who sail their ships through rough waters every day they show up for work. In their ongoing struggles to keep us all healthy, they are discovering that more than just the physical self is involved. Increasingly, they're seeing that mental and spiritual wellness contribute to a patient's recovery as well. In his book, *Head First: The Biology of Hope,* Norman Cousins outlined some of the positive emotions that are needed to promote healing: love, hope, faith, the will to live, festivity, purpose, and determination.[2] Sounds like the fruit of the Spirit to me.

Seeking Strengths, Finding Weaknesses

The list Cousins proposed includes the very qualities most of us want in our lives. As a means of determining our strengths and weaknesses, I asked women, "What is the one character trait you'd really like to change about yourself?" Some of the things we wrote down included:

"Have more fun"
"Less grumble, grumble, grumble"
"Listen more"
"Less quick to judge"
"More trusting that everything will work out"
"Less serious about everything"

"More passionate"
"Less procrastination, but not right now" [very funny]

Many expressed a need for increased confidence, to be "more self-assured," as Carol from Maryland put it, or as Patty wrote, to have less "self-doubt . . . right?"

Four responses seemed to surface again and again, in no particular order:

- Impatience
- Poor self-esteem
- Procrastination
- Perfectionism (what Barbara from Ohio called "nit-picki-ness")

The way I see it, all four stem from the same root problem, aptly expressed by Jan from Washington: "too high expectations of others and myself."

Expecting Too Much from Ourselves and Others—maybe we should label it the "ETMOO Syndrome!" It's safe to say that the majority of us suffer from it. Because we want things done *perfectly,* we *procrastinate* rather than do something wrong. Our realization that we are not perfect leads to *poor self-esteem.* Then, because we want others to be perfect, too, we are *impatient* with their imperfection. It's a vicious cycle, this ETMOO.

The only antidotes I can offer for this malady are grace, love, and laughter. Grace, to assure us we are forgiven for our imperfections. Love, to remind us that we are indeed valuable "as is." And laughter, to help us relax and find the humor in our less-than-perfect condition.

What Will They Think of Next?

For those of us who long to do a better job of, say, staying in touch with loved ones, there's a new software program billed as a "relationship management program designed to help you stay up to date in nine areas of your personal and business relationships." (FYI: The *perfectionists* will love this; those of us with *poor self-esteem* won't think we deserve it; the *impatient* among us may think relationships aren't worth managing; and the *procrastinators* will think it's a great idea, but will never get around to ordering it!)

Here's how it works. After we program in the necessary date information for the presumably dozens, even hundreds, of people in our lives, the computer program prompts us to review data on a person when, say, their birthday is coming up. Then, a handy database gift catalog "allows you to fax, mail, or call toll-free to order products ranging from flowers to tropical cruises with just a click of a button." Amazing. (Should my birthday produce a prompt on your screen, please click "tropical cruise.")

In theory, it's a great idea. How many times have we forgotten the birthdays of coworkers, friends, even loved ones because we neglected to check our calendars? Still, it's too calculated for me, too much hardware (the computer) and not enough software (the heart). I would hate to think that I received a birthday card generated by a PC and signed by an ink jet.

My father has a method that produces the same results—remembering important days in the lives of those he cares about—but with a much more human approach. The first of each year, he takes his long birthday list—there are more than thirty of us in his immediate family, not including great-grandkids!—and heads for the card shop. He carefully chooses a greeting card for each person, one that says exactly what he would like it to say, brings the cards home, puts on stamps, addresses them, and files them into a desk calendar by the date they should be mailed. Voila! Now that's "relationship management." Although I have yet to get a tropical cruise, a birthday card on time is a real treat.

Encouraging One Another—Even Yourself!

There's another important relationship that deserves to be nurtured: your friendship with yourself. In January 1993, I wanted a different sort of resolution for the year ahead. Instead of focusing on the usual, specific, gotta do stuff—get up earlier, walk thirty minutes, eat more fiber—I wrote down one simple goal. Three words that could be applied daily, as I saw fit. Words that would produce a changed life, which is really what we're looking for when we resolve to do something new.

Here is what I wrote:

I know. You were expecting something . . . deeper, more significant sounding. But listen to what happened.

First, to give my phrase-for-the-year emphasis, I typeset it on my computer in a lovely, flowing typeface and printed it on pristine white paper. Then, taking a green ink pad and an ivy rubber stamp, I surrounded the words with colorful greenery and framed them in a silver, heart-shaped frame. (I felt like a third grader working on a school project, but what the heck . . . it was *fun!*) I placed the frame on the shelf in my bathroom, right next to the blow dryer and the velcro rollers.

Experience Beauty Daily. Each morning it hit me differently. Take an extra five minutes for a facial scrub and mask was one day's interpretation, and so I did. Pick fresh blackberries for breakfast was the thought that came to mind another morning. (Okay, Bill did the picking, but I ate them—out of an exquisite stoneware bowl.) Beautiful. Shave above the knee was yet another day's choice.

One morning, I spent ten indulgent minutes reading a favorite book that had nothing to do with work, child raising, or getting "buns of steel." It was just for enjoyment, just for me. Now on my third year of this method of motivation, I'm still experiencing something special each day (in 1994 it was Grace, in 1995, Peace.) Why is this simple reminder working, when all those to do lists over the years did not? Several reasons.. . .

1. There's plenty of room for creativity and no room for *should* or *must*.

2. The goal is experience, not perfection.

3. The measure of success is aesthetic, not numerical.

4. The reminder notice itself brings pleasure and a gentle, daily nudge in the right direction.

Sometimes we just need to encourage ourselves. I was delighted with the responses from women who have developed that strength of character that says, as Janet from Nebraska phrased it, "I'm okay the way I am." "I am not perfect, but there is nothing I want to change . . . right now!" admitted Sheila. Or, as JoAnne said, "Being forty, I finally like my character traits."

While we all long to remain flexible, if we've come to a place of peace and acceptance, the time for adapting and contorting may be over and the time for knowing and sharing our strength may be at hand.

14
Using the Sense(s) God Gave You

She perceives that her merchandise is
good (NKJV).
She senses that her gain is good
(NASB).
She sees that her trading is profitable
(NIV).

Proverbs 31:18

We need all three translations to make sense out of
this verse (pun intended). The "sense-ible"
woman uses all five of her senses—sight, hearing,
smell, taste, and touch—to determine if her labors and the fruits
they produce are worth the effort. We've heard about women
having a sixth sense, or intuition, but we are also called upon to
use the five senses that God gave us more effectively to determine the profit of our efforts.

The Eyes Have It
Yogi Berra said, "You can observe a lot just by watching."
Women watch everything but especially people's faces. We're
looking for clues, for shades of meaning. We process all the
visual messages, the body language, the facial language, the
telltale signs of stress, fear, or anger. Some men are able to carry

on a conversation behind a newspaper. Women cannot. We have to watch others' faces while they speak to us; we want to look into their eyes to make sure we're communicating, no matter who is talking.

When she went back to school to become a nurse-practitioner, Cindy from Iowa "had to live two hours away, Monday through Friday for sixteen weeks, and my children were two and six at the time. When my daughter was playing with her doll house, I would watch as she put the family at the dinner table—Dad, brother, sister, but no Mom!" Instead, her daughter had the other doll sitting on the roof of the house. "Mom's at school," she explained.

Cindy reported, "I guess she adjusted to the situation pretty well after all. I'm happy to say that Mom is now sitting at the table with the rest of the family!" This wise mother could see for herself that her labor was neither in vain, nor did it have any long term ill effects on her family.

There are times, however, when we miss things that happen right before our eyes. Monica from Texas remembers when her grandfather passed away, and she and her eight-year-old daughter went to the funeral. The casket was open at the front of the church, and the two of them sat in a nearby pew, crying. While Monica was looking through her purse for a tissue, the casket was quietly closed and rolled to the back of the church. The young girl looked up first, noticed the casket was gone, and whispered to her distracted mother, "Where did Granddad go?"

Monica whispered as she blew her nose, "Honey, Granddad has gone to heaven to be with the angels."

Her wide-eyed daughter replied, "Man, that was fast! I didn't know they took the casket too!"

Do You Hear What I Hear?

When I ask my female audiences, "Do you think women hear better than men do?" the groan of agreement is deafening. We can all think of instances when men heard the words that were spoken, but *not* what was being communicated.

When Thanksgiving was supposed to be celebrated at our house a few years back, my in-laws kindly suggested we eat at a historic local restaurant on Thanksgiving Eve instead, so Bill and I could spend the long weekend working on restoring our new/old house. My guess is they also remembered another holiday at our house when it took me until 9:00 P.M. to get dinner on the table. In any case, off to that fancy restaurant we went on Turkey Eve to enjoy a delicious multicourse meal, with not one dish to wash. I was in heaven.

Near the end of dinner, Bill's dear grandmother, then in her early eighties, murmured softly, "Well, I don't know what I'm going to do tomorrow. Eat a turkey sandwich, I guess."

Driving home later that evening, I said, "Oh, Bill, we must never do this again. Nanny was so disappointed."

He looked at me in complete shock. "No, she wasn't! She said she was going to eat a turkey sandwich."

Did he hear the words? Every single one. Did he hear what she said? Not exactly. Women listen between the lines, between the words, for the tone, the energy, and the nuance of expression that really tell us what's being said. This isn't a fault-finding mission, just a fact-finding one: we women hear better. Most of the time.

Patty from Utah was confused when her four-year-old daughter came home from a friend's house, insisting that she wanted a zucchini.

"A what?" Patty asked.

"You know, like you wear when you go swimming. A zucchini!"

Then, there's the daughter who went home from Betty's class in North Carolina and told her mother, "I must have permission to take your slip to school tomorrow!" Sure enough, the next day, the child showed up at her teacher's desk carrying a brown paper bag with a pale pink size 38 undergarment inside, rather than what the teacher really wanted: a permission slip.

A Fragrant Aroma

And how well developed is our sense of smell? Bill buys me Estee Lauder's *Beautiful* perfume, not for his benefit, but for mine: I adore it. It's always under the Christmas tree, and to be a good steward, I make that bottle last a whole year. I get six squirts a day, then duck under the "fallout" to try and catch every little drop.

Women can always tell what fragrance their friends are wearing. "Oh, is that *White Shoulders*? Is that *Obsession*? Is that *Giorgio*?" We can "name that scent" with one whiff. On the other hand, if we extended a forearm featuring the six finest scents that a perfume department offered, some of our men would sniff their way past all six, get to our fingertips with the faint scent of onions from last night's dinner, and say, "Mm-m-m . . . that's delicious! Can you bottle that?"

I tried to wear an inexpensive musky thing one summer because I'd been too extravagant with my *Beautiful* all spring. The discount scent got tossed in the trash when Bill stepped into our bedroom right after I sprayed my sixth squirt of the cheap stuff and said, "Is that a new room deodorizer?"

A Matter of Taste

On the question, "Do men have as finely developed a sense of taste as women do?" it's tougher to get consensus. After all, there are famous male chefs the world over who do, indeed, have terrific tasters.

I can only go by my own limited, yet thorough, understanding of the American male taste buds that I have had to cook for over the years. That is to say, they ate my food, so they must have no sense of taste at all. Bill, bless his heart, will eat anything. We often have what at our house is affectionately called, "Chicken Done Some Tricky Way." These are boneless, skinless chicken breasts (aren't you proud of me?), done on the top of the stove in a non-stick pan with something thrown in for flavor. Could be mustard, could be ginger, could be honey, could be minced garlic, you just never know. For that matter, I never know. Which means if I hit on a really tasty combination, and Bill says, "This is wonderful! Can we have it again?" I have to be honest with him: "No. I'm not sure what it is." *And he eats it anyway*. File this under no taste or blind trust. Or maybe, true love.

Even Esther Didn't Wear Polyester!

What of our sense of touch? Consider two fabrics: 100 percent silk and 100 percent polyester. The first is ultra smooth, airy, liquid, floats on air, yet has a depth and texture all its own. The color and sheen, both dull and vibrant at the same time, are a dead giveaway. We can pass a woman at the mall, smile and say, "Lovely silk dress!" and she nods her thanks. Silk looks like nothing else but . . . silk.

Not to say that silk-like 100 percent polyester doesn't give it a valiant try. It, too, is smooth. A bit too smooth. Also light, but not quite the same sense of substance. Wonderfully washable and very tough, it has many qualities silk does not have, including the higher price tag. But we can tell, even with a glance, and definitely with a touch, which one is which.

Yet, if I hold up an expensive silk nightgown and a slinky polyester version for Bill to touch, he simply says, "Ooooh!" and wants to know how quickly I can slip into either one, bless him.

 *She senses that her gain is good.*

The Sixth Sense: Intuition

So how should the perceptive woman utilize her five finely developed senses? Among other things, I use them to monitor my family carefully for signs of distress. Yes, my career is successful, but what effect does it have on my home life? This is not in any way to suggest that troubles at home stem from Mom going to work, of course. It's just our responsibility to perceive and assess and, sometimes, adjust. Working dads must do this too.

Using her eyes, ears, and heart, Leesa from Kentucky knows that the choices she has made for herself and her family were positive ones. After earning a five-year engineering degree and working for the government for three years, she retired to start her family. When her youngsters went off to school, they traveled in Mom's van, not the bus. Back and forth they went, day in and day out. "In the car," she said, "you have your kids' undivided attention. We have had many meaningful hours of conversation—about 1,800 hours in ten years! When we finally traded in our van, it had 158,000 miles on it." For Leesa, every mile was worthwhile. She "sensed that her gain was good."

Our children also use their five senses to assess the world around them. Donna Otto, author of *The Stay at Home Mom*, suggests that "there are three major qualities our children need to see in our lives: truthfulness in words or actions, faithfulness, and gratitude."[1] Her advice doubly suits the working mother, who must display those same three attributes at home *and* at work. Our children's eyes and ears are attentive in both arenas.

Sally from Indiana described the time her ten-year-old daughter was at home after school, waiting for both her working parents to get home.

> We had cautioned her to *never* tell anyone on the telephone that she was home alone, and that if anyone asked for one of us, she should reply, "Mommy/Daddy is in the shower." One day, a friend called and asked for me. My daughter dutifully replied, "Mommy is in the shower." Then the friend asked for my husband! Obviously we had failed to prepare her for this possibility. After thinking it over, she finally told the caller, "Daddy's in the shower with her."

Sally signed her story, "Living a kinky lifestyle in front of the kids!"

Sensory Overload

Even if I'm on hand during the after-school hours, I sometimes use the television as a convenient "keep 'em busy" tactic while I finish a project or start supper. Such shows or videos are chosen with great care because my eyes and ears tell me that most television is an utter waste of time for children. In fact, it's worse: it's a waste of *mind*. Dee Brestin, in *The Lifestyles of Christian Women*, commented that "television not only exalts the transitory and is blind to the eternal, but it saturates us with a flow of lies concerning how to be fulfilled."[2]

Instead, at our house we focus on shows that are positive, fun, creative, and share a good message. Initially, I was tempted to hide our television in a spare bedroom (or better still, in the barn), but a need to monitor every show made putting it right next to the kitchen in the family room the best choice for us.

As often as possible, we watch shows together—I'm a big kid at heart, anyway, so I enjoy all the animated programs. When things come up that are inappropriate, we turn them off and talk about why. I'm careful to say, "This is not healthy for *anyone* to watch," rather than, "You are too young to see this stuff." Matthew and Lillian, at five and seven, are still very compliant about my intervention. I intend to enjoy control as long as I've got it!

Recently, when a commercial for a very violent movie flashed on the screen and I hit the "off" button, I turned around to find Matthew diving to the floor, hands over his ears, saying, "I didn't look, Mom, I didn't look!"

Homeward Bound

In *The Woman Who Works, The Parent Who Cares,* coauthored with John Kelly, Sirgay Sanger, M.D., outlines what our children need from us and where we can focus our intuitive radar: "Security, trust, a sense of mastery and competence, humor, curiosity—all the qualities that matter to a child's future—originate not in what a woman does with her child but in how she does it; in other words, in the sensitivity of her interactional and relationship skills."[3]

Sometimes we don't trust our intuition, our sensitivity, or our mothering skills. Linda from Alaska wrote a lovely, long letter filled with wisdom for such among us:

> I went to work when my kids were small because I couldn't stand being home and I didn't know how to properly run a household. When I was growing up, I was very much into my music and did not learn how to clean, cook, handle money, etc. I was in total shock when I married and had a home of my own. Work was an escape because I am a very organized person and had control and satisfaction at the office, unlike at home.

When I moved to Alaska, I had the opportunity to take a class on home organization from a woman who went from slob to totally organized. I discovered that I could run my home a lot like I ran the office, with time management, files, etc. Wow! What a discovery! I actually began to *love* caring for my home. Looking back, I would give anything to have known this information when my boys were small. I can plainly see that my life would have taken a different course, including that I probably would not have divorced my first husband.

I guess the bottom line is, please urge women who do not know how to care for their homes, and to whom it is important, to seek help! There are a number of excellent books, classes, videos, etc. It can be learned and it can be enjoyed!

Her words were echoed in the story of a woman who left her incredibly demanding newspaper career behind to reinvent home with her husband and five-year-old daughter. She realized that at last she had "put my house in order. What I'd feared the most, what had once looked like a huge, gaping void, gave me solace. In others words, my home life healed me."[4]

Falling in Love with Lillian

Interesting that her daughter was five when that healing occurred. For Miss Lillian's fifth birthday, I arranged a trip for the two of us to Disney World in Orlando. I'd taken her older brother there two years earlier when he was five; now, it was her turn. Just the girls, for two days. She talked of nothing else for weeks, which Matthew endured simply because it was, after all, only fair.

I was excited about the trip, too, but part of me was silently lamenting the sacrifice of time, of many precious hours I knew I should spend writing this very book, or preparing my summer speeches, or responding to some long past due correspondence. The financial sacrifice was real, too, since a day at the Magic Kingdom cost roughly the same as half a dozen of their classic videos. Oof.

Ready or not, the Big Day came and off, via Delta, we went. Without the need to compete for anyone's attention, Lillian was an absolute angel. She flirted with the pilots, entertained the passengers, and carried on a nonstop conversation with her stuffed pony, Brownie, who got the window seat. I was so proud of my little girl, who seemed to be growing up with each minute we were together.

Our first afternoon in Orlando, it was SeaWorld. My animal lover was beside herself with joy, watching Shamu and friends leap and splash. The next day dawned gray and rainy. "Not today, Lord," I thought, as Lillian and I climbed into our special new Disney World outfits. "Not the Magic Kingdom in a thunderstorm!"

Yup. There were no ponchos to be found for miles around, so a little fold-up umbrella was all we had between us and the monsoon. If I was worried that all the rain would dampen my daughter's enthusiasm (and I was), I hadn't counted on her amazing ability to go with the watery flow.

We did Dumbo the Flying Elephant in an absolute downpour, laughing all the way, then headed for dry land with two sailing trips through It's a Small, Small World, where every turn produced a "Wow! Look at that!" We fought a tempest in the Teacups and made our way through the Haunted Mansion with Lillian's head firmly buried in my chest. Big mistake, that one. Yet through it all, she was a trooper. With sheets of rain running down her face, she looked up at me, eyes sparkling, and said, "Mom, we're having a great time, aren't we?" Yes, dear one, we are.

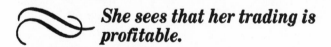 ### She sees that her trading is profitable.

The sun suddenly appeared for Mickey's 3:00 parade, and she wiggled and charmed her way up front and center to take it all in. I watched her shout with glee as the band came by, and found tears sneaking down my cheek. Oh, that pixie! So full of joy, such an unflagging spirit. By 7:00 that evening, she was finally running out of gas, and we made our way back to the hotel as the rains returned in earnest.

That night, fresh from her bath and wrapped in her cotton pajamas, she fell asleep instantly in my arms as we curled up for bed. I watched a movie, but mostly I watched Lillian: skin as smooth as satin, not a line or wrinkle; long lashes across her pink cheeks; curly dark blonde hair ringed around her sweet face. If you look up *cherub* in the dictionary, this is the face you see pictured there.

I had never felt such Mother Love as I felt that night, not just because she is beautiful (which, of course, she is!), and not just because she is clever and creative and charming, though she is those things too. At that precise moment, I fell in love with my daughter as if she were a long lost friend that finally had found her way to my door.

In her, I discovered my own childhood self, long buried; and in me, I found a new wellspring of love for precious little Lillian, and even for little Liz.

It was easy to use my five senses that day to perceive that the cost of this trip was money well spent, and that indeed, our "gain was good."

15

I Am Woman, Hear Me Snore

~

. . . and her lamp does not go out by night.

Proverbs 31:18b NKJV

W e're talking about a real lamp here, the kind that the genie came out of in *Aladdin*. It's long and slender, with a handle, a spout, oil, and a wick. Apparently, the ideal woman literally left her lamp burning, long through the night.

My own mother did the same thing, except her lamp was a fluorescent kitchen light. She often stayed up after the dishes were done, playing solitaire to relax. She earned it, believe me. As a child alone in my big, upstairs bedroom, my five siblings already having flown the coop, I would take solace in the faint light that filtered up the stairwell. It meant Mom was awake and all was well. Later she confessed to me that she often left the light on and went to bed. Yet the light was there when I needed it.

So I come by my night owl tendencies honestly. Many a woman has found that after the kids and/or husband are tucked in bed, she finally has a peaceful moment to herself. As Julie from Kansas noted, "It's hard to cope when you feel you're always at the bottom of the list. Calgon, take me away!" A bubbly bath might be just the ticket, or a good read that puts our hardworking brains on Park for an hour, or some R & R time with hubby. The truth is, those late hours are when most of us finally get the chance to work without interruption. As one scholar phrased it, "she keeps her light burning at night in order to attain maximum production."[1]

Remember how early she started her day, rising while it is still dark? Now we know the truth: the night before was short too. And that's where we can get into trouble.

We call this pattern burning the candle at both ends. The '90s malady known as burnout comes from just such disregard for our body's genuine need for rest. Jill Briscoe cautions us that godly women are to "burn on, instead of burning out."[2]

How can we know when we're burning out? We find ourselves saying, "Nobody else can handle this but me," or "No one understands," or, after sheer exhaustion hits, "This is too much for me!" Of course it is; it's too much for any one woman. It would be like trying to actually do *all* the things described in Proverbs 31. Hm-m-m.

In her perceptive analysis of the problem of burnout in *Perfect Every Time,* author Paula Rinehart revealed that "some part of me felt that a calendar with empty spaces and a phone that didn't ring were proof of not being much in demand."[3] My eyes flew open like windows when I read that: that's me to the max!

For speakers, consultants, and other professionals whose success is indeed measured by how many spaces in the calendar are filled and how many times a day the phone rings, the potential for burnout is exceedingly high. Unlike the standard Monday through Friday, 9:00 to 5:00 sort of schedule, a small business owner can find herself filling up every one of those calendar spaces, week after week, month after month. I empathize completely with Paula's statement, "I tried to find the 'off' button inside me, but I couldn't reach the switch."[4]

Lots of us can identify with too-full calendars. Linda from Pennsylvania remembers one year when she got too busy:

> Spring had rolled into fall and I had somehow never seen the summer. One day as I was rushing through the local supermarket, I

saw a neighborhood woman who lived with her mother. "Hi, Alice!" I said. "How's your mother doing?" She looked at me, gasped, and said, "Linda, she passed away in July!" Embarrassed, I said, "Oh, I'm so sorry, I didn't know!" Again she looked at me, very perplexed, and said, "But Linda, you came to her viewing!" I realized then, it was time to slow down and smell the coffee!

Burning the Midnight Oil

Newspaperman Kin Hubbard wrote, "A bee is never as busy as it seems; it just can't buzz any slower." Some of us are still buzzing, but we can't move around as fast as we used to; furthermore, we aren't sure where the honeycomb is. The physical symptoms of burnout are easy to spot: crying, exhaustion, getting sick more easily and more often, losing our sense of humor, finding it hard to concentrate, becoming forgetful, always running late, wanting to sleep (or not being able to). Rinehart said, "I felt as though I were speaking through a plate glass window, and had someone possibly peeked around the edge, they would have found no one there."[5]

My friend Terry, who works at a local Christian radio station, once started his early morning show still dragging from the day before. The call letters of the station are "WJIE ... Where Jesus Is Exalted." But that particular day, his first attempt came out, "WJIE ... Where Jesus Is Exhausted"! Thank goodness all our overcommitments never truly wear *him* out. Yet, when we leave our light burning too long without trimming the wick, it can leave us with precious little of the oil of gladness.

One of my daughter Lillian's favorite toys is her pink plastic flashlight. She loves to climb into dark spaces and flash it on and off. However, if she neglects to turn it off and leaves it in a corner somewhere, shining away, it quickly wears the batteries down and the light goes out completely.

Pay attention, Liz!

I am always asked by friends and audiences alike, "How do you do it all? Be a mother, a wife, travel, write, run a speaking business ... how?" Time was I would toss out a funny one-liner, like "Good drugs!" or "No sleep!" They weren't true statements, they were just funny.

Reality was not so humorous. I would slide out of bed at 4:00 A.M. and work until my family started waking up for breakfast, then join them at the table for a grand total of thirty minutes before they were off to school and office, where they would all remain for the next *eleven hours* while I worked feverishly in my home office. Finally, in the door they came, for hugs and homework and dinner (after a fashion), then I would slither out to the office for another hour of labor. Bath time gradually became Daddy's job, and I would show up for kiss and tuck-in time, another thirty-minute quickie. After lights out in the house, it was lights on in the office while I worked until midnight or 1:00 A.M. on some "gotta get it done now" project.

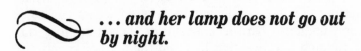 *. . . and her lamp does not go out by night.*

Occasionally, we all do that sort of thing. I received a letter recently from my fifty-two-year-old sister describing her latest wallpapering spree, in which she wrote, "The 2, 3, 4, and 5 A.M.s are catching up to me." Every now and again that kind of overtime activity is fun; it even feels rather daring. But as standard procedure, it can be deadly, if not to a body, perhaps to a marriage or any number of other vital relationships. As Lee from Wisconsin put it, "No matter how many balls we juggle, or how successful we look, we aren't always as we appear!"

I once overheard Bill explain to a mutual friend who had asked the familiar "How does Liz do it all?" question: "For Liz, sleep is an option." I smiled inside, thinking how amazingly productive a woman I was. The Bible calls that pride . . . and it came before a fall, all right. Because my heart fell to my knees when I saw that Bill was not smiling when he said it. I wasn't just wearing myself out. I was wearing my beloved out too.

Time for a Change

Here is what happens when we work 80+ hours a week ("I love my job!"), don't get enough sleep ("Isn't four hours enough?"), get almost zero exercise ("What? Stop working to go for a walk?"), eat less than healthy foods at strange hours ("Oh boy! Pizza again!"), pop antacids like candy ("Where is that bottle of Extra Strength TUMS?"), and drink coffee like water ("Could you make a fresh pot?").

What happens is we lose all perspective, most of our friends, some of our hair and, eventually, all sense of meaning and significance in our lives. Carlysle said, "Nothing is more terrible than activity without insight." Not long ago, I realized that I had plenty of the first and none of the second.

The day comes when we find ourselves yelling at our kids, throwing stuff around the room, slamming doors, and screaming at anyone within earshot. If we have someone in our lives who loves us, we also may find ourselves walking through the door of a therapist's office.

Mother Teresa said it best: "To keep a lamp burning we have to keep putting oil in it." For those who are spiritually minded, that oil is the single most important ingredient in our lives. We can't manufacture the oil, we can't buy the oil, we can't even earn the oil. We just have to ask for it, so that we can burn brightly and clearly see the path ahead. "For Thou art my lamp, O LORD; / And the LORD illumines my darkness" (2 Sam. 22:29 NASB).

Therapy was the oil God used to relight my lamp. It is one of the best gifts I've ever given myself, even though I went through some of the worst days of my life to get there. The weeks that followed were no picnic, either. However, I rest in the truth of the old spiritual: "There is a balm in Gilead to make the wounded whole."

I am not the only one among the walking wounded, trudging through each day with little sense of purpose or passion and no clear view of the Big Picture anymore. We are legion. Consider the words of these women who offered an explanation of why they might want to seek more satisfying work, if not quit working completely:

"I would like to practice my profession—not manage papers."
              Nurse for twenty-six years, age forty-six

"I feel unsatisfied and bogged down in monotony with no encouragement from my employer."
> Bookkeeper for twenty-one years, age forty-four

"The supervisors treat us like children."
> Telemarketer, age thirty-seven

"I feel unappreciated."
> Teacher for twenty-three years, age forty-four

"No job is worth all this incredible stress and time away."
> Nurse manager for twenty-six years, age forty-six

"I hate my job; too detail oriented, very little 'big picture.'"
> CPA for seven years, age forty-three

"After twenty-three years at one place, I'm tired of it."
> Nurse, age forty-two

"Enough already. Up every day, work all day, etc., etc."
> Marketing/PR for fifteen years, age thirty-eight

Do you hear your own voice among these? I don't on this day, but I sure have in the past, many times. You are worth taking care of, and there may never be a better time than this one to trim the wick and seek some fresh oil for your lamp.

In a book aptly titled, *Women's Burnout,* the authors offer a twelve-point checklist for avoiding burnout, including "avoid isolation," "learn to pace yourself," and "take care of your body." Number Twelve was my favorite: "Keep your sense of humor! Begin to bring joy and happy moments in your life. Very few people suffer burnout when they're having fun."[6]

The Paper Chase

We know laughter and a sense of play is what we need. It's also what we want more of in our lives, paired with less stress.

We Want More ...   And Less ...

Humor	Negativity
Play	Anxiety
Happiness	Sadness
Dancing	Eating
Laughter	Heartache
Serenity	Stress

If we do not choose to look for humor, believe me, it will look for us. One exquisite day in May, I had a luncheon program in Ocean City, New Jersey. After my presentation was over, the morning fog lifted and the oceanside resort was bathed in late spring sunshine ... glorious! A wise and balanced woman would have given herself permission to take a stroll on the beach, but not this woman. No, I had work to do, a book to write, and no lollygagging allowed. My only concession to the beautiful day was to open the windows and invite the ocean breezes to gently fill the room.

Dutifully, I sat down with a huge file folder of papers and began to divide them carefully into ten neat piles: this goes in this chapter, that goes in that chapter. After four hours, my hard work neatly spread out before me on the bed, I got up to stretch and head out for an early dinner. Not a leisurely trip to a nice seafood restaurant—that would require *time!*—just a quick zip through the nearest drive-thru, then back to work.

Twenty minutes later, heading into the hotel with my paper sack dinner, I noticed the wind had picked up. Had I left those windows open? Hm-m-m. As I turned the key in the door and began to push it open, I noticed a strange "whooshing" sound and had a sense of the door opening on its own power. When the bed full of papers came into view, still in neat piles, I breathed a sigh of relief ... until the door was fully open and a big gust of wind found a way of escape.

In seconds, nearly two hundred pages of notes were blowing everywhere, including through the door and down the hall.

"W-a-a-aaa!" came from my lips as I dropped my dinner sack and began chasing and stomping on runaway slips of paper.

A few minutes later, papers clutched willy-nilly in my hands, I made my way back to my room to survey the damage. The sea breeze had created a sea of papers, and all my afternoon labors had been in vain (the perfect word for it, since the word means, "a breath, a vapor"!).

I should've cried. I could've stamped my foot. I would've been justified in letting out one good scream. None of the above happened. I started to chuckle. Then a whole laugh sneaked out. Soon I was doubled over with laughter. I almost missed the bellman clearing his throat behind me as he held out a piece of paper with a bewildered expression on his face. "Ma'am? Did you lose something?"

Yes, I did. Thank goodness.

And I found something too. Annie Chapman, in *Smart Women Keep It Simple,* reminds us that in the Greek games, "The winner of the race was the one who came in first—with his torch still lit."[7]

16
Hands to Work, Hearts to God

~

She stretches out her hands to the distaff, / And her hand holds the spindle.
Proverbs 31:19 NKJV

*A*nd you thought we were finished with wool and flax! For those of us who haven't a clue about how a spinning wheel works (including me), the distaff is attached to the wheel and holds the flax. The spindle is the hand-held rod on which the thread is wound as it's spun. Clear as mud, I know.

It's hard for us almost-twenty-first-century women to glean much wisdom from an ancient method of spinning thread. But we can surmise two things:

1. **She was exceptionally skilled.** Why even mention it if spinning flax were not a skill coveted by mothers for their sons' future wives?

2. **It was a necessary and important task** for running both a home and a business. As we'll see later, the wool and flax that were spun on that wheel went into fabrics that clothed her family, and, by producing income, fed them as well.

We may not spin flax, but the women who filled out our surveys perform nearly every other job one could imagine. Among our ranks I found a private investigator, bill collector, research librarian, conference planner, stained-glass artist, math professor, school bus driver, art gallery owner, pharmacist, owner of a floor covering business, and one woman who was both an attorney *and* a flight attendant. What a mix of careers we have selected for ourselves!

Many times, women I meet almost apologize for their chosen field: "I'm just a teacher . . . just a secretary . . . just a nurse." Wait a minute. Education, clerical work, healthcare—those were the Big Three when I was growing up, careers of choice for a working woman in the '50s, '60s, and beyond. The work was, and is, difficult and, without a doubt, not as financially rewarding as it could and should be.

Yet these positions fit the above two stated criteria for our Proverbs woman—exceptional skill and definite need—perfectly:

Teachers are exceptional, and their work is the key to our future.
Thirty of the women who completed our surveys are teachers. My family is filled with teachers, from kindergarten through college. At last count, there were nine in my immediate family who are

in the business of changing lives through education, with more on the way. As more and more children at risk show up at school-house doors, the job of a teacher gets more difficult. Yet they persevere. I could not be more proud of them and of all of those among us who have dedicated themselves to the teaching professions.

Secretaries are gifted, and their skills are crucial to business.
Of those who responded to our surveys, more than 120 are secretaries. My years as a bookkeeper, a bank teller, and a receptionist taught me plenty about the business world and about life. My experience taught me that if the boss were out, no problem; the secretary knew everything. But if the secretary were out . . . run for the hills! Even though my paychecks were on the light side, I am proud of what I brought to those jobs and what many of us bring to our work in the clerical professions.

Nurses are highly trained and deeply committed to their vital jobs.
We heard from nearly one hundred nurses for our survey, plus fifteen women in other healthcare positions. Nearly half of my presentations these days are to healthcare audiences, some of the finest folks in the world. Many of us have entrusted our lives to nurses. These are the pros who keep their cool in a very stressful, life-or-death environment. They are continually learning new skills and technologies as they "stretch out their hands" to help a hurting world through the healing professions.

All this to say, the Big Three require great skill, much training, and are necessary to society's survival. No more "I'm just a . . ."! It's our job now as women to convince society of these truths, in order to bring the salaries of these professionals up to the level of their obvious competency.

What's in It for Us . . . Other Than Cash?

The Women's Bureau of the U.S. Department of Labor issued a national questionnaire in 1994: "Working Women Count!" They wanted to know, among other things, what we like best about our jobs. Which three would *you* check?

Good pay	Good coworkers
Good benefits	New skills
Flexible hours	Enjoyment
Training	Teamwork
Job security	Authority to make decisions
Productive work	

These are all valuable components of job satisfaction, certainly, but what I find interesting is that this list does not include the two things that most people—thousands of people from all over America, from all walks of life—have told me they want from their jobs, which are:

1. To create great products or provide superior service
2. To make a positive difference in the lives of others

The government's list is, sad to say, focused only on self: "what's in it for me?" Few potential employers would respond positively to an applicant walking in with the above long list of requirements, saying, "This is what you owe me." In our tough economy, employers are looking for team players who arrive with a list of skills and goals that they want to *bring* to the workplace, not that they hope to take from it. In the best work settings, bringing your best to your job *should* produce the kind of results you want as well. (We've all been around the block often enough to know this is not always the case.)

If we honestly expect management to focus entirely on making us happy, we will be sorely disappointed. Usually their efforts are aimed, first and foremost, toward creating a marketable product or service. This means that if we're looking for satisfaction from our work, we will need to look internally, not externally. George Bernard Shaw said, "This is the true joy in life: being used for a purpose recognized by yourself as a mighty one." Twenty-five years in the marketplace have taught me that Shaw is right, that true job satisfaction comes from knowing that you are the *best* person for the job and giving it your *best* shot every day. Not only for "them" but also for you.

Legend has it that after the death of John D. Rockefeller, someone asked his accountant, "How much did John D. leave?" The reply was brief: "Everything." When you're gone, few people will know or care how much money you made in your lifetime. But they will know if you made a difference.

Who Are Our Role Models?

Most of us have succeeded in the workplace because of specific individuals who mentored, encouraged, promoted, or demonstrated for us what it means to be a professional in our chosen field. Some of us learned, appropriately, from educators. Pat from Florida honored a teacher who "encouraged me to be more than I ever thought I could be." Pat from Michigan mentioned "three high school teachers who taught me to do the best job I could do the best way I could do it."

Many of us pointed to a particular boss or supervisor who showed us the path to professional achievement. Kathie said of her boss, "She adopted me (not on paper!)." Libby chose "a capable, yet feminine and kind vice president of administration." Sue has learned lots from her "general manager—she sees potential in everyone!" And Julie thinks highly of her boss, who is "comfortable with herself and accepts her limitations."

The biggest category for professional role models was our peers at work. Sylvia looks up to "my office mate—she's so balanced." Cindy admires "a nurse practitioner I work with," and Marilynn looks for encouragement from "my peers—they are givers." Gayle wrote glowingly of a coworker who is "spontaneous, encouraging, [and] good for my soul." And Christine respects those who work for her: "Some of the nurses on my staff embody *caring.*"

Two things stood out as I studied the surveys: almost no one said, "This person helped me make more money," or "They gave me huge raises." The people we chose as role models in our work lives were people who cared, who were willing to go the extra mile, who gave freely of themselves.

The second thing I noticed was that, while the major women's magazines always list celebrities as the most admired women, real women like us chose each other, people who are not household words, do not make big bucks, and are not in the limelight.

> ### *She stretches out her hands to the distaff, / And her hand holds the spindle.*

The only celebrity acknowledgment listed on the eight hundred surveys I read was a tip of the hat to Eleanor Roosevelt by Terry from Pennsylvania: "She was a *worker*, futuristic in her thinking and generous with her time." Even in this case, it was Eleanor's heart for service, and not her money or fame, that impressed Terry.

Mothering Is a Profession Too

I've always nodded with understanding when I see the T-shirts that proclaim, "Every Mother Is a Working Mother." Truer words were never said. I have to fight the urge to laugh when I hear younger women say, "I'm going to stick with this job until I'm thirty, then quit working and have children." "Don't worry," I say, smiling, "you'll still be working!"

Mothering definitely embodies the two job criteria mentioned earlier—exceptional skill and definite need—with a special definition of the word *labor-intensive*. Deborah Fallows, author of *A Mother's Work*, wrote, "At its best, work can offer a kind of spiritual satisfaction—a special feeling of achievement, a special wholeness, a sense that it is worthwhile, important, irresistible. This is the lesson about work from which women at home should draw."[1] She is so right. All work, done well, has value, regardless of the size, or existence, of a paycheck.

One thing the surveys demonstrated clearly: our parents are often role models for us, which means we may be the role models of choice for our children. Now, *that's* a scary thought! Our kids are watching us more closely than we can imagine as they make decisions about the value of work, both in and out of the home. I, for one, believe they deserve a good show.

When the kids see my suitcase at the door or find me all

dressed up in pantyhose and heels, they know I'm off to give a speech. (Believe me, I don't wear pantyhose unless absolutely necessary, since putting them on qualifies as an aerobic activity!) Because I have such an excellent track record for returning home within a day or so, the children seldom display any misery about Mother leaving. In fact, for years they thought I spoke at the airport. After all, that's where they would drop me off and pick me up. They probably decided that I simply rode to the top of the escalator and spoke to anyone who would listen! So when they see the heels and hose, Matthew gives me his biggest smile and says, "Mama . . . have a good speech!" I am fully aware that this enthusiasm may not last much longer, but I am enjoying every minute of it.

When I land at the airport the next day and run into their waiting arms (which sometimes are waiting for me at home), what do you suppose Matthew asks me right away? "Mama . . . did you have a good speech?"

Now what am I going to say to that angel of a boy? "No! I just showed up, put in my time, collected my check, and left." Obviously not. He deserves better than that, and so do my audiences. It is my goal each time to be able to come home and look my children in the eyes and say, with a clear conscience, "Mama did her best."

My high school drama coach used to say, "There are no small roles, only small actors." Whatever role God has given us to play out on the stage called life, we need to stretch out our hands and grasp the spindle, the chalk, the telephone, the computer, the thermometer, the microphone, and go for it. Without apology. Without compromise. Without giving less than our best because the money could be better or because we'd rather be somewhere else. Our children, our husbands, our parents, our friends, our peers, and our role models are in the audience . . . let's take a bow!

17
Reaching beyond Ourselves

~

**She extends her hand to the poor, /
Yes, she reaches out her hands to the
needy.**

Proverbs 31:20 NKJV

An excellent woman not only stretches out her hands to spin thread, she also stretches beyond the walls of her home to meet the needs of the less fortunate. Our pastor once said, "Maturity means growing less self-centered and more other-centered."

Nancy from Illinois and her husband are other-centered. They saw a need for a good preschool that also offered before- and after-school care and summer day camp for children of working parents. So, they built a nonprofit facility, financed in part with their own dollars. Nancy wrote, "We both work hard and are not rich. Our commitment to each other and this project has made us very close. We cut out a lot for our family to make this project go for our community."

This family's need for material goods is apparently balanced out by the intangible good they receive. According to The Institute for the Advancement of Health, "People who volunteer regularly—at least once a week for two hours—are ten times more likely to be in good health than people who don't. Benefits range from an increase in their overall sense of well-being to a decrease in stress-related problems." By sharing her "filled hands," as the Amplified version says, an excellent woman in turn receives a full heart. I've never known anyone who volunteered time, talents, or money who walked away empty-handed.

Help! Not "One More Thing!"

My heart's desire is to find more opportunities to give myself away and teach my children the joy of service at the same time. One little problem: *when?!* A friend of mine once moaned, "There's just not enough of *me* to go around." Lots of us feel the same way and can't bear the thought of adding one more activity, one more to do item to our list, however worthy it may be.

For busy women like us, who don't know how we could manage the added role of volunteer, psychologist Virginia O'Leary offers a word of encouragement: "The more roles women have, the better off they are, and the less likely they are to be depressed or discouraged about their lives. When we have a lot to do, we complain that it's driving us crazy—but, in fact, it's what keeps us sane."

It's ironic that one of the best remedies for impending burnout is to give yourself away. To pick one time and place each week where you stretch out your hands for the pure joy of doing it. Not to earn brownie points or extend your professional network, but just to give something away, for their sake and your sanity.

What usually suffices for giving around our house is Mom writes a check. Sure, a generous one, but still it's only paper. Our angelic role model from Proverbs didn't stretch out her wallet—let's face it, that's often the easy way out—she stretched out her hands and got involved in the lives of her needy neighbors. The studies on the benefits of giving are clear on this: It is the sacrifice of our time and talents that produces results for both parties, something the sacrifice of our dollars alone can't accomplish.

Not that financial gifts don't have their merit. As the Amplified Bible states, "She reaches out her filled hands . . ." Since Lemuel was King, he was also wealthy, so the ideal wife for him would've been generous with their riches. She knew that their prosperity was to be shared not hoarded. "To whom much is given, from him much will be required" (Luke 12:48 NKJV).

A family I know in Louisville keeps a big, clear jar on the kitchen table to collect all the excess change everyone has in their pockets at the end of the day. When the jar is full, the family chooses an appropriate charity to receive their gift. It's simple but very effective, and each one gets to "stretch out their hands," not just Mom.

A Chinese fortune cookie recently told me that "generosity and perfection are your everlasting goals." Not quite accurate. I'll leave perfection to the angels, and keep generosity as my target.

Stretching Out

Paul from Kentucky offered some words of wisdom to all of us who feel called to share our abundance with others. He said, "We can have our cake and eat it, too . . . but please, let's chew with our mouths closed and never talk with our mouths full!" We need to remember his good counsel when we are offering encouragement to someone whose life is not a piece of cake, whose burdens are heavy and needs are many. It's imperative that we not rub it in about how good we may have it (for the moment!), but instead be sensitive to the situations others find themselves in and give as generously as we can.

Something we found in the surveys caught me by surprise. Several women said they wanted to quit their jobs but *not* primarily to be home with family *or* to take a much-deserved break. No, they wanted to give their time away! As MeLynda from Utah phrased it, "I have enough volunteer work to keep me busy into the next life." And, when asked what they wanted more of and less of in their lives, some women wanted "more money to help the ones who really need it" and "more time to help others."

Shirley from Illinois "extends her hands" on the job every day but insists she gets back much more than she gives. Her advice to us? "Don't ever pass up the opportunity to visit with residents of a nursing home. It will be a day you'll never forget. There is so much love and joy in their hearts, and you can learn so much from them, just by sitting and talking. In fact, it will become addictive!" There's one addiction we won't need a cure for

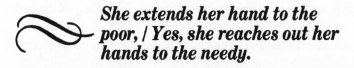

She extends her hand to the poor, / Yes, she reaches out her hands to the needy.

A dozen years ago, my first friend in faith, Evelyn, taught me a valuable lesson about being generous. She and her husband Tim did the morning show at the same radio station where I was doing the midday program. While I came to work at the reasonable hour of 8:00 A.M., they had to show up no later than 5:00 A.M. At that hour, they had to walk through a back alley and pass our big dumpster to enter through the back door. One morning, they found a woman with a grocery cart and ragged clothes digging in the dumpster for something to sell or eat. Evelyn offered her some money, but the woman shot her a nasty look and said, in effect, "I don't need your money!"

Ev knew better, of course, but didn't want to destroy this woman's pride. So the next morning they came to work a few minutes earlier so Ev could stuff cans of food all through the dumpster, hoping they would look like they were accidentally thrown away. Sure enough, when they came out later that morning after their show, the cans were gone. I've heard of collecting canned goods for the needy, but Evelyn took that idea one step further!

A Friend in Need . . .

Speaking of friends, there are times when they need our "filled hands" too. Or our "empty ears." A 1993 Louis Harris survey indicated that some 60 percent of us have between two and ten friends, and nearly 18 percent insisted they had more than twenty friends. Must have been men. Men could easily know twenty guys they think of as buddies, people they work with, hang out with, and so forth. But twenty close friends? The experts say you can only maintain three to five intimate friendships at any one time. My own definition of a *real* friend is someone you can call and sob, "It's me!"—at 3:00 A.M.—and they don't hang up on you! Or say, "Who is this?" Instead they say, "I'll be right over."

My friend Janie Jasin once said, "I believe everyone around us is needy and that we can truly minister to them only when we are fairly well ourselves." The people in our circles of influence are seldom in need of food or clothing, although such people exist by the millions and deserve all the help we can provide. But the deeper, greater needs of people often go unspoken, yet can clearly be heard by those with listening hearts.

"Liz, how many grandmas are out there in situations similar to mine?" asked a woman named Mary. Her daughter has returned home with two toddlers in tow and no money, so Grandma is raising a second generation while her daughter goes to school. She wrote, "If this is where God has me, then I'll just 'bloom where I'm planted' although I sure do wilt quickly!"

Nancy had a simple request: "Let me know that even though I failed in my marriage, I'm still an okay person." Definitely okay. Another woman submitted three funny stories about her family life, but it was the handwritten note at the bottom that slid through my heart like a dagger. "Liz, I have recently gone through a real painful divorce. My husband of twelve years left me for a woman half his age. He's put the girls (five and seven) and me through some real hurt, and we're still not settled due to his greed. Please pray for us!" Consider it done.

The truth is, the needy are all around us. Like the Proverbs 31 woman, we can stretch out our hands and find those who need our healing touch waiting right at the ends of our fingertips. A kind word, a nod, a squeezed hand can keep them going (and meet our own neediness as well).

Putting It All in Focus

At a recent presentation I gave for cancer patients and their families, one young woman told me, "Cancer really puts life in focus for you, and prioritizing gets easy." Dauna, whose young daughter was battling cancer, offered these words of wisdom: "Every single holiday after a cancer diagnosis is more meaningful. Christmas is merrier, birthdays become more important than a national holiday, and Thanksgiving comes 365 days a year."

My presentation for those cancer patients, by the way, was on the benefits of *humor* for both the survivor and the supporter. Surprised? They were wonderful laughers, and they especially appreciated the story of Gilda Radner, who fought ovarian cancer to the end by using her best weapon: humor.

When it was time for Gilda's first radiation treatments, she did all the necessary reading and brought her last three questions on 3" by 5" cards:

1. "What are the possible side effects?"

2. "How do I treat them?"

3. "Do you validate for parking?"[1]

Monica from Pennsylvania declared that "every bad happening has some good in it." When her husband was struck by a speeding car a few years ago, she realized that "in thirty years of marriage, Andy and I never found time to say 'I love you' to each other. We now say it 100 times a day, no matter how busy we get!"

Each of these stories is a gentle reminder that the needs around us—whether financial, practical, emotional, or spiritual—are many. We can't meet all those needs, but we can do something. For our own sake as well as theirs.

After hearing me present a program in her town, Dorothy from Iowa wrote a letter of encouragement telling me "how wonderful it was to share a happy day with you." Then she revealed a bit of her life's journey with me: when she was eight, her parents divorced; at fourteen, she had to quit school and go to work; at fifteen, she married a man "who loved me very much," and together they had six children before her husband's death at the young age of forty-nine; three of her six children suffered traumatic illnesses; she was recently diagnosed with Chronic Fatigue Syndrome, and her seven-year-old grandson has cerebral palsy. She closed her letter, "Sending my love and prayers for your happiness."

And for yours, Dorothy. You've reminded me, and perhaps many others, of how little we have suffered on this earth compared to many. How humbling, even embarrassing, to think of the little things we've complained about, when we should be on our knees in gratitude for all that has been given to us.

Forgive me, Lord, for not grasping the real definition of *needy*: someone who keeps her full hands in her pockets and misses the joy of stretching them out.

18
Let It Snow,
Let It Snow . . .

~

When it snows, she has no fear for her
household; for all of them are clothed
in scarlet.

Proverbs 31:21 NIV

I've spent my Christian life trying to live up to the woman
described in Proverbs 31, but when it comes to this
verse, I'm left out in the cold. Could it be she's not worried
about her family being out in the snow because they're all dressed
in bright red so she won't lose track of them against the white
backdrop? Not quite. "Scarlet" was the best cloth available, a
doubly thick fabric that kept her family warm on cold winter nights.

"How Cold Was It?"

Growing up in eastern Pennsylvania, I saw my share of bad
winters, so neither snow nor cold struck fear in my heart. Until
January 1994, when Louisville had the biggest snowfall on record—ever—an amazing sixteen inches. The next day we had
the coldest temperature on record—ever—right at twenty-four
degrees below zero. Or as the TV meteorologist cheerfully
phrased it, "Fifty-six degrees below freezing!"

The kids were bouncing off the walls, anxious to go out and play in all that white stuff, but cautious Mother kept looking at the thermometer and saying, "No way!" By the third day, the snow hadn't budged an inch, and we'd been stuck in the house together for seventy-two solid hours. I was ready to let the kids out, period, cold or no cold. As our minister said the following Sunday, there was absolutely *no* crime that week in Louisville, but domestic arguments were way up!

More than anything, the kids wanted to make snow angels. I dressed them up as if they were embarking on the Iditarod and followed them out into the snow. *Note:* Do not let a five-year-old lie down in sixteen inches of snow to make an angel. *Angelic* is *not* how she behaved when all that snow and cold made its way into her boots and mittens. After spending nearly an hour locating all our winter paraphernalia, I think we stayed outside a grand total of twelve minutes.

One Ohio mother remembers "a series of wintry, blowy, snowy days" when her three children were suffering from cabin fever and "were absolutely out of sorts." After dressing them from head to toe, she sent them outside with strict instructions to walk around the house three times, "while I ran from window to window to make certain they were all still alive and still moving!"

Reminds me of the story my father-in-law tells of a little girl in Lexington who announced to her family that she found out why ice looks just like glass. "The weatherman said there's a *windshield factory* out there!"

Spectacle on Ice

The Proverbs woman wasn't worried about snow because she was ready for that nasty weather. We, on the other hand, were *not* ready for sixteen inches of snow and were caught with our mittens off. It was weeks before the snow and ice finally disappeared, but we were soon back to business as usual in my office behind the house.

Most of our books, tapes, and toys are stored there, but one product item was so big it had been exiled to the barn: 5,000 bright red kazoos packed in ten huge cardboard boxes. Luckily, kazoos don't melt or rust or attract silverfish. I mean really, what would a silverfish do with a kazoo? So they were perfectly safe in the drafty old barn, though hardly convenient when needed.

Naturally, we ran out of our office supply of kazoos the week after the Big Storm. Since I'm the boss, it was my job to get a fresh box. "I hope you all appreciate this!" I grumbled, yanking the door shut behind me. I stomped through the snow to the barn, only to discover that the steep ramp that led up to the doorway was covered with ice. No problem. By reaching up and grabbing the door handle, I managed to pull myself up the slippery ramp, shove open the door, and fall into the barn. There! Made it.

Once my eyes adjusted to the dim light, I found a box of kazoos, brushed off the dust and cobwebs, and made my way back to the doorway. Now the same ramp that had posed no challenge going up, on the down slope looked like some maniacal amusement park ride: "Terror on Ice."

"I'll just put my feet sideways and slide down," I thought, and off I went. For the first few seconds, it felt like an exhilarating ride on a skateboard. "Whee!" I called out. Then, the gravity of the situation swept over me, and my round bottom headed south. The kazoos flew north. My legs went east and west, respectively. A shriek hung in the frozen air like a large icicle suspended from a tall branch.

Ka-thwomp! All points converged at the foot of the ramp,

where kazoos, round bottom, and both legs were reunited. I ran a quick body check for broken bones and, finding none, replaced the frozen shriek with the warm, toasty sound of human laughter. Just my own, thank goodness.

Gathering up the box of kazoos and what was left of my dignity, I marched through the snow toward the office, head held high. I had survived, and for that I was grateful, if not graceful. Besides, my staff would never know about my slippery trip, I thought, breezing through the door. Their burst of laughter told me differently. "Liz, there's a big, muddy circle on the back of your coat!" My body may not have been "clothed in scarlet," but my face was.

Yes, Bucky, There Really Is a Santa Claus

Snow means winter, and winter means Christmas, which means with children, there's always the issue of Santa Claus. One afternoon close to the holidays, Beverly from Tennessee came home to find her then six-year-old son very upset. "Mom, Bobby said there is no such thing as Santa Claus!" he said. "He did?" she said, sounding surprised. "Well, what did you say to him?" With great conviction, her son replied, "I told him there was so a Santa Claus because my mother would never spend that much money on me!"

In the Buckeye State some years back, another two young boys who were checking on Santa's status got themselves in a heap of trouble. Kelly had two sons, eighteen months apart. "The oldest, Scott, was the leader of most of the anarchy around our house. Unfortunately, the second son, Bucky, was usually a willing follower."

Christmas 1975 dawned with the usual 6:00 A.M. alarm. But when Kelly stepped into the living room "an incredible sight met my eyes. Shreds of wrapping paper, ribbons, and tissue were piled to the ceiling. Opened gifts for grandparents, aunts and uncles, cousins, friends, everybody, littered the room. It was a horrifying sight. Thoughts of all the time I had spent wrapping and curling ribbon swam through my mind, as well as the awful realization I would have to do it all again before lunch. I had to remind myself that murder was against the law."

The dialogue with her six-year-old son, standing amid the ruins, went as follows:

Kelly: "Oh, Bucky! How did this happen?"

Bucky: (get ready, he had quite a lisp) "Well, Thcott thaid, 'Letth go down and thee if Thanta came yet.' We came downthtairs and then Thcott thaid, 'Leth jutht open one gift.' Then we wotht contwol."

Twenty years later Kelly admits she almost "lost control" herself. "I thought my holiday was ruined. Now it's one of the few Christmases that I specifically remember, other than the one when the tree fell over."

Which brings us to Sandy from Pennsylvania:

When I was a child, my father always required us kids to hang each piece of silver tinsel perfectly straight, perfectly spaced on the Christmas tree boughs. For twenty years of my married life I never used tinsel on the tree, afraid Daddy might criticize my results. The year he died, we pulled out an antique box of tinsel and "threw" it on the tree, saying "Daddy, this is for you!" It was so much fun!

That Christmas morning, we were relaying the tinsel story to our many assembled guests when all of a sudden, with no one near the ten-foot tree, it fell onto the floor without breaking one ornament. Mother spoke first. "Well, your father always _did_ have the last word!"

O Tannen-bomb!

In our own family, every Christmas is identified by one specific memory—the Christmas I made smoked turkey without meaning to, the year I gave everyone their gifts in brown paper bags with bows drawn on them, the Christmas Day we spent on the Pennsylvania Turnpike. But 1992 will always be remembered as the year I spoke our Christmas tree into existence.

I don't mean like, "And then God said, let there be ..." I mean

I gave a speech for a charitable organization, and my honorarium was a ten-foot Christmas tree, decorated from top to bottom.

Usually we made a trip to a nearby tree farm and cut our own fragrant spruce. But that year, a ready-to-go artificial tree was a welcome gift since we were in the process of moving to our new/old house. Tree cutting had been pushed aside by painting, papering, and unpacking, and besides it might have taken weeks to find the ornaments. I was thrilled at the thought of receiving our "free tree."

When Bill's parents and grandmother arrived for our traditional bowl of homemade soup and bread, we hurried them in to see our tree. "It's lovely!" my mother-in-law exclaimed. "It was free," my son Matthew declared proudly. Like his father, he appreciates a good bargain.

Our first Christmas in the old house with the new tree went without a hitch. When New Year's Day came, traditionally the day for taking down a cut Christmas tree and sweeping up the dried needles, I came to a wonderful "aha!" realization: this tree would never lose its needles. I could enjoy it right through Epiphany.

By mid-January, still cozy in one corner of the dining room, the tree continued to look fresh and green, though a tad off-season. I removed all the yuletide ornaments and left only the twinkling lights and white snowflakes on the branches. "It's a January tree," I informed the family, and there the tree stayed.

When February came along, it seemed appropriate to replace the snowflakes with valentines, so the kids and I had a ball covering the tree with paper hearts. Not every family has a valentine tree, I thought warmly.

Frankly, the shamrocks in March got lost amid all the green, so on the first of April we moved quickly to Easter eggs of every hue and multicolored grass dripping from the branches. It was my favorite month so far.

Friends were less impressed. When my in-laws came for Easter dinner, they took one look and said, "Well!" I said, "It's an Easter tree," and they said, "Yes, it is."

By May it was getting harder to keep the branches dust-free and, though lovely, the sunflowers couldn't overcome the

Christmas-in-July look. Visitors would roll their eyes, and even the kids were weary of explaining to people that "Mom thought it would be fun to have a holiday tree all year."

By August, it was history: a two-piece memory shoved back in the corner of the garage. November rolled around, and it was time for my annual holiday presentation for that very charitable organization. With a request for my speaking services came their generous offer: "Liz, may we give you another tree again this year?"

"No thanks," I said. "I'll take a wreath."

The Reason for the Season

There were years when I didn't even have a Christmas tree, those single adult years through my twenties and early thirties when money was tight and a tree-for-one didn't sound like much fun. Usually, I worked Christmas day. Radio stations are an every-day-of-the-year kind of business, so rather than let my married friends work and miss time with their families, I always volunteered to do the morning show on Christmas. (Don't be impressed ... I also got paid double-time!)

It was December 25, 1984, and there I was on Christmas morning, standing in the studio, the only person in the building other than a security guard and a news reporter. I was feeling very sorry for myself—all alone, no phone callers, no visitors, just me spinning carols and hymns on the turntables while big tears ran down my cheeks.

"Nobody loves me, Lord!" I said aloud in my most forlorn voice. "Nobody loves me!" I was sobbing by this point, feeling the most alone I'd ever felt in all my life. Then I heard his voice speaking to my heart as clearly and distinctly as the words on this page: "I love you, Liz. I love you."

My response was immediate and instinctive; I dropped to my knees. What love is this, that he would speak to me, his child, on Christmas morning! At that moment, the words of the music blasting out of the studio speakers penetrated my heart: "Joy to the world! The Lord is come!"

He came to us then, he comes to us now, and his message is still the same: "Have no fear of the cold. I love you!"

19
Step Aside, Laura Ashley

She also upholsters with finest tapestry.

Proverbs 31:22 TLB

I can handle a woman who sews her own clothing. With the help of Simplicity and a good zigzag sewing machine, even an inept seamstress like me can crank out something to wear—maybe not in public, but wearable. But here we have a woman who "makes for herself coverlets, cushions, and rugs of tapestry" (AMPLIFIED BIBLE). Now, that's a house of a different color!

Growing up in a small town nestled among Amish farmlands, I had only one friend whose mother was employed. She worked for an upholstery shop, and she was amazing. Old couches turned into beautiful, new-looking sofas under her able hands. Pillows got plump again, and drapes were created to match the upholstery. I was in awe of her powers with needle and thread and mighty machine.

But when Proverbs was written, Elias Howe had not yet ushered in the sewing machine age. So our magnificent woman from centuries ago not only created the thread, not only wove it into fabric, but she also hand-stitched her exquisite tapestry into fine coverings for her home. It makes me tired to think about it.

One might decide that this Queen of Upholstery was a figment of Lemuel's imagination, except I know her twentieth-century counterpart. One Saturday morning I phoned my friend Doris, whose name brings to mind the biblical seamstress Dorcas. "Whatcha doin'?" I asked. "Oh, I just bought some fabric this morning, and I'm going to cover my couch," she said.

I stifled my laughter. "Get serious!" I said. "I am serious," she assured me. And she was. She covered a queen-size sofa bed in one day. Six pillows. Arm covers. Scary.

Inferior Design

It's not that I don't adore home decorating. That love affair began at the dawn of puberty when I turned twelve and my two older sisters had vacated our big bedroom. Mother decided I was old enough to choose a new decorating scheme myself. Did I do a safe pale blue, a feminine pink, a slightly daring lavender? No, I went for a Mother Nature look: navy blue walls (think sky) with *bright* yellow floral wallpaper on the ceiling (sun), brown painted floors (dirt) with green throw rugs (grass, of course). And to think Earth Day hadn't even happened yet. I was ahead of my time. Way ahead of my time.

Mother, being a gardener, thought it was dandy. She even helped me antique the desk and bookshelf—remember that look? We used yellow paint for the base color then brushed on dark blue stain and wiped half of it off. It looked as bad as it sounds: green and yellow striped furniture. My friends made gagging sounds when they walked in the room.

I've traveled the interior design highway many times since then. My first apartment furniture consisted of one metal pole shelf earned with S & H Green Stamps and a dreadful plaid sofa bed bought with a credit card. Next came the early '70s hippie look with oversized floor pillows in earthtone colors: tans, browns, and rust. (Did we really decorate with olive and orange?) Stores sold huge pillows for hundreds of dollars, but penny-pinching apartment dwellers like me went the homemade route, creating enormous pillows that took up lots of empty floor space.

I bought remnant fabric for a song, and ordered loose foam rubber by the fifty-pound bag, which I had to tie on top of my car just to get home. You haven't lived until you've watched a 5'9" woman stuff a 7' by 7' pillow—from inside the pillow. The foam rubber pieces created their own static electricity after a while and insisted on sticking to my clothes and hair. Exasperated, I finally locked all the doors, pulled down the shades, took off all my clothes, put on a shower cap, and stuffed my floor pillows in the nude, hoping no one would ask me how I spent my weekend.

"What did you do Friday night, Liz?"

"Well, I peeled off all my clothes and climbed into a pillow."

"Naked?"

"That's right. Cuts down on the static electricity."

Since the pillow years, I've limited my adventures in sewing to curtains. One casing, one hem, hang it up—that's my speed.

Playing with Blocks

The other mainstay of the struggling-college-student apartment was the bookshelf: long pine boards on cement blocks. So attractive. I had lots of books and lots of records and lots of stereo equipment, so I naturally needed lots of cement blocks. At thirty-two cents each, I thought they were the deal of the century. The man at the quarry looked at me sideways when I pulled up in my '67 Volkswagen and ordered twelve large blocks. "In that car?" he asked. "No problem, I've got plenty of room in the back seat!" I assured him, jumping out.

One by one, he lugged the large, gray blocks over to the car and heaved them into the back. I wondered why he wasn't carrying two or three at a time. They looked so light, what with the two holes in the middle and all. They couldn't be that heavy. But as each one disappeared into the back of the Bug, the tires sank lower and lower. "Better put some up front," he advised, dropping the last two in the passenger seat. I happily paid him his $4.00 and headed for home, proud of my bargain-bookshelf-to-be.

I lived on a steep hill. I lived on a second floor. Parking by the curb, I whipped open the passenger door and grabbed the first cement block with one hand, just like the guy at the quarry had. It didn't budge. The steep downhill slant of the street meant I had a double fight with gravity. With two hands and a big grunt, I got the block onto the sidewalk. Good grief, I thought, this job will take an entire hour. Another "oof!" and we made it to the grass. I continued with an end-over-end tumble move to get it to the front steps. I looked like an unhappy hippie doing the Watusi with a cement block.

Finally, there was no getting around it. I had to pick up the block and march up those steps. Seven steps on the outside of the house, a twenty-step staircase on the inside. Circular.

The fact that I am alive to write this book means I survived, but I don't know how. It took an entire afternoon of huffing and puffing to get those dozen cement blocks up to my apartment. I knew then that I would have to seek more fruitful employment so that I could afford movers so that I would never, ever have to touch those blocks again. They traveled with me for five more apartments in four more states, and indeed, I never "oofed!" again.

In the Pink

When it came to decorating, I found my best bet was paint. It was inexpensive, came in a zillion colors, and required no sewing, stuffing, or hauling. There wasn't any shade I wasn't willing to try: dark green, paper bag brown, turquoise, even feldspar.

Feldspar? The dictionary will tell you it's something found in igneous rocks, but I'm telling you this is *not* a color found in nature. Picture the deepest, brightest coral imaginable, then multiply it by ten. That's feldspar: a color one should use in *very* small doses, which is why it seemed the perfect choice for my tiny, 6' by 7' laundry room.

Never one to rush such projects, I waited until the night before the delivery men would arrive with my new washer and dryer to start painting. How long could one little room take? Anyway, the hardware store insisted it would cover in one coat. I popped open the can and gasped. Feldspar my foot, this was flamingo pink! With trepidation, I poured it into the paint tray and was soon rolling it onto the walls.

Flat and vertical, the color was more coral than pink, and I sighed with relief as I rolled and trimmed, rolled and trimmed. By 1:30 A.M., I had finished three walls and was pleased with the progress, except for one minor point: it was going to take two full coats to cover the old paint. Filling up the paint tray for the last wall, my tired arms stretched the tray up onto the shelf that perched on the side of the ladder.

Maybe it was the late hour, the lack of sleep, or too many paint fumes, but my next move was a terrible one: I moved the ladder. The forgotten paint tray, filled with a quarter of a gallon of bright pink latex, came raining down on my horrified head. If my mouth had been hanging open as usual, I might have drowned. Instead, the metal paint tray landed right on my chest, cascaded paint down the front of my T-shirt and jeans, and landed with a clang at my feet.

Now, the good news: for the first time in my natural life, I had used a drop cloth. On previous painting expeditions, I'd taken one page of newspaper and scooted it around the room with my foot, painting as I went. But because this laundry had a nice hardwood floor, I had wisely covered it with a vinyl drop cloth, a fact that at that moment gave me great solace: it could have been worse.

Had I been a married woman then, I would've called out, "Honey!" and some kind man would've come to my rescue. But I was a single woman when I bought that house, and the only other creature under my roof was my large cat, now perched on the laundry doorstep, looking mighty curious.

I know what most of us would've done: we would've stopped right then and there and gotten ourselves all cleaned up before continuing. But I was not about to waste all that paint, and anyway I had a job to finish. So, I stepped up to the fourth wall and smeared myself all over it, trying to make use of every drop of feldspar on my body. By this point, the clothes were a write off, so I wiggled out of them, turned them inside out and dropped them in the trash can. (I know what you're thinking: does she always do her decorating projects in the buff? No, but when you live alone, you can get away with a lot!)

It was now 2:00 A.M., the first coat was complete and would have to dry for two hours before the second coat could be applied. Certainly at this point a sane woman would have taken a moment to jump in the shower and wash off all that pink paint, but it seemed so pointless. In two hours, I'd be back into the mess all over again, I reasoned, so I simply pulled back the comforter on my bed, pulled back the sheets, pulled back the mattress pad, and positioned myself on top of the mattress. The paint had only landed on my front half, remember, and it was completely dry by now, to boot.

I set the alarm for 4:00 A.M. and immediately fell into a deep sleep. Two hours later, I woke up on the first ring, rolled and trimmed with feldspar abandon, then showered and dressed for the day and was drinking coffee at 8:00 A.M. when the delivery men showed up at my door, appliances in tow. Despite my late night latex disaster, I was going to have a lovely laundry after all.

But later that morning, driving to work, a terrible thought came to mind: what if I had died in my sleep? After all when you're single, weeks can go by before anyone notices you're not around. I could imagine my coworkers finally beginning to ask, "Has anyone seen Liz this month?" until at last the police would break into my house and find a stiff, half-naked pink woman with a starving cat perched at the foot of her bed. Gives me the willies to think about it. Ever since then, my color choices have been more subdued, a favorite being Heirloom Beige, which matches my aging skin perfectly.

Home Sweet Home

By the mid '80s, I was steeped in antiques (a fancy name for used furniture) and had hit my stride in interior design. You'll find *Country Living* stacked high in my magazine basket, quilts of every size and pattern hanging on the walls, and bargain "finds" from many a Saturday scavenger hunt. The sign I saw on the lawn outside a country collectibles store says it all: "Gifts and Goodies: Prepare to Shop."

When we moved to this, our *last* house, I finally tossed the curtain fabric from two houses ago. Now, more than ever, I love decorating my home because I get to go *shopping* to do it. Unlike our super seamstress in Proverbs 31, you and I don't have to make everything homemade . . . we just need to make it home.

20
Queen-Size Couture

~

Her clothing is fine linen and purple.
Proverbs 31:22b NKJV

*I*t was neither fine linen nor purple, but it was a lovely dress, one of my favorites for traveling. The first of four hours on the 727 had just begun as I settled into my coach seat, shoes off, glasses on, intent on tackling some long-neglected paperwork.

Everything was going smoothly until I got an itch in the center of my back. I tried first one hand, then the other, but couldn't quite reach that one place that was itching more with every second. Finally, I put the cap back on my felt-tip pen and poked it down the back of my dress, maneuvering it to the exact spot. I began to scratch . . . ahhh! The relief was immediate. That is, until the top of the pen came off in my hand, and the business half dropped down my back. Visions of the damage a black felt-tip pen could do to the back of an ivory dress began swimming before my eyes. The pen had stopped abruptly at the seat belt, so I leaned forward to point the dangerous end toward my back and away from my dress.

Now what? Ask the man next to me to unzip my dress and retrieve my pen? Hardly. Leave it there for another three hours? Not likely. There was no option but to stand up and try to get it out. I gingerly unbuckled the seat belt, slid forward and stood up, remaining bent over as I stepped into the aisle. A flight attendant who was witnessing all this hurried toward me.

"Miss, are you ill? The seat belt sign is still lit, and you really must be seated." All eyes were fixed on me as I straightened up, gulped and wiggled my hips. Plop! The errant black pen dropped through my dress and onto the carpet, to the astonishment of the flight attendant and two dozen nearby passengers.

I couldn't resist playing to such a captive audience. "Say!" I exclaimed, bending over to pick up the pen. "I've been looking for this for weeks!"

Perfectly Fitting

Although our Proverbs 31 woman didn't wear ivory with an occasional black splotch, she did wear purple, the color of royalty, fit for a queen. Her material was linen, the fabric of the priests, used in the temple. In other words, the "ideal woman" dresses well (hooray!) but sews it all herself (boo!).

If time permitted and I had more talent, I, too, would be sewing my own clothes. Not only out of economic necessity, but also because it's the one way to assure a perfect fit—very important for those of us with abundant bodies—as well as better quality fabric at a better price and seams that hold together for more than one trip through the wash cycle.

Instead, I shop at those stores with clothes especially designed with big, beautiful women in mind. I'm grateful for the pretty clothes, but the names are sometimes a bit much. In North Carolina, I stumbled on a store called, "The Stout Hut." Can you imagine floating into a gathering where you might want to dress to impress and admitting your queenly attire of "fine linen and purple" came from The Stout Hut?

As my last book assured each of us, *"One Size Fits All"* truly is a fable. Tammie from Ohio spotted this sign at her local dry cleaners: "Some stretch pants don't have a choice." Amen. Everyone's favorite funny lady, Erma Bombeck, nicely summed up the pantyhose needs of the full-figured woman: "We're looking for some nice firm sausage casings that sack up the legs and cut our losses around the waist area."[1]

I take great solace in the fact that according to 1 Corinthians, when we get to heaven, we get a new body (I've checked and it's a size 6). More good news can be found in Matthew, where we learn that "many who are first will be last, and the last first" (19:30 NKJV). Which means if you wear a 6 now . . . you'll be wearing a 24 for eternity.

No wonder we love to sing, "When we all get to heaven, what a day of rejoicing that will be"!!

A "Come As You Are" Party

It's worth noting that nowhere in this Proverbs 31 passage do we learn what an excellent woman might look like. She is not called "fair of face" or "lovely of form" or any such biblical language. No mention of her dress size either. Clothing color, yes. Fabric, sure. But size, no. Interesting.

My sweet Bill assures me he has always found my "face and form" to be attractive, even without makeup or a fancy hairdo. But when it comes to clothes, he loves it when I'm all spiffed up. "How do you want me to dress around the house, though?" I asked one day, a bit huffy. Surely he didn't expect me to wear nylons and heels at home. Shades of Donna Reed.

"No, my request is simpler than that," he said. My eyebrows shot up in anticipation. "Let's just say that pajamas are not appropriate after 10:00 A.M."

His comment has a historical basis. Since my writing and speaking office is in a cottage behind our home, going to work means walking out the back door with a cup of coffee. It also means our office dress code is, shall we say, loosely defined.

One morning I headed out to the office early, wearing my favorite p.j.s: an oversized T-shirt. I fully intended to take a shower and dress for the day, but at 7:30 I wanted to take advantage of a nice quiet place for writing.

Nine o'clock came. Pam, my office manager, came. No big deal; she'd seen me in pajamas before. Then the exterminator came. As he helped himself through the front door, I jumped behind the copier. The Minolta was no match for my bountiful body. As he made his way around the room, swishing his bug spray wand along the baseboards, I inched along the wall, eyes glued to the door. Four steps to go, then freedom. As I reached for the handle, he drawled, "Ma'am, I'm just as embarrassed as you are."

Okay, Bill, you win. No more pajamas after breakfast.

All Sown Up

But what about *your* husband? Does he have any particular requests concerning appearance or attire? Since our Proverbs passage didn't feature much along those lines, I didn't include questions on such topics in the survey. Even so, a few women mentioned adjustments to their appearance when asked what their husbands might appreciate most. Betty said, "My husband would be so proud of me if I would let my fingernails grow." Ann was sure he'd be happy if she "lost weight and grew longer hair." "Shaved my legs every day!" said Julee from Kansas.

I, for one, am thrilled that our Proverbs woman was beautifully adorned and busy doing important things but was apparently not caught up with that which does not last—earthly beauty—in order to focus on that which is eternal—heavenly character. She was not only sewing fabric, she was sowing seeds, seeds of righteousness that would bear fruit for generations, even our own.

21

Breadmaker or Breadwinner?

**Her husband is known in the gates, /
When he sits among the elders of the
land.**

Proverbs 31:23 NKJV

Brenda and her husband Roy have a most unusual
sentence at the top of their checks: "This Money Is
Made from Mugging Bugs." Turns out, Roy has his
own exterminating business. Their son hopes to carry on the
eighteen-year tradition, but Brenda wants to know when the
time comes, "Will there be bugs in heaven?" We hope not, but
the rest of your family is welcome. Meanwhile, you can be sure
when she cashes a check in that town, everybody "in the gates"
knows what her husband does for a living.

This verse from Proverbs might bristle the neck hairs of some
of us. "Why isn't *she* known in the gates?" we might ask. "Why is
she always in the home, and her *husband* goes where the action is,
where the business of government and society are conducted?"

No need to get our pantyhose in a knot. The Proverbs woman
will indeed be "known in the gates" for her good deeds by the
time we hit verse 31. The fact that her husband is respected
there, too, is just another feather in her cap. They make a
dynamite team, just like Brenda and Roy.

Bill and I have an interesting situation in that I left my full-time job at WHAS-AM in 1987 and he started at WHAS-TV two years later, in 1989. Although they are now owned by two different companies, our radio and TV stations were in the same building and shared several staff members. When I went to his first Christmas party, I was taken aback that so few people remembered me, but everybody knew Bill, of course. I was introduced again and again as "Bill's wife." Now, *he* was "known in the gates," and I wasn't. Bah, humbug! The evening turned out to be a fairly severe ego squash for me.

It was also a reminder that the world does not ascribe much value to the stay-at-home mother. People said things like, "Didn't you used to be Liz Curtis?" or the old standby, "What do you do all day?" My customary response was to look at them with my head held high and say, "I'm molding, shaping, and influencing the next generation. What do *you* do all day?"

Psychologist Dr. Layne Longfellow observes that in our society, historically, "we have assigned love to women and work to men." Of course, today we have women who love working and men who are working at being more loving. Dr. Longfellow suggests, "We have to create permission for women to find their own individual balance between work and love, intimacy and competency."[1] My intent here has been to affirm both the stay-at-home mother and the mother who works outside the home. If a woman is in tune with her God and her partner, then her choices about gates or no gates is in good hands.

"Iron John" or the Tin Man?

Since this verse focuses on what the husband of the ideal wife is about, suppose we train our camera on the men for a chapter or so and see how they measure up to her standards, as well as ours.

Breathes there a man on this planet worthy of being called perfect? Joanne admits that "even though he is not perfect, my husband is perfect for me!" Vivian cautions, "There are no perfect husbands, only men who make the most of positives in their mates and ignore the negatives." From Anita come these words of wisdom: "The older I get, the more I accept that there is no perfect husband, and that has helped our relationship."

Her husband is known in the gates, / When he sits among the elders of the land.

We had all sorts of stereotypes for describing the "perfect wife"—Donna Reed, June Cleaver, Betty Crocker, Mae West—but no names popped up in our descriptions for the husband. We didn't profess a desire to be married to John Wayne, Rhett Butler, the Galloping Gourmet, or Fred Flintstone. Not even Mel Gibson's name came up as an example of Mr. Perfect (though now that we've mentioned it . . .).

What we *did* find appealing is a man who "loves unconditionally, can handle 'mood swings,' and is involved with the children," said Rebecca. Someone who is "always there for you, even when you let the fuel injected car run out of gas (that's a bad thing to do)," wrote Linda from Arkansas. Sheri thinks "perfect" would be a man who "wouldn't grumble because things are out of place and the kids are whining."

Susan from Alabama remembers how helpful her husband was late one night:

> When my son was teething, he woke up several times crying, and my husband finally volunteered to get up and care for him. As he got out of bed he asked me where the teething ointment was. "In the diaper bag," I told him. He never turned the light on, just reached in the bag, got out a tube and squeezed it, and smeared it on the baby's gums.
>
> My husband thought it felt funny—"too sticky"—so he turned on the light and discovered he had coated the baby's gums with diaper rash ointment! Here the two of them came, running into our bedroom, my baby's mouth covered with white stuff as he licked his lips! We called the poison center, and they assured us that there wasn't enough zinc in the ointment to harm the baby. They also wanted to know if it helped his teething pain. It must have—he slept the rest of the night!

I think she means the baby. I'm not sure about the husband.

I like Bea from North Dakota's wish list for a man: "Partial hearing loss. Suggests eating out often." A man who *"fixes* what needs fixing!" appeals to Sonya. Finally, there's Sherri from West Virginia and her version of the ideal sweetie: "Caring, good listener, loving, respectful, honest, plus can kill *all* types of 'creepy-crawlies'"!

In response to this "describe the perfect husband" question, the legal department of a large company in Charlotte faxed to me a list of "Seminars for Men" that, ostensibly, female staff members would be offering to the men in their company:

Course #104: "How to Fill the Ice Tray"
>   (I wonder if they'd have a correspondence course for Bill.)

Course #123: "The Remote Control—Overcoming Your Dependency"
>   (I just hide it!)

Course #130: "Real Men Ask for Directions"
>   (Helpful women take maps.)

The sign-up sheet reminded interested parties that "class size will be limited to ten as course material may prove difficult."

Now this kind of spoof is funny, no doubt about it. When I showed the list to Bill, he laughed as he read it but then handed it back to me and said, "If the men in our office circulated a similar list of seminars for women, the females would raise the roof." Of course, he's right. Hm-m-m.

All Hail the Working Father

Patty from Indiana believes she married the perfect husband—"or at least he's as close as men come!" She wrote, "From the time I went back to work following the birth of our son six years ago, my husband has been a full-time working dad. Right from the start he took our son with him on visits to hospitals and shut-ins (he's a minister). My son learned social skills that most children his age never get the opportunity to learn."

Not only does this wonder man help with childcare, but "his roasts and chickens are great! He also sometimes cleans and runs the vacuum. Since we've been married, we've tried to operate our household under the idea of whoever has the most time pitches in to do what needs [to be] done."

For my money, Patty and her husband have the best kind of contemporary marriage: a team. She obviously adores him, he is committed to her, and they both love their son. Undoubtedly, all three of them are "known in the gates" as a fine example of family.

22
Delivereth Us from Girdles

She makes linen garments and sells them, / And supplies sashes for the merchants.

Proverbs 31:24 NKJV

*T*he good old King James translation says she "delivereth girdles unto the merchant." Great idea. Let the merchants wear them. I was delivered from those instruments of torture back in 1968 with the advent of pantyhose. A blessing, I think.

Our Proverbs role model chose the best of both worlds: working at home, then delivering her girdles—uh, sashes or belts—to the gates for the merchants to sell. Very clever woman, this. In the current vernacular, we would say she had a cottage industry.

Brenda Hunter, author of *Where Have All the Mothers Gone?* said, "Women who use their gifts or hobbies to create their own businesses are among the most satisfied working mothers I know."[1] Lots of us are seeking that satisfaction these days. According to LINK Resources, "The number of self-employed women working full time at home tripled between 1985 and 1991, from 378,000 to 1.1 million."[2] *Tripled!* That's more than a trend, that's an avalanche.

Mind Your Own Business

The survey question that produced some of the most interesting results was this one: "If money were not at all a consideration, I would . . ." (circle one)

Quit working

Find a more satisfying job

Keep the same job

Start my own business

One option I did not offer, and should have, was "Go back to school," but several wrote that one in anyway.

Here's what we chose: Thirty percent wanted to quit working; of those, half were mothers with children, who preferred to be home with their kids. Forty percent were happy to keep their current job, either from a high degree of enjoyment or a sense of job security. And, 9 percent were ready for greener pastures and would seek more satisfying work.

That left a full 21 percent of us who would, if money were available, start our own businesses. Add to that the dozens of women who filled out the survey and already owned their own businesses, and that's an impressive number! And what if some of the 30 percent, rather than quit work altogether, could come up with a creative way to earn money at home? And what if those looking for more satisfaction decided they would find it by working for themselves? That would add up to more than 60 percent of us! The potential for women working at home is viable, exciting, and certainly the direction many of us are headed for in the twenty-first century.

What home businesses come to mind? In her wonderful collection of advice called *The Mommy Book*, Karen Hull suggests several: home typing (or data entry), proofreading, music lessons, dressmaking and alterations, crafts, home baby-sitting, catering.[3] These are what we might call the traditional home-based businesses for women, and they are still very legitimate pursuits. After all, our Proverbs 31 woman is qualified to do *all* of them—though not at the same time, of course.

On the surveys, we found that women dreamed of being: an interior designer, a consultant, an artist, a travel writer, a horse breeder and trainer, and "a party planner for working moms." (Where do I sign up for *her* services?)

Two different women in Texas expressed a desire to own their own craft stores and fill them with their creations. I'm tempted to put them together and watch what might happen if their mutual dream took shape! Another woman wanted to run a clothing store, and Gloria dreamed of owning "a wildly success-ful wedding catering business." My favorite answer was the woman who circled "Start my own business," then listed her dream occupation as "astronaut." Boy, the start-up costs on *that* one would be . . . astronomical!

First, the Bad News

For those women and thousands more among us who have seriously thought about working from home, let me gently dispel three myths about the advantages of owning a home business:

1. Flexible Hours

When someone asks me where I work and I say, "I have a speaking business with an office behind my house," their immediate reaction is, "It must be so nice to make your own hours!" I sure do . . . *all* of them. A home-based business takes quite a while to establish, so in the first twelve to thirty-six months, you are working every chance you get. When the kids nap, Mom works. At school? Mom works. Asleep at night? Mom works. Although you won't need to punch a time clock, it might be worthwhile to jot down your hours each day to get a feel of how much this "little business" requires of your life. Most self-employed women I know put in fifty to seventy hours a week and don't sleep much.

2. Convenience with No Commuting

The phrase "run your business out of your home" can

easily be reversed to, "your business runs you out of *your* home!" What began in the back corner of our back bedroom soon engulfed the room so completely we had to take the bed out and put in a second desk and storage shelves. Soon, all my paper supplies—cards, letterhead, envelopes, brochures, articles, and so on—began flowing out of the bedroom-turned-office and into the living room. At first, the boxes were just going to be there for a few days, and a month later, three more were stacked on top. We tried moving the boxes to an upstairs closet . . . *not* good. The plaster ceiling in our dining room collapsed under the weight of all that paper! Suffice to say, a business at home is handy but hard to contain.

3. Big Bucks

It *is* nice to know that whatever money you bring in is all yours. Well, almost all yours. The IRS will take a big chunk, especially with that nice self-employment tax on top of paying all your other taxes yourself. Plus there are no benefits, such as health or life insurance, unless you buy them. Then, add in office supplies, printing, marketing, advertising, long-distance phone calls—the list goes on and on, depending on the business. The more it grows, the more it costs to maintain. Nothing will mess up your profit margin like success! Many of our "one woman shows" grew such that we had to hire an employee or two, which for many of us turned out to be our single greatest business expense. Somewhere on that spreadsheet is a perfect balance between the top line—gross—and the bottom line—net. Unfortunately, many small businesses struggle to find that optimum spot between profit and loss.

Now, the Good News

If I've discouraged you from starting your own business, that's good! It is not for everyone and should not be entered into lightly.

But there are some distinct benefits that don't carry to the bottom line but do connect nicely to the heart line. Working in the back bedroom when my children were little, I would play footsie with Matthew as he crawled about on a quilt at my feet. He was a very happy baby and stayed that way as long as Mother was in view. Especially in the first year, children really do sleep a lot, so finding time to make phone calls and type letters was not difficult.

After Lillian came along twenty months later, things got noisier, and clients would occasionally ask, "Who is making all that racket in the background?"

I would reply cooly, "Senior management."

When he was old enough to reach the keys, I taught Matthew how to push the buttons on the calculator to make the place sound more like a busy office and less like a busy nursery. The children always went with me on errand runs, to the post office or the printer, and solved the one problem that often plagues a sole proprietor: isolation and loneliness.

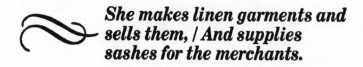 ***She makes linen garments and sells them, / And supplies sashes for the merchants.***

As they are growing, the kids are able to help me with some of the busy work that goes along with any small business: putting stamps on envelopes, attaching mailing labels, putting packing peanuts in boxes, and so forth. We make it a game (which means it takes twice as long), but they *are* the reason I wanted to work out of my home in the first place!

When you have your own business in your home, you have a hard time explaining what you do for Career Day at school. Telling five-year-olds that you're a speaker draws a Big Blank, so I started drawing them into the discussion by asking, "What are *you* going to do when you grow up?" One angelic-faced child turned very pink and stammered, "I'm not going to do *anything* until I get married!" This child has been well trained.

If the survey results are representative, our husbands would love to see us enjoy career success, too, especially if it greatly increases the family's bottom line. Denise said her husband would be so proud of her if she "accomplished a major task, like write a book." As long as he understands that you'll probably never get rich that way, go for it! Judy thought her hubby would be happy if she "made $100,000 a year or more." Right. Finally, Brenda from Hawaii just knew her husband would be pleased if she were "chief money earner and sex kitten." (The only way she could have the energy to be both is if she were a money earner *as* a sex kitten, and that's probably out!)

Whether we make those girdles for the merchants at home or on a job site, some of us have found our husbands may enjoy the extra income but resent our commitment of time and energy to the task, "particularly when they feel their wives aren't giving them the kind of attention they want," noted author Bebe Campbell. She also discovered many instances when women who carefully selected a mate who promised to aid and support them in their professional goals "were angry because their husbands withdrew the support just when they needed it most."[4] It's especially important when home is our place of work that our families be included in the decision making. I've always said that talking quietly now prevents talking loudly later. Bill's goal for our marriage-family-work combo is to land somewhere between Ozzie and Harriet and separate vacations.

Encouragement, Please!

The most important ingredient for success when working at home is to have a network of friends to encourage you, pitch in when needed, and spread the word. Precious is the friend who understands that this *is* a real job—with hours, commitments, and deadlines—yet knows that your family responsibilities come first, and supports your attempts to combine the two.

Debbie from Ohio included a plea for encouragement about going back to work. "I know I can do it," she wrote. "I know my family will survive. It's just taking the plunge that is difficult." No question, it will require some days (weeks? months?) of adjustment, but your family may thrive, not just survive.

What we need most from one another as women is support and positive reinforcement for our businesses, our choices, and our balancing acts. I spoke at a church one Sunday evening, with the children and Bill seated in the front pew. I was so proud of them: they didn't make any faces at me, and even Bill laughed at stories he'd heard a dozen times. When I went to the back of the church at the close of the program, a dear woman came up to me, took my hand, and looked me in the eye. I was certain she was going to join the chorus of, "I thoroughly enjoyed your message," or (oh dear!), "I've never heard a woman speaker before. What did you say your name was again, honey?"

But here's what she said: "Liz, I watched you with your children this evening. You must be a pretty special mom."

Thank you, thank you, thank you. As much as we all enjoy praise for our work, most of us could really use some encouragement in those less visible arenas. Mark Twain said, "I can live for two months on a good compliment." Better than that. So far, I've lived on her kind words for four years!

On the Road with Mom

I found lots of words to encourage us in a nifty book by Katherine Wyse Goldman called *My Mother Worked and I Turned Out Okay*. It's the kind of book you read and say, "Boy, I wish I'd written that!" Since she did, and I didn't, here are two of her brilliant observations:

• Children who know what their mothers do all day at work are more inclined to tell their mothers what they do all day at school.

• Working mothers are masters at including the kids and making everybody think it was a good idea.[5]

I especially love to include the kids when we travel. When I spoke in Montana, Alaska, Michigan, Ohio, and Missouri, the whole family went. *Big* fun. When I spoke in Orlando, five-year-old Matthew went along, so when the speech was over we could visit—where else?—Disney World.

Lillian was the star attraction on a speaking jaunt to Pennsylvania, where various relatives amused her while I spoke and my mother-in-law came along to be of service. I still remember changing Lillian's diaper during our tour of the Lancaster County countryside. We were way out in the middle of nowhere, and there wasn't a dumpster in sight. The only containers to be found were rural mailboxes. Just for a second, we considered slipping our little "bomb" in one of them, putting the flag up, and hitting the gas! You'll be relieved to know we did no such thing.

Sometimes I do have to travel alone, but those trips are generally twenty-four hours long, and I'm back home before too much damage is done to the house. Although the travel is the most challenging part of my business, it's also my best source of stories. Staying at a hotel in Mason City, Iowa, I called down to the front desk and asked them to kindly send up an iron and an ironing board, which they dutifully did. Attached to this big ironing board was a little tag to remind me it belonged to the Sheraton. But, on the flip side of the tag it said: "If carried away inadvertently, drop in any mailbox."

In all my years of staying in hotels, I have never found myself in the lobby saying, "Oh, my word, there's an ironing board in my purse!" Nor have I ever seen a woman trying to stuff one in a mailbox. A diaper maybe, but never an ironing board.

The truth is, I don't work at home. I *play* at home and get paid for it—which should be the goal of all our labors, wherever and however they take place. Katharine Graham said it perfectly: "To love what you do and feel that it matters . . . how could anything be more fun?"

23
Dressed for Success

~

Strength and honor are her clothing.
Proverbs 31:25 NKJV

*B*oy, could this woman dress!

Not just in linen like the priests, not just in purple like royalty, not just in her own fabulous handmade creations, but she wore strength like a shield. In the Hebrew, the word means "mighty fortress" and "powerful stronghold." Sounds like the hymn that Luther wrote: "A mighty fortress is our God."

And she was clothed in honor, meaning "dignity, splendor, majesty, and beauty," from head to toe. The truth is, when you are attired in such timeless virtues and that's what people see first, you really are dressed for success.

What makes her godly attire especially attractive is the combination: strength *and* honor. We've all known women who were strong, but not very honorable. Our television screens are filled with them. And there are women who are honorable, but frankly, not very strong. The first setback or the first perceived threat, and they fold up like a card table.

The kind of women most of us long to be are both strong and honorable, clothed with the kind of power that comes from on high, certain of our value in God's eyes, definite in our calling, and moving forward with complete assurance. Francis De Sales said, "Nothing is so strong as gentleness, nothing so gentle as real strength."

Strong, Honorable . . . and a Little Nervous

Gale from Kentucky needed all the strength and dignity she could muster to get her through this experience. When her son was fourteen, he wanted to have some friends over to "camp out" behind the barn.

As the planning and telephone calls began, I had the feeling he had something else up his sleeve. Finally he told me some girls might come by but only for a little while. "Okay," I said, trying to be a cool mom while knowing I was going to watch them like a hawk!

The evening came and so did the guys. We visited with them for a while and asked where the girls were. Disappointed faces and shrugged shoulders told us the guys had been stood up. I must say, I was relieved, and my husband and I went on to bed.

Around 11:00, I heard the gravel in the driveway. I couldn't believe it! The girls had arrived. What should I do? I didn't want to make a scene, so I decided to watch from the upstairs bedroom window. The kids stood around and talked, and after about ten minutes, the car pulled out. Good!

The next morning, I went out to see if everything was cleaned up, and other than a few plastic cups, they'd done a nice job. I bent over to pick up a napkin and saw what I had hoped I'd never see. There it was, a small square package with a round indentation in the center. The edges were torn back. No doubt about it—there was a condom in my yard!

A million thoughts crashed through my mind: "Maybe it was longer than ten minutes? Maybe one of the girls had stayed behind? What would I say to my son? How should I handle this?"

All this between seeing the package and bending down to pick it up. Then I turned it over to read the label: "Alka Seltzer." Can you believe it?! I almost ended up in the coronary unit because some kid had an upset stomach!

Yes, we can believe it.

"Strong Enough for a Man, Gentle Enough for a Woman"

Notice that our Proverbs woman is not dressed for battle. In the '70s and '80s women wore business attire like a suit of armor as we headed out to slay dragons in the business world. "I can dress like, think like, and work like a man," our clothing said. "I can fit into Corporate America." Reminds me of an old pack of stick-'em notes I found in the deep recesses of my desk, which showed "The Career Woman's checklist for success: look like a lady, act like a man, work like a dog." That was "strength" to us not long ago.

Now wisdom and balance are creeping back in, and we are finding out what it really means to "dress for success." As the Amplified version says, "Strength and dignity are her clothing and her position is strong and secure."

Since I am a woman who is, shall we say, strong-willed, forthright, not afraid to state her mind, aggressive, powerful, and other words folks have used over the years that are *not* appropriate to print, I have always questioned how to use my strong personality in a dignified way. Teresa from Kansas stated it exactly: "My assertiveness sometimes sounds aggressive."

For Teresa and me, and maybe you, Peter Guber advised, "The trick is to use the least amount of power to create the maximum amount of change. Someone who has elegance can apply power selectively like a laser," and do so "carefully, almost unobtrusively, so that you don't feel you're being overpowered. You feel like you're being motivated."[1]

Another mark of dignity is our ability to use strength for the good of others, and not simply for our personal advancement. Kate Halverson once said, "If you are all wrapped up in yourself, you are overdressed."[2]

Dressed for All Eternity

If, as the original Hebrew words suggest, this woman's strength and dignity are grounded in her spirituality, it might be worth looking into who our spiritual role models might be.

On the surveys, many left the question, "Who is your spiritual role model?" blank. Others wrote: "unsure," "never gave it much thought—I really don't know," "I don't have a spiritual role model," "?? I guess I don't have or want one," "it's strange, I've never thought about this," and "big vacuum here—I've lost it."

I always appreciate the honesty of someone willing to respond to such a personal question at all. Until a dozen years ago, I would've answered with a big question mark myself. For many of us, when we moved into our thirties, into marriage, or into motherhood, the questions those new roles raised triggered a desire within us to explore the spiritual side of ourselves again, or perhaps for the first time.

Strength and honor are her clothing.

Our role models in the area of spirituality are both wide and deep. More than one hundred of us specifically wrote down "God." Nancy looks up to "the Lord—his understanding, his strength, everything." Doris wrote, "Jesus—his ability to love and forgive." Molly chose, "God the Father—he has never given me bad advice."

Others of us listed role models with flesh on them, such as Sandy who admires her pastor whose "life is glowing with God's light and love." Anita mentioned "a Sunday school teacher of years ago," and Joan described a woman whom I also greatly admire, "Mother Teresa . . . she is so caring and giving."

Gayle honored "St. Jude (for lost causes) because that's almost the state of our house!" Cara turned to friends with fur on them for spiritual nurturing, listing "animals in general and young children." Indeed, their innocence and closeness to their Creator point us in the right direction.

Then, there's Mary Anne who included among her spiritual role models, "Angels—for reassurance." Besides, everyone knows that angels wear the most heavenly wardrobe around!

24

A Laugh a Day Puts Wrinkles in the Right Places

She smiles at the future.

Proverbs 31:25b NASB

Any woman who can, as the Hebrew declares, "smile, laugh, make merry, celebrate, rejoice, and have no fear" about the future is my kind of role model. She didn't just smile, she snorted. She didn't just giggle, she guffawed. She didn't just snicker, she roared. What a woman! As Bonnie Altenhein wrote in *How Angels Get Their Wings,* "An angel adopts grinning as a second language."[1]

My role models growing up were all funny women. First, I loved Lucy. And Ethel. Then, I longed to be Carol Burnett and was jealous for years that Vicki Lawrence got to be on her show and I didn't. Phyllis Diller, who said, "A smile is a curve that sets everything straight," was always a favorite, talking about her husband, Fang. Lily Tomlin is brilliant and off-beat, and Gilda Radner was a sprite who still twinkles in our hearts.

The funniest women to me are the ones who initiate humor, rather than follow after it or play the straight person: that is to say, Bea Arthur as Maude, rather than Jean Stapleton as Edith Bunker (though she is as fine a comic actress as they come!). It takes a certain kind of woman to shake off the "women can't tell jokes" stereotype and venture out on her own into the humor limelight.

Society values a sense of humor, consistently ranking it in the top five desirable attributes for an employee or a spouse. Among the Navajo Indians there is a tradition known as "The First Laugh Ceremony." The friend or family member who witnesses the baby's first laugh is given the privilege of throwing a celebration in honor of the occasion, considered to mark the child's entrance into society.[2]

Our sense of humor may assert itself at a young age but may not always be applauded. Bette Midler once said, "If only I'd known that one day my differentness would be an asset, then my earlier life would have been much easier."[3] So true! Yet, if I were "normal," I wouldn't be a humorist. Finding humor requires the ability to see life through glasses that aren't so much rose-colored as they are bifocals; they throw us off balance and so provide another view of things.

Take the advertisement I found for Johnson's Swabs in a woman's magazine. The copy read: "Johnson's Swabs now come in beautiful decorator canisters. . . . One for every room of the house." Immediately, my curiosity was aroused; I must have missed this in home ec. Are we supposed to have swabs in every room? Tissues, maybe, but *swabs?* I suppose you could choose a decorator canister to match your dining room set, just in case your guests want to clean their ears before dinner.

I like George Burns's philosophy: "If I get big laughs, I'm a comedian. If I get little laughs, I'm a humorist. If I get no laughs, I'm a singer." Believe me, when I perform, I have a song ready, just in case!

Too Busy to Laugh Is Too Busy

Of course, to be like our Proverbs woman and smile at the days to come, we need to do more chuckling in the present. Our modern sisters are not doing nearly enough merry-making, I can tell you that. When I encourage women to laugh more, they tell me in tight-lipped, terse tones, "I'm too busy to laugh. I don't have time to rent a funny video, and even if I did, I don't have time to watch it. I don't have time to buy a funny book, and even if I did, I don't have time to read it. I just don't have time for foolishness!"

That's us, all right. Poor dears, we are missing the Big Picture, which is that all work and no play makes Jill not only a dull girl, but also a sick one. Laughter is good for our hearts, souls, and minds. It costs virtually nothing, yet its therapeutic effect tops many an expensive medicine.

In theory, we know what we need: "more laughter, less mail!" "more fun, less worrying"; "more chocolate, fewer complications"; and my favorite, from Laura in Ohio, "more private bathroom time and less saturated fat!"

Laughing is the one time we express our true selves, our true nature. There is *no* such thing as "image laughing." You can learn how to walk, stand, sit, eat properly, but when you laugh, you lay all pretense aside and just let go. That's why laughing is so good for you. Anyway, Fred Allen says, "It's bad to suppress laughter. It goes right back down and spreads to your hips."

We know we need to lighten up: "After a bad day at work, a poopy diaper, and six trips for a glass of water at bedtime . . . I need a laugh!" wrote Pam. Carol said, "Make me laugh at things we sometimes take too seriously—like housework." Oh, that's always a laugh at our house. And, concerning this book, Marsha from New Mexico wanted to hear about "both the fun and the *not* so fun aspects of life" as well as how we can "survive it all with humor." The truth is, we can't survive *without* humor.

Children Have Funny Bones Too

Few things make us smile more than children and the things they say. Sandra from Mississippi stifled a laugh when they brought home a cocker spaniel puppy and their youngest asked if that meant it would bark in Spanish. On another occasion, when their car was just turning over 50,000 miles, she was showing her boys where to look on the dash, to which the youngest said, "We'll have to get gas soon, huh, Mom?"

Molly from North Dakota remembered the evening her six-year-old came in from playing with a friend. He was "talking very fast, his eyes like saucers. 'Mom, Mom, Joshua was telling me all about the boogey monster, and I got the willies!'" She asked him, "What are the willies, Daniel?" to which he replied, "You know, when you get willy scared and willy nervous!"

Once those little ones grow up, not everything they say is so cute and funny. One woman admitted, "I hope the Lord comes back before my son turns thirteen!" Meanwhile, if we have husbands, we can count on their sense of humor remaining childlike—or is that juvenile?—forever. Comedian Jay Leno admitted, "All men laugh at the Three Stooges, and all women think they are dumb. When Moe hits Larry with a shovel, the guy cracks up; the woman will get up, mutter 'Stupid!' and turn the set off. When was the last time you saw two women go, 'Nyuk, Nyuk, Nyuk'?"[4]

My Husband, the Humorist

Come to think of it, Bill's sense of humor is very different from mine. His is a dry wit, quiet and clever. Mine is all bold and physical and pratfalls and big grins. As in all things, we are very different when it comes to what makes us laugh and how we make others laugh.

To this day, I'm not sure whether Bill meant this to be funny or not. For my first Mother's Day, instead of getting something sweet for the nursery or something romantic, he got me a fishing license.

This was not on my wish list for Mother's Day, but it was on *his* list for Father's Day. When he checked into it, he found out that Kentucky sells a husband-and-wife fishing license. It's a little cheaper that way, and Bill, remember, is tight. The license must show the exact height and weight for both spouses, so Bill filled out my half for me. He told those nice people in Frankfort that I am 5′9″ (correct), 132 pounds (not correct). Not even close. Even taking a stab-in-the-dark guess, you would come up with a higher number. A much higher number.

So, I'm looking in his eyes for a clue. Is he kidding, or is he serious? He's so analytical, maybe he thought to himself: "I wear a size 44 suit, and Liz wears a size 22 dress. Maybe she's about half my size?"

Finally, the gleam in his eye suggested that I had been had.

"You turkey!" I said with a wink. "What am I going to say when the Fish and Game Commissioner stops us and wants to see our license? 'Sorry, sir, I stopped at Hardee's!'?"

Holy Humor

I have a soft place in my heart for the good old days of television: of watching Carol Burnett transform herself into a washer woman, of watching Jack Benny fold his arms just so, of hearing Red Skelton, a man who once said, "If I can make people smile, then I have served my purpose for God," end his show by whispering, "God bless." We can still watch Dick Van Dyke fall over the ottoman on late night reruns, but I miss the variety shows, the live television comedy hours, even the early years of _Saturday Night Live_.

Of course, as Griff Niblak in the _Indianapolis News_ said, "If you're yearning for the good old days, just turn off the air conditioning." Maybe not. Maybe we need to be like our proverbial sister and smile, not at the past, but at the future. One commentator wrote, "She has full confidence in her ability and resources to meet the challenges of the future. Perhaps, this is her most enviable characteristic."[5]

Reinhold Niebuhr, best known for penning the Serenity Prayer, also wrote: "Humor is a prelude to faith, and laughter is the beginning of prayer." For those who love God, laughter isn't optional, it's scriptural. As we all love to repeat, "A merry heart doeth good like a medicine" (Prov. 17:22 KJV). As a woman who believes in the power of faith _and_ humor, I am heaven-bent to bring more laughter into our lives.

Joy shows up in the Bible more than two hundred times, but I wish there were more in there about laughter. After all, we know "Jesus wept" (John 11:35 NKJV). Why not another nice short verse to assure us, "Jesus laughed"? Cal Samra, founder of the Fellowship of Merry Christians, of which I'm proud to be a member, offers valid proof that Jesus did indeed laugh. "We know that Jesus loved children, who laugh frequently and spontaneously." Samra rightly suggests that he also laughed "at the bumblings of his all-too-human disciples, who were missing the point and messing things up."[6]

I wonder if the big blast of sound we call laughter today might not have been what the psalmist had in mind when he wrote, "Shout joyfully to the LORD, all the earth" (Ps. 98:4 NKJV). After all, they had other words for singing. And if two million Israelites stood around shouting "Hooray for God!" at the top of their lungs, somebody had to start laughing sooner or later.

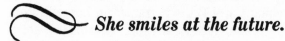 *She smiles at the future.*

We all see and hear things each day that make us shout joyfully. For her job as an educational consultant, Stacy from Kansas does some home visits with families. "I asked one lady for directions, and she promptly replied, 'I live in the third house on the passenger side of the street.'" Oh, that's helpful.

Or there was the sign I saw in the window of a music store: "Used Organs for Sale." Are we talking spleens and kidneys in the piano benches, or what?

Another favorite sign appeared on the outskirts of a small town with one fast food restaurant—not McDonald's. This was "Skeeter's: Home of the Big Biscuit." The big hand-lettered sign hanging out front said, with no punctuation: "Drive Thru 50 Item Salad Bar." I pictured a family of four, all leaning out of their Suburban, trying to keep the croutons from blowing off their salads. "Dad, back up, I missed the dressing!"

Driving through western Kentucky recently, I found myself on the Pennyrile Parkway, a toll road. When I came to the first exit, the Department of Transportation folks had posted a big sign: "Do Not Exit Without Exact Change."

Sure doesn't give you many choices. I'm thinking, *Why didn't they put that sign up before I got on?* People have been driving the Pennyrile for weeks, just hoping to pick up a hitchhiker with the exact change.

When the Laughter Stops

When you are the one people turn to for laughter—the life of the party, the class clown, the raconteur—people expect you to always be on, to be funny all the time. Even those of us who make people laugh for a living can't live up to that expectation. My first pastor, Bob Russell, tells the story of a man who had fallen into such a deep depression that he finally placed himself in the hands of a therapist.

"I have an unusual prescription for you," the therapist told him. "The circus is in town, and last night I saw the funniest clown there ever was. Thirty minutes of watching the Great Rinaldi, and you'll feel 100 percent better."

With tears in his eyes, the patient replied, "I am the Great Rinaldi."

I have yet to meet a humorist, a comedian, or a clown that didn't have some deep hurt at the heart of his or her humor. When we laugh at something, we are in essence saying, "I identify with that!" If someone stood up and described all their blessings, we would be disgusted. When they stand up and share all their faults and foibles, we laugh and love them for it. Rosita Perez kindly encouraged me in a letter with these words: "Whoever says laughter isn't healing just hasn't hurt enough."

Laughter does not mean you are ignoring pain, living in denial, or just not aware of the troubles around you. Solomon said, "Even in laughter the heart may ache" (Prov. 14:13 NIV). For me, laughter is how we take a much-needed break from the heartache, such that when we turn to face it again, it has by some miracle grown smaller in size and intensity, if not disappeared altogether.

An Oklahoma woman wrote, "Laughter was the prescription to help me deal with the unfaithfulness and abandonment by my husband for a woman younger than our two oldest daughters. A laugh a day—a good belly laugh—made me well."

We women need to help each other heal our hurts with laughter. That's really my mission in life, why I speak, why I write. I've watched women who were almost bent over with arthritis laugh until they forgot to hurt. "Look at this!" they call out, waving their arms in the air with glee. "No pain!"

And I've known women who've shared their deepest sorrows with me, how they've lost touch with God and with themselves, then I watch them, sitting in the audience, tears of joy streaming down their faces. "Are you laughing or crying?" I ask them.

"Yes!" they reply.

25
Open Mouth, Insert Kindness

**She opens her mouth with wisdom, /
And on her tongue is the law of kindness.**

Proverbs 31:26 NKJV

She parted her lips to smile, laugh, and make merry; now it's time for her to speak! After fifteen verses describing her glorious talents, her skillful hands and her sacrificial schedule, the woman is finally going to open her mouth and tell us what is on her mind and in her heart: wisdom and kindness, of course.

We are not surprised. Her actions have already spoken loudly on her behalf. Her husband, children, friends, neighbors, even those elders at the gate paid attention when she opened her mouth.

When Brandy from Oregon described a perfect wife, she hit the old nail on the head for this Proverbs woman: "She's patient, intuitive, patient, kind, patient, thoughtful, patient, strong, and has the patience of Job!"

A Little Whine with Dinner

Most of us, however, do not have the patience of Lot's wife, let alone that of Job. Looking over some of the things we would like to modify about ourselves, it's comforting to know that many of us share the same struggles with loose lips. With the names removed to protect the guilty, here's what we'd like to change when we open our mouths:

"Be less critical"

"Talk less"

"Communicate in a more positive and mature way"

"Do less criticizing and yelling"

"Think before I speak"

"Less whining"

"Stop yelling for no reason"

"Control my tongue"

All I can say is: "Me too!" As one who speaks for a living, I shudder to think of how many wasted words, empty phrases, and meaningless mumblings I've gone through in my career. To help me improve my skills, I've dutifully sat through numerous professional development seminars to teach me how to be a more effective speaker, when the answer was here in Proverbs 31 all along.

By example, our ancient sister provides a simple three-point, how-to presentation:

1. First, she spoke with actions, doing good deeds with great skill.

2. Therefore, her "audiences" sat up and paid attention.

3. Then, she was able to offer words of wisdom and instruction.

Mark Twain had her pegged: "Few things are harder to put up with than the annoyance of a good example!" It was because she spoke from a position of strength and firsthand knowledge that people were willing, even eager, to listen to her wisdom, steeped in kindness.

Where does wisdom come from, anyway? We get it from people we trust and admire, like parents, teachers, leaders, role models. Wisdom comes from experience too. A fact, lived out, becomes experience. An experience repeated becomes wisdom.

Good Books

I find wisdom in books too. *Jacob the Baker* by Noah ben Shea is filled with wisdom. The book of Proverbs is even called "Wisdom Literature." *Mere Christianity* by C. S. Lewis and *Practicing the Presence of God* by Brother Lawrence are books I turn to again and again because of their wisdom.

There's one problem with books. I'll read something wonderful, close it up, put it on a shelf, and not have the faintest idea where I read that great idea. Short of reading the book again, I have no way of locating it.

The solution is obvious: I am learning to write in my books—to underline, circle, make notes, do whatever I please. See, I always thought books were stamped "Fragile." No bending down the corners, no highlighting, and no writing in the margins. So much for that. When I'm through with a book now, it looks read. Dogeared pages, two and three colors of pens, scribbled words, and totally stray ideas jotted in the back cover. Mercy!

Now, not only has the book become part of me, but I've also become part of it. We have history together. When I take it off the shelf, I can see clearly the wisdom I've gained not only from the book itself, but from the days I've lived since the last time I read it.

What Children Say

Diana from Kentucky remembers when a book figured in to her daughter's costume for Career Day. "When my daughter was in fifth grade, she showed up in the kitchen one Tuesday morning dressed in her finest Sunday attire. 'Where's my Bible?' she asked. 'On the shelf in your room,' was my quick but baffled reply. 'Why?'

"She replied sweetly, 'It's Career Day, and I'm going as a mistress.' Being a wise mother, I knew that if she truly was going to school as a 'mistress,' she most certainly needed that Bible. 'Do you know what a mistress is?' I inquired. 'Of course I do!' she stormed. 'It's a female minister!'"

Our children expect us to be full of wisdom and know everything. Penny from Alaska's four-year-old once announced, "Mom, God made us!"

She was thrilled and said "That's right, son! God made us."

Then he asked, "But, how do they put heads on?"

Their seven-year-old daughter, equally interested in spiritual things, asked her father, "Will everybody who goes to church go to heaven? You know, like the Jehovah's Witnesses and the Ft. Lauderdale Saints?"

 She opens her mouth with wisdom, / And on her tongue is the law of kindness.

Crystell from Oklahoma remembers when her four-year-old son discovered "toe jam," that mysterious lint that hides between our toes. She told him, "That's why it's so important that you take a bath every night," to which he replied, "How come? It will just come back again."

Jessica, also four, was obviously very frustrated when her mother told her, "Honey, your shoes are on the wrong feet." The child replied with an exasperated sigh, "But, Mommeeee, they're the only feet I have!"

What Children Shouldn't Hear

Our children probably hear more of our words than anyone else. In the first two years, they are listening to vowels and consonants and words, so they can imitate us and say something we'll recognize: "Ma-ma!" Such music to our ears. In the pre-school years, they're listening for grammar and usage and sentence construction, to make their needs known more clearly. Once in school, language becomes a means of getting an "A" with a star on your paper, or getting a "D" with a lecture. Words, wisdom, and kindness are what a child's life is all about.

Which is why I am so disappointed in myself when I think of how often I open my mouth to criticize, gossip, make a catty remark, praise myself, speak in anger, or offer some unsupportive comment.

It was Ben Franklin who said, "Anger is never without reason, but seldom with a good one." For no valid reason whatsoever, many people live on the edge of anger, ready to explode at any moment. These are the ones who cut us off in traffic and make an ugly face at us to boot.

The more anonymous our society becomes, the easier it is to speak anger rather than kindness. Some people spout off on e-mail while they're hopping mad, then regret it after the message has arrived at its destination a mere nanosecond later. More than once, I've wished I had a reverse button on my fax machine, so I could "woosh" something back that had already been transmitted. In the old days, we would write a letter to vent our anger, then throw it away—a much better methodology, I think.

Since it is my unedited mouth, and not my carefully edited written words, that get me in trouble, I now have a plan for catching spoken bloopers too. I first stumbled on the germ of this idea in Allen Klein's marvelous book, *The Healing Power of Humor,* then customized it for my peculiar purposes.

You see, having spent ten years immersed in the wilder ways of the world, I had developed a vocabulary that was, shall we say, "colorful." Since I wanted to move past that foolish period of my life and never expose my children to those particular shades of blue, I made a list of the "Ten Things I Could Say, if I Would Say, but I *Won't* Say." Use your imagination.

Then I gave each one of these words or phrases a number, one through ten. Now when the urge to say something less than kind strikes, I let 'em have it: *"Four!"* Sometimes I even flash them all four fingers, which really confuses drivers on the highway. I can read their lips—"What is she saying to me?"—as their faces contort with confusion.

Meanwhile, the kids think this is hysterical. "Boy, Mom is really having a *seven* kind of day!" they'll sing out. It works like a charm. No one is offended, not my children, not God, nor anyone in earshot. Since I've more or less forgotten which number goes with what, I'm not offended either. And, of course, when you behave so ridiculously, you can't help but laugh at yourself.

It's not a perfect solution, but then again, I'm not a perfect woman. Just one who is aiming for the goal set before us: "When she speaks, her words are wise, and kindness is the rule for everything she says" (TLB).

26
Any Way You Slice It . . .

She watches over the ways of her
household, / And does not eat the
bread of idleness.

Proverbs 31:27 NKJV

When it comes to watching over our households, some offspring need watching more than others. Nancy from Florida has a daughter who was quite the independent girl at age two. She would get up in the middle of the night and help herself to anything she could find in the cabinets or fridge. They finally had to put a rope around the refrigerator at night to keep her out (which their friends thought was hysterical).

Very early one morning, this determined little girl made the block-and-a-half trek to a convenience store, dressed in her nightgown with bare feet. At 7:00 A.M., Nancy was awakened by a police officer knocking at her front door, daughter in tow. "I was totally speechless and very embarrassed, while my two-year-old was very proud of herself and smiled the whole time! As the officer was leaving, he advised me that I owed the convenience store fifty-nine cents for donuts."

We're watching, we're watching, but sometimes they're too fast for us!

Warning! This Section Includes Tips and Ideas

If you're going to watch over your household, you might as well do it in the most efficient manner possible. Kate Redd's book *52 Timesavers for On-The-Go Moms* is the perfect book for those of us who actually *like* lists, tips, and practical how-to ideas on getting it all done. (True Confession: I enjoy them myself occasionally and was relieved to discover I was already following some of her good suggestions.)

These are the ideas she offers that I know from experience are winners:

- Keep one big calendar (I make photocopies for Bill, fridge, and purse)

- Order from catalogs (this can be dangerous; I'm in a "toss before opening" probation period right now)

- Cluster appointments (why blow a whole morning for just one trip?)

- Streamline grocery shopping (my computerized list comes in handy here)

- Choose child-friendly places (we know 'em all, and they know us!)

- Have a back-up childcare plan (what mom in her right mind wouldn't?)

- Choose no-fuss clothing (if only I didn't find such nice things in rayon!)

One word of caution: a book like that can push our guilt meter up a notch. "I should be doing *all* these things," we think, "starting immediately!" Relax. Choose *one* idea that appeals to your current needs the most and try it for three weeks. Hide such a book until you've mastered, altered, or discarded that plan, then try one new one. Little steps add up to big leaps, eventually.

Patricia Sprinkle, author of *Women Who Do Too Much,* said, "God doesn't want you busy about everything, but He does want you busy about something. He even knows what it is."[1] Which makes me want to shout to the heavens, "What *is* it, Lord?!" To which he would probably say, "Stay tuned, Liz."

"Enjoy Them while They're Young"

Patience not being one of my strong suits, I found the first few months of motherhood, of "watching over" the newest addition to our household, to be exhausting. Of course, well-meaning souls who observed my bloodshot eyes and down-turned mouth told me two things:

1. **"Enjoy this time."**

   Give me a break. What's so enjoyable about infants who stay up all night, cry nonstop, constantly demand food, and have erratic mood swings?

2. **"It will never be like this again."**

   Hogwash. When kids become teenagers, they do the very same things only louder.

My friends mean to comfort and encourage me, I know, but what I really needed was an understanding mother to say, "You're right, it's beastly in the beginning, but soon it will be much better, I promise. Why don't you take a nap, and I'll watch your baby for an hour and clip his little nails while I'm at it?" Bless you, Pat, who did just that.

Of course, now that my children are long past this stage, what did I find myself saying to a young mother yesterday, who was holding a screaming infant and looking frazzled? "Oh, enjoy this time, because it will never be like this again!"

Debbie from Kansas would know better than to say such a thing. She was eight months pregnant and full of baby when her two-year-old crawled under a locked stall in the public rest room at the mall. She couldn't bend down, she couldn't crawl under.

All she could do was "watch over." After much talking and coaxing, her voice became more stern. "Shane, come out of there now!" she insisted. Much to her embarrassment, he replied loudly, "No, you'll knock me over like you did yesterday!"

Some of us, like Rebecca from Kentucky, yearn for "more rainbows" and "fewer clouds." With kids, you get both, usually at the same time.

Fresh from the Oven

Bill is the breadmaker in our family. It's therapy, he tells me as he kneads away at the dough. Plus you can serve it with soup.

But the kind of bread that's described in this verse isn't fit to eat. The Amplified translation draws out its true meaning: the bread of idleness is "gossip, discontent, and self-pity." Only Garfield might find that edible, since he once declared, "I'm tired of being bored, I think I'll make a lateral move to self-pity." That's the bread of idleness, all right.

In *A Mother's Heart*, author Jean Fleming included a list she wrote in her diary when her children were younger:

"What Bothers Me about Being a Mother"

1. The demands on my time

2. Serving them over and over

3. Never finishing my work

4. Frustration of not knowing how to handle problems

5. No time for my interests[2]

She hastened to add that this wasn't good, it was just the truth. I can almost hear the whine in her words because I've said every one myself.

Sometimes, in spite of our imaginary halos, we serve up the bread of idleness to our families. At our house, it culminates in a sound I make that we've all agreed would qualify as Power Whining. Call it what you will—grumbling, complaining, or permanent PMS—it is dangerous stuff and can infect an entire household in the time it takes to tear open a package of Pop Tarts.

Maybe the sound at your house could be described as "yammering." To yammer is "to whine or complain in a loud voice." Oh yes, I've done that. I've even gone around feeling disgruntled, which is odd because when I'm in a good mood, I never say I'm feeling gruntled!

"B-O-R-I-N-G!"

Sometimes, like Garfield, we're just bored with ourselves, and we've allowed that frustration to seep into everything we do. Sharon from Utah still laughs about the day her son Mike came running through the door on the last day of school, having just finished the third grade. After going out to lunch to celebrate with his siblings and playing a board game with Mom, he sat in front of the television for a total of three minutes, tumbled off the couch, stretched, rolled his eyes, and announced, "This is the most boring summer I have ever had!"

 She watches over the ways of her household, / And does not eat the bread of idleness.

Kids aren't the only ones who can get bored with the routine of life. We know that our mates might be happier if we stopped nibbling on that bread of idleness. Ellen Glasgow wisely observed that "the only difference between a rut and a grave is their dimensions." If we've dug ourselves into a rut and are feasting on "stale bread," it's time to climb out and find some healthier food.

Leslie said her husband would be so proud of her if she "didn't mope around," and Sandy admitted she should probably "quit nagging!" Another woman knew just what she wanted less of in her life: "Less poor pitiful me and less laziness."

Pet Cemetery III

Which brings us to Fran from Ohio, who knows her husband

would be happier if she'd "stop complaining about our dog and learn to love her." A true mark of sacrifice, that.

Linda from Missouri admits it has not been a great year for pets at her house either.

It began with our four-year-old goldfish leaping to his death from the bowl. Then the dog got hit by a car after he made his break from the "big house" in his quest to mark every bush on the block.

Next, my daughter's birds mistakenly thought their food bowl was a nest, began laying their eggs in their bird seed, then proceeded to peck them open. The lady at the pet store said they would do that if they felt their eggs weren't safe. They probably didn't, with the cat trying to pull the cage down on a daily basis.

Finally, my daughter's prized hamster got loose one night, and the dog licked it to death. At 5:00 A.M. I opened the bathroom door, and the light fell on the hamster's lifeless body. If I had stepped on that thing in the dark, I think I might have joined it in hamster heaven. I couldn't find a shoebox for it, so I put it in a big butter bowl with a lid, and turned the fridge into a hamster morgue until I found time to bury it that evening. I still don't understand why the girls wouldn't eat dinner.

For Linda's sake, when it comes to "watching over the ways of our household," I hope they didn't mean pets too. May the hamster, the eggs, and the goldfish rest in peace.

27

It's Never Too Late to Have a Happy Motherhood

Her children rise up and call her blessed.

Proverbs 31:28 NKJV

*T*o be blessed, according to the Amplified Bible, is to be "happy, fortunate, and to be envied." My mother may have been happy and might have considered herself fortunate. But I did not envy her.

The last day I saw my mother alive was Mother's Day 1978. Four days later, she was gone, a victim of emphysema. For the next nine years, Mother's Day was the most painful day of the year for me, followed closely by every other holiday. No matter what your age, when your mother dies, part of you dies with her.

Yet, at the same time, something was born inside me too. I began to realize that motherhood, the role I had scorned through my teen years, the job I never wanted, might be a pretty special task after all. My longing to be reunited with her was a constant reminder that mothers are one-of-a-kind VIPs. It was then that the desire to become a mother was born in my heart.

The seeds were also planted for another harvest to come: to

finally know God, my heavenly Parent, in a real and personal way. At Mom's funeral, I sang her favorite hymn, "Jesus Makes My Heart Rejoice," though in truth I had no heart knowledge of him at all at that time. It would be four more years before the words of that hymn—"I'm his sheep and know his voice"— would ring true in my heart.

My mother's death, then, led to rebirth for me. Thank you, Mom. Again. Still. "Her children rise up"—wake up, grow up, stand up, speak up, even sing out—"and call her blessed."

The Turning Point

So it was that in 1987, it was my turn to be a mother. That May, on Mother's Day, I was six months pregnant and delighted to finally be able to celebrate that special day again. When the mothers in church were asked to stand up and be recognized, I thought I was far enough along to at least raise my hand (besides, getting up took me six or seven ungraceful minutes!)

Matthew's birth in August 1987 made it official, and I had a new set of letters behind my name: Liz Curtis Higgs, MOM. Twenty months later, in April 1989, God gave me Lillian and probably "smiled at the future" a bit himself. I had just given birth to my mother's pronouncement: "Someday I hope you have a daughter who is *just like you!*"

Now that both have reached school age, I'm breathing again, sleeping better, and waiting for them to "rise up and bless me." How long does this take? Maybe King Lemuel's mother meant her *grand*children would do the rising and the blessing. Maybe when our kids have kids, that's when they'll understand all we've sacrificed for them. As Jennifer from Utah wrote, "The older my children become the more love I feel for my parents. I appreciate my mother more every day."

See, they come around eventually.

Her Children Rise up and Call Her *Stressed*

An eight-year-old boy in Illinois literally "rose up" to bless his mother, Debbie. He was entranced by Mary Poppins and her magical umbrella, so one day while Mom was at work, Dad was playing golf, and his fifteen-year-old sister was in charge, "He took an umbrella up to the roof of our house and jumped off to see if he could fly. The umbrella reversed and he came crashing to the ground. Scared his sister to death! But a few sutures and he was good as new." Good thing Mom was a nurse and had seen such things before.

When I asked women what they wanted more of and less of in their lives, one woman wanted "more vacations!" but "less stress from family members." For my money, few things can be more stressful than vacations with family! Maxine from Iowa shared her experiences on a family camping trip.

Here we were in a Winnebago, packed to the gills—three kids, a dog, and a ten-pound sack of potatoes that immediately broke loose and started rolling around. Two miles out of town, the kids opened up a jumbo bottle of Hawaiian punch, we hit a bump, and dumped sixty-four ounces of red punch all over the carpet. A sign of things to come. That evening we stopped at Jellystone Park. It was 101 degrees as we swam in a tiny pool with a thousand campers, watched outdoor 16mm movies, and slept body to body on our camper's dining room table—and the kids loved it!

Meanwhile, how do moms keep going? When I asked women to complete the sentence, "The one thing that makes mothering worth the effort is . . . " Shelley replied, "*Nothing.* It's just that you fall in love with them before you know what an effort they are and you *want* to do everything for them." That's God's wisdom at work: they are so loveable and so needy that they melt the heart of their mother beyond all recognition.

Every woman has different "buttons" her children push that release a fresh wave of Mother Love in her heart. For Kathy, it's "seeing them turn into people I like to be with." Kabee loves "watching my child sleep." I like that, too, because they are, for the moment, quiet! I find myself sneaking into their bedrooms almost every night to catch a glimpse of my two sleeping cuties. Like Kathy said, "One look at their faces and it's all worth it!"

"Whoever Humbles Himself as This Little Child . . ."

Jo from Colorado loves "hearing their prayers." Specifically, Barbara from Illinois has fond memories of the night she was praying with her three-year-old son. They'd had his favorite dish for supper that night—macaroni and cheese. He remembered to thank God in his prayers for the yummy casserole, "But (pause) I don't know how we'll get your dish back to you."

My Matthew learned the power of prayer soon after his sixth birthday. I was tooling into the family room, which is one step down from the hall landing, except I didn't step down onto carpet. I stepped onto a six-inch rubber ball, which sent me skating around for several wild seconds before I tumbled to the floor with a mighty thud, tossing my armload of books in every direction.

Matthew's eyes were wide with horror. Not only had he just witnessed his mother flailing about like a Raggedy Ann doll on roller skates, but now she was on the floor, groaning in pain, and unable to move her ankle. Worst of all, it was *his* rubber ball that had put this disaster in motion, which must mean it was *all his fault!*

I bit my lip to keep from crying and upsetting him even more, but I knew he could see the pain in my eyes when I said, "Go get Pam, honey, tell her Mama is hurt." Out to the office he dashed, returning with a frantic Pam just moments later. She took one look, and headed to the freezer for ice, while Matthew dropped to the floor in a heap, crying for all he was worth.

"It's not your fault, sweet boy. Mama will be fine," I kept

saying, stroking his hair. "I just twisted my ankle, nothing is broken, nothing is bleeding, I'll be okay." He was not convinced, and frankly, neither was I. My ankle was throbbing, and even the thought of standing up made me dizzy. With each moment, the pain was getting worse. Tears keep slipping out of the corner of my eyes.

With Pam's help, and none too gracefully, I made my way to the chair and sank down in its soft cushions while she pulled the ottoman underneath the afflicted ankle, which she wrapped in a bag of ice. "Mom, what can I do, what can I do?" Matthew sobbed, his cheeks wet with fresh tears. "You can give me a big hug," I said, reaching out as he buried his wheat-colored hair in my chest.

Pam seized the opportunity to help Matthew (and me) handle all this. "Matthew, how about if you pray for your mom's ankle? She has a speech tomorrow in Atlanta and she'll need to be able to walk through the airport, so let's start praying right now that it will get better."

I wish I'd had a tape recorder handy, because this young man put his little hands on my ankle and prayed a prayer that would've made angels swoon. His words were so sincere, his faith was so pure, that instantly I knew that his prayers would be answered. To assist in the healing process, I kept my antsy self planted in that chair all evening as Matthew added more ice and more fervent prayers to my ankle. By the next morning, the swelling was completely gone and the pain was minimal, so off to Atlanta I went. Matthew was beaming all over as I thanked him for his special help. "Hey, Mom!" he said, giving me the thumbs up sign, "Prayer works!" Indeed. The words of Isaiah rang in my heart as I headed out the door, blinking away tears: "And a little child shall lead them" (Isa. 11:6 NKJV).

Kids *Do* Say the Darndest Things!

Marcia loves their "sticky kisses and sweaty hugs," while Jacki enjoys "hearing them say 'I love you' and not ask for money in the same breath!" Every mother knows how Dawn Marie feels "when they say or do something that just makes your heart sing," though with my Lillian, more often than not, she makes my heart laugh! Soon after her fifth birthday, as "my" holiday approached, Lillian asked me, "What are you getting me for Mother's Day?" I reminded her that was the one day of the year when presents were supposed to flow in my direction. "But you wouldn't even *be* a mother if it weren't for me!" she said, stomping her foot. She does that a lot. Can't imagine where she got it.

The honesty of children produces amusing results. One day a group of us moms gathered in the first-grade classroom for an awards ceremony, and one of the children called out for all the class to hear, "Oh, Look! Mrs. Blake has make-up on!" Whereupon a dozen young girls began cheering and dancing about while Mrs. Blake turned the color of her blush.

 ### Her children rise up and call her blessed.

Children really do have an opinion about our appearance. Judith from Florida wore her hair very short back in the '60s, but bought a long hairpiece to wear to a party. When her three-year-old son saw her sporting that glamorous new hairdo, he squealed with delight, "Mom! You're a *girl!*"

Darla tells the tale of a grocery shopping trip: "As we were going down the soft drink aisle, three-year-old Lindsey yelled at the top of her little lungs, 'Hey Mom, let's get some gingivitis!'" (Make that ginger ale.)

Cheri from Washington's six-year-old niece was headed to the barn to bed down her new pony when she asked, "How does my pony know when to get up in the morning?" Aunt Cheri explained that "animals have alarm clocks inside of them that tell them when to go to bed, when to get up, and when to eat." The little girl was quiet for a few moments, pondering this information, then she asked, "Do they have night lights too?"

Not All Fun and Games

Being a mother has many fun moments, but sometimes it's just plain work. Having held down at least one job, if not two or three at a time, since 1970, I am here to say that as jobs go, mothering is the hardest one of all. The work schedule is grueling (twenty-four hours a day, seven days a week), the pay is nonexistent (in fact, it's the only job you pay to do), and the benefits can seem few and far between.

Bonnie spoke from the heart when she confessed, "Mothering does not seem worth the effort during the teen years." To her, and all of us, I offer these words of wisdom from Renee: "Eventually they become nice human beings!" Eventually.

Of this I am certain. None of my earthly activities—not my writing, not my speaking, not my singing, not my teaching— none of those "good works" carry the eternal significance that mothering does. One hundred years from now, when I am long gone to glory, no one will be listening to my tapes or telling my funny stories. (I hate the thought of it, but it's true!) Yet, the Lord willing, my children's children's children will be doing wonderful things on this earth *if* the love I have for my young ones today has been communicated, demonstrated, acted upon, and passed on to future generations. As Josh Billings once said, "To bring up a child in the way he should go, travel that way yourself once in a while."

Shirley captures a sense of her calling: "My children are gifts from God. Doing my best with his help is something that makes me feel whole." Cynde delights in seeing her children "grow to become beautiful souls!" For Ruth, what makes mothering worthwhile is "seeing your children blossom into mature, caring adults with successful marriages and faith in God."

"Give Me Patience, Lord . . . *Now!*"

Children, by their very nature and existence, test us as human beings. As one mother phrased it, "When you have a child, you learn a *lot* about your emotional range. Parent and child are bound by emotion, not intelligence."[1]

In becoming a mother, I discovered that all those nasty little character flaws that I'd learned to hide so well from my friends and coworkers came out at night when I got home. My lack of patience and lack of discipline would be the two most glaring shortcomings I'd mention first.

What a comfort to read hundreds of surveys that all said the same thing as women put into words those imperfections we all identify with:

"As a mother, I'm not so good at . . ."

"Being patient with noise and silliness"

"Taking time out to play"

"Always controlling my temper"

"Recognizing their individuality"

"Relaxing my standards for them"

"Really listening to them"

"Disciplining the kids consistently"

"Remembering to praise them"

"Trusting myself as a good mother"

(Note the names were not included—I'm here to *encourage*, not discourage!)

There were also moms like Linda who fretted at her inability to "keep dental appointments," or Isabel's concern over her lack of skill at "hosting pajama parties." What *all* the mothers seemed to share was the ability to laugh at their less-than-perfect selves, which in my opinion is the key ingredient to good mothering: a sense of humor!

Karyn from Missouri was intent on helping her sons develop positive self-esteem. When she would hear them belittling themselves ("I'm so stupid," "I'm ugly," "I can't do anything right") she would give them a special hand signal, and they would begrudgingly change their tune to "I'm very smart, I'm very talented, I can do anything I put my mind to, and I love myself." One morning when she was getting ready for a community conference that she was in charge of, she was mentally reviewing the day's activities:

A thought began to gnaw at me: "Does the meeting start at 9:30 or 8:30?" Surely, I would have remembered. Still, the doubts hung on. I climbed from the shower and phoned my co-coordinator. Her husband answered, "Cyndi's long gone. The conference started an hour ago." My worst fears snapped to reality. How could I have committed such an oversight? I screamed at my children, "Throw on your clothes—quick! We gotta go, *now!*"

Splashing on my make-up, I was muttering aloud, "I'm such an idiot. I don't deserve to be in charge. What a dumb thing to do . . ." While I rambled on, verbally kicking myself, my youngest son walked up, put his hands gently around my face, locked his gaze with mine and said, "You're beautiful, you're smart, you're talented, you can do anything you put your mind to, and *we love you!*"

Always and Forever

The reality is, our children rise up and bless us every day, if we're listening. Judy delights in hearing, "I love you, Mommy." Jo rejoices when she sees "the light in their eyes when they learn something new." Kelly draws strength from those "hugs at the end of a frustrating day."

As Jean Fleming wrote, a mother is "a woman of influence. I impart values, stimulate creativity, develop compassion, modify weaknesses, and nurture strengths. I can open life up to another individual. And I can open an individual up to life."[2]

While I cannot rise up and bless my mother, I can honor her memory by giving my best effort to mothering my own children. Not by being a perfect mother, nor necessarily a patient mother, nor by any means a totally disciplined mother, but certainly by being a mother who loves God, her husband, and her children, and looks for as many ways as possible to communicate to them, "I'm glad you are part of my world!"

28
Husband Sings Wife's Praises! Film at 11:00

. . . Her husband also, and he praises her: / "Many daughters have done well, / But you excel them all."

Proverbs 31:28b-29 NKJV

While reading a local small-town newspaper, my eyes were drawn to an unusual advertisement, which in large print said: "Hubert and Larry are proud to say that their wives, Brenda and Kaye, are finally playing Rook better. They won a few games over the weekend. It's about time!"

Gentlemen, this is not what was meant by rising up and saying, "You excel them all."

If most husbands knew how little it takes to make us feel loved and appreciated, I believe they would say kind things more often. Flowers and chocolate have their place, but a daily (hourly?) dose of praise would be the best gift of all. It doesn't have to be much. "Thank you for folding my undershirts," would be a great start. "I noticed you scrubbed out the tub," sounds good. How about, "I'll cook all weekend"? Now *that* would be music to our waiting ears!

Productive Praise

Sandy from Pennsylvania is willing to skip the roses, romance, and "rise and shine" compliments. "Actions speak louder than words," she wrote, "and when the dear blessed soul is out there on an icy morning warming up my car and scraping ice so I can go to work, *that's* romantic as far as this kid's concerned. Even though 'only angels can wing it,' there *are* some 'angels' out there who have baseball caps instead of wings!"

When some of us conjured up our image of the perfect husband, it was how he demonstrated love, rather than how he vocalized it, that spoke the loudest. Jeanine from Michigan was hoping for a little of both: "Sensitive at the right times and strong at the right times."

Well, I think I found him! Among the letters, stories, and surveys I received from hundreds of women, I also received one story from a married man in Connecticut, who quit his job of ten years and agreed to move to a new town, buy their first house, and take care of their brand-new daughter Katie. He wrote: "I spent two years at home with our daughter while my wife remained at her job at a local hospital. I did all the 'Mommy' things like the YMCA pool, gym class, shopping, and so on. I coupon-shopped, compared diaper brands, struggled with laundry, and went to Discovery Toy Parties."

Raise your hands if you'd like us to explore a possible cloning of this fine gentleman. His version of "rising up and blessing his wife" was not only to speak well of her, but also to support her in dozens of other practical, hands-on, productive ways.

"You Don't Have to Be Crazy to Live Here But . . ."

Sharon from Michigan, tongue firmly in cheek, thinks her husband might sing her praises more if he were married to "Bo Derek instead of Erma Bombeck." Funny, because at our house, Bill would go for Erma in a heartbeat. What a woman! Humor in the household means a greater potential for the sharing of grace, forgiveness, even sincere praise. When I moan that the house isn't clean enough, that dinner wasn't tasty enough, that my body isn't firm enough, Bill gently reminds me that he didn't marry Martha Stewart or Jane Fonda. "Just be yourself, Liz," he always says. "After all, that *is* who I married." (I think that's supposed to be a compliment!)

 ... Her husband also, and he praises her: / "Many daughters have done well, / But you excel them all."

The sense of humor and play that many of us try to bring to our marriage relationships has some of our husbands literally jumping for joy. The following story requires a little background.

Toni and Ellen were two outrageously fun women I met at a retreat in southern California. One evening, they were sitting in their hotel room, and Ellen was a little discouraged. Toni got this crazy idea (she does that regularly) to start jumping up and down on the bed. "I'll bet you were good at this as a kid!" she said to Ellen, coaxing her to give it a try.

Soon, Ellen got on her own bed and gave a little jump. Then a bigger one. Pretty soon, both women were leaping with child-like abandon, with their hands cradled over their heads in case they hit the ceiling! An hour later, exhausted from all the aerobic laughing and leaping, they collapsed in a heap. Ellen was, to say the least, no longer in the doldrums.

But it doesn't stop there. Toni went home "and explained the art of bed-jumping to my reserved husband and my very cool high-school-aged son. It only took a five-minute demonstration before we were all on the queen-sized bed together. What joy and laughter entered that room!

"When my husband's heart rate slowed, he said that he had forgotten what it felt like to be alive, and that it was a wonderful feeling. 'Life is *fun* again!' burst from my son's lips as he headed for his room for the night. The lesson for me in all of this is that it is life's simple pleasures that bring us the greatest joy."

Amen, Toni!

She added, "P.S. We are up to twelve different ways to jump on the bed and are working on dismounts!"

"Rise Up" and Buy Us Presents, Please

Some of us like to watch our husbands jump for joy over our contribution to their lives.

Some women desire romantic expressions of praise: candlelight dinners, beautiful flowers, soft music, green cash.

Others among us like to see more practical expressions of admiration: lawns mowed, weeds pulled, floors mopped, dishes done. We're talking above and beyond their usual "Honey Do" list, naturally.

Still others would be content if their husbands just got them what they requested for Christmas! Patricia from Ohio remembers her first yuletide season with her husband, twenty-two years ago:

It was a holiday of high expectations. I had hinted, none too subtly, about my desire for a bronze wall hanging. You remember how popular they were—three-dimensional scenes of an outdoor European cafe or a young boy flying a kite in a field. I'd shown them to my husband in stores and catalogs, had the wall picked out, and really didn't care which scene I received.

Under the tree a week before Christmas was a box—three feet long, three feet high, six inches wide. My wall hanging! It was going to be a grand holiday.

Finally, on Christmas morning I confessed to my husband that I knew what my gift was and I could hardly wait to see what scene he'd chosen. He gave me a funny look, like he wished I hadn't guessed.

When it came time to open our presents, I began ripping the gift wrap off the box. Clearly printed on the side of the carton was "Folding Laundry Cart with Wheels."

"Hah!" I laughed, "You've tried to fool me by putting it in this box!" In my frenzied tearing of paper to get into the box, I missed his growing look of despair.

My husband remembers 1972 as the coldest winter on the family record The wall remained bare for months.

Of course, the story has a happy ending. Twenty years later, she was still using the laundry cart on wheels. And, for Christmas 1973, her husband was sent to the mall with ten index cards, listing the item, color, size, store, department, clerk's name, *and* a picture. Patricia assures us, "He's never again had trouble finding that perfect gift!"

Faint Praise . . . Very Faint

Our surveys told us that for lots of us, our husbands serve as role models in our family lives. Gayle from Montana said, "It's because he's very patient and even with our kids." Sue mentioned her husband's "patience and encouragement." Doris appreciates "his calmness and ability to see beyond the immediate." And Marilynn says she plain "lucked out!"

I'm not certain that Debbie from Illinois felt very lucky about her husband's involvement in this little family escapade:

Early one cold, rainy spring day, my husband, three children, and I went off to the woods to hunt mushrooms. We didn't find many mushrooms, but we did find a three-foot green snake. After much screaming, shrieking, and chasing each other with this snake dangling from a stick, the kids killed the snake with the stick and put it in a paper sack.

During the twenty-minute ride home, the dead snake rode in the floor of the car by the heater. As we neared Grandma's house, I opened the sack and out shot the much-alive snake, rigid as a yardstick!

It was like a Chinese fire drill. The car stopped dead in the middle of the street, all four doors opened simultaneously, and out tumbled my husband (all 230 pounds of him), me, and three screaming teenagers. After we composed ourselves and caught the snake, the whining began.

"Can we keep the snake? All boys need a snake for a pet. Do you want us to grow up to be sissies?" We had a lot less company after Mr. Green joined our family.

I'm sure her husband patted Debbie on the back for being a "good sport," one of the greatest compliments some men ever give. But it might have been less traumatic if he'd just said, "There are many fine women in the world, but you are the best of them all!" (Prov. 31:29 TLB).

29
Charm School Is for Snakes

~

**Charm is deceitful and beauty is passing, /
But a woman who fears the LORD, she
shall be praised.**

Proverbs 31:30 NKJV

No one I know ever went to charm school, but I still
grew up knowing what such places were, in theory:
a place to develop manners, to learn which fork to
use first, how to sit correctly, and maybe even how to curtsy
(which obviously I don't know how to do properly, since I just
had to use a dictionary to find out how to spell it!).

Thanks to this verse in Proverbs, excellent women like us are
excused from attending charm school, because every translation
agrees: "Charm is deceptive."

In the Hebrew, *charm* means "showing favor for your own
gain." Having a hidden agenda, as we would say. We know this
kind of woman. She has talked us into baking cookies, carpooling
kids, and lugging lawn chairs out for picnics we didn't even want
to attend, let alone host.

When they say "flattery will get you everywhere," that's the
kind of charm we're talking about. I, for one, prefer to never give
or receive that sort of charm again. Picture a snake charmer, and
it should cure us of ever wanting to be known as charming.

Think of those telephone solicitors, who call us right in the middle of dinner and say cheerfully, "Hello! How are you this evening?" They remain charming as all get out until it becomes clear that you are not going to give them what they want: a signature on a lifetime contract for lawn care service. Suddenly, that overly cheerful, friendly sound is gone from their voice. "You mean you are going to let aphids take over your lawn?!"

Bill received a call from a woman trying to sell him long-distance service recently. As she went happily along, doing a sing-song rendition of the obvious script before her, Bill finally interrupted her and said, "Ma'am, I'm afraid I don't have time for this conversation right now, I'm very busy." The charming chatter abruptly quit, replaced by a cool voice that said, "We are not having a conversation, Mr. Higgs, I am telling you about my product."

That's what this verse means by, "charm is deceptive" (NIV). It looks and sounds like one thing but is another completely. In the Hebrew, it means "falsehood, disappointment," literally "molten wax," an imitation of the real thing.

Those of us who are in sales can learn something from our proverbial sister. Charm does not lead to sales . . it leads to lost revenue!

Beauty Is As Beauty Does

Fine, we don't have to be charming, just sincere. But beautiful now *that* would be fun, if only for a weekend. Just to stroll through the grocery aisles and have someone say, "Wow!" instead of "Do you know where the Ultra Slim Fast is?" Oh, please.

Most of us look in the mirror and see what American humorist George Ade observed: "Her features did not seem to know the value of teamwork."

By fashion magazine standards, I've probably only met two or three flawlessly beautiful women, face to face, in my lifetime. (I tried not to stand too close to them.)

But by the standards of *real* beauty—a woman who celebrates the face and figure she has today, adorns it in style and taste, and gets on with life—there are thousands of beautiful women. My guess is, the woman holding this book is one of them!

In my own life, I've come to a place of peace about my abundant body and would encourage you with all my heart to do the same with whatever size and shape you may be. Minnie Smith took the words right out of my mouth: "I am as my Creator made me, and since He is satisfied, so am I."

My next challenge, as it is for many of us, is to embrace the inevitability of time and its effects on our forty-plus bodies. As Faith Baldwin expressed it, "Time is a dressmaker specializing in alterations."

No Fear of Forty

For the record, I turned forty in July 1994. The ground did not shake. Parts of me did, of course, but they shook when I was thirty-nine too. Author Susan Katz read my mind (or looked at my body!) when she wrote, "I feel the tug, my flesh molding itself to gravity; closer now to the soil than ever to the sky."[1]

A friend sent me an encouraging list of reasons why we should look forward to turning forty based on statistical evidence. For example, the over-forty woman will be less likely to divorce, more immune to colds, and less likely to spend time in a penitentiary. We need an hour's less sleep than we did at twenty and are less likely to develop mental instability. Isn't that comforting?

Of the many fun cards I received on my Big Day, a favorite has to be from my sister Sarah (who crossed over that line a long time ago). It said: "Look at the bright side of being forty—you've already had as much fun as two twenty-year-olds!"

Actually, my thirty-ninth birthday was much more traumatic: all that angst about leaving behind another decade, all those Jack Benny jokes (most of which I told myself), all that ribbing all year long, "Thirty-nine? Oh, sure you are!"

Lin from Ohio remembers the day before her own thirty-ninth birthday. She was seated at a child-size table, stapling together some papers for her young students. The stapler jammed then suddenly opened and staples flew everywhere.

She wrote, "We cleaned them all up and got back to business

when five-year-old Carson said, 'Mrs. G., there's a staple in your hair.' I brushed at it, but nothing fell out. 'It's still there!' he said. I brushed again, but still nothing. He insisted, 'Well, there's something silver up there!'" Indeed.

I really don't mind gray hairs. I married a silver-maned man, and I rather enjoy finding a few grays in my own hair, since the Bible clearly states, "The silver-haired head is a crown of glory" (Prov. 16:31 NKJV). Such encouragement! No, it's not the gray hair that bothers me, it's the hair that's disappearing altogether that I'm not happy about. My doctor assures me that all is well, it's just hormonal and hereditary. A little thinning out on top, no big deal.

Watch my lips: it's a big deal when it's my hair! I've teased, sprayed, moussed, swallowed vitamins, rubbed in conditioners and scalp treatments, and read the Rogaine ads very closely. All to no avail. Welcome to your forties, Liz. Remember how in your teen years, you prayed for "thin"? Ta-da.

Ripe for the Picking and Grinning

I could handle hair falling out of the top of my head, if at the same time it hadn't started poking out of my chin and neck! Good grief, where did those come from? I speak to women's health groups all the time and have never in all of their literature even found a reference to "forty fuzz." What a nuisance. Now I've got to carry tweezers with my lipstick.

We have to look at it like the beautiful Brigitte Bardot does: "It is sad to grow old but nice to ripen." Fine, if you are shaped like a young pear, which takes forever to turn ripe and takes on a golden sheen when it does. Not so good if you are a banana, which has no shape at all, ripens in about three days, and turns dark and mushy.

We heard from Sandy from Hawaii, who recently went through a "hyste-wreck-of-me," and wrote to say "many women need a lot of encouragement and humor when dealing with the influence of estrogen!" Carol hoped to find among these pages, "A light-hearted look at facing life at all ages—middle age and senior years can be overwhelming."

Even more than "face life," let's "embrace life" at any age. And let's move to Florida, where instead of big billboards advertising "Glasses in One Hour," they have billboards for "Dental Express—Same Day Dentures for $199!"

I truly don't mind my body getting older—who has a choice about these things anyway?—but I am fighting to keep my mind young by trying to censor the following phrases *before* they leave my lips . . .

"These younger kids today . . ."

"I remember when . . ."

"Nowadays, they just don't . . ."

"Back in the '60s, we . . ."

If you hear me start to say any of the above, just poke me with my tweezers!

Vanity Not-So-Fair

My mental picture of a vain woman is one standing in front of a mirror, primping and smiling at her narcissistic self. The Hebrew tells a truer tale: *vain* means "something that only lasts a moment."

That's worldly beauty, all right: short-lived! The firm muscle tone and wrinkle-free skin of youth gives way with time, and not much time at that. Mary Anne from South Carolina remembers a visit to her parents' house, when she walked into their bedroom to return a book, right at the same time her dad was changing into his pajamas. With an embarrassed, "Whoops!" she quickly turned around and left the room. Her Dad started to laugh and called out that she'd "almost caught him in his birthday suit."

"Well," she replied, "I'm not sure which suit you were changing into, but it sure needed ironing!"

So, if charm and beauty—the qualities our society finds exceedingly valuable—aren't the trademarks of an excellent woman, what is? We have some ideas, and good ones at that:

"A partner in all matters of the relationship."

"One who has respect for herself and her husband."

"Non-nag, cheerful, creative, helpful, glad to be a woman."

Those of us who seek the timeless, rather than vain, beauty produced by the qualities above will have one happy man on our hands. And, if we are single, we'll have something just as valuable: one happy us!

Scared to Life

Fears and phobias are old news. A little therapy, a little role playing, a deep breath, and onto that airplane we go—or over that bridge, or into that crowd, or whatever fears many women among us may have overcome, or wish to. We're told to "feel the fear and do it anyway."

Although I have few real fears, I'm not crazy about close spaces like a crowded elevator or looking straight down from a very high place. Almost all of us have a fear of appearing foolish. For instance, say I start down the steps leading out of a commuter airplane and accidentally hook the elastic cord from my luggage carrier onto the handrail. I would not only cascade down the airplane steps, but snap back as well. Now, that would be scary. Unintentional bungee jumping, with luggage. Very scary.

But that's not the kind of fear the Proverbs 31 woman had. Not sweaty palms and shaking hands. Nor is it the fear Cybele from Vermont mentioned, when she expressed a desire to have "less fear about taking the 'right' life path." I think we all share a certain amount of that concern.

 Charm is deceitful and beauty is passing, / But a woman who fears the LORD, she shall be praised.

This is "fear of the Lord," which means "to be in awe of, reverent toward." A healthy fear, considering his power. It's a recognition of his magnificence and might which, once grasped, means less fear of anything else. Larry Eisenberg has the right idea: "For peace of mind, resign as general manager of the universe." Why not, the job has already been filled!

For me, to "fear the Lord" means to respect and love God so completely that I want to honor his goodness and grace with my life. While getting my thoughts together for this book, I did a summer Bible study of Proverbs 31, and asked my small but mighty team, "What is your greatest spiritual challenge?" Here's what they said:

"To keep growing in maturity, instead of being too comfortable in my spiritual walk."

"To stay focused on God."

"To have a consistent quiet time."

"To be obedient to God's expressed will for my life."

"To concentrate on producing the fruit of the spirit."

"To have a closer relationship with God in order to survive!"

Singer and author Annie Chapman wrote that "the balanced woman is not out to please some of the people all of the time, or all of the people some of the time. Her strategy for living is to be simply, purely, passionately devoted to the Lord."[2]

On our surveys, I asked a more open-ended question, "What do you wish you had more of in your life?" Some of the same answers came from women from all over America and all walks of life:

"Spiritual awareness"

"Knowledge of the Bible"

"Prayer time"

"Joy of the Lord"

"Time for spiritual growth"

A walk with God is a very private thing indeed, so the honesty of these women is especially generous. Perhaps it could be said of them what author Tony Campolo wrote: "When people rec-ognize God as the ultimate Significant Other, they define their worth in terms of their relationship with Him."[3]

The truth is, that relationship is meaningful to a vast number of people. A 1991 Roper Poll asked a random sampling of men and women, "What is 'success'?" For both men and women, "being a good spouse and parent" was at the top of the list. Second on the list for women was "being true to God," more than twice as important to them as having knowledge, wealth, power, influence, or fame.[4]

There are many in media ministry today, crying out that our nation is going to Hades in a handbasket. And there is no doubt that violence, drug use, family problems, and sexual diseases are on the upsweep. I read and watch the news daily, and so I am not unaware, nor unconcerned.

But then I come back to these verses that offer such hope, that express wise counsel, that give clear direction, and that ultimately provide an exciting promise: "She shall be praised" by her husband, her family, her peers, her community, and her Lord. Once again, I am encouraged.

30
Applause! Applause!

Give her of the fruit of her hands, /
And let her own works praise her in
the gates.

Proverbs 31:31 NKJV

I've always thought that this verse is in the wrong place. The passage should end with the triumphant conclusion of verse 30, "She shall be praised!" Then a trumpet blast and close the book . . . slap! The End. As one commentator concluded his study of the chapter, "May her number increase and the praise that belongs to her be heard in gates all over the world."[1] Brava!

But no, King Lemuel's mother had one more point to make, and anyway, it was an acrostic, a Hebrew A to Z, and she had to say *something* that began with the last Hebrew letter, "tau."

Maybe she was feeling guilty about that "husband at the gates" thing and wanted to assure us that women belong there too. Maybe she wanted to point out that not only would God praise this wonderful wife but so would society. The Living Bible says, "These good deeds of hers shall bring her honor and recognition from even the leaders of the nations."

Or maybe—just maybe—this is exactly how the passage needs to end: with applause. After all, every performer waits for ıt, prays for it, agonizes over it. "Are they clapping as loudly as last night? Are they standing up?" All of us, from all walks of life, need some public recognition now and again, even if the public is just our circle of friends. As Kitty O'Neill Collins said, "What I'm looking for is a blessing that's *not* in disguise."

Harvest Time

The "ideal woman" of Proverbs not only worked hard, but she also tended to her bottom line, her profits, the fruit of her labors. None of these words point solely to money, of course. In fact, the Amplified version of verse 16 says, "With her savings [of time and strength] she plants fruitful vines in her vineyard."

At Laughing Heart Farm, we plant grapes in our vineyard, but for the sole purpose of making grapevine wreaths. The birds get any grapes that the beetles don't eat first. That's pretty much the story of our whole garden, but at least we can say we followed the biblical command to "work the land," even if we do cheat and buy nursery plants that are already half grown.

The men and women of biblical times knew plenty about planting and harvesting crops, about growing and pruning. There are nearly seventy references to vineyards alone. These days, the closest some of us get to growing and pruning is houseplants. Darlene from Kentucky described growing a beautiful jade plant, which her two-year-old daughter turned into Swiss cheese in a matter of minutes using a ball point pen.

> As I felt my anger rise and opened my mouth to let her have it, Kristin started yelling, "It's okay! Mommy, it's okay! See, see I made smiley faces!" Sure enough, on every leaf was carefully poked two eyes, a nose, and a smiley mouth. My anger drained away, and tears over my poor plant mingled with tears of laughter. The plant survived and thrived, ditto for Kristin, and thankfully, so did my sense of humor.

Vines are not the only growing things we care for and not the only things in our lives that bear fruit.

Unexpected Fruit

Sometimes our vineyards bear a painful and bitter fruit, not because of our lack of effort, but because of the weeds that grow up and choke our vines, or because of the seeds from former harvests that sprout up unexpectedly. The following seven women are to be commended for sharing so honestly from their own heartbreaking experiences in the vineyard called Life. To honor their transparency, and protect their privacy, I chose to tell you something about them other than their names.

When asked, "What is the one thing you wish you'd done differently as a mother?" these women said:

"Spent more time trying to educate myself about alcoholism and codependency while I was still married, to help my family."
Billing Clerk, age fifty-five, divorced after twenty-three years

"Had better success in keeping my marriages intact for the children's sake."
Homemaker, age fifty-one, divorced after twenty-four years

"Quit drinking sooner."
Programmer, age forty-two, divorced after twenty years

"Not left their father and broken up their family life, leaving them behind."
Hospital office manager, age forty-two, remarried

"Left an abusive marriage while they were young."
Nurse, age sixty, divorced after thirty-two years

"Tried harder to get help for a problem child. Our oldest son was killed in a drunk driving accident in 1991."
Clerk and student, age forty-one, married

"Kicked out an abusive husband long, long before I did."
Secretary, age fifty-one, remarried

There, but for the grace of God, go any of us. My prayer for these women, and millions of others, is for the healing power of love, grace, and laughter to fill their lives once more and bring forth "good fruit" in their vineyards.

Quiet Works, Thunderous Applause

For many years, I've had the honor of serving as master of ceremonies for a long-term healthcare association banquet. Awards are presented in dozens of categories, and the highlight for me is the statewide Adult Volunteer of the Year Award. In 1993, the winner was Marie Merritt of Campbellsville, Kentucky. As always, I was delighted to announce her name and watch her come forward to receive her well-earned award.

Little did I know that two months later, I would be speaking in her church. She came up and introduced herself, and I realized that she was the embodiment of this verse: "Give her the reward she has earned, and let her works bring her praise at the city gate" (NIV). When I came to that verse in my presentation, I asked her to stand and be acknowledged. As soon as I mentioned her name, hundreds of women from her community burst into applause to honor this dear woman who had given so unselfishly of her time to volunteer 1,700+ hours each year at Medco Center.

"After my husband died," she said, "I didn't work for two years and had no money to speak of, so I began going to the nursing home to encourage the folks there. I've never known a time when I didn't have enough gas in my car to get there and back." Her blue eyes shone with the joy that only years of serving God will produce. Billy Graham said, "Someday we will be as perfect as angels are now."[2] I believe Marie has a head start on most of us.

Fruit That Never Spoils

Olive Schreiner said, "And it came to pass that after a time the artist was forgotten, but the work lived." As I look over my forty years of living, and pray for the grace of enjoying forty more, I wonder what the eighty-year old Liz will wish she had done at forty? I believe I can say without hesitation, I will wish I had been more like the Proverbs 31 woman.

Talk about getting your priorities straight! If you look at the whole chapter, she stacked up her life in this order:

God

Family

Church/Community

Work

I think almost any woman who values those four areas of service would probably say the same thing and feel very righteous as she did so. One slight problem. If I put my calendar next to that list of priorities, it is shockingly upside down:

Work:	ten to twelve hours a day
Family:	three hours a day
Church/Community:	twenty minutes a day (on a good day)
God:	five minutes of prayer at the end of the day (?!)

I promised no lists, tips, or ideas, but I didn't promise not to put before us all a goal: to turn our own lists, even our lives, right side up and begin to actually live what we say we believe.

 Give her the fruit of her hands, / And let her own works praise her in the gates.

Someday I hope I can say, along with one of my most respected role models, Erma Bombeck: "When I stand before God at the end of my life, I would hope that I would not have a single bit of talent left and could say, 'I used everything you gave me.'"

The Fabric of Our Lives

Several years ago, the stage play *Quilters* came to Louisville. It is the story of a group of frontier women who traveled across

America with their families, bouncing along in covered wagons, suffering every hardship known to womankind, but surviving. At every tragedy and every celebration, a woman showed up at the door with a quilt in her arms, intoning, "These quilts is from the ladies of the First Baptist Church."[3]

Quilts. They kept their children warm, kept the rain from coming in, and kept the wolf from their door, even when there was no door.

Quilts made from scraps of their lives, lovingly sewn together with a thousand tiny stitches.

Quilts like the one hanging in front of me now with "1890" carefully stitched at the bottom, made of fabrics that have lived longer than most people. Crazy quilts with no pattern at all, or intricate recreations of familiar old patterns—Bear Paw, Lone Star, Log Cabin, or Nine Patch.

Quilts, then and now, are legacies we leave behind for our children to cherish, and better still, to use.

Back to *Quilters*. The play ends, the stage darkens, and then an amazing thing happens, which the script calls "the last unfolding."[4] The fabric-covered stage, a dull, uneven muslin, begins to lift heavenward on invisible wires and the audience gasps aloud. Before them hangs an enormous quilt, the size of the entire stage itself, huge and colorful and altogether beautiful.

The quilt pattern is, appropriately, the Tree of Life. Sarah, the matriarch, reenters the scene and delivers the final line of the play:

> Give her of the fruit of her hands, / And let her own works praise her in the gates.

[Audience applauds. Stage lights out.]

NOTES

Chapter 1
1. Billy Graham, *Angels* (Dallas: Word, 1994), 60.
2. Kevin Leman, *Bonkers* (New York: Dell, 1987), 10–11.
3. Herbert Lockyer, *All the Women of the Bible* (Grand Rapids: Zondervan, 1967), 274.
4. *Webster's New World Dictionary of American English* (New York: Simon & Schuster, 1988), 104.
5. Barbara Walters, quoted in *The Quotable Woman* (Philadelphia: Running Press), 15.
6. Lockyer, *All the Women of the Bible*, 214.
7. Clifton J. Allen, ed., *The Broadman Bible Commentary* (Nashville: Broadman, 1971), 97.
8. Jean Fleming, *A Mother's Heart* (Colorado Springs: NavPress, 1982), 44.

Chapter 2
1. LaJoyce Martin, *Mother Eve's Garden Club* (Sisters: Multnomah, 1993), 157.
2. Jill Briscoe, *Queen of Hearts* (Old Tappan: Fleming H. Revell, 1984), 9.
3. Allen, *The Broadman Bible Commentary*, 98.
4. Martin, *Mother Eve's Garden Club*, 160.

Chapter 3
1. Luci Swindoll, *After You've Dressed for Success* (Waco: Word, 1987), 67.
2. Paula Rinehart, *Perfect Every Time* (Colorado Springs: NavPress, 1992), 34.
3. Virginia Barber and Merrill Maguire Skaggs, *The Mother Person* (New York: Bobbs-Merrill, 1975), 6.
4. Rinehart, *Perfect Every Time*, 44.
5. Peg Rankin, *How to Care for the Whole World and Still Take Care of Yourself* (Nashville: Broadman & Holman, 1994), x.

Chapter 7
1. Dave Barry, *Babies and Other Hazards of Sex* (Emmaus: Rodale Press, 1984), 12.

Chapter 10
1. Shirley Rogers Radl, *Mother's Day Is Over* (New York: Arbor House, 1987), xv.
2. T. Berry Brazelton, M.D., *Working and Caring* (New York: Addison-Wesley, 1987), xviii.

Chapter 12
1. Leman, *Bonkers*, 188.
2. Elaine St. James, *Simplify Your Life* (New York: Hyperion, 1994), 7.
3. Karen Hull, *The Mommy Book* (Grand Rapids: Zondervan, 1986), 198.
4. Melodie M. Davis, *Working, Mothering and Other "Minor" Dilemmas* (Waco: Word, 1984), 62.
5. Elizabeth Cody Newenhuyse, *The Woman with Two Heads* (Dallas: Word, 1991), 51-52.

Chapter 13
1. Beverly Sills, *The Quotable Woman*, 161.
2. Norman Cousins, *Head First: The Biology of Hope* (New York: E.P. Dutton, 1989), 126.

Chapter 14
1. Donna Otto, *The Stay at Home Mom* (Eugene: Harvest House, 1991), 129.
2. Dee Brestin, *The Lifestyles of Christian Women* (Wheaton: Victor Books, 1991), 138.
3. Sirgay Sanger, M.D. and John Kelly, *The Woman Who Works, The Parent Who Cares* (Boston: Little, Brown and Company, 1987), 177.
4. Carroll Stoner, *Reinventing Home* (New York: A Plume Book/Penguin Group, 1991), 235.

Chapter 15
1. Allen, *The Broadman Bible Commentary*, 99.
2. Briscoe, *Queen of Hearts*, 147.
3. Rinehart, *Perfect Every Time*, 15.
4. Ibid., 21.
5. Ibid., 24.
6. Herbert J. Freudenberger and Gail North, *Women's Burnout* (New York: Penguin, 1985), 232-33.
7. Annie Chapman with Maureen Rank, *Smart Women Keep It Simple* (Minneapolis: Bethany House, 1992), 167.

Chapter 16
1. Deborah Fallows, *A Mother's Work* (Boston: Houghton Mifflin, 1985), 234.

Chapter 17
1. Gildna Radner, *It's Always Something* (New York: Avon, 1990), 205.

Chapter 20
1. Erma Bombeck, *The Erma Bombeck 1992 Desk Calendar* (Kansas City: Andrews & McMeel, A Universal Press Syndicate, 1992), 2 March, Monday.

Chapter 21

1. Layne Longfellow, *Beyond Success: When Ambition's No Longer Enough* (Prescott: Lecture Theatre, Inc., 1993), audio cassette.

Chapter 22

1. Brenda Hunter, *Where Have All the Mothers Gone?* (Grand Rapids: Zondervan, 1982), 120.
2. Patricia Aburdene and John Naisbitt, *Megatrends for Women* (New York: Villard, 1992), 229.
3. Hull, *The Mommy Book*, 194-98.
4. Bebe Moore Campbell, *Successful Women, Angry Men* (New York: Random House, 1986), 19.
5. Katherine Wyse Goldman, *My Mother Worked and I Turned Out Okay* (New York: Villard Books, 1993), 4.

Chapter 23

1. Peter Guber, quoted in Jo Ann Larsen's "Family Corner" column in the *Deseret News*, Salt Lake City, 20 February 1994.
2. Kate Halverson, *The Quotable Woman*, 34.

Chapter 24

1. Bonnie Altenhein, *How Angels Get Their Wings* (New York: Wings Books, 1994).
2. "The Birth of Laughter," *The Laughter Prescription Newsletter*, Box 7985, Northridge, California.
3. Bette Midler, *The Quotable Woman*, 39.
4. Joel Goodman, "Jay Leno's Planet," *Laughing Matters*, Vol. 5, No. 4, 140.
5. Allen, *The Broadman Bible Commentary*, 98–99.
6. Cal Samra, *The Joyful Christ* (San Francisco: Harper & Row, 1986), 8.

Chapter 26

1. Patricia H Sprinkle, *Women Who Do Too Much* (Grand Rapids: Zondervan, 1992), 29.
2. Fleming, *A Mother's Heart*, 147-48.

Chapter 27

1. Barber and Skaggs, *The Mother Person*, 204.
2. Fleming, *A Mother's Heart*, 27.

Chapter 29

1. Susan A. Katz, "New Directions," *When I Am Old I Shall Wear Purple* (Watsonville: Papier-Mache Press, 1987), 71.
2. Chapman, *Smart Women Keep It Simple*, 15.

3. Tony Campolo, *The Success Fantasy* (Wheaton: Victor Books, 1980), 109
4. The Roper Organization Poll, as reported in *The Hope Heart Newsletter*, The Hope Heart Institute, Seattle, Washington, 1991, 8.

Chapter 30
1. Allen, *The Broadman Bible Commentary*, 99.
2. Graham, *Angels*, 45.
3. Molly Newman and Barbara Damashek, *Quilters* (New York: Dramatists Play Service, Inc., 1986), 52.
4. Ibid., 59.

Help!
I'm Laughing
and I Can't Get Up

Dedication

This book is dedicated to the funniest man I have ever known—my handsome, loving, brilliant, dry-of-wit, full-of-fun, fabulous "Foggy" Bill.

Contents

Acknowledgments

Most writers are indebted to so many people by the time a book hits the store shelves that it would require yet another volume to thank them all! Forgive me if I limit myself to one heartfelt page (alright, so I needed a smidge more on a second) of gratitude to some very special people who made sure that I could stand up rather than fall down through the seemingly endless process of putting this book together:

- To more than five hundred fabulous folks from all fifty states, plus Germany, Australia, Canada, Scotland, and France, who contributed their stories and surveys—may the finished product give you half as much joy as you gave me.

- To Gloria Looney and her nimble fingers for putting hundreds of stories, facts, and funnies on disk for me, thereby giving me a fighting chance at hitting my deadline—bless you, Mrs. Looney.

- To Janet Thoma and Todd Ross, my editors and encouragers—thanks for catching my vision for this project.

- To Dennis Hill, whose own sense of humor and playfulness is captured here in delightful black and white (and red all over!)—you, sir, are a hoot.

- To Sara Fortenberry, awesome literary agent, who believes in my dreams and then supports them.

- To some twelve hundred meeting planners across these United States who have invited me to bring a dose of humor to their amazing audiences over the last dozen years—your enthusiasm for this message made every airplane meal (almost) delicious!

- To my humor buddies, on the platform and on the page, who keep me laughing—thanks for helping me practice what I preach.

- To my online LoveKnot sisters—thanks for all your prayers!

- To my precious children, Matthew and Lillian, who put up with a lot of pizza while Mom was screaming, "Help! I'm writing and I can't get up"—extra cheese and lots of hugs for both of you! XOXO

- Most of all, to you, dear reader—bless you for being wise enough to include laughter in your life. Pass it on!

Forewarning: Abandon Soap, All Ye Who Enter Here

Skip the Safeguard, toss the Ivory, give Dial the old heave-ho: This book contains nothing but clean humor!

No need to wash out your mouth with soap after you've read a passage aloud to a friend.

No smarmy innuendos to make you blush, nor four-letter words to offend (unless you count *hoot*).

No put-downs to tickle your funny bone while bruising someone else's.

Nothing but good, clean humor that fills rather than empties, lifts rather than flattens, encourages rather than disheartens.

I agree with Carma from Utah who says, "Laughing feels so good when it's clean and everyone can enjoy the laugh."

Trust me. This book is so clean it squeaks like a duck! Dive right in, my friend, the water's fine.

PART ONE

Encouraging People Through Laughter

You are holding this book for three possible reasons:

1. You enjoy laughing.
2. Someone who knows you thinks you aren't laughing enough.
3. You're visiting a friend's house, and this book was in their reading basket next to the bathtub.

Whether you chose to be here or were dragged into this, I'm thrilled to have you along for the read. Especially since this book won't be funny without you.

That's right. You, babe. All a humorist can do is provide an opportunity for laughter, but you're the one who makes the noise.

Start whenever you're ready.

Chapter 1

Your Jest Is as Good as Mine

I have had a "call" to literature of a low order—humorous.
It is nothing to be proud of, but it is my strongest suit.
—Mark Twain

I make a living encouraging people through laughter. For years I didn't have the nerve to call myself a humorist. Too scary. What if they didn't laugh?

But they did laugh. Even when I wasn't being funny (which was *really* scary).

Then people started making me laugh. (Laughter is, after all, contagious.) I found scribbled notes stuffed in my purse when I wasn't looking. Long, chatty letters arrived in my mailbox. When I included a humor survey with an issue of my free newsletter, *The Laughing Heart*®, more than five hundred people from all fifty states responded with their own funny experiences, many of which landed between the covers of this book.

It's easier to share humor from the platform than on paper because when I'm watching an audience live and in person, I immediately know if something is funny or not. If it's not, I stop! The apostle John said it so well:

Having many things to write to you, I did not wish to do so with paper and ink; but I hope to come to you and speak face to face, that our joy may be full. (2 John 12)

In the meantime, though, we'll share some joy with "paper and ink"!

Our laughter correspondents also offered specific feedback on how important humor is to their well-being. On a scale of 1 to 10, they collectively gave humor a solid 8.9. Susan from Oklahoma rated her need for laughter at a 10, adding that, "Laughter lifts my heart and the hearts of others nearby."

And how often are we laughing in any given twenty-four hours? According to our survey, we're averaging 8.57 big laughs a day. There were those who were off the chart with their number of daily laughs. Stacy from California says she's hitting 600 laughs a day, and Rick must be a mathematician because he clocked his at exactly 143 per day. No more, no less, no kidding.

Most of us hovered in the single digits, though, and as Sherry from Oregon put it, "When I can *count* the number of times, it hasn't been enough." Clearly there's some remedial work to be done, but aren't you clever to realize that fact and to be right here where you belong?

Fly Away Home

Linda related an incident from the years when she and her air force hubby were stationed in California. She was cleaning house one day while their bird was singing away in his cage. Efficient woman that she was, Linda thought, *I have my sweeper out, why not tidy up the birdcage?*

The vacuum proved to be too much for the little bird to resist, and in seconds he was suctioned over to the bars of the cage. Linda quickly turned off the vacuum, but it was too late. The bird jumped on his perch, chirped once, and dropped to the bottom of the cage.

The life had literally been sucked out of him, poor thing.

Bye-bye birdie.

Linda panicked and ran to the phone, called the air force base, and told them it was an emergency and to get her jet-engine technician husband off the flight pad, a major no-no in the military. Her husband ran to the phone, scared to death until she told him what had happened.

As upset as he was about the dead bird, he was more upset about what he was going to tell his commanding officer, who would demand to know what emergency was important enough to call him off the flight pad.

Linda's husband is a clever and resourceful man. He told his CO that his wife was upset because her "Aunt Birdy" had died.

Then the unexpected happened. Flowers and sympathy cards began arriving from their friends on the base. People started asking questions about funeral arrangements for poor Aunt Birdy. Linda and her husband were mortified, but couldn't retract their story or he'd get in serious trouble.

(I imagine that, in lieu of flowers, the family of the deceased requested donations be made to the Audubon Society.)

You're Joking

Like the Aunt Birdy story, almost all of the funny material I received was original stuff from someone's own life. But a few folks shared classic jokes that tickled their funny bones.

Every joke I've ever heard has three things in common:

1. It's fairly brief and to the point, without many specific details.
2. It has a predictable format of setup and punch line.
3. It flies right out of your head two minutes after you hear it.

How many times have we started to tell a joke we just heard and end up petering out halfway through? "No, wait! I think it was the duck that said . . ." People walk away from us, disgusted. The only thing worse than not understanding the punch line is not *delivering* the punch line.

Which is why I never tell jokes. Occasional one-liners, maybe, but they're my own creation so I don't have as much trouble remembering them. I spare myself a lot of social angst by never saying, "Have you heard the one about . . .?" In fact, humorists agree that true-to-life stories work best.

Jeanne Robertson, a former Miss North Carolina and the reigning queen of the humor platform, draws almost all of her humor from her own life experiences. She says, "When a female humorist tries to use those old jokes—the football coach, the traveling salesman—they just don't work." Jeanne observes that while men are happy hearing an old joke, women want to hear stories they can relate to.

Our humor survey turned up exactly the same results: When it's time to laugh, we all agreed that our best resource is personal experience. Psychologist Judith Tingley finds that women especially respond to "anecdotal, conversational stories that deal with people, feelings, and relationships rather than the topics men prefer to laugh about—business, money, and sports."

George Bernard Shaw declared, "My way of joking is to tell the truth; it's the funniest joke in the world."

Amusing truth is everywhere. Dottie from Kentucky faxed me a note that said, "I just came from the store and noticed on the stand a copy of *Prevention* magazine, which said on the cover: FLATTEN YOUR TUMMY; SIMPLIFY YOUR LIFE. Surely they meant those to be two different articles!"

(Surely they did, Dottie, because otherwise it would be a joke about losing weight, and everyone knows there is nothing funny about that . . .)

Real-life humor comes in several flavors. My humor buddy Carl Hurley, Ed.D., subscribes to the theory that every humorous story fits into one of three categories:

1. It happened exactly that way.
2. It happened almost that way.
3. It could have happened that way.

This book will be filled with all three, but here's the scary thing: Neither you nor I will know for sure which one is which. The good news is, it doesn't matter! Artistic or comedic license requires that we stay within the bounds of truth while still producing the results that everybody wants—laughter. As long as it fits our guidelines for good, clean humor, I won't sweat the details if you won't.

I get tickled when an audience participant comes up to me after a program and asks in amazement, "Did that really happen exactly like that?!?" Hmm. *Exactly* meaning "verbatim," "every jot and tittle as it happened," "every detail precisely accurate"? Well, probably not. Since I create stories from weird things that happen to me, some of which occurred years ago, I may not remember my exact words at the time or the exact order of things, but something happened all right!

If you want exact truth, read the Bible. If you're willing to forego accuracy in favor of laughter, then I'm your woman. I must admit, I've wondered what would happen if I answered the did-this-really-happen question with, "No, I made the whole thing up, from beginning to end." Would people ask for their money back? Ask for their laughter back? Ask for my head on a platter?

Why not relax and enjoy the tale? Genuinely funny stories usually have their roots in the truth, because everybody knows you can't beat real life for real humor.

Judy from California shares a story about a woman who was standing in line at an ice-cream store in coastal California when Robert Redford strolled in. (Sigh.) He walked up behind her in line, and the woman decided to play it cool.

She turned, smiled, said hello, then turned back and placed her order. After she paid for her cone and went outside, she realized she didn't have her ice cream.

Robert Redford was still waiting in line when the woman went back in, got the counter girl's attention, and told her she hadn't given her the cone.

The girl answered, "Yes I did, ma'am. You put it in your purse."

Could this have happened? You bet. (Honey, I would probably have put the ice cream in my *blouse* and not noticed.)

Watered Down . . .and Across . . .and Through

Iris and Bill from Pennsylvania were moving their son's possessions from his apartment. To set the scene, Bill was a professional truck driver who'd driven all night for twelve exhausting hours. It was late August, and the temperature outside had hit ninety degrees—it was even worse in this third-floor apartment. The young man owned a queen-size water bed that took up so much space that Iris and Bill had to slosh their way across it just to reach the other side of the room.

Suddenly, the pine box that held the bladder collapsed onto the floor, dropping six hundred gallons of encased water onto their feet. They knew they'd have to drain it before they could ever hope to get it out of the apartment, but they didn't have a siphon handy.

Bill decided they could push this humongous water balloon out the bedroom door, turn a ninety-degree corner, and force it through the bathroom door to the shower, where he could simply hold the spout open and it would drain.

Sounds easy enough.

Bill grabbed onto the end of the waterbed bladder, braced his feet against the wall, and shoved a corner out the door. It slipped from his hand and slopped back, almost knocking him over.

Then he crawled over that full, cold bladder to the other side and tried again, shoving harder, while Iris sat on the floor near the door trying to compress it, hoping to make it more narrow so it would fit through the door.

Six hundred gallons do not a skinny water bed make.

Iris glanced up to see hubby's face the color of a ripe tomato, contrasted with the, uh, "blue" air around them, and she started to laugh when all at once the whole bladder sloshed back—whump!—pinning her underneath it.

Can't you see the headline now? WOMAN KILLED BY FULL BLADDER.

Her husband lifted the edge enough for her to crawl out. Then they shoved and pulled for another ninety minutes, finally forcing the bladder out the bedroom door toward the kitchen. The bladder took advantage of its sudden freedom and took off—slop, gurgle, slurp, plop—not stopping until it reached the far side of the kitchen, traveling ten feet all by itself.

By now Iris was laughing hysterically and Bill was so mad she worried about him having a heart attack. His sense of humor became nonexistent as he feverishly pushed and shoved the six-hundred-gallon body of water, which had a mind of its own. Another hour passed before they forced it across the kitchen—one slop forward, two slops back.

At last they reached the bathroom doorway. They pushed, shoved, pulled, jumped—anything to get it to move through that tiny bathroom door. No luck. Bill leaped like a frog from the kitchen onto the bladder, bounced off, rolled into the bathroom, and hit the wall. "Oh, boy! Whee!!"

All of a sudden the bladder moved. Half of it went through the bathroom door so fast and so hard that it hit the pipes under a little freestanding sink. Slopping back, it pinned Bill to the shower stall. Iris laughed so hard that she was the one leaking now.

Bill whipped out his hunting knife, grabbed that water bed like it was a wild boar, and cut the end off in one fell swoop, prepared for an explosion of water. The water barely moved. It was at best a trickle, and only if they held the cumbersome thing at the correct angle. Out came the knife again. A bigger hole. Even so, it took four hours to drain the bladder, which added up to one very long day.

Iris couldn't stop laughing, and every time she looked at her husband, she'd start anew. The bladder, meanwhile, died a slow, painful death, drop by drop, oblivious—or is that *o-blob-ious?*—of the havoc it had created.

And the laughter. Never forget the laughter.

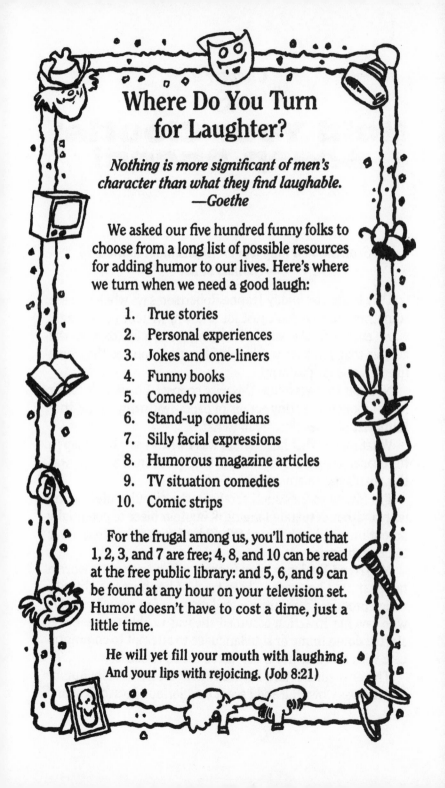

Where Do You Turn for Laughter?

Nothing is more significant of men's character than what they find laughable.
—Goethe

We asked our five hundred funny folks to choose from a long list of possible resources for adding humor to our lives. Here's where we turn when we need a good laugh:

1. True stories
2. Personal experiences
3. Jokes and one-liners
4. Funny books
5. Comedy movies
6. Stand-up comedians
7. Silly facial expressions
8. Humorous magazine articles
9. TV situation comedies
10. Comic strips

For the frugal among us, you'll notice that 1, 2, 3, and 7 are free; 4, 8, and 10 can be read at the free public library: and 5, 6, and 9 can be found at any hour on your television set. Humor doesn't have to cost a dime, just a little time.

He will yet fill your mouth with laughing,
And your lips with rejoicing. (Job 8:21)

Chapter 2

Hold Your Clootie!
Sheep Ahead!

A Scottish mist may wet an Englishmen to the skin.
—Thomas Fuller

My humorist buddy Jeanne Robertson says when you see something funny, don't just jot it down, write it up. A single word, even a phrase, will be meaningless in a few days, so she advises that you keep writing until you've captured the whole funny scene for posterity.

Not that I always follow this wise counsel. I have a file folder full of foolishness, tiny scraps of paper featuring stump-the-humorist phrases like, "Man in hat."

What man? What hat? Where was I when I saw this chap in his chapeau? And the most important question of all: Why was this man's hat so amusing?

I'm forced to toss such scraps in the circular file, gazing with a rather desperate longing at another piece of potentially potent humor, lost between the folds of my gray matter, never to be seen again.

My friend Evelyn, a very funny radio personality, wore a tablet around her neck to keep track of her humor sightings, which produced a few unexpected giggles of its own. Strangers who saw her in action assumed she was unable to speak and started doing mime or sign language to attempt to communicate with her. She never corrected them, of course.

The only time I have faithfully kept a careful daily humor journal was when Bill and I spent ten glorious days in Scotland for our tenth wedding anniversary. Since I was driving (on the wrong side of the road, mind you), I recorded every amusing sight on a microcassette recorder (which made me feel like the spy who came in from the cold). Then each night while it was all still fresh in my jet-lagged mind, I transferred my musings into more decipherable sentences on my laptop computer.

Driving along, microcassette in one hand, camera in the other, I was one happy lassie. Bill was certain that by the end of the ten days I'd be talking into my Kodak and trying to take pictures with my tape recorder.

Oh, ye of little faith. I did no such thing. Not only do I have pages of warm and funny remembrances, captured forever, but now all I have to do to "be there" again is to unfold my photo album, read the words on the computer screen, and it's sheep and tartans, as far as the eye can see.

Granted, I couldn't tell you what I was doing last Monday, but on Monday, May 27, 1996, I was munching on a clootie dumpling at a basement restaurant in Inverness.

Oh, Caledonia!

On paper, it sounded like heaven: Ten days in bonny Scotland, one for each year of our marriage. Just us and no kids, like a honeymoon without the jitters. We'd watched *Rob Roy*, we'd seen *Braveheart*, we were ready.

Eight hours on a plane later, we found out why they call it *jet lag*. Our bodies were in Great Britain, but the rest of us was lagging somewhere over the Atlantic Ocean. Or Greenland.

And what was our first task? Stuff our exhausted, bleary-eyed bodies into a tiny rental car, get behind the wheel on the right side of the car, and drive down the wrong side of the road. Well, wrong to us. Very right to the Scots, and in fact, the only safe option.

It was soon easy to pick out the other tourists—they were the ones using turn signals.

I was driving; Bill was navigating. Correction: I was hyper-ventilating, and Bill was working with a map the size of a table-cloth in a car no bigger than a bread box. On our honeymoon, we'd had a few minor disagreements about where to eat or when to stop for a stretch break. Now, ten years later, the stakes were much higher—we had what the Scots call an *argle-bargle* over which road would get us out of the airport, for heaven's sake.

"It's that way!" I insisted at full volume.

"Stay in the right lane! I mean, the correct lane. No, the left lane!" Bill barked back.

Peace reigned once again when we saw a sign marked WAY OUT, the first of many postings that had us doing double takes. The yield sign read GIVE WAY; a roadside trash barrel became a REFUSE TIP; and highway construction was announced with a simple ! by the road.

We were less certain about the sign that commanded LITTER PLEASE or the enigmatic HEAVY PLANT CROSSING, which suggested a large, leafy ficus being dragged across the pavement. Then there was the petrol station sign that warned NO NAKED LIGHTS. Certainly not, even if we were married.

Businesses announced their trade with equally amusing results: A television repair place was called TELLY ON THE BLINK, an auto body repair place offered SPRAY PAINTING AND PANEL BEATING, and for those who favor self-serve shopping, one market invited you to BAG YOUR OWN MANURE, 70 PENCE A BAG. Your neighborhood pharmacist would be a DISPENSING CHEMIST, the BREAKDOWN MERCHANT handled road service needs, and the most engaging place was the village called YETTS OF MUCKHART.

Driving along the A-75 into Dumfries, we were so taken with the pastoral scenery and the Solway Firth stretched to our south that we hardly spoke at all. On our honeymoon, we'd read aloud every sign to one another and chatted constantly, trying to take in both our surroundings and the strange and wonderful reality of marriage.

Now that our relationship was even stranger and more wonderful, we often communicated silently, holding hands. A gentle squeeze meant "I love you." A tender tap meant "Don't miss what's out the window." A soft caress meant "Only six hours until bedtime." A sudden grip meant "Don't hit the sheep!"

Indeed, sheep rule in Scotland. The edge of town wasn't marked by convenience stores and car dealerships, just sheep grazing in the fields, by the fence, on the road, under our car. Rather than branding their sheep, the Scots spray-paint them. Picture a fluorescent red design on the south end of a northbound sheep. It looked like sheep vandalism.

The little wee ones with their sweet black faces and wobbly knees fairly bleated to the animal lover in me, "Pick me up. Take me home. Baaa." Of course, we couldn't really do that—Delta Air Lines has laws about such cargo—but I considered briefly the merits of a temporary kidnapping.

Perhaps we could keep the baby sheep with us as a backseat pet. Find him a bottle of milk at the naked lights place, maybe. Eventually we'd have to put the little beastie back where we found him, though, and chances are excellent that the mother sheep wouldn't look kindly on this arrangement at all.

When I shared this wooly fantasy with Bill, he assured me we'd have to remain sheepless in Scotia.

We also saw signs posted near farms advertising FREE RANGE CHICKENS, which made us wonder if they laid free range eggs that customers gathered in u-pick-it fashion.

Oddly, neither lamb nor chicken appeared on most Caledonia menus. Haggis, maybe, but not chicken breast. Menus featured mackerel (not holy) served as a pâté on oatcakes; toasties, which consisted of sliced ham and black pickled something; and a sandwich called egg mayonnaise, which we'd just call egg salad. One place served pichards on toast and prawns on baked potato, but we chickened out, so to speak, and got fish 'n' chips.

They had white coffee, filtered coffee, and royal coffee, but what they didn't have was good coffee. Ick! It was a tea-drinkers paradise, but for poor Bill, my own Mr. Coffee, it was a long ten days. Every cup of java he drank was worse than the last one, and thick enough to stain his teeth black in a week. We should have brought our own Maxwell House.

And our own umbrellas. Hadn't we heard Mel Gibson say, "It's good Scottish weather—the rain is falling straight down"? Where were our heads? In the rain. It showered on our honeymoon, too, but we cuddled under one small umbrella and thought it all very romantic. Now we were cruising for a Woolworth store where we could each buy our own golf-size umbrella, an easy feat in a country where golf is so popular it's simply called, "the game."

The Long and Narrow Road

Most of our 1,350-mile adventure was spent on one-lane roads, which appeared to have been created by pouring out asphalt at the top of the hill and letting it find its own trail to the bottom. Imagine driving in the rain at twilight, with an ancient stone wall on one side, a sheer cliff leading to a loch hundreds of feet below on the other side, two nursing lambs with their mother in the middle of the road, and a car coming the other direction, driving faster than, ah, might be prudent.

The most frequently heard phrase in our car was "Waaa!" Soon, though, we got the hang of it. Turnouts along absurdly narrow roads allowed one car to pull aside while the other passed by. Very civilized, really, these lay-bys. When an oncoming car blinked its lights, it meant, "I can wait, you go first." Or as we Kentuckians translate it, "Y'all come on ahead."

The urban routes were much more dangerous. Arrows were painted on the road to show us when to merge, which was very disconcerting when we found them pointed straight at us. Traffic circles had us spinning around and going back in the direction we'd already traveled. Routes were rarely marked, with mere finger signs at intersections pointing in six different directions and written in Gaelic.

The tension was mounting when we hit Ayrshire—and missed the bus. Not missed catching it, mind you, missed *hitting* it. Broadside. To this day, we can't agree whether it was Bill's navigating or my driving that put us between a rock and a Greyhound. Here's where the diminutive size of European cars comes in handy. We squeaked through, with only the angry blast of the bus horn to haunt us. Thank you, Lord, and sorry about that woman's snapdragons.

Speaking of plant life, please note that the only heather we saw was at the gift shop, not on the Highland moors.

But we saw lots of other Scottish flora, fauna, and the like. On the far western shores of Kilchoan, we met our first midges— teensy gnatish bugs that buzz like bees and appear out of nowhere. One minute you're alone, and the next minute you have midges all over you, buzzing around your head, in your ears, up your nose. In no time your teeth look like the grillwork of a Maserati after a cross-country race.

And while there are definitely midges in Scotland, there are not monsters lurking in the lochs. We checked. Went to both of the Loch Ness tourist traps—one was the "original" museum and the other was the "official" museum—and both were pulling our wee legs. Great souvenirs, though, if you like tartan-trimmed teacups and chanters made in China.

The wild life was much more interesting at a local dining establishment (I'd say *pub* but this is a squeaky-clean book, remember), where at 9:30 one Friday night (May 25, to be exact), a local group of musicians gathered for a *ceilidh*, the Scots version of a hoedown.

They certainly gave it their all, they did. Perhaps they shouldn't have convened in a pub and sampled the wares so regularly. The small, multigenerational ensemble labored away on two accordions (which Bill says is three too many), a guitar, an electric keyboard, and a hand-drum called a *bodhran*, none of them tuned to the same pitch. We kept hoping they'd stop playing and have a good argle-bargle, since their voices were much more musical than their instruments.

The next morning we marveled at the Bay of the Pledge on Ardnamurachan (Gaelic for *gesundheit*), which is the spot where the Highlanders pledged their support to Bonnie Prince Charlie centuries ago. The sheer cliff dropped hundreds of feet to the water below, which is why we found it interesting that a sign was posted at the edge of the precipice that stated No CARS BEYOND THIS POINT.

Was this a problem in the past? we wondered. Cars plunging to certain death on the rocks below, just because they'd noticed a little rust at their temples?

Then again, while catching the ferry to the Isle of Skye, a gentleman parked his car in the queue to board the ferry and then wandered off, leaving all of us stuck behind him when the ferry arrived for loading. Apparently cars in Scotland do need their own signs to offset the neglect shown by careless owners.

Our last day in Great Britain found us rubbernecking on our way to the airport in Manchester, trying to determine why two policemen (the first bobbies we'd seen in ten days) had parked their cars nose to nose near a stone fence. Had there been an accident? Should we call the breakdown merchant? Would any panels need beating, perhaps?

Suddenly the morning mist lifted and the scene became quite clear: A cow had wandered onto the sidewalk, and the bobbies had him boxed in between two patrol cars and a stone fence.

What a fitting end to Bill and Liz's Excellent Adventure, all duly recorded in my humor journal, which, as you can see, I milked for all it was worth. Throughout those ten days in Scotland, the beautiful mountains of the Highlands and gentle hills of the Lowlands, echoed our joy-filled laughter. Even wet to the skin, we smiled like the sun.

Trust me, I've got it in writing.

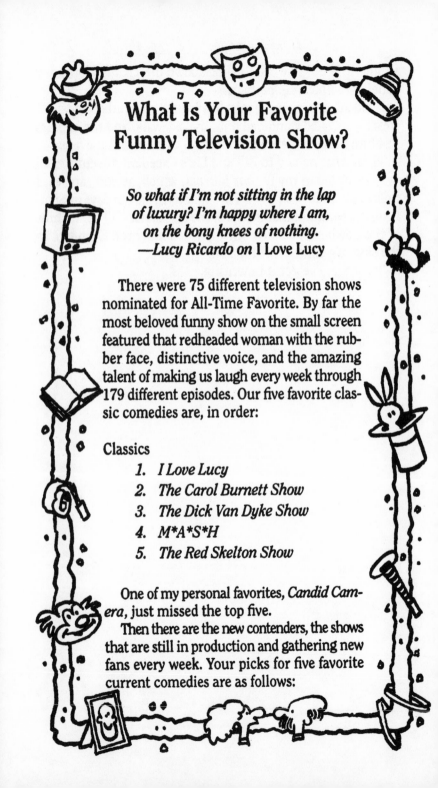

What Is Your Favorite Funny Television Show?

So what if I'm not sitting in the lap of luxury? I'm happy where I am, on the bony knees of nothing.
—Lucy Ricardo on I Love Lucy

There were 75 different television shows nominated for All-Time Favorite. By far the most beloved funny show on the small screen featured that redheaded woman with the rubber face, distinctive voice, and the amazing talent of making us laugh every week through 179 different episodes. Our five favorite classic comedies are, in order:

Classics

1. *I Love Lucy*
2. *The Carol Burnett Show*
3. *The Dick Van Dyke Show*
4. *M*A*S*H*
5. *The Red Skelton Show*

One of my personal favorites, *Candid Camera*, just missed the top five.

Then there are the new contenders, the shows that are still in production and gathering new fans every week. Your picks for five favorite current comedies are as follows:

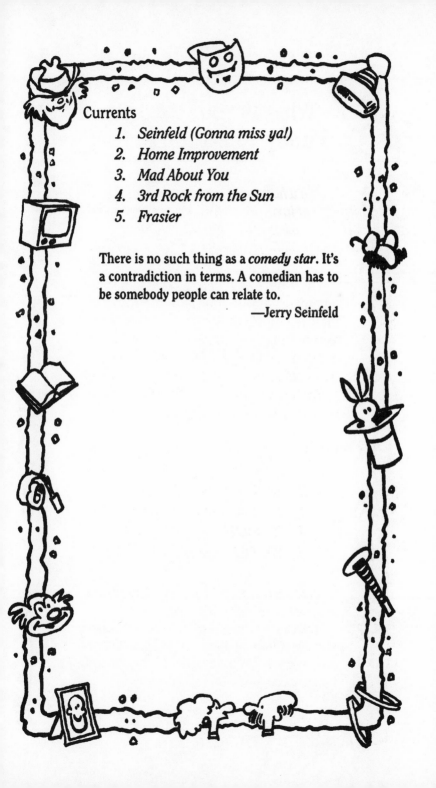

Currents

1. *Seinfeld (Gonna miss ya!)*
2. *Home Improvement*
3. *Mad About You*
4. *3rd Rock from the Sun*
5. *Frasier*

There is no such thing as a *comedy star*. It's a contradiction in terms. A comedian has to be somebody people can relate to.

—Jerry Seinfeld

PART TWO

Seven Types of Laughter

Why do people laugh in the first place? It doesn't have to be the obvious reason—because we think something is amusing. Off the top of my head (and from the bottom of my heart), here are seven reasons why I think we laugh:

1. We're polite
2. We're clueless
3. We're nervous
4. We're relieved
5. We're frustrated
6. We're tickled (literally)
7. We're amused

In this part of the book we will look at the different laughs that result from these situations—the polite laugh, the clueless laugh, the nervous laugh, the relieved laugh, the frustrated laugh, the tickled laugh, and the amused laugh, each with its own chapter.

Chapter 3

The Polite Laugh: Grin and Bear It

*Politeness is one half good nature
and the other half good lying.*
—Mary Wilson Little

What's a *polite laugh*? It's the laugh we offer on cue. When it's clearly our turn, we make the appropriate noise, especially if the person trying to be funny is someone we hope to impress. No matter how faint their little quip, out comes our polite, political laugh.

Heh-heh-heh.

Our lips are curled upward, sound comes out, but nothing moves below the chin. That's the polite laugh.

It's almost always a welcome sound. The writer of Proverbs reminds us of the value of saying the right thing at the right time:

*A man has joy by the answer of his mouth,
And a word spoken in due season, how good it is!
(Proverbs 15:23)*

Indeed, a well-timed word—or a polite laugh—is a social skill worth cultivating.

For a teenage girl, the person she's giggling politely for might be a boy she's had a crush on for weeks. (Please tell me girls still have crushes, yes?) Or it could be the new Latin teacher she's buttering up so he'll score her test on a grading curve the size of Mount Vesuvius. Before the eruption.

When you hit the workaday world, polite, political laughter is the rule of the day. The CEO makes a comment with a spoonful of humor hidden among all the corporate hyperbole? *Ha-ha-ha.* It's expected. A client makes a significant contribution to your bottom line, then shares a supposedly funny story? *He-he-he.* It's necessary.

And on Sunday mornings, when the minister in the pulpit sneaks in a little smiler, we shower him with polite laughter, grateful for his efforts to bring levity along with Leviticus. *Ho-ho-ho.* It's a blessing.

The polite laugh is the sound we make when we hear an old joke and the joke teller hits the punch line. Even when we know what's coming, we hit the HA button at the appropriate moment.

Q: Why did the elephant cross the road?

A: It was the chicken's day off.

It's a timing thing, and clearly it's your turn. *Ha-ha-ha.*

Polite laughter comes in two forms: (1) A slight noise when you know something is expected of you, even if at heart you don't find the comment particularly funny, or (2) the polite grin that masks a less genteel *grrraaakkk!* that's dying to get out but which good manners won't allow.

That second kind of politically correct behavior was at work when Deanna from Kentucky went on a memorable date two decades ago.

Pasta Prima Vera Funny

Deanna's date was several years her senior, well-established in his career and much more sophisticated and dashing than her usual dates. Much to her chagrin, he suggested his favorite place for dinner—an Italian restaurant. Deanna confesses, "I don't know about other women, but I think eating spaghetti, particularly before you know someone well enough to comfortably make a mess of yourself, is a daunting task."

Daunting is an understatement. I always wear a busy print when I eat Italian cuisine, and I still end up at the dry cleaner's the next day. I don't even have to tell them where the spot is. Bill says food falls at right angles when I'm wearing a dry-clean-only outfit. And Italian food is the worst culprit of all.

Deanna was dressed to the nines. Actually, to the seventies—a navy three-piece suit and a satin, pale-baby-blue blouse with a long flowing tie that knotted at the neck and hung the length of her torso.

Yes, we remember those.

"Throughout the meal I was most prim and proper, carefully twirling my spaghetti on the spoon, taking ridiculously small bites, and delicately touching the corners of my lips with my napkin while attempting to sneak swabs at the rest of my mouth.

"My date sat across from me at this elegant restaurant and grinned for no reason whatsoever. I decided he must have fallen for me hard. Just as I finished my meal, I reached into my lap to get the napkin I'd used to wipe my mouth and discovered—horrors!—that the cloth napkin had gotten under my pale-blue satin tie and that I had used my tie as a napkin! It was covered with bright red lipstick and pasta sauce. No wonder he was grinning."

Ah, but politely so.

Awkward situations like this often produce polite laughter, since it's slightly more acceptable than sobbing hysterically, screaming in terror, or running in the opposite direction. What poses as polite laughter may simply be a cover-up for the full-tilt explosion we're holding back until a more appropriate moment.

Dog Bites Man in the Funny Bone

Sharon from Ohio had a surprise for her veterinarian. Sharon's beloved dog had been very ill, and the family made numerous trips and calls to the vet before having to end the dog's suffering. Sharon's first child was due about a month later, which helped to ease the pain of losing their dog and gave them something thrilling to look forward to.

The evening of their blessed event finally arrived. As her husband got things ready for the hospital, Sharon excitedly called the doctor's office. A very poised answering-service attendant answered the phone. When Sharon proudly announced that her water had broken and that she would need to meet the doctor at the hospital, the woman politely replied, "Honey, unless you're having a litter, I'm afraid Dr. Smith can't help you. You've called your veterinarian."

Bobbie, our South Australian contributor who has a son with autism, offered another example of polite laughter. Along with her son's particular disability goes a very loud voice with no volume control. He was nearly six feet tall when she took him on his favorite holiday treat to buy ice cream.

As Bobbie tells it, "We joined a large crowd of mothers, aunties, grandmothers, and small children, all there for the same reason. While we were waiting, a pregnant woman passed by us, which brought to my son's mind a book he had thoroughly read and committed to memory, *How Babies Are Made*."

It seems he could recite it word for word.

"His loud voice boomed over the assembled gathering. 'We don't know what it's going to be, Mum. It all depends on what's between its legs. If it's like mine it's a boy, if it's like yours it's a girl.'

"Slowly, quietly, the stunned crowd melted away and we were left to confront the two young assistants who appeared to be in dire straits. We got our ice cream quickly, then made our way down a side alley to the car while my son continued with the rest of the narrative from his book." In polite but full voice, of course. The polite thing to do in this scenario is swallow one's laugh—hook, line, and sinker—right along with the ice cream.

Know When to Fold 'Em

Recently I got myself in a pickle, and I watched Bill try very hard not to be impolite and laugh out loud. We were on a long trip, and I'd brought my laptop computer with me to get some writing done.

Understand, when it comes to bodies, I've been, uh, abundantly blessed. But laptop manufacturers must have a one-size-fits-all lap in mind because this thing does not stay on my lap—it slides off the end of my knees. That's not a problem at home or in hotels where it sits on a desk. In the van, however, I have to prop my long legs up on our elongated dashboard to make a desktop. It isn't very graceful looking, but it works like a charm at night when no one can see inside the van.

The kids were fast asleep, a CD of soft Celtic music was playing, and I was tapping away at my keyboard when I suddenly decided to recline my seat ever so slightly so I could have even more lap room. The seat snapped back faster and farther than I expected, which sent me scooting forward, dangerously close to the edge of the seat.

Gravity now began taking its toll on my carefully positioned "desk." My legs began pointing due north. The computer slipped onto my tummy, making it difficult to move without the risk of my expensive equipment tumbling onto the car floor. Sitting up was out of the question, as I had no leverage by this point.

My round bottom was responding to the inevitable and heading toward the floor. Imagine a fan, half open, slowly but surely being squeezed closed. Nose to knees, I started folding up while Bill, driving along a dark highway at sixty miles per hour, was unable to help me.

Not that he could've anyway, the rat. I could tell by his breathing that he was stifling a laugh that threatened to fill the car. I did the polite thing and laughed first.

Haawww!

Set free from his inhibitions by my own explosion, Bill did his best to keep breathing and driving, while I just tried to keep breathing with a laptop pinned to my diaphragm and no relief in sight. Finally we pulled into a gas station. There was nothing to do but have Bill open the door on my side, rescue the laptop, yank me out of the bottom of the car, and unfold me onto the pavement.

The people milling around the gas pumps were very polite. They didn't start laughing until we pulled back onto the highway. We could see them in the rearview mirror—bent over, throwing their hands in the air, shrieking.

Let's face it, it's hard to use a laptop computer when you don't have a lap!

Who Do You Think You're Talking To?

One final story about a daughter who didn't mean to sound cruel. Honest.

Jeanne's daughter moved to a small town that didn't have a recycling program. She'd been used to saving her recyclables, so she continued to do so and asked her mother to take them along home with her whenever she visited.

One day when Jeanne visited, they loaded a huge sackful in her trunk just before she left. When Jeanne headed down the street, her daughter waved good-bye and turned to her husband, who'd just strolled out of the house.

"Boy," she sighed in relief. "Am I glad to get rid of that old bag!"

He looked at his wife in shock. How could she speak about her mother like that?! It took some time to sort it all out, and the family still laughs about Jeanne, the Old Bag, and her daughter who had no intention of being impolite.

Chapter 4

The Clueless Laugh: Never Fight a Battle of Wits with an Unarmed Man

It takes a lot of things to prove you are smart, but only one thing to prove you are ignorant.
—Don Herold

We not only laugh to be polite. We also laugh because we haven't the faintest idea what's going on. I call it the *clueless laugh*. It's how we respond when we're confused, don't have all the facts, or want people to think we're "in the loop" when in truth we haven't even seen the loop since 1983.

Laurie from North Carolina watched a homeless Siamese cat in her backyard for a few weeks. She began to feed it, hoping to catch the cat and find its owner. "I saw it crawl into a pile of wood and went outside with a bowl of food to try to coax it to come to me. I stood for several minutes with the bowl in my hand calling, 'Here kitty, here kitty,' not realizing that I was being observed by a man next door digging a new gas line."

He couldn't stand it any longer, turned off the backhoe, and walked over to her. "Lady," he explained, "you don't have to coax that woodpile to eat—it's dead already!"

I'm not sure if he thought she was crazy or if she decided he was a little off. Forrest Gump would say, "Stupid is as stupid does," but then again, what does that mean, anyway?!

Time for the clueless laugh.

Illogical but Lovable

Gracie Allen was a master at the non sequitur (Latin for "it does not follow"). She may have appeared clueless, but don't you believe it. She was a woman with a steel-trap mind, brilliantly disguised as a beautiful airhead.

Gracie would have been proud of this unintentional non sequitur from pregnant Pam:

Shari from Nevada loves celebrating her birthday on June 21, officially the longest day of the year. When her friend, Pam, was expecting a baby around that time, Shari tried to convince Pam that the twenty-first would be the perfect day to deliver.

Pam looked her square in the eye and said, "Why would I want to be in labor on the longest day of the year?"

Duh.

And Duh One, and Duh Two

The fifth-grade class at my son Matthew's school has a perfect method for handling all those ignorant moments in our lives: Each student is permitted one *duh* per day.

I'm not sure one duh would hold me, but I suppose I could stockpile them on good days, in case I ever needed five in a row.

Like the song says, "Here are a few of my favorite duhs . . ." It's only fair that I share one of my own duh moments first.

Duh #1: One of my dear friends in speaking, Sue Thomas, is a consummate pro on the platform—and is also profoundly deaf. While visiting in Louisville, she spoke at my children's school for their chapel service. I'd spoken there myself, and I knew how hard it was to keep the attention of several hundred kids, kindergarten through fifth grade, as they wiggled all over the gym.

"Were they quiet for you?" I asked Sue, careful to look in her direction so she could read my lips.

With a perfectly straight face and a twinkle in her eye, she said, "Oh, yes. They were very quiet."

Duhhh, Liz!

Duh #2: Jennifer from California was busy at work coming up with a new letterhead style for her company. Her head was filled with design ideas, which is why when the phone rang, she answered it, "Pleasant Valley Hospital, this is letterhead."

Duh #3: Albert from Kentucky had just started his new job as an assistant county farm agent. They had a training session for all the 4-H club officers in the county, including a practice meeting to learn parliamentary procedures.

The president said, "We will now have the reading of the minutes."

The secretary looked puzzled at first, then checked his watch and announced, "Looks like about twenty after."

(Albert confesses the real duh is on him, since he was the one who trained the secretaries.)

Duh #4: After a long day at work, Ginny came home for a late dinner, turned on the television, and was cleaning up the kitchen when the phone rang.

"I've been wondering where you and Rick were," laughed her good friend on the other end of the line.

Thinking she was being funny, Ginny bantered back and forth with her until her friend finally said, "No, I mean it, where are you?"

"In the kitchen," Ginny answered, confused. "Where are *you*?"

"I'm on my cell phone on your back porch. I've been pounding the door and ringing the bell for five minutes!"

Duh #5: Modern communication technology doesn't guarantee that the message gets through. Even years after Beverly's mother passed away, the family still received a piece of mail addressed to her. Her sister wrote DECEASED across the envelope and returned it to the sender.

A new letter was promptly sent, addressed to Lois E. Deceased.

Foreign Matters

Melissa moved north from Wilmington, North Carolina, to Raleigh, where the weather is decidedly colder. Her parents, Becky and Fred, visited her there and noticed in the parking lot of her apartment complex a sign that featured a picture of a faucet dripping and the words FREEZE WARNING. LEAVE WATER DRIPPING.

Fred, being the dutiful father, asked, "Melissa, did you leave your water dripping in the apartment?"

A look of total confusion crossed Melissa's face. "What does the water in my apartment have to do with the water in the parking lot?"

"Honey, what do you think that sign means?"

"The water dripping from the leaves causes the parking lot to freeze, so you need to be careful driving. Right?"

Far be it from me to throw the first stone. I'm the woman who just got back from Germany, including repeated trips up and down the autobahn near Frankfurt. Signs pointing to many familiar cities kept popping up along the busy, high-speed highway—Heidelberg, Koln, Munich—but I was amazed how many times we turned off a road with a sign pointing to Ausfahrt.

I finally got the nerve to ask my bilingual driver, "This Ausfahrt must be a very big place."

She grinned from ear to ear. "Oh, all roads lead to ausfahrt."

"But, I've never even heard of that city!" I protested.

"Oh, you have *ausfahrt* in the states too," she insisted. "It means 'exit.'"

There went my duh for September 10.

Ann from Vermont visited Germany by mail, since her in-laws lived there. As a new bride, she wanted to write them and describe all their wedding gifts. Dictionary in hand, Ann started to list their wedding presents—casserole dishes, a hamper, blankets, cooking utensils, all easily found in her English/German dictionary.

Then she came to toaster. Hmm. No word for *toaster*.

She found German words for *electric, toast,* and *maker,* which came out *electrisch trinkspoof fabricans.* When her new husband came home, she proudly showed him her list. He laughed until tears ran down his face. Finally, he explained that their toaster was now "an electric man at a wedding making a toast to the bride and groom."

Caution! Unplug toaster before giving electric man a drink.

The language barrier works both ways, of course. Sally in Ramstein was amused by the German businessman who had cards printed in English for his American customers: AFTER YOU BUY NINE CAR WASHES, YOU BECOME ONE FREE.

English Bloopers

Even when we stick with English, we can say one thing and mean another. Deanna from Indiana described the breakfast scene at her house one morning. Her father was trying to discuss something with her mother who was mumbling to herself while adjusting the toaster button and not listening to him at all.

Finally he said in disgust, "Where is your mind?"

Still turning the light-dark button, her mother responded, "I think it's on medium."

My friend Sue is a missionary in France, where many things are outrageously expensive—a gallon of gas costs about four dollars. She admits, "Now that I've lived out of the country for thirteen years, I've almost completely lost touch with what things cost in the U.S. and tend to think that American expenses are so low."

When Sue and her family were home on furlough, a family member took them all shopping at her expense. Sue's husband absolutely insisted that they pay for lunch at McDonald's, knowing he had twenty U.S. dollars in his wallet. Surely that would be enough to cover lunch for six at a hamburger joint, right?

You know the rest of this story. He had to borrow another ten dollars from their generous family member or consider becoming a kitchen missionary at Mickey D's.

Leigh Ann remembers well the day her parents bought their first dishwasher. Her father liked to inspect every new thing that came into their house, so he stayed in the kitchen and watched the display count down all forty-four minutes of the dishwashing cycle.

As Leigh Ann tells it, "I was upstairs with my mother and older sister when my dad came running up the stairs shouting, 'The dishwasher is useless; it's useless!'

"The three of us looked at one another, amazed that our newest appliance would be broken after only one use, but he insisted that because we had a water softener, the dishwasher was useless."

She decided to look for herself, and there it was, on the inside door, next to the detergent dispenser: Use less with soft water.

Mechanically Challenged

Vicki from North Carolina was washing cars, not dishes—or at least she was trying to. She couldn't get her car on the tracks that would pull her car into the wash bay. "I missed the tracks and my car was poking way up in the air, so high I couldn't even get out of the car. I kept blowing the horn until the manager came out."

He took one look at her car, pointed skyward, and said, "How on earth did you do this?" After helping her step down out of the car, the frustrated man told her, "Just stay out of the way."

"Did I hurt my car?"

"No!" He got the car down on the tracks and washed it himself, much to her chagrin.

The next time Vicki visited a car wash—a different one—she was driving back and forth, back and forth, trying to hit the track, when a nice man waiting behind her, dressed in his Sunday suit, got out of his car and stepped in front of hers to direct her. Seconds later, the wash cycle started and water came pouring down on the nice man in his nice suit.

How about we chip in and buy Vicki a bucket?

Splish Splash

Even trying to get myself clean proves to be a humbling experience. I was staying at a snazzy older hotel in Illinois. The gray, chilly weather outside was quickly forgotten when I saw the cozy fireplace in my room, the tall poster bed draped in a thick, downy comforter, and the luxurious terry-cloth robe hanging in the closet.

But the real surprise was the Jacuzzi in the exquisitely appointed bathroom. Amid mirrored walls and marble floors rose an oversize beauty of a tub, jets at the ready. A whole basket of fancy bath products sat perched on the edge, inviting me to indulge in an afternoon bubble bath.

I didn't have a presentation until much later that day. So, why not?

I followed the directions to the letter, pushing the silver button to start the jets at the appropriate time and giggling to myself at the last instruction on the posted sign: IF PREGNANT, SEE YOUR DOCTOR FIRST. Hmm. Wouldn't your husband be the more likely suspect? *Tee-hee.*

I eased down into the steaming water, feeling the cares of the world slide off my shoulders. This is it; we're buying one of these. Tomorrow.

Using the loofah the hotel generously provided, I lathered it up with a big dollop of almond-and-aloe foaming gel and scrubbed it into my skin. If you've grown an aloe plant, you know this is pretty slimy stuff, like okra, or worse. Soon I was one slick chick, sliding around the tub feeling wonderfully relaxed and silky smooth, ready to dry off and get dressed for my program.

I scooted my feet under me and tried to grab the edges of the bathtub. A faint sense of foreboding crawled up my spine. The tub was surrounded with a foot-wide flat edge of marble, and there were glass walls on three sides. In other words, nothing to hang on to. My feet shot back out from under me—ker-splash!—and I displaced a few gallons of sudsy water, sending them spilling over onto the marble floor.

Maybe a tiny woman could have slithered her way out of this dilemma without incident, but this woman of substance was in trouble.

I tried pulling myself over the edge, seal-like, but feared creating a tidal wave that would engulf my dry clothes draped mere feet away. I considered draining the tub, but then worried about slipping and cracking my cranium wide open, thereby missing my evening program, my family, and the rest of my life. I toyed with filling the tub to the tippy-top, then spilling over the edge with the first few bubbles. I would drown in the process, of course, but at least I'd be out of the tub.

Looking around desperately, panic tightening my throat, I spied a possible solution across the room—a telephone, the latest accessory for swanky bathrooms. Hmm. Whom would I call? "Hello, Front Desk? Could you send a weight lifter to Room 207? That's right. Oh, and blindfold him first, okay?"

The water was getting chilly, and time was quickly ticking by. Slippery or not, I had to get out of that tub. I slithered one leg over the edge and started pushing against the opposite side of the tub. Like a submarine surfacing on the sea at a 45-degree angle, I aimed my leg northeast and shoved my arms southwest and prayed the maid wouldn't pick that exact moment to appear for turndown service.

Before I was fully seated on the marble edge, there was one precarious moment when I could have gone either way—falling back to certain disaster or splashing out with the tsunami—but the Lord smiled on my sorry state and guided me safely, if not gracefully, to the fuzzy rug below.

A sudden knock at the door had me scrambling for the hotel's terry-cloth robe. "Who is it?"

A muffled voice responded, "We've had a report of water dripping in Room 107 below yours. Is there a problem with the Jacuzzi?"

I buried my face in a towel to stifle a loud guffaw. "Gee, a problem?" I sang out. "I haven't got a clue."

Chapter 5

The Nervous Laugh: It's Hard to Laugh Up Your Sleeve When You're Wearing Your Birthday Suit

*I could see that, if not actually disgruntled,
he was far from being gruntled.*
—P. G. Wodehouse

We laugh to be polite, we laugh because we're clueless, and we laugh because we're nervous and hope to shake off our anxiety with a high-pitched, uncontrollable giggle I call the *nervous laugh*.

See the bride at the altar with her veil bobbing up and down? She could be crying, but it's more likely that she's gotten a case of the giggles, brought on by sheer terror. Nothing genuinely funny may be happening, but when you're strung tighter than a violin string, it doesn't take much to make you vibrate with laughter.

The minister stumbles over a word? *Tee-hee-hee.*

Your groom has his cuff links on backwards? *Tee-hee-hee.*

The flame on your unity candle just snuffed itself out? *Tee-hee-hee.*

The more fear involved in a situation, the more our mind and body demand some form of release from the tension. We might shiver with fright (like heroines always do in mystery novels), or we might quiver with unexpected—even inappropriate—laughter as we try to cope with some anxiety-producing circumstance.

Years ago, I came across a list of the top ten things people fear most:

1. Speaking to a group
2. Heights
3. Insects
4. Money problems
5. Deep water
6. Sickness
7. Death
8. Flying
9. Loneliness
10. Dogs

As a professional speaker, I believe it's possible to experience all ten of these fears simultaneously.

Suppose that **speaking to groups** is part of your job description and that those who are **higher up** have been **bugging** you to do more speaking. Since you don't want to **lose your income** and therefore get into **deep water** at home, you step up to the platform, feeling **ill** and **scared to death**, especially when your notes go **flying** off the lectern. You realize you've never felt so **alone** and forlorn because you know this speech you're about to present is a real **dog**.

See? And you thought you had a few fears to deal with.

The Bible says, "Perfect love casts out fear."

So true. And I might add, a perfect *laugh* casts out fear too. Our contributors had a plethora of phobias to conquer with humor, including a fear of flies, snakes, and guns, or a fear of some awful thing happening to them, like fainting in public or being robbed.

When Cathy was four years old, she was scared silly of flies. A common little housefly was more terrifying to her than the nastiest beast or the darkest night on earth. One day while she was riding her tricycle, a fly landed next to her and she started wailing.

Cathy's mother decided she'd had enough. She sat at the picnic table with Cathy and convinced her to wait for a fly to land. When a fly dutifully showed up, Cathy's mother told her to take a good close look and encouraged her that nothing bad would happen if she did.

Cathy got as close as she could to the horrible creature, then raised her head to joyfully announce, "That fly has little pink pedal pushers on!" She was never afraid of flies again.

It's not clear what kind of drug Cathy's mother slipped into her child's lemonade to make her see pink pedal pushers on the fly, but the key is, humor helped Cathy laugh away her fears.

When Eve Met the Snake, She Wasn't Dressed Either

It was a hot, dry summer on Betty and Lloyd's Kansas farm, so hot that everyone was looking for a cool, shady place to camp out, including the snakes. Betty lived in an old rock house, and they were in the process of adding a bathroom. One evening as she was toweling off after a refreshing bath in the unfinished bathroom, Betty heard something scritch, scritching across the bathroom floor.

Glancing in the direction of the noise, she spotted a spine-tingling, fear-inducing sight: A snake was headed right for her! With a leap and a bound that would put Superman to shame, she raced through the bedroom, dining room, and kitchen and was out the door, across the porch, and to the end of the walk, where her husband intercepted her mad dash.

Betty admits, "Coming to my senses, I realized I did not have on a stitch of clothing. Modesty overcoming fear, I sheepishly and cautiously went back in the house, covered myself with a tea towel, and perched on the kitchen table until Lloyd disposed of the harmless garden snake."

Were her troubles over? Of course not. She began fretting about their neighbors, John and Mattie, who lived across the road. Had they been sitting on their screened-in porch? Betty's exit had been fast but far from quiet. Had she attracted their attention?

She would soon find out, since she worked with Mattie. She avoided her at work the next day, and instead described her great snake adventure to her best friend, Wilma, including her fear that she might have provided a free "peep" show for her neighbors.

Betty explains, "Wilma soothed me as a good friend would and assured me she would discreetly find out if Mattie was aware of any goings-on at our house. Lunchtime came, and Wilma gave me the bad news. Mattie and John had been sitting on the porch. They heard the shrieks and saw the whole thing."

Betty avoided her neighbors for the next few weeks until one day Wilma finally confessed the truth: Mattie knew nothing, heard nothing, and saw nothing!

I think I'd be more afraid of Wilma than a garden snake.

Hired Gun

Linda from Colorado laughs every time she sees their custom-made gun cabinet, remembering how it ended up in their house. Her father-in-law, a member of the Texas Cattleman's Association, had purchased a beautiful commemorative rifle that was engraved with his ranch's brand as well as other historic Texas brands. Hubby Paul had often admired the rifle, and when his dad offered it to him, Paul was beside himself with joy.

The first thing Paul did was call a local cabinetmaker and ask him if could design a special display case for it. The cabinetmaker agreed but forgot about the conversation. A few weeks later, Paul called the cabinetmaker back, rifle in hand, and blurted out, "Hi, this is Paul—"

The cabinetmaker missed the introduction and only heard an excited stranger say, "—I've got a gun and I'm coming over." Terrified, the cabinetmaker anxiously awaited the unknown gunman's arrival, mentally reviewing his list of clients, trying to decide if any of them felt disgruntled about their new cabinets.

When teddy-bearlike Paul showed up with the commemorative rifle, you can bet the cabinetmaker breathed a laugh of relief.

"Stop, Thief"

He wasn't the Jason of *Friday the 13th* fame, but for Ann from Texas this Jason was just as ominous. Ann's husband advertised two big-ticket items in their local newspaper. Ann told him she wanted no part selling these items because (1) she'd heard horror stories of strangers calling and coming to your home, and (2) the items were stereo speakers and a work-out gym that she knew virtually nothing about. He assured her he'd handle it all.

The phone immediately started ringing. An extremely polite young man named Jason showed up on their doorstep to look at the speakers. The two men agreed on $450 for the speakers, but Jason would not have the full amount till payday on Friday. He left a twenty-dollar deposit, and they arranged a pickup time.

On Wednesday, Jason called while her husband was at work and explained he'd gotten the money early and wanted to pick up the speakers that evening. Ann's mind raced. "I did not want to do this, and knowing he would arrive shortly after dark made me more leery. I thought about alerting our neighborhood twenty-four-hour police patrol that I was having this stranger come over, but I decided I was just being paranoid."

At 8:30, Jason appeared and handed her a wad of money folded in half. "I'm two dollars short. Can I give it to you in quarters?"

She held out her hand, not counting the wad in her other hand, but sliding the corners enough to see that it looked like four hundred dollar bills, two tens, a five, and some ones. Within minutes the speakers were loaded in his Jeep and Jason was out their driveway and gone.

Ann counted the money more carefully and discovered to her horror that while a normal-looking Ben Franklin bill was folded in half on the outside of the wad, inside the other three hundreds were odd. The face of old Ben was huge, not centered on the bill. *It is counterfeit money!* she realized. *It isn't even a good forgery job; it is blatantly fake.*

"It was Monopoly money and I'd fallen for it," Ann moaned to herself. "I was diverted by the old count-the-quarter scam." She grabbed the phone and called their neighborhood security, frantically describing the vehicle and the criminal who'd just left her house. They told her to call 911 and alert the city police, which soon had officers searching the main roads leading out of their subdivision and the closest pawn-shop locations.

Ann's head was spinning, thinking about the criminal who would undoubtedly return to rob them any minute. She paged her husband repeatedly. No reply. Twenty minutes later an officer arrived at her door. Still shaken, she explained the whole story.

"This is a terrible print job," she declared. "See for yourself."

The officer looked it over, and in a very serious voice said, "Ma'am, did you know they changed the hundred-dollar bill?"

Her jaw dropped. "What?"

"About two years ago, the government changed the hundred-dollar bill."

Her face got hot and turned various shades of red. The change in currency must have occurred while they were living overseas. "Look," she stammered, "I'm a stay-at-home mom. When would I ever have my hands on a hundred-dollar bill?"

They immediately called off the manhunt for Jason, and Ann didn't bother to page her husband again. Meanwhile, fake-Ben sightings have been reported over many parts of the U.S.

Finally, Judy from Kentucky wasn't nervous or laughing, she just needed to sit down. Pregnant at the time, she was standing in line at a shopping-mall food court when she began to feel dizzy and light-headed. She walked a few steps but suddenly got tunnel vision. She knew she was going to faint.

She grabbed the first handy chair, sat down, and put her head between her legs for several minutes. When she sat up, she realized that she'd joined an elderly couple at their lunch table. She apologized and tried to stand up, but felt dizzy again. Not wanting to stay at their table all day, she dragged a chair across the mall and *sat* in line until her food was ready. Someone called security. "Either to make sure I was okay or because they thought I was a nut."

No way, not unless she tried to pay for her lunch with a hundred dollar bill featuring Big Ben's off-center face.

When fear and apprehension strike, your funny bone is your most powerful weapon.

Chapter 6

The Relieved Laugh: By Jovial!

A good time to laugh is anytime you can.
—*Linda Ellerbee*

Okay, so you're not polite, clueless, or nervous. Then why are you laughing? Ohh, I get it. Whew!

You're relieved.

The *relieved laugh* comes out in a breathy *woosh*. You probably weren't even aware you were under that much tension when suddenly out of nowhere the situation resolves itself and—*Ha!*—you feel decidedly better.

Eilene from Maine longed for a little relief from the embarrassment she felt while visiting a school and orphanage in Kenya. Dozens of children who spoke only Swahili pressed around her, trying to see if the white of her skin would rub off. They were all yelling "Jumbo!" and "Super!"

Eilene grumbled to her interpreter, "I know I need to lose weight, but I didn't think I was that fat and large."

He burst out laughing, then explained, "In Swahili, *jumbo* means 'hello' and *super* means 'hello very much.'"

What a relief. I thought Jumbo was an elephant.

The Key to the Crime

Whenever I misplace something, I find I always laugh when I find it (unless looking for it makes me late, in which case the sounds I make are nothing at all like laughter).

Pat shared the time a coworker was carrying a single, loose, office key in her dress pocket, then later in the day realized it was missing. They tried retracing her steps for almost an hour and were about to give up when the woman turned and walked away—and revealed the missing key, safely trapped inside her pantyhose, plastered against her left calf.

Pat says, "Now whenever anything is missing at work, we do a pantyhose check."

What if the missing item is a filing cabinet?

Shop 'Til You . . .

Jan from Nevada can laugh with relief now, but I'd love to have seen the look on her face when it happened. She and her hubby-to-be were on a skiing jaunt together and stopped at a minimarket on the way for snacks.

Her man was standing in front of her in line when she saw some goodies that she wanted and stepped away to gather them from the shelves, not knowing her honey had gone off to do the same thing.

Like any dating couple, they were affectionate in public, so when she turned back in line, she put her hand on his bottom and gave it an affectionate caress. As Pat tells it, "I was shocked when this strange man turned around and looked at me." Meanwhile, the man destined to become her husband saw the whole thing, along with half the customers, who were all laughing.

The man she mistook for her boyfriend said to her, "Wow, lady. At first I thought you were trying to steal my wallet, but the truth is, you made my day."

Jan says her husband now calls those little markets *Grab and Go*.

It's Snowing Up North

Look, these things happen. Life's most embarrassing moments and all that. Laughing about them not only relieves your own tension, but gives everyone around you permission to giggle too. Good thing, or otherwise they might have to excuse themselves and go explode with laughter on the front porch.

Which is precisely what three Navy sailors must have desperately wanted to do when Karen served them spaghetti dinner. Karen's hubby was a Navy officer who invited three single sailors over for dinner when Karen's first child was just two months old. The house looked great, Karen served a lovely meal by candlelight, and everything was fine until she returned to the table after nursing little Ashley.

Within minutes, hubby was making frantic motions, trying to get her attention. Karen was busy serving the food and asking who wanted bread. Finally she realized that all four men were blushing and staring pointedly at her scoop-necked dress.

No wonder.

One of her nursing pads had walked its way up and out of her neckline, and was waving to everyone in sight. Karen, ever the quick thinker, swiftly pulled it out and said, "Anyone need a coaster?"

Sandy was in the midst of serving dinner when things got interesting at her house. Hamburgers were on the menu, and Sandy decided to shake the ketchup bottle. She was halfway across the kitchen, flipping her wrist side-to-side "like a baton twirler on speed," when the top flew off.

Do I need to describe this for you? A big glob of ketchup on her head, more dripping off her eyebrows and nose, ketchup on the table, the walls, the ceiling, the carpet, even on two newly upholstered yellow brocade dining-room chairs, ketchup clear into the corner of the living room and up the side of the yellow-flowered Queen Anne wing chair, and in the stereo headphones that just happened to be in the wing chair at the time.

"There was ketchup everywhere—except in the ketchup bottle." Sand confesses, "With my weirdly warped sense of humor, I promptly burst into fits of hysterical laughter, which brought the whole gang running from the living room. After they had determined that I was not mortally wounded—if I'm laughing, how serious can the injuries be?—they joined in the hilarity of the moment."

Yes, the hamburgers got cold and the chairs may never be quite so pristine a yellow again, but it makes quite a story. If everything went exactly according to plan, life would be a dull, humorless disaster.

Now it's my turn to tell a true tale of an embarrassing moment.

The Bombing of Newport Beach

February 1993. Newport Beach, California. The National Speakers Association, my peer group, was gathered for their winter educational workshop, and I was invited to be their Saturday evening speaker.

Big honor. Big blessing. Big ego alert.

Several details contributed to the outcome of this particular evening. For starters, I spoke in Columbus, Ohio, that same morning, and so had to fly out at 1:00 P.M. for the West Coast, hoping and praying my flight would land on time. I arrived at 5:00 with the main event just two hours away and my nerves stretched to the limit. Toss in a three-hour time change and a little jet lag for good measure, and you get some sense of my level of energy at this point. But it gets worse.

The huge meal (for some, with wine) took a l-o-n-g time to serve. Beef—heavy, sleep-inducing beef—was on the menu. And baked potatoes. And cheesecake. *Zzzzzzz*.

A thirty-minute slide presentation of fine art preceded my program. Oh, that perked people right up.

It was late—well after 9:00—when I stepped on the stage. By my body clock, it was midnight, as it was for many attendees.

The room was too dark, with large mirrored posts blocking both my view and theirs. Everywhere I looked, I saw Liz, and Liz looked nervous.

The five hundred attendees were, for the most part, speakers, fully capable of doing what I was about to do, and anxious to see why I was invited to do so instead of them.

If you are, say, a salesperson, this would be like having five hundred other reps standing around watching you make a sales pitch while talking among themselves—"I wouldn't do it that way, would you? Gee, I'd never have said that."

You get the idea. Pressure City.

If it sounds like I'm making excuses, you're absolutely right. Even though I'd prayed, prepared, and practiced, I laid an egg in Newport Beach. It was the longest hour I've ever spent on the platform. The few times folks did laugh, it had a strained, let's-help-her-out quality.

Groan.

One of the veterans of our association was sitting right in front of me, fast asleep, snoring away. (If I'd had a pocketful of mini-marshmallows, I'd have tossed them at his teeth like bean-bags at a clown face.)

There is no death like dying on the platform. I could feel my hair turning gray as I spoke. Everywhere I looked, I saw mir-rored images of myself. Bombing.

When, blessedly, I finished the last word, the audience leaped to their feet—and ran out the door. I'd hoped for a standing ovation; this was more like a running ovation. I made a bee-line for my room, where I collapsed on the bed, crying like a baby.

It was 2:00 A.M. in Louisville, so I couldn't even call Bill for moral support.

Can you feel my pain?

I'd wanted to give them a performance they would never forget. Sure enough, I had.

Monday morning back in Kentucky, the phone in my office started ringing with words of encouragement from my peers.

"Liz, it wasn't that bad."

"I think people were just tired."

"I'd give you a 12, but the audience was a 4."

Nice try, but I knew the truth: On a scale of 1 to 10, I was the one who deserved the 4. Comedian David Brenner says when you do humor, you can't get good without bombing. But, David, did it have to be that night?!

I was licking my wounds in Louisville, certain that I'd never show my face at another Association gathering again, when the unthinkable happened. The program chair for the big National Convention in Washington, D.C., called and asked me to do a program to kick off the whole event.

I was stunned to silence. The committee members must not have been in Newport Beach.

The obvious solution was to say no thanks, but it's such an honor to be asked that speakers almost never refuse.

My heart was in my throat (or was it my shoes?). I needed help and fast, so I faxed a dear friend of mine, Rosita Perez, a consummate pro in the speaking business and the one who'd introduced me that fateful night.

"Rosita," I wrote, "how am I going to get back up on the platform? You were in Newport Beach, you saw me bomb, what am I going to do?"

She faxed me back. "Liz, you did not bomb, it just wasn't magic." (Rosita is a motivational speaker. They say things like that.) Her fax went on, "Let me ask you something: Do you like Dustin Hoffman?"

I'm thinking, *Dustin Hoffman?! Was he in Newport Beach?*

Her fax continued. "He's a brilliant actor, yes? Award-winning, an incredible talent, a Hollywood legend, yes?"

Yes, yes.

"Did you see him in *Ishtar*?"

Oh, yes, I'd seen *Ishtar*, back when I reviewed movies for a local radio station. I declared it the single worst movie I'd ever paid money to see. That distinction still stands. Forty million dollars, Warren Beatty, Dustin Hoffman—a bomb.

A big bomb.

In fact, one of my favorite cartoons from *The Far Side* showed a video store in Hades, with nothing on the shelves but *Ishtar, Ishtar, Ishtar . . .*

"So, Liz," her fax concluded, "if Dustin Hoffman can survive an *Ishtar* in his career and come back and win an Oscar for Best Actor in *Rain Man*, can't you get back up on that platform?"

The woman had me there. The more I thought about it, the more excited I got. Yes, I would get back up on that horse, and if I fell off again, at least I knew I could survive.

Inspired by her words, I sat down at my computer and created a graphic reminder of my meaningful discovery:

ISHTAR HAPPENS.

It happened to Dustin, it happened to me in Newport Beach, and when/if it happens to you, now you'll be ready. There's a Japanese proverb that says, "When you stumble, don't get up empty-handed." Indeed, if you stand up with your head full of wisdom, your heart full of laughter, and your arms full of encouraging words like Rosita's, who knows what might happen.

Are you wondering what happened in Washington, D.C.? I marched into that meeting room full of my peers, with my ISHTAR HAPPENS sign safely tucked in the back of my notebook to remind me that failing beats not trying, every time. And on a scale of 1 to 10, it was . . . well, I'll sound like I'm bragging if I say a 15, so I'll simply tell you what a delight it was to call Bill and say, "Ta-da!"

What a relief.

God doesn't have Ishtar days, but he understands them only too well. That's why he gave us laughter, so we can survive them with our sense of humor and confidence intact.

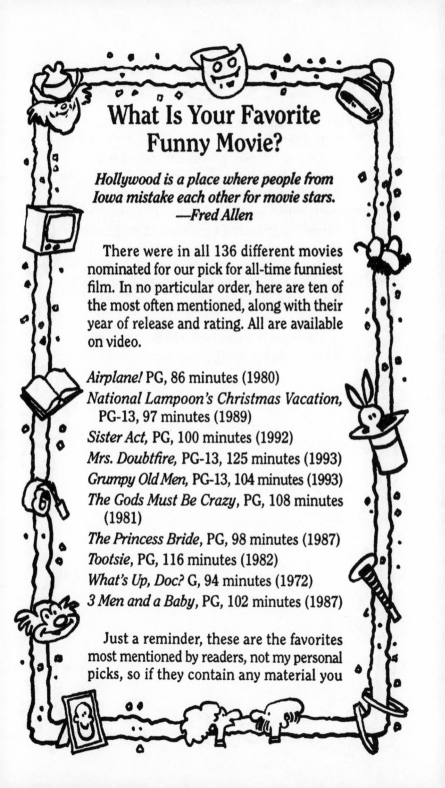

What Is Your Favorite Funny Movie?

Hollywood is a place where people from Iowa mistake each other for movie stars.
—*Fred Allen*

There were in all 136 different movies nominated for our pick for all-time funniest film. In no particular order, here are ten of the most often mentioned, along with their year of release and rating. All are available on video.

Airplane! PG, 86 minutes (1980)

National Lampoon's Christmas Vacation, PG-13, 97 minutes (1989)

Sister Act, PG, 100 minutes (1992)

Mrs. Doubtfire, PG-13, 125 minutes (1993)

Grumpy Old Men, PG-13, 104 minutes (1993)

The Gods Must Be Crazy, PG, 108 minutes (1981)

The Princess Bride, PG, 98 minutes (1987)

Tootsie, PG, 116 minutes (1982)

What's Up, Doc? G, 94 minutes (1972)

3 Men and a Baby, PG, 102 minutes (1987)

Just a reminder, these are the favorites most mentioned by readers, not my personal picks, so if they contain any material you

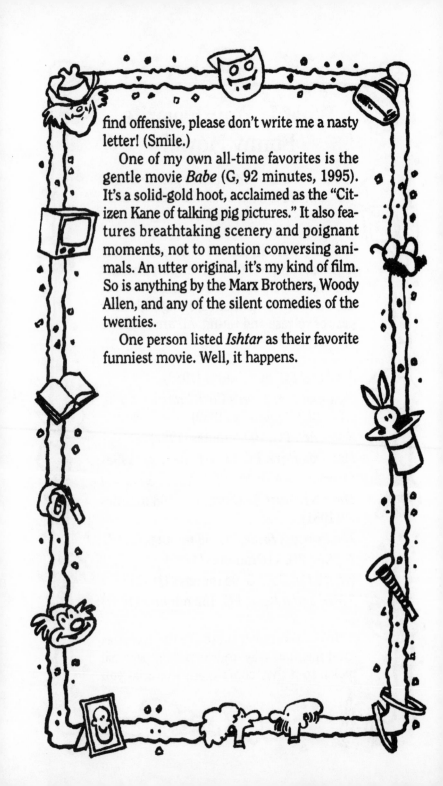

find offensive, please don't write me a nasty letter! (Smile.)

One of my own all-time favorites is the gentle movie *Babe* (G, 92 minutes, 1995). It's a solid-gold hoot, acclaimed as the "Citizen Kane of talking pig pictures." It also features breathtaking scenery and poignant moments, not to mention conversing animals. An utter original, it's my kind of film. So is anything by the Marx Brothers, Woody Allen, and any of the silent comedies of the twenties.

One person listed *Ishtar* as their favorite funniest movie. Well, it happens.

Chapter 7

The Frustrated Laugh: How to De-Tangle a Bad Humor Day

Everything is funny, as long as it is happening to somebody else.
—Will Rogers

We've looked at polite laughs, clueless laughs, nervous laughs, relieved laughs, and now—*grrr!*—the *frustrated laugh*, a cross between a growl and a grin.

Like Ishtar, it happens. You wake up on the wrong side of the bed, the wrong side of the room, the wrong end of the country, and no matter how much you try to laugh away your frustration, it rears its ugly head.

Bad humor days are hairy, and all the shampoo and cream rinse in the beauty-salon world won't solve the problem.

Whenever I'm tempted to grumble that I'm having a bad day, I remember the wise words of a friend: "There are no such things as bad days, only bad moments in good days."

The next time your whine-o-meter is pegged in the red zone, it's helpful to remember:

1. It's only a bad moment.
2. This, too, shall pass.
3. It's still a good day.

4.   Everything is funny eventually.

Bad (Hair) Days

Azriella, a speaking buddy of mine from Pennsylvania, was having a bad hair day. A real one. She asked her husband if he might give her hair a slight trim and spare her an expensive trip to the salon, saving the family some much-needed cash. He'd been cutting their children's hair for years, so he blithely said, "Sure."

With the first snip of the scissors, she realized that she and her husband had very different notions of what trim means. As Azriella describes it, "I wanted to scream as I felt the scissors press against my neck and saw my shoulder-length hair fall to the floor. But after that first snip, what good would screaming do? So I closed my eyes, took a deep breath, and waited for him to finish."

Finally, he snapped his scissors shut with a flourish and asked, "What do you think?"

In the mirror she saw a shocked woman wearing a brand-new pixie cut. She detangled her bad-humor day with a heroic turn of mind. "My first instinct was to scream or cry, but I quickly found the humor in it and said calmly, 'Well, dear, it's quite a bit shorter than I had in mind, so we'd better cut my bangs to match.'"

Then she complimented him on giving her a fabulous haircut.

(Never mind Dustin Hoffman. This woman gets the Oscar for Best Performance by a Wife Under Duress.)

Azriella admits the moral of the story is: Define *trim*. She is clearly a woman who values a great man over a bad haircut. Very smart.

A Hairy Story

I personally wouldn't let my dear Bill anywhere near my hair. The truth is, the woman I pay to hold the scissors sometimes gives me pause. Oh, there were a few days back in 1988 when I thought we'd really hit on something, but the rest of the time it's too long, too short, too curly, too flat, too red, too blonde, or decidedly too gray—though that last one is not my stylist's fault.

As for the cutting and styling itself, that's where I do depend on Carol. I've known her longer than I've known my husband. Our paths crossed in 1984, and I've faithfully sat in her chair ever since. When Carol switched salons, I followed her across town.

"Whither thou goest, I will go," I assured her.

Who wouldn't declare lifelong loyalty to someone who combines amateur therapy skills with the latest techniques in blunt cutting?

Carol listened patiently through my career and dating woes, nodding sympathetically as her scissors snipped away. Those were the perm years—natural color, unnatural curl. Then when hubby-to-be Bill came into my life, Carol and I dumped the perm in favor of longer locks to please my sweetie.

What is it with men and long hair?

Months later, it was Carol who styled the tresses of my wedding party, and Carol again who gave me a pedicure the week before my first child was slated to arrive, so I'd have fashionable toes in the delivery room.

Talk about a labor of love!

Our relationship isn't one-sided, either. I sang at Carol's wedding and rejoiced when she began taking college courses at night. We've laughed, cried, and compared notes on husbands, kids, and cleaning services. You can't simply walk away from that kind of dual commitment over something as frivolous as a few frizzy perms or doubtful dye jobs.

Besides, the mere thought of trying a new stylist gives me the willies. Make that will-he's. As in, "Will he understand about my sparse spots?" or "Will she know how to tame that strange cowlick in the back?" Someone else might do a better job, but then again, what if it's worse? What if my hair comes out five different lengths and three different colors?

Hey, it can happen. Carol once had to rescue a poor high school senior who'd dyed his hair purple to match his prom tux. He spent five hours (and untold dollars) in her chair while she corrected another stylist's nightmare-in-violet creation.

But he probably never darkened her chair again. Men are fickle when it comes to hair. Any five-dollar barber will do. The way my Bill sees it, why bother making an appointment with a pricey stylist when he can drop in Buck's Barber Shop unannounced, thumb through a few issues of *Field & Stream*, plunk down a ten, and leave with change and short hair?

"But what do you and Buck talk about?" I once asked him.

He wrinkled his brow in confusion. "I dunno. The weather? Reds baseball, maybe?" Bill sighed. "Look, the whole thing takes ten minutes, tops."

Aha! There's the difference. Women spend a minimum of forty-five minutes in a salon; two hours with color; three hours for a perm with a manicure. Toss in a facial or a wax job, and we're approaching half a day with our smocked sister.

We spend more money with them too. Lots more money. Bill was aghast the first time he saw a credit-card receipt from a visit with Carol. "Sixty dollars?!? You look the same as you did this morning. Can't you find someone less expensive?"

Less expensive, sure. But that's not the point. Carol and I are friends. Girl buddies. Partners in the fight against dark roots and stray chin hairs. She's seen me in no makeup. No clothes, for that matter, stretched out on a massage table wearing nothing but a towel and a smile.

Who could say sayonara to a soul sister like that?

One January, however, I came frighteningly close to committing hair-care infidelity. Just the memory of it makes my scalp itch. I was facing a photo session for a local magazine cover, and arrangements were made for Jacobson's to do my makeup and hair. After the cosmetician did a bang-up job on eyes, lips, and cheeks, it was time to put my thinning hair in the hands of a stranger named Steve.

Steve the Stylist rested his hands lightly on my shoulders, and my stomach tightened. I felt like a nervous teenager on a first date.

"Is there a particular way you'd like me to style your hair?"

Yes, I wanted to say. Carol's way! Instead, I gulped. "Nooo, just make me look ten pounds thinner and I'll be happy."

His graceful hands danced around my head, comb in one hand, industrial-strength hair spray in the other. I watched in amazement. I was getting thinner!

Gee, Carol never parted it like that. How did he do that lift-and-poof thing on the side? Fascinating.

Steve finally whipped off my plastic cape with a flourish. "There you are, Liz. What do you think?"

I think I'm in love. No, no, not with you, just your hands. Are you this good with scissors? Know your way around a bottle of peroxide? I realized the dangerous path my imagination was taking me down and mentally swatted away the little voices saying, "He's the one! He's the one! Leave Carol and cleave to Steve!"

When he slipped me his card and suggested I give him a call sometime, I stuffed it in my pocket, mumbled a red-faced "thank you," and hotfooted it for the door.

Whew! That was close. I'd resisted temptation, but barely. How could I even think of breaking up a friendship that was in its second decade, just for the thrill of a zippy new do? Sure, Steve might have some fresh ideas for my stale tresses, but what would I say when I saw Carol at the grocery store after being absent from her chair for six months and sporting a new color or cut? Even without a big red *A* on my chest, she would know: I'd been unfaithful.

I knew I should have tossed Steve's business card in the circular file, but I couldn't resist tucking it in my Rolodex, "just in case." In case Carol moved away or quit the business. Or was eaten by sharks. Otherwise, I would not defect to Steve. Would not, could not.

But my fingers kept flipping past his name. Hmm. Would Carol notice if I did one little color weave with Steve? Maybe a teensy trim, between real haircuts? If I timed it right, she'd never be the wiser. I reached for the phone and dialed Steve's salon.

The receptionist was sharp, cool, professional. Yes, Steve had an opening on Tuesday. A trim? Of course, no problem, 2:00 is fine. See you then, Mrs. Higgs.

I almost slammed the phone down. What was I thinking?

As the calendar marched toward Tuesday, I spent more time on my hair than usual, trying to convince myself to undo our risk-filled liaison. It's not that bad a cut, I told myself. In fact, it's a very good cut, or Steve couldn't have styled it so nicely.

Tuesday morning dawned gray and menacing. Cowardice leaped from my heart and into my fingers as I dialed the Other Salon's number and canceled my appointment, muttering a feeble excuse about my too-full schedule.

I waited for my racing heart to slow back down to normal and then hit the speed-dialing button that instantly put me in touch with my regular salon. My salon, Carol's salon. Home.

"A cut with Carol at 2:00 o'clock? No problem, Liz. See you then. Hug the kids for me."

Ahh. I hung up the phone in blessed relief, silently slipping Steve's card in the wastebasket. No more flirting with temptation; I'd stick with a place where everybody knows my name.

Especially Carol, the one woman who can (almost) guarantee me a good hair day.

Chapter 8

The Tickled Laugh: Tickling Permitted (Funny Bones Only, Please)

If you tickle us, do we not laugh?
—Shakespeare

It's not a polite laugh, nor clueless—since we know exactly what causes it—nor is it stimulated by nerves or relief or sheer frustration. It's the sound we make when we're tickled—the *tickled laugh.*

I don't get tickled pink, I get tickled beet red. When I was a kid, my brothers and sisters loved nothing better than twiddling their fingers in my most ticklish spots—behind my knees, under my elbows, on the soles of my feet—until I was lobster red and wheezing.

Don't you just love siblings? This is not what Paul meant when he wrote, "Yes, brother, let me have joy from you" (Philemon 20). Joy, yes, but not via tickling!

When I became a mother, I'm ashamed to admit that I, too, became a mad tickler. My children giggled so adorably, and their tootsies were so soft and cute. Surely it wasn't all that bad.

The problem is, they didn't laugh because it was funny, they laughed as a reflex action, even as their body jerked away as if under attack. Such uncontrollable laughter on their part—and very controllable twiddling on my part—is the problem with tickling.

It's a control issue.

I decided I'd rather have people laughing at me voluntarily, so the only thing I try to tickle now is someone's funny bone.

In my spare time, I tickle my own.

Sometimes we get tickled, not physically, but mentally. And that results in the tickled laugh.

Duck, Duck, Goose

We have a lovely lake next door that belongs to our neighbors (seems only fair—it's on their land), but which we also enjoy through the window. Canada geese come whooshing out of the sky in season, and a whole family of ducks makes its home there as well. One spring we watched a mother mallard lead her ducklings along our driveway, under the fence, and over to the lake. Charming.

Then a few days later, Bill called me over to a spot in the grass, finger to his lips. "Shh! Come see," he whispered.

I peered down at the small hole in the ground, where a tiny baby animal was obviously hiding. All I could see was a soft, downy brown. "Ohh!" I gasped softly, pointing. "Duck!"

Bill's eyebrows shot up into his forehead. "A what?"

At that moment, a large, brown mother rabbit hopped over, looking agitated.

Was she unhappy because I was near her baby, or because I falsely accused it of being fowl-y rather than furry?

We tiptoed away, and as soon as it seemed safe, exploded with laughter. Bill, who almost never laughs out loud, was bent over.

He could only say one thing. "Duck?! Duck!?"

Now whenever either one of us identifies something incorrectly, we just shrug and say, "Duck." And get tickled all over again.

What a Cutup!

Kathleen managed to tickle her funny bone quite by accident while sitting in an elegant hotel lobby in downtown Seattle and waiting for her husband to come out of a seminar. The magazine article she was reading included a photo of an X ray of a man's throat. It seemed he had swallowed a table knife while eating peas.

Suddenly, the very idea of such a ludicrous thing happening washed over Kathleen and she got tickled. "It struck me so funny, I hugged the walls to keep upright while I found my way outside, passing a lobby filled with people staring at me like, 'That woman has lost it!'"

Sitting outside on the front steps in her pretty spring dress, Kathleen laughed hysterically for the next twenty minutes. Meanwhile, her husband heard about the crazy woman outside, and when he realized it was his wife, he simply walked past her. Once she could compose herself enough to walk a straight line, she followed him—at a safe distance—to their car.

Bless her heart, the woman couldn't help herself. She literally had no control. Just like the child getting tickled physically, she got tickled mentally, with the same results: *Haa!*

This happens occasionally among audience members. I'll see a person bending over, red faced, obviously having trouble breathing, and even as I continue telling some tale, I keep an anxious eye on her. What is going on? Is she okay?

Then my eyes widen. Oh, no. The woman next to her is doing the same thing. It's contagious, and it's headed this direction! One by one, people bend over, lean back, fall sideways, turn red, and gasp for breath.

Sneezing and hiccuping are not contagious. Yawning and laughing are.

I've seen some individuals go off the deep end and not be able to get back. Everyone around them begins to draw away, fearing the contagion. Try as they might, though, they can't pull themselves together. Their loud whooping eases up for a breathless moment, then off they go again.

Their friends shrug their shoulders. "She's not usually like this," they mouth carefully.

The rest of the audience stares at me. Can't you do something about this?

Gee, do I have to? If I was the one who brought all this on, I love it. In truth, it was their own fearfully and wonderfully-made mind that went off on its own tangent. That's why they got tickled, never to return. I was merely a mirror, allowing them to discover something funny inside themselves.

When the tickle takeover happens to me, I never see it coming. Some lightly amusing thing happens, and out comes this "Harrr!"

We're talking waaay past hoot.

I start slapping the table, the dashboard, whatever is handy and can withstand my pounding. No sooner do I reign it in than it washes over me again like the waves at Ocean City, knocking me off balance.

Bill just shakes his head. The kids love it, of course.

Northern Disclosure

Several years ago, when Matthew and Lillian were six and four, they saw me at my all-time silliest. We went on a moose-hunting trip to Alaska. No, not that kind of hunting, with guns and trophies and such. This was an "Oh, look! A moose!" sort of hunt as we traveled the highway between Anchorage and Talkeetna.

Moose-viewing was the main selling point that helped our kids sit still on the plane for some dozen hours. The minute we took off in our rental car, we kept our eyes glued to the woods along the roadside, slowing down at the moosiest looking spots, certain we'd spot one any minute. Sadly, day one came and went without a single sighting.

Dinner that evening at the Klondike Café featured salmon (what else?) for Mom and Dad, burgers for the kids. When I suggested they try the reindeer, four-year-old Lillian's eyes teared up at the very idea of serving Donner and Blitzen with ketchup. Bill then spotted moose on the menu, but Matthew just rolled his eyes.

"Dad, we'd like to see a live moose, not a cooked one."

By our last day, we were in major moose-hunting mode, desperate to see one of Alaska's most famous citizens. Pointing our rental car toward the airport, we were coming up on a busy intersection when, without warning, a huge moose—A MOOSE!—came crashing out of the bushes.

She bolted across the four-lane road, inches away from becoming our hood ornament. We got a bird's-eye—make that moose's-eye—view of very long legs in motion, a hump behind her head just like in the pictures, no antlers (she-moose don't have 'em) and more body than head, with more legs than anything else.

Our only moose, in downtown Anchorage, of all places!

No one honked, no one braked, no one seemed the least bit surprised.

But those drivers were Alaskans. We were tourists. We were in hysterics. I was laughing so hard I had to lay my head on the steering wheel to catch my breath as our celebrity Alaskan cow disappeared into the nearby woods.

Raining Cats (Not Dogs)

Another animal altogether managed to elude Janis from California, despite her most valiant efforts.

Janis's aging, mellow marmalade feline, Francis, was being repeatedly harrassed by the neighbor's nasty cat, Pepper. The bully cat's owners were not too concerned, but Janis's vet bills were rising.

She didn't want to hurt Pepper, of course, only scare him away from their yard, so she decided a Bazooka Liquidator was the answer. We're talking one of those enormous water guns that squirts fifty feet. Janis explains, "I stomped into Toy World, pointed to the display of water guns behind the cash register, and announced, 'I need a gun—a *big* one!'"

The young woman behind the counter looked concerned. "Wouldn't you like to go home and discuss this with your husband?" she asked, but Janis assured her that her husband approved the weapon purchase.

Every time Janis saw Pepper in her yard, she ran out and blasted him with water, but he always got away. One morning, hearing some noise in the yard, Janis grabbed her Bazooka and charged out the back door, firing. "I'd forgotten this was the morning the mow-and-blow guys came" she confessed. A thoroughly terrified gardener narrowly escaped the Bazooka's furious flood.

He wasn't tickled about it, but Janis was.

The good news is, Pepper and his family moved away. The bad news is, a new family moved in with three cats. Stay tuned.

Slip Sliding Away, Part One

When it comes to getting tickled, nothing makes me laugh harder than physical comedy. No words, no story line, just a great sight gag or pratfall, the kind where nothing gets hurt but your dignity. Not the Three Stooges. That's a guy thing. We're talking Chevy Chase or *Airplane!*

Or Karla on skis.

"I'd been taking lessons on the beginning slope," Karla says, "and I got to where I wasn't falling too much. Then I decided to go down The Big Hill."

When she got up to the top, she had second thoughts, but no choice. "I couldn't stay up there forever, so I started down. Everything I'd learned disappeared from my mind. I yelled, 'Get out of the way! Get out of the way!' as I went straight down the hill. At the bottom was the lodge with a fence in front of it. Somehow, I dodged the fence and ran smack into the side of the building."

When Karla hobbled inside a few minutes later, she found her twin sister rolling on the floor.

"What is so funny?" Karla asked.

Holding her sides, tears running down her face, her sister gasped, "You missed it. Some idiot just ran into the lodge!"

Slip Sliding Away, Part Two

It was summer, not winter, and it was an inner tube, not a pair of skis, but the end result (pun intended) was much the same. One hot day I got really brave, put on a bathing suit (a navy-blue, no-nonsense, industrial-strength number), and went with Bill and the kids to a water park, the kind with wave pools and huge slides. One of the rides, as it were, was a water slide that twisted and turned from a dizzying height to a splash pool at the bottom.

You rode the slide in a huge inner tube by draping your arms over one side and your legs over the other and parking your bottom in the doughnut hole, so to speak. Easy enough for a young, agile mom, perhaps, but this fortysomething mother doesn't bend as well as she used to, and the rubber inner tube was less than cooperative.

Even with the hunky lifeguard-type helping me, I couldn't seem to get situated. The tube scooted one way, I scooted the other. Frustration quickly gave way to laughter, and then I was really in trouble. As you know only too well, when you start laughing, your muscles relax. Coordination is a thing of the past. The water flowing around the tube sent it spinning in a circle, which made me dizzy and tickled me even further.

My arms were hanging on to the soft, slippery inner tube for dear life, my long legs were sticking straight up in the air, and my ample bottom was parked deep in the doughnut hole, such that I was folded up tight as a card table and couldn't breathe.

But boy, could I laugh.

I was whooping in near hysteria as my family waited in line, pretending they had no connection to the wild woman in the navy-blue suit. The lifeguard gave my inner tube a shove, and down the slide I went, tossing caution and dignity to the winds. Gales of laughter followed me as I plunged sixty miles per hour down to the pool below.

Ker-*splash!*

I hit that landing pool with such force that my own bottom went straight to the pool bottom and the inner tube shot up in the air some fifty feet, according to dozens of wide-eyed spectators. The lifeguard, who'd been listening to this traveling circus as it careened down the slide, now watched in horror as a large, laughing navy-blue woman disappeared beneath the foamy surface of the water.

"Are you okay, ma'am?" he hollered, grabbing my arm to pull me up for air.

I was still laughing, though it sounded more like gurgling. "I'm fine," I assured him, trying to get my breath. "I just got tickled at the top and couldn't stop."

"You did what?"

Another *haawww!* exploded from my lips. "Tickled," I gasped, "I got—oh, never mind. Here come the rest of my family."

Three more laughing Higgses hit the water. They looked tickled too.

"Mom, let's do it again!"

Sorry, one tickle a day is all I can handle.

Chapter 9

The Amused Laugh: Keep Your Wit About You

We're all pretty much alike when we get out of town.
—Kin Hubbard

Finally, the seventh reason—the real reason—we laugh is because something is genuinely funny. These are the best laughs, the heartiest chuckles, the ones that catch us by surprise.

Laughter is not a cerebral decision. No one looks at their watch with a dour face and says, "I think I'll laugh in thirteen seconds." Laughter isn't something you choose to do or not do, unless you've become adept at stuffing every other emotion as well.

The *amused laugh* travels the short distance from brain to mouth and, propelled by the diaphragm, explodes through the lips, bringing a smile not only to the face of the laugher but usually to the faces of all within earshot as well.

When I tell audiences, readers, and friends, "You gotta add more laughter to your life," they shake their heads.

"You just don't understand, Liz. I don't have your sense of humor."

Lucky you.

"You don't need to be funny," I assure them gently. "You need merely to appreciate the humor that's all around you."

"But I don't have time."

No time for laughter?

Mary from Kentucky admits as much. "I like to laugh but am too busy sometimes to find the humor in things."

What about popping a good clean comedy in the VCR tonight?

"I don't have time to rent a funny video," people whine. "Even if I did, I don't have time to watch it."

I've been there, haven't you? Rented a funny video on a Friday after work, with the best intentions of giving myself a humor break. When Sunday night rolled around, the tape was due back at the store by 8:00, so at 7:50 I desperately try to watch ten minutes of the movie to justify the $2.99 I paid to rent it.

Silly me.

You really don't have to buy or even rent humor, when God has graciously planted it all around you. "Seeing the silly side makes life fun," declares Annette from South Carolina.

Funny stuff is everywhere, if you know where to look. Out your car window, for instance. You can add lots of healthy humor to your life merely by slowing down to the speed limit (especially if your state is like Kentucky, where the speed limits are just a suggestion). Tighten your seat belt to be safe, then keep one eye on the amusing scenery along the road.

And do drive carefully. Carol from Alabama picked up her husband for a lunch date and got behind every awful driver on the road. She was ranting and raving about one driver's inability to use a turn signal or another one's decision to stop in the middle of the highway for no apparent reason.

Finally, she fumed, "You know, if I ever have a stroke, it will be while I'm driving."

Her husband didn't miss a beat. "Honey," he said, "if *I* ever have a stroke, it will be while you're driving!"

Sign Language

If you're ready to include more amusement in your laugh life, the first place to look are those roadside signs.

Lori from Indiana saw a sign posted outside a row of stores and offices shared by an OB/GYN and a carpet shop. It's not clear which one put the sign out front that boasted FREE DELIVERY.

A used car lot in Racine, Wisconsin, featured a sign that gave Betty a good laugh: WE SELL NO CARS ON SUNDAY AND PRECIOUS FEW DURING THE WEEK.

Cindy's friend Steve saw a sign in Montana: VETERINARIAN/TAXIDERMIST—EITHER WAY, YOU GET YOUR DOG BACK.

Judi from Georgia got a giggle when she saw a sign displayed at the gate of the Atlanta Open Golf Tournament that said, GOLFERS' WIVES—NO DOGS ALLOWED.

Well, the very idea.

Some signs strike an ominous note, like the one we saw in Alaska that hinted of the long, dark winter that was only weeks away: HAVE YOU HAD YOUR BATTERY CHECKED? THE NIGHT IS COMING.

Around Christmas time, a Hoosier woman spotted a sign that offered BALD CHRISTMAS TREES. (Just a trunk with bare branches, do you suppose?) I saw a similar sign posted at a booksellers convention that announced TODAY AT 3:00, MEET YOUR FAVORITE BALD EAGLE PAINTER.

Bless his heart—and his shiny head.

Here's a cryptic pair of signs found on a Florida highway. The first sign said, PANTHER CROSSING, NEXT 11 MILES. Then three miles later, the second sign read, PICNIC AREA, 6 MILES.

Who's having the picnic—people or panthers?

Speaking of ferocious animals, a friend noted a sign that cautioned FORGET DOG—BEWARE OF OWNER.

And here's a frightening "Father's Day Special" offered by a local restaurant: ADULTS $6.95/CHILDREN $4.95—SERVED HOT TODAY FROM 11:00 A.M. TO 10:00 P.M.

But where was the sign—any sign—when Alice needed one?

Crusin' for Amusin'

Alice from Texas moved to the small town of Andrews and decided to explore her new surroundings. She ventured out, soon became disoriented about which direction she was driving, and found herself turning onto a small country road that was only wide enough for one car.

As Alice tells it, "Then I realized I was on the golf-cart path of the local country club!" Not wanting to ruin their manicured fairways and greens, she quickly proceeded past the clubhouse (where onlookers were doing double and triple takes) and on up to the northern end, trying to find a short escape route.

Alice continues, "Finally finding a wide paved area, I turned off, only to find I was now on the airport runway."

It didn't take her long to find her way back into town from that popular spot. Shortly thereafter a bar gate with a large sign appeared at Alice's new entrance: NO TRESPASSING.

Brenda from Florida was taking the shuttle from La Guardia Airport to the Marriott and passed several signs along the road that warned CAUTION: LOW FLYING AIRCRAFT.

"I wasn't quite sure what we were supposed to do," Brenda admits. "Duck our heads? Veer off the road when a plane was approaching?"

Then there's the one I've spotted on my visits to San Diego, and Linda from Missouri saw it too. On Route 5 near downtown is this sign that gives one pause: CRUISE SHIPS—USE HOTEL EXIT. Just for the record, I've not been passed on the San Diego freeway by a cruise ship yet, but if it happens I'll try to act natural.

And, beware when you are traveling in the suburbs of Oklahoma City, where a sign warns DANGEROUS PEDESTRIAN INTERSECTION.

Finding humor in print is simple enough. Just look in the classified ads, which is where the following unintentional laugh lines were found:

- Dog for sale—eats anything and is fond of children.
- Tired of cleaning yourself? Let me do it.
- Now is your chance to have your ears pierced and get an extra pair to take home too.

Here's an unusual excerpt from a church bulletin, inviting members to the Beginning Again Seminar:

Help for the Formally Married.

Sherry caught this blooper in her own Sunday bulletin:

Hearing assistance devices are available. If you need one, please an usher.

Travel-Size Humor

Gayle was spending a rare night away from home, attending an educational conference. "It was about one in the morning and we girls had just finished our slumber-party talk in my hotel room. I slipped into my navy silk nightshirt, brushed my teeth, and decided to tidy up my room, including disposing of my room-service tray."

Those of us who travel often may see what's coming next.

"I opened my door and gently lowered the tray to the hall floor when I heard the heavy thud of the room door closing behind me. I was now stranded in the hotel hallway in my nightgown. I didn't have the nerve to knock on a neighbor's door at 1:00 A.M., so instead I leaned over the lobby railing of this grand hotel and hollered, 'Is anyone down there?'"

A bewildered bellhop looked up, and Gayle explained her predicament. He promised to send someone up, and after what seemed like an eternity, the manager arrived. As he opened the door he merely smiled and said, "Well, lady, at least you had some clothes on."

Gayle wanted to know, "Liz, with all your travels, has this ever happened to you?"

Not yet, but I've come v-e-r-y close. I usually stand safely inside my room and push the tray of dishes out into the hallway with my big toe. Late one night, garbed in the silliest excuse for pajamas you've ever seen, I was carefully guiding the room-service tray inch by inch across the threshold of my door, trying my best not to knock over the stack of dishes.

So focused was I on moving this tray, I never looked up until it was safely clear of my doorway. My gaze landed on half a dozen couples returning to their rooms, dressed to the nines from a party, staring at big Liz in her too-short, too-tight Daffy Duck pajamas and nothing else, playing footsie with a tray.

Gayle, next time, let's leave the dishes in the room.

Traveling literally keeps you on your toes, and since you're more aware of your unfamiliar surroundings, you often see humor that might escape your notice at home.

One major hotel chain has a little tent sign on the nightstand with this encouraging invitation: PLEASE CALL THE FRONT DESK IF YOU LEFT ANYTHING AT HOME.

I eye the phone, wondering if I dare press 0 and do as they've requested—"Yes, this is Room 502, and I left behind my husband, two children, one cat, a couple of couches, a fake eucalyptus tree . . ."

Of course, we know what such signs really mean, but humor comes from meaning one thing and saying altogether another.

Another little sign appeared on the desk: PLEASE DO NOT IRON ON THE FURNITURE. Golly, it didn't even look wrinkled. If it did, I certainly wouldn't feel compelled to iron it, would you?

In the pool area of the hotel, the sign clearly stated, NO WET SUITS. Yes, yes, we know what they mean, but it's hard to imagine going swimming without getting your suit wet.

In the bathroom of a rural hotel room were some unusual signs: DO NOT PLACE CIGARETTES ON TUB. Again, it's obvious what they were getting at—don't sit in the tub with a lighted cigarette, then lay it down on the edge and ruin the surface—but the temptation was too strong for me.

Deciding it was worth the two-dollar investment, I visited the vending machine down the hall and bought a pack of Marlboros. I didn't light them, of course, but instead stood all twenty of them on their filtered ends, marching around the edge of the tub.

Then I waited till the maid showed up.

Another surprise waited for me when I climbed in this same bathtub and saw the sign above the shower nozzle: PLACE CURTAIN IN TUB. Good heavens, what a lot of trouble. With a sigh, I took down the drapes and stretched them out in the tub, hoping I'd managed this task to their liking.

Honestly, you'd think they'd have their curtains professionally cleaned.

Another hotel apparently wearied of people stealing all the little bars of soap, and so put two soap dispensers in the shower instead. Fine, but which was which? I didn't need deodorant soap on my face, thank you very much. My lips almost never sweat.

It was a moot point, since these soap dispensers were like every dispenser you've ever seen in a public place—empty.

PART THREE

Laughing Moments

Humor is a universal tool for relating to others. Helen from Glasgow, Scotland, who insists the funniest woman she knows is "my mum!" wrote, "A male friend tried to chat up a girl who wasn't too keen. He invited her for dinner on Friday night, to which she replied, 'I'm not going to be hungry on Friday night!'"

I hope the chap had a sense of humor. When it comes to relationships, it's a must-have component for compatibility. Humor breaks the ice, builds rapport, and heals hurt feelings. As Dana from Ohio sees it, "Humor is like a credit card: Never leave home without it."

Chapter 10

Humor and Marriage: Are You Married to a Funny-Baked Ham?

Groucho: *Are you married?*
Guest: *No, I'm separated.*
Groucho: *Maybe you've been using the wrong kind of glue.*
—*Groucho Marx on* You Bet Your Life

This chapter title assumes you have a Honey-Baked Ham store in your neck of the woods, though since I'm cooking impaired, anything I pull out of the oven will be "funny-baked."

My wonderful Bill, first and only husband of a dozen years, is definitely sweet as honey and anything but half-baked. But he is a ham radio operator and he is funny, as in ha-ha funny. Those who only see his quiet side never believe me, but it's true: Bill is much funnier than I am. His one-liners are a work of art; his spin on life is clever beyond measure. Blessed woman that I am, I get to bask in his good-natured humor every day of my life.

Considering how long I looked for my Prince Charming, it's only fair that I found a prince after such a l-o-n-g line of toads. (Say, if you meet a toad sitting on a barstool, would that make it a *toadstool*?)

When you're seventeen years young, men and marriage are a thrilling, frightening prospect in the distant future. Oh, but we planned, we prepared, we made lists of all the qualities our mate-for-life was required to have before we'd even give him a second glance. At seventeen, the list was very long indeed. It filled a legal pad, which we happily covered with ink during study hall.

Everything matters at seventeen.

When I reached twenty-one, still single, I crossed a few things off my long list. For starters, my dream man no longer needed long, curly eyelashes. I could skip that. He didn't have to drive a Camaro, either. A Nova would do. A Pinto, even.

At twenty-five, I went back to my list and ripped off the bottom half. Let's just stick with the core stuff, I told myself.

By thirty I was working with a Post-it note. By thirty-two I had one word left—*breathing*.

Bill breathes well. He also has everything I had on my long list, except hair. Who cares about such things when you're thirtysomething? I love his slippery scalp and the humorous outlook on life that lives under it.

One of the secrets to a happy marriage, we think, is remembering the Source of our joy, which isn't each other. The Source of our joy is the Lord. Yes, we share tons of joyous moments, but we don't expect, let alone demand, joy from our partner. Lot of pressure there. Instead, we look to the same Source, and find the Lord ever available.

In Your presence is fullness of joy;
At Your right hand are pleasures forevermore. (Psalm 16:11)

Happily Ever Laughter

Bill and I are not only partners in life and in parenting, we're also partners in business. June from Pennsylvania was in business with her hubby, too, but before they were married; in fact, before they were even dating. Andy still lived with his parents in Brooklyn but didn't want any of the women he dated to know that, so he gave them June's phone number, which doubled as their business phone.

Hmm, not very romantic. Yet.

After a year of taking messages for him, June was painting a garage floor side by side with Andy one day when she blurted out, "We see each other every day anyway, we might as well get married."

He said okay, and the rest is history! June and Andy celebrated ten years of wedded bliss on October 17, 1997, with four children—ages seven, five, four, and two. Concerning her unusual proposal, June quipped, "Is this biblical? Well, I think God had it planned all along!"

Cindy from Georgia is a happily married woman—twenty-two years and counting. The receptionist at the school where she teaches wants to keep it that way. When the school psychologist called to discuss a student they were evaluating together, he asked, "Is Cindy available?" to which the witty receptionist responded, "Certainly not! She's married."

Snail Male

Dan and Mary were in the early days of courting when he took her to a romantic seacoast spot to spend a warm spring afternoon. They watched the tide go in and out and tried to impress one another with their confidence, cleverness, and charm.

Dan gallantly held her hand as they gingerly stepped from one slippery rock to the next and soon found themselves quite a distance out from shore. Since they'd been gazing into each other's eyes, they'd neglected to notice that they'd run out of rocks and were actually stepping on snails, thousands of snails!

Mary confesses, "There isn't much that shakes me, but when I recognized the crunch underfoot to be newly deceased snails, and all I could see for what seemed like miles was a sea of live snails coming at me, I froze in absolute terror. There I stood, eyes filled with tears, laughing hysterically one minute, whimpering the next, silently begging myself to not lose my composure or ask Dan for help."

Dan is four inches shorter than Mary and of slighter build, so carrying her to safety was not an option. The tide was returning and their choices were limited, so brave Dan confidently grabbed her hand [the hero's theme rises to crescendo here] and with one decisive swoop he began kicking the snails out of her way so she could step on solid, sandy ground while he lovingly encouraged her. "Hold on, you can do it, I'll get you to safety."

In a good romance novel, the story would end with them serving escargot at their wedding reception, but I'll settle for "they lived happily ever after." And they have.

Ronda from New Mexico had a wedding to remember. The bride and groom were dressed in turn-of-the-century costumes complete with top hat, parasol, and bustle dress "that brought snickers and all-out guffaws from family and friends." When the moment came to share their own words of love and commitment, the groom pulled his notes from his pocket and shook out a l-o-n-g list that rolled down the aisle of the church.

Well, why not include humor during your wedding ceremony? The Lord knows you'll need it on your honeymoon. "The quality I love the most about my husband is his dry wit," says Cathy from Oklahoma. "It's made hard times much more bearable."

Rain Falling on Cedars

Regina started dating Ted in April, and by Christmas she was a little depressed about missing her family and their traditions. One of those customs was a cedar Christmas tree, which Ted from the East Coast had never heard of.

On his way home from work one day in December he spotted a grove of cedar trees around an abandoned home. Perfect! They waited until dark, got their flashlights, and drove forty-five minutes back to the grove of trees.

Regina points out, "It was much darker and scarier at night, especially when the wind blew and made strange sounds." They decided to take only the top half of a tree, but it still took Ted a full hour to get the treetop off. Hiding from all the car lights slowed things down, too, and then it started to rain. When they dragged the treetop to his car, they realized the key to the trunk was missing.

They left the tree—grumbling all the way, we're certain—and returned the next night with a bigger car. Regina and Ted got scratched and bruised loading the cedar tree in the trunk, and again when it fell out on the way home. Finally they maneuvered the tree up a tricky staircase and dragged it into her apartment.

Ta-da! and Merry Christmas, right?

Not quite.

They placed the tree in a new, expensive stand and faced the awful truth. As Regina put it, "It was the ugliest, skinniest Charlie Brown tree you ever saw. We laughed until we cried."

In Silliness and in Health

Marriage is more manageable with humor. Laughing relationships last longer, and couples who cut up create ties that bind for a lifetime. Sandy from Pennsylvania sees it this way: "After all these years of marriage, there's a sense of 'this-oughta-be-good!' in our approach to each other's idiosyncrasies. Laughter is just another way of saying I love you."

Cathy was sitting on the couch when she heard the dryer go off. She knew the clothes couldn't be dry yet, so since her husband, John, was in the kitchen, she called out to him, "Honey, please turn on the dryer, would you?"

Soon she overheard him saying: "Ooh, Ba-by, I love you so much. You're so beautiful. I love your lint trap."

"What on earth are you doing?" Cathy called out.

"Turning on the dryer."

First Comes Love, Then Comes Marriage, Then . . .

Bill from New Jersey confesses, "I hate hospitals. In fact, when my wife, Jan, was expecting our first child, I got sick just taking the tour of the maternity floor. The very thought of going into the labor room was enough to send me over the edge."

The night Jan went into labor, Bill sat in the waiting room anticipating the moment when he would assume the role of coach. When the nurse came with his hospital attire, she instructed him to go through the double doors and enter the first room on his left.

Bill says, "I was a wreck but was determined I could do this. I marched through the doors and entered the room, only to find my bride, legs draped in a sheet, already in the stirrups. I lovingly reached over, rested my hand on her leg, took a deep breath, and peered over the sheet—it wasn't Jan! I'd turned to the right instead of the left."

The humiliation continued when later that week at the special couples' dinner provided by the hospital, Bill sat next to the same woman and her husband. A year later, standing behind the counter of his bookstore, waiting on customers, Bill watched with dismay as this woman approached the counter and smiled. "Haven't we met someplace before?"

As some anonymous soul wisely said, "A husband is one who stands by you in troubles you wouldn't have had if you hadn't married him."

Not-So-Silent Night

This wasn't Dana's hubby's fault, but he was there when it all happened.

Dana fell asleep dreaming and woke up screaming, certain that a man had broken into their hotel room. She says, "As my dream became more intense, I began stirring in my sleep. When my sensitive husband lovingly embraced me, I thought I was being attacked by the man in my dream and started fighting for my life."

Suddenly she heard a loud crash and woke up. "My heart was racing out of control, and I shouted out my husband's name. A voice from across the room said, 'I'm over here.'"

In her nightmarish panic, she'd launched her husband out of bed and sent the nightstand lamp flying as well. Dana says, "The people at the Sheraton were very nice when my husband explained about the broken lamp."

It wasn't a good night for Pat from Missouri either. Falling into bed exhausted, she'd no sooner slipped into a deep sleep when "a loud thunderous noise woke me, and I bolted upright. It took me a moment before I realized the noise was my husband snoring. I gently nudged him and he stopped so I dropped off to sleep again. This time the noise was much louder, and there was no doubt of its source. I pushed him on his side, sure that would do the trick."

Seconds later, she was awakened to the loudest snoring she'd ever heard. "I woke him up and insisted that he stop snoring. He kindly obliged and then drifted back to sleep. But within seconds of my sleep the noise started up again. How could he snore so loud?"

It was only then that the shocking realization hit her: *She* was the one snoring, not her husband. "I was so embarrassed. Then I started laughing out loud because of the wonderful joke I'd played on myself. I couldn't stand to have all this joy without sharing it, so I woke up my husband for the fourth time and shared the news with him."

Pat insists she snores only when she has a cold. Her husband isn't talking. Or snoring.

Lord, Give Me Strength and a Good Sense of Direction

Because our driveway stretches a l-o-n-g 600 feet from door to street, my hubby, Bill, avoided paving our driveway for two years, hoping the price of asphalt would suddenly plummet to an all-time low. But when yet another summer downpour washed away the gravel that masqueraded as our driveway, frugal Bill succumbed to the inevitable—a visit from Blacktop Man.

The estimate was ugly. Bill felt too faint even to write the check, so I filled in all the zeros. With payment now assured, half a dozen gruff and grimy men began pouring tar and pebbles down the length of our drive, which suddenly appeared to stretch for six or seven miles from house to mailbox.

To get our cars out of the asphalt zone, we parked them in a ditch at the end of the lane, figuring, Hey, we're out in the country. No one will mind.

They minded.

"Don't leave those cars here overnight!" said the police.

"But where else can we park them?" we whined.

"On a side street with a curb." They seemed very firm on this point, so while asphalt rained down on our gravel drive, Bill prowled the neighborhood for unsuspecting side streets until he stumbled on a distant subdivision with ample parking. The hike back home took nearly half an hour, but the car was safely curbside and was no longer in danger of being arrested for vagrancy.

Meanwhile, my own car and I had vacated the ditch and headed downtown for a dinner meeting. Returning home long after sunset, I absentmindedly turned into our freshly-paved driveway—horrors!—before yellow sawhorses screamed Warn-ing: Fresh Blacktop.

Hastily backing out, I eased down the street. Where had Bill told me to park? I drove around in squares (who drives around in circles?), wishing I'd brought my cell phone, until I spotted Bill's car and parked behind it, relieved to clear the first hurdle of the evening. Now came the tricky part—finding our house in the dark. On foot.

The night was mild, a blessing since I'd forgotten a coat, but the moonless sky was inky black. Up and down the street, lights glowing behind curtains made me long for our own cozy house somewhere out there in the darkness. My high heels, designed only for looking smashing while seated, now made their painful, precarious presence known. "Ouch!" I grumbled under my breath, teeter-tottering down the rough pavement.

That's when I saw it: There, between two houses, beyond a cornfield, was the familiar outline of our barn. As the crow flies, I wasn't far from home after all.

Too bad I wasn't a crow.

Instead, I was a determined woman in horrible shoes bent on finding the shortest distance between two points. I marched up the nearest driveway, paying no attention to the child staring out the window and pointing at me, and started across the backyard.

A vague discomfort settled over me. *Was this trespassing?* I wondered, gingerly stepping around flower beds and garden tools. Is the penalty for this worse than leaving your car in a ditch?

Grateful that tall fences weren't popular in our end of the county, I crossed over to the next yard when suddenly from a corner of the darkness came a loud *grrrgghhh*. An invisible dog was guarding his territory, no doubt. It sounded like a very large breed with not-so-invisible teeth.

"Nice doggie," I said, not meaning a word of it. More growling. High-heeled or not, I hustled into the next yard and prayed I wouldn't find another four-legged security guard.

No such luck. This one was a howler. Long, mournful, wolfy whines filled the air as a screen door banged open. "Who is it?" a male voice demanded to know.

"I'm Liz," I called back, feeling foolish and sounding like Dorothy from Kansas. "I live over there," I added, waving in the general direction of our barn, still far off in the distance. "We, uh, we had our driveway paved."

Even the canine howling stopped with that one.

"You what?" The man in the doorway was trying to sound very authoritative, but the lurking smile in his voice gave him away.

I sighed, desperation beginning to set in. "I had to park my car along your curb because I couldn't park in my own driveway." What kind of an explanation was that? Thank goodness it was enough for him.

"No problem, ma'am, just watch out for T-Bone there. He doesn't cotton to strangers."

I gave T-Bone a wide berth and pressed on through the darkness until a slatted wooden fence presented a momentary obstacle. I fumbled along for a latch for a gate. When the rusty hinges groaned in the night like a scene from a grade-B horror flick, I let loose a nervous giggle. *Get a grip, Liz.*

Our barn now beckoned like an oasis across the harvested cornfield. *This should be easy enough to cross.* Silly me. The field was a land mine of holes, rocks, and cornstalks. My shoes were soon up to their insteps in loamy earth. I resorted to marching along like a four year old at the beach, trying not to sink in any deeper lest I end up in China.

Only a hundred yards or so stretched between me and our dear, dilapidated barn. One more fence and I was home free. A hasty inspection brought bad news: The fencing was wire and had no gate. Launching my larger-than-average body over sharp metal seemed foolish, even dangerous, but launch it I would.

I found a discarded wooden crate, prayed it would hold me, and climbed on. The absence of splintering sounds buoyed my confidence. Guessing the distance and hoping for a soft landing, I took a deep breath and leaped over the fence, high heels in hand.

Thwommpp.

It was a soft landing, all right. Too soft. Squishy, even. I was soon up to my knees in whatever it was. Not manure, thank goodness, but not dirt, either. Too soft for leaves, too warm for sand. *Oh, my, it couldn't be . . .*

I had landed in our neighbor's compost heap. It had to be four feet deep and ten feet wide. Getting out was going to be problematic at best. One wrong move and I could tumble face first into the muck. Yuck.

"Help!" I whispered faintly to no one in particular. My arms were the only thing I could move safely, so I flapped them up and down like a big chicken, hoping someone, anyone, might happen by and rescue me. "Help, help," I said again with less enthusiasm. Who was I kidding? Nobody visits their compost heap in the dark. *Except . . .*

No! I refused to think about the various critters that probably spent many a happy night in a compost heap. I was in the midst of devising the best route of escape from my compost prison when, out of the corner of my eye, I spied a light bobbing along in my direction. Just a few feet off the ground and seemingly attached to nothing, it slowly grew brighter, weaving along an eerie path of its own making, hovering in the night, like a . . .like a . . .

"Aahhh!" The scream wasn't a planned thing, it just happened. "Aahhh!" I screamed again before my throat tightened completely. Suddenly the light was moving toward me and picking up speed. It seemed to be part of something bigger, something with legs.

The legs had a voice. "Liz? Are you okay?"

I almost dropped seat first into the compost. Bill, my beloved Bill, had come to rescue me. "Oh, honey, help me out," I stammered, feeling weepy and light-headed with relief.

Bill put down his big flashlight, practically lifted me out of the mountain of compost—no easy feat—and brushed the worst of it off my legs.

"How did you hear me way out here?" My voice was shaking like a woman who'd just had a close encounter with an alien.

"I didn't hear you, Liz." He tracked down his flashlight and began moving toward the barn. "I saw your car pass by the end of our driveway thirty minutes ago and knew you should've been home by now." Even in the darkness, I could see his grin. "I figured you'd try to find a shortcut."

"Yeah, well, I found one all right." I started to follow him across the grass and realized I was in my stocking feet. "I'll take my shoes now, honey."

"Uh, your what?"

"My heels. Don't you have them?"

We both turned back and gazed at the compost heap, now a shapeless mountain in the darkness.

I found my voice first. "Look, I never liked those shoes. Mister Gardening Guru is welcome to them. How long does it take patent leather to decompose anyway?"

Hardly noticing the sticks and stones tearing up my pantyhose as I tiptoed toward the house, I sent up a silent prayer of thanks for my ever-watchful mate and recalled the verse from Ecclesiastes that appeared on most of our anniversary cards for the last decade:

Two are better than one. . . .
For if they fall, one will lift up his companion.
But woe to him who is alone when he falls,
For he has no one to help him up. (Ecclesiastes 4:9–10)

Amen to that, girlfriend. Especially when you fall in a heap.

Chapter 11

🐝

Humor and Children: Cute, Very Cute

Families with babies and families without babies
are sorry for each other.
—Ed Howe

I have three children under four years of age," writes Cathy. "I love them, but I *need* to laugh because sometimes I feel like screaming."

Yes, we understand completely.

Ellen from Pennsylvania remembers stopping at a family-run café while on vacation. The manager's six-year-old son, apparently accustomed to having the run of the place, plunked himself down at their table and immediately began a one-way conversation, describing the most intimate and embarrassing details of his family life.

After this went on for several minutes, the boy began yet another topic. "My daddy has a pain—"

Goaded beyond endurance, Ellen's husband retorted, "And I know just who it is!"

Good News/Bad News

Lori from Texas was just learning to walk when her mother put her in a pair of shoes and stood her up. Lori took one step and fell down. Her mother picked her up, and again, little Lori took one step and tumbled down. This went on all day.

The new mother panicked and dragged her off to the emergency room, certain her daughter was paralyzed. The doctor took off the toddler's shoes and she promptly took off across the room. One peek in the shoes revealed the problem—a rock.

Lynne from Pennsylvania had a quiet little kindergartner. Her daughter's teacher insisted the shy student would raise her hand in class, "When she's good and ready."

One day, she was ready.

Officer Friendly came to class to teach the children about saying no to drugs and alcohol. As the teacher explained after school, the young girl had finally raised her hand to tell Officer Friendly, "My mom drinks and drives."

Lynne gasped, "She did what? I don't drink and drive."

Her daughter insisted, "Yes, you do, Mom. Every day you drink your coffee when you drive me to school."

Pearls of Wisdom

Lori from Illinois has a sister-in-law who's a high school counselor and thus knows all the signs of emotional upheaval. One morning her preteen daughter showed up for breakfast, dragging her feet and rubbing her eyes. The young girl flopped down in her chair and told her mother she was sick of life.

All of her mother's high school counselor alarms went off as she rushed around the breakfast bar, put an arm around her daughter, and began to explain to her why life is worth living.

The daughter looked up at her with a confused look on her face. "Mom!?! I meant Life cereal."

Who ever thought cereal could be such a cause for concern?

Young David was only two when he looked down at the milk in his cereal bowl and exclaimed, "The cereal ate my milk." His mother Kathy admits, "I think he was a little anxious about cereal after that. It looks harmless, but don't turn your back on it!"

Thanks, I Didn't Need That

Our offspring know just the right thing to say or do to make us smile—most of the time. Glenda's sixteen-year-old daughter watched her mom moping around with a glum face the week before reaching the big 5-0.

"What's wrong, Mom?" the teenager asked.

"I'm depressed about my birthday because it means half my life is over."

"Oh, no, Mom," she assured her. "It's probably more than half your life because most people don't live to be a hundred." Then seeing the look of horror on her mother's face, she started backpedaling. "Unless, of course, you live to be as old as Grandma Carrie, who was 101 when she died. So, let's see, that gives you another six months until half your life is over."

As Glenda says, "There's no comfort like having a teenager in your old age."

Cindy from Georgia values humor in her house. Since she's "a special education teacher and the mother of two teenage boys," laughter helps her cope. Or as Deana put it, "I'm a social worker and a single parent of a fourteen-year-old daughter—need I say more?"

No, that does it.

Marilyn from Michigan hasn't had much support from her teenagers, either. She recalls a time when her thirteen-year-old daughter was taking critical inventory of her mother's fashion sense.

"Mom, that outfit you're wearing looks like it's from the sixties. And your hair needs some work. It looks greasy. And your complexion is awful!"

My, how affirming. Then her eleven-year-old son leaned forward and said very seriously, "Yeah, you ought to use some Oil of Old Lady."

Guarding Our Reputations

Rick from California worked side by side with Gary in police work, and their families became very close. "But as the years passed, our careers went in different directions—Gary's to vice and narcotics enforcement, mine to robbery/homicide investigations. It wasn't long before Gary had the long hair and beard of an officer in deep cover, and our families didn't get to see each other as often as we wanted to."

One day their five-year-old daughters were playing together. Rick's daughter, Erin, passed by a picture of her friend's father as a rookie police officer in uniform—all spit, polish, and short hair. "Kerry, who is that?"

"That's my daddy, back when he used to wash his face and comb his hair."

Sanctified Silliness

Since we usually think of church as a serious place, it's doubly funny when humor happens there.

We all know what the Good News is, but in Susan's South Dakota household, it has additional significance.

Her preschooler had an extreme case of constipation. The doctor suggested all the usual remedies, including mineral oil, enemas, and finally a saline solution, which did the trick.

"Mom, I have good news," her son called out. *Good news* became his phrase to signal a successful bowel movement.

During the children's sermon one Sunday, the minister asked, "Does anyone know what *Good News* means?" Susan's son quickly raised his hand.

The really good news is, the minister called on someone else.

At Molly's church, it was traditional when someone had a birthday to sing "Happy Birthday to You" as that person went forward and put a penny for each year of age in the offering plate.

Their four-year-old son, Bren, had his four pennies, but he also had a problem. Molly writes, "When it was time for the great event, I turned to him and smiled, motioning toward the front of the church. Then I looked down and saw that Bren had hooked the toy handcuffs he got for his birthday to one hand and one leg."

No birthday offering, no song, no going forward for Bren, while his parents laughed hysterically and tried to locate the key.

After the service was over, they finally found it. In his pocket.

Yet a third minor challenge at church turned Suzann's day into a blush fest. Her seven-year-old daughter, Megan, had gone to Sunday school that morning, where her teacher presented a lesson on servanthood.

"Have any of you been helpful recently?" the teacher wanted to know.

Megan nodded and raised her hand. "My mother lost her bra this morning, and I helped her look for it. I finally found it in the dirty clothes, but she said it wasn't really that dirty, so she put it on and wore it to church today."

Oh, now that was helpful.

Just as Bill and I don't put all our "joy expectations" on each other, we don't insist that our kids bring us a reason to laugh every minute either. We're simply grateful when they do make us laugh, which is delightfully often.

Kinda balances things out, don't you think?

THE FAMILY CIRCUS⊛   **By Bil Keane**

"Anytime you're ready, Daddy, I'll be
sitting outside growing older."

Growing Up with Humor

The healthiest families have lots of inside jokes, humor that's communicated with a single word, an expression, a gesture. I remember a basket that my mother often used for serving dinner rolls and such. The person who designed it obviously never tried to pick it up by the handle, which was shaped like the letter *C*.

The first time my brother Tom grabbed the basket to pass the rolls at Thanksgiving—woops!—down swung the basket and down went the rolls, right in the gravy bowl. It became a "trick" basket we loved to use when company came. I've inherited it, along with all the happy memories.

Children are born with a sense of humor already built into their hard drives. But more serious-natured parents and siblings can sometimes belittle that playfulness until it quietly gets deleted like an old computer file. What weary parent hasn't at one time or another squashed the spirit of a noisy, giggling child by intoning, "Wipe that smile off your face . . ." or "You think you're sooo funny" . . . or "It's not polite to laugh here."

The kids get the message: Don't be funny around Mom and Dad. They don't get it!

Our disciplinary ways can be pretty amusing, though, and not necessarily by intent. Sandy's mother was always mixing metaphors and would often toss them into her lectures. Sandy remembers, "One day she was giving us three girls a stern talking to about patience, and she said, 'Don't count your chickens until they get across the bridge.' Naturally, we all dissolved into laughter while our poor mother was mystified and more than a little miffed that we weren't taking her lecture more seriously."

Now as adults, the don't-count-your-chickens thing has become one of their family watchwords. Sandy explains, "If one of us is trying to rush God's timing for our lives, another of us will say, 'Don't count your chickens until they get across the bridge,' and it immediately tells us to chill out and wait for God. In his time, those old chickens will get across that bridge and so will we, with no need to worry about the troubled waters underneath! Besides, it always makes us laugh, and that usually fixes whatever's bothering us. Mom is gone now, but her joy and laughter live on. Humor is one of the few things in life that endures."

Sibling Rivalry in the Making

Bonnie had seven brothers, none of whom came to her rescue when she got in deep water on the family farm. As she tells the tale, "One day as my father was leaving for work, he told me to water the rabbits. I hated the barn and everything in it, including the rabbits, so I paid one of my brothers a dollar to water the rabbits for me."

When her dad returned home from work, he asked, "Did you water the rabbits?"

"Yes," Barbara fibbed.

"What did you use to water them?" he wanted to know.

"I used the same bucket we always use."

"Oh, really? And how did you manage to get the bucket out of the trunk of my car while I was at work?"

The Bible says, "Your sin will find you out." In this case, the rabbits survived and so did Bonnie's sense of humor. She also assures us, "I don't think I ever told him another lie!"

Elaine's family didn't mean to get her in hot water, either, but did they ever. She was the director of religious education at her church, and since it was late November, she was going to show "A Charlie Brown Thanksgiving," which she'd taped.

She popped the video in for the children, then went to help another teacher. Suddenly the teen helpers came running to get her, shouting about naked people on the video.

Snoopy without clothes, maybe, but Charlie Brown?

Elaine ran back into the room to find an R-rated movie on the screen with a man and a woman naked in a Volkswagen. Her face turned red, and she jerked the offensive video out and promptly put in a cartoon video of the creation story. "That way," she reasoned, "if the children remembered a naked couple, I hoped it would be Adam and Eve. I learned two valuable lessons: (1) Stay in the room until the show starts, and (2) never let your family record a movie on a tape you plan to use for church!"

We'll certainly make a note of that.

Squeaky Clean

One evening after a particularly trying day at work, Jeanne was preparing dinner to the sounds of her two sons picking at each other and calling each other nasty names. She kept telling them to quit arguing and reminding them, "We don't call each other names." Did this stop them? "Get real," Jeanne advises.

Finally she'd had enough. "I flew back to their room and told them in a very loud tone of voice that if I heard one more person call anyone a name other than their given Christian name, I was going to wash his mouth out with soap! I warned them that my mother had done this once to me and it was not pleasant."

As she tromped back through the dining area toward the kitchen, she thought she heard her husband make some sort of comment from the TV room. She whirled back into the doorway, fixed him with a glare, and demanded, "Would you repeat that comment?"

"Honey, I didn't say anything."

"Yes, you did," she insisted. "What was it?"

But she didn't really need to hear it again. She had heard him say the first time that he didn't want soap in his mouth.

This only threw fuel on her fire, and she started berating this poor hapless man for making fun of her when she was trying to correct the boys.

Her husband suddenly started rolling with laughter, tears streaming from his eyes.

"Now what's so funny?" she demanded to know.

"I didn't say 'I didn't want soap in my mouth.' What I said was, 'I didn't once open my mouth."

Jeanne laughed until she cried. "It was just what I needed to get rid of the stress of the day. This little story has been told throughout my family, and whenever someone really needs a laugh all we have to say is, 'I didn't want soap in my mouth!'"

All in the Family

Siblings do lose their sense of humor on occasion. One such occasion comes to mind immediately. It was Friday evening and we were on a family outing. Why are these supposed to be fun? Four people, various suitcases, jammed together in a car at the end of a wearying week.

To add to the angst, I was not in good spirits. Was, in fact, cranky, which turns up the volume on Bill's whine-o-meter too. But hey, the kids started it. They were in the backseat, behaving like kids:

"Eeeek, she touched me!"

"Did not!"

"Did too. Move your leg!"

"That's your leg on my side of the car."

Life as usual, in other words. Bill and I were not doing much better in the front seat. I love this man with all my heart, but he was getting on the one nerve I had left. Things heated up to such a pitch that I finally zipped my lips and swung my head around to look out the window of the car.

I was not looking for anything in particular, I just didn't want to look at him. The next words he says better be *I'm sorry*, I fumed to myself.

We passed a Wal-Mart, and the letter *l* had fallen off the sign. That's where we oughta shop tonight, I thought. *Wa*-Mart. Because that's exactly what this car sounds like. Wa-wa-wa!

Suddenly, the kids got quiet in the backseat, and an ominous silence filled the car. You know how it is when you've had words with someone. The tension fills the atmosphere around you with a heaviness that you can almost touch.

Wise Bill decided to cut the tension with the knife of humor. He turned to my back and gave me a full-throttle raspberry. *Thhhwwwppp!*

Bill later told me it was the riskiest thing he'd ever done. Introducing humor at a stressful family moment is dangerous, but the rewards can be well worth the risk.

Since I literally did not see it coming, I cracked up. Exploded with laughter. Relieved, so did Bill. You could feel the tension between us leak out the bottom of the car. We were in love again. We were even in like again.

Meanwhile, in the backseat, the kids kept right on whining. But the two passengers up front had learned a valuable lesson: Life with children goes better with laughter. Betty from Pennsylvania says, "Humor is a bond in my family. My children all say we didn't have much money when they were growing up, but my husband passed on our sense of humor to them."

Dollars and cents pale in value next to a sense of humor.

If you're a laughing parent, your children will be laughing siblings, who marry laughing spouses, who give birth to laughing grandchildren. It's worth the investment.

CHAPTER 12

Humor and Friendship: Friends Laugh with Their Elbows

You can always tell a real friend: When you've made a fool of yourself he doesn't feel you've done a permanent job.
—*Laurence J. Peter*

"I tend to surround myself with friends who have been generously blessed with the art of humor," says Leslie from North Carolina. "They keep me in stitches most of the time, but also help me to stay grounded and feeling great."

And friends do laugh with their elbows. I've watched 'em out there in the audience, elbowing, rubbing shoulders, leaning into one another, playing footsie, even just winking across the table. "Are you getting this?" their eyes say silently to one another. When something funny happens, we always turn first to a friend to share it.

Friendships occur at different levels, from acquaintances to colleagues to best buddies. They differ in number, from the packs we traveled in through school, to the deeper, one-on-one friendships that lasted long past graduation.

A schoolteacher in Florida knows the value of laughter to both build friendships and overcome peer pressure at its most painfully embarrassing. Twyla teaches high school, "where every student must be cool at all times."

Yes, we remember those days.

As she describes it, "The bell was ringing, and one of my students ran blindly down the hall to make it to class on time. As she crossed the threshold, she stumbled on the carpet edge. Books, arms, and legs flew in every direction. Here was this poor child, prostrate in front of her peers."

We feel her pain. Ouch.

"The room was deadly silent, and suddenly my laughter broke the tension. As we laughed and then cried, we finally remembered to see if the girl was okay—she was! The important lesson for that day was not learning U.S. History, but learning to stop taking ourselves so seriously."

I remember all my friends through the years, those one-at-a-time special friends. Through school, it was Elaine, Donna, Judy, and Sue. Through my single years, it was Melinda and Debra. More recently, it was Kathy and Pam, when we each shared a pregnancy together. Now *that's* a humor-based experience.

When women marry, their friendships go through a transitional stage. The new bride drops out of circulation for a season, until the honeymoon is over—both literally and figuratively! No matter how great a man she married, eventually she may discover that her husband just isn't "wired" to meet all her emotional needs.

Example: Let's say I'm chewing over something that happened, some little unpleasant thing that keeps turning over and over in my mind. I tell my dear Bill about it, blow by blow: "Then she said . . .then I said . . ."

He listens for about four minutes, gives me a simple solution, and changes the subject.

Wait! I didn't need a solution. I've already thought of six of those myself. I just needed to talk it over with someone.

Exactly. What I needed was a friend. A woman who understands precisely the scenario I'm describing and gives me the only thing I really needed—her ears and her nodding head.

And her laughing lips.

Shared Funny Experiences

I'm convinced the primary glue in a woman-to-woman friendship is a compatible sense of humor, the ability to steer each other through the deep waters of life in a tugboat called *Shared Funny Experiences*. Usually you each take turns at the helm: You cry, I'll laugh, then I'll remind you when you laughed, and pretty soon, we'll both be in stiches again.

Aren't you intuitively drawn to someone who looks at life with your same warped sense of humor? My friend Frani, who has a smile that can light a room like a 100-watt bulb, says, "I love seeing a person laugh. It changes their entire appearance, makes them accessible. You look forward to being with people who can see the humorous sides of life because they make life fun."

Lisa from Kentucky thinks the only thing more enjoyable than remembering something funny that happened "is reminiscing with a witness, someone who was there when it happened. The story always gets more embellished that way and seems more hysterical."

Andrea from Pennsylvania remembers the year a group of friends went to a small camp for a weekend retreat. "We arrived after dark, so we couldn't see any of the grounds other than where we shone our flashlights.

"Five of us set out to find the girls' rest room. The building was very dark, but as we got closer, a motion light came on. Mere feet away stood a doghouse with a huge black dog lurking in the shadows. We all started screaming and ran past the dog into the bathroom. Our screams turned to laughter when, by the light of day, we realized that the ferocious dog was only a wooden silhouette!"

It's Four O'Clock—Do You Know Where Your Friend Is?

Ronda from New Mexico had friends standing by when she arranged a date with a man she met through a classified ad in the newspaper.

She explains, "My list of the perfect mate was narrowed down to five points: (1) a Christian, (2) cares about other people, (3) loves his parents, (4) likes to travel, and (5) has a sense of humor."

In his first message to her, he explained that he (1) was active in his church, (2) was a volunteer fireman and EMT, (3) had parents in Pennsylvania, (4) was retired Navy and owned a motor home, and (5) definitely had a sense of humor.

They met for lunch at 1:00, while her friends fretted about her safety. When Ronda and her date didn't leave the restaurant until 4:30, she had to "race home to call my two friends who were alerted to where and what I was doing. They were to call the police if I wasn't home by 4:00, fearing that I'd been abducted, raped and murdered," in that order!

Susan from Oregon watched a friend turn green one Easter, right before her eyes. Susan and Karen were dying Easter eggs with the kids and warned them to "be careful or you'll get dye everywhere."

Susan was on one side of the table, with Karen directly across from her. Susan decided there wasn't enough green dye in the water, so she squirted some food coloring in the direction of the bowl.

Oops.

She squeezed too hard, the end of the bottle came off, and Karen became green. And as everyone knows, it's not easy being green.

Susan confessed, "She had to go to church the next morning, still green. We laugh about it to this day. I think that's the only time I've seen her turn green over anything!"

Same holiday, whole different story.

Judy from Texas, along with her husband, flew to Washington, D.C., to visit their daughter, Laurel, for Easter. Judy and hubby rented a car and had Laurel drive them everywhere sightseeing, including Mount Vernon, Georgetown, and Old Alexandria, where Judy bought her daughter a beautiful Easter basket filled with bath products.

After a nice dinner, they headed back to Laurel's townhouse. As they approached the door, Judy saw a strange look appear on her daughter's face.

"What's wrong?" Judy asked.

Laurel gulped. "My keys are in my house, and my roommate is in New Jersey."

"Do your neighbors have a key?"

"Yes, but they are in West Virginia for Easter."

"Call a locksmith," said her father, sounding fatherly.

But no one would come until Monday morning. Meanwhile, it was 11:00 on a Saturday night, Easter eve, and the snow was deepening.

Then Laurel remembered that there was a Realtor lockbox on their door because the house was for sale. Laurel called the Realtor and arranged to get the key. Now the other shoe dropped.

"For safety reasons the lockbox has a timer on it," the Realtor explained, "and it will not open between 10:00 P.M. and 8:00 A.M. See you in the morning."

Cold, tired, and frustrated were just a few of the things they were feeling. The threesome drove to a nearby Holiday Inn and threw themselves on the mercy of the desk clerk, who gave them a room at a discount because of their dilemma.

By the time they got to the room, hubby was fuming, daughter was on the verge of tears, and Mom began to laugh. They looked at her in astonishment

"What is so funny?" they demanded.

"We are," she said. "Look at us. We're on an adventure that was not of our choosing, so let's make the best of it. Thou shalt not whine."

She emptied her purse on the bed and began to dig. "My God shall supply all our needs," she insisted, pulling out three minted toothpicks (unused), three Certs to save for morning, two aspirin (she gave them to her husband at once), a sample night cream, and three chocolate mints, which she placed on the pillows.

Plus, there were all those lovely bath things in the Easter basket. They bathed (one at a time, of course) in fragrant style.

Judy shares, "The last sound I heard as I drifted to sleep was my husband's chuckle. We awoke to a beautiful Easter morning, met the Realtor, and got in the house in time to dress and get to church. As we entered the sanctuary my daughter said, 'Look at these people. I wonder if any of them had as much trouble as we did just getting here?!'"

This trio will never be the same after such an experience. We'd never choose these challenges, but when they happen and we make the most of it, like Judy did, it creates memories that build strong families and strong friendships. As Jan from Nevada sees it, "Laughter creates a powerful energy that connects people and situations."

Blown Away

Speaking of powerful energy, Karla from Texas went to see the movie *Twister* with two friends. She was nervous about the whole thing, since she'd been through three real tornadoes.

Yikes.

Karla worked up her courage, walked into the theater with her friends, and was soon engrossed with the edge-of-seat action on screen. The biggest challenge was the soundtrack, which was a little too realistic in volume and intensity for Karla.

During an especially dramatic scene, a sudden flash of lightning shot Karla out of her seat, jumping, hollering, and unintentionally kicking the seat in front of her. Startled, the man sitting there yelled and launched his popcorn across the aisle, hitting another woman, who in turn jumped up and tossed her soda in the air.

This started a chain reaction along the entire right side of the theater, sending people and popcorn flying with abandon.

The producers of *Twister* didn't know they had a comedy on their hands, but that day in that Texas movie theater, the laugh was on them.

When we rent the video to watch at home, I'm inviting Karla.

Cathy from Oklahoma is welcome to join us, since she agrees, "I love humor, and I love people with a good sense of humor. I think life would be pretty dull without it."

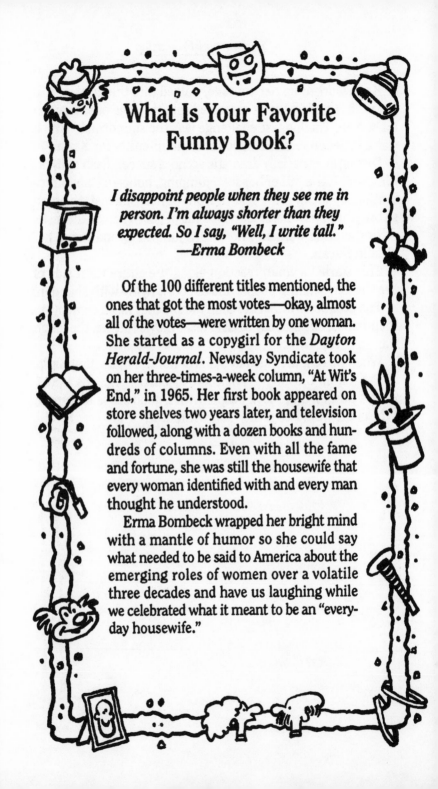

What Is Your Favorite Funny Book?

I disappoint people when they see me in person. I'm always shorter than they expected. So I say, "Well, I write tall."
—*Erma Bombeck*

Of the 100 different titles mentioned, the ones that got the most votes—okay, almost all of the votes—were written by one woman. She started as a copygirl for the *Dayton Herald-Journal*. Newsday Syndicate took on her three-times-a-week column, "At Wit's End," in 1965. Her first book appeared on store shelves two years later, and television followed, along with a dozen books and hundreds of columns. Even with all the fame and fortune, she was still the housewife that every woman identified with and every man thought he understood.

Erma Bombeck wrapped her bright mind with a mantle of humor so she could say what needed to be said to America about the emerging roles of women over a volatile three decades and have us laughing while we celebrated what it meant to be an "everyday housewife."

The Erma Bombeck Bookshelf

At Wit's End

"Just Wait Till You Have Children of Your Own!"

I Lost Everything in the Post-Natal Depression

The Grass Is Always Greener over the Septic Tank

If Life Is a Bowl of Cherries, What Am I Doing in the Pits?

Aunt Erma's Cope Book

Motherhood, the Second Oldest Profession

Family, the Ties That Bind . . . and Gag!

I Want to Grow Hair, I Want to Grow Up, I Want to Go to Boise

When You Look Like Your Passport Photo, It's Time to Go Home

A Marriage Made in Heaven . . . or Too Tired for an Affair

All I Know About Animal Behavior I Learned in Loehmann's Dressing Room

Forever Erma

Books by other humorists were mentioned, to be sure. Several folks sang the praises of my dear sisters in humor Barbara Johnson and Patsy Clairmont. Funny fellas like Dave Barry, Jeff Foxworthy, and Lewis Grizzard were touted too.

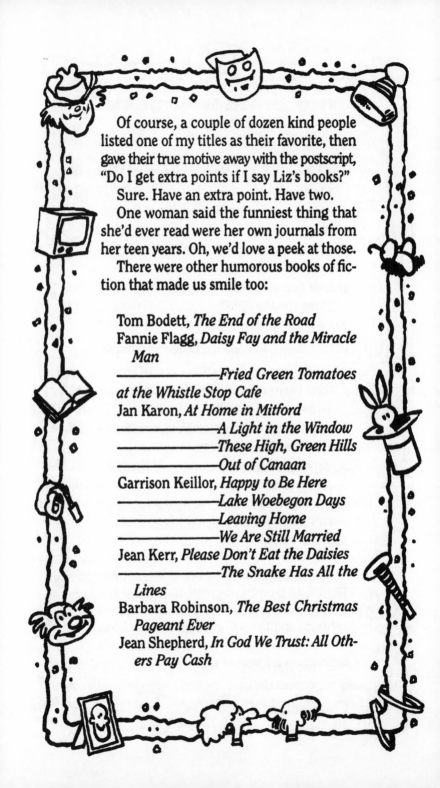

Of course, a couple of dozen kind people listed one of my titles as their favorite, then gave their true motive away with the postscript, "Do I get extra points if I say Liz's books?"

Sure. Have an extra point. Have two.

One woman said the funniest thing that she'd ever read were her own journals from her teen years. Oh, we'd love a peek at those.

There were other humorous books of fiction that made us smile too:

Tom Bodett, *The End of the Road*
Fannie Flagg, *Daisy Fay and the Miracle Man*
——————————*Fried Green Tomatoes at the Whistle Stop Cafe*
Jan Karon, *At Home in Mitford*
——————————*A Light in the Window*
——————————*These High, Green Hills*
——————————*Out of Canaan*
Garrison Keillor, *Happy to Be Here*
——————————*Lake Woebegon Days*
——————————*Leaving Home*
——————————*We Are Still Married*
Jean Kerr, *Please Don't Eat the Daisies*
——————————*The Snake Has All the Lines*
Barbara Robinson, *The Best Christmas Pageant Ever*
Jean Shepherd, *In God We Trust: All Others Pay Cash*

CHAPTER 13

❦

Humor and Work: Funny Business Is Good Business

Did you hear about the cannibal who was fired from his job?
He got caught buttering up the boss.
—Gail from Texas

What's so fun about going to work? Everything, if you take your sense of humor with you. "Give me laugh lines any old day rather than two exclamation marks in the center of my forehead from frowning over a computer screen," laughs Frani from California. "I love to laugh," agrees Brenda from Florida, who works in a health-care setting. "We laugh a lot at work. A good sense of humor helps everybody—patients and staff."

Good thing that Brenda didn't work for the same employer that Brenda from Indiana did: "My sour supervisor told me I laughed too much. I was pleased with that 'fault'!"

She laughed too much? How much is too much? Too much to get her work done? Maybe not. Since laughter relieves stress and promotes communication, it brings more productivity to the workplace, not less. Too much to keep customers happy? Are you kidding? As long as employees know what they're doing, people who make doing business fun will always attract customers.

The key is that the humor be inclusive of the customer, as opposed to employees standing around cutting up with coworkers rather than taking care of business. If you can make it fun for you and for the other person across the counter, across the desk, or on the other end of the phone, then customers will beat a path to your door.

Although my clients hire me to help them laugh, sometimes they toss a giggle in my direction. Pat in Michigan wrote to inform me that I would be met at the airport by a limousine service. "They also operate a funeral home," she warned me, "so make sure you are upright at all times. We don't want them to get their wires crossed!"

What, and die laughing?

Leading by Example, Sort of

No wonder my brother had an I-Like-Ike button in the fifties. Dwight D. Eisenhower is the one who said, "A sense of humor is part of the art of leadership, of getting along with people, of getting things done."

Jody from Iowa led with laughter in her stint as a supervisor over several floors of a major department store in Cedar Rapids. "It was not uncommon for me to put in ridiculous hours and at odd times. One night I stayed late and decided to rearrange everything. Once I get an idea, I'm off and running and can't stop. I was moving clothing racks, switching wall displays, taking pipes off walls, you name it. Clothes were everywhere. It was a mess!"

Her buddies in the janitorial service knew she was doing her usual goofing around and so didn't keep track of her while they were busy cleaning. She disappeared into one of the many back rooms to put away some of the mess and didn't notice the door close behind her. She found the new fixtures she was looking for, went back to the door and, "You guessed it. The door was locked."

She did what anyone would do at 3:00 in the morning, locked in the back room of a department store: "I pounded and pounded and pounded and, well, you get the picture."

Yes, we do.

"I heard vacuuming in a nearby department, so I found the phone and called. It rang and rang and rang and, well, you get my drift."

Yes, we do.

"Now panic set in. I have been at the store for eighteen hours, so you can imagine what I looked like, especially after dragging around clothing and fixtures for the last six hours. Not a pretty sight.

"What were my options? I could call and wake up my sister and brother-in-law, so one of them could come down and try to get the janitors' attention from the front entrance." Maybe not. "There was a window in the back room, and I could get it open, but it's a long way down. What if I fell and hurt myself? What if someone saw me and called the police?"

Her imagination was running full tilt by this time. "Why aren't they worried about me out there? What about the mess I still have to clean up? What will they say when they see me looking the way I do? Is there any way I could just slip out in the morning?"

She tried the phone again, pounded on the door again, and worried some more. "What will my superiors say when they find out? What if the newspaper gets wind of this story, because 911 may be the only way out."

Jody finally decided to get on her knees and pray. "Within minutes, the one woman who was in charge came yelling my name. I jumped up and yelled 'I'm in here!' I did not know whether to die of embarrassment or rejoice. I decided to rejoice."

She has a kindred spirit in Laurie from North Carolina who says, "I've been a manager for almost thirty years. It is a very stressful job. Humor has been my stress relief—after prayer, of course."

Humor and the Trickle-Down Theory

It wouldn't hurt to pray for a sense of humor for your own boss. Loretta is grateful her supervisor had one in her time of need. The year was 1961. As Loretta says, "All the characters are now deceased except me. Therefore, I can tell the story for the first time.

"I'd just graduated from college and was executive secretary to the plant manager of the Tappan Company. The plant manager asked that I write a letter to President Tappan and Vice President Webster asking them and their wives to attend a weekend celebration for the top salespeople. First I typed the letter to Mr. Webster (keep in mind that there were no word processors in 1961), asking that he and Mrs. Webster attend the special event. Then I typed the letter to Mr. Tappan, inadvertently forgetting to change the wife's name.

"We soon had a response to the invitation from Mr. Tappan. I was called to the big corner office, and my plant manager let me read Mr. Tappan's letter: 'We will happily attend the weekend gathering. Even though my wife and I are very fond of Mrs. Webster, my wife is narrow-minded and will not let me spend the weekend with Mrs. Webster!'"

Here's to any CEO who can tee-hee-ho.

Lawyers have a reputation for being humor impaired, but Pamela from Tennessee is happy to toss that stereotype out the window. "I was representing the plaintiff, and the defendant insisted he didn't need an attorney and would represent himself."

His first mistake.

"Every time I asked him a question, he asked me a question. I explained very nicely that he was required to answer my questions but that I did not have to answer his questions. The defendant became so agitated that the judge had to give him the same instructions about answering my questions."

His second mistake.

Finally, she asked the defendant, "What is your reputation for truthfulness in the community?"

At this point the man was so unnerved that he turned to the judge and asked, "What does the truth have to do with this?"

Case closed.

Don't Go Away Mad, Just Go Away

Pam and her husband were newlyweds when they went to one of those home-and-garden shows, with vendors from landscaping to mortgages, insurance to water systems. "We signed up for all the free stuff we could get. One guy we talked to for a really long time—not our choice, we couldn't get away—was named Mike Moss, who sold insurance. We finally gave him our phone number just to get away from him."

Uh-oh.

"Sure enough, a day later we got a call from Mike Moss. My husband was out in the yard, so I decided to do the 'grown-up thing' and ask him not to call again. I told him in no uncertain terms we were not interested in hearing from him or having anything to do with his company."

"Does your husband know you are saying this?" he had the nerve to ask.

"Of course he does; it was his idea!" she declared, her feathers ruffled, and hung up.

"I went out and told my husband what had happened and waited to hear how proud he was of me. All I got was a really strange look."

"Who called?" hubby wanted to know.

"Mike Moss."

Her husband suddenly ran inside to use the phone. Seems that one of his foremen—a Mike Moss—had said he might call that weekend for overtime work. "And I'd told my husband's boss we weren't at all interested in his company!" Pam frets. "Finally, my husband was able to straighten it all out, but his boss—the *real* Mike Moss—never did see the humor in it."

Techno Babble

I've always been the last woman I know to "go techno" about anything. I resisted personal computers until I married Bill— Dr. Geek—who assured me that when I turned the PC off at night, all the words would not leak out. Then when everyone started wearing beepers, I was left out in the cold—hey, I'm self-employed, who would beep me? At corporate speaking engagements, where audience members were constantly getting beeped, I felt so intimidated that I considered wearing my garage door opener.

Next I dragged my feet about going online, until I realized that it's a way to talk long-distance for (almost) free. Sign me up.

Then I fought the cellular phone phenomenon, finally succumbing when a slick salesman rattled off dozens of benefits. The only advantage I can find is one he didn't even mention: If someone calls me, I can find my purse.

Girlfriend, I'm so low-tech, I didn't even have a color television until I married one in 1986.

So when the facsimile machine showed up in my Christmas stocking a few years ago, I wasn't convinced that I had any use for it. Hadn't we been doing business for centuries without one?

It was unimpressive looking at best. A big phone with too many buttons and an appetite for expensive rolls of oddly scented paper. "Just wait," my friends assured me. "When you put a piece of paper in it, it comes out in California."

"No, it does not," I argued, pointing down. "It comes out all over the floor, which is not in Pasadena."

Like I said, I'm slow on the techno.

From the moment I received my first incoming fax, though, and realized what a handy device this would be, I was sold.

My home office would never be the same. With a beep and a flourish, memos, letters, and—how lovely—product orders slithered out of our phone-on-a-box at all hours of the day and night. No charge, no fuss, no trip to the post office.

The first few days after our machine arrived, I would dash to its side at the first telltale tone, anxious to see who was "talking" to me, fax to fax. Like the calculator, the PC, and the VCR before it, the facsimile machine had me walking around shaking my head, saying, "How did we survive without it?"

I'll tell you how we survived. Beautifully. In the pre-faxable era, procrastinators like me could always buy a little time with, "I'll put that in the mail first thing tomorrow" or "Gosh, I don't know where that paperwork could be. Have you checked your mailroom?"

Such stalling devices are history, my dear. In the archives. A fond memory. Never mind Two-Day Air or Priority Overnight, everybody wants it right now, if not yesterday.

Pressure City.

And, remember those *C*s we earned in penmanship? We figured we'd quickly graduate to a typewriter, then a PC, and never look back. Mr. Fax has fixed us good. Those *C*s look like honor-roll material compared to some of the handwritten coversheets that have glided silently out of my machine. More than once I've had to call the sender (long distance, of course) to ask for their secret deciphering code. Sometimes you wonder if a simple phone call, human to human, might have been more efficient in the first place.

What really worries me is the insistence of today's techno-wizards that soon we'll all have fax machines in our homes. A chicken in every pot, a fax in every family room.

A nightmare, I'd say. All that beeping and swishing at odd hours. Junk faxes spilling all over the carpet. Spouses faxing each other the latest entries in their Day Runners. Desperate calls from the school lunchroom, "Mom! I forgot my band uniform. Can you fax it to me?"

Never mind late-night trips to the store for baby food or tp, soon it will be midnight runs for fp—fax paper—at the local convenient mart, where two rolls are just $5.99 with your purchase of a Big Gulp. Before long, they'll have fax paper in decorator colors or country floral prints or with inspirational sayings in the margin. Scarier than HAL, I'd say.

When the day of the ubiquitous fax comes, I'll be ready. I have figured out how to tame the thermal paper beast. If someone whines that they've faxed something to me with no response, I'll smile sweetly and say, "Oh, you did? So sorry. I forgot to check the floor."

CHAPTER 14

Humor and Yourself: Coulda Fooled Me

An onion can make people cry, but there has never been a vegetable invented to make them laugh.
—*Will Rogers*

Your best source of humor is right at the end of your nose. Especially if you're looking in a mirror. Karla from Texas said it best: "If I can't laugh at myself, who will? I love to laugh!" And Julie from Michigan insists she has to laugh "so I don't lose my mind—or what's left of it."

The ability to laugh at ourselves is a sign of maturity, of healthy self-esteem, of having our priorities straight, which is to say, God on the throne, us on the ground. *Humble, humus, human, humor* . . . words well suited to our earthly imperfections compared to God's heavenly perfection. Our richest resource for laughter can be found in our own merry hearts and lives.

Karen, who is vertically challenged (i.e., petite), says, "My philosophy in life is to laugh at yourself. Don't take yourself so seriously. One of my favorite remarks I make as I'm leaving is, 'See you shortly—but then I do everything that way!'"

A Vegetable Faux Pas

Marsha from New Mexico was a young captain in the Air Force. "In other words, college educated and supposedly somewhat intelligent," she explains with chagrin. "Our office planned to have a picnic. Not being a seasoned cook, I volunteered to bring potato salad, figuring it would be easy to make." She called her mother to get her favorite recipe and was all set.

The day of the picnic came. Someone said, "Hey, Marsha, where did you get this potato salad?"

"It's my mother's recipe. How do you like it?"

"Well, the potatoes are awfully crunchy. Could you have undercooked the potatoes a bit?"

Marsha asked in a puzzled voice, "How could that be? I followed my mother's recipe exactly."

"What was the recipe?" asked another.

Marsha proudly began to recite it: "Dice four to six cold potatoes . . ."

"Did you cook the potatoes?"

"Nooo. The recipe called for cold potatoes, so I put them in the refrigerator to get them cold."

The laughter went on for a long time. Poor Marsha was confused, as there'd never been any mention of cooking them first.

She admits, "The joke was on me. I called my mother to relay the story. She, too, laughed, and asked whether I had ever actually seen her make the potato salad. Apparently not!"

A Floral Faux Pas

Even more emotionally healing than laughing at yourself the moment something happens is continuing to laugh about it as the story is told, year after year. Mae from Texas admits, "My humorous story is embarrassing to me, but my friends enjoy it and love to tell it.

"A few years ago we invited a couple to our home for dinner and they brought me a pot of tulips. They weren't particularly pretty tulips—they were in a clay pot with the bulbs partially sticking up out of the soil and they were an ugly color—

but these were friends whom we saw often, so I wanted to take care of the tulips simply because they were from them.

"I nurtured this plant, watered it faithfully, fed it plant food, set it outside in the spring, and brought it back into the house before the first freeze. I couldn't throw it away as long as it was blooming."

One afternoon about two years later, her youngest son absent-mindedly reached over and rubbed the tulip petals.

"Don't touch those, honey, it could cause spots."

She was stunned by his reply. "Mom, this plant isn't real!"

Sure enough, he was right. For two years Mae had nurtured a silk plant. "It did seem exceptionally hardy," she confesses.

Have a Seat

It was a holiday party the guests would never forget. Brenda from New Jersey arrived at her cousin's apartment, which was packed with partygoers. "The apartment was so small that most of us sat on the floor." How small was it? There was a six-foot hero sandwich standing up in the shower stall!

"Unfortunately, the party was very dull," Brenda reports. "I struck up a conversation with one man in a white leisure suit who looked like an Elvis impersonator. He was a big man and sat on a wooden chair all afternoon. He finally got up from the chair, and I sat down in it. The chair was rickety, but I figured if 'Elvis' sat in it for a few hours, I should be safe.

"I don't remember the joke that was said, but I started laughing, and everyone else laughed even harder when I landed on the floor in the middle of the room! The back of the chair came off, and all four legs went flying across the room in different directions. I landed on the floor, with the only evidence that I was ever sitting on a chair pinned beneath me.

"My cousin called a year later to tell me that he finally found the fourth leg to the chair—behind the couch!"

An Award-Winning Performance

The greatest potential for a humbling, humoring experience may come at the exact moment we are being honored for some outstanding accomplishment. That's the Lord's sense of humor at work, don't you think?

Camille's daughter traveled to Boston to receive a special award from her employer, a pharmaceutical company. Camille tells us, "After my daughter, Liz, received the award, one of the vice presidents of the company stepped over to her table to congratulate her. She reached up to shake hands with him and caught her bracelet on her pantyhose! A friend had to cut a hole in her hose so she could get the bracelet loose. She was so embarrassed—but these things happen to a woman named Liz, right?"

(Gee, I can't imagine having such an embarrassing thing happen to me while wearing pantyhose . . .)

Making a Splashy Entrance

Dennis didn't wait until his employer gave him an award to have his most embarrassing moment—he got it out of the way his very first day on the job.

"Of course, I was unfamiliar with the building, so I had to ask my new supervisor where the rest rooms were located. I found the men's room, put the toilet seat down, and unbuckled my pants, etc. Apparently for hygiene reasons, the toilet seat raised up automatically. So when I sat down, fully expecting the toilet seat to be where I had placed it, instead I plunged end-first into the toilet, splashed water everywhere, and got stuck! It took me thirty long minutes to unwedge myself from the porcelain throne.

"By the time I returned to my desk, I was sweating and my polyester leisure suit was drenched. How embarrassing to have to tell my new supervisor that I got stuck in the toilet!"

We couldn't agree more, Dennis.

The Ball Is in Your Court

"Before I was a true believer, tennis was my god," Karen admits. "It was so important to me that I stuffed skirts under the seat of my car so I wouldn't be caught playing again. Finally I gave up tennis, opting instead for Bible study and walking in the park.

"One day while walking around the track, I saw a group of 'serious' tennis players volleying. The ball came over the top of the fence and onto the track. Wanting to be of assistance, I ran to get the ball, giving them a look of, 'Don't worry, I've got this whole situation under control. Just watch this star athlete in action!'

"I picked up the ball, and while the relieved foursome watched me wind up to throw it, my hand accidently released the ball. It shot backward into the path of a moving truck tire and blew up on impact.

"The five of us stared in disbelief. I finally did what I do best—laugh uncontrollably—while the ladies in snazzy tennis attire shook their heads at the poor fool on the other side of the fence!"

Crime Does Not Play

Rick is a robbery-and-homicide detective in California. He was dispatched to a residential neighborhood where uniformed officers had a robbery suspect in custody. As Rick describes the scene, "The culprit had robbed a popular doughnut shop, then fled on foot as several patrons pursued him. The customers had spaced themselves along the street to direct the police officers, who found the robber hiding in his bedroom."

The crook may not have had much sense of humor about himself, but the doughnut-shop customers thought he was a hoot. "The suspect had skulked into the shop door during the busiest time of the morning. He spun through the door and pulled his disguise over his head—a pillowcase—in which he had neglected to cut out the eye holes!"

Oh, now that is funny.

This living pillowase "stood there and waved a sawed-off shotgun at the clerk as he demanded all the cash. Realizing his error, the crook occasionally lifted the front of the pillowcase from his face, told the patrons to remain seated, and then pulled the pillowcase back over his face."

Gee, what a perfect disguise.

"After securing his ill-gotten booty, the bandit fled on foot, only to be followed home by the plethora of patrons who could easily identify him from the several times he raised his mask!"

Beware of Containers That Burp

Louisiana Patty was a brand-new Tupperware consultant, eager and excited about her second in-home demonstration. "The hostess wanted a baking theme, so I began to demonstrate Tupperware's wonderful piecrust recipe—you simply dump in the ingredients and shake."

In went flour, shortening, and 7UP (!), then she sealed the container and started to shake it. "Everything was going great and I had everyone's attention, when suddenly the top came off and flour and shortening went everywhere—all over the nine guests, all over the hostess's gorgeous emerald carpet, and all over me.

"I was totally stunned and will never forget fluttering my eyelashes with shortening and flour dripping off them."

They always play ice-breaker games at Tupperware parties. Maybe Patty could suggest that one to the home office.

Some Sundays Are Like That

Toni knows all about having one of those pie-crust-in-your-hair kind of days. She explains, "I'm a music director for the 8:00 service at our church. One Sunday I found myself driving to mass in a hurry (I'm perpetually late), rushed into church with my music bag in one hand and guitar in the other, and promptly tripped as I climbed the altar steps, a church full of people watching behind me.

"During the mass, I started to play a song in the wrong key and had to start over, and then, after mass I went to my car only to find it still running with my keys in it! And it was only 9:30 in the morning.

"I hope I will always be able to laugh when I blunder," Toni reflected. "I hope in my busy life I will remember to take time to enjoy life as it speeds by. One day my son, four, asked me, 'Mommy, why do we sing lasagna at church?'

"It took me a minute before I realized what he was referring to. Then I laughed and said, 'We don't sing *lasagna*, we sing *hosanna*. It means "praise God."'"

Make a joyful shout to the Lord, all you lands!
Serve the Lord with gladness.
(Psalm 100:1–2)

PART FOUR

What's Your (Weather) Sign?

We now know seven reasons why we laugh—from being polite to being genuinely amused to everything in between—and we know where we laugh—at home, at play, at work. The time has come to discover how we laugh, along with the varied ways we weather life with our unique humor personalities.

Speaking of weather, there must be a reason why in Eustis, Florida, the local paper displays a weather map with "Yesterday's Temperatures." What exactly would one do with this information?! To whom would one address their complaints? "Sorry, but the thermometer on my porch read two degrees hotter yesterday."

I'm much more of a prognosticator who uses today's information to predict tomorrow's behavior. Meteorologists can do that with the weather, and to the best of my ability, I try to gauge how someone will respond to a particular form of humor based on their distinct personality type.

CHAPTER 15

What's Showing on Your Weather Channel?

*Everybody talks about the weather,
but nobody does anything about it.*
—*Mark Twain*

Josh Billings said, "Laughing is the sensation of feeling good all over, and showing it principally in one spot." The spot he's referring to must be our faces, and more specifically, our mouths, but I beg to differ. A dozen years of watching people laugh has convinced me that they laugh in many spots, not just one.

Rainbows and Earthquakers

Some people can be having a great time, yet not a sound leaks from their lips. They may turn a different color—pink, red, and purple are favorite hues among silent laughers. We'll refer to them as *Rainbows*. Other people indulge in vigorous shoulder action or tummy jumping. I call those folks *Earthquakers*, because that's how they laugh, with movement rather than sound. Having been through five earthquakes (albeit at a safe distance from their epicenters), I know the quakes themselves were silent, but the furniture was noisy.

"My biggest laugh is quiet," agrees Tracy. Dollena from Indiana describes her laugh as "deep, long, and past the point of sound." Joanna from Georgia also says her laugh is "silent, with my mouth wide open." Stella from Indiana experiences "complete body shakes," and Stephanie from Michigan admits, "the funnier the story, the more quietly I laugh. People look to see if my shoulders are shaking."

Weather Systems

For the rest of us who are indeed more vocal with our laughter, here are ten ways we'd describe those sounds, in order of popularity among our 500 survey respondents and grouped by the weather system they most resemble.

1. Cumulus Clouds: The Giggle

More than one hundred of us are gigglers. Giggles, like cumulus clouds, pile up and accumulate. The giggle is the most infectious of the bunch. Elaine from Washington says, "My childhood friends would tell me to laugh, and then they would laugh at my laughter."

Sherry from Oregon's "contagious giggle" has been passed around for many a delightful year. And Pat from Michigan's giggles go on and on "until I have tears running down my face." Indeed, if you give cumulus clouds enough time, they'll rain on you as well.

Men and women both giggle, though we often think of it as a girlish sound, simply because it's often high-pitched and cascades like a gentle waterfall. In print, we might capture it as *tee-hee*, though it's more musical than that. Without a doubt, the giggle is one sound that says, "I'm having fun, please join me!"

2. Squall Line: The Howl

Although this is our second most popular style of laughing, only half of us are howlers, compared to the large number of gigglers. The howl is a noisier laugh, sure to draw more attention and elicit all manner of rubbernecking. Howls aren't very short—Karen from Kentucky admits her howl "goes on and on." Another Karen from the Bluegrass State describes her laugh as "a screaming howl, where I lose my breath and wet my pants, all in one motion."

Sorry, we don't have a specific category for that, however weather-related moisture may be.

I'd have to confess that my own laugh is a cross between a howl and a hoot—not to be confused with a hoot owl—and like all howls, it does cause a scene. Sherry from Colorado considers her own howl "totally out of character." In fact, she will perform it "only with family." Even so, onlookers usually exclaim "Oh, no!" or "Oh, dear!"

Loud, sustained, and *unrestrained* are the watchwords here.

3. Wind Shear: The Blast

Of equal frequency with the howl, the blast is usually of shorter duration and—here's the key—is totally unpredictable, showing up out of nowhere, just like the wind shears I've traveled through while hot-air ballooning. (The hot air I've released for the last fortysomething years is another issue altogether.) Iris from Pennsylvania is a blaster, and she says her husband tells her she sounds like Scooby Doo.

Nancy thinks she and her daughter could make a tape of their bouts of blasting. "It would make the whole world laugh with us, as we hit various notes according to how hard we're laughing."

Do they make sheet music for this? "Two Blasts with Oboe," perhaps?

Think *sudden, violent outburst* for this one.

Portia's blast also moves to silence, and she "usually can't breathe." All weather styles contain that possibility, of moving rapidly from one climate to another without warning. It's almost impossible to predict, from a meteorological standpoint, what sound the laugher will return to when the laugher is finally able to breathe again. Stay tuned.

4. Jet Stream: The Whoop

I know what you're thinking: Howls, blasts, whoops—aren't they all the same? Clearly they aren't to our participants, who selected one over the other, for the most part. Then there's Cheri from Florida and her "melodic, whooping blast," which sounds like its own weather system, as does Leigha from Montana's blended laugh that's "between a whoop and a howl."

The very word *whoop* comes from the sound you make when you do it (*onomatopoeia*, for you English majors). It has a sense of eagerness and enthusiasm about it, a war cry for laughter, if you will. Whoop! Let's go! is the sense of it. Pam from Idaho calls her laugh "a burst of happiness," which sounds like *whoopee* to me.

Becky from Ohio thinks her whoop sounds like "a wild turkey"; Wanda from Texas celebrates the "young, vibrant" nature of her own whoop; and Miriam from Indiana says her laugh leaves her in "no man's land"—that silent place again, I suspect, the place between laughing and breathing.

5. Tornado: The Snort

I have a special place in my heart for snorters because, of course, I count myself among them. This isn't a club you join by choice. Rather, the particular way your nose is structured has something to do with it. I think.

Rose from Hawaii is not pleased about her status as a snorter either. "Appalling! Most embarrassing!" she insists. I'll say this about a snort. It isn't contagious, in that others around you will start snorting, but it is so hilariously distinctive that it usually launches those in earshot off on another squall of their own.

A snort stands out in a crowd because of its unusual timbre. While most laughs are in the soprano range, snorts are baritone. Although I prefer to think of them as musical rather than animal, those of us who snort are not the only laughers who draw our inspiration from the barnyard, as these contributors indicate when describing their own laughs:

- A sheep—Shirley from New York
- A woodpecker—Bryan from Alabama
- A horse—Susan from Pennsylvania
- A hen, before and after laying eggs—Deana from Kentucky
- A braying mule—Marbeth from Kentucky

(This last example of four-legged laughter was suggested by Marbeth's husband. Well, the very idea.)

6. Warm Front: The Chortle

Lewis Carroll was fond of this blend of chuckle and snort, which, like the warm front it resembles, is filled with moist air and genuine warmth. One never chortles in disdain. It's a friendly sound, like a chuckle with attitude.

Sue from Ohio describes her own chortle as a "Hee, Hee, Hee" sound, probably with a bit of spacing between them and punctuated by shoulder shakes.

Three dozen of us chortle regularly and seem no worse for wear.

7. Forked Lightning: The Hoot

Here we have the thunderhead of the bunch and, of the ten styles of laughter, the most explosive and sometimes derisive, as in "They hooted their disapproval."

In more recent usage, though, and especially in the South, you'll hear people respond favorably by saying, "What a hoot!" I once had a pastor introduce me to his congregation with, "Please welcome our speaker, Liz Curtis Higgs, a blessed hoot."

Now there's a quote for the next brochure.

8. Sea Breeze: The Melody

There are two dozen singers among us, whose melodic laugh could be captured on a musical staff. Barbara from Washington describes her musical laugh as "like her mother's." Oh, if only we had them both on tape, to compare! But we'll take her word for it.

The lyrical laugh resembles a flute or, even better, a piccolo.

9. Dust Devil: The Gasp

Shorter than all the other laughs described to this point, the gasp has an oh-no! quality. If you're not watching the gasp in progress, you may swing around to be sure the gasper is okay.

Especially if Ann from Kentucky is the one gasping, since she says it's quickly followed by silence. Sheryl from Oklahoma might make you nervous with her gasps, too, since they are, she admits, "multiple."

10. Unstable Air Masses: Seven Varieties

Karen from California shares that she has "a vertical laugh, depending on the intensity of the humor. It can go from a *tee-hee* to a *har-har* in the twinkling of an eye and a simple pratfall."

When you're under a lot of barometric pressure, often referred to as stress among nonweatherheads, your laughter may be unstable, veering back and forth between some of the following less popular but highly dramatic sorts of laughs:

- The Wheeze (the preferred laugh for fourteen of us)
- The Hiccup (how Clara from Minnesota ends her laughs)
- The Groan (has its own humor line: "Groaners")
- The Cackle (Allison from Idaho favors these)
- The Honk (especially popular with Canadians)
- The Sneer (more visual than audible, and rather unkind)
- The Hiss (for people who laugh through their teeth)

Garlena from Montana had a hard time putting her laugh on paper. "I really don't know what I sound like, but people always recognize me by my laugh."

Laughs are as individual as weather systems, each one created by shifts in temperature—moods, in our case—and affected by the environment around them.

Venus and Mars in the Weather Lab

Do men and women laugh in the same way, at the same things?

I could either write an entire book on the subject, or cut to the chase—no, they do not.

As a woman who speaks primarily to female audiences, I've noticed an interesting phenomenon: If there is even one man in the room, sitting in full view, women will curtail their laughter slightly. If the audience is 25 percent or more men, the effect is even more noticeable. Given half a roomful of men, the women wait hesitantly, watching the men and one another for cues: "Now? Should I risk looking foolish?"

The younger the woman, the more likely she is to stifle her laughter when men are present. On the other hand, a more mature woman often laughs with abandon, which is one of the many benefits of maturity.

Many other humorists have seen this phenomenon as well. Rosita Perez, my *Ishtar* conspirator, finds that "we women spend a lot of our time waiting until whatever feels right to us also feels right to everyone around us." She has discovered that "when a husband is present, the dynamics are very different; women censor themselves."

Judith Tingley, who has a doctorate in psychology, speaks and writes about male-female communications. She has assessed the problem of women who withhold their laughter as "a high need for approval coupled with a low risk-taking propensity." She notes that women are more restrained in most of their nonverbal communication, but especially so in a mixed group.

Clifford Kuhn, a psychiatry professor who does stand-up comedy on the side, sees things a bit differently. He believes that men enjoy humor more when their wives are laughing and that women actually control the audience. "Some comedy writers create material with the woman in mind," he added.

Humorist Hope Mihalap, a veteran of the platform, observes that "men enjoy one-liners, short things, that seem vaguely tough coming from a woman." Women, she's discovered, love a broader style of delivery, with well-developed characterizations, wide gestures, and animated facial expressions.

I say, let's not take any chances. Women need to laugh till they cry and cry till they laugh, slap the table, and throw their hands in the air. Women must give themselves permission to gather together in the name of good health, and laugh the mascara right off their faces, without even one man present to interfere with their fun!

Many of these male-female dynamics aren't present in the home, though. Bill and I laugh with equal abandon around the house, as do most couples. It's the public display of laughter where invisible lines may be drawn.

Of course, I've always been a woman who colored outside the lines, especially when it comes to having fun.

The Four Humor Personalities

So many wonderful books have been written on the subject of personalities or temperaments—Tim LaHaye and Florence Littauer are two of the very best authorities on the four basic types. You may be familiar with their excellent materials or with the D-I-S-C model at your workplace, or the Myers-Briggs Type Indicator, or Hippocrates's theories of the Sanguine, Melancholy, Choleric, and Phlegmatic fluids of the bodies and how they affect our behaviors.

But I'm sure you've never heard of the Four Weather Personalities, my friend, because I made them up! They are easy to remember, highly visual, and *fun*—key word, here. Since people are as variable as the weather, especially when the winds of change blow them off course, I thought these words would lend atmosphere (pun intended) to our consideration of not only how we laugh—what we look and sound like doing it—but what makes us laugh.

Each weather type will have its own chapter, with plenty of humor to illustrate and illuminate. Following are the four weather personalities in a nutshell—Sunny, Cloudy, Stormy, and Foggy.

1. Sunny. Fun-loving, people-oriented, enthusiastic, and energetic, the *Sunny* soul loves life and enjoys being center stage, but hates getting organized, often arrives late, and never remembers names! Sunnies laugh no matter what the weather. Of those surveyed, 32 percent shone like the sun.

2. Cloudy. Serious, purposeful, logical, and neat, the *Cloudy* person is conscientious, thoughtful, and altogether wonderful—as long as you don't mind having a moody perfectionist in your midst. Cloudies are saving their laughs for a rainy day. Among our contributors, 28 percent are not convinced every cloud has a silver lining.

3. Stormy. The born leader of the bunch, the *Stormy* sort is a hard-working visionary who gets things done and keeps things moving, someone who isn't too difficult to get along with, as long as you do it their way! Stormies laugh wherever and whenever they feel like it. Some 23 percent of us insisted on being identified with lightning and thunderbolts.

4. Foggy. Everybody's friend, the peace-loving *Foggy* would rather watch than get involved, is a great listener and mediator, and has a dry sense of humor—when they're not being a wet blanket! As laughers go, Foggies are great smilers. Because they're so quiet, you might not notice the 17 percent among those surveyed who are in a fog.

Which one are you? Only time and reading will tell. Even with the brief introduction above you may be concerned. Can a person be more than one weather personality? Most assuredly. Most of us are a solid mix of two—after all, party sunny/partly cloudy days are common weather patterns. Because of the personality types that surrounded you in your growing years, you may even dabble in a third style, but if you think you are all four, you have a serious personality disorder.

Seek professional help at once.

On second thought, this is a book about humor, so just laugh about it and keep reading. Know this beyond a doubt: All four personalities have strengths and weaknesses, but all are a valuable addition to the human race. We need the Sunnies to be in charge of cheerful, the Cloudies to be in charge of details, the Stormies to be in charge—period—and the Foggies to be in charge of keeping the rest of us from killing one another.

The most important concept here is this: All four weather personalities have a sense of humor. All have the capacity to laugh out loud, and all need as much humor as possible in their lives. What makes us laugh and how we respond to humor is what keeps life interesting—as do cold fronts and dry spells.

CHAPTER 16

🐝

The Sunny Sense of Humor: Let a Smile Be Your Umbrella

A good laugh is sunshine in a house.
—William Makepeace Thackeray

Of the four weather personalities, without question the one who has the most fun, day in and day out, is the Sunny, the warmest weather personality.

Sunnies, as the name implies, share many qualities with Mr. Sun himself—they're dazzling, warm, and bright. But yes, you can get a Sunny-burn if you stand too close!

According to the five hundred kind people who responded to the survey, 32 percent of us are Sunnies. Theme song? "Don't Worry, Be Happy!" Slip on your shades and let's take a look at eight traits of the Sunny and their unique spin on humor.

Warm and Outgoing

See that woman at the checkout counter? The one talking to the person in front of her, behind her, the clerk, the bag boy? That's a Sunny in action.

If nobody's listening, she talks to the candy rack.

"Oh, look! I didn't know they had that flavor. Excuse me, Miss, could you hand me one of those, on the bottom? Oh, and look what's in her basket!"

Sunnies make friends instantly. If the Sunny woman at the grocery store has her husband with her, he'll whisper in her ear, "Do we know these people?"

She does now. Sunnies have more signatures in their high school yearbooks than any other weather type, because they know everybody—or at least act like they do.

The Sunny treasures humor because of its social value. What better way to reach out to people than by saying or doing something amusing?

Attention-Getting and Talkative

The minute her teacher asks a question, my daughter Lillian's hand is the first one up. Of course—she's a Sunny. With a bright mind and childlike curiosity, Sunnies love to ask and answer questions, which is why they have no trouble talking to themselves. I always tell people I'm praying under my breath, but half the time I'm carrying on my own conversation. For the Sunny, this isn't psychotic, it's survival. We're always happiest when we're talking.

In fact, the Sunny is the only weather personality that likes voice mail. After all, what does the machine say? "Talk at the beep." We love that. Voice mail beats getting no answer or a busy signal, though I hate the ones that shut off after thirty seconds. I'm just warming up, haven't even said my full name or phone number yet, and then *click*. So embarrassing. I have to call back and say, "Hi, me again . . ." and hope I can get the rest in before I'm beeped into oblivion a second time.

True Confession: I recorded my outgoing voice mail message in a hurry one day and didn't realize until I called back for messages that I'd recorded this message: "At the tone, please leave your beep."

Your what?!

Exactly as requested, there were seven messages in a row, one friend after another, laughing hysterically and shouting, "Beep!"

Miriam from Indiana must be a Sunny.

"I always loved to talk. When I was twelve years old sitting in the backseat of our rather large church, I was talking away when my father, the minister, stopped his message and said, 'Miriam, since you want to talk so much, either come to the pulpit and do my sermon for me, or come to the front and sit with your mother.'"

Miriam admits, "That walk to my mother in the second row was the longest walk I ever took."

Radiant and Friendly

Not only do Sunnies reach out to others, they also draw people to them like a magnet. Their blue-sky view of life and eternal optimism make them a joy to be around—unless you're trying to get a word in edgewise.

Sunnies are generally morning people, eager to start the day, unless they're night owls who talk long after dark. Then their Sunny self hides behind the clouds until midday. Even half-awake they remain friendly, though. Sunnies are people-pleasers and won't risk losing a friend merely from losing sleep.

Sunnies in my audiences like to participate when they get the chance. One time I asked a large group of conference attendees to tell us what unusual things their husbands brought into their honeymoon cottage. One woman raised her hand and said, "Three stuffed moose from Wyoming!"

The audience and I were quite astounded at this unusual decorating challenge. When she came up to me after the event, blushing furiously and looking very guilty indeed, I wondered if she'd not exaggerated just a tad. "You really didn't get three moose from Wyoming, did you?" I said gently.

"No, Liz." She shook her head, eyes downcast. "What I really got were six stuffed ducks from Mexico, but I didn't think anyone would believe me."

Energetic and Spontaneous

The sun is energy itself, and so is the Sunny personality. Ready to try something new at the drop of the hat, and with enough physical and emotional energy to get them through the project, Sunnies embrace change and welcome innovation. They really get excited if those changes include new forms because they can't find the old forms!

If you get the urge to see a movie and it starts in an hour, call a Sunny, especially if it's a comedy. Need instant feedback on an idea? See a Sunny. Want to redecorate your guest room and need a buddy to visit the mall with you? Sunnies are often gifted in color and design. Need someone to proofread your annual report? Oops. Not the Sunny's strong suit.

But shopping? Now there's where we shine. I met a woman named Mary Ann who'd recently moved to Albuquerque. When

I asked her what she thought of the dry southwest, she exclaimed, "Oh, in our neighborhood, we have both a Sam's Club and a Price Club. That's what I call a good climate!"

Colorful and Expressive

You can't have a rainbow without the sun to reflect all the colors in the spectrum. Sunnies are nothing if not colorful, both in style of dress and in vocabulary (not blue language, of course!). Their facial expressions are animated, their body language goes a mile a minute, and sight gags are one of their favorite forms of humor.

Back in high school, Linda from Pennsylvania drove "an old, decrepit Volkswagen Bug. The poor thing was falling apart, mostly because I kept trying to make it fit into spaces that were too small for it, but I loved it. The horn consisted of a big silver disc in the middle of the steering column that looked more like a hub cap than a horn. Many times this apparatus would fall off onto my lap, as other sundry parts did with regularity.

"One day my best friend, Sandy, and I were cruising, and she saw a friend of ours. She said, 'Ooh, there's Ralphie. Blow the horn.'"

Linda couldn't resist the urge. She took off the horn disc and said, "Here, blow it yourself."

"Sandy wasn't aware that the horn came off, and she thought I'd handed her the whole steering wheel! We ended up laughing so hard I nearly wrecked my precious Bug."

Light and Silly

According to Catullus (c. 60 B.C.), "There is nothing more silly than a silly laugh."

I've always loved the word *silly*, until I found out that among other things it means "stunned, dazed, and lacking common sense."

Gee whiz.

The silly Sunny only appears dazed and confused, when in truth they're just easily amused. We love slapstick, visual humor, broad comedy, and pratfalls. It's not that we don't have taste, we just can't help falling down laughing when others . . . fall down.

Deloris from Kansas worked at a home for the elderly with a Sunny friend. "We'd always think of silly things to do to cheer up the residents," she explained. "I bought the biggest shirt and shorts that could be found. She climbed into half the outfit; I climbed into the other half. We're not small gals, so these were big clothes. The residents smiled and laughed and it was so fun!"

Very proud of themselves, they decided to walk around the campus outside. "We didn't stay in step and fell into a ditch right by the highway. We could not get up! Cars would slow down, and we'd laugh harder and harder."

If you've ever been in a three-legged race, you've got a clear picture of this whole silly scene.

Janice from Minnesota didn't fall herself, thank goodness, but everything else did. While maneuvering through a crowded restaurant, Janice accidentally bumped her purse on the sneeze guard over the salad bar. "That's when the chaos began. The guard was not permanently attached, so when I bumped it, down it came along with the baskets of croutons, sunflower seeds, and so forth, that were sitting along the top. I tried grabbing the baskets as they slid past me, only to watch them explode when they hit the ground.

"The worst—and loudest—moment was when the glass guard hit the floor and shattered at my feet. Talk about a red face! I still look for my picture at the entrance along with a warning sign: DO NOT ADMIT THIS PERSON."

Bright and Creative

Sunnies are the very definition of right-brained, creative types. If there's a clever, offbeat way to solve a problem, the

Sunny finds it, even at a young age. Sheena from Texas was a mere toddler when her mother put her to bed and firmly told her, "I love you, but if you get out of bed before morning, I'm going to have to spank you."

Dr. Spock hadn't considered creative Sheena.

Twenty minutes later, her mother heard the pitter-patter of little feet coming down the hall. Sheena poked her head around the corner and said, "Good morning, Mama!"

I'm not sure if the stranger in the next story was a clever Sunny or just plain strange.

Peggy from Texas was eating at a restaurant with her sister and two young children when out of nowhere a woman came up behind her and started talking in her ear like Donald Duck.

"I turned to look at her, and the stranger was gone. A few minutes later, she passed behind me and did it again. I asked my family if they'd heard her, and they cracked up—so hard, my sister almost wet her pants."

Cheer up. If the woman had walked by my table, she probably would've talked like Porky Pig, and then I'd have been forced to follow her to the salad bar and push her face in the cottage cheese!

The Brightest Star in the Sky

When Sunnies enter a room, they fill it with sunshine and laughter. And noise. Phyllis Diller's laugh was once described as the sound of an old Chevrolet starting up on a below-freezing morning.

Yes, Sunnies are loud. Sitting in bed having a conversation with Bill one night, he cut me off with, "Shh! You'll wake the kids!"

"How could I wake two sleeping children?" I demanded in a loud voice.

Oh, I see.

The Sunny's ever-performing approach to life can become tiresome for those around us who long for a few quiet, overcast days. The truth is, the Sunny needs to hide behind a few clouds from time to time. Being "on" all the time is exhausting. In some cases, the ha-ha funny side of the Sunny comes from what my friend Rosita calls "a deep need not to cry."

Joanna from Georgia says, "Humor brings me out of depression and helps me see the brighter side of a situation. Almost all clowns have a sad past."

I've used humor as a coping mechanism myself a time or two (or three or four). But it's so much better than all the other choices, don't you think? It's free, legal, clean, safe, and available twenty-four hours a day.

It's also addictive, but in the most positive sense.

Mary from Oregon is a classic Sunny: "It started out as a sunny summer's day, perfect for getting out my three-wheeler and heading off to a yard sale. My bargain of the day was a large palm plant. I plunked down my two dollars and loaded my plant in the basket in the rear of the three-wheeler, which is like a big adult tricycle."

But Mary hadn't counted on the quizzical looks and amused stares she received as she pedaled along the streets in the pouring-down rain with a very large palm plant behind her.

"One driver slowed down to gape as I was passing in the opposite direction, so I yelled out, 'Well, don't you ever water your plants?!!'"

The Sunny in Review

Favorite career:	Sales
Favorite hobby:	Spending money
Favorite sport:	Cheerleading
Favorite humor:	*Candid Camera*
Favorite clothing:	Colorful, casual

Favorite city:	Phoenix (214 sunny days a year!)
Favorite magazine:	*People*
Favorite color:	Red
Favorite day:	Saturday
Favorite season:	Summer
Favorite holiday:	Fourth of July
Favorite hymn:	"There Is Sunshine in My Soul"
Life verse:	"He who is of a merry heart has a continual feast" (Proverbs 15:15).

CHAPTER 17

The Cloudy Sense
of Humor:
On Second
Thought, Take
the Umbrella

One misty, moisty morning,
When cloudy was the weather...
—Nursery Rhyme

Deep is the word that comes to mind when we think of the *Cloudy* personality. A deep thinker, a deep digger for truth—and a deep well of tears from which to draw bucketfuls as needed.

The Cloudy goes to the well often, as the wettest of the four weather personalities.

Since 28 percent of us are Cloudies, how wonderful of God to create just a few more Sunnies to keep Cloudies from drowning in deep, depressing water. Of course, it works both ways. The Sunnies need the Cloudies to keep them from consuming themselves in a fiery flame of misplaced enthusiasm.

Cloudies touch a cool finger of water to our Sunny lips and say, "Calm down. Be still. Make a list."

Here's our list of eight traits that often appear on a Cloudy horizon, taking special note of the Cloudy sense of humor.

Cirrus-ly Speaking

In cloud lingo, cirrus clouds are the lofty ones, reaching for the highest of heavens, with wispy curls like angel's hair. That's our Cloudy, an angel to all who know them. Often deeply spiritual, Cloudies love nothing better than studying, researching, and seeking after truth.

They've done all five years of Bible Study Fellowship—twice.

Their copy of *Vine's Expository Dictionary* is dog-eared.

The somber Maundy Thursday service is their favorite part of the Easter season (unlike their Sunny sister, who can't wait for the trumpets and ta-das of Resurrection Sunday).

The Cloudies take life seriously, as well they should. Somebody should, and the Cloudies are good at it. What they're not skilled at is giving themselves permission to laugh. The Cloudy definitely has a sense of humor—every healthy person does—but allowing that side to come out and play requires patience and encouragement from the sidelines.

Sherry from Colorado admits she needs lessons on "how to laugh at myself more often. It's so hard because I'm such a serious person." The Lord has a way of humbling us, even if only to help us develop that sense of our humor-filled humanity.

Just after her thirtieth birthday, Sherry "received a pleasant surprise. A cute guy asked me to go skiing. The fact that he had been on the ski patrol for four years during college didn't faze me, even though I'm only a beginner/intermediate skier.

"I hadn't been on a date in almost a year and was really trying to impress him. I bought a new ski suit, hat, gloves, and goggles and insisted on driving my four-wheel drive."

Impressive.

"As we were heading down the highway, I was talking so much to ease my tenseness [ooh, big step for a Cloudy!] that I didn't notice how fast I was going.

"The highway patrolman asked, 'Did you realize you were going 57 in a 50 mph zone, and at a dangerous intersection at that? Let me see your driver's license.'"

Sherry gulped and handed it over.

"Ma'am, did you know your license expired three months ago?"

No, she didn't.

"Well, Miss Dixon, I was just going to give you a warning for speeding, but because your license has expired, I'm going to write a citation for speeding. The gentleman there can drive you both home."

Steve could not drive stick shift.

Steve never called Sherry again.

She says, "All I could do was laugh at all my mishaps. Maybe perfectionists aren't always perfect."

Stratus Listus

Like the low, gray blanket known as the stratus cloud, the Cloudy covers every base, checks every detail, crosses every *t* and dots every *i*.

Cloudies actually use those daily planning guides that most of us bought with the best intentions but have yet to take out of the box. Their neat, legible handwriting covers each page with carefully thought out ideas and plans for the days, weeks, months, and years ahead.

I am a closet Cloudy, meaning when no one is looking I make lists, too, but on my computer where no one will ever stumble on them and laugh at the very notion of me trying to get that much accomplished in one day. You see, putting an enthusiastic Sunny with a Cloudy-style Day-Timer is a dangerous thing. We Sunnies fill each tiny fifteen-minute segment with tasks like "get caught up on laundry."

In fifteen minutes? Very dangerous.

The Cloudy would never do such a thing, because they are efficiency experts, having calculated exactly how long each chore will take to finish, allowing for both best and worst case scenarios.

Worst case scenarios are a Cloudy forte.

Ms. Responsible

Every family needs someone to be responsible, and the Cloudy gets the job every time. She or he keeps the calendar up to date, packs the lunches, checks the homework folder, gets the library books back on time (and probably volunteers there twice a month).

Cloudies know what it takes to make the world go around, and it's one word—*organization*. Unless the Cloudy literally writes "do something fun" on their list of "Things to Do Today," it might not happen. Cloudies genuinely want to include more fun in their lives, if only because they've read eleven articles recently on the health benefits of humor, but they aren't sure where to begin.

Gale from Kentucky works with a woman named Debbie who, if not a Cloudy, certainly jumps in to be helpful in typical Cloudy fashion. "It was a busy day at the doctor's office," Gale begins. "People were scurrying around, pulling charts, weighing patients, and making appointments.

"Debbie decided to do some filing in the huge lateral files we use to house thousands of file folders. A security feature of the file cabinets is a cable in the back that is supposed to keep more than one file drawer from opening at a time. This cabinet's cable was broken, and as luck would have it, two file drawers opened at once, which caused the entire cabinet to tip over!

"Debbie caught the cabinet and was keeping it from falling any further, but she couldn't stand it upright. The beautiful plants on top of the cabinet started sliding off. Some crashed to the floor, but one plant landed right on top of Debbie's head.

"There she stood, muscles bulging, arms shaking, with a pot on her head and soil running down her uniform."

"Helppp!" screamed Debbie.

Gale says, "I immediately sized up the situation and did what I thought seemed appropriate. I took the pot off her head."

[I'm pegging Gale as a potential Sunny at this point.]

The good news is, the rest of the office soon arrived and spared Debbie any additional cloudbursts. The nice thing about a Cloudy is, since they keep a good supply of tears handy, they can water their own plants anytime.

Rain, Rain, Go Away

I'm by no means suggesting Cloudies cry all the time, but I can safely deduce that they don't laugh enough. I know that because they tell me so. When asked on the survey, "On a scale of one to ten, how important is humor in your life?" the responses of women I'd peg to be Cloudies have similar scores—low.

Barbara from Illinois gave her need for humor a 5 and admitted, "I'm too serious, but I was born that way." While she kindly said she enjoyed my particular stories, she insisted, "I hate slapstick."

Yep. Cloudies hate physical comedy. Too demeaning. While Sunnies are hooting in the corner at some poor creature who has tripped over a string in the carpet, the Cloudy glares at her

Sunny sisters, hissing, "How can you laugh at that man? You're so rude!" Then the Cloudy assists the befuddled soul while the Sunnies are sliding down the wall with breathless laughter.

Emilie from California also rated humor a low 5 and confessed, "I need help!" Susan from France only gave it a 3 and explained, "The books I go for are novels or self-help. I'm just not very funny." Patti from Ohio showed a little more propensity for humor, giving it a 6 and agreed, "I want to enjoy life but not be outrageous."

Oh, the self-control of a Cloudy! I love being outrageous, and in fact have little choice in the matter. So it is for the Cloudy and their subdued approach to humor. They definitely see the value of it and don't mind the occasional chuckle, as long as there is absolutely no chance of their being seen as ridiculous, outrageous, foolish, or any other credibility-reducing term.

Changeable Skies

As list-making and organized as Cloudies may be, they also can be moody and unpredictable. Those fluffy cumulus clouds can, without warning, turn into cirrocumulus clouds, a sign of unsettled weather. Authors and artists are often Cloudies, because of their attention to detail, and their temperaments are legendary.

Cloudies may just be having a bad day.

Or they may have spent the afternoon at the dentist.

Mary Ann from Texas had observers trying to figure out what sort of mood she was in after "a long drawn-out affair with my dentist (don't panic). The unexpectedly lengthy tryst left me numb and drooling as I paid the bill.

"On the way home I stopped at the grocery store and reached into my shoulder bag. My change purse popped open and coins spilled all over the floor. A silver-haired gent standing behind me chuckled and said to his younger companion, 'Look at that! Quick, grab as many as you can!'"

They handed over the errant coins, and Mary Ann nodded a polite thanks, not trusting her drooling lips to function. She spied candy bars on a nearby shelf and took two.

Moments later, the cashier said, "That'll be eighty-six cents."

Puzzled, Mary Ann murmured, "That can't be right. You only charged me for the vinegar."

"But that's all that's here. See?"

Thoroughly confused, Mary Ann groped in her purse for money and discovered the two candy bars. Muttering a slobbery apology, she handed the candy over to the cashier while her silver-haired observer laughed out loud, saying "You think that's bad. You should see her work Kmart!"

The Early Cloud Gets the Best Corner of the Sky

This will seem to be a contradiction, but though their moods may be mercurial, their habits are as predictable as the phases of the moon. Cloudies are always punctual. Always. Early, in fact. They don't want to miss anything, nor draw attention to themselves by arriving late (unlike Sunnies, who love it when every eye in the room follows their late entrance).

Cloudies may appear aloof, cool, and distant, but don't you believe it. Mostly, they're shy, waiting for someone to draw them out. Since they are ultra-considerate of the feelings of others and are highly-sensitive in nature, they will wait patiently for someone to notice them rather than wave their arms and shout, "I'm here!"

Lois from Wisconsin shares the old story of an attractive young widow who visited a new church. The pastor met her at the door and made a real effort to help her feel welcome. He went on and on, saying, "We're so happy that you came to visit us. In fact, why don't you choose three hymns today?"

The young widow was overwhelmed with the pastor's generous offer. She promptly strolled into the church, looked over the congregation, turned to the pastor, and pointed: "I'll take him and him and him!"

Whine-o-Metric Pressure

Henri Bergson said it best: "Laughter is the corrective force which prevents us from becoming cranks."

Moody Cloudies can get cranky, but the truth is, they are perfectionists, and life is not perfect, so—bless them—they whine about it. Georgia from Ohio was "getting impatient with my super-picky husband and blurted out, 'Boy, are you a perfectionist!'

"He retorted, 'I married you, didn't I?'"

They have definite ideas of right and wrong, not just in the larger moral sense, but in teeny tiny ways. For the Cloudy, there is a right way to do everything. A right way to attach stamps to envelopes (in the right corner, equidistant from both edges), a correct way to mix frozen orange juice (run warm water over the can first), a definite method for peeling apples (stem to bottom, peel all in one piece).

During break time at a writing seminar I attended, I hunted through the basket filled with tea bags, checking out the different flavors, and was amazed to find all my four weather personalities represented there!

For the Sunny, there was a shiny, bright-yellow packet of tea called "I Love Lemon."

For the Stormy, there was an exotic foreign tea marked "strong, robust flavor."

For the Foggy, there was a pitiful little tea sack—no colorful wrapper, no name, not even a string or a tag.

For the Cloudy—ahh! Lipton Tea, the Choicest Blend, the most dependable of all, with directions on the back "for the perfect cup of tea."

Even the small flap directed one to "pull up gently."

A Cloudy wouldn't think of doing it any other way.

Altitudinous and Cerebral

So what does the head-in-the-clouds man or woman find funny? Does any sort of humor appeal to the Cloudy?

Most definitely, it's cerebral humor. Clever wordplays, puns, and humorous material that makes you think, causes you to pause, or draws on references from literature and the arts.

Or, is just plain quick.

Lee Ann from New Mexico was watching an *Oprah* episode about people's preferences, such as which way they like the toilet paper roll to go.

She asked her brother-in-law, "Are you a sock-sock-shoe-shoe person or a sock-shoe-sock-shoe?"

After thinking about it a few seconds, he decided, "I could go either way."

Lee Ann quipped, "I guess that makes you bisoxual!"

A pun is the lowest form of humor—when you don't think of it first.

—Oscar Levant

And when the Cloudy laughs, it's a garden hose sound—*ssss*. A little bit leaking out at a time. No braying donkeys or howling wolves for this personality. Not hardly. It will be done in good taste, only when and where appropriate, and not at all if one might risk offending another.

Perfectionist Cloudies usually marry loosey-goosey Sunnies, which makes things interesting.

Sally's grandfather was minister of a large Presbyterian church in Denver, Colorado. "Shortly after he became the pastor, he announced that he and his wife would soon have a blessed event with the birth of their second child. All the women of the congregation were anxious to see the baby as soon as it was born.

"Now there is no such thing as an ugly baby, but when that child was born a few months later, he came pretty close. He was tall and thin, bright red, wrinkled up, and totally bald.

"According to family history, my grandmother exclaimed, 'My goodness, how can I show off this baby to all the ladies at church?'"

After thinking things over for a minute, Sally's look-on-the-bright-side grandfather replied, "Well, I guess you'll just have to show them his feet."

The Cloudy in Review

Favorite career:	Library science
Favorite hobby:	Balancing checkbook
Favorite sport:	Chess
Favorite humor:	*Prairie Home Companion*
Favorite clothing:	Coordinated, conservative
Favorite city:	Buffalo, New York (206 cloudy days a year!)
Favorite magazine:	*Architectural Digest*
Favorite color:	Blue
Favorite day:	Sunday
Favorite season:	Fall
Favorite holiday:	Memorial Day
Favorite hymn:	"Rescue the Perishing"
Life verse:	"Sorrow is better than laughter. For by a sad countenance the heart is made better." (Ecclesiastes 7:3)

CHAPTER 18

The Stormy Sense of Humor: It Was a Dark and Stormy Night

Hello! We heard you at the door, but just thought you were part of the bad weather.
—Arthur Baer

With a label like *Stormy*, it's clear we're in for some intense weather! Take shelter in a dry, warm place while we meet the coldest of the four weather personalities. Not to suggest Stormies are heartless and cruel, but they do have the ability to remain more detached than the other three temperaments. And like a cold blast of air, they make a dramatic entrance.

I meet Stormies everywhere I go. If there are sixteen million thunderstorms a year all over the planet, no wonder there's a good bit of thunder and lightning happening under our roofs. Our own informal research here rings true to me: 23 percent of Stormies sounds just right.

And right is what Stormies want to be. I'm a fairly even mix of Sunny and Stormy, so I know this one well. Stand back and observe eight traits of the Stormy weather personality—from a safe distance!

Explosive and Strong-Willed

From the Stormy's point of view, there is one way—their way. Like the bumper sticker says, MY WAY OR THE HIGHWAY.

Stormies have an answer for everything, even if they've never thought about it before. Rather than say, "I don't know," they will make stuff up and then, if necessary, alter history to make certain that the day they made that statement, it was accurate based on the information you gave them.

We Stormies insist "the buck stops here," but in truth, if we can pass the buck and blame someone else, we're even happier.

That's why it's always a good giggle when a Stormy is involved in something where they can't exert their strong will and get the job done. For example, Cathy's husband returned from buying diapers without a coupon (ouch), and announced that it was time to potty train their two-year-old son, Jacob, right now.

"Jacob is too young for this," Cathy patiently explained. "He doesn't have a clue what to do with a potty."

Naturally, this became a challenge for Stormy hubby, who marched into the bathroom, Jacob in tow. Cathy, meanwhile, was outside the room, on her knees, with her ear pressed firmly against the keyhole.

Hubby David discussed the potty and paper with Jacob in typical, no-nonsense fashion. Cathy must have collapsed when David suddenly said authoritatively, "Jake, that is not a hat."

Lightning Leader

In weather words, when a flash of lightning occurs, a *leader* stroke zigzags to the ground, forming a narrow path for the *return* stroke to race back up. How like our Stormy leader, who, in a stroke of energy and decisive action, clears the path for others to follow—whether they want to or not.

Brigadier General Wilma Vaught once admitted, "What I wanted to be when I grew up was—in charge." Go, Wilma. A classic Stormy, as are many military leaders. They command attention, they inspire confidence, and when necessary they pull rank.

Stormies are natural leaders. They walk into any small group and, within fifteen minutes, nominate themselves president. There wasn't an election or anything, they just stood up, pounded the table, and said, "All right, here's what we're going to do."

All heads nodded. "Okay."

Once again, the Stormy sensed the leadership void and filled it. Admirably. Or is that Majorly? Generally? Captainly? You get the idea. The Stormy is in charge.

Decision-making is one of the key distinctives of the Stormy. A television reporter once interviewed a famous Stormy person . . .

Reporter: To what do you attribute your success?
Stormy: Two words: Right decisions.

Reporter: But how did you make those decisions?
Stormy: One word: Experience.
Reporter: But how did you get that experience?!
Stormy: Two words: Wrong decisions.

We Stormies climb the ladder of success wrong by wrong, learning by our mistakes, hoping no one notices, then moving up the next wrong, uh, rung.

Dangerous Business

Stormies love taking risks. They thrive on it, draw energy from it. While a Cloudy might take a walk in the rain, enjoying the gentle caress of each little drop, a Stormy thinks a stroll through a thunderstorm is more interesting. Their sense of invincibility gives them courage—or makes them fools. Either way, when risk is involved, the Stormy is the one who won't shrink back.

Gale was a thrill seeker from an early age. She would climb up their big mulberry tree to get to the roof of their chicken coop and curl up with a good book. "One day, after reading about some adventurers who had rappelled down a mountain, I decided I would try to recreate the experience. I tied one end of a rope to the tree limb and the other end of the rope in a slipknot around my waist.

"I positioned myself on the edge of the sloping roof and jumped off. Seconds later I found myself lying on the ground wondering where I'd gone wrong. In my haste to have the perfect jump, I'd failed to consider the fact that the shed was twelve feet tall and my rope was forty feet long. Miraculously, I only suffered a few bruises. Back to the drawing board."

Stormy children: Do not try this at home! Honor thy mother and thy father!

Since laughing out loud is, in a sense, its own kind of risk, is it any surprise that when the Stormy finally cuts loose, it's one big blast—*ppaaahhh!* Like the fire siren at noon, the Stormy laugh cuts through the atmosphere with deafening sound and with about the same frequency—once a day.

Stormies don't laugh often or easily. They wait impatiently, arms folded over their chest, until something worthy of their response is offered. Make-me-laugh is the look on their faces. This-better-be-good is the body language that goes with it.

That's why it's so fun when Stormies do laugh. Like ball lightning, it's a rare occurrence, worthy of the record books. And, like thunder, it roars through the room and can, in fact, be heard ten miles away.

Since Stormies truly don't care what others think of them, when they're ready to laugh, they do so, whether anyone else is willing to come along for the ride or not. Flying on a plane (how else would I do it?), I was reading something funny, came to the punch line, and let out a laugh blaster. *Pah!* All the people in the aisle seats turned around. What-did-they-put-in-her-roasted-peanuts? was the look on their faces.

Tornadic Activity

Tornadoes are not uncommon in our part of the country, and smart people pay attention when the forecasters say to take cover.

Unfortunately, Stormies don't always broadcast tornado warnings. They simply spin into a room, tossing debris everywhere, and then leave in a huff. When it comes to addressing the volatile issue of our tendency to get angry, we Stormies sometimes justify our behavior by saying, "Sure, I get mad, but it blows over in two minutes."

Right. So does a tornado, but look at what a mess it leaves behind. Will Rogers must have known a Stormy or two when he wrote, "People who fly into a rage always make a bad landing."

Gretchen from Washington deals with a double dose of this at her house. She admits, "My youngest son, Josh, has a temper like his mama—short and difficult to control. One day when he was in the first grade, he brought home a teacher's note saying he had been in trouble several times that week for letting his temper get the best of him.

"I gave Josh a lecture on controlling anger, and decided to show a little empathy. I told him I understood his problem and that his temper was inherited from me—it was in my genes. Later, my husband mentioned the note to Josh and reminded him to keep his anger in check. Josh said, 'Don't worry, Daddy, it's Mama's fault. I only lose my temper when she wears a hair-net and jeans!'"

Sheryl from Oklahoma understands why a Stormy needs humor: "It's God's pressure valve in my life. If I don't get enough laughter, I blow a gasket."

Endless Energy

Ask a Stormy what they do in their spare time, and watch their face go blank. Spare time? What's that? Do you mean when I'm sleeping?

Stormies pride themselves on not requiring much shut-eye, insisting that five or six hours a night is all they need, with a "power nap" or two thrown in for good measure.

Work is what makes the Stormy tick, which explains why they see little need for humor in their lives. How productive is that? they wonder, reaching for another stack of correspondence. Let's have a meeting instead. Taking a laughter break is actually very productive, sending you back to your task with renewed energy, a fresh outlook on things, and increased creative potential. Those things aren't quite bottom-line enough for Stormies, who think Big Picture and skip the details, leaving those for their super-efficient Cloudy administrative assistants.

If you are a Stormy and are still unconvinced about the many benefits of humor, here's an angle you'll understand: Funny means money. The most successful managers are those who create a workplace where fun is part of the strategic mix. It builds loyalty among both employees and customers, reduces stress and all the medical costs that go with it, and lines you up for an even bigger promotion.

See? I knew you'd see it my way.

No Waiting

If you want to humor a Stormy, make it snappy. Literally. Short, to-the-point stories, jokes, and one-liners are the way to reach a Stormy's funny bone, well-hidden inside his or her expensive tailored suit. Get-to-the-punch-line! their eyes will say. Time is money for the Stormy, and long, drawn-out stories cost too much.

Impatient Stormies often marry ultra-patient Foggies (more on that in the next chapter). My Bill has his own ways of handling his impatient wife. When we pull into a parking lot, Bill sighs, "Why don't you go ahead and tell me where to park, I know you've already spotted the space you want."

Smart guy.

Polly from Georgia confesses, "Impatience was my middle name. My husband, Dave, moved at his own pace, but I wanted him to walk faster, especially when it came to cutting the grass."

The mower wasn't repaired and the grass grew, along with her impatience. Finally she prayed that the Lord would motivate Dave, "because I can't." She promised God, "I'll be patient even if the grass grows above my knees"—and it almost did!

One morning their dog began barking, and her husband said in amazement, "There are cows in the yard!"

They had no idea where they came from. Polly begged her husband to get them out of their yard, to which Dave responded, "No, let's wait until they eat the grass."

Not in the mood for a roundup, Polly and Dave located the owner and found out the cows had smelled the grass from a mile away.

Polly says, "Our mower is broken again, but I'll be patient because I don't know who the Lord might send to cut the grass this time!"

Right as Rain

With their traits of always being right, being decisive, and being in charge, Stormies are also always happy to tell you what to do.

Just ask them.

On second thought, you won't have to.

JoAnn from New York remembers the days before children (B.C.), when she'd join her husband for Sunday breakfast at different restaurants. On one occasion, her husband asked his usual question, "What are you getting to eat?"

"A ham-and-cheese omelette."

"You always order the same thing," he said, exasperated.

"I love ham-and-cheese omelettes, and that's what I'm ordering," she insisted.

"But we need to try different things, expand our horizons," he grumbled. With that, he ordered the corn pancakes.

Imagine their surprise when the waitress appeared with a plate with two pancakes on it and a can of whole kernel corn dumped on the top! "When I saw the look on my husband's face, I laughed so hard that I had tears rolling down my cheeks. Every time he took a bite I would start laughing again. The joke was on me when I literally choked on a piece of ham that was in my omelette!"

More than one Stormy has had to eat *crow* when they make a mistake, but eat *corn*?

Taking Charge

Even though they may not have their sense of humor ever at the ready, the Stormy is definitely the one to call when an emergency strikes.

Myra Caye's emergency was really off the wall. Or rather, *in* the wall. Her puppy had climbed out of his crate, terrorized her utility room, jumped on top of the dryer, knocked down the vent, and tried to wiggle through the four-inch hole in the wall, which he managed to do—halfway.

In Myra's words, "The outside of my house looked like a live trophy wall. As the pup tried to free himself, he would literally spin on the wall!

"I tried to stuff him back, but no such luck. I then called 911 and requested help from the fire department. They arrived, and the life squad pulled into my driveway, creating quite a stir in my neighborhood. They tried soapy water, but the dog was stuck fast."

She tried to use a hammer and screwdriver to remove a brick from the house to free the dog, "but every time I struck the screwdriver the dog licked my hand, and I was afraid I'd miss and hit him in the head."

Two hours went by, with many pleas for help directed at various authorities, but no remedy. Frantic, she called a vet who agreed to give her a tranquilizer for the dog, if she would drive the thirty miles to get it. Finally at 9:30 P.M., the puppy swallowed the pill, and by 10:00 he was very relaxed. It took an adult supporting the puppy on each end, one inside, one outside, a chief with a chisel, and lots of soap to get this puppy out of the wall.

The moral of this story is: When life is driving you up the wall, call Myra Caye!

The Stormy in Review

Favorite career:	CEO
Favorite hobby:	Darts
Favorite sport:	Ice hockey

Favorite humor:	*Rowan and Martin's Laugh-In* (Even super-Stormy Richard Nixon said, "Sock it to me!")
Favorite clothing:	Suits
Favorite city:	Biloxi (94 storms and 7 hurricanes a year)
Favorite magazine:	*Forbes*
Favorite color:	Black
Favorite day:	Monday
Favorite season:	Winter
Favorite holiday:	Labor Day
Favorite hymn:	"How Firm a Foundation"
Life verse:	"In all labor there is profit, But idle chatter leads only to poverty." (Proverbs 14:23)

CHAPTER 19

The Foggy Sense of Humor: It Was a Gray and Foggy Day

He was so benevolent, so merciful a man that he would have held an umbrella over a duck in a shower of rain.
—Douglas Jerrold

When I tell you the *Foggy* is the driest of the four weather personalities, you might protest, "But, Liz! Fog is damp, not dry." We're speaking more of wit than weather here. The Foggies have a dry, droll sense of humor that permeates their entire outlook on life. More observer than participant, the Foggy offers a thoughtful response amidst the climatic chaos of the overly enthusiastic Sunny, the oversensitive Cloudy, and the overpowering Stormy.

Foggies are never *over*, they're *under*. Under the covers, under the weather, or under the influence of a strong-willed Stormy boss, spouse, or parent. Our surveys of women pegged the Foggies at 17 percent of the population. Prepare for some fun in the fog with my favorite of the four weather personalities. Of their many touted traits, we'll look at eight.

Well Grounded

Fog hovers near the ground, or rises from the sea when warm air meets cool water on a calm night and collects at the surface. So it is with the Foggy temperament, which is laid back, cool, calm, and collected.

The Sunny and Stormy will both consider the Foggy dull, but that's neither fair nor accurate. Foggies are just quiet, without any desire to draw attention to themselves. Growing up in an all Sunny/Stormy family, I don't remember even meeting a Foggy until I met my wonderful Bill. Okay, maybe I met some and didn't notice. Or, didn't appreciate their finer points.

Then, in my early thirties, I met my future husband and was introduced to the joys of Foggyhood. He is low-key and easygoing, and nothing ruffles his feathers—except me when I'm on a Stormy tirade.

Foggies are steady, predictable, dependable. If Bill says he will meet me at the airport at a certain time, he's there. Not early, mind you, like the Cloudy who always worries, nor late like the Sunny who has a million excuses, nor absent like the

Stormy who would suggest a cab. The Foggy is simply there and waiting.

Will a Foggy be happy to see you? Of course. But don't expect balloons and streamers and a big WELCOME HOME sign. Foggies enjoy parties where they can sit in a corner and watch everyone else, but they aren't likely to throw the party. (They're happy to stay until the end and help clean up, bless them, if you'll just tell them where to put the plates.)

Not only might Foggies forget to bring the confetti, they might also forget to shout, "Ya-hoo!" Early in our marriage, I was all wound up about something while Bill just stared and nodded every few minutes with no change of expression whatsoever. Finally, I paused for breath and blurted out in exasperation, "Just once, I wish you'd get excited!"

His face was utterly blank, his voice flat: "But I am excited."

Okeydokey

On our first shopping expedition together, I saw my Foggy Bill's agreeable personality in action when I held up a textured sweater I was sure he'd enjoy wearing.

"Whadya think of this, honey?"

He shrugged. "That's okay."

"Oh!" I stuffed it back in the pile, posthaste.

Obviously he hated it. In my family, "That's okay" was a code phrase for "That's the most abhorrent thing I've ever laid eyes on. Get rid of it immediately before I faint dead away."

I chose another sweater, this one in subdued stripes, quite different from the first. "How 'bout this one, sweetie?"

He shrugged. "That's okay."

Oh, no! The man was apparently more difficult to please than I'd first thought. I gulped and ditched the second choice in favor of a classic solid that was sure to suit any man.

"Isn't this one nice?" I asked in my tentative-new-bride voice.

He shrugged. "That's okay."

A pattern was forming, and not on the sweaters. I worked my way along the shelves and amassed another dozen more "that's okay" responses before I tossed the last sweater in the air in frustration and whined, "I've run out of options, Bill. Don't you like any of these?"

"No, I like all of them," he insisted.

"But you said they're just *okay*."

"Right."

"Which means . . ."

He shrugged. "It means they're okay. I like them."

"You like them all equally well?!"

What a concept for an opinionated Stormy to grasp!

The man is sooo agreeable. He eats my cooking, he puts up with my grousing, he humors my need for variety when he would be perfectly content eating cinnamon Pop-Tarts for breakfast every day for the rest of his life.

When it comes to amusing Foggies, there are many avenues to choose from, as long as you don't require them to laugh out loud. They'll take the time needed to absorb the cerebral humor of a Woody Allen, yet smile at the quick sight gags of the Marx Brothers too.

Cartoons like *Dilbert* are popular with Foggies because (1) Dilbert is a computer engineering geek and (2) the scenarios reflect workplace humor with hysterical accuracy and (3) they take ten seconds to read, leaving plenty of time for lunch, a nap, etc.

In an effort to be agreeable, Foggies may make assumptions rather than ask questions, which leads to interesting aha! moments. Renee from Florida rented a room in the home of a sweet, elderly lady. "We shared the kitchen and bathroom, which worked out just fine."

She continues, "As our friendship grew, I took on several household tasks to aid my older friend. One morning I was feeling particularly industrious and decided to clean out the bathroom. Never able to find a brush to scrub the toilet, I'd always used a sponge, but since I was about to use a strong new cleaner, I asked if she had a toilet-cleaning brush in the house."

Renee's aha! moment had arrived.

"It's hanging in the shower next to the shower cap and other accessories," the older woman explained.

All those months, Renee had been using that brush as a back-scrubber during her shower.

Was Job a Foggy?

The phrase *patience of Job* fits the Foggy like a moist cloud of air wraps itself around a lighthouse. If we're sitting at a red light and Bill is driving, I'm on the passenger side with an imaginary gas pedal, foot poised, eyes darting back and forth, ready to take off the minute the light changes.

When it does and we don't immediately take off, I realize he just didn't see it.

"Bill. It's green."

He's doing what all Foggies do at red lights: Keeping his hands at ten o'clock and two o'clock and staring at the dashboard. I realize he just didn't hear me.

"Bill. It's green."

He turns to me and says, "There'll be another one."

Sure, in the next millenium, but I didn't want to wait that long. Foggies are wonderful at waiting. And waiting.

Blessed Are the Peacemakers

Foggies have an exceptional ability to calm people down by seeing both sides of an argument and helping the two opponents get together for a truce. Consequently, they make wonderful negotiators and business meeting facilitators.

When tempers flare at work, sending Cloudies off to the ladies' room crying, Stormies stamping off for a caffeine fix, and

Sunnies looking desperately for a funny story to tell to break the tension, the Foggy moves in on little cat's feet, cooling the temperature of the room and, like fog, confusing everyone.

"What were we so upset about?"

"I don't know, I can't even see the problem anymore."

"Will you help me? I am totally turned around here."

It's a purposeful wet blanket, this fog. While it can sometimes dampen enthusiasm, more often it acts as a calming influence at work and at home.

Even in their desire for peace, the Foggies can toss in a few surprises of their own. Cindy from Illinois was amazed when her Sunday school class threw a surprise birthday party for her, and her "shy, stable, but not boring husband" assembled a whole bag of goodies for her "twilight" years. "Things like batteries to keep me charged and sticky-note pads to help me remember things.

"It was special because it was so out of character for my quiet husband to put together something so utterly funny. He doesn't like surprises but knows I love them."

Stubborn as a Rule

The couple next to me on the plane were having a discussion that was so typically *Foggy v. Stormy* that I had to concentrate on the latch of the overhead compartment to keep my composure.

Stormy-she says, "Here, honey, try this mocha-bunga-java coffee. It's delicious."

Foggy-he replies, "No, thanks."

She holds it out to him. "C'mon, try it. You'll love it."

He shakes his head. "I really don't like those tricky coffees."

"You'll like this one," she persists, holding it closer.

"I'll pass."

She now has it right under his nose. "Just one taste!"

"No, thanks," he insists, shaking his head.

"Trust me, this is too good to miss," she says through clenched teeth, getting almost as hot as the coffee.

"I don't want any."

"One taste!" She is pressing the cup against his lips.

He remains cool but stubborn. "I'd rather not."

I clocked it. This went on for seven minutes. We'd flown over an entire state, and they were still going on about the coffee. What was the problem? Stormies are stubborn—but Foggies are even more stubborn. They dig in their heels, and it's all over.

(The people-pleasing Sunny in me almost jumped in and said, "Here, I'll be happy to try it!")

Indecisive? Are You Sure?

Stubborn on occasion, yes. Indecisive, always. If you ask a Foggy, "Do you have trouble making decisions?" they'll consider it for a very long time, stammering and stuttering toward a response.

"Well . . . um . . . gee . . . uh . . . yes and no."

Karen from Nevada admits, "Here is how indecisive I am. I was changing planes in the airport and stopped by the gift shop for something to read. I couldn't decide what to get—a newspaper or a book. Hmm. One book was entitled *How to Overcome Indecisiveness*. I couldn't decide if I should buy it or not and stood there debating about it for ten minutes, back and forth, back and forth.

"Finally I decided not to get it, but by the time I got on board my next flight, I wished I'd bought it."

Wit Served Dry, Shaken Not Stirred

Foggies almost never laugh out loud, but they smile all the time. So much so, you wonder what they know that you don't. Sheri might be a Foggy, since she confesses, "I enjoy humor, but it takes a lot to make me laugh out loud." And Sandra from California says, "I don't laugh often—I smile out loud."

They have a wit that's as dry as fog is moist. We've all heard of a dry wit, but is there such a thing as a *wet* wit? For the Foggy, their favorite form of humor is the harmless practical joke. It fits their sense of time and energy economy to perfection: (1) You can take all the time you want to come up with the prank, pressure free, and (2) once you've pulled it off, you can get years of mileage from it by saying, "Remember the time when . . .?"

I'll bet Jean from Tennessee has enjoyed this memory again and again. "For my brother's fiftieth birthday, I sent notes to friends in different states requesting their help in pulling off a practical joke. I enclosed a birthday card with a stamped envelope and asked them to write a greeting and sign the card with their first name only, address the envelope in their handwriting and mail it well before my brother's birthday."

Then she called him on his big day, and let him ramble on about his apparent memory loss.

"Jean, I received cards from people I don't remember ever meeting," he told her.

"Really?"

"I even got a phone message from a woman named Maggie, who said she'd wait until I came to New York to celebrate my birthday! Jean, I don't know any Maggies."

Jean's inability to speak at this point let him know that she was the culprit. "He was relieved to learn that memory loss doesn't necessarily happen at fifty."

Foggies just love those "Gotchas!"

Jan from Rhode Island tells us, "My dad was a real prankster, and the five of us kids always had to be on the lookout. One evening we were all gathered in the living room when Dad headed to the kitchen. We heard the silverware drawer open and dishes being clanged around. My sister, Elaine, assumed Dad was dishing ice cream and hollered, "I'll have some too."

Dad yelled back from the kitchen, "Okay." He returned to the living room with a dish and gave it to Elaine.

She took a bite and started yelling. "This is awful! What is it?"

Jan explains, "Dad never told us he was feeding the dog. He simply gave Elaine 'some too'!"

Absentminded Professors, Lawyers, Doctors, Indian Chiefs

Foggies never outgrow their delight in such antics, but it's bad form to grow forgetful right in the middle of your own practical joke.

Pat from Indiana shares this story about her parents, now in their seventies. They had a bumper sticker on their refrigerator that read I'M SPENDING MY CHILDREN'S INHERITANCE. One day, unbeknownst to her mother, her father attached the sticker to his wife's trousers—"you guessed it, right on her 'bumper'!"

My, weren't we feeling playful? He soon forgot all about it and wandered downstairs to his workshop.

Pat explains, "An hour later, he came upstairs to find my mom putting away groceries. She had gone up and down the aisles of Winn-Dixie, a store where she knows everyone, wearing the bumper sticker firmly attached to her derriere! She can laugh about it now, but at the time I do believe she threw a package of frozen lima beans at Dad when he shamefacedly confessed what he had done."

Whether sharing a practical joke or a bit of dry wit, the Foggies value humor as much as the rest of us do. Lisa from Virginia says, "Humor has been like a lighthouse to me. Life occasionally gets dark, dreary, and full of stress, like being adrift on the ocean in the middle of the night. Humorous stories can often shed some light and relieve those stresses that bind us.

Humor can also keep us from running aground! Like a beacon in the night, humor offers hope."

The Foggy in Review

Favorite career:	Computer programming
Favorite hobby:	Taking a nap
Favorite sport:	Televised bowling
Favorite humor:	*The Bob Newhart Show*
Favorite clothing:	Jeans, sweats
Favorite city:	San Francisco
Favorite magazine:	*PC World*
Favorite color:	Gray
Favorite day:	Wednesday
Favorite season:	Spring (no snow, no mow, no leaves)
Favorite holiday:	Groundhog Day
Favorite hymn:	"It Is Well with My Soul"
Life verse:	"And having food and clothing, with these we shall be content" (1 Timothy 6:8).

What Is Your Favorite Cartoon?

I get a lot of my best ideas in the middle of the night. I write down two or three words to help me remember. The next morning, I look and it says, "Zup fmph fomph flim."
—*Bil Keane, quoted in* Laughing Matters

Plenty of people turn to the funny pages first each day, and no wonder. What joy can be found there among the familiar drawings and comic captions of America's favorite cartoonists! Always clean, never offensive, as dependable as having the morning newspaper land in the puddle just beyond the porch.

According to our five hundred surveys, here are the cartoons we turn to first:

1. *The Family Circus*
2. *Cathy*
3. *The Far Side*
4. *Dilbert*
5. *Calvin and Hobbs*
6. *Garfield*
7. *Blondie*
8. *Ziggy*
9. *Peanuts*
10. *B.C.*

Bless you for your gentle, true-to-family-life humor, Mr. Keane. (P.S. It's a circus at our house too!)

PART FIVE

Humor and Health

I had a speech in Louisville one chilly Saturday in January. After a whole week of snow, sleet, rain, snow, sleet, rain, the parking lots in town were covered with *snirt*—snow and dirt. Underneath the snirt was *sneet*—snow and sleet, and underneath the sneet was a thin layer of ice, which you couldn't see for all the snirt and the sneet.

In typical Sunny fashion, I arrived late, sliding into the parking lot mere minutes before the opening remarks. I leaped out of the car and grabbed my purse, along with the handouts I'd brought to make the Cloudies happy. I didn't get two feet before I hit a patch of ice hiding underneath the snirt and the sneet, and went sailing across the ice, first in vertical, then horizontal, fashion.

Since Sunnies never zip our purses, the contents went flying everywhere, soon followed by my handouts—paper and snirt are a bad combination. Lying there on the ice, stunned senseless, I contemplated my best options for standing up.

Then from across the parking lot came the voice of an angel, wearing the uniform of a maintenance man. "Are you okay?" he called across the snowy parking lot.

"No, I'm not!" I moaned, assessing the damage while he made his way toward me.

I'd not torn my dress or ruined my hose, and I

had only a few spots of snirt and sneet to brush away. So far so good. But when the kind man helped me get up (I'll spare you the horrid details), I discovered that everything hurt down the left side, from shoulder to ankle. I'd hit that snirty pavement harder than I realized and was now in pretty severe pain, feeling bruises already in the making.

I had no choice. I had to speak. With my angel's guidance, I carefully hobbled across the snirt, brushed myself off, and headed for the front of the auditorium, wincing with every step.

"So glad to be with you this morning!" I said with my lips, but the rest of my body was giving a whole different message. I was listing to the left, only gestured with my right hand, and wondered how I'd make it through the hour-long presentation.

Then an amazing thing happened. They started laughing, on cue, which made me laugh. They laughed, I laughed, and sixty minutes later, nothing hurt! Thanks to the adrenaline flow that always begins when I hit the platform, and an endorphin or two that made an appearance, I had almost no pain at all. I was so excited I ran out in the parking lot and almost fell down again.

When I got home, I exclaimed, "Bill! I thought I hurt myself and I didn't!"

Sure. Until an hour later, when the adrenaline wore off. Yet, I believe the laughter bought me some grief relief, since as Carly Simon sang, "I haven't got time for the pain."

CHAPTER 20

Humor and Your Body: What's Up, Doc?

One of the hardest things for any man to do is to fall down on the ice and then get up and praise the Lord.
—*Josh Billings*

Laughter puts the body in a state of relaxation. Think of it as "Kansas" for your constitution—nothing but gentle, green fields as far as the mind can see. In that physically relaxed state, we take our foot off the pain accelerator and put on the brake—which is the first of seven reasons why I think our bodies were built for laughter:

1. Laughter Is a Natural Pain Reducer

Our bodies were created by an amazing God who knew that we'd get broken and bruised on occasion and would need all the natural painkillers we could get our hands on.

I had a dear woman show up at a presentation in Michigan the very week I was working on this chapter. "Liz, I almost didn't come tonight because I'm in such pain."

"I am so sorry," I assured her, reaching for her hand. "What hurts?"

"Everything. That's why I decided to come. I've heard you before and know how much better I'll feel after all the laughter."

I kept my eye on her during the program and was so thrilled to watch her bending over with laughter, joy beaming from her face. Praise God for his gift of laughter. The only thing it has in common with man's answer to painkillers is, it *is* addictive!

Maybe we could be *joy junkies!*

Karla awoke early one morning to the sound of ice pelting the window. "I was a PBX operator at a department store. If one person had to report to work, it was me, if only to field all the calls from employees saying they couldn't make it in."

She went outside to catch the bus to work, "and a trip that normally took twenty minutes took twice as long. When the bus slid to a stop in front of the store, I asked the driver to please wait until I got on the sidewalk before he started off.

"I stepped down to the ground, and the cane I was using slipped, hooked my foot, and down I went—under the bus."

"Where did you go?" the worried driver called out.

"I'm under the bus," she yelled back.

"You're where?"

"Under the bus!"

"What are you doing there?"

"I'm checking your brakes!"

The good news is, Karla wasn't hurt, "just very embarrassed."

2. Laughter Increases Our Ability to Cope with Pain

If we can't make pain go away, then we can handle it better with humor. It's been said that laughter can increase our threshold of pain as much as 21 percent. Incredible. This calls for some adjustments in those prepared childbirth classes, where their suggested method for coping with pain is to breathe.

Breathe?!

I already breathe several times a day. Every chance I get, in fact. Yet they want us to face the worst voluntary pain in a woman's life—pain that our bodies spend nine months preparing for and our heads spend six intense weeks studying about—this kind of pain is handled by women breathing, women who take an aspirin for a tiny twitch over their left eye?

I practiced my breathing all six weeks, but remained unconvinced.

When the big day came and I went into labor, I dutifully breathed for twelve hours.

"What do you need?" my coach, Bill, asked, sweating profusely. He was breathing, too, but it wasn't cutting the pain one iota.

"Something funny!" I gasped.

Bill rummaged around in the big bag of tricks we'd brought to the hospital with us and came up with Dave Barry's funny book *Babies and Other Hazards of Sex*, the subtitle of which is *How to Make a Tiny Person in Nine Months with Tools You Probably Have Around the Home*.

We were breathing, praying, and laughing, breathing, praying, and laughing until we reached the twenty-sixth hour of labor, at which point all three nursing shifts had come and gone and the first group was back.

"She's still here!" they sang out.

I was singing a happy tune as well when my anesthesiologist, the doctor with the drugs, came in with a big button that said JUST SAY YES TO DRUGS.

Yes. Yes.

When it comes to handling pain, few things go down better than a big dose of laughter.

3. Laughter Massages Our Internal Organs

If you've ever treated yourself to a massage, you know what a delight it is to put your tired muscles and sore joints in the hands of a licensed massage therapist. Ahh.

Now, what about your kidneys? Don't they deserve a massage too? And your spleen. I'll bet you haven't thought about your poor spleen all day, but it's in there saying, "Me too! Me too!"

Laughter massages your inside muscles like a therapist massages your outside muscles. The late Norman Cousins called it *internal jogging*, an exercise for which your organs are most grateful.

You won't have to wrap yourself in a towel or break out in a sweat, either. Just laugh loud and often, with gusto. A smile makes a great umbrella, but for inner massage, you'll need more than a smile. You'll need a solid twenty-minute workout of guffaws and giggles, hoots and honks.

Fifteen big laughs each day is what the experts tell us is our minimum daily adult requirement for laughter. Since toddlers supposedly laugh fifteen times an hour, your prescription is clear: Get yourself a two year old. Oh, you don't have to keep it! Ask any young mother at church if she might loan you her toddler for an hour—trust me, she'll be elated with the plan. Then lock yourself in a room with the little cutie and laugh when they do. Voila! You'll have your allotment of laughter and so will that mom, thanks to this unique Mother's Hour Out program.

Brenda from Indiana gave herself an unintentional workout. She worked in the laboratory of a small rural hospital that required her to sit on a high stool. "I sat down in my chair and immediately realized it had been lowered. This threw me off balance and the chair tipped back, throwing me gracefully to the floor."

When the lab department finally got their laughter under control, Brenda told her coworker, "If I didn't know better, I'd think I hit my head."

"You did!" she told her. "Three times on the way down!"

Upon surveying the damage, not only did Brenda have three bumps on her head, she also had paint on her shirt from hitting the wall so hard. Brenda's intense form of internal and external massage proved one thing, she says: "Germans really are hardheaded."

4. Laughter Exercises Our Facial Muscles

Fifteen facial muscles get involved when we laugh, which is why after a good bout of laughter your cheeks hurt. That's their way of telling you, "Please do this more often, so it won't hurt so much." You know the dangers of being a weekend jogger. The same thing happens when we don't exercise those facial muscles often enough.

Laughter should make us feel wonderful all over. Andrea from Pennsylvania concurs. "It feels so good to laugh. Just like the good feeling after exercising but with less work." Donna from Virginia confesses laughing is "the only exercise my body gets," and Jackie from Colorado insists it's "impossible to live without it. Like oxygen, food, God."

Sustenance indeed.

Was life meant to be fun? Of course. Not every minute of every day, but often enough that it won't hurt when we chuckle. Of all the muscles we're given to work with, our laugh muscles should never be allowed to atrophy.

A merry heart does good, like medicine,
But a broken spirit dries the bones.
(Proverbs 17:22)

The medical community and the spiritual community are (amazingly!) in agreement about the value of laughter. Doctors are known to keep lists of strange words and phrases patients use to describe their ills, for later peer review and aerobic laughing. Patients have complained of migrating headaches, prospect glands, abstract teeth, and hideous hernias. One patient wanted a scat can of his brain, and another sought a better remedy than what he'd been using for muscle pain: Soybean, Jr.

We'd better exercise whatever muscles we have left, because as we age they take on a mind of their own. Linda laughs when she remembers the days of her youth "when we had to have the same garment in different colors. Now, in my menopausal mid-forties, I have to have the same color outfit in two different *sizes*. Hmm. Which one can I get into this week?!"

Gravity and atrophy start much sooner than that, as Cheryl's thirtysomething body has convinced her.

"The other day I was standing half-dressed at the bathroom mirror while my five-year-old daughter watched intently."

"Mommy," she asked, "why is the skin on your tummy all wrinkly like that?"

Cheryl explained, "My tummy had to stretch a lot when I was carrying you and your brothers before you were born, so the skin never quite went all the way back."

Her daughter pondered that explanation for a moment. "Kinda like a balloon that's lost its air, huh?"

"Uh, yes, dear, kind of like that."

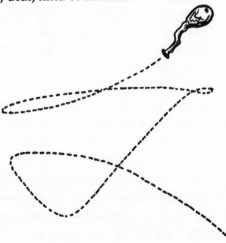

"But, Mommy," she continued, pointing to Cheryl's legs, "Why are your knees all wrinkly?"

Cheryl looked down at her knees. By golly, they were getting wrinkly! Now she was starting to get a bit discouraged.

"Well, honey, that's what happens to your skin when you get a little older," Cheryl replied.

Her daughter eyed her up and down for a few moments more, her blue eyes widening. "Will your whole body get like that? I guess your skin just gets tired and gives up, huh?"

Yes, darlin', that's pretty much how it works. But I'm convinced if we can keep our laugh muscles limber and the skin around our smiles moving, we're going to look gorgeous all the way to glory!

5. Laughter Improves Circulation

It's a common phenomenon I've seen time and again when I'm performing in a chilly room. The women are all folded in on themselves, like beautiful roses freshly delivered from the florist and still cool to the touch—arms folded, legs crossed, a sweater or jacket pulled around their shoulders.

Then they start laughing. Their jacket slips off. Their arms unfold so they can slap the table. Their legs uncross so they can bend over with laughter. Soon their faces are flushed with a warm glow, their fingers and toes are no longer stiff with cold, and they've literally blossomed, just like roses.

Since laughter increases the heart rate, it's only natural that it would increase blood flow and therefore circulation. What a health benefit, especially for those who are cold-blooded! Such was not the case for Charla from Georgia. She and her friend are both minister's wives. "Our husbands always joke that they need to go through and bless the house after we've been together laughing because we get so out of control."

One day they were both laughing so hard that "my friend raised her hand to wipe her eyes, and I doubled over at the same time. We met in the middle. Her thumb jabbed my eye so hard I almost cried—it was scratched and red and hurt for days—but at the time it made us laugh even harder."

When people asked about her bruised red-and-black eye, Charla just laughed. Her friend told people that "if she gets on my nerves again, I'll poke the other eye."

6. Laughter Oxygenates the Body

You were hoping I'd tell you that laughter was aerobic, yes? It's true. You can exhale up to seventy-five miles an hour with a big laugh. Gale warning! It would be prudent not to sit in front of someone with false teeth.

It's pure physiology: To laugh out, you must breathe in. Air is involved, so it has aerobic potential. Whether one could do sustained laughter for twenty minutes at your target heart rate, three times a week is anyone's guess. But think how delightful it would be to try.

Wendy from Colorado was simply trying to find out what the problem was with the air in their apartment. "My husband and I hadn't been feeling well for a week, so I called the gas company to see if there could be a gas leak. They transferred me to 911, and in less than five minutes, we heard sirens near our apartment. The doorbell rang, and five paramedics rushed in to see if we were okay. My husband said, 'What have you done this time?!'"

The paramedics took their blood pressures and checked out their apartment. Everything was fine, except for trying to explain it all to the neighbors who were staring at them through the windows, barely breathing.

7. Laughter Stimulates the Immune System

As a member of the American Association for Therapeutic Humor *and* the Fellowship of Merry Christians, I love discovering the many exciting ways that the Lord has fashioned our bodies to renew themselves. In a spiritual sense, you are to be "transformed by the renewing of your mind, that you may prove what is that good and acceptable and perfect will of God" (Romans 12:2).

Your body renews itself with all the basic necessities—food, oxygen, water, sleep, shelter from the elements, air. But there are many less tangible things that help us stay or get well—hugs, companionship, music, compassion, and, yes, laughter. When our bodies are being cared for properly, we produce T cells, the good blood cells that fight infection.

Laughter is one of the things that produce T cells. I don't have to understand it scientifically to rejoice in the reality that tee-hees make *T*s!

Sharon from Ohio and her husband joined another couple at a convention in Hawaii. "We spent a wonderful week sightseeing and touring the islands. We were amazed by all the open-air architecture. Many places featured lobbies with tropical birds, beautiful ponds with large fish, and intricate fountains made from lava.

"On our last night in Honolulu, we were proceeding through such a lobby, headed for dinner, when we got separated by a large group. My husband turned back to look for us, and suddenly could not feel solid ground beneath his rear foot. He began to teeter and sway, back and forth, struggling to maintain his balance.

"As I moved toward him, I watched him lose the balance battle and tumble backward, right into a rock fountain! He managed to land in a sitting position between the underwater fountain jets and lighting, with only his head unsubmerged.

As he was helped out of the fountain, he nearly pulled his rescuers in with him!

"Other than a few scrapes from the rock, he was uninjured—except for his pride. We couldn't look at him without breaking into laughter. Typical of his good nature, he decided he'd provided a good story for everyone to take home with them from Hawaii."

A fresh floral lei will wither, and photos are stuck in a drawer, but that T cell–producing story will live on and on and on.

CHAPTER 21

Humor and Healing: It Only Hurts When I (Don't) Laugh

There's lots of people in this world who spend so much time watching their health that they haven't the time to enjoy it.
—*Josh Billings*

When I spoke in Louisiana a few years ago, the *Times-Picayune* published a feature article about my visit, with a big headline—LAUGHTER IS GOOD FOR YOUR BODY—and a photo of my abundant body underneath it. People must have opened their papers and said, "Wow! Miracle-Gro!" It's one thing to suggest that humor is good for you in the physical sense. Plenty of research has confirmed that truth, and there are whole books on the subject of the physiological benefits of laughing out loud.

Yes, humor helps, but can it heal? Is it that effective a prescription? Many of us think so. Betty from Oklahoma shares, "Humor has brought me back physically, emotionally, and spiritually. It kept me from going over the edge in a very low, depressed period of my life. Being able to laugh through the tears is a healing process."

Nurses often use humor to gauge a recovering patient's progress. They'll throw out a gentle joke and see how the patient responds. Even a smile indicates they're on the path toward wellness. Wise is the patient who knows humor's ability to assist the healing process and who looks for it at every turn.

Bowed Over

Catherine from New Jersey has a five-year-old granddaughter named Valerie who loves to wear pretty barrettes and bows in her hair. Looking through an old box of odds and ends, Valerie found a huge, pink Minnie Mouse bow with white polka dots.

"Mom, can I wear this to school tomorrow?" she asked.

Her mother cautioned, "It might be better just to wear it at home, Valerie, so the other children won't make fun of you."

But Valerie was determined to wear that bow. The next day after school, her mother met her at the bus stop, and there was that big pink bow on her head, along with a very happy smile.

"My teacher told me she hoped I'd wear it again because every time she looked at me, it made her smile!" Valerie announced.

Young Valerie learned something about humor and healing that day. Her teacher had been going through chemotherapy treatments for cancer, and as Valerie's grandmother sees it, "That big, pink, polka-dotted bow was the best medicine of all."

Judy from Texas fought—and won—a battle with breast cancer. "The Lord and laughter were what helped me to remain strong. After radiation, I developed asthma and couldn't laugh without coughing and losing my breath. I demanded that the doctors fix it! Not being able to laugh was the biggest disaster of my life."

Surviving and Thriving

The first time I spoke to a cancer survivor group on the healing power of humor, I feared that (1) they might argue with me, and (2) they might not have the ability to laugh. Wrong on both counts. They laughed with utter abandon and embraced what many of them already knew to be true: Humor helps us heal.

Beulah's own battle with breast cancer also ended in victory—and a mastectomy. "Since my bra size is 44 DD, it was necessary to get a prosthesis. On Labor Day I was at a family camp where they have a 360-degree water slide into the lake. I didn't have a bathing suit and decided to chance it in street clothes. After my second trip down, I started out of the water and discovered something was missing.

A woman nearby asked her, "What are you looking for?"

"My breast form!" Beulah gasped.

"Does it float?"

"I don't know, I've never lost it before!"

Twenty yards out into the lake they spotted it, floating among the lily pads. The woman offered to swim out and get it for her. Beulah says, "She brought 'Sally' back to me, I put her where she belonged, laughed a lot, hugged the woman, and went back up the hill to slide again and again, each time making sure everything was where it belonged!"

A Laugh or Death Situation

Humor and cancer may seem like odd bedfellows, but in truth, every survivor I've ever talked to confirms the benefits of maintaining, even enhancing, one's sense of humor through the recovery process. Karleen from Indiana shares, "My daughter had just undergone surgery for ovarian cancer for the second time, and upon returning to her room, she found several of us waiting for her, including her husband, Robert."

"Oh, Robert," her daughter said, "don't look so sad. I'm going to be all right. God put me in your life to make you miserable, and I'm not through yet!"

What an incredible testimony to this woman's faith, strength, and ability to overcome adversity with humor. As Golda Meir said, "Those who do not know how to weep with their whole heart, don't know how to laugh either."

Phyllis from Michigan says, "I truly believe laughter is God's pain medicine for the hurts of life. No matter what valley we go through, God provides a way to rejoice in him always, and sometimes that's through laughter."

Lori from Texas is a valley-overcomer as well. When her husband was diagnosed with pancreatic cancer that had spread to his lungs, she was devastated. "My two best friends immediately came to the rescue. Yes, there was some crying, but there was a lot of laughing. They told me everything funny they could think of and made up some stuff.

"My husband is really not a laugher, but since his diagnosis, we've watched funny movies and laughed. We make it a fun day when we have to go to get chemotherapy, and I look for funny things to tell the other patients to get them laughing too."

Marilyn declares, "Humor has seen me through two heart-valve operations and long stays in the hospital. I'm living a life that I was told I had only a 5 percent chance of having. Through all of that, I've learned to laugh at life. If I'm going to be here only a short while, I sure better learn to enjoy it."

What an encouragement when we read the words of our Lord, "Blessed are you who weep now, / For you shall laugh" (Luke 6:21). We do find humor in some of the most unexpected, somber situations.

Kelly from Colorado writes of a friend of the family who lost a loved one. "The brother of the deceased had placed his new, never-before-worn suit in one of the bedroom closets. It came time to dress for the funeral, but the new suit was nowhere to be found.

"When the brother viewed the deceased, guess what the man in the coffin was wearing?! Apparently when they needed clothes for the body, they assumed that everything in the closet belonged to the deceased!"

Death is never funny. But it can be joyous. If a person is set free from pain and suffering, knowing that their Savior waits at the gates of heaven to welcome them home, those of us attending the funeral can smile at one another without apology.

Laughter is exactly what filled the air at Lucille's funeral. Shirley from Indiana loved her "adopted" grandmother Lucille, who was over ninety and nearly blind. As she talked to her on the phone one morning, she heard a man's voice in the background.

"Oh, if you have company, you can call me later," Shirley suggested.

Lucille laughed. "No, no that's just Sam. He was here late last night, so I had him spend the night."

"You did what?!?"

Through her chuckles, Lucille explained, "Sam is my new talking clock." Sam-the-clock was her constant companion in and out of the hospital. She carried Sam at her elbow at all times. Upon her death the family decided to put Sam in the casket nestled in Lucille's arms as he had been for the last several weeks of her life.

At her funeral service, the pastor had just said, "Let us pray," when Sam spoke in his deep, husky voice, "It is now 11:00 A.M."

Shirley confesses, "The room was filled with uncontrollable laughter instead of grief, exactly as Lucille would have wanted it."

There Is a Balm in Gilead

Mary from Michigan took her ninetysomething mother into the hospital for a minor ailment.

"I'm thinking about changing doctors," the elderly woman announced.

"Why, Mother?" a surprised Mary asked.

"I've doctored with this man for forty years, and I'm not a bit better!"

The Lord designed humor not only for our physical well-being, but for our emotional and spiritual health as well. That's exactly how Mary from Kansas sees it. "I believe laughter is a healing gift, for the emotions and the spirit. It feels like a cleansing internal bath to rinse out pain, anger, and self-pity."

Bobbie from South Australia agrees, "Humour has saved my life. Being able to look for a laugh at the everyday quirky, bizarre, and madcap events going on around me—and which I have sometimes created—has provided a healing balm as I've battled grief and mental illness and worked through to healing and peace. And I'm still laughing!"

Donna had 'em laughing in Virginia as the coordinator at her agency for a program that promotes healthy attitudes, exercise, and so forth. "The quarterly regional meeting was being held at a state-operated psychiatric/mental-health facility. Attendees were asked to dress as though we were going to a Hawaiian luau. Out of the fifty people there, I was the only one in costume. You can imagine the looks I received, strolling the halls of a mental-health facility in a grass skirt!"

Cheri from Florida thinks laughter has not only therapeutic value but cosmetic value as well. "I look much better in smiles than frowns." And Sherry from Washington concludes, "There is no life without humor. My very well-being is dependent on humor."

Humor is by no means the only positive emotional experience that promotes healing. Love and affection make all the difference in the world—the love of God and the love of people you care about. Faith and hope walk beside love and laughter, as do the patients' will to live and the unique calling that gives their lives meaning. There is great comfort to be found in glorious music, delicious scents, the beauty of nature, and the warmth of light.

And yes, laughter weaves its carefree way through all those joy-filled, purpose-filled, spirit-filled needs. We humans are a complex bunch. Only the One who knows us and loves us completely has the power to meet every one of those needs in so personal a way that we feel he is ministering to us alone.

The one who knows God can laugh in the face of death because to die with Christ in your heart is to live—and laugh—with him, forever.

As Brenda Sees It

I received a very moving letter from Brenda in Florida. She works with cancer patients, particularly with women who have breast cancer. As a physician assistant in oncology, she explains, "All my patients have refractory cancer of some sort (primarily breast cancer, leukemia, lymphoma, myeloma) which has failed all therapies. Their final chance at a cure is with high-dose intensive chemotherapy followed by bone marrow transplant rescue.

"A high number of patients do not survive the therapy and, unfortunately, a large number relapse after this difficult and prolonged treatment."

Already you are probably shaking your head, as I did, wondering how this woman can go to work every day and face this grim reality.

Brenda wrote, "I love working with these patients and their families, and I really feel this is a ministry for me. I think that the Lord has given me the gift of encouragement. I know that for many people this would be a difficult area to serve, but I really love my work. These patients teach me so much. I definitely am learning which things should be priorities in life—my spiritual life, my family life, and my relationships—and what kind of things are not worth worrying about."

Not everyone who laughs in the face of death overcomes it in the physical sense. Yet humor has a place even in the dying process. Ask Brenda. Ask a hospice volunteer. Ask those who loved comedian Gilda Radner, who died in 1989 suffering from ovarian cancer, which she called "the most un-funny thing in the world."

Brave Gilda told Bob, her radiation technician, that he was the funniest person she'd ever met. (This from a woman married to Gene Wilder!) People always told Bob that he should be on television, but Gilda disagreed. "No, he should be in the radiation therapy department, because that is where his humor is needed most."

You will be sorrowful, but your sorrow will be turned into joy. (John 16:20)

When Laughter and Forgiveness Seem Long Ago and Far Away

Maritza came to hear me speak in Florida recently, and when she responded to our survey for this book, she gave me some crucial insights that I asked her to share with you as well.

There's nothing humorous about this story at all, but it is, in its own way, joy filled.

There are tragic moments that challenge us to the core of our being. Faith and forgiveness appear beyond our grasp, let alone joy and laughter. We doubt, in fact, that we will ever laugh again.

Our only hope and comfort then—as always—is found in the promises of God:

Weeping may endure for a night,
But joy comes in the morning. (Psalm 30:5)

Maritza explains, "One June, while my husband was pastoring a small church in Illinois, our church hosted a Vacation Bible School kickoff picnic at a local park. A woman from the church accidentally drove a malfunctioning van through the pavilion where we were gathered, striking and killing our seventeen-month-old son, Nathan, who was sleeping in his stroller.

"The years that have followed have been extremely painful and difficult. Although always an upbeat and a funny person myself, these years have been filled with many tears and hours of desperation and loss. I hesitated to attend your conference, Liz, afraid you would somehow hint that everything was a laughable situation, and I know all too well it is not."

[I would never do such a thing, of course, but you can easily understand her fears.]

She writes, "I'm so thankful I went, because certainly the laughter was good, and it was so easy to identify with all the examples you gave. You said that laughter doesn't make you forget or dismiss your sufferings, but helps you survive and get through it. Exactly! Thanks so much for a lovely day."

Bless you, Maritza, for sharing your journey with all of us who need that reminder. Suffering is neither fun, nor funny. We stand on his promises, weep with those who will weep with us, and wait for joy to return to our doorstep, as it most surely will.

Those who sow in tears
Shall reap in joy. (Psalm 126:5)

CHAPTER 22

Humor as a Stress-Reliever: Joy Comes in the Morning, Unless You Wake Up on the Wrong Side of the Bed

*With the fearful strain that is on me night and day,
if I did not laugh I should die.*
—Abraham Lincoln

"**O**ne morning, my young son woke up in a terrible mood," writes Sue from Kentucky. "I told him he'd gotten up on the wrong side of the bed."

"But, Mom!" he protested. "The other side is against the wall!"

Offspring Angst

Children and stress—a package deal. Better keep your sense of humor handy. Those of us with younger kids have one sort of stress; those with teenagers smile through gritted teeth and say, "Just you wait!"

Day-to-day stress isn't as dramatic as the stress of facing catastrophic illness or death, but drip by drip, even the daily load of stress we carry can add up.

"It never fails," Sheryl from Oklahoma sighs. "Whenever I go into my boys' rooms to tuck them in for the night, I end up fuming. Clothes here and there, socks on the ceiling fan, toys in the dirty clothes hampers, Big Macs under the mattress, last month's chocolate milk in a glass hidden behind Mr. Bear on the headboard."

We get the picture.

She tells them, "Boys, I hate to come up here and find this mess all the time! Why is it so hard to keep your rooms picked up?"

Her middle child of three boys calmly looked up at her one evening after one of her tirades about the messy rooms and simply said, "Well, Mom, just don't come up here then."

Sheryl laughs. "The simple solutions of a child! I laughed and laughed. God eased my distressed conditon even if just for a few moments at the end of my hectic day."

Ellen from Pennsylvania, also the mother of three boys, had a particularly rough and tiring day. "I went upstairs to rest while my husband fixed supper. Thirty minutes later, my three sons—ages eight, six, and three—trooped into my bedroom.

"Usually a rambunctious crew, they stood quietly by the door, eyeing me cautiously. Trying to muster some energy, I exclaimed, 'Well, isn't this nice! Did you come to get me for supper?'"

They looked at one another, then the oldest ventured, "Nah. Dad said you were stressed out, and we just wanted to see what that looked like."

Choose Joy, Question Boy

When stress arrives at your doorstep (actually, it may live there, but let's not dwell on that), you have a choice in how you respond to it:

1. Scream with anger
2. Cry with anguish
3. Laugh with abandon

The best choice is so obvious. There is a time and place for righteous anger, and tears are wonderfully cleansing too. But in the face of daily stress, Option 3 wins by a country (s)mile.

Linda from Oklahoma stumbled on a great stress-relieving way to handle the horrors of having a dating daughter. She sent me *An Application to Date Our Daughter*. Requests on the detailed, one-page form included a demand for "a complete financial statement, history, lineage, and current medical report from your doctor."

What else did they need to know about prospective dates for their daughter? Here's the hilarious list:

Do you own—
   A van?
   A truck with oversize tires?
   A water bed?
   An earring, nose ring, or belly-button ring?
   A tattoo?
   (If yes to any of the above, discontinue application and leave premises immediately.)

Their "application" also required short essays on:

What does *late* mean to you?
What does *abstinence* mean to you?
The one thing I hope this application does not ask me about is . . .

It concluded with:

Please allow four to five years for processing.

Maybe Susan from Pennsylvania should have created a similar questionnaire for her eight-year-old son who brings wildlife of another sort home, "all types of wildlife, tame or otherwise," she explains. "He'd recently bought a snake from a pet store, a very snakey-looking snake.

"I use my feet to propel my wheelchair. One day as I was wheeling down the hardwood floors in the hall, our son said, 'Mom, stop with the noise. You're scaring my snake.'"

Wait . . .who is scaring whom here?!

Fowl Play

Sometimes parents experience humor by watching their children mature. Lucille from New Mexico finds fun in how her parents are maturing. "After they retired, my mother and father lived out on the California desert with a little orchard, a small vegetable garden, and a pen full of guinea fowl. Though guinea eggs are smaller than chicken eggs, my parents claimed guineas had much more personality than chickens."

I didn't know chickens had any personality at all, did you? And do eggs from high-personality guineas—Sunnies, no doubt—taste better than those from, say, Foggy fowls?

Lucille continues, "Often the guinea hens expressed their personality through a raucous squawk. My mother was convinced the guineas understood words. And sometimes they gave that impression. They had two favorite calls that they frequently screeched. Every time anyone went out the back door, one guinea or another would begin to squawk something that sounded like, 'Stupid! Stupid! Stupid!' or 'Go back! Go back! Go back!'

"One day my mother washed a sheet and took it out the back door to hang on the clothesline. A guinea started a warning squawk, 'Go back! Go back! Go back!' A stiff breeze was blowing from the Pacific Ocean. When my mother opened up the sheet to toss it over the line, a gust of wind suddenly grabbed the sheet, slapped it against her face, and wrapped it all around her.

"While she was struggling to get out of the wet sheet, she heard a raucous squawk, 'Stupid! Stupid! Stupid!'"

It is not clear who is the most stressed out here: (*a*) the daughter with the guinea-loving parent, or (*b*) the sheet-draped mother, or (*c*) the bright mind trapped in the body of a guinea hen.

Kodiak Moments
(In Other Words, a Bear)

Laughter as a means of stress release is hardly a new discovery. In 1860 Herbert Spencer called laughter a "safety valve" for excess energy in the nervous system. For me, the first sign of stress is losing my sense of humor, and the first sign of relief is a loud guffaw.

Carol from Kentucky is the kind of woman who spares herself the stress and sees the humor in the moment ASAP. The second-floor bathroom pipe broke, on her birthday, no less, and her house was flooded all the way to the basement. "Floors buckled, two ceilings caved in, the heat went off, and for a while I didn't have running water. My friends had given me a surprise party the weekend before, so when the construction crew (wrecking crew?) arrived, all the decorations were still hanging from the remaining ceilings and walls. The crew was very polite and wished me a Happy Birthday!"

And, we can only hope, offered a birthday discount.

You never know what stress will make you say or do. Arlene from Michigan was in a car accident. While riding in the ambulance, the attendants asked her some simple questions to see if she was okay.

"How old are you?" the EMT asked.

"I don't know," Arlene admitted.

"How much do you weigh?"

"A hundred and thirty pounds."

"You weigh less than that."

"Good."

"Who is the president of the United States?"

"Mrs. Clinton."

Sometimes medical personnel giggle under their masks at a stressed-out patient, but it does work the other way around as well. Barbara from Georgia worked as a nurse in a busy intensive care unit. "One day things were particularly chaotic and busy. The nurses were running around tending to numerous crises that were all occurring at the same time, doctors were shouting out orders, the phone was ringing off the hook, patients were calling for help, meal trays were arriving, family members were trying to get the nurse's attention to ask questions . . . it was a madhouse.

"One nurse in our unit tended to be a little scatterbrained to begin with. She was running to and fro when she stopped to answer the buzzing intercom. With exhaustion and exasperation in her voice, she pushed the intercom button and said to the entire family-waiting-room area, 'Can you help me?'"

She quickly corrected herself and said, "I mean, can I help you?"

The staff could hear laughter coming back over the intercom from the waiting room as a man's voice responded, "I think you were right the first time."

A Real Flag-Waver

"Unexpected humor has a way of making me feel more positive and healthier," suggests Barbara from Texas. "It is a wonderful stress buster and helps me keep my life in perspective."

Forgive me for one more funereal example of unexpected humor, but Gloria from Washington offers a story we can all identify with. "At my father's funeral, God bless his soul, my siblings and I gathered with fifty other mourners at the graveside. As the bugle blew taps, four young military men solemnly folded the American flag."

Or tried to.

"These men could not fold the flag right! The stars of the flag were folding under, not on top. On the third attempt, my family and I broke out into uncontrolled laughter. However, the people behind us thought that we had broken out into uncontrolled sobbing (because in an attempt to control our laughing, we had covered our faces).

"Meanwhile, the poor young military men did not even crack a smile, which made us laugh even harder. The fourth attempt was their last. I have not seen four young men disappear from a scene so fast."

My own two sisters and I made it through my mother's funeral without laughing, but not without crying. What a sad, sad day, more than twenty years ago. But that evening back at the house, the three of us were sitting around talking about what Mom would have thought of the service and got tickled. I have no idea now what it was that set us off, but that's not the point. The point is, three adult women went from crying to laughing in a matter of seconds. I don't think the tears even shifted gears, they just kept flowing.

When you laugh until you cry, or cry until you laugh, the effect is pretty much the same—red face, scrunched up expression, drippy mascara, wet cheeks, wrung-out tissue, stress gone.

Humor As Oops-Catcher

Jeanette from Ohio has a daughter who sounds much like our sweet Lillian, which is to say, "quite dramatic. Everything requires Scarlett O'Hara-type acting. One day when she was told that she couldn't play until her homework was done," Jeanette says, "she wilted to the floor, moaning and covering her face.

"When it was obvious we weren't budging, she crawled up the stairs and flung herself facedown on the bed. Moaning and crying was all we could hear, which made her father and me start laughing. When we looked in on her, she seemed to be struggling to keep up the act.

"I repeated my directions to finish her homework and added, 'No matter what you do, don't laugh! Don't do it!' She got quiet and wiggled. We kept saying, 'Don't laugh!' and of course she couldn't keep a straight face. Soon, we were all laughing."

Many parents use this time-honored technique (we sure do), and it truly does work, for all the parties involved.

Bonnie's son worked in the produce section of a grocery store where he was approached by a woman asking for half a head of lettuce. "My son said he almost went bonkers and dashed back behind those flip-floppy doors to consult with his manager."

He told his manager rather loudly that there was a "first-class nut" out there who wanted half a head of lettuce. As he and his manager walked back out into the store, there stood the little lady, who'd obviously heard the whole conversation.

Bonnie's brilliant son bent down, put his arm around the lady's shoulder and said to his manager, "And this is the sweet, precious lady who wants the other half!"

CHAPTER 23

🐝

Humor and Perspective: Someday We'll Laugh About This

It would be argument for a week, laughter for a month, and a good jest forever.
—*William Shakespeare*

We've all been in high-stress, low-strength situations where we turn to the next person and sigh, "Someday we'll laugh about this."

I say, why wait? If you can see the humor potential, dive right in. The time and distance between the dastardly deed and your ability to laugh at it is what I call the *stress zone*. You can't hurry the time, but you can decrease the distance, emotionally and mentally, between the first and last moment you spend in the stress zone.

You have to stand back, literally sometimes, to see the Big Picture, to put the thing in perspective, to chop the problem back down to size. It's a universal need, this perspective business. Melinda from Texas thinks "humor lets us see ourselves and others in a different light." A more flattering light, I'd say. "It makes me relax and realize that most crises are not really that important," says Betty from Missouri. Marguerette from Maine wisely points out that laughter "makes bad times and good times both better," and Barbara from Kentucky offers the ultimate challenge: "Why take life so seriously? You're never going to get out of it alive anyway."

Well, there's always that.

Our favorite funny fella, Bill Cosby, said, "If you can find humor in anything, you can survive it."

Someday We'll Laugh About This

The following ten true stories are exactly the kind of situations that must have produced that someday-we'll-laugh-about-this response at the moment of impact. Obviously, the principal players did laugh about it eventually, or they'd never have sent their tale to me for a book about humor!

Take 1

LaRee from Washington was visiting southern California and decided to drop in to surprise her aunt and cousin. "We arrived unannounced. The front door was open, so I quietly walked in. A man was asleep on the couch with a pillow over his head. Certain it was my cousin, I jerked the pillow off his head and said, 'All right, get up!'"

Boy, was he surprised. LaRee too. Her aunt and cousin had moved.

Take 2

New neighbors had moved next door to Bonnie from Michigan. "They moved in around March and, sad to say, it was June and I still hadn't introduced myself.

"The first nice weekend of the summer, I went out to work my flower beds, wearing a perfectly good pair of shorts I'd discovered in my giveaway pile, not at all sure how they ended up in there.

"My new neighbors pulled up, and I decided to greet them and make up for lost time. I was my most friendly outgoing self, but they appeared a little standoffish."

Later, she shared her assessment of the new neighbors with her husband, who offered an observation: "Honey, maybe they acted odd because the zipper in your white shorts is completely undone."

Maybe so.

Bonnie confesses, "It's been hard for me to look them in the eyes ever since!"

Take 3

"My mother bought my father a birthday cake," shares Kim from Alabama, "and she invited some relatives over to celebrate, hiding the cake in her bedroom to keep it as a surprise. Later, being the helpful daughter I was, I took it upon myself to bring the cake out.

"Just as they realized I was missing, I came out of the bedroom, tripped, and dumped the cake upside-down on the floor. Lucky for me the cake was in a box. Mom picked it up, scraped the frosting off the inside of the lid, and kept going like nothing happened."

Go, Mom.

Take 4

Dinner was at a Chinese restaurant for Marilyn from Michigan and her family, including Sheryl, her twelve-year-old daughter. "Sheryl ordered the *human* pork, and our dignified Oriental waiter very politely told her she must mean the *Hunan* pork. Her brothers were less polite and didn't let her forget it all through her teen years.

"Then Sheryl had the privilege of spending a summer teaching in China. She waited eagerly for her assignment, hoping it might be in one of the northern provinces so she could see the Great Wall. Instead, it was in one of the southern provinces.

"God does have a sense of humor!" Sheryl declared. Her assignment? Hunan!

Take 5

Jo from California had every mother's worst nightmare come true. "My three-year-old son was playing in the yard while I got ready to go shopping. When I went outside, there was no sign of him.

"I calmly told myself that he'd probably gone to visit one of our neighbors, but after making the rounds and finding that no one had seen him, I began to panic. There were numerous construction sites on our block that posed many dangers. Even worse, someone could have taken my son.

"I got in my car and began looking for him, asking every person I met if they had seen a little boy with a red shirt on. Several times I got the same answer, 'Yes, he was headed that direction. He said he was trying to find his dog.'

"If I didn't find him soon I realized I would have to call the police to report my child missing. By now I was nearly hysterical. I continued to drive up and down various streets, but my eyes were so blurred by tears that I could hardly see.

"Finally, as a last resort, I stopped my car in the middle of the street and screamed my son's name. A small voice answered, 'I'm right here, Mommy.'

"As my eyes came back into focus, I couldn't believe what I was seeing. There sat my son on some stranger's lawn, happily playing with a toy their youngster had left out in their front yard."

Apparently it never occurred to her son that he was lost.

"I ran to him and scooped him up into my arms, not wanting to ever let him go. Between sobs and kisses, I told him how much I loved him, how worried I had been that something horrible had happened to him, and how happy I was that he was safe.

"Still shaking, I drove home and told him repeatedly never ever to leave our yard without a grown-up again. Even after we got home, I was so shook up that I could not stop crying.

"After about twenty minutes of this, my son looked at me and said matter-of-factly, 'Mom, if you can't stop crying, just go to your room.'"

Take 6

Shari's father-in-law was a minister at two country churches in southern Indiana. He'd had many medical complications in his life, but he also had a wonderful sense of humor. He was fully sighted in one eye and had a glass eye in the other.

Traveling through a busy intersection, his car was hit in the rear end by another driver. Both men got out to assess the damage.

Shari says, "The other driver was a wreck. He was an emotional basket case and started to carry on about his bad heart. My father-in-law said very calmly to him, 'Well, buddy, I don't know what you're complaining about. I'm blind.'"

Take 7

It was the kind of summer that memories are made of. Karla from Washington was twelve when her family spent a long summer vacation roaming around the countryside in a camper.

They'd just spent the night in the Canadian Rockies, and Karla awakened to find that her mother and father "had outdone themselves preparing breakfast. The outdoor picnic table at the campsite was loaded with all kinds of good-looking, wonderful-smelling goodies.

"My sister and I helped set the table, and everything was ready. The rest of the family were still getting dressed, so I sat down on one side of the picnic table (the kind with benches attached), and my mother sat down right beside me on the same bench.

"In all this time, no one had noticed that the table was situated on a slope, and my mother had just added herself to the downhill side of the equation. The next thing either of us knew, we were sprawled on our backs with our feet up in the air and wearing the entire breakfast!

"Both my mother and I were stunned for an instant until we looked at each other and a low rumble of laughter began building. You gain new respect for your mother when you see her with gooey banana-bread frosting on her face! And I admit, I looked quite special with a bowl of peach slices in my hair.

"We laughed for at least ten minutes before we even attempted to get up from the mess, and our entire family joined in. We've repaid the cost of the lost food thousands of times over in the laughter we still share over that one instant in time.

"We also check to make sure the picnic table is on level ground."

Take 8

"The Bicentennial Class of 1976 silently awaited their diplomas. The dignitaries sat in the front row—the principal, vice principal, coaches, and so on."

Garlene from Montana continues, "I was sitting a few rows behind these powerful people, and our row was called to accept our diplomas. I concentrated on not stepping on someone's robe or messing up the procession.

"Then it happened. I tripped into the person handing out the diplomas and knocked over the podium, the flowers, and the microphone. It all happened so fast that all I could do was laugh and turn beet red.

"The audience roared with laughter. Evidently I wasn't the only one experiencing anxiety that day. There was laughter everywhere except that first row.

It was, however, the main topic of conversation at Garlene's twentieth high-school reunion.

Take 9

Mary from Manitoba was coming home late from a meeting in town. "I noticed a car following me as soon as I turned off the highway onto a country road. Since my cousin had been held up under similar conditions I got scared.

"I slowed down to let the car pass, but it kept on following me. I imagined they would follow until we got a little farther from the highway and then attack.

"I panicked and decided to turn in to the first farmyard I came to and pretend I lived there. No use—they kept following! All was dark in the house, so what could I do but turn around?

As I did so, I came face-to-face with the people following me—the couple who lived there!"

Take 10

Kim from Louisiana learned a hard but funny lesson on her very first job as a registered nurse. "I'd had my three-day paperwork orientation and was now set to start on the ward. The hospital had given me a red ribbon to tape to my name tag to indicate, 'Hey, don't count on me for anything, I'm new.'

"The charge nurse's first words to me were, 'That red ribbon doesn't mean anything, you're taking a patient.'"

Gulp.

She gave Kim an elderly lady in her nineties who needed total care. The woman wasn't doing well, but the family wanted full measures taken to resuscitate her if she should stop breathing. "I must have looked really scared because Myrene, the LPN on duty, leaned over and said, 'It'll be okay.'

"About this time the maintenance man stuck his head in and announced that the call-light system was being repaired and couldn't be used. I was really starting to get upset because that system was the way to indicate an emergency when a nurse needed help. I asked Myrene, 'What should I do if I have problems?'"

Myrene answered, "Throw a bedpan in the hallway."

So off Kim went with her big metal bedpan to take care of her patient. "I thought I'd start with something safe and began to give her a bed bath. I finished the front. So far, so good. I turned her on her side to bathe her back, and she suddenly took one big breath, shuddered, and stopped breathing!

"I watched and watched and still no breath. With adrenaline pumping, fueled by fear, I threw the bedpan out the door."

Bad timing.

"The elderly woman's doctor was walking through the door just as I let go. The bedpan bounced off his temple, and he crumpled out cold in the doorway. The rest of the nurses had arrived with the code cart. They hauled the doctor into the hallway, left him there, and tried to resuscitate my patient.

"All I could do was stand in the corner and sob because I knew I had just lost my job!

"My patient, rest her soul, died. The doctor ended up in the hospital overnight with a hairline skull fracture and concussion. Meanwhile, as we were walking down the hallway, my mentor, Myrene, put her arm around my shoulder and said, 'I was just joking!'

"For months I couldn't carry a bedpan anywhere without people yelling, 'Incoming!'"

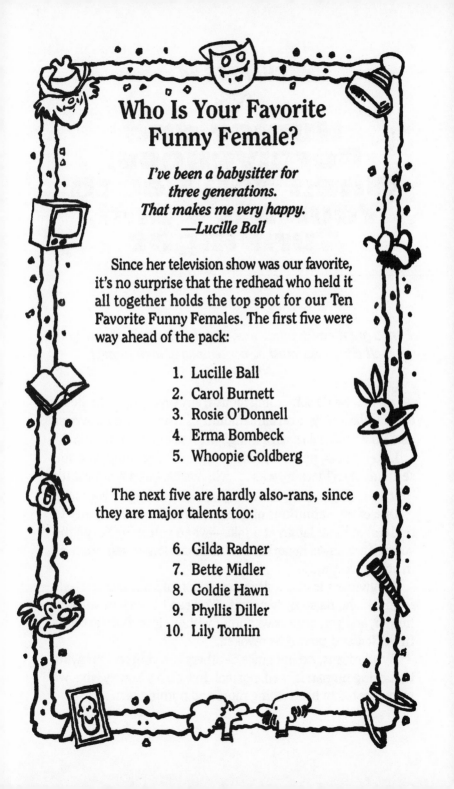

Who Is Your Favorite Funny Female?

I've been a babysitter for three generations. That makes me very happy.
—Lucille Ball

Since her television show was our favorite, it's no surprise that the redhead who held it all together holds the top spot for our Ten Favorite Funny Females. The first five were way ahead of the pack:

1. Lucille Ball
2. Carol Burnett
3. Rosie O'Donnell
4. Erma Bombeck
5. Whoopie Goldberg

The next five are hardly also-rans, since they are major talents too:

6. Gilda Radner
7. Bette Midler
8. Goldie Hawn
9. Phyllis Diller
10. Lily Tomlin

CHAPTER 24

✿

Humor and Forgiveness: When You Reach Your Wit's End, Turn Right

I am a great and sublime fool. But then I am God's fool and all His works must be contemplated with respect.
—Mark Twain

When we do something foolish, embarrassing, ridiculous, or just plain silly, a certain amount of shame may wash over us. "How could I do such a thing?" we'll say, or "I am so stupid!"

Listen to Liz, now: Anybody could do such a thing, and you certainly aren't lacking wits . . . wit, maybe, but not brains! It's time to grab your wit, then laugh, pray, and forgive yourself.

One of my definitions of a sense of humor is the ability to understand and laugh at a joke—when you're it! Forgiving yourself is a way of honoring God's ultimate forgiveness extended in your direction.

Forgiveness is also a deep expression of love, and as Gayle from Oklahoma so aptly puts it, "You can't have love without humor, and you can't have humor without love. Both are gifts from God and cannot be revoked."

By all means, extend grace to others and yourself, knowing that being human is, well, normal. In fact, it's exactly what we were created to be, nothing more and nothing less.

The Handwriting Is on the Wall

"This is as funny as I get," wrote Dianne from Illinois. I'm not sure if that was an apology or a warning. She's a bookkeeper in a nursing home. "Some of our residents are not in tune with reality any longer (bless them). I was walking down the hall, and one of the cute little lady residents who usually lives in her own world asked me for an ink pen. I did not have one with me, so I made a special effort and hunted down a pen for her."

Uh-oh.

"I didn't think to ask her what she was planning to do with the ink pen. She'd sounded so normal, so with-it, that I just gave it to her without another thought.

"I found out later what she'd planned to do with it: She wrote part of a Scripture verse on our fresh, new wallpaper."

The bad news is, she wrote "Love is patient." The good news is, she didn't continue with the rest of 1 Corinthians 13!

"Let it be known that I have learned my lesson," says Dianne. "If anyone asks me for an ink pen, I ask what, where, when, who, why, and how is this pen going to be used before handing it over!"

Dianne wisely forgave the resident and herself. No word yet on her supervisor.

Cruisin'

Edie from Michigan was on a cruise with her husband. As she confesses, "I bought a special new outfit, sure to impress the others at our dinner table. I was convinced only the most influential people took cruises. Our first evening came, and I was seated next to a very distinguished-looking man who reminded me of Perry Como. We chatted through the first three courses until my curiosity wouldn't allow me to go on without inquiring about his occupation."

A Wall Street banker? Corporate CEO, perhaps?

"He was a farmer. I know the Lord had to be rolling with laughter. After my 'attitude check,' we had a wonderful voyage. One of the other 'farmers' at our table was a great tenor. He and I entered the talent contest later in the week and won first prize!"

Edie also gets first prize for humbly admitting her own mistaken impression, forgiving herself, and pressing on toward the fun.

How Old Did You Say You Were?

We've all had those down-in-the-dump days that refuse to go away. Sheila's mother-in-law was having one of those, and "decided to get her hair done and buy herself a new outfit."

After a productive visit to the salon and the mall, she stopped by the grocery on her way home. As Sheila describes it, "It was a beautiful summer day, and she was beginning to feel much better about herself. Her favorite bag boy helped her with the groceries as they carried on a bit of small talk."

She said to the nice young man, "I hear it's going to be eighty today."

He replied, "Oh, really? Well, happy birthday!"

Rumor has it she still shops at that grocery, but avoids small talk with the bag boys.

Rainy Day People

Ever had your ladies' retreat at a rustic campground in the pouring-down rain? I've attended a few, I've spoken at many, and that was the situation for Shirley, the keynote speaker on this particular rainy weekend.

She confesses, "As I sloshed through the rain, my spirit was as drenched as my hair. I whispered to God that I was not grateful for the situation he had put me in!

"After being introduced, I stood up to face my audience and realized none of them looked any better than I did. I told them so, we all laughed, and then we were ready to listen to what God had to say—especially me."

Once again, extending forgiveness to oneself is step one on the road to recovering your wit.

Hot Plates

My house is full of Fibber McGee closets. Crack the door open at your own risk, because who knows what might come tumbling out.

Paula from Wisconsin is my kind of woman. "One time when I was getting ready for a date with a new boyfriend, I didn't have time to do the dishes, so I just threw them in the oven temporarily.

"At the end of the date, we stopped at Shakey's for pizza. Since they were closing up for the night, we brought the pizza back to my place."

Where they could heat it up in her oven.

Her date was the one who flipped open the oven door and found the dishes. "I had to confess I wasn't the perfect housekeeper. He still asked me out after that anyway."

Most men would rather have a woman with a sense of humor than a clean house anyway, don't you think?

Tiger by the Tail

Cathy and Joe want to make sure you do not try this at home. We promise, we won't. Besides, it would require a big, fourteen-pound cat named Velcro for the starring role, and only Cathy and Joe have one of those.

"I had a helium-filled balloon out in the yard one day," Cathy begins. "Velcro, the curious cat, had to check out this balloon. For no reason I can explain, I loosely tied it to his tail. He didn't seem to mind since I would often tie a piece of yarn to his tail that he would chase for a long time.

"Joe and I were amused by this cat walking around the yard with his balloony tail up in the air when suddenly our terrier, Step, came around the corner and gave chase to the sporting Velcro, who made a fast run toward our nearby car.

"Before I could stop anything, Velcro dove under the car with his balloon in tow, which gave a very loud POP! Velcro flew out the other side and didn't stop running until he was way up in the woods. Joe and I were laughing so hard we were both lying down in the yard crying."

Cathy admits with great remorse, "Velcro was a little skittish for an hour or so after we got him to come back home, but otherwise he soon forgot the whole incident."

Forgive and forget—hey, if cats can do it, we humans should be able to manage to forgive ourselves, forget our follies, and find the humor that's hiding in our own backyard.

Merry-Go-Round Is Right!

Nancy was in her mid-twenties when she rode the merry-go-round at King's Island near Cincinnati. Lest you think she was a little old for that particular ride, I'll point out that her husband and mother-in-law had joined her.

"I hate heights," says Nancy, "and my horse was quite tall." Someone helped her up, but at the end of the ride she looked waaay down at the floor far beneath her and thought, *I guess you get off this thing like you would a real horse.*

She had her left foot in the stirrup and swung her right leg over the back of the horse. "Unfortunately, at this point the left stirrup flew up in the air with my foot stuck in it, and I landed under the horse's stomach with both legs wrapped in a death grip around the saddle and my hands hanging onto the pole!"

This is quite a picture.

To make matters worse, her horse was stationed at the entrance where people were winding in and out, so "there were probably three hundred people in total hysterics with a perfect view of all this.

"I yelled for my husband who hurried to my side, but he couldn't figure out what to grab hold of to get me off, and he was laughing so hard—along with the three hundred other people—that he was in a state of total relaxation. People were crying, tears rolling down their faces, many doubled over, and some laughing so hard that no noise came out at all, as I swung there, upside down, for a full five minutes.

"My greatest fear was that my horse would start back up with me still under it! Finally my left hand, from sheer exhaustion, slid down the pole, and I dropped off in a huge heap at the bottom. Every drop of blood in my body was in my face, both from hanging upside down and from sheer embarrassment.

"I thought, *Okay, well these people will never see me again anyway.* Boy was I wrong! Everywhere I went for the rest of the day somebody from the group of three hundred would recognize me and double over laughing when I came to a new ride."

I was there . . . weren't you?

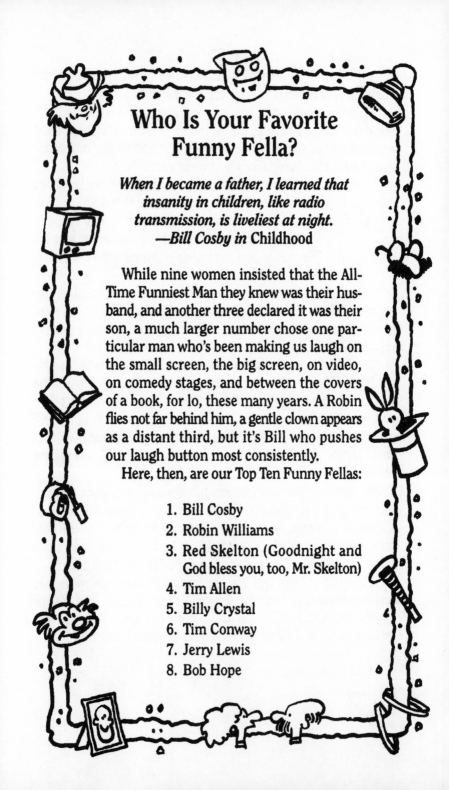

Who Is Your Favorite Funny Fella?

When I became a father, I learned that insanity in children, like radio transmission, is liveliest at night.
—Bill Cosby in Childhood

While nine women insisted that the All-Time Funniest Man they knew was their husband, and another three declared it was their son, a much larger number chose one particular man who's been making us laugh on the small screen, the big screen, on video, on comedy stages, and between the covers of a book, for lo, these many years. A Robin flies not far behind him, a gentle clown appears as a distant third, but it's Bill who pushes our laugh button most consistently.

Here, then, are our Top Ten Funny Fellas:

1. Bill Cosby
2. Robin Williams
3. Red Skelton (Goodnight and God bless you, too, Mr. Skelton)
4. Tim Allen
5. Billy Crystal
6. Tim Conway
7. Jerry Lewis
8. Bob Hope

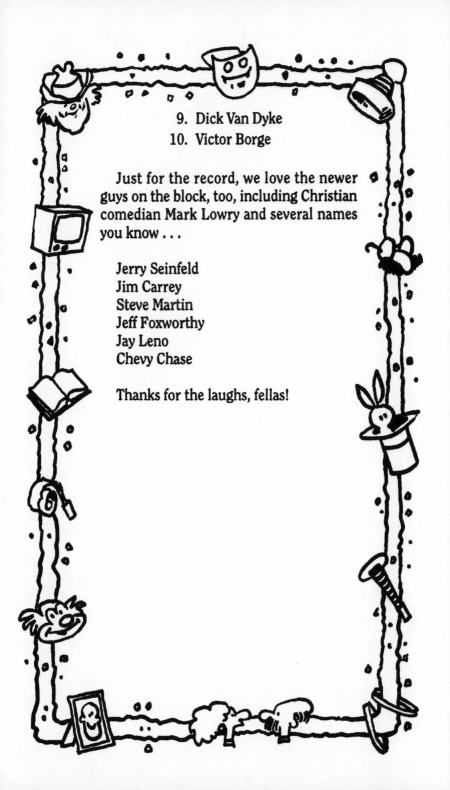

9. Dick Van Dyke
10. Victor Borge

Just for the record, we love the newer guys on the block, too, including Christian comedian Mark Lowry and several names you know . . .

Jerry Seinfeld
Jim Carrey
Steve Martin
Jeff Foxworthy
Jay Leno
Chevy Chase

Thanks for the laughs, fellas!

PART SIX

Humor and Eternity

One Sunday morning Mary's pastor was preaching about heaven, and he said that money wasn't important in the afterlife because in heaven there is no money.

Whereupon her friend Helen whispered to her husband, "You hear that, Bill? We're already in heaven."

There won't be money in heaven, nor marrying, nor tears. But there will be worship and music and praise and joy unspeakable. And, I believe, there will be laughter. It was Martin Luther who said, "If you're not allowed to laugh in heaven, I don't want to go there." Since the many Lutherans among us know their fearless founder will be there, we can surmise that laughter probably will be too.

And grace, Martin. Glorious grace.

CHAPTER 25

Humor and the Lord: Glad Tidings of Great Joy

I have never understood why it should be considered deroga-
tory to the Creator to suppose that he has a sense of humor.
—William Inge

Sandy from Pennsylvania quipped:

He made us in his image,
So he must want us to laugh;
He, no doubt, had a chuckle
When he made the first giraffe!

What makes God laugh? We do, of course! As much as we
laugh at our children, knowing so well their personalities,
strengths, and weaknesses, why wouldn't God be amused at
our antics, even knowing in advance what we're going to say
and do? "I just know God has a wonderful sense of humor,"
insists Mae from Texas. And Karen from Kentucky says, "I firmly
believe God has a very strange sense of humor, but then, I've
been accused of that myself."

Since God is Spirit and Truth rather than flesh, the laughter might be silent—or it might rock the gates of heaven.

Won't it be fun when we find out?

Some among us already have a sense of what tickles the Lord's funny bone, as it were. Donna from Arkansas writes, "During a very special time in his presence, I sensed God placing a picture of himself in my heart and we laughed together. His eyes were full of love and laughter, and he had a smile so full of joy, I just had to hug him . . . what a moment!" Perhaps she heard what Sir Thomas Browne in 1658 called "that unextinguishable laugh in heaven."

Mary from Michigan affirms, "I'm so glad the Lord laughs at me, with me, in me, and through me," and Donna from Virginia says, "At times when I've done something really ridiculous, I'm sure God is sharing the moment with me."

Sanctified Silliness

Does your church have a sense of humor? Many traditions seem to view humor as the opposite of spirituality. Everything associated with the religious experience is serious, from sermons to orders of service to worship styles. At the other end of the spectrum is the Toronto Blessing, where laughter is part of the revival expression.

How one laughs with the Lord is as individual and private a decision as how one prays, observes communion, or celebrates in worship. My only goal here is to encourage you to consider ways to incorporate more laughter ("expressions of joy," if that sounds more spiritual!) into your daily walk with God.

One church reaches its hand toward the community with a "joy buzzer" hidden in their palm, so to speak. The sign advertising the weekly sermon featured this title: ETERNITY: SMOKING OR NONSMOKING?

Cheryl from Oklahoma spotted this sign on her daughter's office wall: JESUS IS COMING! LOOK BUSY!

Then there was the young woman attending an all-girls Christian school. On her floor of the dorm, they had one rest room that offered four toilets—three with privacy doors and one without. Pat from Utah explains that someone cleverly wrote over each stall: 1 JOHN, 2 JOHN, 3 JOHN, and REVELATION!

Elemental Humor

It's not just the signs of the times that make us laugh in church. It is our own foibles that often tickle us most.

Doris from Texas remembers a recent Christmas Eve service where Communion was served in a special way. Rather than just passing the elements down the pews, the deacons were stationed in the aisles. Participants got up when they were ready and collected their "crackers and grape juice," as Doris calls it.

"I reached in the plate for my cracker and ended up with three stuck together. I returned to my seat with juice and crackers in hand, not knowing that my daughter, Jennifer, had told my husband not to get a cracker because 'Mom had them.'"

Doris popped her three-fold cracker in her mouth, followed by the juice. "It's always a very meaningful time of reflection, made extra special on Christmas Eve. Then I looked at my daughter, who had an expression of horror on her face because I had eaten all the crackers. We got tickled and had to turn away from each other so we wouldn't laugh.

"Meanwhile, my husband has told everyone how I shortchanged their Lord's Supper. He said it would've been too embarrassing to get up and get a cracker, since he didn't want anyone thinking he needed seconds."

Speaking of Communion, I had a hard time not spraying my tiny cup of grape juice all over the pew in front of me one Sunday. I'd invited several of my coworkers to visit my church that particular day because I was singing a solo. It seemed a natural way to share my faith with them and let them be embraced by our warm, loving church fellowship.

One friend from work, Jack, was really made welcome that morning. I was sitting in the front row, preoccupied with getting mentally prepared for my solo, when Jack came in the sanctuary and found a seat at the end of the last pew.

Since our church is so big, with so many new faces, it's hard to know who's been around awhile and who's new or visiting. Apparently the deacons were short a man or two that first service and were desperate for help serving the elements.

Someone leaned down and whispered in Jack's ear, "Could you help us serve Communion?"

"I don't attend here," Jack informed them.

"We don't mind, if you don't. We could really use your help."

In marched Jack with the other deacons, and of course, they started at the first pew. I was busy reviewing the words to my song, oblivious to the Communion crisis going on in the back of the sanctuary, and looked up to see my own guest, Jack, handing me the elements with a huge grin on his face!

Do you suppose the Lord was laughing, too?

Vi from Texas must have had a terrible time keeping a straight face when she accompanied her husband, who was filling in for a much younger pastor one Sunday morning. "As I sat in a pew in the back, an older lady sitting next to me said, 'Honey, are you a visitor?'"

"Yes, I am," Vi assured her.

"Oh, I'm so sorry. We have an old retired preacher filling in today, but you be sure and come back next Sunday. Our pastor will be back, and it will be much better."

Vi has also seen a few hundred baptisms in her time, I'm sure, but the one Dixie is about to describe must have been memorable for all in attendance.

Dixie from Illinois says, "I had never seen a baptism before, and I was so excited. There stood our stern, solemn pastor, waiting at the bottom of the baptistery, not smiling, just waiting for me to descend.

"Bounding down the slippery steps in my excitement, I fell in with a large splash, covering the pastor with water that now dripped from his face. He baptized me—again—still not smiling. Since no one told me to wear white underclothes, I had on my brand-new red bra with panties to match. When I came up out of the water, I wasn't the only one wearing red!"

Pint-Size Humor

Robin thinks, "Some things children do to make you laugh you know are directly from God." Amen, sister, and here's proof:

Exhibit #1: Billie from Oklahoma was taking her grandson, Jeff, to Sunday school and gave him a small offering to share. "Here's your money for Jesus," she said.
His eyes opened wide. "Is he gonna be there?"

Exhibit #2: Katrina was tucking her seven-year-old son in bed Easter night and asked him, "What are you thankful for?"
"I'm thankful it's Easter," he declared.
"And what does Easter mean to you?"
"It means Jesus died on the cross for our sins and he was raised again so that we could have *alternative life*."

Exhibit #3: Marian was saying grace and took the opportunity to ask God to grant her five-year-old daughter various qualities that Marian had been suggesting the girl should develop.

When Marian finished, her daughter made a *harrumph!* sound and said, "You weren't praying to God; you were praying at me."

Humor is a prelude to faith and laughter is the beginning of prayer.

—Reinhold Niebuhr

Out of the Mouths of Babes

Renee's mother had only recently come to know Christ as her Savior, and so had much to learn about the Christian faith, about the Bible, and all the myriad facets of her new life in Christ. When her mother came to visit her in Florida, Renee took her to one of the historic churches in the area with a large crucifix. Nailed above it was the sign, written in Greek, Latin, and Hebrew, saying, THIS IS THE KING OF THE JEWS, just as described in Luke 23:38.

"Look, Renee!" her mother exclaimed, pointing at the sign. "In God we trust!"

On another occasion, Renee was discussing various Bible stories with her mother, realizing again how little her mother yet knew about Scripture. Later that day they left for a long car ride, and Renee thought she'd make good use of the time. "So, Mom, what do you know about Adam and Eve?"

Her mother, bless her, looked confused and said, "What were their names? Is that the couple we met yesterday at Walt Disney World?"

Renee could barely get out, "No, Mom, like in the Bible," before her mother caught on. Both laughed hysterically, weaving through traffic with tears streaming down their faces.

We were all babes in the kingdom once. Kinda fun when you're an adult in "spiritual diapers." Humbling yes, but joyful for all.

Does Laughter in the Pulpit Count?

A question I've often posed to the Lord in prayer is simply this: "Is it okay if I'm funny, Lord? In my presentations, in my books, am I truly honoring your name when I cut up and carry on?"

Of course, the humor is clean, never offensive, and that's good. But my query goes deeper than that. I long to know if humor is encouraging and edifying to the body of Christ. Does it count, in terms of glorifying God and building his kingdom? Should I instead be pouring my energy into leading Bible studies and sharing meaningful insights from life and Scripture?

At a Michigan speaking engagement, I was fully prepared to share a strong, meaty message about "Ten Tips for Lifestyle Evangelism." Oh, was it deep stuff. Much note taking would ensue. God will be so proud of me, I thought.

My presentation was on Sunday morning, and there I was at midnight on Saturday, wide awake, stretched across my bed, feeling very uneasy about the next morning. "But, Lord," I said in the direction of the ceiling, "what am I anxious about? This is such a good teaching. A serious Bible study, Lord. Important stuff, right?"

The ceiling wasn't talking, but the Lord was. His still, small voice echoed in my heart. "Liz, think again. Where are your gifts, where is your calling, and what do women respond to most?"

"Oh, yeah," I sighed. "They do like to laugh, and I love to watch it happen. But Lord, does it count? I want to be deep. Deep, like Jill Briscoe or Gloria Gaither or Elisabeth Elliot. Deep, Lord, can't I be deep?"

"You're forgetting the song, Liz: 'Deep and wide. Deep and wide.' You handle the wide part, okay?"

For a minute, I thought I heard him smile.

His words to my heart continued.

"The woman who pours the grape juice into little cups on Saturday night. Is her work deep? Does it honor me?"

"Of course," I assured him.

"The women who sew the costumes for the Easter pageant. Do their labors count deeply for the cause of Christ?"

"Certainly!"

"The man who mows the lawn around the church every Saturday morning. Are his efforts in vain, or do they please my heart?"

I was crying by now. "Okay, okay."

"Put away your Bible study, Liz. I've called others to do that who are, frankly, better at it than you are. But your calling, my child, is to make women laugh with fullness of joy, so that their hearts might be opened to the love and forgiveness I've prepared for them."

"Is that it, Lord?" I sniffed. "It seems so . . . shallow."

Now he reminded me of a Scripture: "Whatever you do, do it heartily, as to the Lord and not to men" (Colossians 3:23).

"Whatever?" I said, then laughed. "I get it, Lord. Laughter comes under the category of whatever!"

Sunday morning dawned with an air of anticipation. I had some wild, scribbled notes and a vague sense of where the message was going, but I'm usually much more organized when I speak. This was scary. "Whatever, Lord," I whispered under my breath. "Hope you enjoy the show."

It seems he did. A dear woman there named Mary slipped me a note: "Thank you for being obedient to God today! The stress in my life has been immense . . . I broke free this weekend through laughter! You were a physician, bringing medication to the afflicted. Psalm 2:4 says, 'He who sits in the heavens shall laugh'!"

Suzi also handed me a note that read, "Even your name begins with *l*—like laughter! You sure do tickle my funny bone and bring me to my knees to face things I need to look at."

Oh, Lord! That's deep!

After that Sunday, my speaking started taking a new turn. I found myself sharing even more humor (without guilt!) at church events, and more of my faith (without fear!) at general events. Kelley heard me at a women's health event sponsored by a hospital in Indiana and wrote me to say, "You truly exhibit the joy, the passion, the adventure of the Christian life!"

Yes! It's wonderful to be walking in the will of the Lord and have it be such a hoot. I'm hardly alone in this. Carol from Alabama says, "I love showing others that it's fun to be a Christian!" Karen thinks "funny Christians witness so much better than sour ones," and Natalie agrees: "If others don't think Christians can have a little fun, they lose interest."

The key is that the humor of one who knows God should be decidedly different from the humor of this world:

Worldly Humor

1. Glorifies sin
2. Puts down others
3. Ridicules righteousness
4. Hurts the spirit

Godly Humor

1. Avoids offense
2. Pokes fun at ourselves
3. Honors the Lord as our source of joy
4. Heals the spirit

Since I believe laughter and music are two of God's finest gifts to his people, I wanted to share this little ditty that I sometimes sing to close my programs.

I wrote it on a plane. (No, not on the side of it! I mean, while flying.) Since I'm an *encourager*, which means in a literal sense, "to fill the heart," and since I love to fill hearts with laughter, it's only fitting that the Lord put this song in my heart for you . . .

Laughter Is the Language of the Heart

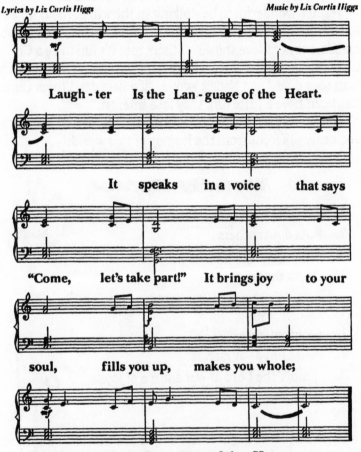

Lyrics by Liz Curtis Higgs

Music by Liz Curtis Higgs

Laugh - ter   Is the Lan - guage of the Heart.

It   speaks   in a voice   that says

"Come,   let's take part!"   It brings joy   to your

soul,   fills you up,   makes you whole;

Laugh-ter,   It's the Lan-guage of the Heart.

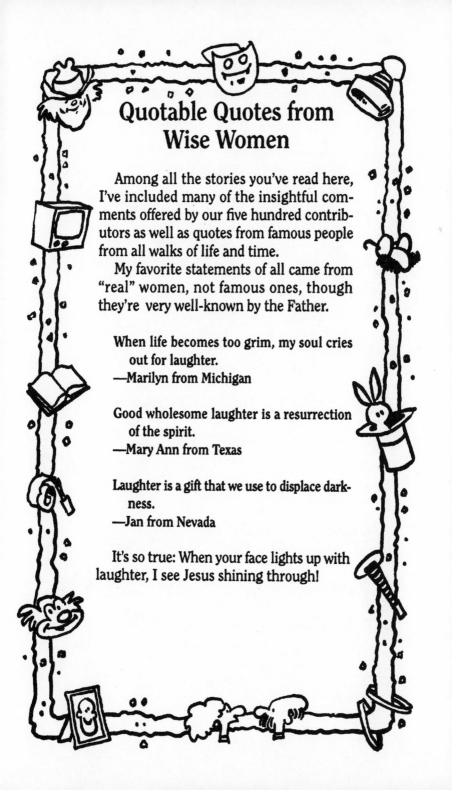

Quotable Quotes from Wise Women

Among all the stories you've read here, I've included many of the insightful comments offered by our five hundred contributors as well as quotes from famous people from all walks of life and time.

My favorite statements of all came from "real" women, not famous ones, though they're very well-known by the Father.

When life becomes too grim, my soul cries out for laughter.
—Marilyn from Michigan

Good wholesome laughter is a resurrection of the spirit.
—Mary Ann from Texas

Laughter is a gift that we use to displace darkness.
—Jan from Nevada

It's so true: When your face lights up with laughter, I see Jesus shining through!